Macroeconomics
A European Text

Macroeconomics
A European Text

SIXTH EDITION

Michael Burda
and
Charles Wyplosz

OXFORD
UNIVERSITY PRESS

OXFORD
UNIVERSITY PRESS

Great Clarendon Street, Oxford, OX2 6DP,
United Kingdom

Oxford University Press is a department of the University of Oxford.
It furthers the University's objective of excellence in research, scholarship,
and education by publishing worldwide. Oxford is a registered trade mark of
Oxford University Press in the UK and in certain other countries

Third edition published 2001
Fourth edition published 2005
Fifth edition published 2009

Impression: 1

British Library Cataloguing in Publication Data

Data available

ISBN 978-0-19-960864-5

Printed in Italy by
L.E.G.O. S.p.A—Lavis TN

Preface to the Sixth Edition

The sixth edition of *Macroeconomics: A European Text* comes at a frightening, but exciting time in modern economic history. The global financial crisis that began in 2008 with the collapse of Lehman Brothers, one of Wall Street's most prestigious investment banks, caused the most severe economic downturn since the Great Depression. Europe was hit hard, but in the aftermath has been hit with its own crisis: one of government finance in a common currency area. As we write this preface in July 2012, Europe is facing unprecedented challenges. Many countries—both those who use the euro and those who do not—are in recession, some for several years now, while millions of Europeans are feeling the pain of high unemployment and bleak future prospects. For macroeconomists, these events represent a deep intellectual challenge, in the same way that the Great Depression gave birth to macroeconomics as a field in its own right. Many see the current state of affairs as a humbling failure of the field.

Did macroeconomics fail? It will take time to understand fully the implications of the crisis, yet we are convinced that macroeconomics has enough tools to analyse and understand the events of the past decade. The fault lies with the users of those tools. Policymakers either used those tools incorrectly or took the eye off one of the many balls of sound policy. The principles developed in the current and previous editions of this textbook can help organize our thoughts on a very complex situation, and allow us to evaluate the adequacy and appropriateness of current policy responses. Because the study of economics, especially macroeconomics, tends to be countercyclical, a key objective of the sixth edition is to give our readers the ability to assess the current European crisis in a structured way. The result is a large number of changes from the previous edition.

As with every new version of our book, we have reviewed the text word for word to improve readability and stimulate interest. While we have retained the overall structure from the fifth edition, we have replaced many examples with discussions of recent events, in the text or new boxes. In particular, a new version of Chapter 19 offers a comprehensive treatment of the euro sovereign debt crisis. We also present changes in the world's financial architecture following the global financial and European crises, including the emergence of new global players as reflected in the creation of the G20. With a fast changing landscape, we have faced the risk of early obsolescence by focusing on principles, showing their relevance to grasp the on-going challenges that Europe faces.

The fifth edition took the major step of showing how the *LM* curve could be replaced with the Taylor rule to better describe what central banks actually do. In response to the enthusiastic response of teachers who have adopted our book, we have now completed that transition, abandoning the *LM* curve completely. We took advantage of the freed space to clarify some aspects of monetary policy that were dealt with a bit too quickly in the previous edition. We are convinced that students who discover macro through *IS–TR* will feel thoroughly comfortable with this apparatus. The transition from *IS–TR* to *AD–AS* has been reworked to clean up some loose ends. The result is a graphical treatment of the modern New Keynesian synthesis that is now the consensus in the profession and is being used in central banks and international institutions around the world.

In addition to the elimination of the *LM* curve from Chapter 10, a number of chapters have undergone important revisions. Chapter 9 presents the new challenges to monetary policy posed by the financial crisis.

It explains quantitative easing, describes the decision to peg the Swiss Franc to the euro and discusses the controversial role of the European Central Bank as lender in last resort. Chapter 11 simplifies the introduction of international capital flows by simply removing respectively the IS or the TR curve from the analysis, depending on whether exchange rates are flexible or fixed. The result is, we hope, a clear-cut graphical treatment which makes it easy to apply the same framework to both countries that are inside the Eurozone (with irrevocably fixed exchange rates) and those that let their exchange rate float. The improved derivation of the AS–AD framework directly from the IS and TR curves and from a non-formalized version of the new Keynesian Phillips Curve is now much clearer. Chapter 14 contains much new material on asset prices with a discussion of some of the financial instruments involved in the global financial crisis. Chapter 15 has been rewritten to reflect new thinking on the exchange rate. Chapter 16 has added material on the role of demand policy in fighting the Great Recession. Chapter 17 uses the euro-sovereign debt crisis as a foil for studying the dynamics of government debt, with explicit reference to both fundamental and non-fundamental explanations of the surge in sovereign bond yields in late 2009. Chapter 18 has also been rewritten to explore long-run, supply-side policies which have been successful in the Netherlands, Ireland, Denmark, Sweden, UK and Germany and which are currently being called for in southern European countries.

This textbook can be used in second or third-year BA courses, as well as courses offered in business schools, public policy and political science programmes. While every chapter contains important knowledge about macroeconomics and offers important insights into the European context, some instructors may prefer to use only those parts that fit into their teaching plans. While designed for a full year, two-semester course, *Macroeconomics: A European Text* can be used for shorter courses as well. Here are three suggested tracks:

Full course All 20 chapters	Medium-length track 15 chapters	Short track 10 chapters
General introduction Chapters 1 and 2	*General introduction* Chapter 2	*General introduction* Chapter 2
The long run and the real economy Chapters 3 to 6	*The long run and the real economy* Chapters 3, 4 and 5	*The long run and the real economy* Chapters 3 and 5
The short run Chapters 7 to 13	*The short run* Chapters 8 to 13	*The short run* Chapters 8 to 13
Financial markets and the exchange rate Chapters 14 and 15	*The exchange rate* Chapter 15	*The exchange rate* Chapter 15
Policies and debates Chapters 16 to 19	*Policies and debates* Chapters 16 to 18	
History of macroeconomics Chapters 20		

Oxford University Press has always provided valuable support at various stages of the editorial process and the sixth edition was no exception. We are indebted to Alexandra Lazarus-Priestly, Joanna Hardern, and Kirsty Reade for expert guidance in keeping the book close to schedule. Graham Gill provided careful copy editing, and I would like to thank Maike Burda, for her invaluable proofreading. We are also grateful for our many adopters for offering feedback on adapting and restructuring our book to the new challenges posed by the current crisis.

Our textbook has always been a data-intensive enterprise, and this edition would not have been possible without the help of an army of students. We are very grateful to Maren Brede, Lilli Bombei, Christina Resniscek, Nawid Hoshmand, Evgenij Komarov, Marko Ringmann, Femke Schmarbeck, and Stefan Tübbicke for diligent research assistance.

Brief Contents

Detailed Contents

List of Tables

List of Figures

List of Boxes

PART I

Introduction to Macroeconomics

Part I of this textbook sets the stage for macroeconomics as a subject. Chapter 1 explains the objectives and methods of macroeconomics, its history and usefulness, as well as its controversies and open questions. It provides a number of essential definitions and offers a preview of what will follow.

Macroeconomics is about measurement as well as analysis. Chapter 2 introduces the methods of measurement used in macroeconomics. In particular, we will explore the national income accounts, the language economists use to describe and communicate the economic activities of a region or a nation, and the balance of payments, which summarizes its transactions with the rest of the world.

What is Macroeconomics? 1

The Theory of Economics does not furnish a body of settled conclusions immediately applicable to policy. It is a method rather than a doctrine, an apparatus of the mind, a technique of thinking, which helps its possessor to draw correct conclusions.

J. M. Keynes

1.1 Overview of Macroeconomics

Whether we like it or not, economic themes tend to dominate the news. A day seldom passes when we do not hear about unemployment, inflation, economic growth, stock markets, interest rates, or foreign exchange rates—either at home or somewhere else in the world. We hear and read so much about these phenomena because, directly or indirectly, they affect our well-being. It is perhaps mostly for this reason that **macroeconomics**, the study of these economy-wide phenomena, is so exciting. Macroeconomics is more than just headlines, however: it is a fascinating intellectual adventure. The breadth of issues it covers is evidence enough of its inherent complexity. All the same, we will see that simple economic reasoning can take us a long way. And it is often surprising how well a few simple ideas can explain complex situations.

Macroeconomics can also be useful. The economic well-being of all consumers, rich or poor, is affected by movements in interest rates, exchange rates, the rate of inflation, and other macroeconomic variables. Businesses can gain or lose large amounts of money when their environment changes, regardless of how well they are managed. Being prepared for such changes in macroeconomic fortunes can have considerable value. More generally, it makes us all better citizens who are able to grasp the complex challenges that our societies face. Macroeconomics is relevant to voters who wonder what their governments are up to, but also can help governments avoid severe economic crises that have afflicted modern industrial societies over the past century—depressions, when overall economic activity is very far below average, and hyperinflations, when prices are increasing at monthly rates of 50% or more. These extreme situations can tear at a society's social fabric, yet can be prevented when policy-makers apply sound economic principles.

1.1.1 Income and Output

The most important indicator of a nation's economic well-being is a measure of its output and income, the **gross domestic product (GDP)**. At this point, it is enough to think of the GDP simply as an indicator of the goods and services which an economy produces in a year for final uses; the concept will be discussed in greater detail in Chapter 2. For example, in 2011 the GDP of the UK amounted to about 1.51 trillion pounds; in Germany, 2.57 trillion euros; in France 2.02 trillion euros; in Italy 1.59 trillion euros; in the Netherlands 614 billion euros; and in Denmark 1.81 trillion kroner. These are very large numbers. Yet on a per-head basis in a common currency, they are much closer, ranging from 25,000 to 40,000 euros per capita. Comparing these data over time is difficult because prices also change; we will see in Chapter 2 how to deal with that issue and produce so-called *real* GDP numbers – we say *at constant prices*. Table 1.1, which corrects for this effect, displays the development of GDP over the past century.

Macroeconomics is concerned with many aspects of the GDP, which simultaneously signal income and production. The two most salient features are that (1) most countries are characterized by the steady growth of GDP over time, but that (2) there are significant and recurring fluctuations of GDP around its trend, called **business cycles**. We return to these themes in separate sections later. In addition, one might be concerned whether GDP or GDP per capita is a good indicator of individual well-being. In any case, it says little about the distribution of income in the economy, which may also matter to its residents. Many researchers are now examining issues related to happiness and quality of life, not just economic output. One of the robust findings on research in this area is that while GDP is not everything, it is certainly an impor-

Table 1.1 Real Income per Capita (GDP in euros, 2000 prices)

	1900	1913	1929	1950	1987	1992	1999	2002	2007	2010	Av. growth rate
Austria	2,462	2,961	3,160	3,167	13,085	14,937	17,145	17,920	20,289	20,280	1.9
Belgium	3,188	3,606	4,319	4,667	13,280	15,078	17,010	17,987	20,069	20,071	1.7
Denmark	2,578	3,343	4,337	5,933	15,401	16,192	19,017	19,717	21,414	20,346	1.9
Finland	1,426	1,804	2,322	3,634	13,144	12,837	15,931	17,152	21,051	20,008	2.4
France	2,457	2,978	4,025	4,504	14,144	15,774	17,549	18,610	19,040	18,562	1.9
Germany	2,550	3,117	3,462	3,316	13,417	14,433	15,737	16,399	18,066	18,018	1.8
Italy	1,526	2,191	2,643	2,992	12,771	14,216	15,612	16,339	17,229	16,329	2.2
Netherlands	2,925	3,459	4,861	5,124	13,447	15,165	17,966	18,493	20,854	20,489	1.8
Norway	1,604	2,091	2,895	4,639	15,521	16,715	21,019	22,093	24,399	24,096	2.5
Sweden	2,188	2,646	3,306	5,759	14,483	14,509	16,962	18,144	21,688	21,192	2.1
Switzerland	3,275	3,645	5,410	7,745	16,912	17,800	18,590	19,179	21,175	21,534	1.7
United Kingdom	3,838	4,205	4,703	5,930	13,154	13,785	16,650	17,817	20,183	19,158	1.5
Canada	2,488	3,800	4,328	6,231	15,678	15,511	18,347	19,654	21,619	21,292	2.0
USA	3,496	4,529	5,895	8,170	18,618	19,908	23,669	24,383	27,052	26,348	1.9
Argentina	2,355	3,245	3,732	4,261	6,237	6,406	7,443	6,083	8,803	9.310	1.3
Bangladesh	417	443	445	461	515	574	708	778	960	1,088	0.9
China	466	472	481	383	1,484	1,822	2,702	3,586	4,857	6,299	2.4
India	512	575	622	529	961	1,146	1,568	1,719	2,402	2,847	1.6
Japan	1,008	1,185	1,731	1,641	13,887	16,648	17,597	17,918	19,505	19,005	2.8

Source: www.eco.rug.nl/~Maddison/ and The Conference Board and Groningen Growth and Development Centre, Total Economy Database, January 2011, http://www.conference-board.org/economics/

tant factor, if not a necessary condition, for economic and social well-being.

Some evidence is provided in Figure 1.1, which displays on the vertical axis the results of coordinated public opinion polls. People were asked how satisfied they were with their lives. The horizontal axis corresponds to that year's GDP per capita in each country. The figures show that deep unhappiness is only found in poor countries. Yet, people in some countries seem to be poor and happy (e.g. Bhutan) while the French and the Japanese seem less happy than the Austrians and the Canadians who have similar standards of living. Some explanations are being explored, but this is an entirely different topic!

1.1.2 Unemployment

One important phenomenon associated with cyclical fluctuations is **unemployment**, the fact that people

seeking paid work cannot or do not find it, sometimes even when the economy is growing rapidly. The **unemployment rate** is the proportion of unemployed workers in the **labour force**. The labour force consists of those who are either working or are actively looking for a job. In comparison with the total population, it leaves out young people who are not yet working, the old who are retired, and those who cannot or do not wish to work—or have given up hope of working.

There are many reasons to be concerned about unemployment. A first reaction to the image of idle workers is lost production and income. At the same time, we need to ask whether the unemployed are receiving offers of work, whether they are turning down job offers, and if so, for what reason. Are the jobs that workers are searching for available at all, or are workers truly available for the jobs on offer,

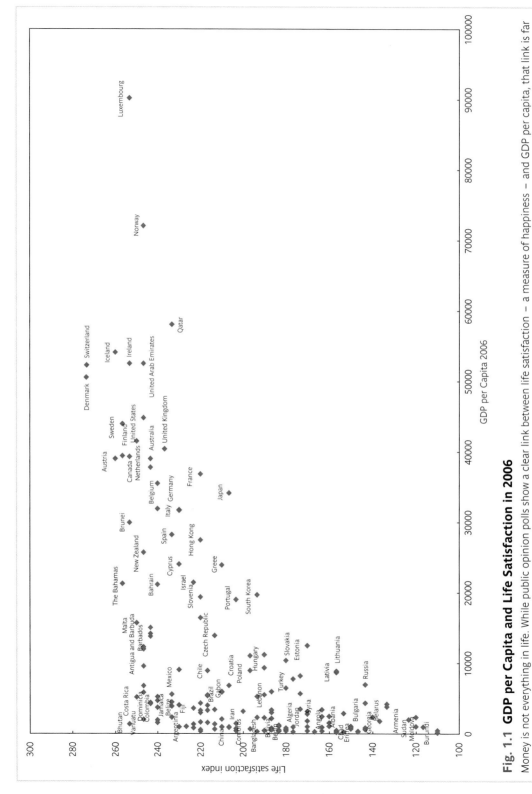

Fig. 1.1 GDP per Capita and Life Satisfaction in 2006

Money is not everything in life. While public opinion polls show a clear link between life satisfaction – a measure of happiness – and GDP per capita, that link is far from tight.

Sources: GDP per capita from World Economic Outlook, IMF; Index of satisfaction with life: http://en.wikipedia.org/wiki/Satisfaction_with_Life_Index

perhaps because their expectations are unreasonable? Or rather, are they desperately frustrated not to find a job? The answers to these questions will help us better understand this complex phenomenon.

Unemployment is generally not a pleasant affair. Even with well-developed and efficient unemployment assistance programmes, long-term jobless workers can experience emotional stress and their skills may deteriorate. Even if they are not measurable, the social and psychological costs of unemployment are high for the affected individuals and for society as a whole. By that criterion, Europe has not done well over the last decades, as Figure 1.2 shows. The average rate of unemployment has grown inexorably to reach double-digit numbers. In the USA, in contrast, unemployment has closely followed the business cycle, rising in periods of slowdown, declining when growth returned. At the same time, not all European countries have shared this misery, as the case of Switzerland shows. Chapters 5 and 18 will present explanations for these different outcomes.

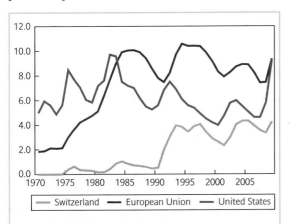

Fig. 1.2 Unemployment Rates in the European Union, Switzerland, and the USA, 1970–2009

The unemployment rate, measured as the proportion of workers who do not have a job but are looking for one, varies considerably across countries. In the USA, the unemployment rate moves tightly with the business cycle. In the European Union it rose markedly in the 1970s and 1980s and stayed there for a long time. In contrast, Switzerland avoided high unemployment for the entire period, but has also suffered a significant increase over the past two decades.
Source: OECD.

1.1.3 Factors of Production and Income Distribution

The output of an economy, its GDP, is by and large the result of work effort by men and women combined with equipment—'machines', but also buildings and other structures. **Labour** and **capital** are the technical names given to the two main **factors of production**, or inputs.[1] The distribution of total income between these two factors of production is often a political matter, even if it is largely determined by economic forces. Understandably, wage-earners wish to enlarge their share of the pie. In stock markets, ownership of companies, or shares, are traded in open markets and valued on the basis of the firms' profitability, or what is left after wages and other costs are paid. Figure 1.3 shows the share of income in manufacturing that goes to labour, the **labour share**. It also plots the evolution of the stock market **index** over the same period, which tracks the value of shares in companies traded on the stock exchange or bourse. An index is an indicator of the evolution of some phenomenon over time, designed to take a standardized value (e.g. 1 or 100) on a particular date to highlight relative changes. The figure reveals a clear, but not perfect, inverse relationship between the labour share and average stock prices. When the share of income going to labour is high, less is available for the firms' owners, and stock prices tend to be lower. While it would be premature to assert that one causes the other, it is certainly plausible that both are driven by common economic phenomena. In Chapter 8, we will see that depressed stock prices may adversely affect the accumulation of productive equipment and, ultimately, the growth and size of the economic pie itself.

1.1.4 Inflation

Inflation refers to the rate of change of the average level of prices. For comparability, the inflation rate is usually stated in terms of percentage change per year, even when it is measured more frequently, such as every quarter or every month. Most of the time,

---

[1]   Land, energy, intellectual property, and many other inputs also matter, but are quantitatively less important in macroeconomics and will be ignored to make matters simpler.

Fig. 1.3 Labour Share of Income in Manufacturing and Stock Prices, Four Countries, 1951 – 2007

Labour and capital share the fruits of the economic activity. The labour share is the fraction of economic output which is paid to workers in wages and other forms of compensation. The valuation of companies, reflected in stock prices, is negatively associated with the labour share.

Sources: OECD; IMF; US Department of Labor.

inflation is low or moderate at rates ranging from just above 0% to 4%. In the 1970s, many European countries experienced double-digit inflation, with rates rising to 10%, 20%, or even more. In a number of countries, for example in Latin America or in the transition countries of Eastern Europe, inflation rates of several hundred per cent were quite common in the 1980s. When inflation is very high it is usually measured on a monthly basis; the term **hyperinflation** describes situations when this monthly inflation rate exceeds 50%. A sign of exceptional economic distress, hyperinflation has been observed in Central Europe in the early 1920s, in Latin America in the 1980s, and in many countries which emerged from the collapse of the Soviet Union in the early 1990s.

In normal times, inflation is related to the business cycle. Figure 1.4 shows how the rate of inflation changes when the rate of **capacity utilization** varies. The rate of capacity utilization measures the degree to which companies are truly employing their available plant and equipment, and it serves as a good indicator of cyclical conditions. The inflation rate is generally **procyclical**: it tends to rise in periods of high growth and declines in periods of slow growth. In contrast, the unemployment rate is **countercyclical**: it moves against the cyclical behaviour of output,

falling when output is growing rapidly and rising when output is growing more slowly or falling. The behaviour of inflation is investigated in Parts III and IV of this book.

1.1.5 Financial Markets and the Real Economy

Financial markets play a central role in modern economies. Either literally or with the help of sophisticated communications technologies, they represent arenas where buyers and sellers of financial assets such as bonds, stocks, currencies, and other financial instruments meet to trade. Together with banks and other financial institutions, financial markets gather resources from households in the form of savings and lend them out to others who will spend them. One specific feature of these markets is the extreme day-to-day variability of prices at which financial instruments are traded.

Physical investment, the accumulation of productive capital by firms, is intimately related to financial conditions. It is one channel through which financial markets affect the **real economy**. The other channel is consumption spending by households. Stocks—shares in corporations—represent one form of private wealth. When share prices rise, people feel richer and consume

Fig. 1.4 Capacity Utilization Rates and Inflation, USA, 1962–2009
When measures of the utilization of capacity indicate a high level of activity in factories, the rate of inflation tends to increase. Conversely, low levels of activity are accompanied by declining rates of inflation.
Sources: IMF; OECD, Main Economic Indicators.

more. The real economy is contrasted with the financial or **monetary economy**: the former concerns the production and consumption of goods and services, and the incomes associated with productive activities; the latter deals with trade in assets, i.e. monetary and financial instruments. Chapter 10 brings the real and the monetary spheres of the economy together to understand how output and interest rates are determined from year to year. Chapter 11 explores these short-run linkages in more detail when the economy is open to international trade in financial assets. Chapters 12 and 13 bring together the issues of inflation, output, and exchange rate determination.

1.1.6 Openness

In the modern world, all countries engage in international trade by exporting and importing goods and services to and from each other. In addition, an increasing number of countries are also connected through trade in financial assets. One measure of a country's **openness**, or exposure to the various economic influences coming from the rest of the world, is the ratio of the average of its exports and imports to its GDP. Table 1.2 shows that openness has considerably increased over the past decades. This process of increasing trade and trade integration in goods, services, and financial assets over time is frequently called **globalization**. Smaller countries tend to be more open than larger countries, and indeed the USA and Japan are fairly closed by international standards. This is also the case of the European Union vis-à-vis the rest of the world, even though considerable trade integration has taken place among its member countries and with the rest of the world. Since mid-2004, the European Union has expanded to 27 nations to become an economic region of more than 500 million inhabitants. These substantial enlargements have further accentuated the importance of

 Table 1.2 Openness (ratio of average of exports and imports to GDP, %)

	1960	2010
European Union	6.1	16.8
United States	5.2	14.2
Japan	10.7	13.1
China (1)	—	15.3
Belgium	38.3	83.4
Denmark	32.7	54.4
Germany	19	47.7
Hungary	—	132.2
Ireland	30.6	87.0
Netherlands	46.3	83.4
Poland	—	40.3
Portugal	16	35.8
Russian Federation	—	25.9
Spain	8.9	32.7
Sweden	22.7	47.7
Switzerland	27.7	51.9
Ukraine	—	51.6
United Kingdom	20.9	28.4

(1) 2008 instead of 2010
Sources: IMF; OECD.

international trade, financial, and policy links between EU member countries.

As a consequence, no country's fate is truly independent of events that occur elsewhere, sometimes very far away. A good example is the financial crisis that began in the summer of 2007 in the USA but has spread not only to Europe and Asia but also to remote parts of Africa and South America. Chapter 19 looks more closely at these problems and potential solutions.

1.2 Macroeconomics in the Long Run: Economic Growth

Figure 1.5(a) displays estimates of GDP for France, Germany, and the UK since 1870. A positive long-run general tendency, or **trend**, clearly dominates shorter-run fluctuations. The trend rate of growth has been

Fig. 1.5 **Gross Domestic Product (GDP), France, Germany, and the UK, 1870–2010**

National output and income, as captured by the gross domestic product, exhibits a robust growth trend. Growth tends to be exponential; that is, annual percentage increases are reasonably stable in the long run. This does not preclude significant year-to-year variations. When the data are displayed on a logarithmic scale instead (panel b), the slope of the curve measures the annual rate of growth.

Source: The Conference Board and Groningen Growth and Development Centre, Total Economy Database, available at <www.conference-board.org/economics/database.cfm> and <www.eco.rug.nl>.

fairly stable, perhaps with a slight increase after the Second World War. Another way of seeing this is to plot the natural logarithm of GDP against time, as in panel (b) of Figure 1.5. With this so-called **logarithmic scale** the slope of the curve is a direct measure of the annual growth rate: a constant growth rate would yield a straight line.[2] In the long run, on average, we seem very close to a rather robust and steady trend.

This trend growth in total output implies remarkable increases in living standards. Let's take another look at Table 1.1. Note that per capita, or average, income increased to more than sixfold in Belgium since 1900, ninefold in Sweden, and 18-fold in Japan. Yet the growth phenomenon is not shared by all countries at all times. In Bangladesh, real income per capita rose by only 120% over the same period. Some countries have faced serious setbacks, such as wars and famines, while others have expanded rapidly. Some, like China and India, stagnated for many decades before suddenly entering a period of rapid

---

[2]   For mathematically inclined readers, if $x(t)$, the value of x at time t, grows at constant rate g, which is defined as $(1/x)dx/dt$, then $x(t) = Ae^{gt}$ and $\ln x(t) = \ln A + gt$, where A is a constant.

increase in living standards. China poses a particularly interesting case because its explosive take-off was so recent, and because it was the world's most advanced economy 700 years ago.

Because of the diverse nature of experience when studying the wealth of nations, **economic growth** is one of the most exciting issues in macroeconomics. Chapter 3 explores in detail the reasons why economies grow. One reason is an increase in population, since more people can work and produce more output. Another is the accumulation of means of production: plant and equipment, roads, communication networks, and other forms of infrastructure make workers more productive. Most important is the development and harnessing of knowledge and technology to economic ends. The sharp acceleration of scientific discoveries towards the end of the eighteenth century is thought to have triggered the industrial revolution, and some believe we are now witnessing the onset of a new wave of advances related to information and telecommunications technology.

1.3 Macroeconomics in the Short Run: Business Cycles

While output and income have increased by staggering amounts over many decades, this growth is not constant or even steady. A second important message contained in Figure 1.5 is that real output tends to fluctuate around its trend. This is even more apparent in Figure 1.6, which plots the quarterly rate of change in GDP for the UK. Quarterly data tend to accentuate the relative importance of short-run fluctuations. These sustained periods of ups and downs are called

business cycles. One important challenge of macroeconomics is to explain such deviations of GDP from its underlying trend. Why do these fluctuations occur and persist over periods ranging from three to ten years, and what can be done, if anything, to avoid the disruptions that are associated with them? This is the common theme of Parts III and IV of this book.

Macroeconomics has come to recognize that while business cycles are hardly identical across countries

Fig. 1.6 Quarterly Gross Domestic Product, UK, 1962:1 – 2010:4
With growth rates, fluctuations of economic activity become more apparent.
Sources: IMF; OECD.

and across time, they have a number of common features. These features can be summarized statistically, but they can also be represented in diagrams. The **Burns–Mitchell diagram** can help us organize our thoughts about these common features of the business cycle. The idea is simple. Imagine cutting up a series like those depicted in Figures 1.5 or 1.6 into a set of cycles. To do this, it is necessary to identify calendar dates for cyclical turning points of output (GDP)—here we will be concerned with peaks, but the procedure can be used for troughs as well. Having identified those cyclical peaks, simple numerical averages of other macroeconomic variables of interest can be calculated around the calendar date of the output's peak. The behaviour of those variables around the turning points of output tells us something about whether the variables are leading—meaning that they can help forecast future turning points in output. More importantly, they can help inform the formulation of theories which will help us better understand how business cycles arise and develop over time. Box 1.1 provides more details on the Burns–Mitchell methodology.

Box 1.1 Burns–Mitchell Diagrams, Now and Then

The sharp fluctuations of economic activity in the rapidly industrializing economies of Europe and the USA attracted the professional interest of many economists in the early part of the twentieth century. In the 1920s and 1930s, the National Bureau of Economic Research (NBER) in New York was a centre of such research, associated with Gottfried Haberler, Simon Kuznets, Wassily Leontief, Allyn Young, and many other economic luminaries of the day. A common view of these researchers was that the emergence of powerful statistical methods made it possible to study economic phenomena in general, and the business cycle in particular, in a more scientific fashion.

Two NBER researchers, Arthur Burns and Wesley Mitchell, were somewhat sceptical of the statistical approach but committed to a data-driven, descriptive assessment of business cycle regularities. Mitchell had already written a book in 1927 that more or less laid out the research programme, but together with Burns the project ultimately came to fruition after the Second World War. The idea was to reduce the time series of data to a sequence of cycles and then study the *average* behaviour of other important variables a number of periods before and after the peak of the average cycle. This highly data-intensive empirical approach was considered modern and useful, even if it was criticized in some quarters as 'measurement without theory'.

The identification of business cycles is always a tricky procedure with some element of arbitrariness. We employ a particular method which has gained acceptance in recent years and apply it to eight advanced economies over about 35 years of quarterly data.[3] The result is a reference cycle which appears in the first panel of Figure 1.7. The cycles identified by procedure are used to produce the other panels of Figure 1.7, which give the behaviour of variables 10 quarters before and 10 quarters after the cyclical peak, usually stated in proportion to the average value over that period. In Figure 1.8, we present the original findings of Burns and Mitchell, who worked on primarily monthly US data from the late nineteenth and especially the early twentieth century.

---

[3] The method is due to Harding and Pagan (2001) and can be summarized as follows. For a 4-quarter moving average of the original series, define a peak as the quarter for which GDP is higher than the two preceding and the two successive quarters. In case two or more consecutive peaks are found, only the highest is retained. Next examine the highest and lowest points in a neighbourhood of the peaks. Now repeat the procedure using an unweighted short-term moving average of the original series. In the neighbourhood of these intermediate turning points, troughs and peaks are determined in the unsmoothed time series. If these pass a set of additional restrictions on the magnitude of the fluctuation, they are selected as the final cyclical turning points.

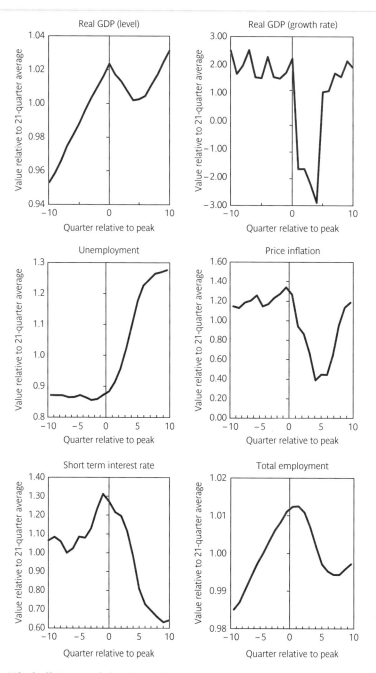

Fig. 1.7 Burns – Mitchell, Now: Eight Countries, 1970 – 2006

These six figures display the average behaviour of variables around cyclical peaks, where the cycle is measured using a procedure described in the text. The vertical line around zero shows the quarter in which real GDP hits its peak (upper left panel). The peak is followed on average by a sharp drop in the growth rate of output (upper right panel). Unemployment is countercyclical, rising most after the peak in GDP has been passed, but is rising across cycles, indicating that unemployment rates in the sample were increasing on average. The inflation rate is procyclical but lagging, peaking in the quarter after output. Short-term interest rates and employment are strongly procyclical.

Sources: OECD; authors' calculations.

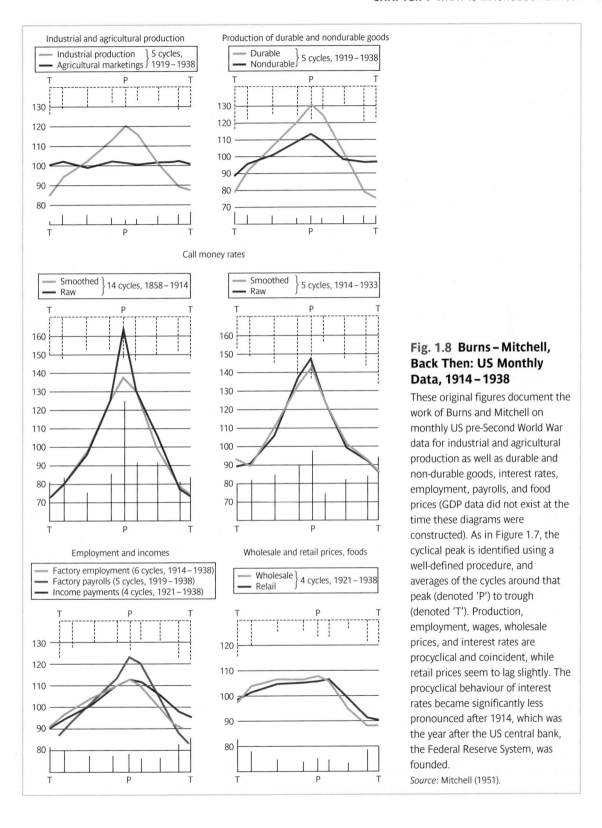

Fig. 1.8 Burns – Mitchell, Back Then: US Monthly Data, 1914 – 1938

These original figures document the work of Burns and Mitchell on monthly US pre-Second World War data for industrial and agricultural production as well as durable and non-durable goods, interest rates, employment, payrolls, and food prices (GDP data did not exist at the time these diagrams were constructed). As in Figure 1.7, the cyclical peak is identified using a well-defined procedure, and averages of the cycles around that peak (denoted 'P') to trough (denoted 'T'). Production, employment, wages, wholesale prices, and interest rates are procyclical and coincident, while retail prices seem to lag slightly. The procyclical behaviour of interest rates became significantly less pronounced after 1914, which was the year after the US central bank, the Federal Reserve System, was founded.

Source: Mitchell (1951).

1.4 Macroeconomics as a Science

1.4.1 The Genesis of Macroeconomics

Why do we observe cyclical fluctuations—ups and downs—in the level of GDP around its trend? Why is unemployment generally countercyclical, while changes in inflation appear procyclical? For a long time, economists paid little attention to such phenomena. In fact, it was believed that properly functioning markets would deliver the best possible outcome, to a good approximation at least, and that there was no point in looking into their aggregate behaviour. This principle was called '**laissez-faire**'. Laissez-faire was opposed by proponents of **interventionism**, who advocated government support for particular markets and industries, including subsidies and protection from foreign competition.

This does not mean that business cycles were ignored completely. In fact, cycles of varying lengths were identified and studied, ranging from inventory cycles of one or two years' duration to long-wave cycles lasting half a century. Box 1.2 provides details on these cyclical movements. Such cycles were seen as the cumulative outcomes of disturbances such as discoveries, inventions, exceptionally good or bad crops, wrong bets by firms on goods that customers want to buy, or even changing tastes of consumers at home and abroad. Inflation was seen as the consequence of rapidly growing money stocks, first because of gold discoveries in the nineteenth century, afterwards because of reckless paper money creation by central banks. As will be seen in Chapter 16, much of this wisdom remains valid today. Yet the Great Depression of the 1930s, which spread throughout the world and sent millions into unemployment and misery, seemed too severe to be simply bad luck. Reflecting upon the Great Depression in 1936, British economist John Maynard Keynes published *The General Theory of Employment, Interest and Money*, a book that is often said to have started the field of macroeconomics. Keynes stressed the role of aggregate demand in macroeconomic fluctuations. His followers later persuaded policy-makers to engage in **aggregate demand management**, that is, to manipulate government demand

 Box 1.2 All Kinds of Cycles

Business cycles, like comets, bear the names of their discoverers. Simon Kuznets (1901–1985) was a Russian-born US economist who received a Nobel Prize for his work on growth. Russian economist Nikolai Kondratieff (1892–1938) developed his theory of long-wave cycles in the 1920s before he was arrested and disappeared; the official Soviet Encyclopaedia then wrote about his work: 'this theory is wrong and reactionary'. It was also in the 1920s that Joseph Kitchin (1861–1932), a South African statistician and gold trader, uncovered his own more rapid cycles of 2–4 years periodicity, which are associated with inventory movements, bank clearings, and wholesale prices. Clement Juglar (1819–1905), a nineteenth-century French physician, first studied cycles in human births, deaths, and marriages before turning his skills to interest rates and credit conditions. These Juglar cycles—which involve fluctuations of investment spending, GNP, inflation, and unemployment—are perhaps the closest thing to the business cycle that we will study in this book.

Interestingly, one of the most robust and regular cycles in economic activity is the seasonal cycle, which coincides with the seasons of the year. Movements of output in agriculture, manufacturing, construction, and tourism have obvious seasonal components which sometimes swamp business cycle fluctuations in magnitude, as do patterns in overall output associated with bank holidays, summer and winter weather, and harvests.

in order to smooth out fluctuations, mainly to avoid protracted recessions.

An evaluation of the success of demand management policies, presented in Chapters 16 and 17, suggests that there have been both benefits and costs. Since the Second World War, the amplitude of the business cycle appears to have diminished considerably, as can be seen in Figure 1.5. Of course, the global recession of 2008–9, sometimes called the 'Great Recession', is a major setback and a challenge to conventional wisdom. For centuries, earlier generations assumed that favourable periods of growth were inevitably followed by periods of declining activity;

current generations worry mostly about slowdowns of growth. At the same time, economists have also begun to think hard about the **supply side**—meaning the productive capacity of an economy—and more efficient utilization of labour and capital resources. This applies especially to unemployment, which remains a big problem in Europe. These topics are the subject of Chapter 18.

Another remarkable change in the behaviour of the post-war economy concerns the general **price level**, or the cost of goods in terms of money. Until the First World War, prices were as likely to rise as they were to fall, as can be seen from Figure 1.9.

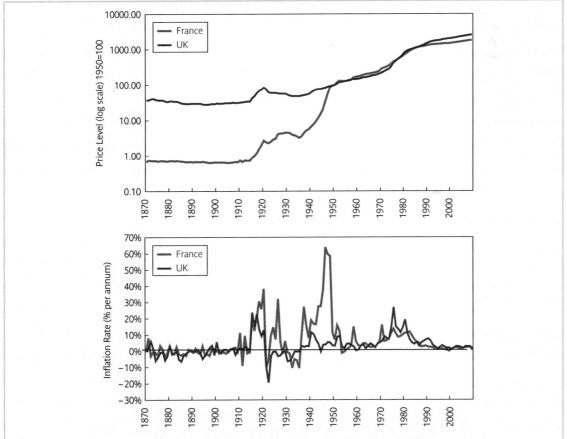

Fig. 1.9 Price Levels and Inflation Rates, France and the UK, 1870–2009

Until the outbreak of the First World War, the price level was stable, and inflation was close to zero on average. Since the Second World War, the price level has risen secularly, average inflation has been positive, high in the late 1970s and much of the 1980s, declining over the 1990s.

Sources: Maddison (1991); OECD.

Apart from war periods, the price level was trendless; over long periods of 20 to 50 years, the cost of living—a measure of the average price level—was remarkably stable. One interpretation of the post-war era—a controversial one, as we shall see—is that macroeconomics has led to more steady output growth at the cost of inflation. In the mid-1980s, concern with high inflation triggered a change of heart. In particular, most central banks have toned down Keynesian policies and refocused their energy on keeping inflation low. The crisis that stared in 2007 is now forcing central banks to recognize that they have a broader duty than price stability; in particular, they have to be concerned with financial stability and the health of the banking system.

1.4.2 Macroeconomics and Microeconomics

The macroeconomy is just the sum of hundreds or thousands of markets, each of which is explained by microeconomic principles. Microeconomics is devoted to the study of prices of individual goods and of the markets where these goods are produced and sold. Why do we need two separate disciplines? To a great extent they are linked. Microeconomics is dedicated to the analysis of market behaviour of individuals. Macroeconomics is concerned with collective behaviour, the outcome of individual decisions taken without full knowledge of what others do. Keynes stressed the notion of **coordination failures**, which arise in decentralized markets as illustrated in the following example.

A consumer wants to purchase a car, but his income is insufficient for him to do so. A car manufacturer could actually hire him to build cars, and with his salary he would then be able to buy one. That one sale, however, would not suffice to pay his salary, so other buyers would need to be found. In order to generate sufficient demand for his employment, several other individuals would need to be hired, perhaps in different industries. For this scheme to work, a considerable amount of coordination among producers and consumers would be required. The laissez-faire principle is that prices and markets automatically and perfectly perform this coordinating role.

Keynes' critique of markets was that sometimes they fail to produce the desired result as quickly as we would like to see. There may be many consumers wishing to buy goods and willing to work to produce them, and many firms that would benefit from hiring them if only they could be persuaded that their sales would increase. But this potential may not be realized and we have both recession (fewer sales) and unemployment (fewer jobs). Even if market forces tend to correct this imbalance—which they eventually do—the period of time necessary may be long enough to involve significant social costs.

Macroeconomics started with the idea that prices and markets do not continuously resolve all the coordination requirements of a modern economy. As microeconomics has moved in this direction too, the sharp distinction between the two fields has faded. Modern macroeconomics starts from sound microeconomic principles, and we follow this approach in the early chapters. We then focus on market failures to study business cycles and what can be done about them.

1.4.3 Macroeconomics and Economic Policy

Early macroeconomists argued that governments have the means and the duty to correct market failures. The experiences of the past decades have shown that governments too may fail. Indeed, one major dividing line among macroeconomists is between those who primarily fear market failures on the one side, and those who primarily fear government failures on the other. Yet, in nearly every country, governments are held responsible for the good health of the economy. At election times incumbent governments are judged, first among many other issues, on their economic performance. This is largely a consequence of the **Keynesian revolution**. It explains why the study of macroeconomics is so intertwined with policy and politics.

1.4.4 Demand and Supply

In its most concentrated form, macroeconomics boils down to separating events into two categories: (1) those that affect the demand for goods and services, and (2) those that affect the supply of those goods and services. The **demand side** relates to spending decisions by **economic agents**—households, firms, and government agencies—both at home and abroad. The principle of aggregate demand management policies is that the government can take actions to offset or smooth out those of private agents—firms and households—in order to dampen or eliminate fluctuations in total spending. The idea is to take the edge off recessions as well as booms. Two traditional demand management instruments are fiscal and monetary policy. **Fiscal policy** manipulates government expenditures or taxes in an attempt to affect the volume of national spending. This subject is studied in detail in Chapter 17. **Monetary policy** is directed at influencing interest and exchange rates, and more generally conditions in financial markets. This in turn affects spending on goods and services. Chapter 9 provides an in-depth analysis of money and monetary policy.

The **supply side** relates to the productive potential of the economy. The choice of hours worked by households, the productivity of their labour, and in general the efficiency with which resources are allocated in generating output, all affect an economy's aggregate supply. Accordingly, supply-side policies represent government's effort to increase an economy's long-run capacity as well as its overall efficiency. Frequently, this effort is about reducing or eliminating government-induced inefficiencies, which were introduced before the importance of the supply side was understood, or as the result of successful lobbying by interest groups. It is also about bringing idle or underutilized resources into productive uses. Unemployment policy—designed to fight the scourge of market economies—occupies a key role in the supply side. Chapter 18 explores these issues and shows how the government can improve or worsen the economic climate.

1.5 **The Methodology of Macroeconomics**

1.5.1 **What is to be Explained?**

Macroeconomics is concerned with aggregate activity, the level of unemployment, interest rates, inflation, wages, the exchange rate, and the balance of payments with other countries. As a scientific undertaking, macroeconomics deals with phenomena which can have highly complex channels of causation. Let's consider an example. In this book you will learn that inflation affects the **exchange rate** (the value of our currency). You will also learn that the inflation rate is also affected *by* the exchange rate.

Before beginning to think about these questions, it is essential to be clear about what we want to explain and what we take as given, or outside the realm of analysis. The variables to be explained using economic principles are called **endogenous** variables. The other variables—those we do not try to explain—are called **exogenous** variables. This distinction is represented in Figure 1.10. Examples of variables often considered exogenous are policy instruments (the tools of fiscal and monetary policies), economic

conditions abroad (foreign levels of activity and interest rates), the price of oil, and sometimes even domestic social conditions such as business optimism or trade union militancy.

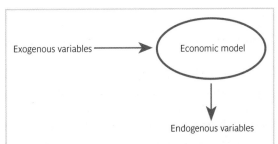

Fig. 1.10 Endogenous and Exogenous Variables

Endogenous variables are the object of analysis in an economic model. Exogenous variables are determined outside the economic model. The weather, political decisions, and the onset of time are examples of variables generally considered to be exogenous.

The distinction between endogenous and exogenous variables is necessarily arbitrary. Many exogenous variables are not strictly independent of the endogenous variables. Because the analysis occurs in steps, many variables initially considered exogenous are later made endogenous, or endogenized. For example, fiscal and monetary policy decisions are often responses to the course of inflation or unemployment. While it is convenient to take policy variables as exogenous, it is sometimes interesting and useful to understand how these exogenous variables themselves are determined. We will treat monetary policy as a systematic response to economic conditions.

1.5.2 Theory and Realism

Macroeconomics proceeds by making simplifying assumptions. We never literally believe in our assumptions, but we need them in order to see through the vast complexity of an economy. This is why the distinction between endogenous and exogenous variables is artificial. Truly exogenous variables are rare. Two examples are climatic conditions (and even these may be affected by economic events, such as the greenhouse effect) and scientific discoveries and inventions (which also may result from economic decisions). The task of systematically linking the behaviour of endogenous variables to changes in exogenous variables is accomplished by specifying relationships between all the variables of interest. You might say that economics—and in particular macroeconomics—is in the business of establishing relationships involving causality.

All these relationships, when brought together, constitute a theory. Almost by definition, in social sciences, theory must be an abstraction, an intentional departure from realism. If the real world could be understood without simplifying assumptions, theories would be unnecessary. The problem is not with economics, but rather with the world's inherent complexity. Karl Marx, who was no friend of conventional political economy, seemed to hit it on the head:

The body in its entirety is easier to study than are the cells of that body. In the analysis of economic forms, moreover, neither microscopes nor chemical reagents are of use. The force of abstraction must replace both. ((1867) Foreword to Volume I.)

Progress is made by weeding out those assumptions and theories that lead us to false conclusions. As time passes, some theories prove to be unfounded, while others gain acceptability. This process is long and complex, and far from complete. Because macroeconomics is a young discipline, a number of controversies continue to dominate, and this aspect is discussed in Section 1.6.

1.5.3 Positive and Normative Analysis

Macroeconomic analysis and policy are closely linked. Because a number of exogenous variables are under the control of government, it makes sense to ask what is good and what is bad policy. At its best, macroeconomics can explain the economy. For example, it can link particular events to exogenous events or policy decisions. This is **positive economics**: it refrains from value judgements. **Normative economics** takes a further step and passes judgement or makes policy recommendations. In so doing, it must specify what criteria are used in arriving at particular conclusions. This inevitably implies a value judgement. Economists generally like to make policy recommendations. As long as they are truthful about their own preferences and reveal their criteria, this is part of their professional activity. In this textbook, we will generally refrain from normative economic analysis.[4] At the same time, we believe and hope that many readers will make use of their newly acquired knowledge to indulge in the normative side of macroeconomics: this is what makes it fun.

1.5.4 Testing Theories: The Role of Data

The generally accepted way of evaluating theories is to subject them to scientific testing. In macroeconomics, this means looking at the facts, i.e. at data. This is easier said than done, and there are a number of unusual difficulties. First, data correspond to sometimes elusive concepts, as Chapter 2 will show. Second, constructing aggregate data implies enquiring into the behaviour of millions of individuals, who sometimes have good or bad reasons to misrepresent

---

[4] Many are motivated by 'social conscience' to study economics. Much like idealistic health professionals who want to cure the sick, economists can also be interested in ways to provide relief to the disadvantaged and suffering.

the truth. Third, economics shares the predicament common to other social sciences that experimentation is not really possible—when observed, people often change their behaviour. Not only is it possibly immoral—no macroeconomist would wish to start a hyperinflation just to test a theory—but more crucially, many important variables simply are not observable. This is the case of people's expectations of the future, for example. Macroeconomists are forced to conduct empirical tests with the data that they have. They develop statistical techniques, often sophisticated ones, to deal with observation and measurement errors. They refine their techniques for gathering and analysing data. This allows the elimination of inadequate theories and the modification of others. The surviving theories will be those that withstand the test of time in this scientific process.

1.5.5 Macroeconomic Modelling and Forecasting

Economists are frequently asked to make forecasts. Governments, international organizations, and large financial institutions frequently employ large teams of economists to prepare forecasts. If macroeconom-

ics were to be judged by the performance of forecasts, the verdict would not be unkind. However, the respectable track record of forecasters has been sullied by some large historical errors. Box 1.3 illustrates this fact by examining the accuracy of forecasts, after the fact, for the disastrous crisis years 2009 and 2010.

There are several reasons why economic forecasting is inherently difficult. First, even an excellent understanding of an economy's structure—how its endogenous variables interact—can fall victim to unexpected changes in exogenous variables. Good examples of this are the oil price increases of 1973 and 2000, the high-tech crash of 2001 and, of course, the latest crisis. Second, expectations—which are volatile in nature—wield an important influence over the economy. Governments sometimes react to their own forecasts by implementing policies designed to prevent those forecasts from happening. Political changes occur quickly and can disrupt the economic environment. Finally, it takes time—often several months—to know what has really happened at any given point, so forecasts are always based on provisional information which becomes more precise only with time.

 Box 1.3 Forecasting the Crisis Years

Economic forecasts can be wrong, and often spectacularly so. Table 1.3 presents a few examples about the crisis years. The collapse of the investment bank Lehman Brothers in September 2008 triggered banking crises in the US and Europe. The result was a deep, unforeseeable recession in 2009. Determined action by governments and central banks often limited the recession to just one year. The table shows how forecasts of GDP growth have changed over time. We use the forecasts published every six months by the Organization for Economic Cooperation and Development (OECD), an organization of industrialized countries. These forecasts usually reflect the consensus of professional public and private forecasters. The eventual outcome is also shown.

The Year 2009

The financial crisis began in mid-2007, but was hardly noticed and downplayed by most analysts at the time.

This explains why the initial GDP growth forecasts, produced in December 2007, were fairly optimistic. Six months later, in June 2008, concern started to grow for the US and Europe, but it was perceived that the rest of the world (here Japan and Korea) would not be much affected. The December 2008 forecast, after the Lehman collapse, became alarmist but, with hindsight, still much too optimistic.

The Year 2010

The initial forecasts, in December 2008, correctly expected that the recession would only last one year; they projected relatively modest but positive growth rates for 2010. However, as 2009 turned out much worse than expected, in mid-2009 forecasters became overly pessimistic and revised downward their numbers for 2010. The last forecasts, from December 2009, show that pessimism had declined, yet they remained too pessimistic.

Table 1.3 **GDP Growth Forecasts, 2009 and 2010 (% per annum)**

2009	France	Germany	Japan	Korea	UK	USA
Forecast (December 2007)	2.0	1.6	1.8	5.1	2.4	2.2
Forecast (June 2008)	1.5	1.1	1.5	5.0	1.4	1.1
Forecast (December 2008)	−0.4	−0.8	−0.1	2.7	−1.1	−0.9
Actual Outcome	−2.7	−4.7	−6.3	0.3	−4.9	−2.6
2010	**France**	**Germany**	**Japan**	**Korea**	**UK**	**USA**
Forecast (December 2008)	1.5	1.2	0.6	4.2	0.9	1.6
Forecast (June 2009)	0.2	0.2	0.7	3.5	0.0	0.9
Forecast (December 2009)	1.4	1.4	1.8	4.4	1.2	2.5
Actual Outcome	1.4	3.5	4.0	6.2	1.3	2.9

Source: OECD, Economic Outlook.

Most forecasts are generated by computer-based models. These models resemble those that we present in this book. They are made of hundreds, sometimes thousands, of equations. Constructing these equations is a long and difficult task. The exogenous variables must be guessed by forecasters before they can ask their computers for an answer. This introduces many margins of error. The models can never be fully reliable, and the exogenous variables may be difficult to pinpoint. For these reasons, the forecasters themselves take their results with a grain of salt, and often, when the outcome is not completely satisfactory, 'drop in' their own subjective factor to the results.

1.6 Preview of the Book

1.6.1 Structure

The book proceeds in steps. Parts I–III build up an understanding of the measurement and the behaviour of the underlying economy. Part I is concerned mostly with defining terms and constructing a macroeconomic vocabulary. Part II studies the behaviour of the economy in the long run: growth and output, labour markets, and prices and exchange rates. Part III develops our understanding of macroeconomy in the short run, that is, from quarter to quarter or from year to year. This part spans many subjects, ranging from the demand of households and firms for goods and services, the financial system, the short-run determination of output, interest rates, and the exchange rate. It also extends the analysis to include the analysis of inflation, output, asset prices, and exchange rates over a longer horizon. It introduces a framework for thinking about inflation and the business cycle. Part IV then uses this framework to explore policy issues facing governments: demand management, fiscal policy, and macroeconomic policies designed to enhance long-run performance. The book concludes with an extensive look at the world international financial system, and the state of economic thought late in the first decade of the twenty-first century.

1.6.2 Controversies and Consensus

Economists often make a bad name for themselves by quarrelling in public. Visible disagreements among economists frequently have to do with finer points, if not outright hair-splitting. This discourse is intellectually healthy, but misleading to outside observers, whose opinions are often based on accounts in the popular press and more apt to recall sensational talk-show appearances rather than sober analysis of theory and data. It is unfortunate that many disagreements have important policy implications. Perhaps as a result, politicians often see economics as a sort of debating event, with economists acting as advocates for one particular ideology or another, and may even abuse economists' opinions to get a stamp of approval for a particular policy.

In this textbook we do not shy away from presenting some of the most important disagreements among economists, leaving the reader free to judge. Yet we do not dwell upon these controversies either, choosing to focus rather on the common ground. Because there is so much that is not controversial, it is best first to understand the broad areas of consensus. Box 1.4 provides more details.

1.6.3 Rigour and Intuition

The only possible scientific approach to the complexities of the real world is the rigour of reasoning. However, to be useful, macroeconomics must be versatile and easily put to work when we want to understand particular events. This is why a great deal of macroeconomics amounts to the organized accumulation of intuition about particular phenomena. Our objective is, therefore, to leave readers with a natural understanding of how the economy functions. We do this by trying to draw robust yet simple conclusions from the various and often intricate principles presented. Such intuition is never completely rigorous, but can be useful in practice. Rigour plays a crucial

---

 Box 1.4 Macroeconomic Schools of Thought: A Primer

Almost from the beginning, macroeconomics has been divided into two main schools of thought. Keynesians (and their neo-Keynesian heirs) and monetarists (and neo-monetarists) continue to pursue the old debate about the role of the marketplace and government in society. Keynesians are more likely to believe that markets function imperfectly and that governments can and should use economic policy actively to combat recessions. Monetarists[5] tend to reject this view, seeing politics and the power of bureaucracies as barriers to government efforts to steer the economy away from business cycles and more generally market failures, which they see as either unavoidable or of lesser importance. Given these premises, each school uses theories and data to build and support its case.

These labels are not exclusive. In the USA reference is sometimes made to saltwater versus freshwater macroeconomists. Saltwater economists come from universities located on the two US seaboards (Harvard, MIT, Yale, Stanford, Berkeley) and tend to defend the Keynesian legacy. Freshwater economists are more frequently associated with monetarism and laissez-faire; they hail from universities located near the Great Lakes, e.g. Chicago, Rochester, or Minnesota. In Europe, similar controversies characterize national, and increasingly European, debates. National traditions tend to make British and French economists more Keynesian, while German or Swedish economists are more monetarist. Dutch, Italian, and Spanish economists are hard to classify, having as many exceptions as examples for any rule. In recent years, the differences have tended to diminish, both among researchers and policy-makers and a synthesis was in sight. Then the Great Recession came, which for predictable reasons led to a new polarization of views on theory and policy.

---

[5] The term 'monetarist' derives from the Latin '*moneta*' signalling their original emphasis on excess money growth as the sole cause of inflation. Now the term is sometimes applied to those who advocate unregulated markets and criticize government intervention at both the microeconomic and the macroeconomic level.

role in telling us when our intuition is correct, and when it is leading us astray.

1.6.4 Data and Institutions

Macroeconomics is fascinating because it tells us a great deal about the world in which we live. It is not merely a set of abstract principles with interesting logical properties. Many theories will look odd at first sight, yet they capture key aspects of the real world. This is why at each important step we pause to look at facts. Facts can be data or particular episodes. Studying them carefully shows how theories work and shape our understanding of macroeconomic phenomena. It broadens our knowledge of important events that have shaped the lives of millions of people.

On the other hand, a graph or a table is no substitute for more rigorous analysis of the data. Merely demonstrating that two economic variables move closely together is a far cry from proving that one causes the other. Our motive in using data to illustrate economic phenomena is to give readers a feel for economics itself. On our website we offer a list of suggested reading for each chapter—which is by no means meant to be exhaustive—for those who want to learn more about the theory and practice of macroeconomics.

Finally, good economic theories must be valid under different conditions. At the same time, the response of different countries to economic shocks is often shaped by their particular economic and political institutions. These include their form of government, the existence of labour unions and employers' associations, and regulations. The interplay of macroeconomic principles and institutions is an essential part of a proper understanding of the field, and this is why we spend a lot of time reviewing them.

The economics of these institutions is, however, far beyond the level of this textbook.

1.6.5 Europe

Our textbook bears the subtitle 'A European Text'. Does this mean that we think that macroeconomics in Europe is fundamentally different from macroeconomics in the USA, Asia, or Latin America? Most certainly not! To the contrary, we take the view that macroeconomics is sufficiently global in scope to apply to economies around the world. This includes the transforming economies of Central and Eastern Europe as well as the newly emerging economies of Southern and Eastern Asia. On the other hand, we do wish to send a more subtle signal: we believe strongly that European economies have important distinguishing features that make them hard to study through the lens of, say, the leading textbooks from North America.

There is much in Europe that warrants such a European emphasis. Rather than a collection of states under a federal government, Europe is a mosaic of nation-states, each with a sovereign macroeconomic policy-maker, but also with distinct preferences and endowments. The completion of the Single European Market, the creation of a monetary union, and the significant enlargement of the European Union will increase the pressure towards integration, raising specific new challenges along the way. To varying degrees, European countries also share a common view of the relationship between market forces and social justice. The attachment to fairness and economic solidarity is deeply ingrained in Europe's traditions and history, which explain why her labour markets differ so much from those in the USA. This observation alone warrants a markedly different perspective, even if the underlying theory is the same.

🔑 Key Concepts

- macroeconomics
- gross domestic product (GDP)
- trend

- logarithmic scale
- economic growth
- business cycle

- **Burns – Mitchell diagram**
- **unemployment**
- **unemployment rate**
- **labour force**
- **labour**
- **capital**
- **factors of production**
- **labour share**
- **index, index number**
- **inflation**
- **hyperinflation**
- **capacity utilization**
- **procyclical and countercyclical**
- **real economy, monetary economy**

- **laissez-faire versus interventionism**
- **aggregate demand management**
- **price level**
- **coordination failures**
- **Keynesian revolution**
- **demand side**
- **economic agents**
- **fiscal policy**
- **monetary policy**
- **supply side**
- **exchange rate**
- **endogenous**
- **exogenous**
- **positive and normative economics**

→ Media

Students can greatly benefit from reading daily the economic section of their newspaper. Some publications with high-quality analyses (but not free of prejudices) are (in English): the *Financial Times* and *The Economist*. There is also a wealth of information on the internet. See our website for further hints.

Data are produced by national statistical institutes and central banks. Some international institutions produce comparable data and are of easy access: the IMF's *International Financial Statistics* and its biannual survey *World Economic Outlook*, the OECD's biannual *Economic Outlook*, the World Bank's *World Development Report* and *Global Economic Prospects*, the European Commission's *European Economy*, and the European Bank for Reconstruction and Development's annual *Transition Report*. All maintain websites, more or less generous in allowing access to their data and publications.

Macroeconomic Accounts | 2

Facts and theories meet in analysis. The combination of the two is essential if economics is to progress, since it is neither a pure subject, like mathematics, of which one does not ask that the theories should be applicable to actual phenomena, nor is it a collection of facts, like the objects on a junk heap, of which one does not ask how they are related.

Richard Stone[1]

2.1 Overview

Every science has its own special language; not necessarily to exclude non-experts, but to make discussion more meaningful and precise. In this chapter we will start learning to speak the language of macroeconomics. We first provide a quantitative description of the economy and definitions of more frequently used concepts. As a natural point of departure, the chapter begins with a discussion of the national income accounts and **accounting identities**—how magnitudes we are interested in relate to each other, by construction. The national income accounts play a central role throughout the study of macroeconomics.

Chapter 2 will be limited to a description of what happens in an economy. Knowing the facts and how these facts are measured are essential for understanding the underlying behaviour of aggregate magnitudes. The distinction between description (this chapter) and analysis (the rest of the book) is similar to that found in biology. As was already noted in Chapter 1, it is important to know that living organisms consist of a collection of different cells; yet this biological description is only a first step. Analysing and understanding how cells function and affect each other is vastly more important. In a similar way, decomposing the gross domestic product into its components and examining the external accounts describe interactions and relationships without explaining how or why. That is the job of subsequent analytic chapters. It is thus unavoidable to spend time with these definitions. As we shall frequently see, there is much more to them than first meets the eye.

2.2 Gross Domestic Product

2.2.1 Three Definitions of Gross Domestic Product

The **gross domestic product** (GDP) is a measure of productive activity. It is defined for a particular geographic area—usually a country, but possibly a region or a city, or a group of countries such as the European Union (EU) or the euro area. It is also defined over a time interval, usually a year or a quarter. This is because the GDP is a **flow variable**, much like the amount of water flowing down a river. Flow variables differ from **stock variables**, which are always defined with reference to a particular point in time, such as the quantity of water held back by a dam.[2]

It turns out that there are three ways to measure GDP, and a different definition corresponds to each. Our first definition of GDP is the sum of all final

[1] Sir Richard Stone (1913–1991) of Cambridge University received the Nobel Prize in Economics in 1984 and is generally regarded as the father of national income accounting.

[2] Another example of a stock variable is a company's balance sheet, which measures its financial state at a single point in time, say 31 December. A corresponding example of a flow variable is an income statement, which records the profit or loss attributed to the firm over a time period, say 1 January to 31 December.

sales of goods and services sold during the measurement period.

Definition 1

GDP = the sum of final sales within a geographic location during a period of time, usually a year.

This definition refers specifically to **final sales**, i.e. goods and services sold to the consumer or firm that will ultimately use them. For example, the purchase of a loaf of bread or a motor car by a household is a final sale. In contrast, a car sold to a dealer which is subsequently resold during the measurement period, or a loaf of bread purchased by a grocery store which is later sold to a household are not final but **intermediate sales**. Intermediate sales are excluded from GDP to avoid double counting. For this reason, GDP should never be confused with total sales, or turnover. Consistent with this approach, exports are always counted as final sales regardless of how the foreigners use them, because they leave the geographic borders of the national economy.

Our second definition of GDP recognizes that each final sale of a good or service represents the ultimate step that validates all the efforts that have gone into producing and making it available to the buyer. It encompasses a chain of economic activities which are each seen as **value added**.

Definition 2

GDP = the sum of value added occurring within a given geographic location during a period of time.

A firm creates value added by transforming raw materials and unfinished goods into products it can sell in the market place. The firm's value added is the difference between its sales (turnover) and the costs of raw materials, unfinished goods, and imports from abroad. If the firm produces intermediate goods, its sales are costs to its customers, who themselves are producers. This value added should not be counted twice, and it is deducted from those customers' own sales in computing its own value added. When the final consumer purchases a good or a service in the market, the price includes all the value added created at each stage in the production process; hence the consistency between Definitions 1 and 2. Box 2.1 uses a concrete example to show how various productive activities contribute to a country's total value added.

GDP includes all incomes earned within a country's borders—by residents and non-residents alike. Because one person's final spending must be someone else's income, the third definition of GDP is also consistent with the first.

Definition 3

GDP = the sum of factor incomes earned from economic activities within a geographic location during a period of time.

GDP statistics are mentioned constantly in the financial and political press. The GDP, and in particular, its rate of growth, are generally considered to be the most important indicators of an economy's health, and their evolution is closely watched by managers, economists, and politicians. They allow us to study the performance of a single economy over time as well as to compare different countries. Three important points are worth mentioning:

(1) For comparison over time, we want to distinguish two reasons why GDP can increase: (1) more real economic activity and (2) higher prices for the same economic activity. This aspect is taken up in Section 2.2.2.

(2) For comparison across countries, we need to convert all GDP measures into a common currency. But, as we will see later, exchange rates are quite volatile and may give a faulty picture. For that reason, we usually use the concept of purchasing power parity, which is presented in Chapter 6.

(3) Small countries tend to have small GDPs, and yet they may be well-off. This is why we often look at **GDP per capita**, dividing the GDP measures by the population.

The definition of GDP contains a fair amount of arbitrariness, and it is open to debate whether every positive movement in GDP constitutes an improvement in national well-being. All the same, it is the best indicator we have. More details on this controversial issue are provided in Box 2.2.

2.2.2 Real versus Nominal Quantities, Deflators versus Price Indices

Real and nominal GDP

Now that we know what GDP is and how GDP data are constructed, we can immediately see how the

Box 2.1 Value Added and Value Subtracted: Two Examples

Consider the following example of value added. A keg of beer is produced and sold for final use by consumers at the price of €100. It is useful to break up this final sale into the steps of value added which were involved in its production. First, a brewery bought barley from a farmer, paying €10, used and paid for energy in the brewing process with a value of €20, and bought a keg from a keg manufacturer at a cost of €5. (For simplicity, the intermediate inputs of the farmer, energy producer, and keg manufacturer are assumed to be zero.) The beer is sold to a wholesaler for €80, so the brewery's own contribution to value added per keg is €45, given by his sale price (€80) less costs of inputs (€10 + €20 + €5 = €35). Next, the wholesaler sells the filled keg for €90 to a retailer, contributing value added of €10. The retailer sells the keg for €100, generating €10 of value added on his own. Summing up, the final price can be broken down into value added at each stage of production and delivery of the final good:

Value added contributed by the:

Farmer	€10
Energy producer	€20
Keg manufacturer	€5
Brewery	€45
Wholesaler	€10
Retailer	€10
Sum	€100

Each step in the value added chain represents a source of income for factors of production involved. Suppose

for example that the brewer had labour costs of €35 (wages and salaries as well as social security contributions) and €5 in beer taxes. Then the brewery's activity led to profits of €5, which are the income to the owners—assuming there were no further costs such as interest on loans, royalties for brands or trademarks, or rent. Similarly, if the wholesaler had no costs (employees, rent, or interest), the €10 of value added would represent his income, which can also be thought of as the profit which he receives as owner of the business. The example shows how the division of the value added is arbitrary and potentially separable from the issue of whether value added is generated at all.

Because value added is the source of income for labour, capital and other factors of production, few economic activities could survive very long if they *subtracted* value, i.e. if sales did not even cover material input costs. Not only would labour and capital not receive income for their efforts, but also someone would have to pay for the operating loss on each unit of output sold. Yet there are many examples of value subtraction. In the centrally planned economies before the fall of communism, many industries were requested to sell cheaply. As a result, firms produced too little goods of poor quality, exemplified by the Trabant car which citizens of the German Democratic Republic had to wait for years. In capitalist countries, some public services are thought to be worth less than they cost, but this is not visible because they have no price and the costs are covered by taxpayers.

national income statisticians have solved the problem of adding up apples and oranges: the solution is to use *prices* to convert volumes (the numbers of apples and oranges) into values (sales of apples and oranges). Suppose an economy produces only these two goods and requires no imports. Final sales of apples and oranges are obtained by multiplying the quantities of apples and oranges sold, Q^a and Q^o, by their respective prices, P^a and P^o, yielding **nominal GDP**, or GDP at current prices:

(2.1)   nominal GDP = $P^a Q^a + P^o Q^o$.

Yet there is a slight problem: If the price of oranges increases from one year to the next, nominal GDP rises even while the volume of final sales has not changed at all! An increase in nominal GDP can result from either higher prices *or* more output. To separate the effects of output and price movements, national income accountants distinguish between nominal and **real GDP**. Increases in real GDP correspond to increases in physical output, the number of apples and oranges produced and sold. Whereas nominal GDP is computed, as in (2.1), using the actual selling prices, real GDP is computed by using prices observed in some agreed base year.[3] In our example, if prices of apples and oranges were P_0^a and P_0^b in the base year, the real GDP in year t, when net final sales of apples and oranges are Q_0^a and Q_0^b is:

(2.2)   real GDP$_t = P_0^a Q_t^a + P_0^b Q_t^b$

This distinction is very general and applies to all macroeconomic variables: nominal variables represent values at current prices; real variables represent volumes at constant prices. As an example, Table 2.1 reports growth rates of nominal and real GDP for the euro area.[4]

Price deflators and indices

The distinction between nominal and real GDP can be used as a measure of the general price level, or the price of goods in terms of money. The **GDP deflator**, one way of measuring the price level at some particular time, is simply the ratio of nominal to real GDP:

(2.3)   GDP deflator = nominal GDP/real GDP.

In the base year, nominal and real GDP coincide and the GDP deflator equals 1.0. (Sometimes it is multiplied by 100 for ease of comparison over the years.) It can be thought of as an average of all prices of final goods in terms of money, where each price is implicitly weighted by the proportion of the corresponding good in the GDP. As these proportions change over the years, so do the weights.

The inflation rate can be measured by the rate of increase in the GDP deflator, which in turn can be approximated by the following formula:[5]

(2.4) $\dfrac{\text{GDP deflator}}{\text{inflation}} = \dfrac{\text{nominal GDP}}{\text{growth rate}} - \dfrac{\text{real GDP}}{\text{growth rate}}$

Table 2.1 **Growth Rates of Nominal GDP, Real GDP, and GDP Deflator: Euro Area 1999–2010 (% per annum)**

	Nominal GDP	Real GDP	GDP deflator
1999	4.6	3.0	1.6
2000	5.2	3.9	1.3
2001	4.3	.9	2.4
2002	3.4	0.9	2.5
2003	3.0	0.8	2.2
2004	4.1	2.2	1.9
2005	3.6	1.7	1.9
2006	5.0	3.1	1.9
2007	5.3	2.9	2.4
2008	2.3	0.3	2.0
2009	−3.2	−4.2	1.0
2010	2.6	1.7	1.0

Source: Eurostat.

For example, Table 2.1 shows that in 2005 the nominal GDP of the euro area rose by 3.6% while the real GDP increased only by 1.7%. On average, therefore, prices rose by roughly 1.9%.[6]

An alternative measure of inflation is based on an average of prices with fixed weights, called a **price index**. A basket of goods is selected and the amount of each good, or category of goods, in the basket is used to weight the corresponding prices. An example is the **consumer price index (CPI)**. This is based on a basket of goods consumed by a representative or average individual.

Figure 2.1 shows the growth rates of the GDP deflator and of the CPI in Italy. Differences between the two measures of inflation are usually not very large,

---

[3] Problems arise when new goods are introduced (MP3 players), or existing goods improve in quality (personal computers). National income accountants have devised procedures to deal with such effects.

[4] In previous decades, it was common to update the base year for prices used every five or more years. Rapidly changing product mixes and globalization have increased the value of redefining base years more frequently. It is now EU national income accounting practice to redefine the base year *every* year, effectively rendering real GDP a so-called chain standard index. With this change, growth rates in real GDP are more reliably measured. As a result, some national statistically authorities have even stopped publishing real GDP levels, using an index number without units instead.

[5] Box 6.3 in Chapter 6 provides the arithmetical background for this formula. If we denote nominal GDP as Y, real GDP as Q and the GDP deflator as P, we have $Y = PQ$, which means $P = Y/Q$. Then, using the results from Box 6.3, we have $\Delta P/P = \Delta Y/Y - \Delta Q/Q$.

[6] To see why this formula is an approximation, suppose real GDP increased at rate g and inflation at rate π. The rate of nominal growth must be $(1 + g)(1 + \pi) - 1 = g + \pi + g\pi$. For g and π small, $g\pi \approx 0$, so the rate of growth of nominal GDP is approximately equal to $g + \pi$.

Box 2.2   What GDP Measures

The GDP is a measure of recorded market transactions. This leaves out many activities which are not carried out through legal channels or do not reach the market place, like growing vegetables in the garden. Furthermore, since the value of goods and services are measured using their transaction prices, two identical goods may enter the GDP differently if one of them is sold at a discount. Finally, it is not a measure of happiness: painful expenses (having a tooth removed, for example) enter the GDP in the same way as pleasurable ones. When someone dies, GDP rises: the funeral service, the hospital expenses, and the execution of the will by lawyers and bankers all represent additional final sales of goods and services. Despite the fact that they are costs, pollution and other forms of environmental damage are not considered in the GDP, since they are not traded in markets.

Services enter the GDP exactly like goods. Services include medical doctors' fees or an estate agent's commission when an existing house is sold. The GDP also excludes many forms of income. In the case of real estate, if the house's value has increased since it was purchased, the previous owner enjoys a capital gain, but capital gains do not enter the GDP. Used-goods sales, such as cars or antique furniture, do not enter the GDP either. Such transactions represent a transfer of ownership rather than production. These goods entered GDP when first sold, but the fees of the dealers represent a service which is accounted for. Sales by retailers from inventory accumulated in earlier periods actually reduce GDP, as they represent a depletion of stocks.

Public services are part of GDP, even if they are not really sold. Their price is simply measured by their cost of production. For example, public education enters GDP as the sum of teachers' salaries, operating costs such as electricity or heating costs, and equipment including rents. Similarly, the national defence enters the GDP as total expenditure on armed forces.

A related measure is **gross national income (GNI)**.[7] Unlike the location-based GDP, the GNI is *ownership based*. It is the value added attributable to all factors of production owned by a country's residents, regardless of where those factors are actually employed. It thus includes value added or income earned abroad and repatriated by residents. For example, an Italian living in Como and commuting to work in Lugano in Switzerland contributes to the Italian GNI and to the Swiss GDP, but not to the Italian GDP or Swiss GNI. Because GNI is harder to measure, economists tend to follow GDP more closely. We will do the same.

To see how important the distinction between GDP and GNI can be, consider the case of Ireland. After several years of high economic growth, Ireland's GDP per capita rose above that of the UK in the late 1990s. Nevertheless, many of Ireland's factories are owned by foreigners— Britons, Germans, or Americans—or were purchased with money borrowed abroad. Investment income and interest paid to those foreigners was significant enough that until 2005, Irish per capita GNI remained lower than the UK's. Since then, however, Irish residents even have a higher GNI per capita than those of the UK, a remarkable turn of the economic tables!

---

but they can become significant when the import prices—which matter for the CPI but not for the GDP deflator—behave differently from domestically produced good prices. For example, in the late 1980s the price of crude oil increased less than prices of goods and services produced in Italy. In the early 2000s, domestic wage increases put pressure on domestic production costs and the GDP deflator rose faster than the CPI, an evolution that backfired with the financial crisis.

Other price indexes can be tailored to describe the prices of certain types of goods, of certain types of

consumer, or for certain sectors of the economy. Along with price deflators, there is a large menu to choose from, each price index or deflator having its own special emphasis. Box 2.3 presents some frequently used deflators and indexes.

2.2.3 Measuring and Interpreting GDP

The GDP, which represents the economic performance of an entire economy, is not easy to measure.

---

[7] This measure was known previously as the gross national product (GNP).

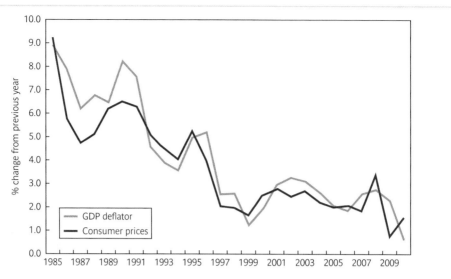

Fig. 2.1 Inflation rates, GDP Deflator and Consumer Price Index: Italy, 1985 – 2010
Both the GDP deflator and the consumer price index (CPI) measure the price level, or the price of goods in terms of money. The inflation rate is simply the rate of growth of one of these price level measures. The figure shows that both GDP deflator and CPI measures of inflation tend to move together over time, with occasional exceptions when the difference in the underlying 'baskets' matters. In the late 1980s, world oil prices declined sharply. Since gas and heating oil are part of household consumption, inflation measured by the CPI declined. Since oil is imported, it does not contribute value added directly in Italy, and has only a small impact on the GDP deflator.
Source: International Financial Statistics.

The task is generally carried out by official statistical offices which draw on various sources of information. One natural source is the tax authorities. Firms report sales (first definition of GDP), individuals report incomes (third definition), and in most countries (all EU countries, but not the USA) value added taxes (VAT) are collected by intermediate and final sellers who then report their value added when they pay the tax (second definition).

The fact that GDP figures are collected through tax returns immediately raises the suspicion that individuals and firms may misrepresent their finances to the fiscal authorities. Such unreported income and output is frequently referred to as the **underground economy**. Box 2.4 presents estimates of how large it could be. It also alerts us to the importance of work that is not paid for in the marketplace.

Another shortcoming associated with the magnitude of the task is the time it takes to get reasonably accurate numbers. Data from tax returns are usually processed with delay. Usually at the end of the first month of each quarter, figures for the preceding quarter are released. Box 2.5 explains how such flash estimates are produced and updated several times over the following years. The inaccuracy of these estimates is unsettling because they are frequently used by governments when deciding on economic policies, by investors when valuing their assets, and by firms deciding on hiring or firing workers and on acquiring new plant and equipment. This is why other indicators are often used to supplement the GDP figures.[8] It is also why analysts tend to concentrate on growth rates rather than levels. As long as the distortions do not change much over time, measured GDP growth rates offer a good picture of average economy performance.

It is tempting to compare GDPs across countries. Because countries have different populations, it is natural to look at GDP per capita, or the average

---

[8] Chapter 16 discusses some of the most frequently used indicators.

Box 2.3 Price Deflators and Price Indexes

The price index closest to the GDP deflator is the producer price index (PPI), with fixed weights corresponding to a basket representative of national production. Similarly, the CPI is closely tracked by the consumption deflator, the ratio of nominal and real aggregate consumption expenditures by households. A price index like the CPI or the PPI is an example of a fixed-weight, or *Laspeyres index*. The consumption deflator, which is based on the actual share of goods in the corresponding year's consumption, is called a variable weight or *Paasche index*. The CPI and the consumption deflator include goods and services produced abroad and imported, while the PPI and the GDP deflator do not, but these latter measures include goods and services locally produced and exported. Figure 2.1 suggests a growing divergence between the PPI and the CPI in Italy in the late 1980s. The reason is that imported goods prices increased by less than those of domestically produced goods.

Other frequently used deflators are related to exports, imports, investment goods, and government purchases. The wholesale price index (WPI) measures the average price of goods at the wholesale stage, and various commodity price indexes track the evolution of raw materials prices. The dizzying diversity of indexes and deflators simply reflects the fact that there is no absolute 'average' price. Different price levels are used for different purposes. For example, wage-earners wish to tie their wages to their cost of living; in this case, the relevant index is the CPI or the consumption deflator. In the case of Italy, linking wages to the CPI rather than to the PPI resulted in higher profits for firms whose sales are better tracked by the PPI. Because the CPI and other Laspeyres indexes are easier to compute, they tend to be used most often in practice.

Box 2.4 The Underground Economy and Unpaid Work

Who hasn't had an offer from a carpenter, a car mechanic, or painter to do some work 'without a receipt'? Agents engage in the underground, or informal economy for straightforward reasons. First, they want to avoid taxes (the value added tax, employment and social security charges, profit taxes). Second, while significant, criminal activities, such as drug-dealing, prostitution, or racketeering, are intentionally concealed and kept underground by market participants. By definition, the size of the underground economy is unknown, but national income statisticians often attempt to guess its importance. They use various approaches such as monitoring household electricity use, which tends to be higher in economies where unreported market activity is more significant, or looking at the amount of large-denomination currency in circulation, since under-

ground transactions do not use bank accounts and profits are conveniently held in large bills. The sale of intermediate inputs related to final production often indicates underground economy activities. For example, a large discrepancy exists between the purchase of construction materials and reported construction activity. Figure 2.2 shows the extent of the underground economy in a number of countries.

Another serious drawback of GDP as a measure of economic activity is unpaid work. Minor repairs around the house, caring for children, cooking for the family and cleaning up take up much time and effort. Wealthier people hire help for these chores, in which case it becomes part of GDP (if reported to the tax authorities). Most people do it themselves, and it is unrecorded.

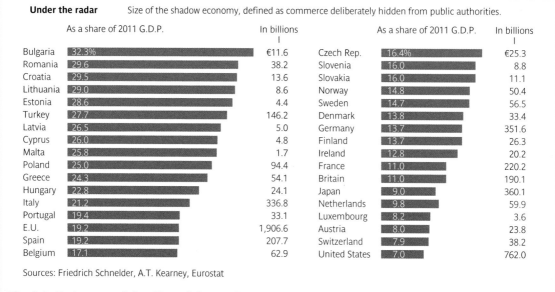

Under the radar   Size of the shadow economy, defined as commerce deliberately hidden from public authorities.

	As a share of 2011 G.D.P.	In billions		As a share of 2011 G.D.P.	In billions
Bulgaria	32.3%	€11.6	Czech Rep.	16.4%	€25.3
Romania	29.6	38.2	Slovenia	16.0	8.8
Croatia	29.5	13.6	Slovakia	16.0	11.1
Lithuania	29.0	8.6	Norway	14.8	50.4
Estonia	28.6	4.4	Sweden	14.7	56.5
Turkey	27.7	146.2	Denmark	13.8	33.4
Latvia	26.5	5.0	Germany	13.7	351.6
Cyprus	26.0	4.8	Finland	13.7	26.3
Malta	25.8	1.7	Ireland	12.8	20.2
Poland	25.0	94.4	France	11.0	220.2
Greece	24.3	54.1	Britain	11.0	190.1
Hungary	22.8	24.1	Japan	9.0	360.1
Italy	21.2	336.8	Netherlands	9.8	59.9
Portugal	19.4	33.1	Luxembourg	8.2	3.6
E.U.	19.2	1,906.6	Austria	8.0	23.8
Spain	19.2	207.7	Switzerland	7.9	38.2
Belgium	17.1	62.9	United States	7.0	762.0

Sources: Friedrich Schnelder, A.T. Kearney, Eurostat

Fig. 2.2 Estimates of the Size of the Underground Economy (% of GDP)

Source: *International Herald Tribune*, 3 November 2011, p.II.

 Box 2.5   How National Accounts Estimates Vary over Time

Because governments, firms, and investors require timely information about the economy, national statistical institutes in advanced economies have devised ways of quickly producing preliminary estimates of GDP. The procedure is based on the knowledge that the value added of, for example, the 100 largest corporations represents a given proportion of GDP. If the proportion were 10%, as these firms fill in VAT tax reports or respond to specially designed questionnaires, multiplying by 10 their combined value added provides a rough early estimate of GDP. A few months later,

revised estimates can be based on data provided by a larger sample of firms. Waiting still longer will allow the incorporation of estimates based on an early and partial analysis of tax returns. Detailed analysis of all tax returns data—using procedures to reconcile differences between measures based on the three definitions—leads to a final figure. Table 2.2 shows successive estimates of German GDP in 2008. The first estimate, published in January 2009, exceeded the final figure by €8 billion, or by about 0.3% of the initial estimate.

income earned within a country's boundaries. Such data must be regarded with caution, however. First, GDP is a measure of income, not wealth. Income is a flow, while wealth is the stock of assets accumulated over longer periods of time. For example, the average income earned in the UK is lower than that of Abu Dhabi. Yet average British wealth is likely to be much higher because Britain has been accumulating

wealth for centuries, in the form of private assets (e.g. houses, factories, jewels, stocks) and national assets (e.g. the London Bridge, paintings in the British Museum, railroads, highways and telecommunication networks, and much more).

Second, a large number of transactions are not recorded, especially in developing countries. They belong to what is sometimes called the informal

Table 2.2 **Estimates of 2008 German Nominal GDP**

Date of publication	GDP (bn EURO of 2000 prices)	% difference from previous estimate	% difference from Jan 2009
Jan 2009	2489.4	—	—
Feb 2009	2489.4	0.00%	0.00%
May 2009	2492.0	0.10%	0.10%
Aug 2009	2491.4	−0.02%	0.08%
Nov 2009	2495.8	0.18%	0.26%
May 2010	2495.8	0.00%	0.26%
Nov 2010	2481.2	−0.58%	−0.33%
Feb 2011	2481.2	0.00%	−0.33%

Source: Estimates as published in the monthly bulletin of the Deutsche Bundesbank, various issues.

economy. For example, much food can be produced within the extended family (a non-market activity), or exchanged for other food (a non-reported market activity). Very low reported per capita income levels in developing economies underestimate true value added and income. Finally, GDPs are measured in the country's local monetary unit, or currency, and are then converted into a common currency using the exchange rate. But local costs are often much lower in poor countries, for reasons presented later in Chapter 15. To correct for this effect, economists often use GDP figures that have been adjusted for differences in purchasing power.

2.3 Flows of Incomes and Expenditures

2.3.1 The Circular Flow Diagram

From final expenditures to net taxes and factor income

Each individual's expenditure necessarily contributes to some other individual's income. The simplified **circular flow** diagram represented in Figure 2.3 is based on this simple truth and goes a long way in tracking the functioning of an economy. Based on the first and third definitions of GDP, it shows how GDP arises as final sales, and how it is paid out to households, the owners of the factors of production. In addition, it shows how firms—around which market activity is organized—households, and the government interact to make GDP possible.

The GDP appears in the left part of the figure. It represents the final net sales of firms. Since firms are owned by households, the GDP represents the gross income of factors of production employed in the geographic region under consideration.[9] To see what firms do with revenues coming from their final sales, we move clockwise. The government, shown as the circle inside the flow diagram, takes (in the form of taxes) and gives (in the form of various transfers). It

---

[9] Technically, GDP also includes 'sales' of labour services by the self-employed. It also excludes sales of households' labour and capital services abroad. In order to keep things simple, we will ignore these latter components of GDP in what follows, so that all value added in the economy represents income to residents.

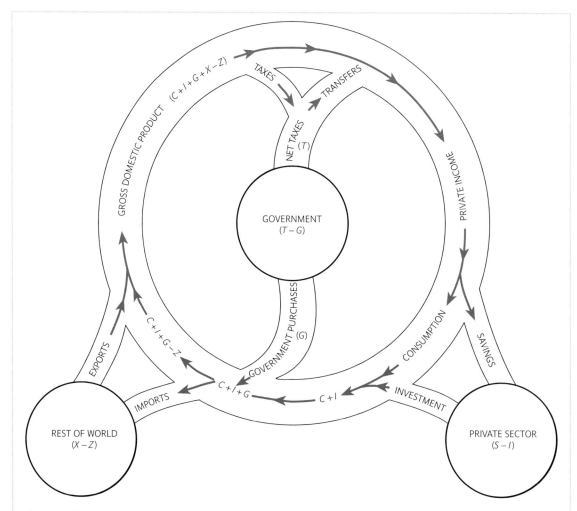

Fig. 2.3 The Circular Flow Diagram
The lower left part of the wheel represents final sales of goods and services which are domestically produced. It is the sum of consumption spending (C), investment spending (I), government purchases (G), and exports (X) less imports (Z). In the upper left part of the wheel this is interpreted as income to residents. This income is taxed by the government, but is also supplemented by transfers to households and firms (T). The remainder is private income, which may be saved (S) or spent (C). The private sector invests in productive equipment (I), which it finances in part by savings (S); the balance S − I is the private sector's net saving behaviour. Similarly, the public sector's net saving behaviour is reflected in its budget surplus T − G. The balance X − Z represents both net exports of goods and services as well as the net import of financial assets (claims against the rest of the world).

also purchases goods and services. Because it needs to pay for them, the government will almost always take in more than it gives away in transfers. The difference between taxes and transfers is called **net taxes** and is represented by T. These taxes are taken in at several points of the value added chain—as indirect taxes such as value added taxes, or as direct taxes on different types of income. Here we consolidate them for simplic-

ity. What is left of GDP after these taxes and transfers are subtracted is called **private income**, $Y - T$.

From private income to absorption plus net exports—GDP

Private income is ultimately earned by those households which own the factors of production involved in creating the value added. The largest part of private income is wages and salaries paid to workers plus payments for rent and royalties, as well as net interest on loans from banks. The residual which remains after firms pay all these other factors is known as gross profit. This profit can either be saved by the firm or redistributed back to firm owners as income.[10] Since all factors of production are ultimately owned by some households, households receive income as employees, as bondholders, as shareholders, as owners of land, and as holders of patents. Households can either save this income, or spend it on **consumption**.

The private sector represents the consolidation of households with the firms that they own. The flow diagram shows how the aggregate savings of the private sector (S) are deposited with the financial sector. The financial sector includes banks, financial institutions, and stock markets whose function is to collect savings and channel them to firms seeking to invest, that is, to purchase productive equipment. This activity, called **financial intermediation**, is represented by the lower-right circle. In the aggregate, the private sector uses its **savings**—the income that it does not consume—to finance, or pay for, the acquisition of new productive equipment by firms. The stock of existing productive equipment, including structures, is referred to as **physical capital**, while the purchase of new equipment is called **investment**. The excess of private saving over investment (S − I) is called net private saving. Net private saving can be positive or negative. Firms and households spend their income— part of it borrowed—to consume (C) and to invest (I).[11]

To private sector expenditures on goods and services (C + I) the government adds its own demand (G). Governments purchase goods (roads, military equipment, newly built buildings, and stationery for the bureaucracy) and services (of civil servants and other employees). While governments transfer lots of income, distribute various subsidies to firms and households, and pay interest on the public debt, these are not purchases of goods and services and not included here. Total national spending, sometimes called **absorption**, is the sum (C + I + G) of private and public spending on all goods and services. Part of absorption includes the purchase of imported goods and services (Z). This is shown as the branch going into the leftmost circle, which represents the rest of the world. It should not be thought of merely as merchandise purchases, but as covering all kinds of services, including labour and capital services, as long as they are rendered within the boundaries of the nation. Similarly, while some domestic income thus leaks abroad, foreigners buy domestically produced goods and services, the country's exports (X). Netting these two flows with the rest of the world gives net exports (X − Z). When positive, net exports increase demand for domestic production above that originating with domestic residents; when negative, demand for domestic production is less than total domestic demand.

The sum of absorption and net exports represents the total final sales that occur within the geographic area, i.e. the GDP. The circular flow of income is closed. This circularity is the essence of economic activity: we (collectively) earn to (collectively) spend.

2.3.2 Summary of the Flow Diagram

The flow diagram can be summarized using the first and third definitions of GDP (Y). As net final sales, the GDP is broken down into four main categories: (1) final sales of consumption goods and services (C), (2) final sales of investment goods and additions to inventory stocks (I), (3) final sales to the government (G), and (4) sales to the rest of the world (X). Since part of domestic income leaks abroad to pay for imported goods, imports (Z) must be subtracted, which gives the first decomposition of GDP by final expenditures:

(2.5) $$Y = C + I + G + X - Z.$$

The flow diagram also shows that GDP can be viewed as net incomes earned by factors of production. What do they do with this income? The three possibilities are given on the right-hand side of the flow diagram: they pay taxes net of transfers (T), they save (S), and

---

[10] The other production costs are mainly land and buildings, financial costs (borrowing from banks and bondholders), and raw materials and intermediate goods which, for the country as a whole, are frequently imported.

[11] There is an important difference between this terminology and that used in the business or popular press, in which 'investment' includes the acquisition of existing assets or financial instruments. Although stocks and bonds are often issued by firms to finance purchases of productive equipment, their simple acquisition or sale does not necessarily imply 'investment' in economics, i.e. the creation of new productive capacity.

Table 2.3 Components of GDP by Expenditure, 1999–2010 (% of GDP)

	Consumption (*C*)	Investment (*I*)	Government purchases (*G*)
Australia	56.4	22.4	17.4
Germany	58.5	18.2	18.9
France	56.8	20.1	23.6
UK	65.0	17.0	21.0
Italy	59.3	20.7	19.9
Japan	57.4	24.0	18.1
Canada	56.4	21.4	19.7
Switzerland	59.1	21.4	11.3
USA	69.8	18.8	15.8
EURArea	57.2	20.8	20.5

Source: IMF.

they consume (*C*). Hence the second decomposition by uses of income:

(2.6) $Y = C + S + T.$

Table 2.3 displays the components of the first decomposition as a percentage of GDP for a few countries. Consumption typically represents about 60% of GDP in Europe, but it is much higher in the US. The investment rate—the ratio of investment expenditures to GDP—amounts to some 20%, with few differences among the developed countries, but it is about twice as much in China. Because investment corresponds to the accumulation of productive equipment, it matters for future economic growth. The table shows that public spending varies quite a bit, but comparisons here can be treacherous. Investment in infrastructure equipment (roads, bridges, public utilities) may be undertaken privately in some countries and publicly in others. In addition, in federal countries, sub-central governments (e.g. the Swiss cantons or the US states) carry a substantial amount of public spending. Much the same concerns many goods and services that are privately produced in some countries while they are delivered freely as public goods in others: these include medical services, schools, child care, and public transport. Finally, the 'size of government' is considerably greater than the share of government expenditures: transfers to firms and households, not

reported in Table 2.3, may be as large as direct expenditures. When total spending is considered, which adds transfers to expenditures, the government often 'handles' more than half of GDP.

The flows of incomes and spending captured by Figure 2.3 constitute the real, as opposed to financial, side of an economy. Parts of these flows leak out to the financial side in the form of corporate and household savings; others leak out to the government in the form of tax payments or social security contributions; others to foreigners through imports. To the extent that withdrawals of resources from the circular flow due to a particular sector is not matched exactly by inflows in the form of spending, then that sector's net asset position must be changing, by definition.[12] If savings of the private sector exceed investment spending, for example, this means that net accumulation of assets in the private sector is positive. The same holds for the consolidated government if net taxes exceed government purchases of goods and services, or for the nation if net export of goods and services, broadly defined, is positive. Asset

---

[12] If the net outflow is positive, net assets owned by the sector must be increasing; if the net outflow is negative, net assets are decreasing. Technically, increasing net assets can occur either by increases in gross financial assets (claims on other sectors), or by reducing gross liabilities (i.e. paying off existing debt to other sectors).

Table 2.4 GDP and Household Disposable Income, 2009

	GDP (billions of €)	Households disposable income	
		Level	% of GDP
Germany	2,395.0	1,554.2	64.9
France	1,907.7	1,293.9	67.8
Sweden	290.9	154.4	53.1
Switzerland	354.5	211.4	59.6
United States	10,122.6	7,911.5	78.2
United Kingdom	1,565.7	1,057.6	67.5

Sources: OECD, *Economic Outlook*; ECB.

accumulation or de-cumulation has economic consequences. How the financial side of the economy functions, and how the real and financial sides are linked,
is studied in Part III of this book.

2.3.3 More Detail

While GDP represents the collective income earned
within a nation's boundaries, not all of it ends up in
the hands of private individuals. What households
actually receive to spend or save is called **personal
disposable income**. Table 2.4 shows that a big share
of GDP does not reach individual households. It
either goes to the government (net taxes) or is saved
by firms (retained earnings).

Figure 2.4 starts with GDP and, moving right,
decomposes it by its ultimate recipient. The first item
is **depreciation**: in the process of producing GDP, productive equipment is subjected to wear and tear and
obsolescence. Properly measured, this depreciation
should be subtracted from GDP to give a clearer picture of the output that is really available as income if
we wish to preserve the value of our productive
capacities. Subtracting depreciation from GDP gives
us the **net domestic product (NDP)**.[13] Moving further
to the right, domestic income is what is left for firms
once indirect taxes are paid out. Indirect taxes vary

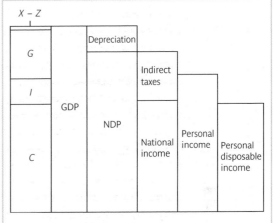

Fig. 2.4 From Expenditure to Income to Personal Disposable Income

Depreciation is stripped away from GDP to obtain net
domestic product (NDP). When net factor income from
abroad is zero, we can subtract indirect taxes from, and
add subsidies of firms to, NDP to obtain domestic
income (NI). (If net factor income from abroad is not
zero, it must then be added at this stage.) Domestic
income can be distributed in a number of ways: firms'
savings (retained earnings), taxes on businesses, and
contributions to social security are subtracted from
domestic income, leaving various forms of income paid
to households in the end. The government also transfers
income to households (social security, unemployment
insurance, etc.). This results in personal income (PI).
After income taxes and some miscellaneous fees, we are
left with personal disposable income (PDI), that is,
resources available to households for spending or saving.

---

[13] In practice, financial accounting of depreciation is determined
by tax regulations. Firms are allowed to subtract from their
revenues a given proportion of the book value of equipment
for computing taxable profits. It may under- or overstate actual
economic depreciation by a wide margin.

from country to country, and include the value added tax (VAT) and excise taxes (on petrol, tobacco, alcohol). They are collected by sellers on behalf of the government.

After indirect taxes, firms pay out the value added they generate in four primary ways. First, wages and salaries and other compensation to their employees represent the largest component. This includes contributions to social insurance, which is paid to the government. Second, they pay interest to bondholders and banks. Third, they pay corporate or business income taxes. What remains is profits to the firms' owners, or shareholders. These profits are either distributed as dividends or held back as retained earnings, sometimes called net corporate saving.[14]

To summarize, what is not paid as corporate taxes or saved by firms is ultimately paid out to households as the firms' employees, their owners, or indirectly as their creditors. When government transfers (e.g. unemployment benefits, disability payments, health care reimbursements, family allowances) are added to labour incomes and distributed profits, the result is personal income. Households cannot freely dispose of their personal income: they must first pay personal income taxes, as well as non-tax payments like parking fines and other governmental fees. The result is personal disposable income, which can either be consumed or saved.

Finally, economic boundaries can be trickier than it seems. GDP looks at a country as defined by its geographic boundaries. In doing so, foreigners (firms and individuals) who are domestic residents are treated as the national residents: their incomes and productions are part of GDP. Another approach is to look at the nationality of firms and people, independently of where they live. The gross national product (GNP), or gross national income (GNI), measures incomes and outputs of a country's citizens and corporations, no matter where they actually operate. Thus GNP = GDP + net factor incomes, adding incomes of national operating abroad and deducting incomes of foreigners operating at home. The logic of Figure 2.4 remains unchanged: simply we have net

national product instead of net domestic product and national income instead of domestic income.

2.3.4 A Key Accounting Identity

The two decompositions of GDP, (2.5) and (2.6), are accounting identities: they hold by definition. Therefore it is always the case that:

$$C + S + T = C + I + G + X - Z.$$

Consumption C appears on both sides of this equality and can be eliminated. When this is done and terms are rearranged, the two accounting identities yield a third one:

(2.7) $(S - I) + (T - G) = (X - Z).$

The last term, $X - Z$, is the balance of exports over imports of goods and services, now extended to include the services of factors of production employed outside the national borders. Parentheses highlight the fact that the corresponding expressions appear in Figure 2.3 as net flows of the private sector (household and business), government, and the rest of the world, respectively. Each of the three net flows can be thought of as a form of saving or withdrawal from the circular flow income and expenditure: a leakage if positive, or

Table 2.5 The Accounting Identity in 2010 (% of GDP)

	S-I	T-G	CA
USA	5.6	−8.8	−3.2
Japan	10.3	−6.7	3.6
Belgium	3.9	−2.6	1.3
Denmark	4.7	0.8	5.5
France	2.6	−4.8	−2.2
Germany	8.1	−2.5	5.6
Italy	−1.3	−2.2	−3.5
Netherlands	11.5	−3.8	7.7
Spain	0.7	−5.2	−4.5
Sweden	4.7	1.6	6.3
UK	5.8	−8.3	−2.5
Euro area	4.1	−3.9	0.2

Source: OECD.

---

[14] Adding depreciation to net corporate savings gives gross corporate savings. It represents the resources that firms set aside to replace used equipment and generally to strengthen their financial position.

an injection if negative. If $S > I$, the private sector in the aggregate is a net saver. If $S < I$, the private sector is a net borrower. Similarly, if $T > G$ the government is saving, and if $G > T$ it is borrowing by issuing public debt to domestic or foreign residents. The identity (2.7) shows how these leakages are linked, by definition.

In Italy that year, both private and public sectors were spending more than they took in; the country as a whole, therefore, had to borrow abroad, which explains why they were running sizeable external deficits, as will become clear in Section 2.4. The Eurozone as a whole was running a balanced current account as budget deficits were about matched by private sector savings. Japan, the USA, and the UK were running huge budget deficits but Japan's net exports were in surplus thanks to even larger net private savings, while the US and the UK had to borrow abroad.

2.3.5 Identities versus Economics

Identity (2.7) is a particular way of stating that all goods and services produced (Definition 3 of GDP) must be purchased (Definition 1). For example, if private savings exceed private investment ($S > I$), either net exports must be positive or the government budget must be in deficit, or both. But identities tell us little or nothing about causation. Without more information, it is impossible to know whether (1) the government deficit is at the origin of positive net private savings, (2) high exports are generating income that is simply saved by residents, or (3) low domestic investment spending is coinciding with a domestic recession, in which both imports and tax revenues are low, bringing either current account or government budget or both into deficit. This is the difference between simply collecting data and interpreting them. This is also the difference between accounting and economics. The identity (2.7) is not only a requirement that accounts be correctly measured; we will see later that, as a market equilibrium condition, it also tells us a lot about how adjustment mechanisms work.

2.4 Balance of Payments

The **balance of payments** accounts record all economic transactions between a country and the rest of the world. Most countries have adopted the same classification, which has been designed by the International Monetary Fund. We also follow this classification. The presentation in Table 2.6 separates out international transactions in goods and services in the broadest sense (the upper part I) from financial transactions (the lower part II). Financial transactions imply the purchase and sale of assets such as stocks and bonds, loans and credit, bank deposits and currency, as well as real estate and other forms of wealth.

A simple rule to help understand the meaning of entries is the following: transactions involving *outflows of our money* are recorded as *deficit* (−) items, while those involving inflows of domestic money are considered as surplus (+) items. Box 2.6 offers a number of examples, which will become clear as we move along.

2.4.1 The Current Account and its Components

The first account to consider in Table 2.6 records exports and imports of goods and services. Imports are entered with a minus sign (deficit item), while exports contribute positively to the balance (surplus item). The net result is line IA, the **balance of goods and services**. The balance of trade in goods (line IA1) includes merchandise trade as well as trade in intermediate inputs, goods repair, goods held in ports, and non-monetary gold. The balance of trade in services (line IA2) incorporates a wide and growing variety of invisibles such as transport and travel, communication, insurance, financial, and other services. It also includes royalties and licence fees.

A second account to consider is the **balance of international income** (line IB). This account summarizes the net income of a nation which

Table 2.6 The Balance of Payments

I. Current account
A. Goods and services
1. Goods
2. Services
B. International income
1. Wages and compensation
2. Investment income
C. Current transfers
II. Capital and financial account
A. Capital account
B. Financial account
1. Direct investment
2. Portfolio investment
3. Other investment
4. Reserve assets
C. Errors and omissions

originates abroad. Two important components of international income are worth mentioning.

- Wages and salaries paid for work by individuals in countries different from their place of residence (line IB1).
- Profits or interest income received by residents *less* profits and interest paid to foreign residents (line IB2).

The third important item of the current account is the **balance of current transfers** (line IC). These are payments which are not associated with commercial or financial transactions. An example is the remittance of guest workers to their home countries. When a Polish plumber living in London sends money to relatives living in Warsaw, this counts as a surplus to the Polish balance of transfers and as a deficit to the UK's. Another example is development or emergency aid offered by one country to another.

The sum of the balances of trade in goods and services, international income, and current transfers is called the **current account balance**. A current account surplus may be interpreted as the net sales of goods and services, broadly defined to include the

services of capital and labour services, know-how, and goodwill ('purchased' with remittances or foreign aid).

The importance of the current account is best seen by returning to the definition of decomposition (2.5). If we define Y this time more broadly as gross national income (GNI), we can rewrite this decomposition as follows:

(2.8) $$CA = Y - (C + I + G) = Y - A,$$

where $A = C + I + G$ is referred to as absorption, or total domestic spending on goods and services, both domestic and foreign, by households, firms, and government agencies. By definition, the current account is the excess of income over spending. It signals whether the country is a net borrower or a net lender. When a country earns more than it spends (i.e. $CA = Y - A > 0$), it is a net lender vis-à-vis the rest of the world. Conversely, a country running a current account deficit spends more than it earns ($CA < 0$ and $A > Y$) and must match the difference by borrowing abroad.

Table 2.7 illustrates the balance of payments accounts for a number of different countries with widely different experiences. The enormous current account deficit in the USA is due to a deficit in goods and services trade. Turkey, Mexico, and China are three countries which receive significant transfers from abroad. In the case of Turkey and Mexico, many citizens work as guest workers abroad and remit their income regularly. Sweden and the UK find themselves in the opposite situation; many foreign workers live there and remit money to their home countries. This is also the case for the EU overall, as well as the USA.

2.4.2 The Capital and Financial Accounts

Part II of Table 2.6 describes financial transactions. As the balance of payments is an accounting exercise, the sum of all entries in the balance of payments must equal zero. This is also a consequence of (2.8): if the current account is in surplus, a country is exporting more to the rest of the world than it is importing. Earning more than it spends, that country must be experiencing a net financial outflow: it is either lending to the rest of the world by acquiring assets abroad, or it is paying down its debts. Conversely, a

Table 2.7 Balance of Payments, Various Countries, 2010 (US$ billion)

	Euro-zone	U.S.	Sweden	Turkey	Mexico	China	United Kingdom
Balance on goods	32	−644	11	−56	−3	254	−151
Balance on service	43	148	16	14	−10	−22	69
International Income	−12	163	8	−8	−14	30	56
Current transfers	−140	−137	−6	1	21	43	−31
Current account	−77	−470	29	−48	−6	305	−56
Capital account	12	0	−1	0		5	5
Direct investment	−1	194	5	9	18	185	44
Portfolio investment	259	613	22	16	39	24	12
Other investment	−46	−240	−43	34	−8	72	−22
Financial Account	212	568	−16	60	49	282	34
Capital and financial account	225	567	−17	60	49	286	38
Net errors and omission	−33	235	13	6	−7	−60	13
Overall balance	6	2	−1	15	23	472	10

current account deficit implies borrowing from abroad, so financial capital is flowing into the country. Accordingly, the remainder of the balance of payments, representing financial transactions, must be equal to, and of opposite sign to, the current account. The remaining question is: Who actually performs the balancing act, and how?

The answer is to be found in the **capital and financial account**, which consists of two components. The capital account (line IIA) registers unusual and sporadic financial transfers such as debt forgiveness of public or private debts. The more important component of the capital and financial account is the financial account balance (line IIB). The IMF defines four categories of financial transactions which affect this account.

(1) Direct investment (line IIB1)—purchases and sales of shares (equity investment) in business enterprises in excess of 10% of the total value; reinvested profits; real estate purchases.

(2) Portfolio investment (line IIB2)—purchases and sales of shares (equity investment) in business enterprises of less than 10% of total value; purchases and issues of bonds, money market instruments, and financial derivatives.

(3) Other investments (line IIB3)—trade credits; loans by banks; deposits held at banks; currency.

(4) Reserve asset transactions (line IIB4)—transactions involving monetary gold, special drawing rights and reserve positions with the IMF, and foreign exchange reserves.

While the first three types of financial account transactions can be conducted by the private or public sector, the fourth item is performed exclusively by the monetary authorities, usually the central bank. This balance is also called the **official account**. The official account captures the fact that the monetary authorities may act as the residual agent in the balancing process. When the official account is in deficit, it means that residents have sent more money abroad than they received, through either commercial transactions—the current account—or financial transactions—the financial account—or any combination of both. This was the case of the euro area in 2010, as can be seen in Table 2.7. In that case the monetary authorities make up the difference, bringing domestic money back home; hence the positive surplus entry in the table. Put differently, the monetary authorities have sold some of their **foreign exchange reserves** (foreign currencies that they own) and

Box 2.6 **Examples of Balance of Payments Accounts**

In the main text we noted that international transactions give rise to deficit items when they involve an outflow of our *money*, and are surplus entries when they imply *receipt* of our money. This includes both 'above-line' or current account as well as 'below-line' capital account transactions. Example: a Swedish company which exports a car to France and receives Kroner for it gives rise to a surplus in the current account (export of goods), while if it sells stock to a French resident it causes a surplus entry in the capital account (capital and financial account, portfolio investment). In Table 2.8 we give some examples of transactions and how they are recorded, using the simple rule. Note that the transactions are always symmetric in their effect, when properly recorded.

 Table 2.8 **Balance of Payments: Some Examples**

Transaction	Surplus (+) or deficit (–)	Country	Account
UK exports chemicals to France to the amount of £1 million	+ £1 m	UK	Goods and services
	– £1 m	France	Goods and services
French school trains German cyclists for €500,000	+ €500,000	France	Goods and services
	– €500,000	Germany	Goods and services
German construction company is paid SF 5 million to build a Swiss bridge	+ SF5 m	Germany	Goods and services
	– SF5 m	Switzerland	Goods and services
Swiss ski instructor is paid salary of €80,000 for work performed in Austria	+ €80,000	Switzerland	International income
	– €80,000	Austria	International income
UK fast food franchises remit £1 million in profits to headquarters in the USA	+ £1 m	USA	International income
	– £1 m	UK	International income
Austrian government gives €3 million in relief aid to tsunami victims in Thailand	+ €3 m	Thailand	Current transfers
	– €3 m	Austria	Current transfers
Estonian worker in Denmark sends DK 100,000 to family in Tallinn	+ DK100,000	Estonia	Current transfers
	– DK100,000	Denmark	Current transfers
Spanish government forgives debt of €10 million owed by Peru	+ €10 m	Peru	Capital account
	– €10 m	Spain	Capital account
Swedish investor purchases a factory in Germany for €100 million	+ €100 m	Germany	Financial account / direct investment
	– €100 m	Sweden	Financial account / direct investment
Portuguese bank buys €20 million of stock in German company from French bank based in France	+ €20 m	France	Financial account / portfolio investment

Table 2.8 **Balance of Payments: Some Examples** **(Continued)**

Transaction	Surplus (+) or deficit (−)	Country	Account
	− €20 m	Portugal	Financial account / portfolio investment
UK bank based in London lends £50 million to subsidiary in Ireland	+ £50 m	Ireland	Other investment
	− £50 m	UK	Other investment
Slovenian resident transfers €100,000 from home account to a bank account in Italy	+ €100,000	Italy	Financial account / portfolio investment
	− €100,000	Slovenia	Financial account / portfolio investment
Bank of England purchases €5 billion from the European Central Bank (ECB) paying with pound sterling	− €5 b	UK	Reserve assets account
	+ €5 b	Eurozone	Reserve assets account

Source: IMF.

received domestic currency for it in return.[15] Such actions are called **foreign exchange market interventions**. When a monetary authority buys back its own currency, it necessarily spends some of the foreign currencies that it holds. The distinction between private and official financing is further taken up in Section 2.4.4.

2.4.3 Errors and Omissions

There is a final item in Table 2.7, 'Errors and omissions' (line IIC), which requires some explanation. By definition, the total of the balance of payments should be zero:

$$(2.9) \quad \underset{\substack{\text{current} \\ \text{account}}}{\text{CA}} + \underset{\substack{\text{capital and} \\ \text{financial} \\ \text{account}}}{\text{FA}} + \underset{\substack{\text{official} \\ \text{intervention}}}{\text{OFF}} = 0.$$

While accounting guarantees the consistency of current and financial accounts in theory, the nature of data gathering for payments statistics virtually guar-antees discrepancies. Trade data originate with customs authorities. Financial data come from the banking system, since international transactions are mediated by financial institutions. Official interventions are known by the monetary authorities, which are often responsible for collecting the data and producing the balance of payments accounts. Because these data come from different sources, relationship (2.9) will never hold in practice. This is why an additional account called 'Errors and omissions' is needed. This is necessary to obtain zero at the bottom of the table. While there are genuine mistakes—the sheer volume of data to be treated is an invitation for errors—there may also be omissions which are less than innocent.[16] Table 2.7 shows that errors and omissions can at times be embarrassingly large.

2.4.4 The Meaning of the Accounts

A current account imbalance must be matched, or financed, one-for-one by either the private financial account or official interventions by the monetary

---

[15] Note that this follows the rule of thumb already mentioned for thinking about the sign of an entry in the balance of payments: ask yourself whether it means that domestic money comes in (a plus) or goes out (a minus).

[16] By definition, the sum of the current accounts of all countries in the world should equal zero. In fact, it is systematically negative, as receipts are 'omitted' more often than expenditures.

authorities. What is the difference between the two mechanisms? A country with a current account deficit makes more payments abroad than it receives. More domestic money must be flowing out than is entering the country. If the private financial account is in balance, the imbalance between inflows and outflows must translate into excess supply of the domestic currency on exchange markets worldwide. This excess of sellers over buyers—or excess supply—will depreciate, or reduce the value of, the domestic currency.[17]

Now two things are possible. First, the monetary authorities may want to prevent the depreciation. They must then step in immediately and buy up the excess supply of the domestic currency—using their own holdings of foreign currency. This transaction represents a positive entry in the official financial account (OFF) in (2.9). The country's current account deficit is financed by sales of foreign exchange reserves.[18]

The second possibility is that the central bank may refuse to intervene (OFF = 0). In this case the domestic currency would be in excess supply on world markets. With an excess of sellers, it would tend to depreciate, or lose value. This exchange rate depreciation works towards reducing the current account deficit, as foreign goods become more expensive and domestic goods become cheaper. It will also prompt capital inflows as foreigners take advantage of the low exchange rate to acquire domestic assets. In the accounting identity (2.9), either the current account deficit disappears or the private financial account is positive, or both. Similarly, a current account surplus can be financed privately (a negative financial account), publicly (purchases of foreign exchange reserves), or both.

The monetary authorities determine if, and to what extent, a current account imbalance translates into a change in the exchange rate. At one extreme, the monetary authorities may be committed to maintaining a fixed exchange rate. If so, they must intervene in the market, purchasing or selling foreign exchange in whatever amount necessary to keep the exchange rate constant. At the other extreme, the monetary authorities never intervene and the exchange rate is determined solely by market forces. This is the **overall balance**—sometimes called the balance of payments (BoP).[19] It is the sum of the current and financial accounts (including errors and omissions). The overall balance attracts special attention because it is the mirror image of interventions by the monetary authorities during the period under study and reveals their behaviour. Ignoring errors and omissions,

(2.10) $BoP = CA + FA = -OFF.$

A balance of payments surplus means that the authorities have acquired foreign exchange reserves. Put differently, they have sold the domestic currency to match an excess demand for the domestic currency, thus preventing or reducing pressure for an exchange rate appreciation (OFF < O). Accordingly, the official account is in deficit. A balance of payments deficit corresponds to a loss of reserves as the monetary authorities buy back the domestic currency to prevent a depreciation (OFF > O). The official account would then be in surplus.

❶ Summary

1 The gross domestic product (GDP) can be defined in three equivalent ways: (1) as the sum of final sales, (2) the sum of factor incomes, or (3) the sum of value added. GDP is a flow variable measured over a well-defined time interval, usually a year.

[17] Later chapters will explore this process in much greater detail. A currency appreciates when its value in terms of other currencies increases. Conversely, if its value decreases, we speak of a depreciation.

[18] Technically, this can be thought of as an official credit from foreign monetary authorities, or the calling in of loans made to them in previous periods.

[19] It is misleading to use this term because, strictly speaking, the term 'balance of payments' refers to the whole set of accounts. The official balance is its bottom line and the one that attracts the most attention. We defer to tradition and use the symbol 'BoP' for the official balance.

2 Because nominal GDP measures final sales at market prices, an increase in the price level leads to an increase in GDP even if quantities sold are constant. Real GDP is computed by pricing current output with constant prices, corresponding to a chosen base year.

3 The GDP deflator is the ratio of nominal to real GDP. It is one measure of the price level. Inflation is approximately equal to the difference between the nominal and real GDP growth rates. Price indexes, also used to compute inflation rates, use constant-weight baskets of goods and services.

4 Measurement of GDP is imperfect, costly, and time-consuming. A large amount of economic activity is unmeasured, such as household services and the underground economy. Yet year-on-year comparisons, such as annual growth rates, are less affected by measurement problems.

5 GDP is equal to the sum of consumption, investment, government spending, and the current account ($Y = C + I + G + CA$). At the same time, GDP is equal to consumption, plus private sector savings, plus net taxes (gross taxes less public transfers received by the private sector) ($Y = C + S + T$). It follows as an identity that the current account surplus is equal to the surplus of the government plus the surplus of the private sector ($CA = (T - G) + (S - I)$).

6 The balance of payments is a record of current account transactions and their financial counterparts, the capital and financial (or simply financial) account. The current account is the sum of the merchandise, invisibles, and transfer accounts. Any surplus or deficit must be matched by an equal and opposite sum of private long-term capital, short-term financial errors and omissions, and official accounts.

7 If the monetary authorities want to maintain the value of their country's exchange rate, they must intervene on exchange rate markets to match any possible balance of payments imbalance. Conversely, the exchange rate floats freely when the monetary authorities refrain from intervening; then all adjustment for balance of payments equilibrium occurs within the private sector, as a result of changes in the market-determined exchange rate.

🔑 Key Concepts

- accounting identities
- gross domestic product (GDP)
- flow versus stock variables
- final versus intermediate sales
- value added
- GDP per capita
- gross national income (GNI)
- nominal and real GDP
- GDP deflator
- price index, consumer price index (CPI)
- underground economy
- circular flow
- net taxes

- private income
- consumption
- financial intermediation
- savings
- physical capital
- investment
- absorption
- personal disposable income
- depreciation
- net domestic product (NDP)
- balance of payments
- balance of goods and services, of international income and current transfers

- ◆ current account
- ◆ capital and financial account
- ◆ official account

- ◆ foreign exchange rate reserves
- ◆ foreign exchange market intervention
- ◆ overall balance

❓ Exercises

1 You are given the following data:

GDP	2,500
Depreciation	250
Before-tax corporate profits	500
Social security contributions	350
Transfers to households and firms	500
Net interest to foreigners	100
Proprietary income	35
Net corporate saving	300
Indirect taxes	500
Subsidies to enterprises	200
Fines and fees	50
Net remittances to rest of world	250
Corporate taxes	50
Consolidated government deficit	50
Personal taxes	750
Household savings	100
Investment expenditure	600

Compute: NDP, national income, personal income, personal disposable income, consumption, government purchases, GDP, the current account balance. State your assumptions clearly.

2 What happens to GDP when a music teacher marries his student whom he was tutoring previous to the marriage, but stops billing her for her private lessons? What happens when a housewife becomes self-employed as her own day-care centre?

3 'Services do not contribute to GDP as much as industry because industry produces *things*—tangible goods.' Comment on this using what you have learned about the national income accounts.

4 I bought my house for €100,000. I have just sold it for €200,000, and the estate agent received a 10% commission from the buyer. What is the effect on GDP?

5 Suppose you have the following data on prices and quantities transacted:

Prices (€)

	Apples	Pears	Petrol
2006	1.0	2.0	5.0
2007	1.0	3.0	6.0

Quantities

	Apples	Pears	Petrol
2006	300	100	50
2007	400	150	40

(a) If the economy produced all three (and only these three) goods, compute the nominal GDP in both periods, and real GDP at 2006 prices. What is the rate of inflation in 2007, as measured by the change in the GDP deflator?

(b) Suppose a CPI is constructed using weights corresponding to quantities produced in 2006. What is the rate of inflation measured by the CPI?

6 Give the three definitions of GDP. Explain whether the following transactions contribute to UK GDP, and, if so, explain how all three definitions apply.

(a) A resident of York purchases a bag of sweets produced in Manchester.

(b) A tourist visiting York purchases a bag of sweets produced in Manchester.

(c) An operator of a Slovakian food chain purchases a large order of sweets produced in Manchester which are sent in the measurement period to Bratislava.

(d) A Manchester businessman purchases a machine to mould the sweets, which is manufactured in the Czech Republic.

(e) A store manager purchases several boxes of sweets from the Manchester sweet company, but stores them in the stock room, where they sit until the beginning of next year.

(f) The city government of York purchases several boxes of sweets from the Manchester sweet company for its reception for the Lord Mayor.

7 Over the past five years, taxes were about 60% of GDP in Sweden. Yet disposable income over the past five years also amounted to 60% of GDP. How can these numbers be reconciled?

8 'Commuters increase GDP because they send home a large fraction of their earnings.' Comment.

9 How would the following transactions be recorded in the *French* balance of payments?

◆ A French resident buys an Austin Mini produced in the United Kingdom.

◆ A French resident purchases stocks in a German corporation from a German bank based in Germany.

◆ A French national living in Switzerland buys stock in a French company from a bank based in Switzerland.

◆ A French resident builds a house in Italy, paying Italian residents to do the job.

◆ A French resident gives money to Greenpeace located in Hamburg, Germany.

◆ A French banker sends a wire transfer of euros to his daughter at the Humboldt University of Berlin.

◆ The same French banker wires euros from his bank account in Berlin to his account in Paris.

◆ A Tunisian worker in Marseilles sends money to his family in Tunis.

◆ Peugeot SA, a French concern, pays dividends to a resident of Finland.

◆ Profits of Owen Corning, a US company, are reinvested in capacity expansion of a factory in Fontainebleau, France.

◆ The Banque de France (a part of the European Central Bank) purchases Danish kroner to prevent the exchange rate (in euro) from falling in Copenhagen.

◆ A French resident of Colmar, a town in Alsace near the German border, smuggles home a stereo purchased in Freiburg (Germany).

10 In Table 2.8, China has a very large surplus in the *overall balance*—many times greater than other countries shown. What does this mean for the official transactions balance? What does this imply for the behaviour of the People's National Bank of China?

→ Essay Questions

1 Evaluate the following statement: 'Bringing the underground economy above ground would increase the GDP, but worsen tax receipts and the balance of payments.'

2 In recent years firms in Europe as well as in the USA have begun to 'outsource' or divest themselves of many traditional service functions, purchasing them on the market instead. Companies are increasingly obtaining computer, catering, legal, consulting, and other business services by ordering them from outside, independent companies. What is the effect of outsourcing on GDP? (Think of the example of a firm which turns its cafeteria into an independent contractor.) How does your answer depend on what the new firm does with its independence?

3 GDP mixes up everything. It includes 'goods' such as apples we eat and theatre shows we enjoy, but also 'bads' such as petrol burnt in traffic congestion and burial costs. It ignores many 'goods' as well: the value of a good neighbour or the free time that we can spend watching a sunset. Comment and explore how you would compute gross domestic happiness?

4 Countries which generate most economic activity from the exploitation of natural resources often experience large fluctuations in their national income and product account results. Explain why this might be the case, carefully defining the terms value added and costs of production. Why might the national income and product accounts lose their relevance for these countries? How might the problem be solved?

5 'The EU member states don't need balance of payments statistics. The individual states of the USA get along fine without them.' Discuss.

PART II

The Macroeconomy in the Long Run

Part II studies the long run. The long run is what economists mean when they talk about the behaviour of an economy over a period of decades, rather than over short time spans of quarters or a few years. The long run describes attainable and sustainable aspects of the national economy, and goes far beyond the short-term perspective of the business cycle fluctuations described in Chapter 1. This includes, most importantly, the evolution of standards of living of present and future generations.

We begin with economic growth, the most fundamental of all long-run macroeconomic phenomena. Economic growth is the rate at which the real output of a nation or a region increases over time. As the ultimate determinant of the poverty or wealth of nations, sustained economic growth is a central aspect of the long run. Because this is such an important topic, two chapters are dedicated to studying it.

Next, we look at the labour market, one of the most important markets in modern economies. In the labour market, households trade time at work for the ability to purchase goods and services in the goods market. We will see how labour is allocated: where it comes from, who demands it, and how to think about unemployment.

The last chapter in Part II introduces the long-run role of monetary and financial variables: money, interest rates, and the nominal exchange rate, which are generally denoted in nominal terms—in pounds or euros or dollars. Nominal variables are used to determine the real terms of exchange between goods within a country, between countries, or over time—the command of resources represented by one type of goods and services over others.

The Fundamentals of Economic Growth 3

The consequences for human welfare involved in questions like these are simply staggering: once one starts to think about them, it is hard to think about anything else.

R. E. Lucas, Jr[1]

3.1 Overview

The output of economies, as measured by the gross domestic product at constant prices, tends to grow in most countries over time. Is economic growth a universal phenomenon? Why are national growth rates of the richest economies so similar? Why do some countries exhibit periods of spectacular growth, such as Japan in 1950–1973, the USA in 1820–1870, Europe after the Second World War, or China and India more recently? Why do others sometimes experience long periods of stagnation, as China did until the last two decades of the twentieth century? Do growth rates tend to converge, so that periods of above-average growth compensate for periods of below-average growth? What does this imply for levels of GDP per capita? These questions are among the most important ones in economics, for sustained growth determines the wealth and poverty of nations.

This chapter will teach us how to think systematically about growth and its determinants. It turns out that the explanation of this fundamental process is rather simple. Fig. 3.1 shows the per capita GDP of the UK since 1920. It is plotted in logarithms because, as explained in Chapter 1, the slope of the curve directly shows the growth rate. The curve reminds us of important historical events: the build-up of a war economy in the late 1930s, the massive destructions and disruptions that followed and, more recently, the excessive growth of the early 2000s that led to the 2008–12 crisis. The figure also plots the trend. The amazing observation is that, in the end of it all, the economy always

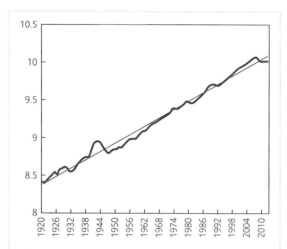

Fig. 3.1 GDP per capita in the UK 1920–2011

Using a logarithmic scale, we show the evolution of per capita GDP along with a trend that corresponds to a 2.1% growth rate. We see important events: the Great Depression in the early 1930s, the build-up of a war economy at the end of the same decade, the sharp fall as a result of the Second World War and the overheated 'bubble economy' of the 2000s. Remarkably, the GDP returns over time to its seemingly immutable growth trend.

Source: Maddison (1995), AMECO

comes back to its trend. No matter how profound are these historical episodes, Britain has been growing at 2.1% per annum. This suggests that there exist some fundamental forces that, if left free to operate, keep an economy increasing indefinitely.

Three main forces can be identified. First, investment can add to the capital stock, and a greater capital stock enables workers to produce more. Second, the working population or labour force can grow,

---

[1] Robert E. Lucas, Jr (1937–), Chicago economist and Nobel Prize Laureate in 1995, is generally regarded as one of the most influential contemporary macroeconomists. Among his many fundamental contributions to the field, he has researched extensively the determinants of economic growth.

which means that more workers are potentially available for market production. This growth can arise for many reasons—increases in births two or three decades ago, immigration now, or increased labour force participation by people of all ages, especially by women. The third reason is **technological progress**. As knowledge accumulates and techniques

improve, workers and the machines they work with become more productive. For both theoretical and empirical reasons, technological progress turns out to be the ultimate driver of economic growth. Because it is such an important topic, a detailed discussion of technological progress will be postponed to Chapter 4.

3.2 Thinking about Economic Growth: Facts and Stylized Facts

3.2.1 The Economic Growth Phenomenon

Despite setbacks arising from wars, natural disasters, or epidemics, economic growth seems like an immutable economic law of nature. Over the centuries, it

has been responsible for significant, long-run material improvements in the way the world lives. Table 3.1 displays the annual rate of increase in real GDP—the standard measure of economic output of a geographic entity—for various periods in a number of currently

Table 3.1 The Growth Phenomenon

	Average rates of growth in GDP (% per annum)							Av. Growth GDP per capita 1820–2010 (% per annum)
	1820–1870	1870–1913	1913–50	1950–73	1973–2001	2001–2010	1820–2010	
Austria	1.4	2.4	0.2	5.2	2.5	2.2	2.0	1.6
Belgium	2.2	2.0	1.0	4.0	2.1	2.0	2.1	1.5
Denmark	1.9	2.6	2.5	3.7	2.0	1.7	2.4	1.5
Finland	1.6	2.7	2.7	4.8	2.4	2.3	2.6	1.8
France	1.4	1.6	1.1	4.9	2.3	1.9	1.9	1.6
Germany	2.0	2.8	0.3	5.5	1.8	1.7	2.2	1.6
Italy	1.2	1.9	1.5	5.5	2.3	1.7	2.1	1.5
Netherlands	1.7	2.1	2.4	4.6	2.4	2.2	2.4	1.4
Norway	2.2	2.2	2.9	4.0	3.4	2.9	2.7	1.9
Sweden	1.6	2.1	2.7	3.7	1.9	1.9	2.3	1.6
Switzerland	1.9	2.5	2.6	4.4	1.2	1.3	2.4	1.7
United Kingdom	2.0	1.9	1.2	2.9	2.1	2.0	1.9	1.4
Japan	0.4	2.4	2.2	8.9	2.7	2.2	2.6	1.8
United States	4.1	3.9	2.8	3.9	3.0	2.7	3.5	1.7

Source: Maddison (2007) 'Historical Statistics for the World Economy: 1–2003 AD'.

Box 3.1   China and the Chinese Puzzle of Economic Growth

At the end of the fourteenth century, China probably was the world's most advanced economy. While Europe was just beginning to recover from centuries of inward-looking backwardness and relative decline, Chinese society had reached a high degree of administrative, scientific, and economic sophistication. Innovations such as accounting, gunpowder, the maritime compass, moveable type, and porcelain manufacture are just a few attributable to the Middle Empire. Marco Polo was one of many famous European traders who tried to break into the Chinese market. According to crude estimates by economic historian Angus Maddison, fourteenth-century Western Europe and China were on roughly equal footing in terms of market output—and many experts claim the Chinese were technically more advanced.[2] Yet over the next six centuries, standards of living increased 25-fold in Western Europe compared with only sevenfold in China.

Most of that sevenfold increase in GDP per capita has occurred in China over the last three decades. After adopting far-reaching market economy reforms in the 1980s, economic growth has averaged a phenomenal 10% per annum since 1990. At this rate, the economy doubles in size every seven years. If this growth continues, China will easily reach the standard of living of poorer EU countries by 2025.

The Chinese growth phenomenon raises a host of intriguing questions. Why did China stagnate for centuries, while Europe flourished? Why did China literally explode in the 1990s? It is widely agreed that the Chinese success story would have been impossible without China's shift from isolationism to a policy of openness to international trade and foreign direct investment. Almost as a converse proposition, some historians associate the economic stagnation of China after the fifteenth century with the grounding of 3,500 great sailing ships of the Ming dynasty in 1433, the world's largest naval expeditionary fleet under the command of Admiral Zheng He. A policy of 'inward perfection', fear of Mongol threats, lack of government funding, and a deep mistrust of merchant classes which benefited most from the international excursions of the Imperial 'Treasure Fleet', all led China to close itself off from foreign influences, with disastrous consequences. For many economists, this is a warning shot about potential risks of an unquestioning anti-globalization movement. In Chapter 4, we revisit the theme of international trade and economic growth in more detail.

wealthy countries since 1820. (The early data are clearly rough estimates.) Over almost two centuries, GDP has increased by 60- to 100-fold or more, while per capita GDP has increased by 12- to 30-fold. Our grandparents are right when they say that we are much better off than they were.

The table also reveals that the growth process is not necessarily smooth. We will see that this variation reflects the effect of wars, colonial expansion and annexation, and dramatic changes in population as well as political, cultural, and scientific revolutions. It also reflects the business cycle. Despite these swings, it is striking that the overall average growth of GDP per capita is remarkably similar across these countries and over time. Indeed, the last column shows that *per capita* growth since 1820 has been 1.5–1.9% per annum.

Small average annual changes displayed in Table 3.1 cumulate surprisingly fast. The advanced economies of the world grow by roughly 2–4% per year. A growth rate difference of 2% per annum increases a gap by 49% in 20 years, and by 170% in half a century. The recent phenomenal growth successes of China and India and the troubling slowdowns in Western Europe and Japan show that growth is by no means an automatic birthright. Moreover, fortunes can change: Box 3.1 reminds us that China was a leading world economy in the fourteenth century, only to fall into half a millennium of decline and stagnation.

3.2.2 The Sources of Growth: The Aggregate Production Function

Growth theory asks how sustained economic growth across nations and over time is possible. Do we produce more because we employ more inputs, or

[2] Maddison (1991: 10).

because the inputs themselves become more productive over time, or both? What is the contribution of each factor? The most important tool we will use to think about these questions is the **production function**. The production function relates the output of an economy—its GDP—to productive inputs. The two most important productive inputs are the physical capital stock (equipment and structures), represented by K, and labour employed, represented by L. The capital stock includes factories, buildings, and machinery as well as roads and railroads, electricity, and telephone networks. Employment or labour is the total number of hours worked in a given period of time. The labour measure L is the product of the average number of workers employed (N) during a period (usually a year) and the average hours (h) that

they work during that period ($L = Nh$). We speak of person-hours of labour input.[3] Symbolically, the production function is written:

$$(3.1) \qquad Y = F(K,L).$$
$${\scriptstyle +}{\scriptstyle +}$$

The plus ('+') signs beneath the two inputs signify that output rises with either more capital or more labour.[5]

The production function is a useful, powerful, and widely used short-cut. It reduces many and complex types of physical capital and labour input to two. In microeconomics, the production function helps economists study the output of individual firms. In macroeconomics, it is used to think about the output of an entire economy. Box 3.2 presents and discusses

---

 ## Box 3.2 **For the Mathematically Minded: The Cobb–Douglas Production Function**

The use of mathematics in economics can bring clarity and precision to the discussion of economic relationships. An illustration of this is the notion of a production function, which formalizes the relationship between inputs (capital and labour) and output (GDP). One particularly well-known and widely-used example is the Cobb–Douglas production function:

$$(3.2) \qquad Y = K^\alpha L^{1-\alpha},$$

where α is a parameter which lies between 0 and 1, and is called the elasticity of output with respect to capital: a 1% increase in the capital input results in an α increase in output.[4] Similarly $1 - \alpha$ is the elasticity of output with respect to labour input. It is easy to see that the Cobb–Douglas production function possesses all the properties described in the text.

Diminishing marginal productivity

The marginal productivity of capital is given by the derivative of output with respect to capital K: $\partial Y/\partial K = \alpha K^{\alpha-1} L^{1-\alpha} = \alpha(L/K)^{1-\alpha}$. Since $\alpha < 1$, the marginal product

of capital is a decreasing function of K and an increasing function of L. Similarly, the marginal productivity of labour is given by $\partial Y/\partial L = (1-\alpha)(K/L)^\alpha$, which is increasing in K and decreasing in L.

Constant returns to scale

The Cobb–Douglas function has constant returns to scale: for a positive number t, which can be thought of as a scaling factor,

$$(3.3) \qquad (tK)^\alpha (tL)^{1-\alpha} = t^\alpha t^{1-\alpha} K^\alpha L^{1-\alpha} = tK^\alpha L^{1-\alpha} = tY.$$

Intensive form

The intensive form of the Cobb–Douglas production function is obtained by dividing both sides of (3.2) by L, which is the same as setting $t = 1/L$ in equation (3.3), to obtain:

$$(3.4) \quad Y/L = y = (K^\alpha L^{1-\alpha})/L = K^\alpha L^{-\alpha} = (K/L)^\alpha = k^\alpha,$$

where $k = K/L$ and $y = Y/L$ are the intensive form measures of input and output defined in the text. Since $\alpha < 1$, the intensive form production is indeed well-represented by Figure 3.2.

---

[3] Since output and labour inputs are flows, they could also be measured per quarter or per month, but should be measured over the same time interval. Note that capital is a stock, usually measured at the beginning of the current or end of the last period. We discussed the important distinction between stocks and flows in Chapter 1.

[4] To see this, note that the elasticity of output with respect to capital is defined as $(dY/dK)(K/Y)$ and is given by $(\alpha K^{\alpha-1} L^{1-\alpha})(K^{1-\alpha} L^{\alpha-1}) = \alpha$. Similarly, $1 - \alpha$ is the elasticity of output with respect to the labour input.

[5] Formally, the first partial derivatives $FK(K, L) \equiv \partial F(K, L)/\partial K$ and $FL(K, L) \equiv \partial F(K, L)/\partial L$ are positive.

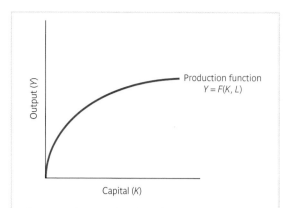

Fig. 3.2 The Production function

Holding labour input L (the number of hours worked) unchanged, adding to the capital stock K (available productive equipment) allows an economy to produce more, but in smaller and smaller increments.

the characteristics of a widely-used production function, the Cobb–Douglas production function.

The production function is a *technological relationship*. It does not reflect the profitability of production, and it has nothing to do with the quality of life or the desirability of work. It is meant to capture the fact that goods and services are produced using factors of production: here, equipment and hours of labour. In the following, we describe some basic properties that are typically assumed for production functions.

Marginal productivity

Consider an economy producing output with workers and a stock of capital equipment. Then imagine that a new unit of capital—a new machine—is added to the capital stock, raising it by the amount ΔK, while holding labour input constant.[6] Output will also rise, by ΔY. The ratio $\Delta Y/\Delta K$, the amount of new output per unit of incremental capital, is called the economy's **marginal productivity**. Now imagine repeating the experiment, adding capital again and again to the existing stock, always holding labour input constant. Should we expect output to increase by the same amount for each additional increment of capital?

Generally, the answer is no. As more and more capital is brought into the production process and the number of hours worked remains the same, each new piece of equipment is allocated less of workers' time. As one might expect, the increases in output become smaller and smaller. This is called the principle of **diminishing marginal productivity**.[7] It is represented in Figure 3.2, which shows how output rises with capital, holding labour unchanged. The flattening of the curve illustrates the assumption. In fact, the slope of the curve is equal to the economy's marginal productivity.

It turns out that the principle of diminishing marginal productivity also applies to the labour input. Increasing the employment of person-hours will raise output; but output from additional person-hours declines as more and more labour is being applied to a fixed stock of capital.

Returns to scale

Output increases when either inputs of capital or labour increases. But what happens if both capital and labour increase in the same proportion? Suppose, for example, that the inputs of capital and labour were both doubled—increased by 100%. If output doubles as a result, the production function is said to have **constant returns to scale**. If a doubling of inputs leads to more than a doubling of output, we observe **increasing returns to scale**. **Decreasing returns** is the case when output increases by less than 100%. It is believed that decreasing returns to scale are unlikely. Increasing returns, in contrast, cannot be ruled out, but we will ignore this possibility until Chapter 4. In fact, the bulk of the evidence points in the direction of constant returns to scale.

With constant returns we can think of the link between inputs and output—the production function—as a zoom lens: as long as we scale up the inputs, so does the output. In this case, an attractive property of constant returns production functions emerges: output per hour of work—the **output–labour ratio** (Y/L)—depends only on capital per hour of work—the **capital–labour ratio** (K/L). This simplification allows

---

[6] Throughout this book, the symbol 'Δ' (Greek delta) is used to denote a step change in a variable.

[7] Following footnote 5, this feature of the production function implies mathematically that the second partial derivatives $F_{KK}(K, L) \equiv \partial^2 F(K, L)/\partial K^2$ and $F_{LL}(K, L) \equiv \partial F^2(K, L)/\partial L^2$ are negative.

us to write the production function in the following intensive form:[8]

(3.5) $$y = f(k),$$

where $y = Y/L$ and $k = K/L$. The output–labour ratio Y/L is also called the average productivity of labour: it says how much, on average, is being produced with one unit (one hour) of work.[9] The capital–labour ratio K/L measures the capital intensity of production.

The intensive-form production function is depicted in Figure 3.3. Because of diminishing marginal productivity, the curve becomes flatter as the capital–labour ratio increases. The intensive-form representation of the production function is convenient because it expresses the average productivity of labour in an economy as a function of the average stock of capital with which that labour is employed. In a world of constant returns, the intensive form production function says that standards of living do not depend on the absolute size of an economy. Indeed, Ireland, Singapore, and Switzerland have matched or exceeded the per capita GDP of the USA, the UK, or Germany.

3.2.3 Kaldor's Five Stylized Facts of Economic Growth

At this point it will prove helpful to look at the data: How have inputs and outputs in real-world economies changed over time? In 1961, the British economist Nicholas Kaldor (1908–1986) studied economic growth in many countries over long periods of time and isolated several **stylized facts** about economic growth which remain valid to this day. Stylized facts are empirical regularities found in the data. Kaldor's stylized facts will organize our discussion of economic growth and restrict our attention to theories which help us to think about it, just as a police

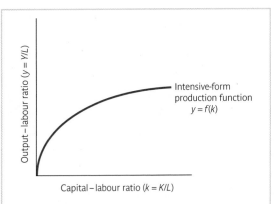

Fig. 3.3 The Production Function in Intensive Form

The production function shows that the output–labour ratio y grows with the capital–labour ratio k. Its slope is the marginal productivity of labour since with constant returns to scale $\Delta Y/\Delta K = \Delta y/\Delta k$. The principle of declining marginal productivity implies that the curve becomes flatter as k increases.

detective uses clues to limit the number of possible suspects in a criminal investigation.

The first of Kaldor's stylized facts concerns the behaviour of output per person-hour and capital per person-hour.

Stylized Fact No. 1: both output per capita and capital intensity keep increasing

The most remarkable aspect of the growth phenomenon is that real GDP seems to grow without bound. Yet labour input, measured in person-hours of work (L), grows much more slowly than both capital (K) and output (Y). Put differently, both average productivity (Y/L) and capital intensity (K/L) keep rising. Because income per capita (Y/N) is closely related to average productivity or output per hour of work (Y/L), economic growth implies a continuing increase in material standards of living.[10] Figure 3.4 presents the

---

[8] The constant returns property implies that if we scale up K and L by a factor t, Y is scaled up by the exactly same factor—for all positive numbers t, it is true that $tY = F(tK, tL)$. In the text we use the case $t = 2$; we double all inputs and produce twice as much. If we choose $t = 1/L$, we have $y = Y/L = F(k, 1)$. Rename this $f(k)$ because $F(k, 1)$ depends on k only. The intensive production function $f(k)$ expresses output produced per unit of labour (y) as a function of the capital intensity of production (k).

[9] It is important to recall the distinction between average productivity (Y/L) and marginal productivity ($\Delta Y/\Delta L$).

[10] If population size N and total hours worked L change in the same proportion, the growth rates of Y/N and Y/L are identical. In developed (mature) economies, people tend to work less hours and less years, so Y/L grows more slowly than Y/N. Formally, $\Delta(Y/L)/(Y/L) = \Delta Y/Y - \Delta L/L$ and $\Delta(Y/N)/(Y/N) = \Delta Y/Y - \Delta N/N$, so the difference between the growth rates of per capita output Y/N and average productivy Y/L is $\Delta N/N - \Delta L/L$. Section 3.6.3 examines this difference.

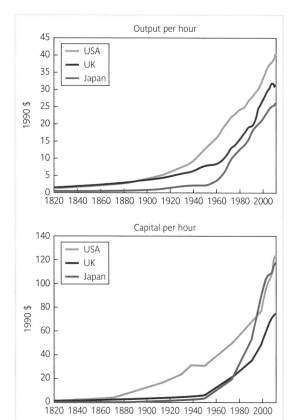

Fig. 3.4 The Output–Labour and Capital–Labour Ratios in Three Countries

Output–labour and capital–labour ratios are continuously increasing. Growth accelerated in the USA in the early twentieth century, and after 1950 in Japan and the UK.

Sources: Maddison (1995); Groningen Total Economy Database, (www.ggdc.net), OECD, *Economic Outlook*, chained.

Table 3.2 Capital–Output Ratios (K/Y), 1913–2009	1913	1950	1973	1992	2009
France	1.6	1.7	1.8	2.3	2.6
Germany	2.3	2.1	2.4	2.3	2.6
Japan	1.0	1.8	1.7	3.0	3.9
UK	1.0	1.1	1.7	1.8	1.9
USA	2.9	2.3	2.1	2.4	2.3

Source: Maddison (1995); 2009 data from *Economic Outlook*, OECD.

evolution of the output–labour and capital–labour ratios in three important industrial economies.

Stylized Fact No. 2: the capital–output ratio exhibits little or no trend over time

As they grow in a seemingly unbounded fashion, the capital stock and output tend to track each other. As a consequence, the ratio of capital to output (K/Y) shows little or no systematic trend. This is apparent from Figure 3.4, but Table 3.2 shows that it is only approximately true. For example, while output per hour in the USA has increased by roughly 600% since 1913, the ratio of capital to output actually fell slightly over the same period. At any rate, the capital–output ratio

may not be exactly constant, but it is far from exhibiting the steady, unrelenting increases in average productivity and capital intensity described in Stylized Fact No. 1.

Stylized Fact No. 3: hourly wages keep rising

The long-run increases in the ratios of output and capital to labour (Y/L and K/L) mean that, over time, an hour of work produces ever more output. Simply put, workers become more productive. It stands to reason that their wages per hour should also rise (the theoretical reasoning will be shown more formally in Chapter 5), and this is indeed the case. Growth evidently delivers ever-increasing living standards for workers.

Stylized Fact No. 4: the rate of profit is trendless

Note that the capital–output ratio (K/Y) is just the inverse of the average productivity of capital (Y/K). The absence of a clear trend for the capital–output ratio (K/Y) implies that average capital productivity too is trendless: over time, the same amount of equipment delivers about the same amount of output. It is to be expected therefore that the rate of profit does not exhibit a trend either. This stands in sharp contrast with labour productivity, whose secular increase allows a continuing rise in real wages. Yet income flowing to owners of capital has increased, but only because the stock of capital itself has increased. Indeed, with a stable rate of profit, income from capital increases proportionately to the capital stock.

Stylized Fact No. 5: the relative income shares of GDP paid to labour and capital are trendless

We just saw that incomes from labour and capital increase secularly. Surprisingly perhaps, it turns out that they also tend to increase at about the same rate, so that the distribution of total income (GDP) between capital and labour has been relatively stable. In other words, the labour and capital shares have no long-run trend. We will have to work a little harder to explain this remarkable fact.

3.2.4 The Steady State

Stylized facts are not meant to be literally true at all times, certainly not from one year to the other. Instead, they highlight central tendencies in the data. As we study growth, we are tracking moving targets, variables that keep increasing all the time, apparently without any upper limits. Thinking about moving targets is easier if we can identify stable relationships among them. This is why Kaldor's stylized facts will prove helpful. Another example of this approach is given by the evolution of GDP: it seems to be growing without bounds, but could its growth rate be roughly constant? The answer is yes, but only on average, over five or ten years or more. In Chapter 1, we noted the important phenomenon of business cycles, periods of fast growth followed by periods of slow growth or even declining output. As we look at

secular economic growth, we are not interested in business cycles. We ignore shorter-term fluctuations—compare Figures 1.5 and 1.6 in Chapter 1—and focus on the long run.

This is why it is useful to try and imagine how things would look if there were no business cycles at all. Such a situation is called a **steady state**. Its central feature is that certain variables, such as GDP growth rates, or ratios of key variables, such as the capital–output ratio or the labour income share—are constant. Just as the stylized facts are not to be taken literally, think of the steady state as the long-run average behaviour that we never reach, but fluctuate about. From the perspective of 10 years ago, we thought of today as the long run, but now we can see all the details that were unknown back then. Given that modern GDPs double every 10–30 years, a temporary boom or recession which shifts today's GDP by one or two percentage points amounts to little in the greater order of things, the powerful phenomenon of continuous long-run growth. Steady states—and stylized facts—are not just convenient ways of making our lives simpler; they are essential tools for distinguishing the forest from the trees.

3.3 Capital Accumulation and Economic Growth[11]

3.3.1 Savings, Investment, and Capital Accumulation

Kaldor's first stylized fact highlights a relationship between output per hour and capital per hour. This link is in fact predicted by the production function in its intensive form. It suggests that a good place to start if we want to explain economic growth is to understand why and how the capital stock rises over time. We will thus first study how the savings by households—foregone consumption—is transformed into investment in capital goods, which causes the capital stock to grow.

The central insight is delivered by the circular flow diagram presented in Chapter 2 (Figure 2.3). GDP represents income to households, either to workers as wages and salaries, or to owners of firms as distributed profits. Households and firms save part of their

income. These savings flow into the financial system—banks, stock markets, pension funds, etc. The financial system channels these resources to borrowers: firms, households, and the government. In particular, firms borrow—including from their own savings—to purchase capital goods used in production. This expansion of productive capacity, in turn, raises output, which then raises future savings and investment, and so on. This is the machinery behind the growth phenomenon.

To keep things simple, let us first assume that the size of the population, the labour force, and the numbers of hours worked are all constant. At this stage, we ask some fundamental questions: can

---

[11] This section presents the **Solow growth model**, in reference to Nobel Prize Laureate Robert Solow of the Massachusetts Institute of Technology.

capital accumulation proceed without bound? Does more saving mean faster growth? And since saving means postponing consumption, is it always a good idea to save more?

3.3.2 Capital Accumulation and Depreciation

Let us start from the national accounts of Chapter 2. Identity (2.7) shows that investment (*I*) can be financed either by private savings by firms or households (*S*), by government savings (the consolidated budget surplus, or $T − G$), or the net savings of foreigners (the current account deficit, $Z − X$):

(3.6) $I = S + (T − G) + (Z − X).$

As a description of the long-run or a steady state, suppose that the government budget is in balance ($T = G$), and the current account surplus equals zero ($Z = X$). In this case, the economy's capital stock is ultimately financed by savings of resident households.[12] More precisely, we reach the conclusion that, in the steady state, $I = S$. Investment expenditures are financed entirely by domestic savings. This is a first explanation of the growth phenomenon: we save, we invest, we grow. As a first approximation, let *s* be the fraction of GDP which households save to finance investment. Equality of investment and saving implies:

(3.7) $I = sY$ and therefore $I/L = sY/L = sy = sf(k).$

This relationship is shown in Figure 3.5 as the **saving schedule**. It expresses national savings as a function of national output and income. The saving schedule lies below the production function because saving is just a fraction of GDP.

We next distinguish between **gross investment**, the amount of money spent on new capital, and **net investment**, the increase in the capital stock. Gross investment represents new additions to the physical capital stock, but it does not represent the net change of the capital stock because, over time, previously installed equipment **depreciates**—it wears out, loses

12 This need not be true for a region within a nation: the capital stock of southern Italy, eastern Germany, or Northern Ireland may well be financed by residents of other parts of their countries. Yet even these financing imbalances are unlikely to be sustainable for the indefinite future.

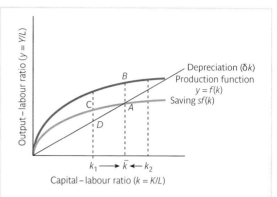

Fig. 3.5 The Steady State
The capital–labour ratio stops changing when investment is equal to depreciation. This occurs at point *A*, the intersection between the saving schedule *sf(k)* and the depreciation line *δk*. The corresponding output–labour ratio is determined by the production function *f(k)* at point *B*. When away from point *A*, the economy moves towards its steady state. Starting below the steady state at k_1, investment (point *C*) exceeds depreciation (point *D*) and the capital–output ratio will increase until it reaches its steady-state level $\bar{k}$.

some of its economic value, or becomes obsolescent. The fraction of the capital stock that is routinely lost each period is called **depreciation**, and the proportion of the total stock lost each period δ is called the **depreciation rate**. The depreciation rate for the overall economy is fairly stable and will be taken as constant. Logically, this implies that the more capital is in place, the more depreciation will occur. Because it is proportional to the capital stock, depreciation is represented in Figure 3.5 by a ray from the origin, the **depreciation line**, with slope δ.

Whenever gross investment exceeds depreciation, net investment is positive and the capital stock rises. If gross investment is less than depreciation, the capital stock falls. While it may seem odd to imagine a shrinking capital stock, it is not uncommon to observe in declining industries or regions. Net investment is therefore:

(3.8) $\Delta K = sY − \delta K$

or equivalently, written in intensive form:

$$\Delta k = sy − \delta k.$$

We see that the net accumulation of capital per unit of labour is positively related to the savings rate s and negatively related to the depreciation rate δ. How about the link between capital accumulation Δk and capital intensity k? It is ambiguous. On the one hand, a larger capital stock means a higher income level ($y = f(k)$), and therefore more savings and more gross investment. On the other hand, more capital means more depreciation and less net investment. This ambiguity is a central issue in the study of economic growth and will be addressed in the following sections.

3.3.3 Characterizing the Steady State

Let us summarize what we have done up to now. The production function (3.5) relates an economy's output to inputs of capital and labour. Its intensive form, presented in Figure 3.4 and Figure 3.5, relates the output–labour ratio to the capital–labour ratio. According to equation (3.8), capital accumulation is also driven by the output–labour ratio. Putting all these pieces together, we find that capital accumulation (Δk) is determined by stock of capital already accumulated up to that point (k):

(3.9) $\Delta k = sf(k) - \delta k.$

In Figure 3.5, Δk is the vertical distance between the savings schedule $sf(k)$ and the depreciation line δk. It represents the net change in the capital stock per unit of labour input in the economy. The sign of Δk tells us where the economy is heading. When $\Delta k > 0$, the capital stock per capita is rising and the economy is growing, since more output can be produced. When $\Delta k < 0$, the capital stock per capita and output per capita are both declining. At the intersection of the saving schedule and the depreciation line (point A), gross investment and depreciation are equal, so the capital–labour ratio (point B) no longer changes. The capital stock is thus similar to the level of water in a bathtub when the drain is slightly open: gross investment is like the water running through the tap, while depreciation represents the loss of water through the drain. The newly accumulated capital exactly compensates that lost to depreciation—the water flows into the bathtub at the same speed as it leaks out. This is the steady state.

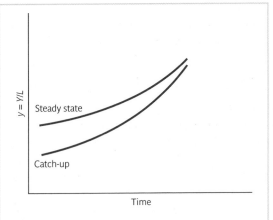

Fig. 3.6 Catching up

Catching up occurs when a country starts below its steady state GDP (lower curve) and embarks on a faster growth path, approaching the steady state (the upper curve) from below.

Wherever it starts, the economy will spontaneously gravitate to the steady state and stay there. Suppose, for instance, that the economy is to the left of the steady-state capital–output ratio $\bar{k}$, say at the level k_1.[13] Figure 3.5 shows that gross investment $sf(k_1)$ at point C exceeds depreciation δk_1 at point D. According to (3.9), the distance CD represents net investment, the increase in the capital–labour ratio k, which rises towards its steady-state level $\bar{k}$.

Can the capital stock proceed beyond $\bar{k}$, going all way to say, k_2? It turns out that it cannot. As the economy gets closer to point A, net investment becomes smaller and smaller as the steady state is approached; it equals nil precisely when $k = \bar{k}$. This process, called catch-up, is represented in Figure 3.6 and illustrated in Box 3.3. To see how the economy behaves when capital is above its steady state, consider $k_2 > \bar{k}$. Gross investment $sf(k_2)$ is less than depreciation δk_2, the capital–labour ratio declines, and we move leftward towards $\bar{k}$, the economy's stable resting point. Later we shall see that the result that capital per capita and output per capita eventually stabilizes carries over when we account for population growth.

---

[13] In general, steady-state values of variables will be indicated here with an upper bar, e.g. $\bar{k}$, y, etc.

Box 3.3 Growth Miracles Eventually Come to an End

In each period, we see 'growth miracles', countries that go through a period of rapid growth. The USA in the late nineteenth century and Australia in the early twentieth century went through this catch-up phase. For historical reasons, a country with a low capital–labour ratio unleashes the process described in Figure 3.6. The USA and Australia were initially poor colonies. Table 3.3 show some more recent examples. Europe recovered in the 1960s from wartime destructions. The next wave included Japan, also recovering from the war and economic backwardness. Then came China, a very poor country after centuries of economic and political repression. Catch-up started once it adopted fundamental economic reforms and opened to international trade in the late 1970s under the leadership of Deng Xiaoping. More recently, India and Vietnam have joined in. Much of Latin America has also started to catch up over the last decade or two.

Africa, finally, seems about to extricate itself from poverty as well.

These are amazing episodes. A 10% annual growth rate means that standards of living double every seven years. Why do these growth explosions take off, and how long do they last? Growth theory tells us that catch-up occurs spontaneously when people save and firms borrow these savings to invest and raise the capital stock, and when firms can adopt state-of-the-art technology. This requires adequate financial systems and economic openness. Importantly, it requires a reliable system of property rights, which in turn requires effective legal systems and the absence of armed conflict. As for the latter question, Figure 3.6 confirms the answer given by theory: until the economy reaches the steady state. This happened to Europe in the 1970s, to Japan a decade later. China is still poor and should keep growing for a decade or two, albeit at a decreasing rate.

3.3.4 The Role of Savings for Growth

We now show that the more a country saves, the more it invests; the more it invests, the higher is its steady-state capital–output ratio; and the larger its capital–output ratio, the higher its output–labour ratio will be in the steady state. This long-run proposition implies that countries that save and invest a lot have high per capita incomes. Is this true? Figure 3.7(a) looks at investment rates and GDP per capita for the whole world and is suggestive of such a relationship. For example, the poor countries of Africa typically invest little, in contrast to the richer countries of Europe and Asia. Yet, the link is hardly strong. In addition, Figure 3.7(b) shows that the investment rate fails to account for differences in economic growth between countries. Obviously, our story is too simple and we will soon put more flesh on the bare bones that we have just assembled.

Still, at this stage, we reach an important result: savings and investment are more closely linked to

 Table 3.3 Average Annual Growth Rates of GDP per Capita since 1960

	1961–1970	1971–1980	1981–1990	1991–2000	2001–2010
France	4.6	3.1	1.8	1.5	0.5
Japan	8.5	3.3	4.1	0.9	0.8
China	2.4	4.4	7.8	9.3	9.8
India	4.1	0.8	3.4	3.6	6.3
Vietnam			2.3	5.9	6.1

Source: World Development Indicators, The World Bank.

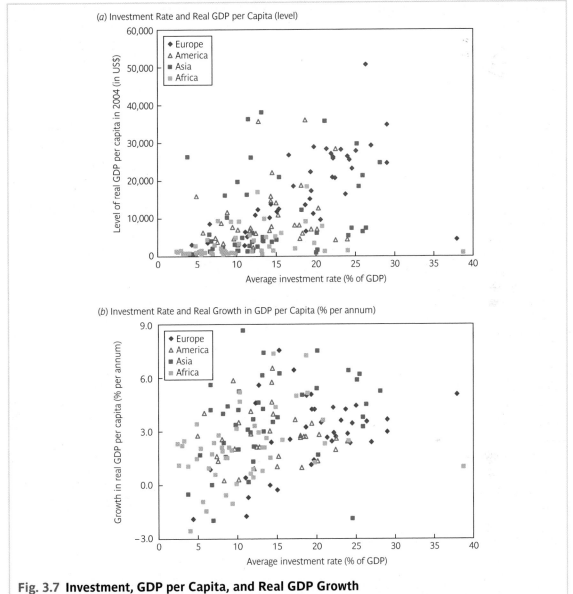

Fig. 3.7 Investment, GDP per Capita, and Real GDP Growth

For a sample of 174 countries over the period of 1950–2004, the correlation coefficient between the investment rate (the ratio of investment to GDP) and the average per capita GDP over the period is high and positive (0.51). The correlation of the investment rate in the countries with real GDP growth is also positive but less striking (0.31).

Source: Penn World Table Version 6.2 September 2006.

steady-state *levels* of output rather than their growth rates. This means that nations which save more should have higher standards of living in the steady state, but they do not grow faster, indefinitely. This is an important result which may seem counterintuitive. Yet it is implied by the simple Solow model.

To see this, consider Figure 3.8, which illustrates the effect of an increase in the savings rate from s to s′. The savings–investment schedule shifts upwards while the production function schedule remains unchanged. The new steady-state output–labour and capital–labour ratios are both higher at point B than

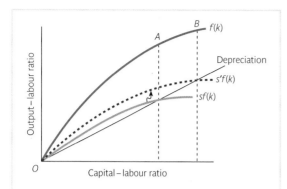

Fig. 3.8 An Increase in the Savings Rate

An increase in the savings rate raises capital intensity (k) and the output–labour ratio (y).

they were at point A beforehand. It will take time, however, for the economy to reach that new steady state. At the initial steady-state position (point A), an increase in the saving state causes gross investment to rise. Since depreciation is unchanged, net investment must be positive. The capital–labour ratio starts rising, which raises the output–labour ratio. This will go on until the new steady state is reached at point B. During this interim period, therefore, growth is higher, which can give the impression that higher investment rates cause higher economic growth. The boost is only temporary; once the steady state has been reached, no further growth effect can be expected from a higher savings rate. We still need a story to explain growth in output per capita. This is the story told in Sections 3.4 and 3.5.

It may be surprising that increased savings does not affect long-run growth. That result is an implication of diminishing returns. An increase in savings causes the capital stock to rise, but this also means that more capital depreciates and thus needs to be replaced. Increasing amounts of gross investment are needed just to keep the capital stock constant at its higher level. Yet the resources for that increased investment are not sufficiently forthcoming because the marginal productivity of capital decreases. Further additions to the capital–labour ratio yield smaller and smaller

increases in income, and therefore in savings and investment, while depreciation rises proportionately with the capital stock. Put simply, decreasing marginal productivity implies that, at some point, saving more is simply not worth it.[14]

3.3.5 The Golden Rule

Figure 3.8 contains an important message: to become richer, you need to save and invest more. But is being richer—in the narrow sense of accumulating capital goods—always necessarily better? Saving requires the sacrifice of giving up some consumption today against the promise of higher income tomorrow, but does saving more today always mean more consumption tomorrow? The answer is not necessarily positive. To see why, note that in the steady state, when the capital stock per capita is $\bar{k}$, savings equal depreciation and the steady-state level of consumption $\bar{c}$ (the part of income that is not saved) is given by:

(3.10) $$\bar{c} = \bar{y} - s\bar{y} = f(\bar{k}) - \delta\bar{k}.$$

In Figure 3.9, consumption per capita is given by the vertical distance between the production function and the depreciation line.[15] If we could choose any saving rate we wanted, we could effectively pick any point of intersection of the savings schedule with the depreciation line, and therefore any level of consumption we so desired. Figure 3.9 shows that consumption is highest at the capital stock for which the slope of the production function is parallel to the depreciation line.[16] The corresponding optimal steady-state capital–labour ratio is indicated as $\bar{k}'$. Now remember that the slope of the production function is the marginal productivity of capital (MPK) while the slope of the depreciation schedule is the rate of depreciation δ. We have just shown that the maximal level of consumption is achieved when the slope of the production function, the marginal

---

[14] In Chapter 4, we will see that the outcome is very different when the marginal productivity of capital is not decreasing in capital.

[15] Note that everything, including consumption and saving, is measured as a ratio to the labour input, person-hours. As already noted, if the number of hours worked does not change, the ratios move exactly as per capita consumption, savings, output, etc.

[16] An exercise asks you to prove this assertion.

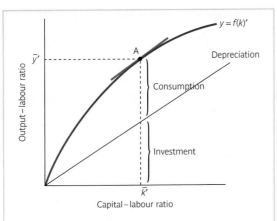

Fig. 3.9 The Golden Rule

Steady-state consumption $\bar{c}$ (as a ratio to labour) is the vertical distance between the production function and the depreciation line. It is at a maximum at point A corresponding to the situation where the slope of the production function, the marginal productivity of capital, is equal to δ, the slope of the depreciation line.

product of capital, is equal to the slope of the depreciation line:

(3.11) $$\text{MPK} = \delta.$$

This condition is called the **golden rule**, and can be thought of as a recipe for achieving the highest consumption per capita, given existing technological capabilities. In this case, with no population growth and no technical progress, the golden rule states that the economy maximizes steady-state consumption

when the marginal gain from an additional unit of GDP saved and invested in capital (MPK) equals the depreciation rate.

What are the consequences of 'disobeying' the golden rule? If the capital–labour ratio exceeds $\bar{k}'$, too much capital has been accumulated, and the MPK is lower than the depreciation rate δ. By reducing savings today, an economy can actually *increase* per capita consumption, both today and in the future. This looks like a free lunch, and indeed, it is one. We say that the economy suffers from **dynamic inefficiency**. Dynamically inefficient economies simply save and invest too much—in order to maintain a capital stock which is simply too large—and consume too little as a result.

A different situation arises if the economy is to the left of $\bar{k}'$. Here, steady-state income and consumption per capita may be raised by saving more, but not immediately; consumption can be increased only in the long run, after the adjustment has occurred. No free lunch is immediately available. More consumption in the future—in the steady state—must be 'earned' by increased saving and reduced consumption at the outset. Moving towards $\bar{k}'$ from a position on the left requires current generations to sacrifice so future generations can enjoy more consumption which will result from more capital and income in the steady state. An economy in such a situation is called **dynamically efficient** because it is not possible to do better without paying the price for it.

The difference between dynamically efficient and inefficient savings rates is illustrated in Figure 3.10,

Fig. 3.10 Raising Steady-State Consumption

In a dynamically inefficient economy (a), it is possible to permanently raise consumption by reducing saving. In a dynamically efficient economy (b), higher future consumption requires early sacrifices.

which shows how we move from one steady state to another one with higher consumption. In the dynamically inefficient case (*a*), it is possible to permanently raise consumption by consuming more now and during the transition to the new steady state. In the dynamically efficient case (*b*), a higher steady-state level consumption is not free and implies a transitory period of sacrifice.

Dynamic inefficiency—in short, too much capital—may have characterized some of the centrally planned economies of Central and Eastern Europe. We say 'may' because the proof that an economy is dynamically inefficient lies in showing that the marginal productivity of its capital lies below the depreciation rate, and neither of these is easily measurable. What we do know is that communist leaders often boasted about their economies' high investment rates, which were in fact considerably higher than in the capitalist West. Yet overall standards of living were considerably lower than in market economies, and consumer goods were in notoriously short supply. Box 3.4 presents the case of Poland.

In dynamically efficient economies, future generations would benefit from raising saving today, but those currently alive would lose. Should governments do something about it? Since it would represent a transfer of revenues from current to future generations, there is no simple answer. It is truly a deep political choice with no solution since future generations don't vote today. A number of factors influence savings, such as taxation, health and retirement systems, cultural norms, and social custom. Importantly, too, saving and investment are influenced by political conditions. Political instability and especially wars, civil or otherwise, can lead to destruction and theft of capital, and hardly encourage thrifty behaviour. As we discuss in Chapter 4, in many of the world's poorest countries, property rights are under constant threat or non-existent.

 Box 3.4   Dynamic Inefficiency in Poland?

From the period following the Second World War until the early 1990s, Poland was a centrally planned economy. Savings and investment decisions for the Polish economy were taken by the ruling communist party. The panels of Figure 3.11 compare Poland with Italy, a country with one of the highest saving rates in Europe. The first graph shows the increase in GDP per capita between 1980 and 1990 (the GDP measure is adjusted for purchasing power to take into account different price systems). While Italy's income grew by 25%, Poland's actually shrank by about 5%. The second graph shows the average proportion of GDP dedicated to saving over the same period. Clearly, Poland saved a lot, but received nothing for it in terms of income growth.

The third and fourth panels of Figure 3.11 show that the situation was reversed after 1991, when Poland introduced free markets and abandoned central planning. From 1991 to 2004, per capita GDP increased by 68%, with a lower investment rate than Italy's (which grew by 17%). However, our theory predicts that savings affect the steady-state level of GDP per capita, not its growth rate. In 1980, Poland invested 21.6% of its GDP. By 1990 this rate had fallen to 18.3%. In the period 1990–2004 per capita consumption rose in Poland from $2,908 to $7,037, an increase of 142%, compared with 61% in Italy over the same period. Is this proof of dynamic inefficiency, i.e. that a significant part of savings was used merely to keep up an excessively large stock of capital? Anecdotal evidence would suggest so. Stories of wasted resources were common in centrally planned economies: uninstalled equipment rusting in backyards, new machinery prematurely discarded for lack of spare parts, tools ill-adapted to factory needs, etc. One important cause of wastage was a reward system for factory managers. These were often based on spending *plans*, and not on actual output. An alternative interpretation is that the investment was in poor quality equipment, which could not match western technology. No matter how we look at it, savings were not put to their best use in centrally planned Poland.

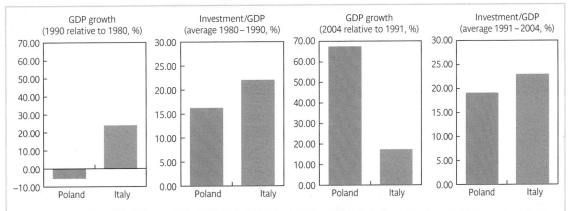

Fig. 3.11 Was Centrally Planned Poland Dynamically Inefficient?
Despite a high investment and savings rate, Polish per capita GDP shrank during the period 1980–1990 while Italy's grew. During the transition period, Poland grew much faster, with a lower investment rate than in Italy.
Source: Heston, Summers, and Aten (2006).

3.4 Population Growth and Economic Growth

A major shortcoming of the previous section is that it does not explain permanent, sustained growth, our very first stylized fact. Capital accumulation, we saw, can explain high living standards and growth during the transition to the steady state but the law of diminishing returns ultimately kicks in. Clearly, some crucial ingredients are missing. One of them is population growth, more precisely, growth in the employed labour force. This section shows that, once we introduce population growth, sustainable long-run growth of both output and the capital stock is possible.

Recall that labour input (person-hours) grows either if the number of people at work increases, or if workers work more hours on average. Later on in this chapter and Chapter 5, we will see that the number of hours worked per person has declined steadily over the past century and a half. Figure 3.12 shows that, despite this fact, employment has been rising, either because of natural demographic forces (the balance between births and deaths), increasing labour force participation (especially by women) or

immigration. Overall, more people are at work but they work shorter hours, so the balance of effects is ambiguous. Because the number of hours worked per person cannot and does not rise without bound, we will treat it as constant. Then any change in person-hours is due to exogenous changes in the population and employment, and output per person-hour changes at the same rate as output per capita.

Even though population and employment are growing, the fundamental reasoning of Section 3.3 remains valid: the economy gravitates to a steady state at which the capital–labour and output–labour ratios ($k = K/L$ and $y = Y/L$) stabilize. If L grows at an exogenous rate n, output Y and capital K will also grow at rate n. The relentless increase in the labour input will be the driver of growth in this case. Quite simply, if income per capita is to remain unchanged in the steady state, income must grow at the same rate as the number of people.

The role of saving and capital accumulation remains the same as in the previous section, with

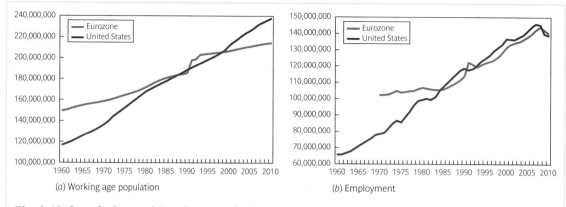

Fig. 3.12 Population and Employment in the Eurozone and the USA, 1960–2010

Population of working age (between 15 and 64) has been growing both in the USA and the countries of the Eurozone, the part of the European Union that uses the euro. Employment has also been growing, albeit less fast in Europe. Note the jump in the euro area in 1991, the year after German unification.

Source: OECD, *Economic Outlook.*

only a small change of detail. The capital accumulation condition (3.9) now becomes:[17]

(3.12) $\Delta k = sf(k) - (\delta + n)k.$

The difference is that, for the capital–labour ratio to increase, gross investment must not just compensate for depreciation, it must also provide new workers with the same equipment as those already employed. This process is called **capital-widening** and it explains the presence of n in the last term of the equation.

The situation is presented in Figure 3.13. The only difference with Figure 3.5 is that the depreciation line δk has been replaced by the steeper **capital-widening line** $(\delta + n)k$. The fact that the capital-widening line is steeper than the depreciation line captures the greater need to save when more workers are being equipped with productive capital. The steady state occurs at point A_1, the intersection of the saving schedule and the capital-widening line. At this intersection $\bar{k}_1$, savings are just enough to cover the depreciation and the needs of new workers, so $\Delta k = 0$.

The role of population growth can be seen by studying the effect of an increase in the rate of population growth, from n_1 to n_2. In Figure 3.13 the capital-widening line becomes steeper and the new steady state at point A_2 is characterized by a lower capital–labour ratio $\bar{k}_2$. This result makes sense, since we assume that savings behaviour is unchanged and yet we need

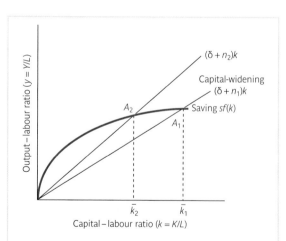

Fig. 3.13 The Steady State with Population Growth

The capital–labour ratio remains unchanged when investment is equal to $(\delta + n_1)k$. This occurs at point A_1, the intersection between the saving schedule $sf(k)$ and the capital-widening line $(\delta + n_1)k$. An increase in the rate of growth of the population from n_1 to n_2 is shown as a counter-clockwise rotation of the capital-widening line. The new steady-state capital – labour ratio declines from $\bar{k}_1$ to $\bar{k}_2$.

---

[17] The proof requires some calculus based on the principles presented in Box 6.3. The change in capital per capita obeys $\Delta k/k = (\Delta K/L) - (\Delta L/L)$. After substituting $\Delta K = I - \delta K$ and $\Delta L/L = n$ and setting $I = sY$, the equation simplifies to $\Delta k = sy - \delta k - nk = sf(k) - (\delta + n)k.$

more gross investment to equip the constant inflow of new workers. The solution is to provide each worker with less capital. Of course, a lower $\bar{k}$ implies a lower output–labour ratio $f(\bar{k})$. The Solow model with population growth implies that, all other things equal,

countries with a rapidly growing population will tend to be poorer than countries with lower population growth. Box 3.5 examines whether it is indeed the case that high population growth lowers GDP per capita.

Box 3.5 Population Growth and GDP per Capita

Figure 3.14 plots GDP per capita in 2008 and the average rate of population growth over the period 1960–2009. The figure could be seen as confirming the negative relationship predicted by the Solow growth model—and might even be interpreted as support for the hypothesis that population growth impoverishes nations. Thomas Malthus, a famous nineteenth-century English economist and philosopher, claimed exactly this: population growth causes poverty. He argued that a fixed supply of arable land could not feed a constantly increasing population and that population growth would ultimately result in starvation. He ignored technological change, in this case the green revolution which significantly raised agricultural output in the last half of the twentieth century. As we confirm in Section

3.5, technological change can radically alter the outlook for growth and prosperity.

Yet the pseudo-Malthusian view has been taken seriously in a number of less-developed countries, which have attempted to limit demographic growth. The most spectacular example is China, which has pursued a one-child-only policy for decades. At the same time, we need to be careful with simple diagrams depicting relationships between two variables. Not only do other factors besides population growth influence economic growth, but it may well be that population growth is not exogenous. Figure 3.14 could also be read as saying that as people become richer, they have fewer children. There exists a great deal of evidence in favour of this alternative interpretation.

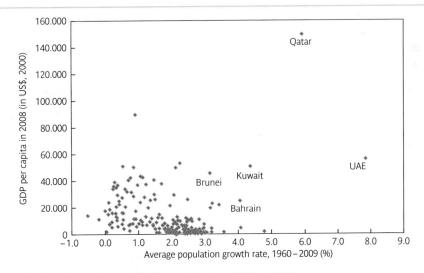

Fig. 3.14 Population Growth and GDP per Capita, 1960–2009

The figure reports data on real GDP per capita and average population growth for 190 countries over almost a half century. The plot indicates a discernible negative association between GDP per capita and population growth, especially when the rich oil-producing countries (United Arab Emirates, Qatar, Kuwait, Bahrain, Oman, Brunei, and Saudi Arabia) are excluded. The sharp population growth observed in these countries is largely to due to immigration.

Source: Alan Heston, Robert Summers and Bettina Aten, Penn World Table Version 7.0, Center for International Comparisons of Production, Income and Prices at the University of Pennsylvania, May 2011.

At what level of investment does an economy with population growth maximize consumption per capita? Because the number of people who are able to consume and save is growing continuously, the golden rule must be modified accordingly. Following the same reasoning as in Section 3.3, we note that steady-state investment per person-hour is $(\delta + n)\bar{k}$, so consumption per person-hour $\bar{c}$ is given by $f(\bar{k}) - (\delta + n)\bar{k}$. Proceeding as before, it is easy to see that consumption is at a maximum when:

(3.13) $\text{MPK} = \delta + n.$

The 'modified' golden rule equates the marginal productivity of capital with the sum of the depreciation rate δ and the population growth rate n. The intuition developed here continues to apply: the marginal product of an additional unit of capital (per capita) is set to its marginal cost, which now includes not only depreciation, but also the capital-widening investment necessary to equip future generations with the same capital per head as the current generation. A growing population will necessitate a higher marginal product of capital at the steady state. The principle of diminishing marginal productivity implies that the capital–labour ratio must be lower. Consequently, output per head will also be lower.

3.5 Technological Progress and Economic Growth

Taking population growth into account gives one good reason why output and the capital stock can grow permanently, and at the same rate. While this satisfies Kaldor's second stylized fact, the picture remains incomplete: so far, we conclude that the capital–labour and output–labour ratios are *constant* in the steady state. That standards of living are not rising is inconsistent with Kaldor's first stylized fact and the data reported in Table 3.1. We still need to account for the fact that per capita income and capital stock grow, *and* grow at the same rate.

As it turns out, we have ignored **technological or technical progress**. Over time, increased knowledge and better, more sophisticated techniques make workers and the equipment they work with more productive. With a slight alteration, our framework readily shows how technological progress can explain ever-rising living standards. To do so, once more, we reformulate the **aggregate production function** introduced in (3.1). Technological progress means that more output can be produced with the same quantity of equipment and labour. The most convenient way to think of technology is as an additional factor of production. In the production function, we add a measure of the state of technology, A, which raises output at given levels of capital stock and employment:

(3.14) $Y = F(A, K, L).$
$\qquad\qquad\quad\; {\scriptstyle +\;\; +\;\; +}$

When A increases, Y rises, even if K and L remain unchanged. For this reason, A is frequently called **total factor productivity**. Yet A is *not* really a factor of production, but rather a method or technique of production. No firm pays for knowledge; each firm just benefits from it. It is best thought of as 'best practice', which is assumed to be available freely to all. Innovations of all sorts continuously raise productivity. At this point, it will be convenient to assume that A increases at a constant rate a, without trying to explain how and why. Technological progress, which is the increase in A, is therefore considered as exogenous.

It turns out that it is possible to relate our analysis to previous results in this chapter in a straightforward way. First, we modify (3.14) to incorporate technical progress in the following particular way:

(3.15) $Y = F(K, AL).$

In this formulation, technological progress acts directly on the effectiveness of labour. (For this reason it is sometimes called *labour-augmenting* technical progress.)[18] An increase in A of, say, 10% has the same impact as a 10% increase in employment, even though the number of hours worked hasn't changed. The term AL is known as **effective labour** (or labour in efficiency units) to capture the idea that, with the same equipment, one hour of work today produces more output than before because A is higher. Effective labour AL grows for two reasons: (1) more labour L, and (2) greater effectiveness A. For this reason, the rate of growth of AL is now given by $a + n$.

Now we change the notation a little bit. We redefine y and k as ratios of output and capital *relative to effective labour*: $y = Y/AL$, $k = K/AL$. Once this is done, it is only a simple step to recover the now-familiar production function in intensive form, $y = f(k)$.[19] Not surprisingly, the ratio of capital to effective labour evolves almost exactly as before:

(3.16) $\Delta k = sf(k) - (\delta + a + n)k.$

The reasoning is the same as when we introduced population growth. There we noted that, to keep the capital–labour ratio K/L constant, the capital stock K must rise to compensate for both depreciation (δ) and population growth (n). Now we find that, to keep the capital–effective labour ratio $k = K/AL$ constant, the capital stock K must also rise to keep up with workers' enhanced effectiveness (a). So k will increase if saving $sf(k)$, and hence gross investment, exceeds the capital accumulation needed to make up for depreciation δ, population growth n, and increased effectiveness a. From there on, it is a simple matter to modify Figure 3.13 to draw Figure 3.15. The steady state is now characterized by constant ratios of capital and output to effective labour ($y = Y/AL$ and $k = K/AL$).

Constancy of these ratios in the steady state is a very important result. Indeed, if Y/AL is constant, it means that Y/L grows at the same rate as A. If the average number of hours remains unchanged, then income

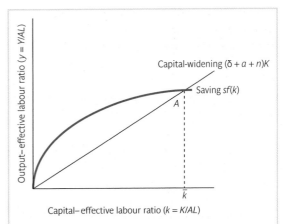

Fig. 3.15 The Steady State with Population Growth and Technological Progress
In an economy with both population growth and technological progress, inputs and output are measured in units per effective labour input. The intensive form production function inherits this property. The slope of the capital accumulation line is now $\delta + a + n$, where a is the rate of technological progress. The steady state occurs when investment is equal to $(\delta + a + n)k$ (point A), which is the intersection of the saving schedule $sf(k)$ with the capital-widening line $(\delta + a + n)k$. At the steady-state A, output and capital increase at the rate $a + n$, while GDP per capita increases at the rate a.

per capita must grow at the rate of technological progress, a. In other words, we have finally uncovered the explanation of Kaldor's first stylized fact: the continuous increase in standards of living is due to technological progress. Since K/AL is also constant, the capital stock per capita also grows in the steady state at the same rate as A, which is Kaldor's second stylized fact.

Figure 3.16 illustrates these results. Because of diminishing marginal productivity, capital accumulation alone cannot sustain growth. Population growth explains GDP growth, but not the sustained increase of standards of living over the centuries. Technological progress is essential for explaining economic growth in the long run. Rather than creating misery in the world, it turns out to be central to improvements in standards of living.

Note that an increase in the rate of technological progress, a, makes the capital-widening line steeper

---

[18] Obviously, technological innovation sometimes also makes capital more productive. It is much simpler to assume that technological progress is labour-augmenting and it is enough to provide a reasonable—if incomplete—interpretation of the growth phenomenon.

[19] Constant returns to scale implies that $y = F(K, AL)/AL = F(K/AL, 1)$.

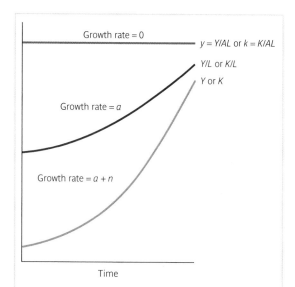

Fig. 3.16 Growth Rates along the Steady State

While output and capital measured in effective labour units (*Y/AL* and *K/AL*) are constant in the steady state, output–labour and capital–labour ratios (*Y/L* and *K/L*) grow at the rate of technological progress *a*, and output and the capital stock (*Y* and *K*) grow at the rate *a* + *n*, the sum of the rates of population growth and technological progress.

than before. In Figure 3.15 this would imply lower steady-state ratios of capital and output to effective

labour. This does not mean that more rapid technological progress is a bad thing, because what counts is income per person (*Y/L*), not income per unit of effective labour (*Y/AL*). The latter is just an accounting device to help describe a dynamic economy analytically and graphically. In the steady state, the higher *a* is, the faster *Y/L* and standards of living will grow.

The discussion can be extended in a natural way to address the issue of the golden rule. Redefining *c* as the ratio of aggregate consumption (*C*) to effective labour (*AL*), the following modified version of (3.10) will hold in the steady state:

$$\bar{c} = f(\bar{k}) - (\delta + a + n)\bar{k}.$$

The modified golden rule now requires that the marginal productivity of capital be the sum of the rates of depreciation, of population growth, and of technological change:

(3.17) $\mathrm{MPK} = \delta + a + n.$

Maximizing consumption per capita is equivalent to making consumption per unit of effective labour as large as possible. To do this, an economy now needs to invest capital per effective unit of labour to the point at which its marginal product 'covers' the investment requirements given by technical progress (*a*), population growth (*n*), and capital depreciation (δ).

3.6 Growth Accounting

3.6.1 Solow's Decomposition

As shown in Figure 3.16, we have now identified three sources of GDP growth: (1) capital accumulation, (2) population growth, and (3) technological progress. It is natural to ask how large the contributions of these factors are to the total growth of a nation or a region. Unfortunately, it is difficult to measure technological progress. Computers, for instance, probably raise standards of living and growth, but by how much? Some people believe that

the 'new economy', brought on by the information technology revolution, will push standards of living faster than ever. Others are less optimistic that the effect is any larger than other great discoveries which mark economic history. Box 3.6 provides some details on this exciting debate.

Robert Solow, who developed the theory presented in the previous sections, devised an ingenious method of quantifying the extent to which technological progress accounts for growth. His idea was to

Box 3.6   The New Economy: Another Industrial Revolution?

The striking changes brought about by the ICT (information and communications technologies) revolution, which include the internet, wireless telecommunications, MP3 players, and the conspicuous use of electronic equipment, have led many observers to conclude that a new industrial revolution is upon us. Figure 3.17 reports estimates of overall increases in multifactor productivity in the USA, computed as annual averages over four periods. A difference of 1% per year cumulates to 28% after 25 years. The figure shows a formidable acceleration in the period 1913–1972, and again over 1995–1999; hence the case for a second industrial revolution.

While initially there was much scepticism about the true impact of the ICT revolution—Robert Solow himself said early on that 'computers can be found everywhere except in the productivity statistics'—there is compelling evidence that ICT have indeed deeply impacted the way we work and produce goods and services, and have ultimately increased our standards of living significantly. These total factor productivity gains, according to recent research by Kevin Stiroh, Dale Jorgenson, and others, can be found both in ICT-*producing* as well as ICT-*using* sectors.[20] Strong gains in total factor productivity have been observed in the organization of retail trade, as well as in manufacturing and business services. Even more interesting is the fact that not all economies around the world have benefited equally from productivity improvements measured in the USA. In particular, some EU countries continue to lag behind in ICT adoption as well as innovation.

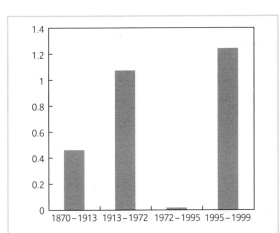

Fig. 3.17 Multifactor Productivity in the USA (average annual growth, %)

The average annual increase in *A* (multifactor productivity) accelerated sharply after 1913, almost came to a halt in the years 1972–1995, and seems to have recovered vigorously at the end of the 1990s.

Source: Gordon (2000).

and labour *L*. Once we know how much GDP has increased, and how much of this increase is explained by capital and hours worked, we can interpret what is left, called the **Solow residual**, as due to the increase in *A*, i.e. $a = \Delta A/A$:

$$\text{Solow residual} = \frac{\Delta Y}{Y} - \text{output growth due to}$$

growth in capital and hours worked.[21]

We now track down the **Solow decomposition**.

3.6.2 Capital Accumulation

Table 3.4 shows that, typically, capital has been growing at about 3–5% per year over most of the twentieth century in the developed countries. Capital accumulation accelerated sharply in the 1950s and 1960s as part of the post-war reconstruction. Many European countries accumulated capital considerably faster than the USA and the UK up until the mid-1970s, the reason being that continental Europe was poorer at

---

[20] See the references at the end of the book.

[21] Formally, the Solow residual is $\frac{\Delta A}{A} = \frac{\Delta Y}{Y} - \left[(1 - s_L)\frac{\Delta K}{K} + s_L\frac{\Delta L}{L} \right]$, where s_L is the labour share, defined as the share of national income paid to labour in the form of wages and non-wage compensation, and $1 - s_L$ is the income share of capital. The WebAppendix shows how this formula can be derived from the production function.

start with the things we can measure: GDP growth, capital accumulation, and hours worked. Going back to the general form of the production function (3.14), we can measure output *Y* and two inputs, capital *K*

Table 3.4 **Growth of Real Gross Fixed Capital Stock, 1913–2010 (% per annum)**

	1913–50	1950–73	1973–87	1987–2010
France	1.2	6.4	3.7	3.3
Germany	1.1	7.7	2.7	1.9*
Netherlands	2.4	6.9	2.2	2.5
UK	1.6	5.7	2.3	3.6
USA	1.7	3.8	2.6	2.8

* 1991–2008.
Sources: Maddison (1991); OECD, *Economic Outlook*.

the end of the Second World War. These sustained periods of rapid capital accumulation fit well the description of catch-up, when the capital stock is below its steady-state level.

3.6.3 Employment Growth

The most appropriate measure of labour input is total number of hours worked. For several reasons, however, growth in population or the number of employees does not necessarily translate into increased person-hours. To understand this, we can rewrite the total number of hours in the following way:

Total hours worked = (hours/employee)

× (employee/population) × population.

The total number of hours worked can increase for three reasons:

♦ Obviously, population growth. Everything else unchanged, more people provide more working hours. But many things can and do change.

♦ The proportion of people who work. Some working-age people are unemployed and others voluntarily

Table 3.5 **Population, Employment, and Hours Worked, 1870–2010**

	Population growth (% per annum)	Employment growth (% per annum)	Growth in hours worked per person (% per annum)	Hours worked per person in 1913	Hours worked per person in 2010
France	0.4	0.3	− 0.5	2,588	1,561
Germany	0.5	0.7	− 0.5	2,584	1,418
Netherlands	1.1	1.3	− 0.5	2,605	1,372
UK	0.5	0.5	− 0.4	2,624	1,647
USA	1.5	1.6	− 0.4	2,605	1,690
Japan	0.9	0.9	− 0.4	2,588	1,713

Sources: Maddison (2006); Groningen Growth and Development Centre and the Conference Board, Total Economy Database, January 2011.

stay out of work for various reasons. In addition, people live longer, study longer, and retire earlier. Furthermore, women have increased their labour force participation over the past 30 years.[22]

◆ Hours worked per person. Over time, those who work tend to work fewer hours per day and fewer days per year.

Table 3.5 shows that these effects have roughly cancelled each other out so that, in the end, employment and population size have increased by similar amounts in our sample of developed countries.

Table 3.5 also documents the sharp secular decline in the number of hours worked per person in the developed world. The long-run trend is a consequence of shorter days, shorter workweeks, fewer weeks per year, and fewer years worked per person. This is why the number of person-hours has declined across the industrial world. The dramatic decline in hours worked per person is a central feature of the growth process; an average annual reduction of 0.5% per year means a total decline of 40% over a century. As societies become richer, demand for leisure increases. The last two columns of the table reveal a massive jump in leisure time available, which is as important a source of improvement of human welfare as increases in material wealth.

3.6.4 Technological Change

Table 3.6 presents the Solow decomposition in two different contexts. The first employs historical data for the period 1913–1987. The second examines the same countries over the last two decades. We see that growth in inputs of labour and capital account for only one-half to two-thirds of total economic growth in these economies. The rest is the Solow residual, and confirms the importance of technological progress. Technological change appears to be remarkably steady, contributing to growth about 1% per year. We see a tendency to an acceleration of technological change since the late 1980s, with the notable exception of the UK, which makes a comeback over the last decade.

[22] Chapter 5 explores these and related issues in more detail.

Table 3.6 The Solow Decomposition (average annual growth rates)

(a) 1913–1987*

Country	GDP	Contribution of inputs	Residual
France	2.6	1.1	1.0
Germany	2.8	1.4	0.8
Netherlands	3.0	2.0	0.4
UK	1.9	1.2	0.5
USA	3.0	2.0	0.7
Japan	4.7	3.0	0.5

* An adjustment is made to account for the modernization of productive capital.

Source: Maddison (1991:158).

(b) 1987–1997

	GDP	Contribution of inputs	Residual
France	2.0	1.1	1.0
Germany*	1.4	0.2	1.2
Netherlands	2.9	1.8	1.1
UK	2.2	1.4	0.7
United States	3.0	2.5	0.5
Japan	2.7	1.4	1.3

* 1991–1997.

(c) 1997–2006

	GDP	Contribution of inputs	Residual
France	2.2	1.3	1.0
Germany	1.4	0.6	0.8
Netherlands	2.3	1.4	0.9
UK	2.7	1.7	1.0
United States	3.0	1.9	1.1
Japan	1.2	0.1	1.1

Sources: Maddison (1991); authors' calculation based on Groningen Growth and Development Centre and the Conference Board, Total Economy Database, January 2007, available at <www.ggdc.net>; OECD, *Economic Outlook*.

❗ Summary

1 Economic growth refers to the steady expansion of GDP over a period of a decade or longer. Growth theory is concerned with the study of economic growth in the steady state, a situation in which output and capital grow at the same pace and remain in constant proportion to labour in effective terms. This approach reflects key stylized facts.

2 The aggregate production function shows that output grows when more inputs (capital and labour) are used, and when technology improves the effectiveness of those inputs.

3 The capital stock, the sum of productive equipment and structures, is accumulated through investment, and investment is financed by savings. When savings are a stable proportion of output, the steady-state capital stock is determined by savings and capital depreciation.

4 The assumption that the marginal productivity of capital is declining implies that output, and therefore savings, grow less proportionately to the stock of capital, in contrast to depreciation, which is proportional to capital. The steady state is reached when capital accumulation exhausts the productive potential of additional savings and comes to an end.

5 In the absence of population growth and technological change, the steady state is characterized by zero output and capital growth. Adding population growth provides a first explanation of secular output growth, but standards of living—measured as output per capita—still do not increase. It is only when we allow for technological progress that permanent growth in per capita output and capital is possible.

6 The golden rule describes a steady state in which consumption is as high as possible. It occurs where the marginal productivity of capital equals the rate of depreciation (so as to replace lost or worn out capital) plus the rate of population growth (to provide new workers with adequate equipment) plus the rate of technological change (adjusting capital to enhanced labour effectiveness): $MPK = \delta + n + a$.

7 An economy is dynamically efficient when steady-state consumption can be raised tomorrow only at the expense of lower consumption today. An economy is dynamically inefficient when both current and future steady-state consumption can be increased. In the former case, the capital stock is lower than the golden-rule level. In the latter case, the capital stock is above the golden-rule level.

8 Saving does not affect the steady-state growth rate, but only the level of output per capita.

9 The Solow decomposition is a method of accounting for the sources of economic growth. It breaks down growth in GDP into the sum of growth attributable to changes in the factors of production and growth due to improved production. The latter is called the Solow residual, and is usually interpreted as technological change.

🔑 Key Concepts

- **economic growth**
- **technological progress**
- **Solow growth model**

- **stylized facts**
- **steady state**
- **capital accumulation**

- **aggregate production function**
- **marginal productivity**
- **diminishing marginal productivity**
- **returns to scale (constant, increasing, decreasing)**
- **output – labour ratio**
- **capital – labour ratio**
- **saving schedule**
- **gross investment**
- **net investment**

- **depreciate, depreciation rate**
- **depreciation line**
- **capital widening, capital-widening line**
- **golden rule**
- **dynamic inefficiency, dynamically efficient**
- **effective labour**
- **Solow decomposition**
- **Solow residual**
- **total factor or multifactor productivity**

❓ Exercises

1 Draw intensive-form production functions $f(k)$ with decreasing, constant, and increasing returns to scale.

2 Use graph paper (or a computer spreadsheet) to plot the following intensive-form production functions (expressing y as a function of k) from the interval [0, 100]:

(a) $f(k) = 2k$;

(b) $f(k) = 10 + k^{0.5}$;

(c) $f(k) = k^{1.1}$;

(d) $f(k) = 10 + 2k - 0.5k^2$;

(e) $f(k) = \max(0, -10 + 2k)$.

Which of these functions has constant returns? Decreasing or increasing returns? Are your answers always unambiguous, i.e. do they hold for all $k \in [0, 100]$?

3 Define the steady state. How is a steady state important in the context of the Solow growth model? Explain why stylized facts are necessary to organize the discussion of economic growth.

4 Suppose K/Y is constant at 2. (a) Assume first that there is no population growth and no technological progress. What is the steady-state saving–output ratio consistent with a rate of depreciation of 5%? (b) Now allow for positive economic growth, due to either population growth or tech-

nological progress. What is the steady-state saving–output ratio consistent with a rate of depreciation of 5% and 3% real growth?

5 Consider a country with zero technological progress and $K/L = 3$. Its population grows at the rate of 2% per year. What is the steady-state rate of growth of GDP per capita if the saving rate is 20%? If it is 30%? How do your answers change if depreciation occurs at a rate of 6% per year?

6 Suppose the aggregate production function is given by $Y = \sqrt{KL}$. Does it have increasing, decreasing, or constant returns to scale? Show that the marginal products of capital and labour are declining. Show that they are increasing in the input of the other factor.

7 Define the concept of a golden rule. Explain why it is achieved at $\bar{k}'$ in Figure 3.9. To establish this result, imagine that you start to the left of $\bar{k}'$ and explain why moving to the right increases consumption. Similarly show that consumption decreases when moving rightwards from a position to the right of $\bar{k}'$.

8 The golden rule (3.17) is MPK = $\delta + a + n$. In comparison with the no-technological change case, we now require a higher marginal productivity of capital. With diminishing marginal productivity, this means a lower capital stock per effective unit of labour. Is that not surprising? How can you explain this apparent paradox?

9 Draw a graph showing the evolution of Y/L in the catch-up phase and then in the ensuing steady state when the economy starts from a capital–effective labour ratio below its steady-state level. Draw a diagram showing investment (not the capital stock).

10 Explain, formally or informally, the difference between average labour productivity and output per capita.

11 In the steady state, output per effective labour Y/AL is constant. What happens to output per capita when the average number of hours worked declines, holding all else constant?

→ Essay Questions

1 Japan in the 1960s, Korea in the 1980s, China in the 1990s, and India in the current decade have experienced periods of rapid growth, in effect catching up on the richer and more developed countries. How can you explain this phenomenon, and why did it not happen earlier?

2 In earlier centuries, colonial expeditions were launched to increase a country's land and population. How might such activities make a country richer?

3 'Globalization is bad for growth since it means that countries invest abroad and expand the capital stocks of other countries instead of their own. The Solow model would consider this a decrease in the savings rate, thus leading to lower GDP per capita.' Comment.

4 Examining the panels of Figure 3.7, one immediately notices that African countries are bunched in the lower left-hand part of the diagram, while the European countries are clustered in the upper right-hand region. What explanation of this fact is offered by the Solow growth model? Do you think this is a sufficient explanation? Explain.

5 It is often claimed that the defeated nations after the Second World War grew faster than the victor nations. Is this hypothesis consistent with the Solow growth model?

Explaining Economic Growth in the Long Run

4

No one could have ever intended to deny that technological change is at least partially endogenous to the economy. Valuable resources are used in the pursuit of innovation, presumably with some rational hope of financial success.

Robert M. Solow

4.1 Overview

In Chapter 3, we identified three sources of economic growth: (1) increases in the working population, (2) capital accumulation, and (3) technological progress. Its message was that two countries with identical economic characteristics should have equal output and income per capita in the long run, regardless of their initial conditions. In effect, the Solow model predicts that countries as diverse as Algeria, Bangladesh, Paraguay, or Zambia can all hope to reach the living standards of the wealthiest nations of the world in reasonable time. Yet reality is not as clear-cut or encouraging. Rather than converging to a common growth path, we observe very different outcomes around the world—wealthy, middling, and poor—and they don't seem to be pulling together in the way theory predicts. While the Organization for Economic Cooperation and Development (OECD) countries continue to converge to a common (high) standard of living, other countries have diverged or congregated around common, stagnating regional averages.

To begin to understand the diverse growth experiences across the world, we need to recall that another conclusion of Chapter 3 was that technological progress—as measured by the Solow residual—is the only true engine of growth. The most convincing explanation of divergence of economic development in the modern world must therefore lie in explaining differences in levels and growth of total factor productivity. But what is total factor productivity? Can anything be done to better understand, harness, or even accelerate this formidable source of economic prosperity?

Chapter 4 delves into these fascinating and important questions. First, by extending our description of the aggregate production function to account for labour quality, we can explain a great deal of the differences in per capita income levels across countries. Labour is not homogeneous: some workers are highly skilled, others much less so. Human capital (skills acquired on the job or through investment in education, and kept in use through good health care) contributes a great deal to explaining why workers in wealthy countries are so productive. Second, countries have different levels of public capital or physical infrastructure—streets and highways, bridges, hospitals, airports, to name just a few examples. Third, intangible aspects such as law and order, efficient court systems, and transparent governmental administration also contribute to income differences around the world and cannot be ignored. Here it makes sense to speak of social as well as physical capital.

Yet to explain economic growth over many decades, we must return to technological progress. In Chapter 3, technological progress was the engine of growth because it never runs out of fuel. Productivity was assumed to increase exogenously, irrespective of economic and social circumstances. This is unsatisfactory for both intellectual and practical reasons. Technological progress is the result of costly efforts at research and development (R&D). R&D combines pure production of knowledge (research) and making that knowledge work for us (development). In fact, R&D represents an economic activity in its own right. Yet why doesn't R&D fall victim to decreasing returns, as is the case with other factors of production? The question of whether the evolution of technological progress itself could be endogenous is an open area of macroeconomics. It also raises the question of whether government policies can improve the long-run growth performance of nations.

4.2 The Convergence Hypothesis

4.2.1 The Boundless Optimism of the Solow Model

In Chapter 3, output per capita in the long run was explained by (1) the savings rate and (2) the state of technology as summarized by the vertical 'height' of the production function at any given level of capital per capita. All other things being equal, countries with higher savings rates and more productive technologies will have higher output per capita than those with lower saving rates and less productive technologies. Countries with similar savings rates and comparable technological sophistication should have the same income per capita in the long run. Moreover, even if countries have different savings rates, they should grow at the same rate, if they have access to the same technology as the leading economies—either by copying international best practice or by allowing foreign corporations to transfer their know-how by investing in or trading with the domestic economy.

The Solow growth model thus contains a fundamentally optimistic view of economic development. Given the similar underlying conditions, GDP or income per capita should converge in level and growth rate across countries. Furthermore, the more distant a country's GDP is from its steady state, the faster it will grow in subsequent years. These predictions are known as the **convergence hypothesis**.

Panel (a) of Figure 4.1 plots the average growth rate of 34 advanced countries over the period 1960–2009 against their real per capita GDP in 1960. The convergence hypothesis predicts that countries with low initial per capita GDP will grow faster than those that started richer, that is what catching up is all about. Under the assumption that these countries have more or less the same steady state value of GDP per capita, it makes sense to expect a negative relationship between initial conditions (per capita GDP in 1960) and the growth which followed. This does indeed appear to be the case. As Box 4.1 explains, among these countries, it takes about 35 years to

eliminate half of the gap between any nation and the richest ones. While the optimistic message of the convergence hypothesis is that poorer countries should grow faster than average, practical experience teaches us that the process is slow, even under the best of circumstances.

4.2.2 Reality: Growth Clubs and Growth Traps

While panel (a) of Figure 4.1 shows that the convergence hypothesis does remarkably well among the club of richer nations, panel (b) shows that, for the world as a whole, there is little or no evidence of convergence. Evidently, per capita incomes differ considerably and that, for many poor countries, income differences persist or have even widened. While standards of living among the wealthier countries seem to be organized around **convergence clubs**, many poorer countries seem to be 'stuck' in **growth traps** with low per capita GDP and low or even negative growth. How can we explain this apparent contradiction with the principles laid out in Chapter 3?

One possibility is that countries with low income per capita suffer from insufficient capital accumulation because of inadequate saving or destruction by war or natural disaster. Yet low domestic savings alone cannot explain the situation. While we stressed in Chapter 3 that investment must equal savings, this need not be true out of the steady state. It is very possible for foreigners—either individuals or corporations—to invest in poor countries. In this case, investment could be financed through foreign borrowing. In fact, if capital is free to move, we should expect multinational firms, investors, and financiers to move capital to countries where capital–labour ratios are low and, therefore, returns on investment ought to be high. Over time, capital–labour ratios (k) should be equalized across countries. This process may take some time, of course, but a process of convergence towards similar capital–labour ratios, and therefore per capita GDPs should occur.

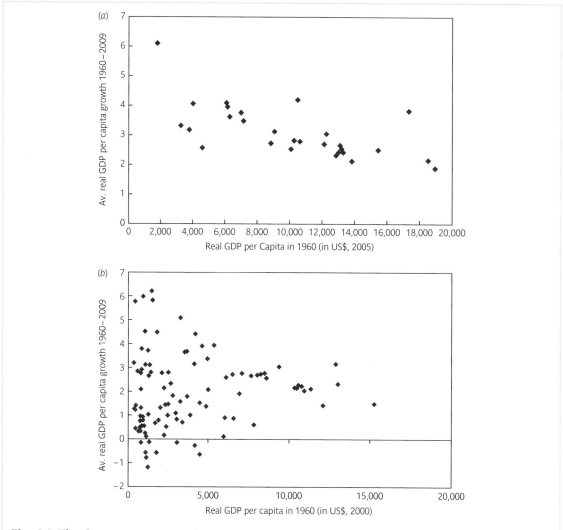

Fig. 4.1 The Convergence Hypothesis in Reality

All things equal, growth theory predicts that poorer countries should grow faster than richer ones. Panel (*a*), which plots the average growth rate for 28 advanced OECD countries over 1960–2009 against initial GDP per capita in 1960, lends strong support to the convergence hypothesis. Panel (*b*), which displays the experience of 100 countries over the same period, does not.

Sources: Heston, Summers, and Aten (2006); authors' calculations.

A second possibility is that chronically poor countries suffer from technological backwardness or a lack of a properly functioning economy. It must be that, for some reason, the poorest countries have not yet been able to reach a steady-state level attainable by rich countries—point B in Figure 3.5. In that case, when and if they eliminate the barriers that prevent them from moving towards their steady states, they should catch up and therefore grow faster than the wealthy economies, which can only grow at the speed of technological progress. A prominent example is China, which has grown by some 10% per year ever since it abandoned central planning in the 1980s. India is following, although not quite as fast.

Plainly, this process may have occurred in China and India recently, but it hasn't occurred in many

Box 4.1   A Snail's Pace: The 2% Convergence Rule

The convergence hypothesis can be expressed in the following way:[1]

(4.1)
$$\frac{\Delta Y_t}{Y_t} - a = \beta \frac{\bar{Y}_t - Y_t}{\bar{Y}_t},$$

which asserts that the *growth rate* of an economy in period t, $\frac{\Delta Y_t}{Y_t}$ will be higher than its steady-state growth rate (a) when current GDP (Y_t) is less than the steady-state *level* (M_t) predicted by savings and technology. The parameter β captures the speed of convergence. The greater the distance is between the current GDP and its steady-state value, the faster the rate of growth. For the countries shown in Figure 4.1, Robert Barro of Harvard and Xavier Sala-i-Martin of Pompeu Fabra University[2] conclude that β is about 0.02, which means that about 2% of the gap in per capita income is closed per year.

This implies that it takes roughly 35 years to eliminate 50% of the difference between a given region and the leading one.[3] As an example, consider the convergence of regions within the USA. In 1880, the US South had a GDP per capita of about one-third of the richer, north-eastern New England region. This very low initial condition reflected the destruction of capital and infrastructure during the Civil War. It has taken more than a century of convergence for GDP per capita of the two regions to move to within roughly 10% of each other. Similarly, the hopes and expectations that southern Italy, eastern Germany, or western Spain will converge quickly to the leading regions of their respective countries have not been entirely fulfilled. We will look at some reasons why convergence may be held in check, an issue of burning relevance to some countries of Eastern and Central Europe.

countries.[4] Poorer countries' inability to close the income gap represents a massive challenge to the international community and to economics as well. It calls into question the basic assumption that all benefit from free markets. It also casts doubt on the

validity of the principles presented in Chapter 3. At the very least, it is suggestive of a systematic factor that we have not taken into account. Could our story just be too simple? Let us try to review what could be changed to better explain the facts.

4.3 Conditional Convergence and Missing Inputs

So far, we have implicitly assumed that all countries have access to the same technology, represented by the production function. What if they were to differ? Figure 4.2 shows an example of dissimilar production functions in two otherwise identical economies, in which households save the same fraction of their

income and with the same capital-widening lines in both. The figure shows that two countries with dissimilar production functions will converge to

---

[1] Interested readers can see in the WebAppendix how this formulation is derived.

[2] See Barro and Sala-i-Martin (1991).

[3] This is the useful rule-of-thumb for computing doubling time or half-lives. Suppose a variable x grows at a constant positive rate of g% per annum, then it will double in roughly $70/g$ years. If it is shrinking at rate g, it will shrink to half its size in $70/g$ years. See the WebAppendix for a derivation of this rule.

[4] Nobel Laureate Robert E. Lucas, Jr of Chicago estimated that if India and the United States had the same production function, the marginal product of capital in the former would have to be about 58 times the marginal product in the latter! In his words, 'If this model were anywhere close to being accurate, and if world capital markets were anywhere close to being free and complete, it is clear that, in the face of return differentials of this magnitude, investment goods would flow rapidly from the United States and other wealthy countries to India and other poor countries. Indeed, one would expect *no* investment to occur in the wealthy countries in the face of return differentials of this magnitude.' (Lucas 1990: 92.)

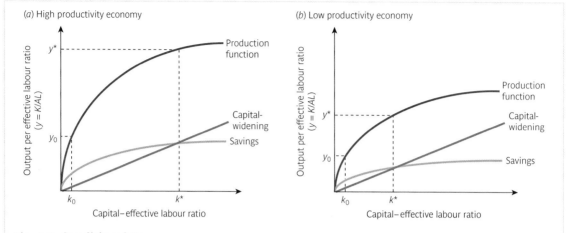

Fig. 4.2 Conditional Convergence

The economies depicted in the two panels are identical in all respects except that the available production technology is more productive at all levels of capital per capita in (a) compared with (b). In the steady state, the more productive economy is richer because it has a higher capital–effective labour ratio. For two countries with identical initial capital stock per effective labour (k_0), conditional convergence will occur to fundamentally different steady states. The richer economy at the outset will also grow faster along its path to the steady state, as predicted by equation (4.1). Conditional convergence means taking not only an economy's initial condition into account, but also its steady state.

different steady states. The notion that convergence occurs, but to steady states that depend on the individual attributes of an economy, nation, or region, is called **conditional convergence**.

But why should production functions differ across countries? International differences are unlikely due to technology in the strict sense. It is hard to see why knowledge or the mere availability of state-of-the-art methods can differ across countries for any period of time. Information is freely available, so producing clothing or electronic chips in an internationally competitive market will necessarily involve the same production techniques whether in Taiwan, Germany, India, or Zimbabwe. Yet, most experts would agree that productivity per head in these countries would be significantly different even if they had the same amount of capital per head to work with.

The most important reason why production functions are different is the existence of other observable inputs to the production function which make capital and labour more productive, just as technological progress does. Research has identified a long list of such influences. While they can be thought of as 'technology' in the broader sense, they are observable and often are quite evident features distinguishing

rich, fast-growing countries from poor, stagnant ones. Which factors are they, exactly? We now examine a number of possible explanations.

4.3.1 Human Capital

Education and training

Just as firms acquire physical capital for producing goods and services, individuals expend time, energy, and money to acquire knowledge and learning how to use that knowledge. These activities range from going to school, learning a skill, or taking a training course. Acquisition of knowledge is an investment. It represents a sacrifice today—foregoing a paid job, or the costs of education—for gains in the future. Such sacrifices are generally made because future gains exceed the initial costs.[5] It is for this reason that one speaks of investment in **human capital**. Better-trained and educated workers are more productive, and more productive workers can earn higher wages. Beyond this, more educated workers tend to enhance the productivity of other factors. Skilled workers are

---

[5] In Chapters 7 and 8 the notion of an investment and the assessment of the desirability of investment will be made much more precise.

better at operating complex machines, and may be used to manage other labourers and organize the production process.

Thus, it makes sense to think of production as combining not only physical capital K and hours of work L, but also a third input, human capital H. The economy's production function becomes

(4.2)
$$Y = A F(\underset{+}{K}, \underset{+}{L}, \underset{+}{H}).$$

Much of the reasoning in Chapter 3 can be repeated using this extended version of the production function. Like physical capital, human capital is accumulated over time and is subject to depreciation as knowledge progresses and people age. This implies that countries that invest more in education and training tend to be better off in the long run—they would tend to have a production function in panel (*a*) of Figure 4.2 rather than in panel (*b*).

Yet, this does not quite explain away all the puzzles. If the production function (4.2) exhibits constant returns to scale in all three factors—capital, pure labour, and human capital—then the marginal product of human capital must be decreasing, just as it was for capital in Chapter 3.[6] Then, again, it follows that, in the steady state, long-run growth rates in economies with low and high 'savings' rates in human capital will still be the same, determined by the rate of technological progress. Of course, the country that invests more in human capital will be richer and more productive.

Health

Human capital is not just education. It includes anything that raises labour productivity for a given capital stock. In particular, human capital also includes the state of health of workers. Freedom from disease and chronic illness as well as access to adequate medical care are considered by many to be fundamental human rights, but they also represent a critically important determinant of economic prosperity. Workers who are ill or must care for relatives cannot be available for productive activities. Furthermore,

in places where health services are poor or access is limited to the richest segment of the population, life expectancy will be low. Reduced life expectancy reduces incentives for individuals to invest in education, and can lead to emigration of wealthy elites.

Poor health services, therefore, are a plausible further interpretation of growth traps. But does good health cause high income, or does high income cause good health, or both? Figure 4.3 shows that the relationship between income and life expectancy is positive, but by no means linear. Life expectancy increases dramatically with income. Not only is life expectancy shamefully low in the very poorest countries, but the growth benefits from improved health are likely to be shamefully high—because the marginal productivity of labour, and therefore of health, is likely to be decreasing. In large parts of the world, existing medicines could cure endemic sicknesses, but people cannot afford them. The AIDS disaster in Africa is a tragic example of a vicious circle in which poverty shortens life expectancy, which further cripples incentives to invest in human capital and future growth.

4.3.2 Public Infrastructure

A second important factor which is missing from the production function is **public infrastructure**. This includes streets, public transport, telecommunication, postal services, airports, systems of water distribution, electricity provision, and sewage treatment, etc. Like the private capital stock, public infrastructure are goods which contribute to general productivity and are widely available to all users, often at low or no cost, and are most often provided by the government. Firms use roads and telephone lines as much as they use their own computers, machines, and lorries. At the aggregate level, the production function can be further augmented to include the stock of public capital, which we will call K^G:

(4.3)
$$Y = A F(\underset{+}{K}, \underset{+}{L}, \underset{+}{H}, \underset{+}{K^G}).$$

The importance of public infrastructure raises a number of questions. Public infrastructure is often free to use, but it is definitely not costless. Like private physical capital, it must be financed. Governments are generally in charge of infrastructure spending, and use taxation or user fees to finance these expenditures.

---

[6] In general, if the production function is subject to constant returns to scale in all inputs, it must be the case that the marginal productivity of each input taken individually is decreasing.

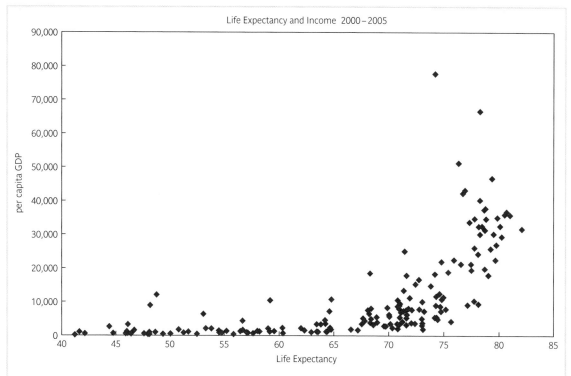

Fig. 4.3 Life Expectancy and Income

In a cross-section of nations, life expectancy declines dramatically at low to moderate income levels. It is difficult to believe that general health conditions do not influence investment decisions, especially in skills and education. At the same time, the demand for health depends on income.

Source: United Nations Population Division, Heston, Summers, and Aten (2006).

While private firms are under constant pressure from their owners to evaluate the balance of costs and benefits from acquiring more equipment, it is difficult, if not impossible, for the government to evaluate the benefits that accrue in millions of ways to millions of users. Furthermore, politicians rarely reap the benefits of infrastructure spending directly. At best, infrastructure enhances tax revenues in the future, and politicians may not be in power to claim credit for those future growth effects. Figure 4.4 shows the average amounts that European governments spent on public capital accumulation over the period 1995–2005. The wide variation across countries signals both needs to modernize their infrastructures (Ireland, Portugal, and Spain) and constraints of fiscal policy (Germany and the UK).

A number of difficulties arise in getting the level of spending on public infrastructure right. Some governments tend to underinvest because other uses of taxpayers' money are more politically rewarding, or because pressures to cut the budget force spending cuts. On the other hand, some other governments might spend too much on infrastructure because political lobbies for public works defend this budgetary item. Growth may be held back for lack of adequate infrastructure in the first case and because of excessive taxation in the second case. In order to reduce the risk of such slippage, a number of governments have increasingly decided to privatize these areas. Indeed, over the last decade, the production of electricity, telephone, water, railways, etc. has been increasingly turned over to the private sector. Yet, we must remember that there is no guarantee that public infrastructure will be adequately provided, an issue to which we return in Chapter 18.

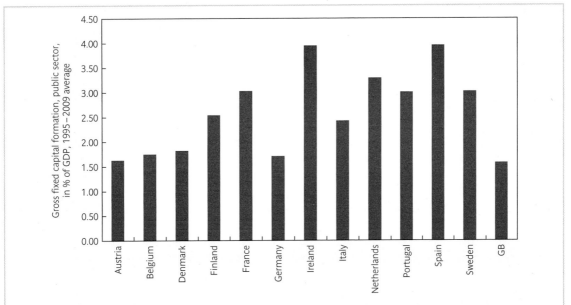

Fig. 4.4 Gross Fixed Capital Formation in the Public Sector, 1995–2009 (% of GDP)

On average, European countries spend 2–3% of GDP on public infrastructure. Yet the variation across countries is high.
Source: OECD

4.3.3 Social Infrastructure

Even accounting for 'hard factors' like education, health, and infrastructure, it remains difficult to account for the enormous differences in total factor productivity between the richest and the poorest nations of the world. For instance, the level of GDP per capita in the USA is roughly 35 times as high as in Niger in Africa. This means that an average US worker works 10 days to produce the *annual* output of a worker in Niger. Naturally, part of this difference is linked to the fact that US workers have better capital equipment, education and skills, and public infrastructure to work with. Yet even if these differences are taken into account, US workers are still almost eight times more productive in per capita terms. Economists attribute this wide gap to 'soft' factors which improve both directly and indirectly the effectiveness of workers.

The first of these is **property rights**. A recurrent theme of Chapters 3 and 4 is that growth is driven by investment. In Chapter 3, emphasis was placed on physical capital, while in this chapter we have seen that the concept of investment is flexible enough to include public infrastructure, health, and human capital. The common feature of an investment,

spelled out in more detail in Chapters 7 and 8, is that it means spending now for uncertain benefits in the future. It is often taken for granted that ownership of capital will be unquestioned both today and in the future, and that individuals will be able to use the skills that they acquire. In both cases, we can speak of clearly defined rights of ownership, or property rights, which are respected by others and systematically enforced by the state. While property rights are well established in the richest countries of the world, they cannot be taken for granted universally.

Property rights require clear, credible, and enforceable legislation or constitutional provisions which guarantee that individuals and firms cannot be dispossessed of their belongings, except if they violate the law and even then, only after due process. The concept of property rights is not restricted to merely retaining one's belongings. In the extreme case, it would guarantee that one's possessions can always be used as intended and disposed of, under all circumstances. Such absolute property rights are rarely observed: landowners are seldom allowed to build 'the house of their dreams' without the implicit or explicit permission of their residential area. More relevant for economic growth, property rights are denied if a firm is taken over by the state, say, to produce weaponry against the will of its owners. Such nationalizations, which occurred in France as recently as the early 1980s, similarly violate property rights, even if the owners are compensated, because they break the link between investment and its intended use. Nationalizations are an example of retroactive legislation, enacted after the original investment was carried out. They damage the fabric of trust between capital owners and the government, which depends on productive economic activity to finance its activities.

At the individual level, property rights should be extended to **human rights**. Being arbitrarily sent to jail, being barred from jobs, or being prevented from performing (non-harmful) economic activities prevents people from using their human capital. Mere threats of imprisonment or assassination also deny

property and human rights. As long as individuals do not have basic freedoms of association, expression, and protection from violence—and these irrespective of sex, race, political opinions, or religious beliefs—their property rights are not established.

It is easy to see why property rights are a precondition for long-run economic growth. If investors cannot be sure that they will own their investments tomorrow, why bother to invest today? This would also explain why capital does not always seem to flow from rich to poor countries. Even if the rate of return on capital in poor countries is much higher, the risk of expropriation or arbitrary restriction of property rights may convince investors to keep their money in richer, more stable places. And if investment is held back, future growth will be too. This elementary proposition is far from being universally accepted. Box 4.2 examines communism, a doctrine

 Box 4.2 Communism and Economic Growth in Communist Countries

In its unrecanted form, communism holds that private ownership of capital leads to the never-ending concentration of wealth in a few hands, while workers are subordinated and kept at the subsistence level of existence. A revolution would ultimately collectivize ownership of the capital stock ('the means of production' in Marxian terminology), by nationalizing large private firms, and in some countries even by banning small ones as well. In several countries, collective ownership was extended to land and housing. While communism or state socialism has been in decline since the mid-1980s, there are still a number of countries which adhere to its tenets (Cuba, Venezuela, North Korea). While undoubtedly one of the most dynamic market economies of the world today, China still claims to be a 'people's republic' and still carries the heavy baggage of decades of socialism in the thousands of state enterprises still in government ownership.

While driven by lofty aims of creating a better society, communism suffers from fundamental flaws. Most economists agree that incentives to work, invest, and innovate are severely attenuated in societies of collectivized ownership and centralized economic planning. To counteract this, communist regimes offered a combination of centrally organized carrots (rewards) and

sticks (penalties). Firm managers negotiated production plans with the central planning office, and were provided with the necessary means, equipment, and salaries. Both managers and workers were also offered various incentives to produce more: more money, medals, better housing, and other benefits. Underperformance was punished, sometimes harshly so.

How did it work? Figure 4.5 shows that, up until the early 1970s, the growth performance was good, certainly on a par with Western Europe. Part of the reason was catch-up after the destruction of the Second World War, which affected both East and West. But then things turned sour, much worse than in Western Europe. Most centrally-planned countries experienced two decades of negative growth rates, an extraordinary failure. Central planning simply did not work, and brought the collapse of the communist regimes. The odd man out is China: a poor performance over the first period, followed by fast growth. The most plausible explanation of the Chinese success story is the gradual relaxation of central planning, accompanied by the introduction of private ownership and openness to trade. But another part of the story seems to be the tight control over human rights imposed by the regime; a puzzling observation.

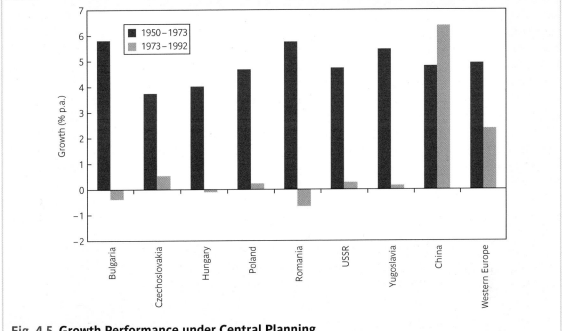

Fig. 4.5 Growth Performance under Central Planning

The impressive growth performance over the first 25 years in planned economies was followed by a catastrophic decline over the next two decades. China stands out as a different and puzzling story.

Source: Maddison (1995).

which explicitly rejected private ownership of means of production. More generally, property rights are routinely denied by arbitrary, undemocratic regimes and by wars, both civil and international.

The relationship between property rights, broadly defined, and growth is more complicated than meets the eye. There is powerful evidence that rich and fast-growing countries tend to be democratic, law-abiding, and peaceful, but it is not clear what comes first—economic well-being or property rights. One view is that property rights are a prerequisite for sustained economic growth. Another view is that affluence makes basic freedoms and property rights more desirable. It could well be that each aspect strengthens the other, generating either virtuous circles of growth and better-established rights, or vicious circles leading to poverty traps which combine economic stagnation and the absence of property (and human) rights.

Indeed, there are cases of countries which embarked on a stable, often fast growth path while enjoying limited property and human rights: the

communist countries, Chile under Pinochet, or some countries of South-East Asia. Conversely, it can be argued that some countries visibly fail to grow because property rights are non-existent. A sobering example is Sub-Saharan Africa, which has grown by a mere 1.5% (GNI per capita) over the years 1965–1997, while the world's overall growth over the same period stood at 50.9%. As Figure 4.6 shows, this average performance conceals a wide disparity, depending on the policy regime.

Another main threat to property rights is armed conflict, which destroys both physical and human capital. If wars are occasional, a catch-up process sets in once they are over. This was the experience of Europe after 1945, which enjoyed rapid growth while building supra-national institutions (the common market, the European Court of Justice, monetary union) and peace-enhancing mechanisms (NATO, the Organization for Security and Cooperation in Europe) to reduce the risk of renewed conflict.

Civil wars can also pose an enormous hindrance to economic development. Africa has been devastated by

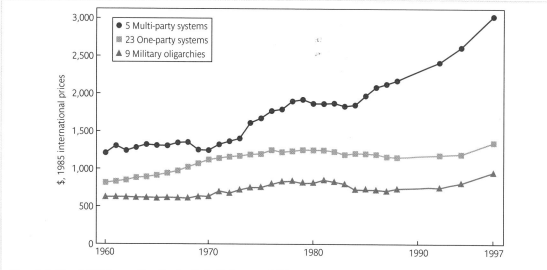

Fig. 4.6 Real GDP per Capita in Sub-Saharan Africa

Over the period 1960–1999, the five countries with democratic political regimes (Botswana, Gambia, Mauritius, Senegal, and Zimbabwe) display a much better growth performance than countries with one-party systems. Countries with military regimes have stagnated.

Source: Ndulu and O'Connell (1999).

civil conflict as states inherited from colonial times have tried to come to grips with ethnic diversity. For example, the index of ethnic fractionalization stands at 67.6% in Sub-Saharan Africa, and at 32.7% on average in other developing countries.[7] Besides the obvious material destruction, investment is held back and human capital declines through the emigration of wealthy and powerful elites. Figure 4.7 establishes an unmistakable link between growth and property rights, where the latter is measured by a legal index of the rule of law prevailing in the country.

4.3.4 Contributions of the Missing Inputs

Alongside capital and labour, human capital, public and private infrastructure should be taken as inputs of the production function. Although precision is obviously limited, most of the missing inputs can be quantified, or expressed in a readily comparable form. Do they account for average growth over a period of several decades, in a type of statistical

'horse race'? Table 4.1 presents estimates of their effects on average annual growth rates.

1 Catch-up (convergence). Starting far below its steady state, a country should be accumulating

Table 4.1 What Drives Growth? Some Estimates

Factor	Effect on annual growth rate
Initial per capita GDP (effect of 1% higher level)	−2.5
Education (effect of 1 more year)	0.4
Life expectancy (effect of 10% increase)	0.8
Fertility rate (effect of a 50% increase)	−0.6
Government consumption (effect of a 10% higher ratio)	−0.6
Rule of law (effect of an increase of 0.1)	0.2
Investment (effect of a 10% increase of ratio to GDP)	0.8

Source: Barro and Sala-i-Martin (2004).

---

[7] This index reports the probability that two people randomly chosen in a country belong to two different ethnic groups; Collier and Gunning (1999).

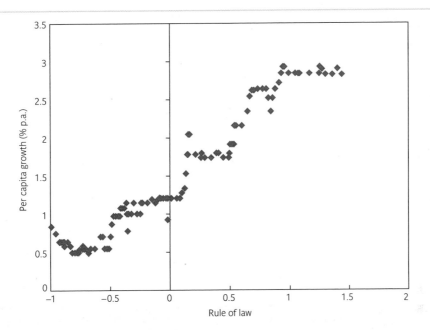

Fig. 4.7 Rule of Law and Growth, 1960 – 1998

Based on a large sample of countries, the figure relates average economic growth over nearly four decades with an index measuring how well the rule of law applies. The index ranges from –2.5 (complete breakdown) to +2.5 (perfect legal protection). It includes political corruption, likelihood of government repudiation of contracts, risk of government expropriation, quality of bureaucracy, and overall maintenance of law. The figure sends a very strong message: the stronger the rule of law, the faster a country grows. Note the beneficial effect only sets in after some minimal threshold.

Source: Easterly (1999).

capital, both physical and human, more rapidly, as well as adopting new technologies. The table indicates that the economic backwardness is closed at a rate of about 2.5% per year (the higher is initial GDP, the less it subsequently grows).

2 Human capital. People's knowledge, ranging from basic literacy to sophisticated skills, represents an additional factor of production. One common measure of investment in education is the average number of years spent in secondary or higher education by males.[8] Raising the population's average

schooling by one year is found to speed up growth by 0.4% per year.

3 Health. A ten-year increase in life expectancy at birth raises average growth by 0.8%—a very large effect indeed. As stated already, the effect is likely to come through investment in human capital and, more generally, more effective labour input and greater work effort. This effect is unlikely to be important in rich countries where it is retirement that limits the length of active lifetime. It may be crucial in the poorest countries where few people ever reach retirement age.

4 Fertility. The negative effect of the rate of fertility (the average number of children per woman) seems related to two main effects: capital-widening and time spent by mothers in child rearing instead of economic activity.

5 Public consumption. Reducing public consumption by 10% of GDP raises growth by 0.6%. This measure excludes spending on public infrastructure. The

[8] This does not mean that female schooling is unimportant, even if the study reported here does not detect any clear *direct* effect. Female schooling is usually found to be more socially productive than male schooling, but this effect is more complex, and mostly *indirect*. In many developing countries, female school attendance is much lower than for males, so a little effort produces large effects. Also better-educated females make better mothers, with considerable impacts on children's education, health, and, more widely, approach to life. Female education also affects fertility.

negative effect probably reflects the fact that high public employment tends to be inefficient and invites corruption, as well as high tax collection, which acts as a disincentive to savings, investment, and innovative activity.

6 Rule of law. Lasting, credible property rights are a precondition for investment in both physical and human capital. Going the full way from the worst to the top ranking raises growth by a whopping 2% annually.

4.4 Possibility of Endogenous Growth[9]

The analysis of Chapter 3 showed that technological change is the ultimate engine that pushes the output–labour ratio—and GDP per capita—ever higher. While differences in human capital, public investments, and social infrastructure can explain differences in long-run levels of national prosperity, they do not change the bottom line. Per capita growth in the long run settles down to the rate of technological change, which is exogenous at rate a. Technological progress is the engine of growth because it is assumed never to run out of fuel; it increases exogenously, irrespective of what happens.

Can the growth process be as simple as that? Might not technological progress itself—or at least part of it—be driven by man-made decisions? Technological progress is related to investment in education and science, to efforts in R&D, and to millions of discoveries, small and large. Might not those discoveries be affected by what others do?

We will find that growth can only perpetuate itself when the marginal product of capital stops falling. As we explore the nature of technological progress, we open up the hunt for possible sources of non-decreasing marginal productivities. **Endogenous growth theory** attempts to explain how growth in the leading economies can vary in the long run—meaning over several decades at a time. Because it represents the boundary of economic research, it is not accepted by all, for reasons we discuss later.

4.4.1 A Sufficient Condition for Endogenous Growth

A hallmark of the analysis of Chapter 3 is that the capital–labour ratio will converge to a steady-state value which is predetermined by the economy's indi-

vidual characteristics. Declining marginal productivity is responsible for this result. Graphically, this feature is captured by the gradual flattening out of the aggregate production function shown in Figure 3.5. As the capital stock in an economy increases, the marginal product of additional investments and additions to the capital stock declines, as do their contribution to generating new income. As the marginal income from investment falls, savings and investment decline and the economy grows more slowly.

But suppose that marginal productivity did not decline enough, and that the slope of the production function schedule always exceeded the slope of the capital-widening line. This would mean that, for sufficiently high levels of the capital–effective labour ratio, the production function schedule would become a straight line. This would remain consistent with output increasing at the same rate as new capital is being accumulated, one of the stylized facts discussed in Chapter 3.

Figure 4.8 shows how things change radically. If the capital–labour ratio is initially at k_1, savings and investment correspond to point A and lie above the capital-widening line (point B). The ratio of capital to effective labour ratio $k = K/AL$ will thus increase by the distance AB. As this ratio grows to reach the level k_2, saving is determined by point C and the capital–effective labour ratio keeps rising even faster as indicated by the distance CD.

Because the marginal productivity of capital does not decline, more of it produces more income and therefore more saving. The striking consequence is that the output–labour and capital–labour ratios

---

[9] The material in this section is somewhat more advanced.

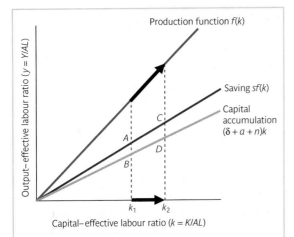

Fig. 4.8 Endogenous Growth with Non-Declining Marginal Productivity

When the marginal productivity of capital is constant, the production function is a straight line. If saving is large enough to exceed depreciation and the need for capital-widening, the capital stock will increase without bound. For example, starting from per capita capital stock k_1, AB represents new capital being installed, which takes the economy to k_2. There, CD corresponds to a further increase in the capital stock, and so on.

never stop growing.[10] This contrasts sharply with the case of declining marginal productivity in Figure 3.13, in which a unique steady state is always reached with $y = Y/AL$ constant, and GDP per capita Y/L growing at the constant rate a. Now y itself is rising secularly, while Y/L is rising even faster.[11] Another implication of non-declining marginal productivity of capital is that an increase in the saving rate makes the saving schedule rotate upwards, leading to faster accumulation of the capital stock and permanent growth in GDP per capita.

[10] A simple example: suppose the production function in intensive form is simply $y = Ak$ where A is a positive constant. Then the capital accumulation equation is $\Delta k = sAk - (\delta + a + n)k$, which implies a growth rate of k given by $\Delta k/k = sA - (\delta + a + n)$. Furthermore, $\Delta y/y = \Delta k/k$, so a higher growth rate of capital per capita (k) forever implies a higher growth rate of output per capita (y) forever.

[11] Note that, in this case, the saving line must lie above the capital accumulation line ($sA > \delta + a + n$). If this were not the case, the capital–effective labour ratio would instead shrink to zero over time, because savings would never be sufficient to make up for depreciation and capital-widening.

We have thus found a sufficient condition for endogenous growth: the marginal product of capital must stop declining. The question is whether this condition is reasonable and whether it occurs in reality. The next two sections outline some possible economic mechanisms which could give rise to endogenous growth.

4.4.2 Externalities and Constant Returns in Accumulated Factors

One important reason that the marginal product of capital ceases to decline is because the law of diminishing returns no longer holds. For some reason, the accumulation of capital—physical as well as human or infrastructural capital—no longer diminishes its marginal product *from the perspective of the aggregate economy*. The English economist Alfred Marshall hypothesized that the perceived effect of an individual's actions can differ substantially from the factual outcome if others act in the same way. In particular, while each individual perceives diminishing marginal returns to investment, it could well be that, when *everyone* engages in the same activity, effective marginal productivity does not fall, but remains constant. Marshall, in fact, was introducing a new concept—economic externality.

An externality occurs when the actions of individuals affect the welfare or productivity of others in ways which are not mediated by the market. For example, someone listening to loud music may disturb those around him; he imposes a cost on others but one for which there is no market. There is no market because a property right is not assigned: it is not clear whether one owns the 'right' to quiet surroundings or to listen to music in an unrestricted way. This is an example of a negative externality, because one's action imposes a cost on others. Externalities can also be positive. For instance, working alongside skilled and educated people may increase your own productivity as they give you tips and provide advice.

That individual activities could increase aggregate productivity, even if the individual does not perceive any effect of his own actions, is called a **Marshallian externality**. If the Marshallian externality creates conditions of constant returns to scale with respect to accumulated factors *only*—physical capital, human

Box 4.3   Constant Returns in Accumulated Factors: Some Mathematical Examples

Using the Cobb–Douglas production function,[12] it is easy to see how constant returns in accumulated factors could arise and lead to the production function shown in Figure 4.8.

The simplest example involves human capital. Suppose that aggregate output of an economy is given by the function $Y = K^{\alpha}(AL)^{1-\alpha}$, and that $A = H$, that is, human capital is the same thing as labour augmenting technical progress. A doubling of human and physical capital will lead to a doubling of output, holding labour input constant. If agents save constant fractions s_K and s_H of their income in physical and human capital, respectively, then K and H will grow along a steady-state growth path at the same rate as Y. In addition, this rate will depend on the savings rates s_K and s_H.

A second example of constant returns in the accumulated factors involves infrastructure. Let K^G be the stock of infrastructure capital described in Section 4.2.2, and is financed by taxation on output at the rate τ: $\Delta K^G = \tau Y$. Let the production function be $Y = AK^{\alpha}L^{1-\alpha}$. Finally, let $A = (K^G)^{\gamma}$, meaning that total factor productivity is increasing in infrastructure, but at a decreasing rate ($\gamma < 1$). Under these conditions, the economy's production function is given by $Y = (K^G)^{\gamma}K^{\alpha}L^{1-\alpha}$. If $\gamma = 1 - \alpha$, the economy has constant returns in K and K^G, the two factors which can be accumulated by saving out of current income, and will behave exactly as in Figure 4.8. Here the tax rate τ acts like the savings rate. Note that a

similar argument could be made for human capital, substituting H for K^G throughout the example. This would lend support to the case for government-financed education.

A third example is a Marshallian externality. Suppose an economy consists of a very large number of identical firms, each producing with the same production function $Y_i = AK_i^{\alpha}L_i^{1-\alpha}$. But now suppose that A depends on the sum of what all the producers are doing, but no single producer can perceive her individual effect on A. To make the point, let $A = Z^{\gamma}$ where Z is an indicator of the sum of all the capital inputs of the individual firms: $Z = \Sigma_i K_i^{\alpha}$ and assume that $\gamma < 1$. Again, if $\gamma = 1 - \alpha$, this economy will have constant returns in capital alone, even though no individual producer perceives this to be the case.

All these examples require restrictive assumptions on the parameters of the model. In the first, human capital acts as labour-augmenting technical progress without any slippage (loss of marginal productivity). The second two cases require the 'knife-edge' condition $\gamma = 1 - \alpha$. These assumptions led Robert Solow, the intellectual father of growth theory, to criticize models of endogenous growth precisely because they lack robustness, i.e. they are sensitive to such assumptions. If there is little reason to believe that these conditions hold exactly, the overall plausibility of the conclusions is easy to challenge.

capital, or infrastructure—then the marginal product of capital need not decline with growth, and endogenous growth is possible. In Box 4.3, the mathematics of such conditions is spelled out in more detail.

4.4.3 Knowledge

The term A has been defined as 'the state of technology', but what is it exactly? A very particular feature of knowledge is that it is a **public good**. Two features characterize public goods. First, they are **non-excludable**, meaning that the consumer of a good cannot

legally or physically prevent others from consuming it at the same time. Second, they are **non-rivalrous** to the extent that the consumption of a good by one person does not affect others' ability to enjoy it. Table 4.2 shows how goods and services we encounter in our economic life can be classified according to their excludability or the rival nature of their use. Knowledge turns out to be both non-excludable and non-rival. It is non-excludable because, once produced, it tends to be freely available. In the form of education, internet, or TV and radio programmes, knowledge is also non-rival; the consumption by one person does not preclude someone else from consuming (or using) it at the same time.

---

[12] The Cobb–Douglas production function was introduced in Box 3.2.

Table 4.2 Non-rivalrousness and Excludability: A Taxonomy of Goods

	Rivalrous	Non-rivalrous
Excludable	Most conventionally marketed private goods	Police protection, patented inventions, copyrighted material, subscription cable television programming
Non-excludable	Parking spaces, public tennis courts, beaches, park benches, congested highways	National defence, good weather, radio/television programming, internet, knowledge

Because knowledge can be used over and over again, it cannot be characterized by diminishing returns. Some mathematical formulae from ancient times (e.g. the area of a circle) have been put to such extensive use since their discovery that they could well be among the most productive investments ever made! Yet, as Box 4.4 shows, the ultimate discoverers are frequently underpaid for their efforts. This crucial observation implies that, under intuitive and plausible conditions, knowledge can be the secret to endless growth.

Innovation and knowledge creation represent a clear case of a positive externality. Social gains resulting from the activities of creative, inventive thinkers generally exceed their private return. But the creation of new knowledge does not come free.

Innovators work hard and invest lots of their own money in their ideas, blueprints, and inventions—as well as money of investors. It is hard to know whether these contributions to economic activity will be remunerated sufficiently. Will the inventors of the next wonder drug or telecommunication device reap rewards for their hard work, or will copycats or 'intellectual pirates' steal the idea? And because they do, will the inventors and investors expend less effort than they should to achieve their goals? Later we discuss how societies encourage this engine of growth by establishing property rights over ideas for some limited time, enforcing them with judicial systems, and thereby seeking to encourage entrepreneurial activity essential to research and development.

Box 4.4 The Origins of Icons

Because it is easy to borrow, copy, or steal new ideas or basic research results, innovative activity frequently yields far greater gains to society than to the clever individuals who first came up with them. A striking new example is the 'technology' of icons, cursors/pointers, double-clicking, and windows. This paradigm for working with information was developed by the Xerox Corporation in their Palo Alto research facility in the 1970s, before personal computers and the mouse were even invented. Apple was able to convert the technology into a usable system and Microsoft, Intel, and other companies were able to make enormous amounts of money on what was essentially a free technology.

Describing the invention, Professor DeLong of Berkeley writes:

The net result? Large benefits to the economy and the society in terms of expanded productivity growth from the work carried on at Xerox's Palo Alto Research Center in the 1970s. But barely a cent returned in revenues to Xerox from this particular drain on its cash flow. Companies that are in business to make money will not long spend a great time and effort on such research projects that do not boost productivity and revenues, even if they boost industry productivity and revenues manifold. Thus there is every reason to believe that the private sector tends to underinvest in research and development.

4.4.4 **Evidence for Endogenous Growth: Long Waves**

Innovations add to our stock of knowledge but they come in many forms and shapes: new ideas (e.g. Newton's discovery of gravity), new techniques (electricity, the steam and combustion engines, computers), new processes (float glass, household appliances, the internet), or new consumer brands, designs, and products. How do these major discoveries really occur?

One view is that discoveries appear more or less randomly. R&D produces innovations, some big, some small, continuously restarting growth by boosting the existing technology. Another view, initially proposed by Harvard economist Joseph Schumpeter, is that big discoveries tend to be associated with long-term waves in economic activity, because they are followed by a number of subsequent, related secondary innovations. Figure 4.9 shows the average annual rate of increase in total factor productivity. We see a sharp acceleration in the UK and the USA early on in the twentieth century, which continues until the early 1970s. This wave is often associated with a succession of great inventions in the latter part of the nineteenth century: electricity, engines, petro-chemistry, pharmaceuticals, telephone, radio, etc. According to Schumpeter's vision of innovations, major innovations were bunched in their occurrence but required decades to diffuse across the economy.

To explain why innovation came in long waves, Schumpeter puts the entrepreneur at centre stage. When growth slows, some enterprising managers react by investing more in risky R&D projects. More research effort eventually pays off, producing a number of innovations that emerge more or less simultaneously, all within a decade or two. As profits rise spectacularly, fierce competition sets in. Competition takes two forms: improvements and **imitation**. Both erode monopoly power of the original innovators,

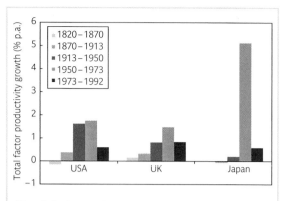

Fig. 4.9 Long Waves
Sustained increases in technological changes seem to come in long-lasting waves.
Source: Maddison (1995).

eating into their profits and reducing their ability and desire to pursue vigorous R&D. Technological progress slows down, ending the big wave of accelerated growth. As profits gradually decline, a new generation of entrepreneurs emerge and prepare the next long wave.

The **Schumpeterian theory of innovation** represents one of the most compelling accounts of the evolution of growth of advanced economies over the past two centuries. Although we still lack sufficient data to firmly establish its validity, the Schumpeter account is supported by the fact that long waves in growth occur across countries together, and that leading nations do tend to grow in a synchronous way. This supports the notion that innovations involve ideas and knowledge which travel rather well across national boundaries, even if they require some time. The leading nations tend to be those which innovate frequently, pushing out the frontiers of technological possibilities, while follower nations adopt later and adapt or perfect the technologies.

4.5 **Growth Policy**

What can governments do to increase long-run economic growth? When the issue of policy arises it is usually a good idea to follow the rule 'if it ain't broke, don't fix it'. In properly functioning economies, it is best to let the interplay of households and firms run its course, unless a convincing case for government policy can be made. A good example is the savings rate. According to the Solow model of Chapter 3, nations which save a greater fraction of their income will have a higher level of GDP per capita, but this certainly does not imply that the government should increase the national savings rate. The golden rule (Section 3.3.5) made it clear that a higher savings rate does not necessarily mean more consumption per capita, or more welfare for that matter.

Much of the discussion of Sections 4.3 and 4.4 centred around missing and possibly non-marketed factors in the production function and externalities. Here it is possible to make a convincing case for government intervention. Among other things, it may pay off to subsidize education, research and development, other innovative activities, and even certain types of investment spending. It may be worth improving the rewards to entrepreneurial activity, but it may also make sense to increase protection of innovators from copycat activity. It is generally a good idea to encourage trade and a stable economic environment. In the following sections we briefly discuss these policy options.

4.5.1 Education and Research

It is well established that education is a key factor for economic growth. Although education is frequently a private investment, it is difficult to borrow money to pay for it. Unlike many investments, human capital does not involve collateral, an asset which can be pledged in case repayment of the loan does not occur. While firms can raise money from banks, stock markets, or their owners to buy equipment, many people cannot pay for their own education, especially in poor countries. The usual response is that governments provide public education, along with scholarships for poorer students. Yet if the returns from education are better salaries, should the state provide public money for private benefit? The answer may still be yes, if human capital creates a Marshallian externality. Being the only one in a country who knows how to read and write is less useful, both privately and collectively, if most others cannot read and write. As noted in Box 4.3, human capital may not face diminishing marginal productivity at the collective level.

Human capital is a linchpin for any theory of growth which is based on inventions and innovation. It raises current productivity and helps speed the **diffusion** of innovations. Figure 4.10 shows that countries that began the growth journey in 1960 with more average schooling generally grew at a faster pace over the next four to five decades, but the correlation is not perfect. One interpretation is the message of conditional convergence in Section 4.2 of this chapter: a low stock of human capital hampers growth, *ceteris paribus*, for reasons expressed by equation (4.2) and Figure 4.2.

As an example, compare the Republic of Korea and Honduras. In 1960, the GDPs per capita of the two countries were roughly equal. By 2005, Korea's GDP per capita exceeded that of Honduras *by a factor of 667%*. The most striking difference between the two countries appears to be education. In 1960, the average Korean had almost twice as much completed years of schooling than the average Honduran.

Naturally, causality could and probably does also run the other way as well. Poor countries simply cannot afford accumulating much human capital, given the costs of education systems. We need not choose between these two interpretations, because *both* can be correct at the same time. Taken together, they suggest the existence of poverty traps: poor countries cannot invest enough in human capital, which in turn hinders growth. For the same reasons, individuals too can be trapped in poverty, even in developed countries. This represents a key justification for means-tested scholarships for bright students.

Externalities can also justify state subsidies for research laboratories. Indeed, a great deal of research—especially basic research—must be funded by government or non-profit institutions. But then, the problem encountered with public infrastructure also arises with knowledge: it is difficult if not impossible to determine the proper level of public financing of research. To make things even more complicated, research is inherently uncertain and often entails very long gestation periods, it is a risky undertaking. This all makes it very possible that not enough is spent on an activity that is obviously not politically attractive and yet, over the long haul, may be an essential source of increases in standards of living.

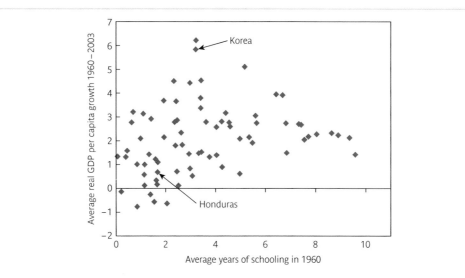

Fig. 4.10 Human Capital and Economic Growth, 1960–2003

The initial endowment of human capital—expressed crudely as average years of schooling in 1960—is strongly positively correlated with real growth over the following 4–5 decades. The cases of Honduras and Korea are striking examples of the correlation between education and growth.

4.5.2 Intellectual Property, Patents, and Competition Policy

Because knowledge is unlikely to face diminishing returns, it is a potential source of endless growth. To encourage the private production of knowledge, governments should protect its excludability for some period. Policies have been designed over the centuries to do precisely this. One is the **patent**. A patent confers the exclusive legal right on its owner to exploit an invention commercially, usually for a limited period of time. While not generally granted to ideas per se, patent protection is reserved for inventions that are sufficiently novel and wide-reaching. Similarly, **copyrights** safeguard artistic expression from plagiarism or outright duplication, and **trademarks** recognize exclusive use of a name or symbol to distinguish a firm's product in the market place. Like patents, copyrights and trademarks establish **intellectual property rights** on certain forms of knowledge.

With the possibility of obtaining intellectual property rights, investing in innovation—R&D, artistic expression, and brand development—can pay off. For some period, the holder of the patent can charge prices which are at least high enough to cover the costs of the research and development of the product.

But there is a side-effect: patents confer monopoly power on their owners and thus allow them to charge much more than development costs. In one sense, monopoly is bad, since it allows the seller to set monopoly prices. Because demand is discouraged, patents limit the full exploitation of useful knowledge. At the same time, patents offer powerful incentives to researchers. Without them, knowledge creation and its contribution to economic growth would probably proceed at a much slower pace. As Box 4.5 shows, the border between fair remuneration and exploitation of monopoly power is arbitrary and subject to considerable legal wrangling.

Even if patent protection confers monopoly power on their inventors, it may be a necessary evil for promoting the production of knowledge and thus for economic growth. If the widely shared benefits of knowledge production are not reflected in their compensation, researchers will not deliver as much innovation as is socially desirable, if only because too few bright students will choose this career. Viewed this way, it is perhaps less objectionable that successful innovators derive extra profits from their temporary monopoly power. Naturally, after an invention is patented, the owner of the patent will charge a high

Box 4.5 Protecting and Punishing Monopolists

To some people, Bill Gates is a bad, mean monopolist. Monopoly rights belonging to the Microsoft Corporation have made him into one of the richest men in the world, since virtually every computer in the world is equipped with its software products. Perhaps this is why many cheered when the US Department of Justice and the European Commission initiated lawsuits against Microsoft. The lawsuits, however, were not about monopoly power derived from legal patents and copyrights. They were aimed at Microsoft's alleged stifling or even elimination of new competitor products and services. While Microsoft has made it possible for hundreds of millions of people to use computers for work and pleasure, history and innovations must continue. New innovators will continue to improve computers' software, and should be encouraged to do so.

Microsoft's encounter with justice is reminiscent of an equally famous trial pitting the US Justice Department against International Business Machines (IBM) in the late 1970s. At the time, IBM dominated the computer hardware industry: PCs didn't exist, and there was hardly a competitor which could produce powerful mainframe computers the way IBM did. The charge was very similar. IBM was accused of using its dominant position to eliminate new competitors. In the end, IBM argued that it retained its lead only thanks to its ability to innovate, and was hard-pressed to do so because of pressure from the competition. IBM won twice. The case against it was dismissed and its argument was soon proved correct as it lost ground to competition, especially with respect to small portable computers and networking machines. In relative terms, IBM is now a shadow of its former self. Microsoft was punished severely by the European Commission for not revealing details about its operating system software to firms which use it. Whether it will soon become a minor player remains to be seen.

An altogether different story involves the pharmaceutical industry. Most wonder drugs are indeed patented, and their inventors reap massive profits. What makes the case different is that drugs are paid for by health insurance, private or public. Insurance agencies agree with the pharmaceutical industry on 'fair' prices, which exceed the marginal cost of producing the drugs by a factor commonly believed to be ten or more. Pharmaceutical firms claim that this is the only way for them to recoup the huge costs of R&D. Critics call the industry's profits excessive, but find it difficult to find solid evidence to back their claim. They correctly note that a significant part of humanity cannot afford these drugs and die or are permanently incapacitated as a result, a fact most recently underlined by the global AIDS epidemic. Even more troubling is the absence of priority in the pharmaceutical research community to develop drugs which could eliminate tropical diseases, such as malaria, which kill or cripple hundreds of thousands. These diseases are ignored because they affect primarily poor people in poor countries with no ability to pay for the R&D costs.

price, possibly even higher than normal costs would warrant. Given that the invention has become public knowledge, governments have a strong *ex post* incentive to abrogate the original patent agreement. This would clearly make everyone better off in the short run, but would probably bring research and development to a standstill, since the promise of a patent would no longer be credible. For this reason, governments generally avoid breaking their promises.

4.5.3 Openness to Trade and Competition

International trade is an engine of growth. First, openness to trade and the resulting competition from foreign firms serves to spread knowledge and technology across national boundaries. Competition encourages domestic firms to adopt leading-edge production techniques and become more efficient. Multinational corporations, which operate in several countries at once, serve as an important channel in the diffusion of innovations. This view is based on the phenomenon of **learning by doing**, whereby people and firms improve their knowledge on the job. When a multinational establishes a production unit in a developing country, it usually brings with it a technology invented in its home country. Individuals who work in such firms acquire the technology and can subsequently create their own firms based on the new technology, or migrate to other firms which can then tool up. This possibility should be kept in mind when considering controversies that surround multinational corporations. From a *social* perspective, they contribute to convergence by accelerating the diffusion of innovations and thus the transfer of knowledge.

Growth and openness to international commerce are known to be positively related. Countries which have large trade exposure—measured as the ratio of exports plus imports to GDP—tend to grow faster. The experience of more open Western European countries, and especially the Asian Tigers of the last two decades, suggest that open economies grow faster, all things considered. This faster growth can be attributed to a number of possible effects. First, closed economic systems impede the transfer of knowledge, effectively excluding some individuals from what should be a non-excludable good. Openness allows for ideas to flow more easily across national boundaries. Second, openness means increased competition from abroad. Domestic producers cannot rely on protection to shield their market positions from the threat of imports. They must constantly remain at the 'cutting edge' of new areas of innovation and development. To use the terminology of Section 4.4.3, this requires either innovation or imitation; either will have positive effects on productivity and growth.

4.5.4 Politics: Democracy, Equality, and Stability

We saw in Section 4.3 that credible property rights and peace are important elements of social infrastructure and are essential for economic development. Beyond property rights, the legitimate scope of government and its behaviour should be directed towards establishing stability and continuity, rather than interrupting it. The system of government can therefore do much for economic growth in a passive way: it can work towards the establishment of stable conditions that improve the business climate. Since it is most likely to represent the wishes of its citizens, democracy should be the ideal means of translating the common will into policy. Democracy should be conducive to a better growth performance, for all the reasons reviewed so far: property rights, economic and political stability, health, and institutions which have broad public acceptance.

Democracies are not perfect institutions, and the relationship between democracy and economic growth is a controversial one. Democratically elected governments may change frequently—with shifting coalitions of smaller parties, for example—and this may lead to constantly changing tax and expenditure policy. This type of uncertainty, especially if it applies to the taxation of physical or human capital, may deter longer-term projects from being undertaken. The rule of majority does not necessarily protect minorities from violations of property and human rights. Such actions may include legal pressure on 'the rich', ranging from nationalizations to heavy taxation, both of which discourage investment. At the same time, well-organized lobbies in many democracies enable wealthy minorities to exert disproportionate influence on decision-making.

Democracies often find it difficult to organize the sacrifices necessary for sustained economic growth. Some salient examples are: (1) increasing the savings rate to accumulate capital for future generations; (2) the restructuring of economic activity, which implies the painful decline of some sectors (agriculture, mining, or heavy industries, for example); (3) reform of the social safety net and labour market regulations, and (4) migration towards cities, which is accompanied by some degree of social and family dislocation. In facing up to such painful changes, democracies can encounter political difficulties. Some have concluded that only dictatorships are capable of suppressing opposition to changing conditions long enough for economic growth to take hold. In their view, democracy is a luxury that only rich societies can afford.

It is for this reason that the best-functioning democracies operate within a widely accepted constitutional framework which is designed to be difficult for simple majorities to change. In such a setting, democracies offer many economic advantages. Only democracies have the legitimacy to guarantee the property rights needed for investment in human and physical capital (see Section 4.3). Inequality, which is an unavoidable by-product of market economies, is better tolerated when the political regime receives legitimacy from a majority of citizens. Such legitimacy is probably necessary to carry out the deep reforms that accompany sustained growth. Dictatorships can impose changes, which may be desirable from an economic viewpoint, but soon become as unacceptable as the dictatorship itself, and may be swept away in painful revolutions. Finally, democracies rarely go to war with each other.

ⓘ Summary

1 The Solow model predicts that countries with identical production functions, savings rates, depreciation rates, and population growth will achieve the same level of production and income per capita, and they will grow at the same rate in the steady state. According to the convergence hypothesis, poorer countries should grow faster than wealthier ones.

2 Empirically, the convergence hypothesis fails in its unconditional form. While rich countries and wealthy regions of the world seem to converge in both level and growth rate of GDP per capita, a large part of the world does not. Many poorer countries appear to be locked in a poverty trap of economic stagnation.

3 The most compelling explanation of the lack of convergence in the data is that production functions are different across countries. Yet these differences are unlikely to be due to different technologies in the narrow sense, since blueprints, information, and techniques are readily transferred across national boundaries. International differences in production functions are mostly due to missing inputs which enhance the productivity of capital and labour.

4 The conditional convergence hypothesis states that nations converge to levels implied by these missing inputs. When they are accounted for, nations do seem to converge to their individual steady states. An important conclusion is that nations can improve their economic condition by increasing their endowments of these missing, complementary inputs: human capital, public infrastructure, and social infrastructure.

5 Human capital is a central missing input in the production function. It ranges from education and training to the health of individuals. Countries with better educated, trained, and healthier workers are more productive, all else constant.

6 Public infrastructure, defined as those public goods which are accessible to all and often provided by the government, include roads and bridges, highways, airports, railways, and hospitals. Public infrastructure is also an important determinant of the position of the production function, all other things being equal.

7 One of the most important missing factors for explaining the poor performance of many nations empirically is social infrastructure. Social infrastructure refers to those 'soft' factors which facilitate economic relations and thereby make all factors of production more effective. These factors include property rights and human rights, but extend to the rule of law and the sustainable absence of armed conflict.

8 Even if missing factors can explain a great deal of growth internationally, explaining the overall evolution of transferable technology in the leading nations remains a central goal of economics. This opens up the possibility of endogenous growth.

9 Endogenous growth is possible when the marginal product of capital or other accumulated factors is bounded from below by a value which exceeds the slope of the capital deepening line. An increase in the savings rate can then lead to permanently higher growth.

10 One of the most promising explanations of endogenous growth lies in seeing research and development as the outcome of economic decisions. This requires understanding the nature of

blueprints, ideas, and knowledge in general. The social return from innovation exceeds the private return on this activity, so the incentives to innovate could affect long-run growth.

11 Growth policy should not second-guess the decisions of firms and households. It should aim to improve the quality of missing inputs in the production function, and to provide conditions which improve innovation. Most importantly, providing limited intellectual property rights for innovations without stifling competition is an important challenge of growth policy.

🔑 Key Concepts

+ convergence hypothesis
+ convergence clubs
+ growth traps
+ conditional convergence
+ human capital
+ public infrastructure
+ public good
+ property rights
+ human rights

+ endogenous growth theory
+ Marshallian externality
+ non-excludable and non-rivalrous goods
+ intellectual property rights
+ Schumpeterian theory of innovation
+ diffusion and imitation
+ patent, copyright, trademark
+ learning by doing

❓ Exercises

1 Explain, using a diagram, why the Solow model with exogenous technical progress implies convergence of both levels and growth rates of GDP per capita.

2 Give a definition of the convergence hypothesis. Explain why the convergence hypothesis in its *unconditional* form is unlikely to hold across countries of the world.

3 Suppose two regions in the same country have identical production functions, savings rates, population growth rates, and depreciation rates. Suppose that per capita GDP differs by 20% between them, but that this gap is closed by 2% per annum. How many years will it take to close the gap to 5%?

4 Define the notion of conditional convergence. Give some examples of factors upon which the convergence hypothesis should be conditioned (i.e. take account of).

5 Suppose output Y is produced with physical capital K, human capital H, and labour L using the production function $Y = K^{\alpha}H^{\beta}L^{1-\alpha-\beta}$. Assume that households save a fraction sH of their income in human capital and sK in physical capital and that $sH = sK = s$ and that both forms of capital depreciate at the rate $\delta\sim$. Solve for the steady-state level of output and output per capita. Why isn't this economy growing?

6 Define a Marshallian externality. Give at least two examples.

7 Why must knowledge not be subjected to diminishing returns if it is to be a permanent source of growth?

8 Use the example from Problem 5, but this time assume that production is given by the function $Y = K^{\alpha}H^{\beta}L^{\gamma}$ and $\alpha + \beta = 1$ and $\gamma < 1$. Explain why growth in this economy will now depend positively on the savings rate s, even if total factor productivity is constant.

9 Define non-excludable and non-rivalrous goods and give examples of both. Can you name some that have both traits?

10 Name concrete ways which governments can use to promote innovation and explain how they work. Why are these measures enacted for only a limited period of time?

→ Essay Questions

1 Why is the acquisition of human capital called an investment, like the acquisition of physical capital? Explain why knowledge and human capital depreciate, like physical capital. What is the link between property rights and investment in both physical and human capital?

2 Explain, with reference to elements of social infrastructure, why much of Africa seems unable to grow and eradicate poverty. What measures are most likely to improve the economic fate of African nations?

3 What aspect of public goods is more likely to inhibit the private production of goods: non-rivalry or non-excludability?

4 'Corruption stunts growth.' Comment.

5 Give arguments for and against democracy as a factor promoting economic growth.

Labour Markets and Unemployment $\quad$ 5

In our present-day complicated economic life we are likely to be confused by the many industrial operations and money transactions. But net income remains exactly what it was to primitive Robinson Crusoe on his island—the enjoyment from eating the berries we pick, so to speak, less the discomfort or the labour of picking them.

Irving Fisher[1]

Labour is the source of all value.

Karl Marx[2]

5.1 Overview

In the last two chapters, we showed how output is a function of the **endowment** of factors of production—capital and labour—as well as technical sophistication. We examined the evolution of the capital stock and of technology in some detail, but we took the supply of labour as given, regardless of the wage or other variables. Even in storybooks, life is not so simple. In the famous novel by Daniel Defoe, the shipwrecked castaway Robinson Crusoe was endowed with a stock of capital (coconut trees) to produce output (coconuts), but needed to expend time and effort to gather and transport the fruits that he would eventually consume. Like most people, Crusoe had to choose whether to work or not, and how much effort he would put into it. Presumably, the rewards to work played a role in his decision. And the decision of how much to work determined how many coconuts would be harvested. This chapter is all about the labour market, which determines how much people work and earn.

To introduce the labour market, we need to think hard about the decisions of households, which supply hours of work to the market, and of firms, which demand them. Households work so that they can consume, but they also want to spend some of their time not working and enjoying **leisure** or free time.

The supply of labour is seen as a trade-off between consumption and leisure. At the same time, someone must be willing to employ and pay for the hours of work that workers want to supply. If firms demand labour, it must have some value to them in production. As we study the interaction of the demand and supply of labour, we will learn how **unemployment** emerges.

We begin by looking at a household that supplies hours of work to the labour market. Then we turn to the demand for labour by firms. This leads naturally to the standard confrontation of demand and supply, which is sorted out by the wage, the price of labour. Yet we will see that labour is not a standard 'commodity'. Workers are not identical, and the quality of labour services is difficult to ascertain and harder to monitor. Unlike machines or raw materials, workers can decide whether they would like to work for a particular employer and under which conditions to sell their labour services. Frequently, the employment relationship involves explicit and implicit arrangements specific to both firm and employee. The functioning of labour markets is also influenced by country-specific institutions, such as labour law or collective bargaining, and is subject to complex legal

---

[1] Irving Fisher (1867–1947) was an American who is often described as one of the greatest mathematical economists of all time. Among other subjects, he contributed to the theory of investment, capital, and interest rates; monetary economics and the theory of inflation; and most notably to the theory and practice of price index numbers. He was founder and first president of the Econometric Society.

[2] Karl Marx (1818–1883) was a German economist and political philosopher whose theories predicted the immiseration of labour and the ultimate crisis and collapse of market (capitalist) economies. Although he clearly got all that wrong, his empirical observations on the plight of the working class at the time and his focus on issues relating to product and labour markets—and his influence on the lives of millions of people who lived and worked under communism and socialism—earn him a central place in the history of economic thought.

rules and customs. Finally, the labour market is dynamic, with suppliers and demanders of labour entering into and exiting employment relationships at a remarkable rate. We show how these interactions help us to understand the concept of equilibrium unemployment, which may differ from actual unemployment observed at a particular point in time.

5.2 Demand and Supply in the Labour Market

While Karl Marx may be out of favour these days, he was certainly right to see labour as the most important factor of production. Virtually everything stems directly or indirectly from labour. Raw materials are brought forth from the earth by human hands. Equipment used in this and other forms of economic activity is made using labour and previously manufactured equipment, itself the output of labourers and capital in a more distant past. Even the knowledge embodied in people—human capital—comes from our own efforts at mastering skills and techniques, as well as the time our teachers spent trying to educate us.

5.2.1 Labour Supply and the Consumption–Leisure Trade-off

In modern societies, consuming goods and services requires income. Earning income most often means working for firms for a wage or salary.[3] But labour has a cost, too: every hour of work means an hour less of free time. Because households value both consumption and leisure, they balance the two the best they can, given the possibilities available to them. This trade-off is known as the **consumption–leisure trade-off**. The consumption–leisure trade-off is best illustrated by the choices faced by Robinson Crusoe.[4]

The Crusoe we consider consumes all the fruits of his labour, which are the coconuts that he picks up on the beach, shucks, and cracks open—hard work by anyone's measure. (We postpone issues related to saving and investment to Chapters 7 and 8.) Crusoe values both the consumption (coconuts) and the free time he can enjoy *not* working to obtain them (resting, contemplating, watching the stars at night). His preferences or tastes with respect to consumption and leisure can be summarized with **indifference curves**. Each indifference curve presented in Figure 5.1 shows combinations of consumption and leisure which make Crusoe equally happy, or to have the same **utility**—the word economists use for a consumer's state of satisfaction.

Indifference curves are designed to tell us something about the preferences of households. Higher indifference curves correspond to higher levels of

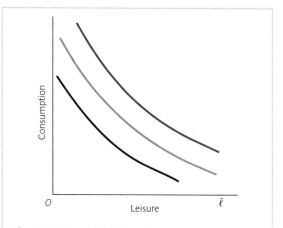

Fig. 5.1 Household Preference

An indifference curve shows how readily a household is willing to substitute consumption C for leisure, N holding its level of satisfaction or utility constant. Curves further out from the origin correspond to higher levels of utility.

---

[3] 'Firms' are understood to include public as well as private enterprises, national, regional, and local governments. It can even mean working for oneself, in the case of self-employment. In what follows we will focus on firms which strive to maximize profits.

[4] The use of this character, based on the classic novel by Daniel Defoe (1660–1731), is traditional in economics and will be seen again in Chapters 7 and 8, in which goods are distinguished by the point in time that they are consumed.

utility or happiness. The negative slope of the curve shows that a trade-off is involved: taking a unit of consumption from Crusoe requires compensation in the form of more leisure. The (absolute) slope or steepness of each curve at a given point shows how readily Crusoe substitutes consumption for leisure, holding his level of satisfaction constant. The bowed shape of Crusoe's indifference curves tells us that the greater his consumption relative to its leisure, the more of that consumption he is willing to give up for an additional unit of relatively scarcer leisure. The rate at which a household is willing to give up consumption for leisure, holding satisfaction constant, is called the **marginal rate of substitution** of consumption for leisure. An important principle is that as a good becomes increasingly scarce, the marginal rate of substitution of other goods for that particular good increases.

On Crusoe's island there is no money, but there is time, in fact, lots of it. Yet even Crusoe's time is in limited supply over a certain period (a day, a month, or year), after sleep and other important functions are accounted for. All scarce resources have a price, and time is no exception. The price of an hour of leisure is its opportunity cost: how much consumption could one otherwise earn in that hour by working in the market? For the representative household with access to a labour market, the price of leisure is the **real (consumption) wage**. In practice, it is measured as a ratio of an average nominal (money) wage (W) to the consumer price index (P), the price of goods. If total available time for work is denoted as N and the hourly real wage is $w = W/P$, the value of Crusoe's total time endowment in terms of consumption is $\bar{\ell}w$. This endowment can be allocated between C units of consumption and ℓ hours of leisure, with value ℓw, according to the following equation:[5]

(5.1) $$\bar{\ell}w = \ell w + C.$$

Equation (5.1) is Crusoe's budget constraint; it states all possible combinations of leisure and consumption that he can afford. It is depicted in Figure 5.2 as

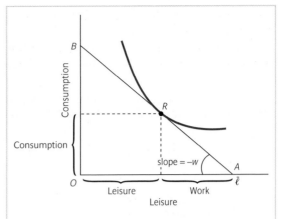

Fig. 5.2 The Household Budget Line and Optimal Choice
The household has a total of N hours at its disposal (measured by the distance OA) for either leisure or work. For every unit of leisure that it gives up, it can earn w consumption goods. The real wage w determines the slope of the budget line AB. Given the budget line, the highest possible utility is achieved at point R, where an indifference curve is tangent to the budget line.

the negatively sloped line AB. The horizontal distance OA is equal to N, the number of hours at his disposal. The distance OB measures the value of that endowment in terms of consumption goods. It is the total amount of consumption attainable when leisure is zero—i.e. if Crusoe were to work all the time.[6]

The negative slope of the budget line ($-w$) measures the trade-off of consumption for leisure ℓ offered by the market: how much consumption must be given up to get an additional unit of leisure, or how much consumption can be 'purchased' with an additional hour of foregone leisure. In both cases it is the hourly wage rate w. It explains why the real wage w is often referred to as the **relative price** of leisure in terms of consumption. If the real wage changes, the budget line rotates around point A, which is the fixed time endowment N. It represents the amount of leisure possible when consumption is zero.

[5] The nominal budget constraint is $\bar{\ell}W = \ell W + PC$. To write it in real terms of consumption goods in (5.1), we simply divide by P, the price of consumption goods.

[6] If Crusoe possessed some initial wealth to begin with, the budget line would be shifted upwards (vertically) by that amount. This would then represent consumption attainable without having to work at all.

Optimal choice and the individual labour supply schedule

Crusoe maximizes his utility by choosing the highest possible indifference curve without moving to the right or above his budget line. This is achieved at point R in Figure 5.2, where the indifference curve is tangent to the budget line. At this point, the marginal rate of substitution of consumption for leisure is equal to the real wage w. Given the terms of trade offered by the market, he cannot make himself any better off (reach a higher indifference curve) by choosing any other point on the budget line, i.e. by trading leisure against consumption.

An important issue is the influence of the real wage on household behaviour. How does the household react to an increase in the real wage depicted in the first panel of Figure 5.3? Graphically, OB increases and the budget line rotates clockwise. Crusoe's optimal choice is now represented by point R'. This point is above R—Crusoe's consumption increases—but it is not clear whether it is to the left—Crusoe works less—or to the right—he works more. This ambiguity is a consequence of two different effects. First, the relative attractiveness of leisure *declines* because its relative price has *risen*. Taken alone, this would encourage Crusoe to take less leisure, work harder, and consume more. This is called the **substitution effect**. Second, and at the same time, each hour of Crusoe's labour is paid better. Holding leisure constant means earning more income overall. A normal reaction to an increase in income should be to enjoy both more consumption and more leisure, which means working less. This incentive to work less in response to a wage increase is called the **income effect**.

So, if the wage rises, will Crusoe work more or less? This question cannot be answered unambiguously without knowing more about preferences. In Figure 5.3, the substitution effect dominates, so the net effect is positive: an increase in the wage leads to a decline in leisure and an increase in labour supply. This is depicted in the second panel of Figure 5.3 as an upward-sloping **household labour supply curve**.

In practice, the response to rising wages varies widely across individuals, depending on tastes, family circumstances, age, etc. It also depends on the

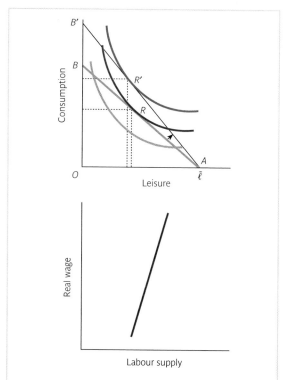

Fig. 5.3 Reaction of the Household to a Wage Increase: Labour Supply

When the real wage increases, the budget line rotates around point A (the endowment of time remains unchanged) and becomes steeper, because a unit of leisure is exchanged for more units of consumption. This allows both consumption and leisure to increase at the same time (income effect). Because leisure is more expensive, however, some is given up (substitution effect). In the case depicted here, the substitution effect dominates.

time horizon under consideration.[7] In the short run, most individuals do not seem to react much to changes in the real wage. Over the very long run, increasing real wages have led to decreasing labour supply as the income effect dominates. Table 5.1 shows that, over the last 100 years, real wages have increased by five- to fifteen-fold, while working hours have declined by one-half. Labour supply behaviour also varies according to sex. For men, the average work-week, the retirement age, and the **labour force**

[7] For details, the reader is invited to look at the WebAppendix.

Table 5.1 Annual Total Hours Worked and Average Wages, 1870–2009

	1870	1913	1938	1973	1992	2000	2007	2009
Annual hours worked per Person								
France	2945	2588	1848	2027	1695	1591	1556	1558
Germany	2941	2584	2316	1870	1566	1473	1430	1390
UK	2984	2624	2267	2016	1874	1712	1673	1646
USA	2964	2605	2062	1797	1716	1739	1709	1681
Sweden	2945	2588	2204	1564	1565	1642	1618	1602
Real Wage (index: 1870 = 100)								
France	100	205	335	1048	1505	1614	1714	1727
Germany	100	185	285	944	1226	1320	1309	1306
UK	100	157	256	439	605	691	770	767
USA	100	189	325	595	696	791	860	871
Sweden	100	270	521	1228	1523	1874	2132	2085

Source: Hours worked are from Maddison (1991) for years 1870–1938 and from Groningen Growth and Development Centre and The Conference Board, Total Economy Database for the years 1973 to 2007; wages are from Mitchell (1978, 1983), and OECD, *Economic Outlook*, German wage data from 1913–38 are approximated using average labour productivity growth.

participation rate have fallen secularly since 1900.[8] In contrast, labour force participation and hours per week of women have risen in the past half-century. One possible interpretation is that the income effect of higher wages dominates for men, whereas the substitution effect dominates for women. Another interpretation is that customs and sociological factors change. Services such as child care and schooling, as well as improvements in the technology of home production, have made it possible for more people, especially women, to take up paid jobs.

The aggregate labour supply curve

We have studied a representative household's decision to work. The next step is to add up the supplies of individual households across the economy, while noting the special aspects of labour and labour markets. In many instances, individuals cannot vary the hours of work that they supply. At best, they can choose between working or not working at all. Most labour contracts specify a standard working time

[8] The labour force participation rate is defined as the proportion of working-age people which is either working or registered as unemployed.

(length of the work-week, days of holiday leave per year). Workers frequently receive and accept 'take it or leave it' job offers. Sometimes workers are better off not working at all. In cases such as these, small wage increases may not be sufficient to motivate households to take up jobs, although large ones might.[9] In any case, the aggregate labour supply remains the sum of many individual decisions (to work or not work, and how many hours to work). While individual labour supply is measured in hours during some period of time (e.g. per year as in Table 5.1), aggregate supply is measured in **person-hours**, the total amount of hours supplied by all workers during that same period.[10] As in Chapter 3, total hours are the product of the number of persons in

[9] These important cases are taken up again in detail in a box in Chapter 18.

[10] Aggregate employment is sometimes measured as the number of people who have a job. Generally, we will use the first definition (person-hours), and make explicit mention when referring to the number of employed workers. Under any definition, when more workers enter the labour force, the labour supply curve shifts to the right independently of the wage level.

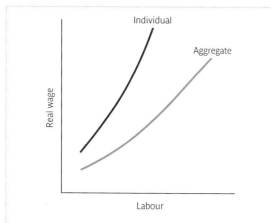

Fig. 5.4 Individual and Aggregate Labour Supply

The aggregate labour supply curve is less steep than that of individual households for two important reasons. First it represents the summation of a great number of upwardly sloped individual supply curves. Second, new workers choose to enter the labour force as wages rise.

work times the hours worked per person. When wages rise, even if those who already work do not modify their supply of labour (the benchmark case), others who had preferred not to work may now decide to join the labour force. Figure 5.4 shows how

it is then possible for a steep or even near-vertical (inelastic) labour supply curve at the individual level to be consistent with a flatter aggregate supply curve.

5.2.2 Labour Demand, Productivity, and Real Wages

The labour demand curve and its slope

Firms use both capital and labour to produce goods and services. As discussed in Chapter 3, the capital stock at any particular point in time is best thought of as given; from month to month firms vary their output by adjusting employment of labour (person-hours). Holding capital constant, we can express the link between output Y and employment L using the production function, as shown in Figure 5.5. The slope of the production function measures the **marginal productivity of labour** (MPL), the quantity of additional output which results from one more unit of labour input (an hour). The shape of the curve reflects the principle of decreasing marginal productivity. With all else held constant, the MPL in a representative firm declines as the amount of labour employed increases.

In deciding how much labour to employ, the representative firm seeks the highest possible profit given the cost of labour, the real hourly wage w. The line OR

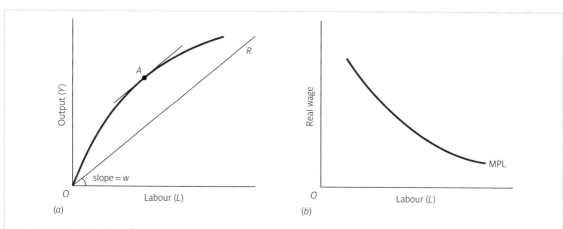

Fig. 5.5 The Production Function and the Labour Demand Curve

When labour input increases, output increases, but at a declining rate. This additional output is the marginal productivity of labour (MPL). In panel (*a*), the ray *OR* represents the labour cost of producing when the hourly real wage is *w*. The vertical distance between the production function and the cost line represents the firm's profit. The firm maximizes its profit at point *A*, where the curve is parallel to *OR*, i.e. where MPL = *w*. Its demand for labour is given in panel (*b*) by the declining marginal product of labour (MPL) curve.

represents the total cost of labour to the firm at different levels of employment. Because L hours of work cost wL, its slope is w. For each level of employment, profit is measured as the vertical distance between the curve depicting the production function and the labour cost line OR. Profit is at a maximum at point A, where the production function is parallel to OR. At this point, the MPL, the slope of the production function, is equal to the real wage, the slope of OR. If the MPL exceeds the real wage, hiring one more hour of work raises revenues by the amount MPL, while raising costs by only w. This implies an increase in profits. A firm interested in maximizing profits would hire the extra hour, and continue to do so as long as the MPL exceeds the wage. But the MPL will decline as more employment is utilized, so the expansion of employment has a natural end: the point at which MPL equals the real wage. Suppose, taking the opposite case, that the real wage exceeds the MPL. Now the firm can increase its profit by *reducing* its demand for labour. Because it is optimal to set labour such that MPL = w, the MPL schedule in panel (*b*) of Figure 5.5 is also the firm's **labour demand curve**.

The slope of the labour demand curve depends on the rate at which the MPL falls. If MPL is relatively insensitive to labour and falls only slightly as labour inputs are increased, then the demand curve will be relatively flat. Small changes in the wage will lead to large responses in the demand for labour. The labour demand curve is **elastic**. In contrast, if the MPL drops sharply as labour inputs are increased, the labour demand curve is steep and the demand for labour is unresponsive to changes in the wage. We say that the demand for labour is **inelastic**.

Shifts in the demand for labour

After studying the slope of the labour demand curve, we consider reasons for the labour demand curve to shift—to change its position. One possible reason is an increase in the capital stock K, which we took as given, i.e. exogenous. At the aggregate level, an increase in the capital stock tends to make additional labour more productive. In panel (*a*) of Figure 5.6 this is shown as an increase in MPL—the production function becomes steeper at every level of production. In panel (*b*), this implies that the labour demand curve shifts out. A technological improvement that makes labour more productive at any given level of capital and labour input will have a similar effect on the MPL. This is identical to an increase in total factor productivity discussed in Chapter 3. Increasing total factor productivity can help account for the fact that wages have grown secularly over time.

Conversely, it is also possible for labour demand to shift back, i.e. to decline holding the wage constant. A decline in the capital stock brought about by war, natural disaster, or technical obsolescence causes the labour demand curve to shift inwards, i.e. down and

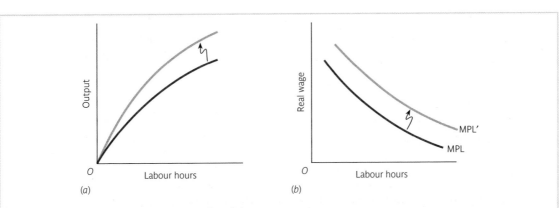

Fig. 5.6 An Increase in Labour Productivity

Labour can become more productive either because more capital is put in place, or because technological progress makes labour more productive using the existing stock of equipment. In panel (*a*), at any level of labour input, more output is produced and the production function is everywhere steeper. The MPL increases and the demand for labour schedule shifts up in panel (*b*).

Box 5.1   Technical Change and Unemployment

What is the effect of technological progress on jobs? A common perception is that technology destroys jobs by making people redundant, i.e. unnecessary for the production of goods and services. Aren't cars mostly produced by robots? Don't computers reduce the need for secretaries? Isn't the internet replacing mail and jobs in the post office? It would be hard to deny that technological advances destroy some jobs, occupations, or even whole sectors of economic activity. At the dawning of the industrial revolution in the early nineteenth century, the Luddites in Britain or the *soyeux* in France agitated against mechanized weaving machines and mobilized mobs to destroy them in large numbers. And indeed, weaving cloth by hand has disappeared as a trade, as have many other technically backward activities. Nevertheless, overall productivity of labour has increased roughly tenfold in the nations of Western Europe in the past 120 years, and if anything, unemployment is somewhat lower now than it was a century and a half ago, so the story must be more complicated than simply technology killing jobs.

Indeed, the story is more complicated. Technological progress does mean that the same output can be produced with fewer person-hours, but this does not mean that overall employment must fall. The key question is: How are technology-induced increases in labour productivity (Y/L) split between growth in output (Y) and employment (L)? Because both employment and output are endogenous, a correct answer requires much more knowledge in order to follow all the mechanisms that influence the final outcome. Sorting this out is the task of macroeconomics. But what do the facts tell us? Kaldor's fourth stylized fact discussed in Chapter 3 says that the wage share is stable long term. The wage share is WL/PY, which can be rewritten as $w/(Y/L)$. For the wage share to remain constant when productivity rises, real wages w must have to keep up with productivity (Y/L).

We also know that, over the decades, the number of hours that people work has been secularly falling, but the number of workers employed in the USA and Europe has increased dramatically—a consequence of increasing labour force participation. Higher real wages, more leisure and more employment—it seems that technological progress has made a positive contribution to our well-being.

The Luddites and their modern-day equivalents are guilty of the 'fallacy of composition': the disappearance of some jobs or the decline of some regions need not apply to the economy as a whole. The demand for secretaries may have fallen, but who builds, programs, and maintains the computers that make secretaries redundant? Who designs, markets, and services the cars built by robots? New jobs replace old jobs. Of course, these are not the same people. At the aggregate level, old skills are replaced by new skills, but some individuals must be retrained, which takes time, and some are sidelined. That some people become unemployed does not mean that total employment declines. Economic progress may be painful for some, but it is by no means a systematic job-killer. And from Chapter 3 we have learned that it is the most important engine of sustainable increases in the standards of living.

to the left. In the case of labour-saving technical change, it is possible for labour demand to decline, even as total output is increasing. Box 5.1 explains the important phenomenon of technical change in more detail.

5.2.3 Labour Market Equilibrium

We now have the building blocks needed to understand the labour market: a supply curve derived from household behaviour, and a demand curve derived from firm behaviour. The interaction of supply and demand for labour is depicted in Figure 5.7. Equilibrium occurs at the intersection of the two curves (point A). At wage w the market clears (there is no excess demand or supply): L is the number of hours firms want to hire and households want to work. Both the real wage rate and employment are endogenously determined in the labour market.

This basic characterization of the labour market is an important part of an economist's toolkit, and its predictions serve as the benchmark for the rest of the chapter. Figure 5.8 provides two examples of its

Fig. 5.7 Equilibrium in the Labour Market

Labour market equilibrium occurs at point *A* where demand and supply are equal. The real wage *w* clears the market at employment level *L*. Since total labour endowment is given by $N\bar{\ell}$ voluntary unemployment is given by the distance $N\bar{\ell}-L$.

usefulness. Panel (*a*) shows the outcome of an increase in labour productivity resulting from capital accumulation or technological advances, already examined in Box 5.1. The labour demand curve shifts outwards; the supply curve remains unaffected. The result is an unambiguous increase in real wages. In the figure, employment increases, but if the labour supply curve is vertical, employment remains unchanged and labour income *wL* rises proportionally with the real wage. It turns out that if the income effects of wage increases dominate the substitution effect, the supply curve can even be backward-bending: employment (person-hours) would even decline. Table 5.1 suggests that this has been the case over the past century.

The second panel of Figure 5.8 shows that an exogenous increase in the supply of labour leads to an increase in employment, but also to a reduction in real wages. Yet, this is a short-run effect. One of the stylized facts presented in Chapter 3 states that, in the long run, real wages grow with productivity. To the extent equilibrium employment increases, an increase in labour supply will initially lower the capital–labour ratio *K*/*L*. A lower capital–labour ratio means that the productivity of capital has risen, which leads to more capital accumulation. As the capital–labour ratio returns to its previous growth path, the labour demand curve shifts outward (not shown). In the long run, an increase in the supply of labour is eventually matched by an increase in the stock of productive capital, and, *ceteris paribus*, no reduction in real wages.

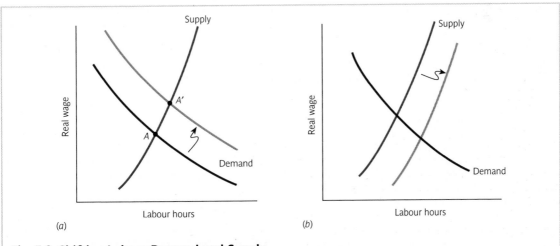

(*a*)   (*b*)

Fig. 5.8 Shifting Labour Demand and Supply

When labour demand increases (panel (*a*)), for example because of additional capital or technological progress, the real wage and the employment level both increase. When labour supply increases instead (panel (*b*))—because of new entries into the labour force, for example—employment rises but the real wage declines.

5.2.4 **The Interpretation of Unemployment**

While the supply-and-demand apparatus allows us to evaluate the effect of various changes on equilibrium employment and real wages, it is disappointing in one crucial respect. At point A in Figure 5.7, labour supplied is equal to labour demanded and denoted by L. Any unemployed labour—literally, labour not employed—reflects the voluntary decisions of households and firms. Indeed, $N\bar{\ell}$ represents total potential labour supply, the maximum amount of hours of work that all the people in the economy can contribute. If L is actual employment, corresponding to point A, unemployment (measured as hours of work not employed) is simply $N\bar{\ell} - L$. Since point A lies on the labour supply curve, unemployment reflects the choices of households. Why then do we see unemployment? The reasoning so far leads us to conclude that unemployment in Figure 5.7 is voluntary. The real wage w is simply too low to persuade all workers to give up all their leisure:

some may wish to work only part-time, others may not want to work at all.

It might be disturbing to think that unemployment could be chosen freely. Yet **voluntary unemployment**—or, more precisely, the decision not to work—is an important phenomenon in modern economies. It is not only the very wealthy who can afford not to work. Those who receive an income from other sources (from a spouse or from the state, for example) may also find that the net wage they can earn does not compensate for foregone leisure or non-market activities, including working at home or raising children. Voluntary unemployment is likely among low-skilled people who cannot earn much, or in countries where taxes are so high that working yields little net gain. The most obvious costs to working are faced by families with children. The high cost of child care—or simply the unavailability of such services—explains why two-earner families are not as common in some countries as in others. Box 5.2 presents more general evidence on how very different patterns of household labour supply can emerge,

 Box 5.2 **Market Hours at Work: Europe versus the USA**

International comparisons should always be taken with a pinch of salt, because data from different countries—especially labour market data—are frequently difficult to compare. Yet often differences are just too large to attribute to measurement error. Table 5.2 compares hours worked per week, on average, per adult of working age (in general, aged 15–65). Evidently, most Europeans spend less time in market work than US Americans or Britons do, 20–25% less in some cases. Yet there are clearly different trends in the data, reflecting the outcome of changing labour supply at two different margins: a decrease in average hours worked by those already in work as documented in Table 5.1 (the so-called intensive margin), versus a trend of increasing labour supply at the extensive margin (labour force participation). In Denmark, the Netherlands, and Sweden, weekly hours per capita actually rose over the past decade, reflecting the successful reactivation of the long-term unemployed and the rising entry of women

in the labour force. In Italy, efforts to increase part-time and marginal employment have begun to bear some fruit. In other countries, such as France and Germany, hours per capita continue to decline, as the negative trend in hours worked per employee dominate the upward trend in participation.

Does this mean that continental Europeans are lazy? Despite such striking international differences, underlying economic behaviour is remarkably similar. Research on time use has given economists important insights into the way people use their time, and it turns out that market work is not the only type of work that people perform. For example, we know that in 2000–2003, when US Americans were working about 45% more in the market on average than Germans, they only worked about 8% more overall. How can this be? The answer is that Germans—both men and women—work much more at home, performing services that many Americans would purchase in the market.

Table 5.2 Weekly Hours Worked per Person of Working Age

	1995	2008
Austria	18.1	18.3
Canada	19.7	21.0
Denmark	18.0	19.8
France	15.3	15.5
Germany	15.8	15.2
Italy	14.8	15.9
Netherlands	14.5	17.2
Sweden	18.3	19.1
United Kingdom	18.6	18.7
United States	22.1	21.2

Source: International Labour Office.

suggesting that labour market institutions may have a more important role for explaining differences across countries than preferences themselves.

The decision for women to enter and remain in the labour force is of central importance for an economy's productive potential. Table 5.3 displays the labour force participation rate (the proportion of women of working age in the labour force, whether employed or not), the female unemployment rate, and the proportion of women of working age actually employed. The variation of these indicators across countries is significant, and points to differences in both cultures and institutions. For example, female participation in the labour force is very high in countries like Denmark and Sweden, which have a highly developed and subsidized child care system. It is lower in societies in which women have traditionally played a greater role at home, but also where taxation may discourage a second earner in the family.

Table 5.3 Female Labour Force Participation Rates, Unemployment Rates, and Employment Ratios, 2009

	Employment/population	Labour force participation rate	Unemployment rate
Belgium	56.0	60.9	8.1
Canada	69.1	74.4	7.1
Denmark	73.1	77.3	5.4
Finland	67.9	73.5	7.6
France	60.0	66.2	9.4
Germany	65.2	70.4	7.4
Ireland	57.8	62.9	8.1
Japan	59.8	62.9	5.0
Netherlands	70.6	73.5	3.9
Norway	74.4	76.5	2.7
Portugal	61.6	69.0	10.7
Spain	53.5	65.7	18.5
Sweden	70.2	76.4	8.1
United Kingdom	65.6	70.2	6.5
United States	63.4	69.0	8.2

Source: OECD, *Employment Outlook*.

5.3 A Static Interpretation of Unemployment

Our first attempt at defining unemployment in the last section is somewhat unsatisfactory. Surely, unemployment is more than simply labour withheld voluntarily from the market. The International Labour Organization (ILO) and the Organization for Economic Cooperation and Development (OECD) define an individual as unemployed if he or she does not have a job during the reference period, is actively looking for one, and is ready to work. Let us start by defining the labour force as those members of the adult population who are either working (L) or unemployed (U). The labour force mainly excludes young people in school, the retired, and those who are not looking for work. It corresponds closely to the amount of labour supplied to the market, given current conditions, including the level of real wages. Denoting the labour force as L^S, we can write:

(5.2) $L^S = L + U.$

labour force = employment + unemployment

The unemployment rate u is the fraction of the labour force which is out of work, or $u = U/L^S$. Perhaps it is now clear why the picture of unemployment in Figure 5.7 is incomplete: according to the ILO definition, it would have to be zero! In the rest of this chapter, we examine alternative reasons for unemployment.

5.3.1 Involuntary Unemployment and Real Wage Adjustment

One interpretation of unemployment in the ILO definition is the excess of labour supply over labour demand. In equilibrium depicted in Figure 5.7 this outcome was ruled out by assumption, because the labour market was assumed to clear. Figure 5.9 considers the important case where the real wage is fixed at $\bar{w}$, which is higher than the level which equates supply and demand, w. At $\bar{w}$, firms are willing to hire $\bar{L}$ labour, while workers supply L^S. Since firms cannot be forced to hire more than they wish, actual

Fig. 5.9 Involuntary Unemployment

At the real wage rate $\bar{w}$ workers supply L^S of labour but firms demand, and hire, only $\bar{L}$. The quantity $L^S - \bar{L}$; which is supplied by households but not demanded by firms, represents involuntary unemployment. If the real wage were to adjust downward from $\bar{w}$ to w, the market would clear at point A.

employment is $\bar{L}$, and $L^S - \bar{L}$ is labour supplied but not demanded by the market. The labour market does not clear and there is **involuntary unemployment**. Involuntary unemployment occurs when labour is willing and able to work at the wage $\bar{w}$ but cannot find employment. At point B, the marginal product of labour (MPL) exceeds the valuation of leisure time by households which are out of work. Put differently, at point B, firms are not willing to hire all labour that workers are willing to supply at wage $\bar{w}$.

The solution to the unemployment problem in Figure 5.9 appears rather straightforward. If the real wage were to fall from $\bar{w}$ to w (point A), demand would increase, supply would decrease, and unemployment would be eliminated. It is the failure of the wage to decline that perpetuates unemployment. This is a key result: the existence of involuntary unemployment must be explained by **real wage rigidity**, which we examine next.

5.3.2 Collective Bargaining and Real Wage Rigidity

For sustained real wage rigidity to occur, involuntarily unemployed workers must be unable, on average, to supply their labour services at wages below $\bar{w}$, or firms must be unwilling to take up such offers, or be unable to make their own.[11] There are many reasons why wages may not adjust, or do so only slowly. The most important features of labour markets which have been neglected until now are **labour market institutions**. Labour market institutions are distinguishing national features of labour markets based on legal, cultural, operational, or organizational characteristics, which are designed to interfere with or modify the functioning of labour markets.

Labour (or trade) unions are one of the most fundamental and universal institutions that operate in modern labour markets today. Unions are organizations of employees which advocate interests of labour in a number of dimensions, including workers' rights, working conditions, and most importantly, wages. They exist because workers have considerably less ability to influence these conditions individually than collectively. Labour unions are often matched by equally powerful **employers' associations**. Bargaining between employers and unions contrasts sharply with the perfect-competition description of labour markets described in Section 5.2. In what follows, we study the motives of negotiators, and how they impact on wage determination. In doing so, we discover how unemployment can be voluntary from the perspective of trade unions, and nevertheless be involuntary from the viewpoint of the individual household.[12] We will also see that unions try to smooth out the ultimate fundamentals of the labour market as determined by supply and demand in Figure 5.7. At the same time, it is impossible to ignore them.

The rationale for labour unions

The employer–employee relationship has inherently conflictual aspects. One is the distribution of income. While economic principles assert that income should be split according to the marginal productivities of capital and labour, marginal productivity in practice is difficult, if not impossible, to measure. Another more subtle reason is that firms cannot observe the work effort, a key element of productivity, which is under the control of each individual employee. Individual workers facing a large employer are in a poor bargaining position. They have little influence over their own wage rate and may not even feel safe discussing working conditions, fearing reprisals in the form of a salary cut or dismissal. They may even feel pressure to accept conditions that would not be acceptable under competitive conditions.

Historically, workers have organized themselves into unions to help resist such pressures, in particular, to achieve higher pay levels and a voice in the day-to-day operation of the workplace. Table 5.4 gives some details on union organizations and their organizational strength (membership) and impact on workers' contracts (coverage). Clearly, labour market institutions vary considerably from country to country. Scandinavian countries have a tradition of centralized unionization. German workers are organized by industry unions; in Britain they tend to be associated with members' craft or occupation. In France, Italy, and Spain, unions are frequently tied to political parties. In the Nordic economies, union membership is generally greater than three-quarters of the workforce and coverage is often as high as 90%, while in the USA unions have more or less disappeared from the private (non-governmental) workplace.

These vast differences reflect social history as well as the costs and benefits associated with union membership. The costs are dues (fees) that members must pay. The benefits vary, ranging from higher wages and protection from arbitrary employer decisions to more specific advantages, including priority for certain jobs and income supplements when unions are on strike. In some countries, many advantages accrue

---

[11] It is important to stress 'on average', since workers are different, varying by occupation, skill level, and industrial affiliation. Thus, real wage rigidity may affect workers with low productivity more than those with high skill levels.

[12] It should be stressed that we limit ourselves strictly to the economic significance of trade unions. As the history of the labour movement amply demonstrates, unions have had an enormous influence on modern society beyond their economic impact.

Table 5.4 **European Trade Unions: Membership and Coverage, 1950–2004**

Country	Structure	Union membership (%)				Union coverage (%)
		1950	1970	1990	2007	2007
Sweden	Umbrella (ILO, TCO, SAGO)	67	67	82	68	91
Finland	Umbrella (SAK, STTK, AKAVA)	30	51	73	74	90
Denmark	Umbrella (LO, HK, FTF)	56	63	75	69	83
Norway	Umbrella (LO, AF, YS)	45	50	56	52	74
Belgium	Party, religious (ACV/CSC, ABVV/ FGTB, ACLVB/CGSLB)	43	42	50	51.5	96
Ireland	Mostly crafts in ICTU, fragmented	42	59	59	31.4	44
Austria	Umbrella/industrial (ÖGB)	62	57	47	35	98–99
Italy	Party, religious (CGIL, CISL, UIL)	45	37	39	35.6	80
United Kingdom	Mostly crafts (TUC)	45	50	43	28	34.6
Germany[1]	Umbrella/industrial (DGB, IG Metall, Ver.di)	38	32	36	22	61
Portugal	Party, religous /Umbrella (CGTP, UGT)	—	—	40	22	90
Netherlands	Party, religious (FNV, CNV, MHP)	43	37	24	24	84
Greece	Occupational/ sectoral (GSEE, ADEDY)	—	—	34	28	100
Spain	Industrial, company level (CC.OO, UGT, ELA, CIGA)	—	—	12	17	60.3
France	Party, religious (CGT, CFDT, CGT-FO, CFTC, CFE-CGC)	30	20	14	8	90
Memo: US	Mostly local plant-level (AFL–CIO)	—	—	—	n/a	n/a

[1] West Germany until 1990.
Source: EIRO, country profiles.
<http://www.eurofound.europa.eu/eiro/country_index.htm>.

to all workers, so there is little point in paying union dues. This is the case in France, for example.[13] In other countries, such as Belgium and in Scandinavia, unions help manage some social benefits systems, including unemployment insurance. In the USA, some unions even issue credit cards and provide other financial services to their members. In the end, the influence of unions is usually much stronger than simple membership statistics would suggest, and is partly related to labour laws which institutionalize their role. This is evident from Table 5.4, which shows the fraction of all workers working under contracts negotiated by unions, whether or not they are union members.

The economics of labour unions

Simplifying somewhat, we can think of two primary economic objectives which motivate unions: higher

---

[13] This is an illustration of the so-called free-rider problem. If no workers pay dues, the union disappears and no one is protected. So some workers must pay the dues for all to have a union. Often workers tend to join unions for reasons related to peer pressure, social norms, or ideology.

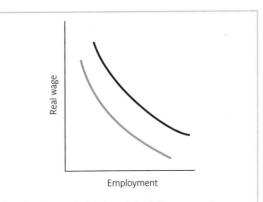

Fig. 5.10 Trade Unions' Indifference Curves

When a trade union values both higher wages and more employment, its preferences are described by indifference curves. A 'hard-line' union is not willing to give up much in lower wages to raise employment. A union mainly preoccupied with employment is represented by steep indifference curves.

real wages, and more jobs.[14] It is helpful to think of union preferences in terms of indifference curves shown in Figure 5.10. The slope of the indifference curve represents the willingness of the union to trade-off employment for wages. It is flat for 'hard-line' unions which are unwilling to trade wages against employment, steeper for unions which care relatively more about jobs than wages.

In contrast to Section 5.2, we now describe a labour market in which union indifference curves replace those of the representative individual as the relevant preferences. This captures the fact that the active agent in the labour market is not the individual, but the labour union, or the collective bargaining process more generally. The 'budget line' faced by the union is simply the labour demand curve. From Section 5.2.2 we know that labour demand is given by the MPL (either a firm's MPL, or that of an industry or the entire economy: if firms are all alike, their individual demand does not differ from the collective one represented by an employers' association).[15]

Given the demand for labour that it faces, the optimal choice for the union is the tangency point of the highest indifference curve with the current demand for labour. This outcome is the best the union can do, given the economic environment it faces, which is the behaviour of firms. Should the demand for labour shift, the union's menu of options will change too. Capital accumulation or technological progress which shifts out the labour demand curve, for example, will increase the wage that firms are willing to pay at a given employment level, or increase the sustainable employment that can be hired on, holding the wage constant. Inward shifts of labour demand are also possible. These are attributable to destruction or obsolescence of the capital stock (e.g. due to wars, earthquakes, the lack of new investment), or new inventions which make some labour unnecessary. They have the opposite effect, shrinking available options to the union. As the labour demand schedules shifts, the set of tangency points map out the **collective labour supply curve** shown in Figure 5.11. The curve describes the most desired joint evolution of real wages and employment from the union's perspective.

The slope of the collective labour supply curve thus reflects the preferences of the union for employment and wages as well as its economic environment. It will also reflect whether demand is shifting outward or inward.[16] Union members who are currently employed, or who enjoy seniority or job protection, tend to fight for a hard-line union. If their influence is high, the slope of the collective labour supply curve will be steep. In contrast, a 'jobs-first' union accepts moderate real wage increases and supplies more labour. It will tend to exhibit a flat collective labour supply curve. (More details on different possible shapes of the collective labour supply curve are discussed in the WebAppendix.)

[14] As noted already, unions care about many other aspects of labour markets, such as safety at work, working time, employees' rights and influence over working conditions and organization. They also care about the size of their membership. To simplify the analysis, these aspects are not considered here.

[15] Here we assume that firms are behaving competitively—each firm on its own. More likely than not, associations of employers will arise in response and exert their own power in the bargaining process, presuming they can organize and discipline enough firms. A more general treatment of bargaining when employers are non-competitive is possible but beyond the level of this textbook.

[16] Note that the collective labour supply curve depends on the successive shifts in the demand for labour that we imagine. Different shifts can change both the position and the slope of the labour demand curve. A number of outcomes are possible. These are described in more detail graphically in the WebAppendix to Chapter 5.

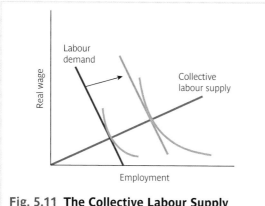

Fig. 5.11 The Collective Labour Supply Curve

The collective labour supply curve is obtained by connecting the points of tangency between the indifference curves and a shifting labour demand schedule.

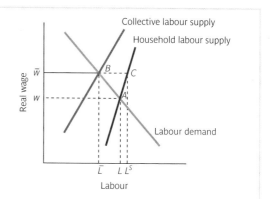

Fig. 5.12 Labour Market Equilibrium with a Trade Union

When a labour union represents workers at wage negotiations, labour market equilibrium occurs at point B. If the union collective labour supply curve is above the individual labour supply curve, the real wage $\bar{w}$ is higher and employment $\bar{L}$ (hours or number of workers) lower than at point A, which would be the outcome if individuals were negotiating individually. The result is the existence of union-voluntary, individual-involuntary unemployment ($L^S - \bar{L}$): it is the difference between actual employment $\bar{L}$ and the amount of work L^S that workers are willing to supply individually at the real wage rate $\bar{w}$ (point C).

Employment effects of collective bargaining

The collective labour supply curve resembles the individual supply curve of Figure 5.3, but has different origins. Collectively, through their unions, workers increase their bargaining power and, accordingly, aim at better outcomes. In particular, for a given amount of labour supplied, they ask for higher real wages: for this reason, it should be clear that the union-driven collective labour supply curve can only lie above the individual labour supply curves. Without the union's influence on wage setting, equilibrium would occur in Figure 5.12 at point A: individuals would be willing to work up to L at wage w. They cannot, however, because the wage is set in negotiations between the firms and the trade union, and individuals cannot simply underbid their employed colleagues. The outcome is $\bar{w}$, and the resulting unemployment ($L^S - \bar{L}$) is involuntary for affected individuals, but voluntary from the union's point of view.

How can unions enforce wage rigidity, apparently against the will of unemployed individual workers? One reason is that the leadership is typically elected by the employed, sometimes called the **insiders**. The employed are always a dominant majority of the membership, even at record high unemployment rates of 10% or 20%. Unemployed workers often give up their membership or lose interest in union affairs. They are called the **outsiders**. Unions end up representing the insiders, who have jobs, rather than the outsiders, who are an unemployed minority. Employed workers lobby for high real wages (for themselves) at the cost of some unemployment (for others). Box 5.3 illustrates how the relentless rise of unemployment in Europe after the two oil shocks can be explained by this effect.

The split between unions and unemployed workers cannot go too far, though. After unemployment increased to high levels in Europe in the 1970s and 1980s, unions became more employment-conscious and real wage growth moderated significantly. There are several reasons for this wage moderation. First, members became worried that they too might become unemployed. Second, there was criticism from the non-unionized workers. Third, the loss in membership revealed in Table 5.4 has meant lower income from union dues as well as less overall influence.

Box 5.3 The European Unemployment Problem

Two major negative shifts to the demand for labour occurred during the past 30 years. Both were associated with the sudden oil price increases of the mid-1970s and early 1980s, the so-called oil shocks. These shocks made many production processes obsolete, because they had been developed on the assumption that oil, and more generally energy, would remain cheap. The consequence was a sharp drop in productivity, which can be represented by a significant inward shift of the aggregate labour demand curve. If a smaller membership leads trade unions to demand even higher wages, the collective labour supply curve shifts upwards. Owing to the behaviour of the 'insiders' who have jobs, employment prospects for 'outsiders' are reduced. After

the oil shocks have passed, the employment level is permanently reduced. That such an effect—dubbed the 'hysteresis effect'—was observed in several European countries is suggested by the step-wise increase in the unemployment rate following each oil shock (Table 5.5). In contrast, unemployment rates in the USA increased at the time of each oil shock, but then reverted towards earlier levels. As unemployment rises, pressure to do something does as well. In a number of countries, measures have been taken to help these countries turn the corner on the European unemployment problem. In addition, unions come under pressure to moderate wage levels, which leads to the re-employment of outsiders.

Table 5.5 Standardized Unemployment Rates (% of labour force)

	1960–1969	1970–1979	1980–1989	1990–1999	2000–2009	2010
France	2.0	3.8	8.5	10.5	8.8	9.8
Germany	0.8	2.4	5.8	8.0	9.0	7.1
Italy	3.8	4.7	7.8	10.2	7.9	8.4
Spain	2.5	4.4	14.6	16.1	11.0	20.1
Sweden	1.7	2.0	2.6	7.2	6.7	8.4
United Kingdom	1.8	4.2	9.5	8.0	5.4	7.8
United States	4.8	6.2	7.3	5.8	5.5	9.6

Source: OECD.

It would be unfair to assert that unions are solely responsible for real wage rigidity. Employers' associations can also contribute to real wages rigidity. These associations represent the collective interests of firms. They represent an additional mechanism for policing collective bargaining agreements reached with unions. In the end, employers' associations do not control the demand for labour: this is the prerogative of the individual companies. So, while it is in firms' interest to keep wages low, it is also in their interest to 'take the wage out of competition'. This

means keeping the wages of their competitors high, or at least preventing them from hiring cheap labour.

5.3.3 Social Minima and Real Wage Rigidity

Beyond trade unions and employers' associations, several other institutional and economic factors can contribute to wage rigidity, and therefore involuntary unemployment. Frequently mentioned in the European context are social minima, or minimum standards for income and earnings mandated by the government for reasons of social equity or protection. Social minima may stem from social or unemployment benefits, since few will work for a net wage which falls below the level available for no work at all. They can also be set at a higher level by **minimum wages**, which are legal limits on how low wages can be.

Minimum wages have been enacted for a variety of reasons. One was to prevent employers with excessive market power from abusing it by depressing wages. Another reason was to protect young people from exploitation. With schooling rudimentary and poverty endemic, for many youngsters on-the-job training was the only way to get started. Unscrupulous employers would offer very low wages, sometimes below minimal survival needs. Social protection was and often still is justified. Even in countries without statutory or legal minimum wages, it is frequently the case that collective agreements are extended to uncovered workers, and contract wages assume the characteristics of a legal minimum wage. With occasional exceptions, this is generally the case in continental Europe.

The primary economic effect of minimum wages is to discourage firms from hiring workers with low MPL, which tend to be the young, the unskilled, those with little training, or those with the wrong skills. Figure 5.13 illustrates the effect of minimum wages. To serve any purpose at all, the minimum wage $w_{\min}$ must be higher than the wage that would be obtained otherwise ($\bar{w}$), and which is itself higher than what individuals would accept with market clearing (w). The result is employment equal to $L_{\min}$; unemployment ($L_{\min}^S - L_{\min}$) is even higher than the level implied by the wage set in collective bargaining ($L^S - \bar{L}$).

Some evidence on the effect of minimum wages is discussed in Box 5.4. Those most likely to be hurt by the existence of minimum wage legislation are poorly educated young people with no job experience and older workers with obsolete skills; their MPL is simply too low to justify the going minimum wage. The minimum wage can also affect jobs paying more than the floor, because once in place, it tends to push up into the higher echelons of the wage pyramid, just like a spring which is compressed. This is because market forces tend to re-establish wage premia between different skill and productivity levels.

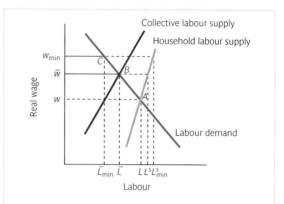

Fig. 5.13 **Minimum Wages**

Minimum wages reduce the demand for labour below the level that would result with either union-negotiated wages or individual-supplied labour.

5.3.4 Efficiency Wages and Real Wage Rigidity

Another reason why real wages may not decline in the presence of involuntary unemployment is that firms themselves may not wish to lower them for various reasons. The phenomenon is often called **efficiency wages**, and it is related to another special aspect of labour. In contrast with other factors of production, work effort is not easily observed by firms, and yet it matters a lot. By paying higher wages, firms may attempt to elicit more work of better quality. If the wage is relatively high, a worker who is dismissed for lack of effort is unlikely to obtain such a good deal elsewhere, especially if dismissals are interpreted as a sign of poor work effort. Firms may also pay higher wages to obtain a better selection of applicants and to keep workers from quitting too often. If all firms behave this way, the outcome will be a wage level which exceeds the market-clearing value w in Figure 5.13.

In capital-intensive industries, where shirking could seriously disrupt the production process and where a high-quality workforce is of primary importance, firms may have a strong incentive to pay efficiency wages. In this case, the function of real wages goes beyond simply equilibrating demand and supply in labour markets. Generally, wages will not be able to satisfy both functions. They will tend to be rigid and lie above the market-clearing level, as in Figure 5.12.

Box 5.4 Minimum Wages and Youth Unemployment

It is striking that teenagers in the USA often work during the summer when their European counterparts go on vacation. One reason might be that wages that must be paid for young, unskilled labour are too high in Europe. The minimum wage amounts to about one-third of the average manufacturing wage in the USA, while in many EU countries it well exceeds 50%. This is one reason why filling station attendants and grocery shop assistants have all but disappeared in most European countries. Table 5.6 shows non-employment and unemployment rates for young people in a number of countries, as well as the average minimum wage, as a fraction of the average overall wage. In interpreting the table, it is important to note that Danish youth under 18 years receive a deep discount from a collectively bargained minimum wage, as they do in the USA, while in France, Belgium, and the Netherlands, the minimum wage as a fraction of the median wage is high, meaning that a great many jobs are paid the minimum wage.

In France, the minimum wage, called the SMIC (Salaire Minimum Interpersonel de Croissance), is an important element of the collective bargaining system. It is set by a council on which both the government and unions are represented. Many government employees receive the SMIC. In recent years, 10–15% of workers in industry, commerce, and services earned the SMIC or near it, a much higher proportion than in the USA (about 3–4%). While the minimum wage in general has a negative effect on youth employment, it may lead to a substitution of adults for youths, even increasing the employment of the former. Recent evidence from Portugal's experience with the minimum wage supports this hypothesis.

We have emphasized the economic effects of minimum wages. The public debate, in contrast, is frequently guided by considerations such as social equity and social norms. A minimum wage is supposed to help the fight against 'working poverty'. Yet it is rarely mentioned that the minimum wage destroys jobs as long as the labour demand curve is elastic. Thus, those who might have held those jobs are implicitly 'financing' the minimum wage—those whose productivity is just below the level necessary to justify the job's existence. The public purse might be a better approach to solving the problem of the working poor.

Table 5.6 Minimum Wages and Youth Labour Market Experience, 2003

	Minimum wage as % of median wage	% affected (at or near minimum)	Youth minimum as % of adult level (relevant age)	Non-employment ratio for youth age 15–24: 2005 (%)	Unemployment rate for youth aged 15 to 24: 2005 (%)
Belgium	47	4	slightly less	74.8	19.9
Denmark	Collective agreements	6	40 (<18)	31.8	7.9
France	61	11	80 (16); 90 (17); 30–75 for trainees	79.9	22.8
Germany	Collective agreements	—	Industry agreements	55.6	15.2
Italy	Collective agreements	—	Industry agreements	74.8	24
Netherlands	51	3	34.5 (16); rising to 84 (22)	38.9	9.6
Spain	29	7	66 (<18)	71.1	19.7
UK	44	—	None	39	11.8
USA	32 s	4	None	42	11.3

Source: OECD.

5.4 A Dynamic Interpretation of Unemployment

5.4.1 Labour Market States and Transitions

Any person in the working-age population is either employed, unemployed, or out of the labour force. Figure 5.14 displays these three states and how flows occur between them. A striking aspect of labour markets in developed economies is the sheer size of these flows. Table 5.7 shows that the flow of individuals moving into and out of unemployment over a year represents several times the stock of unemployment at any particular point in time. In contrast to the static impression conveyed by Section 5.3, labour markets are remarkably dynamic, even when unemployment seems stuck at high levels.

There are three ways of becoming unemployed.

- First, new entrants to the labour market join the labour force before they have found work, but are initially unsuccessful.

- Second, voluntary **separations** of workers from jobs can lead to unemployment. In general, separations occur due to quits, layoffs (redundancies), plant closures, or expiration of fixed-term contracts. Quits represent voluntary separations from the employee's viewpoint. They account for roughly 50% to 66% of all separations from employment in the UK, and up to 70% in the USA. Most workers who quit

one job take up another immediately—a transition from employment to employment. Of those who quit but do not start a new job, most leave the labour force, usually for family reasons (e.g. maternity leave), return to school, or retire. Relatively few workers quit into unemployment.

- Finally, involuntary separations, or job losers, tend to flow into unemployment (although some may just decide not to look for work). Job loss may result from termination of fixed-term contracts (common in France and Spain), unanticipated redundancies or layoffs (more common in Denmark, the UK, and the USA), and closure or relocation of factories (which occurs everywhere).

5.4.2 Stocks, Flows, and Equilibrium Unemployment

In earlier sections, we have ignored the obvious fact that no two positions and no two persons are the same. This has led us to overlook that pairing a worker and an unfilled job opening–also called a vacancy–is not always easy and may take time. The matching of skills, occupation, industry, and geographical location requires a large amount of information. The more efficient the labour markets are, the faster the match is achieved. From this perspective,

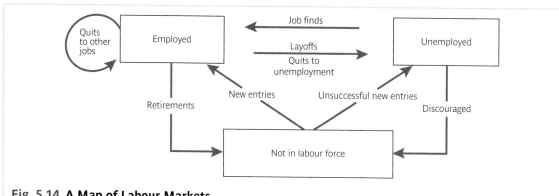

Fig. 5.14 A Map of Labour Markets
Every individual is in one of three states: employed, unemployed, or out of the labour force. Over any period of time, large numbers of workers are flowing from one state to another.

Table 5.7 Unemployment Stocks and Flows, 2010

	Average unemployment stock, millions	Unemployment Flows (millions of cases per year)	
		Inflows	Outflows
Austria	0.25	1.00	1.17
Germany	2.97	8.64	8.83
UK	1.44	3.73	3.84
USA	14.82	33.20	33.93

Sources: AMS (Austria); Bundesagentur für Arbeit (Germany); Department of Employment (UK); Bureau of Labor Statistics (USA).

unemployment emerges as an unavoidable result of the dynamics of labour force movements, and the normal process of job creation and destruction as firms grow or shrink, are born or die.

In addition to the efficiency of the job-matching process, equilibrium unemployment depends on the number of job separations and the number of vacancies. If we ignore the flows from and to 'Not in the labour force' in Figure 5.14, the number of workers who become unemployed (per month or per year) represents a fraction s, called the **separation rate**, of existing employment relationships (L). While sL workers flow into unemployment each period, a number of unemployed workers find jobs and flow out of unemployment. If we use f to denote the job **finding rate**, i.e. the fraction of the unemployed (U) who find employment during the period, the change in unemployment in a given period is given by

$$(5.3) \qquad \Delta U = sL - fU.$$

$$\underset{\text{unemployment}}{\text{change in}} = \underset{\text{unemployment}}{\text{inflows into}} - \underset{\text{unemployment}}{\text{outflows out of}}$$

In the dynamic interpretation of labour markets, unemployment is the stock that results when flows into and out of unemployment are equal, or when $\Delta U = 0$ in (5.3). Expressing unemployment as a proportion of the labour force $L^S = L + U$ and neglecting transitions in and out of the labour force allows us to use the flow perspective of labour markets to write the **equilibrium unemployment rate** u as[17]

$$(5.4) \qquad u = \frac{s}{s + f}.$$

[17] If $\Delta U = 0$, it follows that $sL = fU$. Substituting $L^S - U$ for L and dividing by L^S yields (5.4).

We can think of the proportion s of workers separated from their jobs as the probability of losing a job if currently employed and, similarly, the proportion f of unemployed workers represents the probability of finding a job if unemployed.[18] Equilibrium unemployment is higher, the higher the job separation rate and the lower the job finding rate. The next two sections will examine more closely the determinants of these two indicators—the job separation rate s and the job finding rate f.

5.4.3 Job Separation and the Incidence of Unemployment

The separation rate s is a measure of the incidence of unemployment. It has both structural and cyclical components. The structural aspect is linked to the ease with which firms can dismiss workers, regardless of the business cycle. It is lower in countries where legal and social restrictions on layoffs exist (as in most continental European countries) than in countries where redundancies are more acceptable (e.g. Denmark, the UK, and the USA).[19] The cyclical aspect simply refers to the fact that during recessions the probability of losing a job rises and so, therefore, does equilibrium unemployment.

Table 5.8 shows that in one particular country (the UK) in a given year (2004), job separation rates vary considerably across various characteristics of labour

[18] These figures conceal a large degree of heterogeneity in the labour market: some individuals find a job easily after becoming unemployed, whereas others may have very low probabilities of exiting unemployment.

[19] It is, however, usually the case that outflow rates in countries with employment protection are also lower, because firms are more reluctant to hire new workers. For that reason, the effect of employment protection on unemployment is ambiguous.

Table 5.8 Inflows into Unemployment and Unemployment Rates in the UK, March 2004

	Inflow rate into unemployment (monthly, as % of employment)	Unemployment rate (% of relevant labour force)
By region: Britain		
East Midlands	0.7	2.9
Eastern	0.5	2.3
London	0.8	3.6
North-East	1.0	4.6
North-West	0.8	3.3
Northern Ireland	0.7	4.0
Scotland	0.9	3.9
South-East	0.5	1.8
South-West	0.5	1.9
Wales	0.8	3.5
West Midlands	0.8	3.6
Yorkshire and the Humber	0.8	3.4
Total	0.7	3.1
By demographic group: UK		
Aged 16–17	1.0	21.1[a]
Aged 18–24	2.2	9.9[a]
Aged 25–49	0.6	3.9[a]
Aged 50 and over	0.4	2.5[a]
Male	0.9	4.3
Female	0.4	1.7

[a] Average from Dec 2003 to Feb 2004.
Source: UK Labour Market Trends, March 2004.

market participants. Just as equation (5.4) implies, those specific labour force groups that exhibit higher separation rates of inflow into unemployment tend to have higher unemployment rates.

5.4.4 Job Finding and the Duration of Unemployment

Like the separation rate, the job finding rate f has cyclical and structural components. It is highly procyclical, increasing when output and employment are rising and declining when the economy is contracting. On the structural side, the job finding rate depends on a number of long-run factors, including labour market institutions, the effectiveness of the worker–job matching process, and the suitability of the unemployed for work in the vacancies which firms are posting. It depends on how hard the unemployed look for jobs, how many job openings are available, and how easy it is to spot an opportunity (and how many opportunities are available). It depends on incentives to remain unemployed, and unemployment insurance may therefore slow down the exit rate out of unemployment. Many of these aspects will be discussed in Chapter 18.

Unemployment benefits are intended to assist the jobless while they search for work. Table 5.9 shows that unemployment benefit systems vary considerably from country to country, with respect to eligibility criteria, income replacement, and the period over which they are paid. While **unemployment benefits** reflect a widely perceived need for income insurance, solidarity, and social conscience, they may encourage unemployed workers in declining industries to wait for an unlikely recovery rather than to retrain and change sectors, possibly at a lower wage. They also act as a disincentive for looking for a job, or as an incentive for being 'choosier'.[20] If the benefits are generous, and particularly if they are long-lasting, unemployed workers may take more time to find an acceptable job, a time in which their skills and re-employability may deteriorate. This 'unemployment trap' often applies to unemployed low wage-earners who face loss of benefit upon taking on a new job. The last column of Table 5.9 shows a tendency for people to remain unemployed longer in countries where unemployment benefits are more generous, paying more income over longer periods. As the finding rate declines, equilibrium unemployment rises. This confirms an uncomfortable trade-off between social concern and economic efficiency.

---

[20] Strictly speaking, this applies only to those who already qualify for benefits. Prior work experience is often required before one can receive unemployment insurance benefits. In this case, individuals will be more willing to accept the first job. This is called the 'entitlement effect'.

Table 5.9 Unemployment Compensation: Conditions for Eligibility and Benefit Levels, 2007

Country	Eligibility conditions: Employment	Period	Maximum benefit duration (in weeks)	Replacement rate of net earnings/ Benefit levels[c]	Restrictions	Long term unemployment (>12 months) as % of all unemployed, 2006
Austria	28 weeks	12 months	52	55%	according to wage class	27.3
Belgium	312 days	18 months	indefinite	60%	of max earnings	55.6
Canada	from 420 to 700 hours	last 1 year	45	55%	average covered earnings	8.7
Denmark	52 weeks	3 years	208	90%	of average earnings	20.4
Finland	43 weeks	28 months	100	€25.63	per day	24.8
France	4 months	28 months	103	57.4–75%	of average daily wage	44.0
Germany	12 months	2 years	77	60%	of net earnings	57.0
Greece	200 days	2 years	51	40% (50%)	daily wages (monthly salary)	55.6
Ireland	39 weeks	last 1 year	51	€196.00	per week	34.3
Italy	52 weeks	2 years	34	40%	of gross average daily wage	52.9
Japan	6 months	12 months	47	50–80%	of average daily wage	33.0
Netherlands	26 weeks	36 weeks	months (old), 38 months	70%	of minimum wage	45.2
New Zealand	resident for 24 months		indefinite	NZ$173.92	per week	7.1
Norway	registered employment		104	0.24%	of annual income per day	14.1
Spain	12 months	last 6 years	102	70% (60%)	of average earnings	29.5
Sweden	480 hours or 6 months	12 months	43	320 kr	per day	14.2
Switzerland	12 months	2 years	74	80%	of last earnings	39.1
UK	[a]		26	£65.45	per week	22.1
USA	15–20 weeks[b]	1 year	26	50%	of last earnings, taxable	10.0

[a] Contributions must have been paid on earnings equal to at least 25 times weekly lower earnings limit (£84 from April 2006) in one of two tax years.
[b] Different across US states.
[c] Single household without children.
Sources: Social Security Programs Throughout the World: for Europe, United States, New Zealand, Japan for 2006, OECD
<http://www.ssa.gov/policy/docs/progdesc/ssptw/2006-2007/europe/index.html>.

5.5 The Equilibrium Rate of Unemployment

5.5.1 The Concept

If all unemployment were voluntary, it would hardly attract any attention. The existence of high and evidently involuntary unemployment means that labour markets do not function like other markets. The existence of market imperfections, arising from both economic and institutional factors, makes it necessary to modify the market-clearing paradigm of Section 5.2. We should also consider alternative concepts of equilibrium besides the equality of demand for labour by firms and the supply of labour by households.

The unemployment rates shown in Figure 1.2 clearly fluctuate in the short run over 2–3 year intervals, but also move slowly over a longer horizon. It is these longer-run movements in unemployment which are of interest to us now. Long-run labour market equilibrium can be summarized by an unemployment rate that would occur in the absence of cyclical disturbances. Because of imperfections, labour markets may be in equilibrium and yet unemployment may not be limited to voluntary unemployment. **Equilibrium unemployment** can be thought of as the sum of frictional and structural unemployment:

(5.5)   equilibrium unemployment =
          frictional unemployment +
          structural unemployment.

Frictional unemployment can be thought of the unemployment which is unavoidable, even under the best of conditions, because it takes time for a match to occur between a worker seeking a job and a vacancy needing to be filled. It depends on the efficiency of the labour market, including the eagerness of both parties to find a match quickly. The frictional unemployment rate may well vary over time, but only slowly as the market's efficiency changes and policies make it more or less likely for people to find jobs or to become unemployed in general. Is frictional unemployment voluntary or involuntary? Probably a bit of both. Some laid-off workers do find it genuinely difficult to quickly find a new job. Others may be choosy.

Structural unemployment describes the unemployment caused by inappropriate wage levels that are not allowed to adjust to their market-clearing levels. It has many causes. The common theme is that the demand and supply of labour are influenced by a number of institutions and regulations. Collective labour supply, which is brought into balance with labour demand in equilibrium, is generally inconsistent with individual supply behaviour. Some workers are involuntarily unemployed even when real wages equate the collective supply of labour with the demand of firms. Another possibility is that an economy's industry has suffered a loss of competitiveness, meaning that at any level of wages employment is lower, meaning that the inflow rate (s) and equilibrium unemployment rate (u) are higher.

Estimates of equilibrium rates of unemployment are provided in Table 5.10. The contrast between

Table 5.10 Estimates of the Equilibrium Unemployment Rate (in %)

	1970–1979	1980–1989	1990–1999	2000–2009	2010–2011
Germany	N/A	N/A	7.1	8.0	7.5
Italy	5.5	7.4	9.3	7.4	7.2
Japan	1.7	2.4	3.2	4.2	4.1
Spain	5.8	11.0	14.0	10.5	13.3
United Kingdom	5.3	9.3	8.1	5.5	5.9
United States	5.9	6.6	5.7	5.1	5.4

Source: OECD, *Economic Outlook* No 89.

Europe and North America is striking. The equilibrium unemployment rate was generally very low in Europe in the 1960s. Since then it rose considerably while remaining stable in the USA. A comparison of Table 5.10 with Table 5.4 shows that actual unemployment has followed the same pattern. To begin to understand this dramatic evolution, we return to the two components of the equilibrium rate of unemployment—demand for labour and the supply of labour.

5.5.2 The European Experience

The evidence suggests that European unemployment rose when large numbers of workers lost their jobs at the time of the oil shocks. The expected subsequent return to pre-oil-shock levels was thwarted in many European countries by a fall in the finding rate, so exit from unemployment became increasingly harder. Is the development of the social safety net to be blamed for having provided workers with the incentive to wait out their unemployment? Simple comparisons between Europe and the USA, such as the one in Figure 5.15, seem to confirm the suspicion that an extensive social safety net has become a barrier to more employment.

Yet there is also some striking counter-evidence. The social safety net is even more developed in

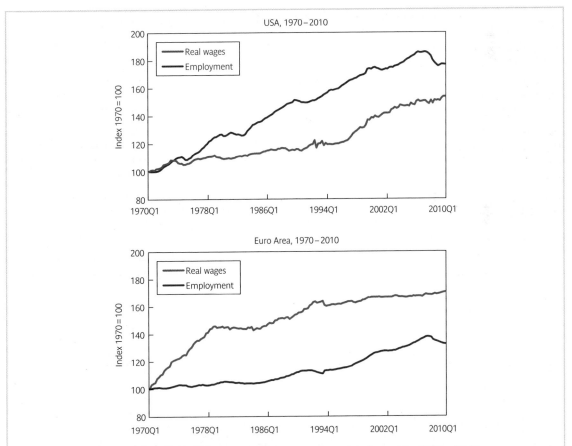

Fig. 5.15 Employment and Real Wages in the Euro Area and the USA, 1970–2010

Over the period 1970–1990, real wages doubled in the euro area, while employment rose by about 10%. During the same period, real wages in the USA increased by only about 50%, while employment rose more than 70%. Real wages are defined as total compensation per employee deflated by the GDP deflator. Since 1990, real wage growth in the euro area has moderated sharply, and growth of employment has increased. The distribution of this growth across Europe is not even, however.

Source: OECD.

Denmark, Sweden, and Norway, where long-term unemployment has remained lower. This implies that what really matters is not the safety net itself, but the disincentives that it can generate. Unemployment benefits, for example, provide an alternative to finding a new job, and help transform temporary unemployment into permanent—structural—unemployment. Long-term unemployment has become increasingly widespread, and as workers gradually lose their human capital and contact with the active labour force, they become unsuitable for any vacancy.

The strikingly different evolution of the equilibrium unemployment rate across countries also points to the importance of wage-setting institutions. The comparison between Europe and the USA in Box 5.5 shows that high unemployment in the EU appears to be related to steep real wage increases, amounting to what has been dubbed the European 'wage shock'. Labour costs consist not only of wages received by workers. In many European countries, labour taxes and contributions to the social security system have also been allowed to rise steeply. Of importance, too, is the regulation of the use of

---

 Box 5.5 **'Eurosclerosis' and 'Euro-Recovery'**

Most European countries—especially France, Germany, and Italy—have experienced chronically high rates of unemployment since the mid-1970s. For many, high and rising unemployment was an accepted fact of life, with average unemployment rising after every economic downturn (see Figure 1.2). Yet it may be surprising that in the 1960s and early 1970s, Europe had lower unemployment rates than in the USA. A number of things happened in the 1970s which were not particularly favourable for countries with an important role for collective wage setting. First, two severe oil price increases—in 1973–1974 and 1979–1980—acted like large negative productivity shocks and shifted labour demand to the left. These 'oil price shocks' were reinforced by a slowdown in investment by firms in response to bad times. Second, a slowdown in the rate of total factor productivity growth shrank the pie over which unions could bargain. Third, the late 1960s and early 1970s were a particularly militant period for European trade unions, with a number of general strikes and labour unrest across the continent and the UK. 'Hard-line' unions pushed real wages higher and increased their downward rigidity. The term 'Eurosclerosis' was coined by German economist Herbert Giersch of the Kiel Institute of World Economics to characterize this period of gloom and doom. Facing this rising tide of unemployment, many leaders simply accepted unemployment as inevitable and as beyond the influence of policy.

Figure 5.15 compares the experience of the euro area (calculated back to include the time before the euro was actually introduced) with that of the USA. Evidently, the USA and Europe had different experiences. European wages shot up in the early part of the period, and employment growth was sluggish. In contrast, the USA showed wage moderation in the 1970s and 1980s, which created the conditions for more job creation. It is tempting to conclude that US labour markets are closer to the market-clearing and took their medicine when it was time to do so. Because the US population and labour supply has increased faster, a direct comparison is not quite fair. Yet the experience of a number of EU countries since the 1990s—Spain, Ireland, Denmark, and the Netherlands for example—teaches us that it is possible to have high rates of employment growth and lower unemployment rates.

What brought about the partial recovery in the EU? After many years, reforms have begun to bear fruit. In many smaller countries, such as the Netherlands, cooperative solutions brought unions and employers together to agree on wage moderation in return for other concessions. It is believed that the introduction of the euro has increased the elasticity of the demand for labour and forced collective bargaining—especially in smaller open economies—to avoid wage policies which price workers out of international markets. The lesson is that Euro-pessimism is unfounded. Unemployment can be brought down, but it takes time, and political will.

labour (length of the work-week, dismissal proce-dures, part-time work, etc.). We return to these issues in Chapter 18.

5.5.3 Actual and Equilibrium Unemployment

It can take many years before real wages adjust to their long-run values in Figures 5.7 and 5.12. In the meantime, actual unemployment can deviate from equilibrium unemployment. Actual employment is below, and actual unemployment above, equilibrium when the real wage is above the equilibrium level, as at point A_1 in Figure 5.16. When the real wage is low, firms may be able temporarily to move away from the union-set collective labour supply curve towards the individual labour supply curve (point A_2), for exam-ple by using agencies specializing in temporary jobs or overtime work. Workers may have overestimated the real wage by underestimating the rise in the price level. Firms may be willing to hire more work-ers at the going wage. In such situations, employ-ment is above, and unemployment below, the equi-librium level. These deviations, while short-term in nature, tend to be associated with fluctuations of the economy that we know as the business cycle. We revisit this important topic in Chapter 12.

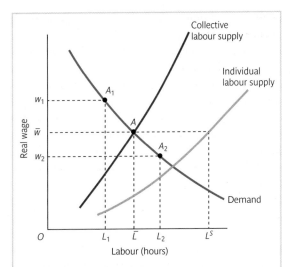

Fig. 5.16 Actual and Equilibrium Employment

When unions negotiate on behalf of workers, market equilibrium occurs at point A, and equilibrium unemployment is $L^S - \bar{L}$. Actual employment and unemployment may differ if the real wage is slow to move to its equilibrium level $\bar{w}$. If it is above the market equilibrium level $(w_1 > \bar{w})$, firms reduce employment to L_1 and actual unemployment exceeds equilibrium unemployment. Conversely, below-equilibrium real wages $(w_2 < \bar{w})$ enable firms to connect with structurally unemployed workers willing to work at lower wages than the collectively bargained level. The resulting unemployment rate is lower than the equilibrium level.

🛈 Summary

1 Households trade off leisure against consump-tion. An increase in wages can induce more labour supply if the substitution effect domi-nates, i.e. labour supply is relatively elastic. It will supply less labour if the income effect dominates. When the two effects offset each other, labour supply is inelastic and does not change.

2 Individual labour supply seems to be inelastic in the short run. But in the long run it is more likely to be backward-bending, as the higher incomes afforded by higher real wages allow households

to enjoy both more leisure and more consump-tion. Aggregate labour supply is more responsive to real wage changes than that of households in the short run, as real wage increases draw new individuals into the labour force.

3 The demand for labour by firms depends on its (marginal) productivity, which is determined by the available technology and the capital stock. Firms hire labour to the point where the marginal productivity of labour is equal to the real wage. The labour demand schedule is shifted outwards

by an improvement in technology or an increase in the capital stock.

4 Equilibrium employment and the wage level are given by the intersection of labour demand and labour supply. Improvements in technology or increases in capital will be reflected in higher wages if labour supply is inelastic, and in higher employment if labour supply is elastic.

5 Involuntary unemployment arises when real wages do not decline to clear the market so that not all labour supplied by households is hired.

6 Labour unions care about real wages and employment. In determining their target wage, given the demand for labour by firms, they ask for higher real wages than if the labour market were perfectly competitive. While the resulting unemployment rate is (optimal and) voluntary for unions, it may be involuntary for individuals.

7 Because firms cannot easily monitor work effort or wish to elicit lower turnover or improve worker quality, they may pay efficiency wages. This is yet another reason why real wages may be set above market-clearing levels.

8 Labour markets are also characterized by widespread government interventions. Minimum wages, designed to protect workers, can actually cause unemployment. Despite this, governments may see minimum wages as an effective means of guaranteeing a socially acceptable minimum income for those who find work.

9 The labour market is characterized by large flows between states of employment, unemployment,

and being out of the labour force. These flows are an important dimension of labour markets and determine equilibrium unemployment.

10 The efficiency of job search can vary across individuals and countries, and is affected by government labour market policies. Unemployment benefits, designed to make unemployment more bearable, provide disincentives to finding a new job quickly, thereby increasing equilibrium unemployment. Other programmes, such as training and relocation subsidies, can reduce equilibrium unemployment.

11 Because there are labour market institutions as well as natural market imperfections, unemployment is never zero or entirely voluntary, even under the best of conditions. Frictional unemployment is the result.

12 Equilibrium unemployment is the sum of frictional and structural unemployment. Structural unemployment is due to fundamental problems related to the demand and supply of labour. Individuals may be willing to work at lower wages than those prevailing in equilibrium, but may not be able to underbid in the market. This is the sense in which real wages are downwardly rigid.

13 Real wages are slow to adjust to disequilibria, if only because they fulfil many other roles. This speed of adjustment will depend on labour market institutions, among other things. As a result, actual and equilibrium unemployment may differ for some time.

🔑 Key Concepts

- endowment
- leisure
- unemployment
- consumption – leisure trade-off
- indifference curves
- utility
- marginal rate of substitution
- real (consumption) wage
- relative price
- substitution effect
- income effect
- household labour supply curve
- labour force, labour force participation rate
- person-hours

◆ marginal productivity of labour

◆ labour demand curve

◆ elastic, inelastic

◆ voluntary unemployment

◆ involuntary unemployment

◆ real wage rigidity

◆ labour market institutions

◆ labour (or trade) unions

◆ employers' associations

◆ collective labour supply curve

◆ insiders and outsiders

◆ minimum wages

◆ efficiency wages

◆ frictional unemployment

◆ separations, separation rate

◆ finding rate

◆ unemployment benefits

◆ equilibrium unemployment rate

◆ structural unemployment

❓ Exercises

1 Suppose that the household in Figure 5.2 receives an inheritance. Show the effect on its decision to work and to consume. According to this result, do rich people work more or less than poor people? Explain your answer.

2 Suppose Robinson Crusoe is paid a higher wage ('overtime pay') if he works more than 8 hours a day, but only has 16 hours at his disposal.

(a) Draw his budget line in this case.

(b) Does the existence of overtime necessarily make him better off?

(c) Show Crusoe's optimal behaviour for 'normal' indifference curves.

Under which conditions will he choose to work overtime? Under which conditions will he refuse?

3 Suppose Crusoe must pay for his work tools (coconut husks?) and must spend an hour a day to climb the trees to get to the coconuts. Think of these as fixed costs which must be paid as long as he is working at all in the labour market.

(a) Draw his budget constraint in this case.

(b) Show Crusoe's optimal choice for the case that he goes to work, grumbling about the fixed costs, but voluntarily. What do you conclude about his utility level compared with staying at home?

(c) Now sketch the case in which Crusoe decides to stay at home. What can you say about his utility

level and preferences in this case? Show that if the wage rises enough, Crusoe can be enticed to leave his tree house.

(d) Now apply this to a modern-day worker who faces commuting cost as well as a monetary/resource cost of working, regardless of how high the wage is or how many hours are worked. Show both cases—the worker who works and the worker who stays at home. How could an 'in-work' grant to those who work any positive amount of time entice the worker to accept a job? Could it fail?

4 It is frequently claimed that Europe's unemployment problem is due to high labour taxes in the form of employer and employee contributions to social security, which are proportional to wages for some range. Assume that individuals care about after-tax wages.

(a) Using the machinery of Figure 5.3, show the effect of a high tax versus low tax environment. What is the effect on labour supply and equilibrium wages? State your assumptions carefully.

(b) What is the effect on equilibrium employment levels resulting from the increased tax for the case of the utility function $U = c^{\alpha} l^{1-\alpha}$ (ignore labour demand).

(c) What changes in your answer to (b) if the tax revenues are rebated to the households as a lump-sum payment, i.e. unrelated to their income tax payments? Given that high labour taxation (social security charges and income taxes) in France, Germany, and Italy coincides with high rates of transfers to households (as opposed to Denmark and Sweden) how could you explain the observed pattern of market labour supply in Table 5.2?

5 Derive the collective labour supply curve graphically. Show how different union preferences can interact with the same shift of labour demand and lead to: (a) rigid wages around some 'target level' with flexible employment; (b) flexible wages around some target level of employment; (c) flexible wages when employment is rising, but rigid when employment is declining.

6 In the 1980s, many European countries tried to tackle the unemployment problem by encouraging early retirement, with arguments that only a fixed amount of jobs are available for job-seekers. Use the supply and demand framework to show how the advocates of such a policy might have argued. Why do you think that most policy-makers have now given up on early retirement as a way of fighting unemployment?

7 It is well-known in Europe that the unemployment rate among well-educated workers is consid-erably lower than for those who left school early or without training. Why might this be the case? How might an 'education offensive' help solve the unemployment problem, even if wages for the low-skilled are rigid?

8 In Japan the bonus system is widespread. Workers often receive 30% of their pay in the form of a profit-contingent payment, which can go up or down depending on the fortunes of the enterprise in which they work. What are the implications of such a system for real wage rigidity and equilibrium employment?

9 It is sometimes claimed that the influx of foreign migrants into the labour force is a cause of unemployment. Show the effect of immigration on the labour market as described by Figure 5.12. What does it mean for real wages and employment?

10 Show the effect of a technological innovation which raises the MPL in a market with an upward-sloping supply curve for labour when: (a) wages are flexible; (b) wages are rigid. Now show the effect of technical change which *reduces* the MPL. Given these differences, evaluate how unions might regard technical change differently, depending on their preferences. Given your answer, assess why unions are frequently in disagreement about the merits of a minimum wage.

⮕ Essay Questions

1 How would you determine whether unemployment is voluntary or involuntary? How do you respond to the criticism that it is virtually impossible to distinguish between the two?

2 Critically evaluate the statement that labour unions should assume responsibility for the administration, financing, and disbursement of unemployment benefits.

3 Severance regulations—government interference with the separation of workers from firms which frequently occurs in modern economies—are universally thought to influence labour markets, but it is hotly disputed whether they increase or decrease unemployment. Discuss. Do you think there are other costs involved in the regulation of redundancies?

4 Discuss both sides of the minimum wage debate. What kind of hard facts might help resolve the argument?

5 From equation (5.4) it follows that all policies which reduce unemployment can be boiled down to two types of measures: reducing the inflow rate s and increasing the outflow rate f. Discuss policies which could affect these two rates. Are they necessarily good for the economy—in the sense of increasing output of the economy or utility of members of society?

Money, Prices, and Exchange Rates in the Long Run 6

It is indeed evident that money is nothing but the representation of labour and commodities, and serves only as a method of rating or estimating them. Where coin is in greater plenty, as a greater quantity of it is required to represent the same quantity of goods, it can have no effect, either good or bad … any more than it would make an alteration on a merchant's books, if, instead of the Arabian method of notation, which requires few characters, he should make use of the Roman, which requires a great many.

David Hume[1]

Money frees you from doing things you dislike. Since I dislike doing nearly everything, money is handy.

Groucho Marx[2]

6.1 Overview

In this chapter we introduce a new actor on the macroeconomic stage: money. Money is a central theme in macroeconomics—in fact, so central that macroeconomics is sometimes even called monetary economics. It may be surprising that we waited until now to introduce this concept! But there is a good reason to do so. The key message from this chapter is the **principle of monetary neutrality**. In the long run, the supply of money does not matter for the real aspects of the economy considered up to now: long-run economic growth, standards of living, employment, and unemployment. Until now, we did not need to bring money into the picture because we were focused on the long run. This chapter therefore represents a critical juncture: it is the last one dealing with the long run and it is the first one dealing with money.

In addition to money, this chapter introduces another innovation that will accompany us for the rest of the book: the open economy, an economy which trades in goods, services, and financial assets. To do this we need to introduce the **exchange rate**, the price of our money in terms of other monies. The exchange rate, appropriately adjusted, can give us insight into the meaning of **external competitiveness**. It will also provide another implication of money

neutrality: in the long run there is not much that monetary policy can do about competitiveness. Short-run changes in the price of one money in terms of another cannot increase our long-term welfare.

We start by presenting the logic behind the neutrality principle. This leads us to derive its central implication—that inflation is a monetary phenomenon. The evidence is compelling. If you wonder why a country undergoes persistently high inflation, you have nowhere else to look but the central bank, which has let money grow too fast in the past. In addition, the overwhelming evidence also shows that high-inflation countries see their currency depreciate at about the same rate.

In order to understand this second result, we will need to define two exchange rates: a nominal and real one. The **nominal exchange rate** is familiar; it is the price of one money in terms of another that is quoted in newspapers and by banks. The **real exchange rate** is a more subtle concept which tries to address the notion of what money can actually buy in the two countries being compared. It involves adjusting the nominal exchange rate for price levels at home and abroad. While the real exchange rate is characterized by both short-run fluctuations and wider medium-

---

[1] David Hume (1711–1776) was arguably Scotland's greatest moral philosopher and economist (although Adam Smith is pretty strong competition). Hume's most noteworthy contribution to economics was his essay *Of Money* (1752), from which this quotation is taken.

[2] Groucho Marx (1890–1977) was a US-American actor and comedian who got many laughs at the expense of the wealthy during the Great Depression. He himself was rumoured to have lost a fortune in the crash of 1929. He also said: 'While money can't buy happiness, it certainly lets you choose your own form of misery.'

term swings, the neutrality of money implies that the real exchange rate is constant in the long run, and independent of monetary factors.

One difficulty with quoted exchange rates in practice is that they always link two monies, very often the home currency and the US dollar. But what about other bilateral exchange rates that relate the home currency to important neighbours and trading partners? In order to tackle this issue, we discuss the construction of effective exchange rates, both nominal and real, which are averages of bilateral nominal and real rates.

In the end, this chapter serves two purposes. First, it presents the fundamental neutrality result and some of its implications. This will serve as a bridge between the long run discussed up to now and the short-run evolution of the economy that is the subject of the next seven chapters. Second, it introduces key variables—money and the exchange rate—which are the bread and butter of macroeconomics.

6.2 Money and the Neutrality Principle

6.2.1 Money

We all think we know what money is, don't we? After all, it is rare to spend a day not having to deal with money in some form or another. Well, it is considerably trickier than it looks and Chapter 9 will provide a detailed definition, or rather several definitions, of money. To make things even more confusing, people tend to use the term 'money' when they mean income (wages, interest, or retirement benefits) or wealth. For economists, money is what you use when you go shopping: cash, your bank accounts, and possibly other forms of purchasing power. It is an asset which is readily accepted in exchange by others.

A related question is where that money comes from in the end. Again, a full explanation will have to wait until Chapter 9. While civilizations have seen money in the form of gold, silver, salt, exotic seashells, cigarettes, or privately minted IOUs of banks or other companies, in modern times money has been ultimately provided by a government or by a government-sanctioned institution. Here it is sufficient to assert that, in the end, the ultimate control of the supply of money is exerted by the monetary authority, the central bank.

A fundamental principle of economics is that money ultimately only affects the price level, leaving the real side of economy untouched. This is what David Hume meant in the epigram to this chapter. Think of money as a numbering system that allows us to express prices of all the goods and services we buy and sell in common terms. The exchange rate can be seen as a way of converting this numbering into a different measurement unit— going from euros to pounds sterling, for example. This suggests that prices and the nominal exchange rate should grow at the same rate as money, in the long run at least. This common-sense idea is called the **neutrality principle**. It is readily illustrated in the left-hand side chart of Figure 6.1, which shows average annual inflation and money growth over about 30 years, a suitably long time period. Later chapters (Chapters 9 and 12) will provide more precision about what we mean by 'the long run'. The chart shows that, indeed, those countries where money has been growing fast have had high inflation rates. Over a period of decades, high monetary growth is no accident or unavoidable fate, but is subject to the control of the central bank. At the same time, the figure also shows that the neutrality principle suffers from many exceptions. We will first look at why the principle makes sense and then at why it is only an approximation to reality.

6.2.2 Money and Prices

Money is held by households and firms to carry out transactions. For this reason, money is often called a medium of exchange. As a first approximation, let us start by assuming that people simply hold cash as a proportion k of their income in each period, measured in money units.[3] In Chapter 9, we will refine

---

[3] One could assume that money is held in proportion to total transactions or nominal spending, but such spending includes purchases by firms of intermediate inputs, which are not counted in GDP. For this we would need much more detailed information on what occurs in the economy on a periodic basis than the information in the national income accounts.

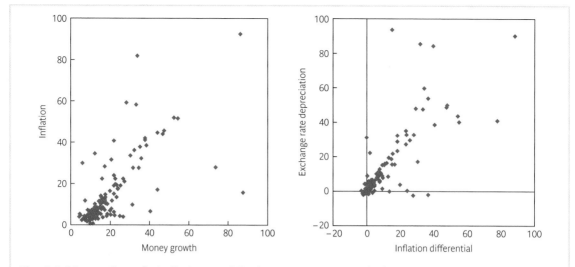

Fig. 6.1 Money Growth, Inflation, and Exchange Rate Depreciation, 1975 – 2006
The left-hand side chart shows the average annual rates of inflation rate and money growth in 155 countries. The average annual depreciation vis-à-vis the US dollar is related to the average annual difference of inflation in the same countries (excluding the USA) and in the USA is displayed in the right-hand side chart. We have excluded the pathological countries where inflation rates have been in excess of 100% per year on average during this period. For most countries, the annual averages are computed over the period 1975 – 2006. For some, the period is shorter, because data are not available for the whole period (this concerns the formerly planned economies until about 1995 and the euro area countries after 1999 since the latter have abandoned their own monies).
Source: International Financial Statistics, IMF.

this analysis. For a country as a whole, total income is measured by GDP. Denoting the real GDP as Y and the price level as P, the nominal GDP is PY, so we now state that the total **demand for money**, denoted M, is simply proportional to the nominal GDP:

(6.1) $$M = kPY.$$

This equation is known as the **Cambridge equation**, and is the simplest and most readily understood formulation of the demand for money.[4] The neutrality principle is easily understood with the fol-

lowing simple thought experiment: Imagine that prices of all goods and services were to double overnight. As a result, a €20 banknote today only buys today what a €10 banknote could buy yesterday. The value of money—the purchasing power of money—has fallen by 50%. In fact, its value is inversely proportional to the price level, which doubled.

Money is the ultimate nominal variable. All nominal variables are measured using the monetary unit: euros, pounds, dollars, roubles, kroners, etc. We will even sometimes use the word 'monetary' as a substitute for 'nominal'. Box 6.1 uses the introduction of the euro in continental European countries as a plausible illustration of monetary neutrality.

Since the purchasing power of money is inversely proportional to the price level, it can be written as the ratio M/P. This is also called real value of money, or real money for short. M/P measures the purchasing power of the money stock M. Dividing both sides

---

[4] This famous relationship is called the Cambridge equation because it was first elaborated formally by Cambridge (UK) economist Arthur Cecil Pigou (1877–1959). A variant is the quantity theory of money, which defines the velocity of money as $V = 1/k$ to obtain $MV = PY$. It is called velocity because it measures how often, on average, one unit of money—say one pound—is used during the year to support spending (indeed $V = PY/M$ relates the total value of all final transactions to the money stock). The quantity theory of money is due to the American economist Irving Fisher (1867–1947).

Box 6.1 Evidence for Monetary Neutrality: The Introduction of the Euro

An excellent example of monetary neutrality was the introduction of the euro, the money currently used by over 330 million Europeans. On 1 January 1999, 11 members of the European Union gave up their national currencies 'irrevocably' and adopted the euro as their new money. On 1 January 2002, euro banknotes became legal tender for transactions in Austria, Belgium, Finland, France, Germany, Ireland, Italy, Luxembourg, the Netherlands, Portugal, and Spain. The adoption of irrevocable exchange rates three years earlier had already rendered these national currencies 'non-decimal units' of the euro. Greece joined in 2001, Slovenia in 2007, Malta and Cyprus in 2008, Slovakia in 2009 and Estonia in 2011. As monetary neutrality would predict, the introduction of the euro and the abandonment of national monies represented nothing but a

mere rescaling of prices, an excellent example of a purely monetary event, with no consequences for the real economy. The short-term impact of the event on the inflation rate has been estimated at 0.2–0.5% and this was a one-off effect, well within the margin of measurement error.

What followed the introduction of the euro is a different story, however. It lies at the heart of the interaction between real and nominal variables. The introduction of a new money means new institutions and agencies— the European Central Bank—as well as new responsibilities for the creation of money. In addition, the introduction of the euro has affected the behaviour of many economic agents in the euro area. This is the exciting subject of the rest of the textbook.

---

of the equation by P, we can rewrite (6.1) in real terms as

(6.2)
$$\frac{M}{P} = kY.$$

This expression relates real money demand to the real GDP Y. This is logical; in the absence of money illusion, real variables ought to be related to real, but not to nominal variables. Now let us go a step further. Money, we noted, is created by the central bank. What happens if the central bank doubles the stock of money overnight and distributes the new banknotes to everyone? People will be happy at first! They will want to buy more goods and services. The question is how producers and sellers will respond. In the short run, they might well supply more goods and services to their customers, a process that we will examine in great detail in Chapters 10 and 11. But this is unlikely to last very long; otherwise, it would mean that growth could be increased simply by printing more and more money! Most would think that this is too good to be true, and indeed it is. Every few years, another country tries the recipe and fails. The unfortunate fact is that, for reasons to be fully spelled out in Chapter 12, faster money growth will ultimately only lead to higher inflation. More pre-

cisely, the neutrality principle asserts that money has no long-run effect on output and, more generally, it has no long-run effect on any real variable.

In the extreme, high inflation tends to lead to higher inflation, which sometimes even leads to **hyperinflation.** A hyperinflation is somewhat arbitrarily defined as a period when the rate of price increase exceeds 50% per month. Hyperinflations occur rarely, but when they do they cause great disruption and social damage, for reasons discussed in more detail in Chapter 16. In the twentieth century, spectacular hyperinflations were observed in Germany (1922–3), Greece (1943–4), Hungary (1945–6), Taiwan (1948–49), Bolivia (1983–4), Yugoslavia (1993–4), and Bosnia-Herzegovina (1994–5). Box 6.2 tells the story of Zimbabwe, which wins the prize for the highest inflation in the twenty-first century.

Let us try to make this reasoning more formal. If the nominal money stock M doubles, the left-hand side of (6.2) also doubles, all other things equal. The monetary neutrality principle says that, in the long run, real GDP is unaffected. This implies that the right-hand side remains unchanged. From a purely logical standpoint, this can only work in equation (6.2) if k or P changes. If k is constant, as we assumed thus far, P must perform the balancing act. Indeed, if

Box 6.2 **Zimbabwe: The Top of the Inflation Heap**

One of the highest inflation rates in modern history and certainly the highest in the last half-century is due to Zimbabwe in southern Africa. By the time the calculation of price indices was halted in August 2008, inflation stood at 231 million per cent. If one counts 22 working day in a month, this means that prices were then rising at a rate of 120% per day. And that was not even the peak! Figure 6.2 presents quarterly measurements of the inflation rate, expressed at an annualized rate of change. The scale is cut off at 800% per year, otherwise we cannot observe anything. In late 2008, banknotes were denominated in the trillions of Zimbabwean dollars, and yet they were nearly worthless! Figure 6.3 shows two banknotes from Zimbabwe, issued in mid-2008.

The root cause of the hyperinflation was the fact that the central bank created money at full throttle, as Figure 6.2 shows. It did so because the government was broke and could not pay for essential services, like the police or the army. The government simply borrowed money from the central bank, the Reserve Bank of Zimbabwe, which gladly accommodated and printed the banknotes. Yet it blamed the underground economy, threatening to 'take stern and unprecedented punitive measures

against the dark forces of parallel market trading and financial disintermediation'. According to the central bank, 'The blossoming cash barons, smugglers and other illicit dealers will threaten the stability of our national payment systems.' In fact, most citizens had stopped using the local currency. As soon as they were paid in Zimbabwean dollars, they converted them into US dollars.

At such high rates of price increase, it becomes difficult even to measure inflation. At some point, President Mugabe forced firms and stores to cut prices by half. Rather than complying, firms sold their goods on the illegal underground market, where prices exploded even further. With shops empty, the Central Statistical Office simply stopped producing the consumer price index. Its chief statistician, who refused to sample prices in the informal markets, candidly explained that 'there are too many data gaps'. Finally, in late 2008, the central bank bowed to reality and allowed trade to be carried out in any currency. The Zimbabwean dollar has effectively disappeared, mostly replaced by the US dollar and the South African rand. In a matter of weeks, inflation stabilized. In mid-2011, it stood at about 3%.

P also doubles, then the real money stock M/P remains constant and nothing has changed. Thus the long-run neutrality principle implies that money and prices must remain proportional to each other in the long run. Formally, the neutrality principle implies that inflation π, the growth rate of the price level, is equal to the growth rate of money:

(6.3)
$$\pi = \frac{\Delta M}{M}$$

inflation = money growth.

We have reached this conclusion by logical means, but there is an important economic story lurking in the background. When we say that the central bank prints more money, we are really talking about an increase in the *supply* of money. When we say that households and firms collectively want to hold cash

in a proportion k of their purchases, we mean the *demand* for money. Then, we can interpret (6.1) or (6.2) as a money market equilibrium condition: demand (on the right-hand side) must equal supply (on the left-hand side). Equilibrium in the money market requires that demand and supply be kept equal. How does money market equilibrium come about? With k constant, M exogenously set by the central bank, and Y unaffected by M as a consequence of the neutrality principle, it is the price level P that brings supply back in line with demand.

This reasoning is represented in Figure 6.4, which depicts the supply of money by the central bank (S) and the demand for money by the private sector (D). Equilibrium occurs at the intersection of the two schedules and determines the price level. An increase in the nominal money supply is met by a proportional increase in the price level.

Fig. 6.2 Annual Inflation in Zimbabwe, 2000–2011

The figure displays the rate of increase of the consumer price index and of the money stock over the previous four quarters. Surprisingly, the price level seems to be growing less rapidly than money since 2006. This is when the government started to impose price controls. Observers report that inflation is much higher than recognized by the official numbers. The figure suggests that the observers are probably right. Since the end of 2008, when the government allowed US dollars and South African rand to be used in trade, inflation has fallen to less than 5%.

Sources: Reserve Bank of Zimbabwe and IMF.

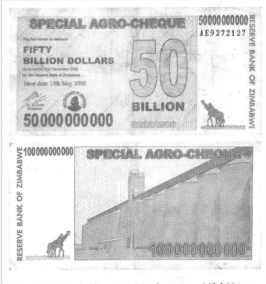

Fig. 6.3 Zimbabwean Banknotes, Mid-Year 2008

6.2.3 Money, Prices, and Output

Let us now be a little more sophisticated. The left-hand side chart in Figure 6.1 provides only limited support for the neutrality principle as stated so far. The various observations tend to line up along the diagonal, but there are many deviations from the general pattern. For example, so far we reasoned as if output is constant but, in the long run, we expect real GDP to grow along the principles developed in Chapter 3. In line with the neutrality principle, money was never mentioned in that chapter. The view that nominal variables do not affect real variables in the long run, also called the **dichotomy principle**, implies that long-run growth is independent of the evolution of money. On the other hand, growth

proceeds at its own path and affects real money demand; this could well explain some of the apparent departures from neutrality in Figure 6.1.

To see why, note that as the economy grows, more transactions will occur, and more money is needed to

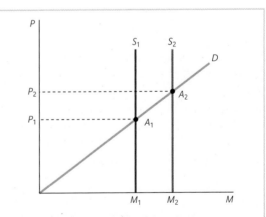

Fig. 6.4 Money Market Equilibrium

Nominal supply, the right-hand side of (6.1), is represented by the vertical schedules S_1 for M_1 and S_2 for M_2. According to the left-hand side of (6.1), demand is proportional to P (for given k and Y), which is represented by the line D. Money market equilibrium occurs at A_1 when the supply is M_1 and at A_2 when the money supply is M_2.

conduct those transactions. Indeed, the logic of (6.1) is that nominal money demand increases proportionately to GDP as long as k remains constant. Nominal money demand also increases proportionately to the price level. Using the arithmetic presented in Box 6.3, we can be even more precise and amend equation (6.3), which was derived by assuming zero output growth—Y was assumed to be constant—to take into account GDP growth. Then we find that the growth rate of money demand is equal to the sum of GDP growth and inflation:

$$(6.4) \quad \frac{\Delta M}{M} = \pi + \frac{\Delta Y}{Y}$$

$$\text{money} = \text{inflation} + \text{GDP}$$
$$\text{growth} \qquad\qquad\qquad \text{growth.}$$

Now, we can reason as before. If the central bank determines the money supply and if GDP growth is driven by other, non-monetary factors, as explained in Chapter 3, this relationship in fact explains inflation. To see this formally, we can rearrange (6.4) to find:

$$(6.5) \quad \pi = \frac{\Delta M}{M} - \frac{\Delta Y}{Y}$$

$$\text{money} = \text{inflation} - \text{GDP}$$
$$\text{growth} \qquad\qquad\qquad \text{growth.}$$

This result can be interpreted as follows. Money demand is driven by GDP growth. Money supply is set by the central bank. If, for instance, the central bank lets the money supply grow faster than GDP, there is too much money around. People, i.e. household and firms, have more money than they wish to hold. Of course, no one throws money away. People spend it. There is now too much money chasing too few goods and services (the GDP) and inflation plays the balancing act. Rising prices reduce the purchasing power of money, i.e. the real value M/P of money, until (6.1)—or (6.2)—is satisfied. Conversely, if money grows more slowly than GDP, inflation is negative. Put differently, the only possibility of reconciling discrepancies between real money demand (M/P) and nominal supply (M) growth is for inflation to be an endogenous

---

Box 6.3 **The Arithmetic of Rates of Change**

In several parts of this book, we use two arithmetic principles concerning rates of changes. If we look at a variable x, we may be interested in its rate of change $\Delta x/x$, where Δx represents the change over a given period (a day, a month, a year, etc.). Rates of change are most often expressed in per cent per annum (per year). For example, if x increases from 10 to 12, $\Delta x = 12 - 10 = 2$, so $\Delta x/x = 2/10 = 0.2$, which is also 20%. The two principles concern the rates of changes of products and ratios. With two variables, say x and y, we can ask what is the rate of change of their product xy. The intriguing answer is that it is the *sum* of the rates of change of the individual variables x and y: $\frac{\Delta(xy)}{xy} = \frac{\Delta x}{x} + \frac{\Delta y}{y}$.

Similarly, the rate of change of a ratio is the difference of the rates of change of the individual variables:[5]

$$\frac{\Delta\left(\frac{X}{Y}\right)}{\frac{X}{Y}} = \frac{\Delta x}{x} - \frac{\Delta y}{y}.$$

As an example, consider the real money stock M/P. Its rate of growth is the difference with the nominal growth rate and inflation, the rate of growth of the price level P:

$$\frac{\Delta(M/P)}{M/P} = \frac{\Delta M}{M} - \frac{\Delta P}{P} = \frac{\Delta M}{M} - \pi$$

If the real money stock M/P is constant, $\Delta(M/P) = 0$ and it must be the case that $\Delta M/M = \pi$.

---

[5] Strictly speaking, these are approximations which are acceptable if the rates of changes are small. Using calculus, this can be shown to be exactly true for infinitesimally small changes:

$$\frac{d}{dt}xy = y\frac{dx}{dt} + x\frac{dy}{dt} = xy\left(\frac{1}{x}\frac{dx}{dt} + y\frac{dx}{dt} + \frac{1}{y}\frac{dy}{dt}\right),$$

so

$$\frac{d(xy)/dt}{xy} = \frac{dx/dt}{x} + \frac{dy/dt}{y}.$$

variable which can help ultimately restore long-run money market equilibrium. Note that (6.3) is a special case of (6.5), corresponding to the situation where GDP is constant.

How does this analysis help explain the left-hand side chart in Figure 6.1? Consider two countries: one grows fast and the other grows more slowly, say not at all. In the second country, in the long run, inflation is equal to the money growth rate, as in (6.3), while it is the excess of money growth over GDP growth that determines inflation in the first country, as in (6.5). Now imagine that money growth rates are equal in both countries. Obviously, inflation will be lower in the first country, by an amount equal to its GDP growth rate. Graphically, it means that the point representing the first country in the left-hand side chart in Figure 6.1 will lie below the point representing the second country. If all countries were growing at the same rate, we would expect to see all the points neatly set along a straight line, parallel to the first diagonal, but below it. If growth rates differ among countries, we expect deviations from this line. These deviations should seem small if the growth rates are not too different. This observation explains much, but not all, of what we see in the chart. To explain more, we need to understand why k is not necessarily constant, which will be shown in Chapters 9 and 16. For the time being, we accept the rule of thumb given by (6.5) and the money neutrality principle.

This rule of thumb is illustrated in Table 6.1, where we assume that real GDP grows in the long run, on

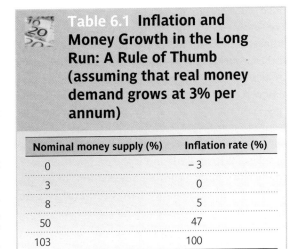

Table 6.1 Inflation and Money Growth in the Long Run: A Rule of Thumb (assuming that real money demand grows at 3% per annum)

Nominal money supply (%)	Inflation rate (%)
0	− 3
3	0
8	5
50	47
103	100

average, at a rate of 3%. This means that the real demand for money also grows by 3% per year. If the central bank allows the nominal money stock to grow at the same 3% per year, demand and supply coincide when the average inflation rate is 0%. Were the nominal money stock to grow at an average annual rate of 8%, inflation would have to be 5%. Only then would the real money stock grow at the same 3% rate as real money demand (8% nominal money growth less 5% inflation). This reflects that, in the long run, inflation is a monetary phenomenon. It occurs when the nominal money supply grows faster than real money demanded by the public.

6.3 Nominal and Real Exchange Rates

The neutrality principle is very general. It applies in particular to the exchange rate, which is an important variable that we have not yet encountered. This section will give a few definitions and then show an implication of money neutrality.

6.3.1 Nominal Exchange Rates

Everyone who ever travelled to a foreign country has encountered nominal exchange rates. These rates are posted in foreign exchange rate booths at airports and border posts and they tell us how much it costs to swap one currency for another. These exchange rates are an annoying aspect of tourism for most of us, yet as the relative price of money, they are an essential part of our lives and it is useful to understand how they work. Nominal exchange rates are set in foreign exchange markets. These markets are studied in detail in Chapter 15, which also explains how markets determine nominal exchange rates.

Exchange rates can be quoted in either of two ways. The first, as the number of foreign currency units per domestic unit, is called **British terms**, e.g. $1.6 per £1 from the perspective of UK residents, or £0.85 per €1 from the point of view of the European Monetary Union. A second way of quoting the foreign exchange rate is sometimes called **European terms** because, before the euro, most European countries used it to quote the US dollar or British pound sterling. It is the inverse of British terms and is the number of domestic currency units needed to buy one unit of foreign currency. For example, we have CHF1.2 per €1 for Switzerland, or DKR7.5 per 1€ for Denmark.

We will adopt the convention of British terms since it is commonly used for quoting the euro and the pound. With this convention, an **appreciation** of a currency conveniently corresponds to an increase in its value in terms of foreign currencies, so the exchange rate rises (e.g. from $1.2 to $1.4 for €1). Conversely, a loss of value, or **depreciation**, implies a decline in the exchange rate.

6.3.2 Real Exchange Rates

Nominal exchange rates compare the relative prices of two different monies. They don't say anything about how much one can buy with each money, that is, real goods and services. The higher is the price level, the less one can buy with, say, one unit of money. However, because domestic prices are measured in the domestic currency and foreign prices in the foreign currency, price levels cannot be directly compared. Before we do any comparison, we must convert prices into the same currency, and this is where the nominal exchange rate comes in.

Consider the following simple example. In Berlin, a haircut costs €20. In New York, you have to pay $36 for the same service. To decide where you will go next time, you must take the exchange rate into account. Assume that it is 1.5 dollars per euro. This tells us that in dollars, the Berlin haircut costs $30, less than in New York. What happens if we compute the price in euros instead? The New York haircut costs ($36)/(1.5$/€) = €24, still more expensive than in Berlin. Obviously, it does not matter which currency we use. The relative price of haircuts in Berlin relative to New York is the ratio of these two prices expressed in the

same currency. It is 0.833, the ratio of €20 to €24 or, equivalently, the ratio of $30 to $36.

Real exchange rates normally compare broad price level indices such as the CPI of the GDP deflator rather than individual goods.[6] Let the price index in the euro area be denoted P, and P^* in the US. The price index represents the cost of a basket of goods; a European basket that is worth €100 in the euro area and another US basket worth $200 (the baskets need not be the same). Denote the nominal exchange as S. In our example, $S = 1.5$, so the dollar value of the European basket is $SP = \$150$. The real exchange rate is the ratio of these two baskets expressed in the same currency. In dollars this works out to be $SP/P^* = 1.5 \times 100/200 = 0.75$. For this comparison, we used the dollar but we could have looked at the euro values of these baskets. The euro value of the dollar basket is $P^*/S = 200/1.5 = 133.33$. The relative price is therefore €100 (P) divided by €133.33 × (P^*/S) which is again 0.75.

Note that in the first example we compared a haircut in both places, and could decide where it is cheapest. Now the real exchange rate is the ratio of two index numbers, or average prices for different baskets of goods in two different places. Thus the value of the real exchange rate does not mean much. The European basket collects goods and services in proportions that represent European tastes and habits. It may be at 100 for a particular reference year. The US basket includes goods and services in different quantities (more baseball equipment, fewer soccer balls) and it may be at 100 in a different year. In the next section, we see that what matters are *movements* in the real exchange rate.

In the end, the real exchange rate is an index defined as

(6.6)
$$\sigma = \frac{SP}{P^*} = \frac{P}{P^*/S}.$$

both prices   both prices
in foreign   in domestic
currency   currency

The real exchange rate can be thought of as the nominal exchange rate 'doubly deflated' by foreign and domestic goods prices. Like their nominal

---

[6] Price indices are presented in Chapter 2.

counterparts, real exchange rates appreciate when σ increases, and depreciate when σ declines.

6.3.3 Movements in Nominal and Real Exchange Rates

We already noted that nominal and real exchange rates move in tandem, as long as inflation is the same at home and abroad, so that P/P^* remains unchanged. Now let us look at the case when the nominal exchange rate S is constant. If inflation at home is higher than it is abroad, domestic prices are rising faster than foreign prices and the ratio P/P^* must be increasing. The real exchange rate σ appreciates. Conversely, a lower inflation at home results in a real depreciation.

The real exchange rate can thus appreciate for two different reasons: (1) when the nominal exchange rate appreciates and inflation rates at home and abroad are equal; and (2) when the nominal exchange rate is stable but inflation is higher at home. More generally, using the arithmetic presented in Box 6.3, we can compute the rate of change of the real exchange rate:

(6.7)

$$\frac{\Delta\sigma}{\sigma} = \frac{\Delta S}{S} + \frac{\Delta P}{P} - \frac{\Delta P^*}{P^*} = \frac{\Delta S}{S} + \pi - \pi^*.$$

rate or change of the real exchange rate = rate of change of the nominal exchange rate + $\underbrace{\text{domestic foreign inflation} - \text{inflation rate rate}}_{\text{inflation differential}}$

This decomposition shows that the real exchange rate σ is driven by two factors: (1) the nominal exchange rate S, and (2) the **inflation differential**, the difference between domestic (π) and foreign (π^*) inflation. The logic is simple. A real appreciation is a loss of competitiveness, as our goods become expensive relative to foreign goods. This happens when the nominal exchange rate appreciates, or when domestic inflation exceeds foreign inflation. In the first case, the foreign price of domestic goods (SP) rises even if the domestic price is unchanged, or the domestic price of foreign goods (P^*/S) declines even if the foreign price is unchanged. In the second case,

even if the nominal exchange rate is unchanged, domestic goods become relatively more expensive since $\pi > \pi^*$ implies that P/P^* increases. These various possibilities are illustrated in Figure 6.5, which presents effective exchange rates—effective rates are explained in the next section—for the Dutch guilder.

6.3.4 Measuring the Real Exchange Rate in Practice

In practice, measuring real exchange rates poses two problems. The first concerns the definition of 'foreign'. 'Foreign' stands for the rest of the world, the various countries with which our country has

Three exchange rates are displayed: (1) the nominal bilateral rate between the Dutch guilder and the US dollar (after the adoption of the euro in 1999, the figure converts the euro exchange rate using the rate at which guilders were then converted into euros); (2) the nominal effective exchange rate; and (3) the real effective exchange rate. All rates are all expressed as indices that equal 100 in the year 2000. From year to year, inflation differentials are relatively small, so the nominal and real effective exchange rates tend to move together. Over the longer run, however, inflation differentials accumulate to sizeable magnitudes and the effective nominal and real exchange rates move differently.

Fig. 6.5 The Dutch Guilder's Nominal and Real Exchange Rates, 1970–2010

Sources: OECD, *Economic Outlook* and International Financial Statistics, IMF.

significant trade and financial relationships. Exchange rates tend to be quoted in terms of the US dollar. This practice reflects both the size of the US economy and the role of the dollar as an international currency. Yet, the USA cannot really stand for the rest of the world. It is convenient because the rest of the world comprises a large number of countries, with which each home country has a bilateral exchange rate. How should one go about aggregating these individual rates? The same question can also be applied to *the* foreign price level P^*: *Which* foreign price level?

The solution to this problem consists of computing an 'average exchange rate' and an 'average foreign price level' using weights that reflect the relative importance of the partner country (ideally, all of them), and 'an average nominal exchange rate' S as a

weighted average of our nominal exchange rate vis-à-vis each of them. The weights assigned to each country are chosen to represent its importance to us, e.g. in trade or in financial flows. Box 6.4 explains how this is done. The corresponding values of S and σ are called nominal and real **effective exchange rates**, respectively. These are indices—we can no longer express the nominal exchange rate in value terms, e.g. dollars per euro—which are normalized to take a simple value, such as 1 or 100, in some base year. Figure 6.5 presents an example.

A second problem arises when deciding which prices to compare. In fact, a real exchange rate is simply the price ratio of two baskets of goods and services, one of which represents domestic goods and services and the other foreign goods and services.

 Box 6.4 Computing and Comparing Effective Exchange Rates[7]

Effective exchange rates are computed using a number of partner-countries. Each partner-country receives a weight typically representing its importance in trade for the country in question. For example, its share of our exports or our imports, or the average of both. Geometric averaging is applied to price indices in these countries and to our bilateral exchange rates vis-à-vis their currencies.[8] If n countries are selected and S_i is the bilateral nominal exchange rate vis-à-vis country i with trade weight w_i, our effective nominal exchange rate is

$$S = (S_1)^{w_1} (S_2)^{w_2} (S_3)^{w_3} \dots (S_n)^{w_n},$$

where the weights are fractions which sum up to 1 ($\Sigma w_i = 1$). The effective foreign price level P^* is computed by applying the same weights to each partner-country's price index P_i:

$$P^* = (P_1)^{w_1} (P_2)^{w_2} (P_3)^{w_3} \dots (P_n)^{w_n}.$$

Then the effective real exchange rate is simply the average of our real exchange rates vis-à-vis each partner-country:

$$\sigma = \left(\frac{S_1 P}{P_1}\right)^{w_1} \left(\frac{S_2 P}{P_2}\right)^{w_2} \left(\frac{S_3 P}{P_3}\right)^{w_3} \dots \left(\frac{S_n P}{P_n}\right)^{w_n} = \frac{SP}{P^*}.$$

The effective real exchange rate is thus a weighted geometric average of the individual bilateral exchange rates which characterize a country's international trade.

This approach can be applied to other price indices besides the consumer price index, for example, traded versus nontraded goods, or domestic versus foreign wages can be used. A frequently used measure of the real exchange rate is the ratio of export to import prices. It differs from the ratio of non-traded to traded good prices in two ways: (1) it suppresses non-traded goods, and (2) it compares the price of traded goods, which are produced domestically and exported, with imported goods produced abroad. In this view, the 'home' goods are exports instead of non-traded, and the 'foreign' goods are imports instead of all traded goods lumped together. The choice between this or that measure really depends on the characteristics of the country at hand and on the question of interest.

---

[7] Nominal and real effective exchange rates are computed and published by various sources. Among them, *International Financial Statistics*, a monthly publication of the International Monetary Fund, presents a variety of real exchange rates (using GDP deflators, export prices, CPIs, labour costs) computed using a sample of 18 advanced economies.

[8] There are two ways commonly used to compute weighted averages. The most common approach is arithmetic averaging, which sums up values of the variables of interest $x_1, x_2, \cdots$, etc., with their respective weights w_1, w_2, etc.: $w_1 x_1 + w_2 x_2 + \cdots$. Geometric averaging uses products: $x_1^{w_1}, x_2^{w_2} \dots$.

Since 'domestic' and 'foreign' are rather vague, many baskets, and many definitions of 'the' real exchange rate, are possible. So far, we have looked at the ratio of consumer price indices, but there are a number of alternatives.

- One frequently used real exchange rate is the ratio of domestically produced exports to foreign-produced import prices. It is called the **external terms of trade** because it indicates how many imports we get in return for our exports.

- Another definition considers the ratio of non-traded to traded goods prices, sometimes called

the **internal terms of trade**. This recognizes that many goods are not traded internationally and measures the price of those goods relative to goods that are.

- Still another possibility is to measure the real exchange rate on the basis of the price of labour, using wages, total earnings, or total labour costs, including employer contributions to social insurance.

In the end, there is no uniformly appropriate measure. Different questions are best answered with different indices.

6.4 The Exchange Rate in the Long Run: Purchasing Power Parity

We now present a second implication of money neutrality, which is displayed in the right-hand side chart in Figure 6.1. For each of the 155 countries, it plots the average annual rate of nominal exchange rate *depreciation* vis-à-vis the US dollar (i.e. $- \Delta S/S$, or the *negative* of the rate of appreciation) against the inflation differential vis-à-vis the US, the difference between the country's inflation rate and the US inflation rate $(\pi - \pi^*)$. The chart suggests that, in the long run, countries which have a high rate of inflation also have currencies which depreciate at the same rate. Conversely, currencies with a low rate of inflation appreciate in the long run. If we treat foreign inflation π^* as a given, the lower the domestic rate of inflation, the higher the rate of appreciation:

(6.8) $$\frac{\Delta S}{S} = \pi^* - \pi.$$

This property is expected to hold in the long run. It carries a pretty striking implication, which can be seen by noting that together (6.7) and (6.8) imply

$$\frac{\Delta \sigma}{\sigma} = \frac{\Delta S}{S} + \pi - \pi^* = 0.$$

In other words, the real exchange rate is constant over the long run. This conclusion should not

surprise those who looked carefully at Figure 6.5. Over 40 years, the effective real exchange rate of the Dutch guilder has fluctuated, but in a narrow margin, and most importantly, the absence of any trend is suggestive of long-term constancy. The conclusion that the real exchange rate is constant in the long run is sometimes presented as the principle of **purchasing power parity (PPP)**.

The logic behind PPP is quite simple. Suppose that monetary policy is permanently more expansionary at home than abroad. We expect inflation eventually to be higher at home. If the nominal exchange rate remains unchanged, the real exchange rate appreciates. This means that domestic goods and services become expensive relative to foreign goods and services. As a result, domestic producers gradually lose competitiveness. This obviously cannot go on forever, and indeed it will not. The nominal exchange rate will depreciate, and this will work towards restoring competitiveness. If it depreciates by the full amount of the accumulated inflation differential, the loss in competitiveness is entirely erased. Thus PPP can be seen as simply asserting that, in the long run, a country must retain its competitiveness.

There are two versions of PPP. The version presented here is called **relative PPP**. It is a natural implication of monetary neutrality. Because they are nominal variables, the nominal exchange rate and the price level are not expected to affect real variables in the long run, including the real exchange rate. This is a manifestation of the dichotomy principle.

An alternative version of purchasing power parity, **absolute PPP**, is a much stronger proposition. It starts with the **Law of One Price**. Not really a law, this hypothesis holds that the same good should trade everywhere at the same price, when prices are expressed in the same currency. If prices were to differ significantly, it is asserted, traders would buy the goods where they are cheapest, sell them where they fetch a higher price and make a profit. Demand would rise where the prices are low, supply would rise where prices are high. **Arbitrage**, as this process is called, should continue until profit opportunities have disappeared. This means that prices have been equalized throughout the world.

Absolute PPP is a much stronger hypothesis than relative PPP. Relative PPP requires that the real exchange rate σ be constant, while PPP wants it to be equal to unity. Indeed, according to the Law of One Price, $P^* = SP$, which implies $\sigma = SP/P^* = 1$. In practice, the Law of One Price is known to be grossly violated, not just across countries but within the same country, using the same currency! In contrast, relative PPP is a pretty good rule of thumb and is supported by empirical evidence, as Figure 6.1 shows.

This discussion highlights the difference between the long run, which has been the subject of the last four chapters, and the short run, which lies before us. While it is a good guess that a continuously depreciating currency reflects persistently high inflation, Figure 6.5 indicates that relative PPP is not entirely robust, certainly not from quarter to quarter. Rather, a closer look suggests that nominal and real effective exchange rates tend to move together. Especially when inflation is low, it does not move one-to-one with the rate of depreciation. Over many years, however, inflation differentials will add up to sizeable magnitudes and the effective nominal and real exchange rates will move differently. This is what happened until the late 1990s. The nominal exchange rate appreciates sharply while the real rate remains trendless. From equation (6.7), we can deduce that inflation in the Netherlands was lower than abroad. In fact, the negative inflation differential and the nominal exchange appreciation offset each other. Since the late 1990s, inflation differentials have vanished and the nominal and effective rates move closely together.

Notice that the dollar bilateral rate is much more volatile than the effective rate. This is normal since the latter is a weighted average of many bilateral rates, one of which, not the most important, is the US dollar. Yet, dollar exchange rates receive considerable attention, which may give an exaggerated impression of volatility.

The nexus between nominal and real exchange rates is one of the most important in macroeconomics, especially for small open economies. There are interesting cases to come, in which the nominal exchange rate is not solely driven by inflation differentials. In the short run, sharp movements of the nominal exchange rate imply sharp movements of the real exchange rate, with implications for the real economy. This represents an important transmission mechanism from nominal to real variables and will be the subject of extensive discussion in Chapter 11. Finally real exchange rates themselves can change, depending on the fundamental real economy. Chapter 15 will explain the conditions under which real exchange rates are constant in the long run.

❗ Summary

1 Money is necessary because we need it to carry out day-to-day transactions. We demand money because we receive income and because we spend it.

2 The Cambridge equation asserts that the demand for money is a constant fraction of nominal GDP, a measure of total income.

3 The monetary neutrality principle asserts that money does not affect real variables. This is a manifestation of the dichotomy principle. The principle is understood to hold in the long run. It implies that, in the long run, prices, nominal exchange rates, and all nominal variables change at the same rate as money is growing.

4 The nominal exchange rate defines the price of a currency in terms of another one.

5 Real exchange rates measure the price of domestic goods in terms of foreign goods.

6 Effective nominal and real exchange rates are weighted averages of a country's exchange rates vis-à-vis the rest of the world—in practice, its main trading partners.

7 Relative purchasing power parity is obtained when the equilibrium real exchange rate is constant. In that case, the rate of change of the nominal exchange rate is equal to the inflation differential, the difference between foreign and domestic inflation. The inflation differential is a fundamental determinant of the long-run evolution of the nominal exchange rate.

8 Absolute purchasing power parity states that the equilibrium real exchange rate is not just constant but equal to unity. The Law of One Price asserts that prices for the same good are the same in different countries. If that were true, absolute purchasing power parity would tend to be verified. The evidence tends to reject absolute purchasing power parity for most countries.

9 While the evidence supports relative purchasing power parity in the long run, there are significant deviations from this proposition in the short run. This suggests that movements in the exchange rate are not immediately offset by exchange rate changes, and that nominal and real variables interact with each other in the short run.

🔑 Key Concepts

- **principle of monetary neutrality**
- **exchange rate**
- **nominal and real exchange rate**
- **external competitiveness**
- **Cambridge equation**
- **hyperinflation**
- **demand for money**
- **dichotomy**

- **British/European terms**
- **appreciation/depreciation**
- **inflation differential**
- **effective exchange rates**
- **external, internal terms of trade**
- **absolute and relative purchasing power parity (PPP)**
- **Law of One Price**
- **arbitrage**

❓ Exercises

1 Table 6.1 implies a relationship between money growth and the inflation rate when the GDP trend growth rate is 3% per annum. Represent graphically this relationship. Show graphically how this relationship would change if the GDP trend growth rate would be 8% instead. What conclusions can you draw?

2 What happens to the real exchange rate between two countries if the price level at home doubles, all other things given? What if the price of foreign goods doubles? What if the nominal exchange rate doubles?

3 The following figure displays the evolution of the nominal and real effective exchange rates of Portugal since 1970. What can you conclude about the rate of inflation in this country?

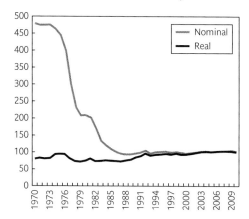

4 Money is neutral in the long run, but is it neutral in the short run? Looking at the Cambridge equation (6.2), how could money increase without the price level increasing proportionately?

5 Consider an economy where the stock of money is growing by 5% per year while GDP expands by 2.5% annually. Assume that inflation abroad is 3.5%. What will be the rate of change of the exchange rate in the long run?

6 Use equations (6.5)—written for both the home and foreign countries—and (6.8) to find an expression that describes the long-run evolution of the nominal exchange rates as driven by the domestic and foreign money and GDP growth rates. Denote domestic and foreign money supply as M and M^*, respectively, and domestic and foreign GDP as Y and Y^*.

→ Essay Questions

1 Most governments regard a depreciation as a sign of weakness. Does it make sense to resist a depreciation when inflation is high?

2 'Money neutrality simply says that there is no way to cheat with money.' Comment.

3 A strong currency is a currency that tends to appreciate. In what sense is this a desirable objective?

4 The Law of One Price does not hold. Can you imagine reasons why?

5 Box 6.2 tells the story of Zimbabwe. It also notes that hyperinflations often occur after a war. In your view, why do governments allow hyperinflation to occur?

PART III

The Macroeconomy in the Short Run

With its emphasis on long-run and sustainable trends, Part II sets a natural stage for the study of what happens in the meantime: in the short run. In Part III, the object of interest is not the development over the next decade, but rather over the next few months or quarters. To do this, we study the short-run behaviour of aggregate demand—the sum of spending decisions by households, firms, and governments. We start by laying out the budget constraints of those economic agents and then examine what shapes their spending decisions.

In the long run, the real and nominal sides of the economy can be studied separately; in the short run, they are tightly intertwined. This interaction gives rise to the phenomenon of business cycles, the succession of periods of rapid economic growth and recession. The central role of interest rates and the financial system leads us to look at money, how it is created, what role it plays in a modern, open economy, and how central banks conduct monetary policy.

Next, we take the most important step: the integration of all these different decisions in a way that ensures their consistency. This type of economic reasoning, which is called general equilibrium, analyses the simultaneous determination of output, employment, the interest rate, and finally the price level and the rate of inflation. The concept of macroeconomic equilibrium is first developed for the case of a country that only trades goods and services with the rest of the world, with capital flows playing a passive role. The next step is to examine how financial openness changes the situation. Next, we turn to inflation, the rate of growth in the general level of prices. After the origins of inflation are explored in Chapter 12, Chapter 13 presents the aggregate demand – aggregate supply (*AD – AS*) framework as a powerful tool for explaining the behaviour of both output and inflation over short-run horizons. Finally, looking at asset markets and the exchange rate rounds out the understanding of the short run. Asset markets are places where financial and real claims are traded. Financial markets, and the market for foreign exchange in particular, look forward to the future when determining the prices at which assets are traded. The exchange rate turns out to be a special and important example of an asset price, one that ultimately connects the short and long run.

Borrowing, Lending, and Budget Constraints

7

Many people despise wealth, but few know how to give it away.

Francois de La Rochefoucauld

What's the quickest way to become a millionaire? Borrow fivers off everyone you meet.

Richard Branson

7.1 Overview

Borrowing and lending is a fundamental act of economic life. Each of the main economic players identified in the circular flow diagram of Chapter 2—households and firms of the private sector, the government, and the rest of the world—have their own reasons to borrow and lend. In doing so, they shift income and spending between the present and the future. Borrowing brings future income forward to be spent today. Lending or, more generally, saving, defers the use of current income to some later date.

Borrowing and lending decisions are motivated by expectations about the future. Those who reasonably expect their incomes to grow will want to borrow and raise their standards of living now instead of waiting. In contrast, the lucky winner of a lottery will probably save a large fraction of the prize, because it is unlikely to occur again. Firms' investment decisions, which means adding capacity for future production, are a gamble on future demand. Not the present, not the past, but expectations of the future exert the greatest influence on firms' investment decisions.

The shifting of spending over time can be seen as an intertemporal trade. One could think of a lender as a seller of money today, and the borrower as a buyer. Like any trading activity, there must be both a price linking the present and the future and each actor must face a budget constraint. Indeed, because people are impatient, time has a price. This price is determined by the interest rate. An **intertemporal budget constraint** requires that liabilities be repaid someday, while accumulated assets will eventually be spent.

The intertemporal budget constraint provides a powerful framework for understanding many fundamental aspects of macroeconomics. Because the future is unbounded, it can be rather overwhelming to think about it. This chapter adopts two simplifications. First, we reduce the course of time to just two periods, called today and tomorrow, the present and the indefinite future. Second, we will continue to employ Robinson Crusoe, already introduced in Chapter 5, as a parable for consumer, producer, and his own government, all at once. These steps will make abstract and complex considerations a bit easier to handle.

7.2 Thinking About the Future

7.2.1 The Future Has a Price

Anything of value must have a price. This includes money and goods delivered at future dates. In fact, markets exist for the sole purpose of pricing future deliveries of commodities. These are the stock markets like Euronext or New York Mercantile Exchange (NYMEX), exchange markets or specialized commodity

markets. Such markets exist in many countries, both developed and emerging. Their common feature is to place a value on future 'things' like company shares, loan repayments, steel deliveries or foreign currencies. They price the future.

Microeconomic principles can be readily used to understand how the future is priced. There is a parallel between *intertemporal* consumption choices (between present and future goods) and *intratemporal* consumption choices (among goods at a particular point in time). When we choose between consuming now or in the future, we effectively decide whether to save or to borrow. As rational households plan spending over time, they take into account their future incomes and needs, and balance these against the interest rate at which they can borrow or save. Similarly, firms need to forecast the profitability of plant and equipment in which they invest. They need a benchmark for that profitability—what could they or their owners have otherwise done with their money? They compare the profit, or return, from those projects with that available from lending their money at some available interest rate, which represents either the cost of funds or, if funds are available, the best alternative use for them.

7.2.2 The Rational Expectations Hypothesis

Expectations about the future are crucial to all this. But how exactly do firms and households form their expectations? Do they get it right or wrong? In this book, we will generally take the modern view that economic agents' forecasts are right *on average*. This is the **rational expectations hypothesis**.

The rational expectations hypothesis does not mean that households and firms never make mistakes, or that they always forecast the future perfectly. It is simply a way to apply the rationality principle to the way economic agents think about the future—we assume that they do not make *systematic* errors. Clearly, alternative assumptions about expectations are possible. In fact, laboratory experiments on human subjects show that we all get sidetracked, sometimes, often responding to emotions rather than to cold calculation. These experiments also show that we have limited ability to process mentally all the information that we have, or should have. So why do we adopt the rational expectations hypothesis? For three reasons:

◆ First, because there are so many ways of being irrational that there is no simple alternative.[1]

◆ Second, standard economic theory is based on the hypothesis that agents 'optimize' in the sense that they behave rationally—that they take the best possible decisions in a logically consistent way. If agents are rational in planning their consumption, work, and production, then they should be rational when thinking about the future.

◆ Third, even if most people are not fully rational all the time, it is unlikely that they are repeatedly and systematically wrong. If they are, they must suffer continuous losses. Isn't it natural to expect them to take steps to avoid such errors in the future?

There is an even better and subtler justification for rational expectations. We are ultimately interested in how prices, interest rates, incomes, and spending interact on the market place. It is often enough that a few well-informed agents behave rationally to drive the markets. If trade unions act on behalf of their members, it suffices that their expectations will be correct on average. In financial markets, all that is required is that a number of professional traders are well informed and have sufficient resources at their disposal. If they perceive that prices are too low compared with their valuation, they will buy, forcing prices upwards. If prices are too high, they will sell. Less well-informed customers end up accepting the market prices because they know that it could be dangerous to disregard them.[2]

As a short cut, this book will frequently use a simplified version of rational expectations known as perfect foresight. Perfect foresight simply assumes that people know everything that will happen in the future. The difference with rational expectations is that we ignore uncertainty. Perfect foresight can be thought of as an exploration of what the world would be like if the future was in fact perfectly known. Of course, no one thinks that this is realistic but, as with rational expectations, if surprises are sometimes good and sometimes bad, perfect foresight is a reasonable starting point.

---

[1] Some alternatives to rational expectations are presented formally in the WebAppendix to this chapter.

[2] This point highlights an important tension between rationality of individual behaviour and aggregate outcome. We will see in Chapter 14 that financial markets can be susceptible to problems when too many people blindly believe the signal thought to be contained in prices.

7.2.3 The Parable of Robinson Crusoe

This chapter sets up the intertemporal budget constraint facing households, firms, the government, and the nation as a whole. We return to Robinson Crusoe as our representative household, already familiar to us from Chapter 5. As we deal with the infinite future,

it is convenient to collapse time into two periods, 'today' and 'tomorrow', where tomorrow is a metaphor for the future. And beyond tomorrow? Crusoe is rescued and will no longer need to concern himself with the economics of his island!

7.3 The Household's Intertemporal Budget Constraint

7.3.1 Consumption and Intertemporal Trade

Let's start by imagining that Crusoe's island does not even have coconut trees. Rather, the coconuts simply wash up on the beach. The number of coconuts that he (rationally) expects to have today and tomorrow is his exogenous **endowment**. This endowment includes both present and future resources. Using subscripts to denote the relevant period in which they become available, we can represent his endowment of Y_1 coconuts today and Y_2 coconuts tomorrow by point A in Figure 7.1.

Until Robinson learns how to plant coconuts, he has no choice but to consume what nature gives him. Since coconuts cannot be carried over to the next period, Crusoe's consumption is also given by point A. This is the **autarky** point. A household or a country operates in autarky when it does not trade and consumes its endowment.

If we bend the story a little and allow for neighbouring islands inhabited by other economic agents, trade is possible. Because Crusoe's coconuts are just as good as his neighbours', we might not expect to observe any trade between them. Yet Crusoe may well be interested in **intertemporal trade**, or exchanging resources across time. He might lend his neighbours some coconuts today, if he expects to find only a few tomorrow, or if he prefers to consume more tomorrow. On the contrary, if today's 'harvest' is abnormally low or if Crusoe is impatient, he could borrow coconuts now and repay later when times are better.

The rest of the chapter will explore borrowing and lending, and the role of financial markets. As a way of moving away from autarky, borrowing and lending is just like selling or buying goods and services. Yet banking and financial markets suffer from reputation problems, and the recent financial and credit crisis hasn't made matters better. Box 7.1 explores these reservations and possible reasons for them.

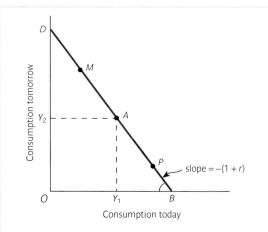

Fig. 7.1 Endowment, Wealth, and Consumption

Resources available today and tomorrow—the endowment—determine wealth and available consumption choices along the budget line BD. In the figure, the same level of wealth (OB) is attainable by a professional athlete (point P) or a university student (point M).

Box 7.1 Neither a Borrower nor a Lender Be: The Economics and the Sociology of Credit

In a well-known scene from Shakespeare's *Hamlet*, Polonius gives his son Laertes some parting advice: 'Neither a borrower, nor a lender be: For loan oft loses both itself and friend, and borrowing dulls the edge of husbandry.' In other famous plays, such as *The Merchant of Venice*, Shakespeare gives lenders a pretty tough time. Is it morally wrong to borrow (or to lend)? And what is wrong with charging interest, if borrower and lender freely agree to it? Although the economic arguments against autarky are convincing, many important religions of the world—including Islam, Christianity, and Judaism—have banned lending at a positive interest rate at one time or another in their histories. Why the ambivalence?

Perhaps it is because lenders have an unconditional claim on the resources of individual borrowers in an inherently risky world. If the fortunes of a borrower go south, those of the lender do not—that is, unless the borrower declares bankruptcy. Perhaps it is because borrowers appear to be in a poor bargaining position, often seeking credit when all else has failed. Perhaps it is because individuals are frustrated when their bank won't give them the loan they think they deserve, because the credit officer deems them 'too risky', which they feel is insulting. And the market has ways of dealing with individual risks which are distasteful to many. One is charging higher interest rates, which appears

opportunistic since the 'risky' poor people pay more than the 'safe' rich. Stories abound in the USA and the UK of indebted families with credit card debt paying interest rates of 30% and more. Then there is loan-sharking, illegal and possibly violent enforcement mechanisms, and 'payday loans', which amount to selling one's own wage packet in advance at effective annual interest rates sometimes in excess of 600%.

And yet, borrowing and lending is as natural as breathing. Even when lending at interest is prohibited as in many Islamic countries, the market finds ways around the ban, for example declaring loans to be 'equity stakes' which participate in profits and losses of the enterprise. The American economist Irving Fisher wrote in 1930 that:

Prohibiting loan contracts cannot prevent interest taking. To forbid the particular form of sale called a loan contract would leave possible other forms of sale, and the mere act of valuation of every property right involves an implicit rate of interest. ... Indeed, as long as buying and selling of any kind were permitted, the virtual effect of lending and borrowing would be retained. (Fisher 1930: 116.)

In the end, the fundamental truth is that the market for loans exists because there are gains from trade: different degrees of patience, different wants, different opportunities, and different information.

7.3.2 The Real Interest Rate

Crusoe and his neighbours must agree on the terms of repayment: how much should he pay (or receive) tomorrow for one coconut borrowed (lent) today? These terms are the **real interest rate**, which we denote by r and will treat as given or exogenous; 'real' because Crusoe and his neighbours do not use money. Borrowing 100 coconuts will require paying back $100(1 + r)$ tomorrow—the principal of 100 plus interest payments of $100r$. If the real interest rate is 3%, or 0.03, interest payments will be 3 coconuts. Another, equivalent way of thinking of this transaction is that Crusoe agrees to sell $100(1 + r)$ coconuts tomorrow for the price of 100 today. Similarly, if Crusoe takes the other role and lends 100 coconuts today, he will receive $100(1 + r)$ coconuts tomorrow;

to buy $100(1 + r)$ coconuts tomorrow he must save 100 coconuts today. The relevant intertemporal trade involves swapping $1/(1 + r)$ coconuts today for each coconut tomorrow. We can say that a coconut tomorrow is worth $1/(1 + r)$ coconuts today.[3]

The price of tomorrow's consumption in terms of today's, $1/(1 + r)$, is called an **intertemporal price**. As the real interest rate r is positive, $1/(1 + r)$ is less than 1, which means that goods tomorrow are cheaper—or less valuable—than goods today. The real interest rate measures the cost of waiting. Valuing future goods in terms of goods today (here, dividing by the interest

[3] As a simplifying assumption, we have assumed that the interest rate is the same, whether one is borrowing or lending. The world is more complicated, but the logic is unchanged, when we consider different rates of interest for borrowers and lenders. Section 7.5 provides more details.

Box 7.2 Discounting and Bond Prices

Discounting is used in economics and finance to value future incomes or expenditures in terms of income today. It is frequently used to put a value on financial assets and debts. It asks: What is the amount of money required today, given an interest rate, to generate some payment or payments in the future? By valuing a coconut tomorrow only as worth $1/(1 + r)$ coconuts today, Robinson Crusoe has successfully applied discounting to a practical problem.

Let us apply discounting to a financial problem, and consider a simple bond that pays €100 in one year's time. (This type of bond is called a *pure discount* bond.) If the interest rate given by the market is 5%, what is the value of this bond today? It is the amount that, if invested now, yields €100 next year. If that amount is B, then it must be true that $B(1 + 0.05) = 100$, so $B = 1/(1.05) = $ €97.24. Similarly, the value of a two-year discount bond is given by $B = 100/(1 + 0.05)^2 = $ €90.70. The further into the future the payout is, the more heavily any amount is discounted, and the lower the discount bond price is.

Conversely, given discount rate r, the present value of a stream of payments a_t over n years, $t = 1, ..., n$ has present value given by

$$\frac{a_1}{1+r} + \frac{a_2}{(1+r)^2} + \frac{a_3}{(1+r)^3} + ... + \frac{a_n}{(1+r)^n}$$

Now consider the case of a consol, a bond that promises to pay a fixed amount a forever. Is it possible to put a price on that income stream, even though the payments are infinite? As long as the interest rate is strictly positive, the answer is yes! The price of a consol C which pays a each period is simply the present discounted value of its payments:

$$C = \frac{a}{1+r} + \frac{a}{(1+r)^2} + \frac{a}{(1+r)^3} + ... + \frac{a}{(1+r)^n} + ...$$

$$= \frac{a}{1+r}\left[1 + \frac{1}{(1+r)} + \frac{1}{(1+r)^2} + ...\right]$$

$$= \frac{a}{1+r}\left[\frac{1}{1 - \frac{1}{1+r}}\right] = \frac{a}{r},$$

where we have applied the formula for a sum of a geometric series to the term in brackets. The price of a consol is inversely related to the interest rate. Other bonds have a finite maturity so the formula is more complicated, but the general principle survives that higher real interest rates imply lower bond prices.

factor, 1 plus the real interest rate) is called **discounting**. Discounting is a very important concept in macroeconomics which is worth studying carefully. It helps explain the inverse relationship between bond prices and interest rates, as well as the fact that surprising changes in market interest rates often move stock prices in the opposite direction. It explains why borrowers—including governments—love to postpone repayment of loans, and why lenders resist such attempts with vigour. Box 7.2 presents the important concept of discounting more generally.

Intertemporal trade allows Crusoe to choose combinations of consumption today and tomorrow which are different from his autarky point. These combinations are represented by the line BD in Figure 7.1. This line must go through his endowment point A, since he can always choose not to trade at all.

At point B Crusoe would forgo consumption tomorrow completely. In that case he would borrow fully against his future endowment Y_2, receive $Y_2/(1 + r)$ coconuts, and consume $Y_1 + Y_2/(1 + r)$ coconuts today. At point D he would fast today and lend all his current endowment Y_1 in order to consume $Y_1(1 + r) + Y_2$ coconuts tomorrow. The line BD represents all the possibilities open to Crusoe, in between the extremes just described. It is called the **budget line.** The budget line is the simplest representation of the intertemporal budget constraint. Its slope[4] is given by $-(1 + r)$. If the rate of interest increases, the budget line becomes steeper. For a given amount of saving today, more will be available tomorrow.

[4] The slope of the budget constraint is negative and is given by −1 times the ratio OD/OB. From the text we know that $OD/OB = [Y_1(1 + r) + Y_2]/[Y_1 + Y_2/(1 + r)] = 1 + r$.

7.3.3 Wealth and Present Discounted Values

If Crusoe's income 'from nature' in the first period is Y_1 and he consumes C_1 in the same period, his saving is $Y_1 - C_1$. If $Y_1 - C_1$ is positive, Crusoe is lending; if $Y_1 - C_1$ is negative, he is borrowing. In the second period, his maximal consumption C_2 will equal the sum of income Y_2 and $(1 + r)(Y_1 - C_1)$, i.e. the interest and principal on his savings from period 1. If saving was negative in the first period, this means paying back principal plus interest. The budget line can be represented formally as:

(7.1) $\qquad C_2 = Y_2 + (Y_1 - C_1)(1 + r).$

This fully describes Crusoe's intertemporal budget constraint. Dividing both sides by $(1 + r)$ and rearranging,

(7.2) $\quad \underset{\substack{\text{present} \\ \text{value of} \\ \text{consumption}}}{C_1 + \dfrac{C_2}{1+r}} \; = \; \underset{\substack{\text{present} \\ \text{value of} \\ \text{income}}}{Y_1 + \dfrac{Y_2}{1+r}} \; = \; \underset{\substack{\text{wealth} \\ \text{derived from} \\ \text{income}}}{\Omega}$

The left-hand side is the **present discounted value** of consumption. It is the sum of today's and tomorrow's consumption valued in terms of goods today. The right-hand side is equal to the present discounted value of income (his endowment). It is the maximum consumption that Crusoe could enjoy today, given his resources today and tomorrow, and is represented by point B in Figure 7.1. Put differently, OB is the present discounted value of Crusoe's total endowment. In fact, it represents his wealth, which we denote by the symbol Ω.

Lending and borrowing enable individuals with the same total wealth but with very different income profiles to enjoy the same menu of possible consumption over both periods. It doesn't matter whether Crusoe is a university student with low current and high future income, as represented by point M in Figure 7.1, or a professional athlete with high current and low future income (point P). As long as these points are on the same budget constraint, the present discounted value of income is the same and intertemporal trade allows income to be shifted across time by borrowing and lending.

Now suppose Crusoe had initial tradable wealth B_1 (an initial cache of coconuts). His wealth will increase by this amount and the budget constraint will be modified as follows:[5]

(7.3) $\quad \underset{\substack{\text{present} \\ \text{value of} \\ \text{consumption}}}{C_1 + \dfrac{C_2}{1 + r}} \; = \; \underset{\text{total wealth}}{Y_1 + \dfrac{Y_2}{1 + r} + B_1.}$

If $B_1 > 0$, Crusoe can consume more in both periods. But B_1 could be negative, if Crusoe began his existence with debt. In that case, he will have to consume less (in present value terms) in order to repay the debt and interest. In general, total wealth Ω is the sum of inherited wealth or debt B_1 and of the present value of income: $\Omega = Y_1 + \dfrac{Y_2}{1 + r} + B_1$. This is shown in Figure 7.2, where the inherited wealth or debt is added to the present value of income. At a given real interest rate, it implies shifting the budget line BD to $B'D'$ (if wealth increases) or $B''D''$ (if it decreases).

7.4 The Firm and the Private Sector's Intertemporal Budget Constraint

7.4.1 Firms and the Investment Decision

Crusoe's income has been exogenous until now. In reality, income mostly comes from planned activities. As we saw in Chapter 3, production requires that resources are diverted from consumption and used to acquire productive capital. Crusoe could plant coconuts today

which would grow into trees bearing coconuts tomorrow. Naturally, once planted, a coconut cannot be consumed: it is useful only for its future production. The use of valuable resources to produce more goods later

---

[5] This is obtained by noting that today's available resources are $Y_1 + B_1$ so that (5.2) is changed to $C_2 = Y_2 + (B_1 + Y_1 - C_1)(1 + r)$.

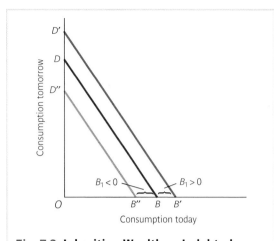

Fig. 7.2 Inheriting Wealth or Indebtedness

When wealth $B_1 > 0$ is inherited, the budget line shifts from BD to $B'D'$. Debt $B_1 < 0$ shifts the budget line to $B''D''$. The lines are parallel because the real interest rate is assumed unchanged.

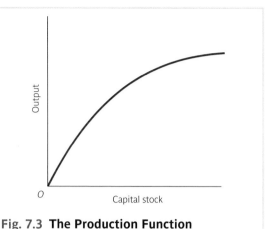

Fig. 7.3 The Production Function

As more input is added, output increases, but at a decreasing rate. This is the principle of declining marginal productivity.

is called **investment** or **fixed capital formation**. Many goods produced in modern economies are designed solely to make future production possible, and have no consumption value at all.

The notion of investment was already explored in Chapters 3 and 4 in the discussion of long-term economic growth. The investment decision also has a fundamentally intertemporal aspect. Firms decide to accumulate capital when it is sensible, i.e. profitable to do so, and profitability depends on expected future outcomes. In order to finance their investments, firms can either obtain resources in the capital market (stock exchanges, bond markets, or banks) or use their own funds (retained earnings). The discussion of this and the next chapter deviates from the growth model in Chapters 3 and 4. In those chapters, capital was accumulated as the result of available savings, which was assumed to be an exogenous fraction of national income. In what follows, investment and savings will be described as conscious choices of firms and households.

7.4.2 The Production Function

The investment decision depends upon the amount of output that can be produced with the available equipment (the number of coconuts to be obtained

from a tree). The **production function** $F(K)$ captures this relationship between capital input and output and is depicted in Figure 7.3. It can be thought of as a special case of the production function of Chapter 3, in which labour input is exogenous.[6] The shape of the curve implies that, as more capital is accumulated, the additional or marginal yield declines. That marginal output decreases when input increases is the same principle of **diminishing marginal productivity** that we encountered in Chapters 3 and 5.[7]

7.4.3 The Cost of Investment

Starting with no capital stock (assuming no coconut trees on the island at the outset), today's investment represents the total stock of capital available for production tomorrow. (Box 7.3 considers the more realistic case when previously accumulated capital already exists.) Crusoe understands that he can either invest K in productive equipment, or lend K in the capital market. In the first case, he will receive output $F(K)$ tomorrow. In the second case, he will receive $(1 + r)K$ tomorrow. The real interest rate measures

---

[6] In Chapter 3, labour supply was also treated as exogenous. If we set $L = 1$, and $Y = F(K, L)$, as in Chapter 3, then $Y = F(K, 1)$.

[7] The reason behind this principle is that, given the existing amount of labour used to man the equipment (here, Crusoe's time), adding new equipment is less and less effective in raising output.

Box 7.3 Gross Investment, Depreciation, and the Capital Stock

When previously accumulated capital already exists in the amount K_1, the situation in the next period is more complicated. The stock of capital may differ in the future from the previously accumulated stock in two ways. First, new capital I_1 may be invested. Second, depreciation—wear, tear, and obsolescence—may remove some of the value of the old capital stock. It is a proportion δ of the capital stock. The new capital stock is:

$$K_2 = K_1 + I_1 - \delta K_1$$

new capital stock = old capital + gross investment − depreciation

The realized change in the capital stock, $\Delta K = K_2 - K_1$, is therefore equal to $I_1 - \delta K_1$, the difference between gross investment and depreciation of previously accumulated capital. For the capital stock to grow, new investment spending must exceed depreciation.

the **opportunity cost** of the resources used in investment. Because of the option of lending at rate r, the investment in this case must yield at least $1 + r$ to be worth undertaking.[8]

Figure 7.4 shows the opportunity cost of invested capital K as the ray OR from the origin, which is given by $(1 + r)K$. As long as the resulting output exceeds the cost, the technology is sufficiently productive and investment is worthwhile. At point A, investment just covers its cost. There is no economic profit possible. To

the right of A, investment uses up more resources than it produces. Positive economic profits occur only to the left of A.

The interest rate r is obviously crucial for the valuation of investments. For example, if the rate of interest were to increase, the OR line would rotate upwards to the left, moving point A to the left and the reducing the volume of investment that has any positive value at all. Capital must be more productive—and therefore lower—to make up for higher borrowing costs.

Another approach, that will prove useful later, is to ask what is the net return V from investing K—what Crusoe gets from planting K coconuts as an irrecoverable expense. The net return is simply the difference between the present value of output tomorrow and investment today:[9]

(7.4)
$$V = \frac{F(K)}{1 + r} - K.$$

Note again that to compare goods available tomorrow with goods available today, we must price the former in terms of the latter, i.e. we discount the former by applying the intertemporal price $1/(1 + r)$.

An investment project is economically justifiable only if it has a positive present value. In terms of (7.4), that means $V > 0$ or if $F(K) > K(1 + r)$. Figure 7.5 illustrates a case when the technology is not productive enough given the real interest rate. In that case it

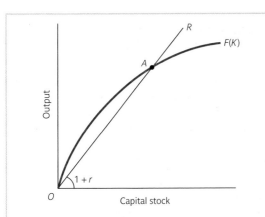

Fig. 7.4 Productive Technology

The cost of borrowing to finance investment is given by OR. As long as output exceeds the cost of borrowing, the technology is productive and the producer makes profit. Beyond A, she makes losses.

[8] Alternatively, Crusoe could borrow coconuts for investment purposes. The interest rate then is literally the cost of this debt-funded investment. This is discussed in the WebAppendix.

[9] By assumption the trees are assumed not to have resale value; they die after the second period. If they didn't, one would need to add back the resale value of the depreciated trees in the second period, which would increase the value of the investment activity. This modification is described in detail in Chapter 8.

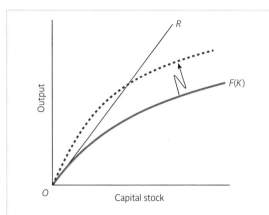

Fig. 7.5 Unproductive Technology

Given the interest rate, no firm will operate with the production function shown in the figure. A technological innovation which shifts the production function upwards can make an unproductive technology productive again.

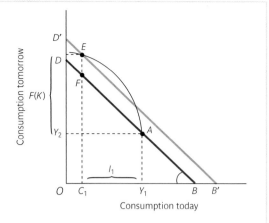

Fig. 7.6 Investment Increases Wealth

Investing I_1 (which becomes K_2) in a productive technology allows a household to increase its wealth over and above that corresponding to the initial endowment A. Here wealth increases by BB' as FE additional goods become available in the second period.

does not pay to invest anything at all: it is more profitable simply to lend at the rate r. It would require either an improvement in technology (the production function schedule shifts upwards as in Figure 7.5) or a decline in the interest rate (the ray OR rotates downwards) for some investment to be worthwhile.

7.4.4 The Intertemporal Budget Constraint of the Consolidated Private Sector

The budget constraint of Section 7.3 took endowments as given by nature as on Crusoe's island. Once investment and production are taken into account, income tomorrow is no longer simply given by nature. The budget constraint now depends on the amount that is invested and on its profitability. As long as the investment project has positive present value, investment increases wealth. Figure 7.6 shows how this happens. Starting from point A, Crusoe can save either by lending, or by investing an amount I_1 up to a maximum of his endowment Y_1. In the later case, Crusoe's saving are equal to investment, which is equal to the capital stock for tomorrow's output production (remember: the island is barren upon his arrival, so initial capital $K_1 = 0$). This is the difference between today's endowment Y_1 and consumption C_1:

(7.5)
$$K_2 = I_1 = Y_1 - C_1.$$

The more he invests—the more we move to the left in Figure 7.6—the larger will be tomorrow's production. This is why the production function AE is now the mirror image of the one shown in Figure 7.4: as consumption declines and saving rises, we move leftwards from the endowment point A, investment increases and tomorrow's output becomes larger. Tomorrow's income—and consumption as it is the last period—is the sum of the endowment Y_2 (the coconuts lying on the beach) and produced output $F(K_2)$:

(7.6)
$$C_2 = Y_2 + F(K_2).$$

The intertemporal budget constraint determines the present value of consumption $C_1 + C_2/(1 + r)$ as equal to total wealth Ω. Recognizing that $C_1 = Y_1 - I_1$ is given by (7.5) and C_2 given by (7.6), the intertemporal budget constraint can be rewritten as:

(7.7)
$$\underbrace{C_1 + \frac{C_2}{1+r}}_{\substack{\text{present} \\ \text{value of} \\ \text{consumption}}} = \underbrace{\Omega}_{\substack{\text{total} \\ \text{wealth}}} = \underbrace{\left[Y_1 + \frac{Y_2}{1+r} \right]}_{\substack{\text{wealth} \\ \text{from} \\ \text{income}}} + \underbrace{V.}_{\substack{\text{value} \\ \text{of the} \\ \text{firm}}}$$

Wealth now consists of two parts.[10] The first part is the present discounted value of the endowment as before in (7.2). The second part is the increase in wealth represented by V, the net value of the investment activity, as in (7.4). In Figure 7.6 the outcome of investment I_1 is shown as point E. Note that E lies above the initial budget line. This is because the production technology is productive at the rate of interest r. The distance OB still represents the present value of the endowment. But now, for a choice of investment I_1 that brings Crusoe to point E, new total wealth is the distance OB'. Since the value of future output is discounted at the same rate r, the new budget line is parallel to BD. The distance BB'

represents the net present value of the investment project.[11]

In the parable, Crusoe stands for the private sector as a whole, which consists of individuals and the firms they own. Firms ultimately belong to their shareholders, and the net return from investment raises their wealth. If shareholders anticipate that a firm will become more profitable in the future—because of a technological advance, as represented by the shift in Figure 7.5—then net expected returns rise and they are richer. This wealth gain takes the form of an increase in the value of the firm. In the real world, this would be reflected as an increase in the firm's value in the stock market.[12]

7.5 Public and Private Budget Constraints

7.5.1 The Public Budget Constraint

There was no government on Robinson Crusoe's island. In the real world, there is a public sector, which collects taxes, purchases goods and services, and makes transfers to households. Yet the government is little different from other economic agents. It can borrow, but is expected to repay its debt with interest; if it lends it will expect to be repaid by its debtors. Consider a government, which spends G_1 today and G_2 tomorrow, and raises net taxes T_1 and T_2.[13] The government has debt outstanding at the beginning of the period in the amount D_1. This debt must be serviced (interest must be paid) at interest rate rG, and must be repaid in the last period.

The government spends $(G_1 + r_G D_1)$ and has net tax revenue (T_1) today. It is running a deficit if spending

exceeds revenue, that is if $G_1 + r_G D_1 - T_1 > 0$. Like anyone who spends more than they earn, the government must borrow to finance that deficit. Total borrowing requirement can be broken down into two parts: (1) the **primary deficit** $(G_1 - T_1)$, the amount by which non-interest expenditures exceed revenues, and (2) interest payments $(r_G D_1)$. While a solvent government cannot avoid making interest payments which are due, the primary deficit can be chosen by changing either spending or net taxes.

In the second and last period, the government must repay its obligations in full. This means that tomorrow's primary surplus $(T_2 - G_2)$ must be sufficient to repay today's deficit $(G_1 - T_1)$ plus interest on

---

[10] To see this, write wealth as the present discounted value of net income and rearrange using $V = \dfrac{F(K_2)}{1+r} - I_1$, which yields

$$\Omega = \left[Y_1 + \frac{Y_2}{1+r} \right] + \left[\frac{F(K_2)}{1+r} - I_1 \right] = \left[Y_1 + \frac{Y_2}{1+r} \right] + V.$$

[11] A subtle, but important point: This valuation of the firm is independent of whether Crusoe finances the investment himself out of savings (or 'retained earnings' in the language of business) or whether he *borrows* funds to finance it (and discounts the project returns using the same interest rate). In this benchmark case it doesn't matter. This result is known as the Modigliani-Miller Theorem, and is discussed in the WebAppendix to this chapter.

[12] Because the production function lies above the new budget line $B'D'$, total wealth could be increased by investing a little bit less than I_1. Chapter 8 shows that, when Crusoe strives to do the best he can— behaves optimally—he will invest to push out his new budget line as far as possible, i.e. he maximizes the value of his total wealth.

[13] Note that G represents government purchases of goods and services. It is not the same as total government spending or outlays, which include transfer payments. In our notation, transfer payments are deducted from taxes to give net taxes T. Although interest payments are treated like transfers in the national income and product accounts, they are such a central component of the intertemporal budget constraint that we will always distinguish them from other transfers throughout this book.

that deficit $r_G(G_1 - T_1)$, but also the inherited debt from the past D_1, *plus* interest $r_G D_1$:

(7.8) $T_2 - G_2 = (1 + r_G)(G_1 - T_1) + D_1 + r_G D_1$

$= (1 + r_G)(D_1 + G_1 - T_1).$

This is the government budget constraint, which can be rearranged as

(7.9) $D_1 = (T_1 - G_1) + \dfrac{T_2 - G_2}{1 + r_G}$

$= \left[T_1 + \dfrac{T_2}{1 + r_G} \right] - \left[G_1 + \dfrac{G_2}{1 + r_G} \right]$

public debt = present value
of primary budget surpluses.

For the government to obey its intertemporal budget constraint, the sum of the present value of primary budget surpluses is equal to initial outstanding debt. This also means that the present value of government income must be sufficient to cover the present value of purchases plus the initial debt. The government budget constraint is illustrated in Figure 7.7 for the case of no initial debt or assets ($D_1 = 0$). The budget line has slope $-(1 + r_G)$ and passes through the origin.

The two-period parable contains a strong message: Governments with debt and deficits *today* must run primary surpluses *tomorrow*; similarly, governments with a comfortable fiscal position today can let go (a little) in the future. Yet do governments really obey their budget constraints? The European debt

crisis—Box 7.4 discusses its genesis—has given many reason to doubt it. In fact, some governments throughout history been faced with budget problems, sometimes resulting in spectacular defaults, or repudiation of past debts. Yet an error commonly made by politicians and the general public is to look only at the current year's deficit as a measure of the government's solvency. Especially when the economy is growing robustly, tax revenues can be expected to grow over time as well, thus easing some of the burden.[14] For that reason, it is always a good idea to measure expenditures and tax revenues relative to GDP. Still, in order to avoid defaults, today's primary deficits require primary surpluses later, and conversely. Given spending plans, lower taxes today are followed by higher taxes tomorrow. Alternatively, for a given path of taxes, more spending today requires spending cuts tomorrow. How long does 'today' last before a government is hit 'tomorrow' by the budget constraint?

Figure 7.8 shows that governments do generally obey their budget constraints. It shows the evolution of primary budget balances for four countries over time, relative to the size of the economy measured by the GDP. Some countries (the UK) show a succession of primary deficits and surpluses. In other cases (Ireland, Italy, the USA) deficits have been sustained over many years, yet eventually the primary budgets were corrected, sometimes moving into spectacular surpluses. The financial crisis of 2007–8 has led to sudden relapses in Ireland, the UK and the US. The case of Ireland is unusual (note that the scale is not the same for all four countries). In 2010, the government had to scramble to save its collapsing banks. With a deficit of some 30% of GDP, the Irish government itself went into crisis and had to be bailed out by the other Eurozone countries with assistance from the International Monetary Fund. Italy, on the other hand, managed to keep its budget roughly balanced. Yet it went into crisis when markets took a dim view of several decades of large deficit and smaller surpluses that left a legacy of a public debt of some 110% of GDP. These examples show how sudden unexpected spending needs or long strings of

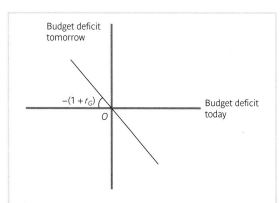

Fig. 7.7   The Government Budget Line

A deficit today must be matched by a budget surplus tomorrow, or vice versa, if the government is to obey its intertemporal budget constraint.

[14] The implications of economic growth for government budget constraints and stabilization policy will be explored in detail in Chapter 17.

Box 7.4 The European Debt Crisis

Many people were surprised by the sudden market panic on the Greek government debt which arose in the spring of 2010 and seemed to spread to other Eurozone countries. At the time of this book's writing (January 2012), several euro area countries are under severe budgetary stress, meaning that economic analysts doubt that they will be economically or politically able meet their budget constraints. This judgment reflects and is also driven by 'current market conditions'—meaning those high current interest rates that the market demands for fresh lending.

History is littered with government defaults, frequently accompanied by sharp political upheavals: the turbulent years of the French Revolution, the October 1917 revolution in Russia, the end of the Weimar Republic in 1933, Castro's revolution in Cuba.[15] In most cases, however, defaults are just the end of a long period of debt accumulation, reflecting a long string of budget deficits which don't seem to reflect any budget constraint at all. This was true of much of Latin America in the 1980s, Russia in 1998, Argentina in 2001, and Iceland in 2008. It could be coming closer to home, to the euro area.

The history of government finance shows that default is a subjective concept.[16] Technically, it occurs when the borrower country has failed to service its debt, meaning that it has missed a payment due—even by a day! Yet financial markets, which finance most of the deficits, can be enormously patient or excessively optimistic. It is always possible to arrange a short-term 'bridge' loan, even on short notice, for a few years time, if there is a high chance that the loan will be repaid. In the end, it is not really possible to know with certainty whether a government is meeting its budget constraint at any point in time. In reality, the intertemporal borrowing constraint features public spending and tax revenue streams that extend into the infinite future. If there are lenders out there with strong nerves and enough patience, current deficits associated with a temporary decline in tax revenues in a recession can be overlooked. This is why the current situation—which will be examined in more detail throughout the rest of the book—is so disturbing. The financial markets, right or wrong, seemed to have lost hope in 2010.

insufficient surpluses can stretch the intertemporal budget constraint to its limits.

7.5.2 The Consolidated Public and Private Budget Constraint

Both households and firms—which are owned by households—ultimately have to pay the taxes. They cannot ignore the public sector budget constraint. Much as they must include the budget constraints of the forms that they own, households must also see through the public sector financing veil. In this section we follow this logic and integrate the private and public budget constraints to face intriguing and important consequences.

For simplicity, we ignore the existence of firms and set initial government debt to zero. The private and

public intertemporal constraints are, side-by-side as follows:

$$(7.10) \qquad C_1 + \frac{C_2}{1+r} = Y_1 - T_1 + \frac{Y_2 - T_2}{1+r},$$

$$(7.11) \qquad G_1 + \frac{G_2}{1+r_G} = T_1 + \frac{T_2}{1+r_G}.$$

In the first budget constraint, the private citizens pay the taxes, while in the second, the government receives them. Note that we do not assume that the government and the private sector face the same interest rates when they engage in borrowing or lending activities. Traditionally, the private sector is considered as less safe than the public sector but the crisis may be changing this presumption. The government sector borrows and lends at rate r_G, while

---

[15] The public debt should be distinguished from the external debt, although in some instances the public debt is held by foreigners and represents the bulk of the external debt. This chapter assumes that the public debt is held by domestic residents.

[16] We will have much more to say about this in Chapter 17, which looks more carefully at government deficits, debt, and the role of the central bank.

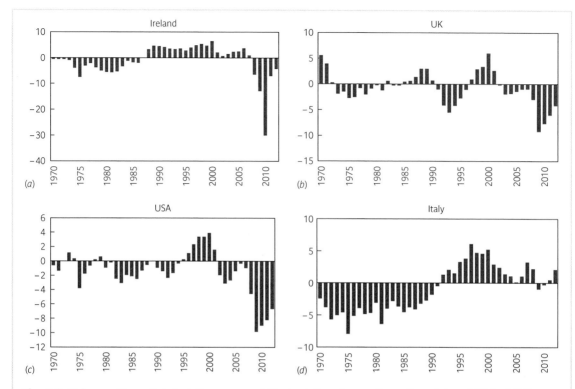

Fig. 7.8 Primary Consolidated Government Budget Surpluses, Four Countries, 1974–2009

Over time, primary budget balances must add up, in present-value terms, to initial public debt. Some governments, like the UK, have maintained primary budget balances on average over many years. Those that have allowed deficits to cumulate into large indebtedness will eventually have to run surpluses, as has been the case in Ireland, Italy, and the USA.
Source: OECD, National Accounts.

the private sector borrows and lends at rate r. Combining the private and public budget constraints yields the consolidated budget constraint[17]

(7.12)

$$C_1 + \frac{C_2}{1+r} = \underbrace{(Y_1 - G_1) + \frac{Y_2 - G_2}{1+r}}_{} + \underbrace{\left[\frac{r - r_G}{1+r}\right](G_1 - T_1)}_{}$$

present
value of   =   present value of   +   present value of
consumption   private resources   the government's
                    net of government   financing
                    spending   advantage.

[17] To derive this result, multiply both sides of (7.11) by $(1 + r_G)/$ $(1 + r)$, and rewrite as

$$G_1 + \frac{G_2}{1+r} + \frac{r_G - r}{1+r}G_1 = T_1 + \frac{T_2}{1+r} + \frac{r_G - r}{1+r}T_1.$$

or

$$T_1 + \frac{T_2}{1+r} = G_1 \frac{G_2}{1+r} + \frac{r_G - r}{1+r}(G_1 - T_1).$$

Substitution of this last expression into (7.10) yields (7.12).

A comparison of the consolidated budget constraint (7.12) with the private constraint (7.10) shows that both link private consumption to private income— remember that to simplify, we ignored inherited debts or assets. Before consolidation, private income is the present value of net of taxes incomes over both periods. After consolidation, (7.12) private income includes two parts. First, the present value of incomes net of public spending, not taxes. This means that households can only consume the output that the government has not taken for itself. As long as the government respects its budget constraint, its spending will be paid for by taxes, now or in the future, and it does not seem to matter when!

Yet it does matter. The second part of private income reflects the difference between the interest rates at which the government and the private sector can borrow. If, as is normally the case, the government can borrow more cheaply than the private sector, $r > r_G$, this part is positive: the more the government borrows, the better off the private sector is. In order to understand this surprising result, consider the case when the government reduces taxes today and raises them tomorrow to meet its budget constraint. This means that it will have to borrow today at rate r_G and pay back tomorrow. The private sector will pay less taxes today but more tomorrow; it makes sense for the private sector to save the correspond amount, at interest rate r. The private sector benefits from this operation because it earns r on its saving and will have to pay more taxes to cover the public borrowing at the lower interest rate r_G. In effect, the government borrows on behalf of the private sector, allowing the private sector to save at a higher rate than it borrows indirectly. Of course, it is also true that if the government borrows on *worse* terms than its citizens, it can *reduce* net wealth of its citizens. Furthermore, is r greater than or less than r_G?

7.5.3 The Ricardian Equivalence Proposition

The story gets even more interesting. Suppose for the moment, that the interest rates of the private sector and the government are exactly equal, so $r = r_G$. In that case, the consolidated budget constraint (7.12) collapses to

(7.13) $$C_1 + \frac{C_2}{1+r} = (Y_1 - G_1) + \frac{Y_2 - G_2}{1+r}.$$

This looks very much like the private sector budget constraint (7.10), except that now it does not matter at all when taxes are levied. Once the government has 'helped itself' to G_1 and G_2 of output, the private sector will take the rest whenever it wishes in the form of C_1 and C_2, borrowing or lending as needed. In fact, the private sector has fully internalized the public sector's budget constraint. The hypothesis that the private sector fully internalizes the public sector's budget constraint is known as the **Ricardian equivalence proposition**.[18] In Figure 7.9, point A represents Crusoe's endowment measured before taxes. Once

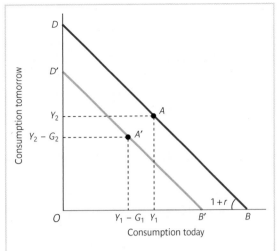

Fig. 7.9 Ricardian Equivalence
The government's spending and taxing activities reduce private wealth. Given government purchases, the precise scheduling of taxes does not matter.

public spending is taken into account as in (7.12), the private endowment is represented by point A'. The government reduces Crusoe's private wealth by an amount represented by the distance BB', which is either the present value of taxes or the present value of public spending—the two are equal because of the government budget constraint. As long as the public and private sectors borrow and lend at the same rate ($r = r_G$), these intertemporal shifts are equivalent and the public borrowing can be matched one for one by private saving along the same private budget line.

The Ricardian equivalence proposition can be stated in a number of different ways. The first is that total national spending—the sum of private and public spending on goods and services—cannot exceed the country's wealth. The country can borrow or lend abroad, but it must respect its (national) budget constraint.[19] The second is that private sector wealth—which can be spent on private consumption—is the difference between the present value of production or income on the one hand and public purchases of goods and services on the other. The implication is that the pattern of taxation over time

---

[18] Named after English economist David Ricardo (1772–1823), who first formulated this idea, only to dismiss it as unlikely. The idea has been revived and championed by Harvard economist Robert Barro.

[19] This can be readily shown by rewriting (7.13) as

$$(C_1 + G_1) + \frac{C_2 + G_2}{1+r} = Y_1 + \frac{Y_2}{1+r}.$$

has no effect on private wealth. What matters in the end is public spending, which represents resources taken away from the private sector. Finally, Ricardian equivalence means that its citizens do not treat government debt as net wealth. Government's indebtedness does not appear as part of private wealth on the right-hand side of (7.13). The private sector sees through the veil of government. It recognizes that the government's promises to pay the principal and interest on public debt are matched by taxes levied to service the debt, today or tomorrow. Public bonds are an asset to households, which is exactly offset by the present value of their future tax liabilities.

7.5.4 When Ricardian Equivalence Fails

For obvious reasons, the Ricardian equivalence result is highly controversial. It means that the path of taxes is irrelevant for the behaviour of the private sector. It implies that public borrowing and the resulting stock of government debt do not, on net, contribute to the wealth position of households. Holding constant the path of government purchases of goods and services, budget deficits do not matter! This controversial Ricardian equivalence result requires a number of assumptions, and this section reviews them critically. In the end, the result of this discussion is that budget deficits probably do matter, and that at least some fraction of public debt is regarded by the private sector as wealth.[20]

Different interest rates

A central assumption behind the Ricardian equivalence result is that the government and the private sector face the same interest rate. Is that realistic? It has long been taken for granted that, in any country, governments borrow at the lowest interest rate. The reasoning is that the government is considered a less risky borrower than most private businesses or individuals because governments can always tax to pay back their debts while private agents may find themselves unable to reimburse some loans. In the developed countries, the difference between the rates at which a government borrows and those that apply to firms in good standing has traditionally been of

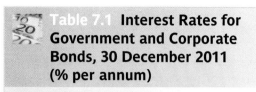

Table 7.1 **Interest Rates for Government and Corporate Bonds, 30 December 2011 (% per annum)**

	10-year government bond	10-year corporate bonds	
		A-rated	BBB-rated
United Kingdom	1.96	6.13	n.a.
United States	1.89	4.38	4.78
Euro area	4.11	5.04	7.03

Source: Macrobond.

some 1–2% more for businesses, and much more for households. Table 7.1 shows that this still holds for the UK, US, and the Eurozone as a whole, but it is definitely not the case for individual countries.

This was a nearly universal observation before the crisis hit the Eurozone. Figure 7.10 shows that when

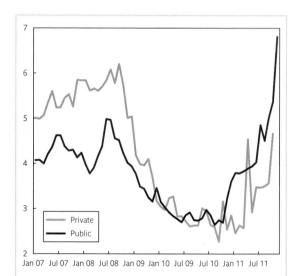

Fig. 7.10 Public and Private Borrowing Rates in Italy, 2007 – 2011

The rates refer to loans of 1- to 5-year maturity for the private sector and of 5-year maturity for the government. The reversal of the traditional hierarchy in 2010 was a potent signal that Italy was entering into a public debt crisis situation.

Source: ECB and Banca d'Italia.

---

[20] Other potential failures of the Ricardian equivalence proposition are related to the behaviour of agents under uncertainty, and go beyond the scope of this book.

the crisis started to unfold in 2009, the Italian government borrowing privilege has gradually eroded. By late 2010, Italian firms with solid credit ratings were paying interest rates on debt that were considerably lower than those demanded of the government. While government and private interest rates are taken as given for the purposes of the analysis, they are in fact endogeonous and depend on a number of factors. Box 7.4 already hinted that the reason for increases in government interest rates could be a perceived increased risk of default. Chapters 14 and especially Chapter 17 will make this case more clearly. In any case, when $r_G > r$ the government should be wary of running deficits, since according to the logic of the budget constraint, they are hurting, not helping their citizens; in this case deficits reduce, not increase, their net wealth!

Mortal or new citizens

Another objection is that Ricardian equivalence must fail because citizens are not all alike when they face the taxman: some pay a lot more taxes than others. So the burden of public debt service is not equally borne by all citizens. Similarly, some hold government debt, and some don't. Yet, this does not imply that the aggregate household sector can escape the implications of equations (7.11) and (7.13). In the *aggregate* some pay more than average, others pay less and, as a first approximation, it does not matter.[21]

On the other hand, citizens are certainly mortal. If they are not alive in period 2, they have little reason to care about the implication of the intertemporal budget constraint of the government. Of course, no one knows whether they will be alive next period but there is always a possibility, unfortunately, that the answer will be negative. Collectively, the private sector currently alive may factor in only a fraction of *all* future tax liabilities. In that case, government debt represents private wealth as we realize that we will not be alive next period and therefore we will not pay taxes to cover the public debt. To those who will not be alive, holding the current debt represents wealth. In a similar vein, new agents—immigrants, perhaps—who enter at some future date will pay taxes to reimburse the public debt issued before they arrived. This too breaks the link between the budget constraint of the presently living generations and future government revenues.

Restrictions on borrowing

Many households cannot borrow as much as future expected income would justify, sometimes they cannot borrow at all. They may be unable to convince lenders—typically banks—of their creditworthiness. For their part, lenders only possess incomplete information on the creditworthiness of borrowers when they apply for credit. In addition, future incomes are never really certain, so lending to households is risky. Borrowing rates exceed lending rates to compensate for this risk.[22] In the worst case, no lending is extended and individuals are said to be credit rationed. The case of credit rationing is represented in Figure 7.11. With a net private endowment represented by point A, the agent can only move along her budget line on the segment AD. The segment AB is not attainable through private borrowing. This means that the consolidated budget constraint—and Ricardian equivalence—is irrelevant for that agent. For instance, consider the case where the government runs a deficit today, so that $T_1 < G_1$, borrowing at rate r_G which we assume equal to r for simplicity. The agent may now reach point A' and could consume $Y_1 - T_1$, which is larger than $Y_1 - G_1$. She benefits when the government does the borrowing that she cannot do.

Most often, individuals face higher and rising costs of borrowing. Lending institutions frequently demand higher interest rates from individuals to compensate for additional risk. The situation is similar to the case studied in the previous section and is also illustrated in Figure 7.11. When lending, the constrained agent can move along AD, but for borrowing she moves along AB'. The budget line is now kinked at the endowment point. In this case, public debt contributes to citizens' wealth, and the time profile of taxes affects the private sector budget constraint. At

---

[21] It is true that poor people do not save and spend all of their income, while rich people only spend a fraction of what they earn. Taking from the rich to give to the poor does raise spending. Yet, the effect is typically very small, hence the 'first approximation' conclusion.

[22] More details on the rates of return paid on risky assets is provided in Chapter 14.

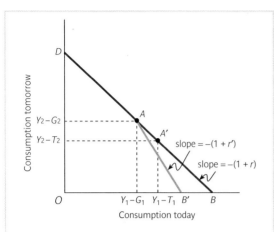

Fig. 7.11 **Borrowing Constraints**

When the household cannot borrow at all, its budget line is restricted to the segment AD, because it cannot consume today more than what is left of the endowment after public spending ($Y_1 - G_1$). If the government reduces taxes and borrows instead (here, from abroad), the household's borrowing line extends to the segment $A'D$. When borrowing constraints take the form of a higher private borrowing rate r', the budget line is the kinked line $B'AD$. A budget deficit at A' at a lower interest rate $r = r_G$ relaxes the private household's budget constraint.

point A' the constrained citizen is better off than any point along AB'. Once again, when the government borrows on behalf of its citizens, it increases the wealth of those who cannot borrow on those terms.

Distortionary taxation and unemployed resources

Another important reason why the Ricardian equivalence can fail is that people change their behaviour in response to taxes. Most taxes are said to be distortionary. For example, taxation on labour income or wages may lead some to work less, and this will reduce output. In the parable of Crusoe, the endowments of coconuts are exogenous, so increasing taxes on them does not affect their supply. In the real world, taxes can reduce wealth because they reduce output. This is especially important in the presence of unemployment. If a tax cut increases the level of economic activity and generates additional income, then the associated fiscal deficit will be associated with higher wealth.

Evidence

Given the long list of qualifications, it would seem quite unlikely that Ricardian equivalence could ever hold in practice. Yet, it receives some empirical backing, especially when the public budget moves by large amounts that are clearly perceptible to the private sector, possibly signalling important policy shifts.

At a very fundamental level, it is unlikely that the private sector would completely disregard what the government is up to. One piece of evidence that supports the Ricardian equivalence is presented in Figure 7.12. Using the case of the UK, the figure shows that changes in the government primary budget balance are partly mirrored by household savings: when the government borrows more, that is when it runs a bigger deficit or smaller surplus, households save more as if they were putting money aside to face future tax liabilities. More formal studies, using advanced statistical techniques, indeed

Fig. 7.12 **Ricardian Equivalence in the UK, 1970–2011**

The figure plots the primary budget balance of the British government (in per cent of GDP) and the household saving rate, the proportion (in per cent) of disposable income that is saved. Remarkably, the two curves tend to move systematically in opposite directions, although not always and not exactly. This suggests that British households are partly Ricardian.

Source: Economic Outlook, OECD.

suggest that households save about half of tax cuts and increases. Ricardian equivalence is thus '50% true'—although this is a dramatic oversimplification but worth keeping in mind.

7.6 The Current Account and the Budget Constraint of the Nation

7.6.1 The Primary Current Account

The consolidation of the budget constraints of the private and public sectors can be thought of as the intertemporal budget constraint of the nation as a whole. In Chapter 2 we saw that national net saving vis-à-vis the rest of the world occurs through the current account. Like the public sector budget surplus, it can be decomposed into a **primary current account** and net investment income:

$$
\text{(7.14)} \quad
\begin{array}{ccc}
\text{current} & & \text{primary} & & \text{net} \\
\text{account} & = & \text{current} & + & \text{investment} \\
\text{surplus } (CA) & & \text{account} & & \text{income } (rF), \\
& & \text{surplus } (PCA) & &
\end{array}
$$

where F represents the country's net asset position (sometimes called net investment position) vis-à-vis the rest of the world, and r, as before, is the real interest rate paid on F. Net investment income is positive when the country holds more assets than liabilities ($F > 0$), or negative in the case of an indebted country ($F < 0$).[23]

It was a lesson from Chapter 2 that the consolidation of the public and private intertemporal budget constraints can be expressed in terms of primary current accounts. In the two-period framework, the budget constraint of the nation requires that the present value of a country's primary current account surpluses be no less than the value of international assets in the first period:

$$
\text{(7.15)} \quad \underbrace{PCA_1 + \frac{PCA_2}{1+r}}_{\substack{\text{present value of} \\ \text{current and future} \\ \text{primary accounts}}} \geq \underbrace{-F_1.}_{\substack{\text{existing net} \\ \text{external debt}}}
$$

---

[23] In Chapter 2, it was noted that when writing (2.8) as $Y - A = CA$, Y is properly measured by the GNI. Equation (7.14) shows that if Y is the GDP, we have $Y - A = PCA$.

If a country has net wealth at the beginning of period 1 (F_1 is positive), it can draw on it to run future current account deficits. If there is external debt (F_1 is negative), the present value of current accounts must be positive, by an amount sufficient to repay the external debt plus interest. Box 7.5 presents the net external position for a few countries.

The implication for the country as a whole is the same as for the private and public sector. A primary current account deficit in the first period ($PCA_1 < 0$) must be repaid by primary current surpluses (in present value) in the second unless there exist previously accumulated assets ($F_1 > 0$). Symmetrically, surpluses in the first period enable a nation to spend more than it produces in the future. It would seem wasteful for a country not to do this; otherwise it is literally giving away resources for claims on the rest of the world, which it will never use. For that reason, it seems likely that the countries of the world with large surpluses today will eventually get wise and start using these surpluses to improve the standards of living of its citizens.

7.6.2 Enforcement of International Credit Contracts and Sovereign Borrowing

If a country fails to satisfy its budget constraint, eventually it will face a tough situation. Many of the crises of the 1990s can be traced back to growing fears that some countries were not going to meet their budget constraints. But ultimately international borrowers have more or less honoured their obligations. Research shows that despite spectacular exceptions, international borrowers more often than not actually repay their debts in present value terms.

Box 7.5 **Global Imbalances**

Figure 7.13 show estimates of net foreign asset positions—exactly what we have called F_1 —for selected countries, expressed as per cent of each country's GDP. At one end of the spectrum, countries like Switzerland, Japan, Germany or China could go on running current account deficits for years and still not violate their budget constraints; in fact these countries are still running surpluses and further accumulating net foreign assets. At the other end of the spectrum, countries like Ireland, Spain, Australia and Poland must eventually start paying back their debts, and yet they are still running current account deficits.

This pattern has been called **global imbalances**, a topic that is a recurrent theme of G20 meetings. This situation cannot go on indefinitely, because budget constraints cannot be violated. The fear is that the constraint will reassert itself through a crisis, pretty much as the government budget constraint eventually led to the Eurozone crisis.

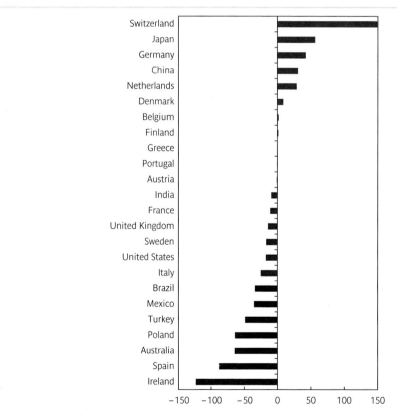

Fig. 7.13 Net Asset Positions, 2010 (% of GDP)
The figure displays the difference between what residents (households, firms and government) own abroad and what they owe to the rest of the world. This includes financial assets and foreign exchange reserves, companies, production facilities and buildings. The net position is measured as a proportion of each country's GDP.
Source: International Financial Statistics, IMF.

Box 7.6 Pyramids: Is it Possible to Beat the Budget Constraint?

Failure to understand the budget constraint can be costly to ordinary citizens and governments alike. The view that debts must be repaid is frequently lost on gullible gamblers who invest in 'pyramids'. A dubious investment promises depositors huge returns. When the time comes to pay out, newly invested money from others is used to pay principal and interest to the earliest investors. Word of mouth spreads news of the wonderful opportunity and more and more gullible people line up to invest, especially when the first depositors are repaid and sceptics are silenced by the 'evidence'. So the scheme grows and grows, as it must if only to pay back maturing deposits. But it cannot grow indefinitely, simply because there is not an infinity of people in a country, or even in the world. Pyramids eventually collapse and the people who set up such schemes know it. So they wait until they think that they have enough investors, and then suddenly disappear with the money, and thousands of investors discover that they have just lost their lifetime savings.

Pyramids are often called Ponzi-schemes, after Charles Ponzi, an Italian immigrant to the USA who operated a grand-scale scheme in the early twentieth century. Poor Ponzi did not run away fast enough; he went to jail, was later released, deported, and died a pauper in a Rio de Janeiro hospital.[24] Most countries ban pyramid schemes, but they flourished in the early years of transition in several former communist countries (with huge ones in Bulgaria, Romania, and Russia). Apparently, most ordinary citizens didn't grasp the mathematics of intertemporal trade and budget constraints, or were convinced by smooth-talking salesmen that they could pass the potato off to others in time. The collapse of an Albanian Ponzi scheme in late 1996 wiped out the savings of tens of thousands of already poor people, many of whom had sold their cattle and houses in response to promises of 300% return and more. Massive street demonstrations and social unrest subsequently brought down the government, which had failed to close down the pyramids after they had collected an estimated €1.1 billion in a country with a GDP of €2.3 billion.

Modern pyramid schemes are not the exclusive property of Eastern European countries. For more than a decade, New York financier Bernie Madoff ran what was probably the biggest pyramid ever. He was able to attract the money of savvy professional investors and old rich grandmothers from around the world. He now sits in a US federal prison and his clients have lost fortunes. The recent 'sub-prime' crisis in the USA, in which low-quality long-term loans for housing, or mortgages, were traded between banks and investors, has many aspects of a Ponzi scheme. Fundamentally, bad mortgages loans were made, then pooled together and repackaged and sold off to other investors, who rationalized the investments with expectations of ever-increasing rising house prices. As long as there is greed and the inevitable overestimation of one's own chances, there will be attempts to beat the intertemporal budget constraint. They are successful only for the few brilliant and greedy criminals who originated the scheme in the first place. Assuming they get away with it.

Governments, just like private households and firms, face an intertemporal budget constraint that limits their ability to borrow at any point in time to the present value of lifetime resources. 'Lifetime' has a clear definition for individuals; for firms and governments less so, since the existence of firms and governments is never guaranteed. Nevertheless, within a legal jurisdiction, private borrowers and lenders will generally be able to rely on special institutions to enforce the budget constraint. Firms or individuals who simply walk away from debts face bankruptcy and possibly jail. Of course, there are always exceptions, but they generally involve fraud, either via outright default ('take the money and run') or more complicated schemes such as financial pyramid schemes described in Box 7.6. These tricks are either illegal or declared to be such as soon as they are detected. In principle, these rules should also apply to governments, regardless of whether they borrow at home or abroad. As soon as they obviously violate their budget constraint, the source of credit should dry up rapidly.

[24] For more details on Charles Ponzi's life see <http://en.wikipedia.org/wiki/Charles_Ponzi>.

All the same, it is important to distinguish between international borrowing by private entities and **sovereign borrowing**, or borrowing by national governments from foreigners. A country cannot be bankrupted or jailed. Unlike private lending within a country, enforcement of sovereign loan contracts is legally difficult. What happens when a country's government is unable to serve its debt? The first reaction is that foreign lending immediately stops, and this often affects would-be private borrowers. The country must at least balance its current account, since it

cannot borrow, which forces painful adjustments in private and public budgets. Thereafter, negotiations start with the creditors to try to arrange a rescheduling of debt service. Rescheduling means that the terms of repayment are changed from the original loan agreement, but without changing the present value of those repayments. Debt forgiveness, in contrast, involves a reduction in the present value of the loan burden to the borrowing country, and a loss to the creditor.

🛈 Summary

1 Because households may borrow or lend, their budget constraint is fundamentally intertemporal. It incorporates all current and future spending on the one hand, and all current and future income on the other. Future spending and incomes are discounted using the interest rate at which households can borrow or lend.

2 Wealth is the sum of the present value of current and future income and inherited assets less debts. The intertemporal budget constraint requires that the present value of spending be less than, or equal to, wealth. It applies to all economic agents, households, firms, the public sector, and the nation as a whole.

3 When firms invest, they forgo—on behalf of their shareholders—current consumption for future output. The profitability of investment depends both on the technology and on the rate of interest. The rate of interest is the opportunity cost of capital that investors apply to investment projects because it is available on other assets.

4 Budget constraints can be added together, or consolidated. Consolidating the households' and the firms' budget constraints gives the budget constraint of the private sector. To a first approximation, corporations are a veil: they provide their owners or shareholders with a means of increasing their wealth.

5 The public sector intertemporal budget constraint implies that, for a given time profile of government purchases, tax reductions today imply tax increases later on, and conversely. Alternatively, given a tax profile, more government spending today implies less spending later on, and conversely.

6 The Ricardian equivalence proposition asserts that the private sector internalizes the public sector budget constraint. Public debt does not represent private wealth, and the path of taxes over time does not affect the private sector budget constraint. If the private sector can freely borrow at the same rate as the government, additional public dissaving is matched one for one by private saving.

7 Ricardian equivalence is unlikely to hold for several reasons. Interest rates are different and usually lower for governments than private agents. Individuals may rightly expect that some current public debt will be repaid after they die. Many households face borrowing constraints. Yet there is some evidence that the private sector internalizes part of government debt.

8 The national budget constraint is the consolidation of the private and public sector budget constraints. It states that the present value of primary current account deficits cannot exceed the nation's net external wealth. It also implies that, all things being equal, higher primary current account defi-

cits today will require primary current account surpluses in the future.

9 Although it must also obey an intertemporal budget constraint, sovereign borrowing by a nation may differ from private international borrowing by its individual residents. One difference is that governments and countries cannot be bankrupted, and the assets of defaulting governments are hard to seize.

✪ Key Concepts

- ◆ intertemporal budget constraints
- ◆ rational expectations hypothesis
- ◆ endowment
- ◆ autarky
- ◆ intertemporal trade
- ◆ real interest rate
- ◆ intertemporal price
- ◆ discounting
- ◆ budget line
- ◆ present discounted value

- ◆ investment
- ◆ fixed capital formation
- ◆ production function
- ◆ diminishing marginal productivity
- ◆ opportunity cost
- ◆ primary deficit
- ◆ Ricardian equivalence proposition
- ◆ primary current account
- ◆ global imbalances
- ◆ sovereign borrowing

❓ Exercises

1 Draw a budget line for Crusoe in a two-period world, assuming an interest rate r of 5% and an income of 100 in the first period (Y_1) and 200 in the second (Y_2). What is the value of total wealth Ω? Why are your answers different when instead $Y_1 = 200$ and $Y_2 = 100$?

2 Use the example given to consider the case of a higher interest rate $r = 10\%$. In terms of wealth, which version of Crusoe has more to lose from an increase in the interest rate? Compare your answer to an individual with $Y_1 = 300$ and $Y_2 = 0$. Explain.

3 Suppose that Crusoe cannot trade intertemporally with his native neighbours, but coconuts no longer spoil completely, so he can store them for consumption tomorrow. Consider the case $Y_1 = 200$ and $Y_2 = 100$, and suppose that 10% of the stored coconuts are lost because of spoilage. Represent this budget constraint graphically. Why does opening the market for loans always make him better off?

4 In the text, Robinson Crusoe does not want to leave any wealth beyond tomorrow because he will be rescued. The situation would be different if he wanted to leave his friend Friday a gift of a fixed amount B_3 in the second period (B_3 might also be thought of as a bequest). Write down Crusoe's budget constraint and represent it graphically.

5 The real interest rate is 5%. What is the value of a new firm which invests €200,000 initially and expects to have profits (sales minus costs) of €100,000 next year, €70,000 the year after, €40,000 the third year, and then to close down

with equipment valued at zero? How does your answer change if the equipment bought initially is instead sold for €50,000? How does your answer change if the interest rate rises to 10%?

6 Sometimes when a firm announces a plan to take over another firm using its cash and not to distribute dividends to its shareholders, its share price decreases; and when the plans are cancelled, the share price rises again. Other times, the opposite pattern is observed. Can you explain why? Under what conditions would you expect such an action to have no effect at all?

7 Suppose the production function has the Cobb–Douglas form: $Y = AK^\alpha L^{1-\alpha}$, and assume labour input is fixed at $L = 1$. Let $\alpha = 0.5$ and $A = 1$. At an interest rate of 5% and no depreciation, what is the level of the capital stock K for which the project is just profitable? How does your answer change when the interest rate is 10%? When the depreciation rate is 5% per annum? When $A = 2$?

8 Write down the value of the firm when the production function is $Y_2 = F(K_2, L)$ with $L = 1$, and the capital stock in the second period is given by $K_2 = I_1 + (1 - \delta K_1)$. How does the initial and given stock of capital in the first period affect the firm's value? The depreciation rate? The rate of investment?

9 Consider a government in a two-period world starting with €1,000 in debt. $G_1 = G_2 = 500$ and $T_1 = 400$. If the interest rate $r_G = 0.05$, what do taxes in the second period need to be to guarantee the solvency of this government? How does your answer change when $r_G = 0.10$?

10 Starting from your answer to the previous problem, show how a tax cut in period 1 can increase wealth if $r_G = 0.05$ and $r = 0.10$? What happens if $r_G = 0.15$? If $r_G = 0.10$?

11 Compare the two measures of the Italian budget in Table 7.1 and Figure 7.8. Explain the difference.

→ Essay Questions

1 Why do you think the interest rate is positive? What would be the consequence of a negative (real) interest rate?

2 For the government to honour its budget constraint, it is sufficient but not necessary that its budget be balanced every year. Why? Why might a balanced budget law not be a good idea? What conclusions do you draw?

3 Some contend that the 'pay as you go' system of social security in many European countries, in which the pension contributions of the currently employed are used to pay the pension benefits of older workers already in retirement, is a pyramid scheme. Do you agree or disagree? Explain.

4 When a country defaults on its external debt, a frequent controversy concerns whether the country is unable or unwilling to honour its debt. Discuss this distinction and why it is difficult to resolve the controversy.

5 In recent years many newly emerging economies— China, Indonesia, and Russia to name a few—have accumulated large net asset positions in the form of foreign government bonds, but have begun to convert these into foreign direct investment positions via 'sovereign wealth funds'. Explain this phenomenon using the intertemporal budget constraint. Are these funds a good or bad thing? From the point of view of these countries, are high interest rates a good or a bad thing?

Private Sector Demand: Consumption and Investment

8

There is often misconception in reasoning about spending and investing. For example, Henry Ford's remark has been widely reported: 'No successful boy ever saved any money. They spent it as fast as they got it for things to *improve themselves*.' In this remark Mr. Ford drew no hard and fast line between spending for personal enjoyment and investment for improvement. And there is no hard and fast line ... Spending merely means expending money primarily for more or less *immediate* enjoyment. Saving or investing is spending money for more or less *deferred* enjoyment.

Irving Fisher (1930)

8.1 Overview

We learned in Chapter 2 that GDP is income paid to production factors, and it also represents value added. Another equally important interpretation is that GDP represents the sum of all final goods expenditures. More precisely, it is the sum of consumption, investment, government purchases, plus exports minus imports in a year's time. These components of total spending represent demand for goods and services by various sectors—households, firms, the government, and foreigners. The sum of these components is often called aggregate spending, or aggregate demand. In this chapter, we focus on explaining the behaviour of the most important private elements of aggregate spending: consumption and investment.

As the epigram to this chapter suggests, consumption and investment are driven by different motives. Private consumption spending, about two-thirds of GDP, is a much more stable component over time than investment, which is volatile and is often thought to be a major reason for business cycle fluctuations. We will see that while consumption represents the ultimate source of worldly existence and satisfaction, investment is only a means to an end, enabling the economy to produce more goods and services in the future. This pattern can be seen in the USA and the euro area as well as in Japan and in the poorer regions of the world. Among other things, this chapter will contribute towards explaining the strikingly different behaviour of consumption and investment. Moving from our long-run model of economic growth to the short-run view of business cycle fluctuations is all about understanding these differences.

As in previous chapters, we will continue to study the decisions of a representative consumer and a representative firm. Both are taken to be rational: they strive to do the best they can, given their available resources and opportunities. We often say that they take decisions to optimize, or achieve the best possible outcome. Although optimizing behaviour is sometimes understood as implying extraordinary intelligence or the ability to perform elaborate calculations, in fact it simply means that agents are rational and, possibly through trial and error, behave in a logically consistent fashion.[1] The final product of the chapter will be a **consumption function** and an **investment function**, two key building blocks of macroeconomic analysis.

---

[1] Introspection often makes us sceptical about such assumptions. Who hasn't given in to the temptation of buying a pastry when not really hungry or a stereo system when short of cash? Such departures from rationality are infrequent enough to be outweighed by a majority of reasoned decisions. This is why rationality in economics is the right way to think about reality—at least to a first approximation!

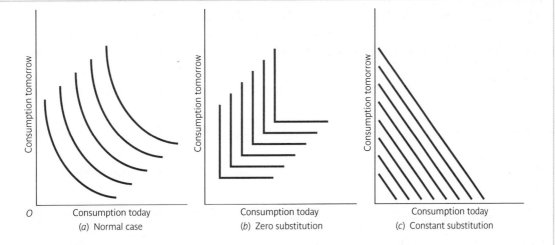

Fig. 8.1 Indifference Curves

Along any indifference curve, utility is constant. In panel (*a*), consumption tomorrow can be substituted smoothly for consumption today, but at a rate which decreases as today's consumption increases. In (*b*), the consumer can be made better off only by increasing consumption today and tomorrow in fixed proportions. In (*c*), consumption today and consumption tomorrow are always substituted at the same rate. In all cases, indifference curves further up in the north-east direction correspond to higher utility levels.

8.2 Consumption

Households receive income from their labour or their asset holdings and have to decide what to do with it. The decision to consume is a decision not to save, and saving is a decision to postpone consumption. It is fundamentally intertemporal: now or later, which is better? *Micro*economics focuses on how households decide *what* to consume, e.g. apples or oranges. For *macro*economics, the emphasis is on *when* to consume. For this reason, we make the simplifying assumption that there is only one good to consume (Robinson Crusoe's coconuts) and the focus is the choice between now and later.

8.2.1 Optimal Consumption

Contemplating what do to with the coconuts that he finds on the beach, Crusoe realizes that he need not consume them on the spot. With access to a capital market, he can borrow or lend: this is called intertemporal trade. In Chapter 7, we saw that the intertemporal budget constraint allows him to choose from many different combinations of consumption today and consumption tomorrow (Fig. 7.1), but were silent about the choice he ultimately made. His optimal choice will depend on his tastes or preferences, which are summarized in Figure 8.1 using **indifference curves**.[2] Each curve corresponds to a given level of **utility**, or well-being. A particular indifference curve represents combinations of consumption today and consumption tomorrow that leave Crusoe equally happy, or indifferent. Higher indifference curves correspond to higher levels of utility.

Two central aspects of indifference curves are their slope and their curvature. The slope of an indifference curve shows Crusoe's willingness to swap

---

[2] Indifference curves were introduced in Chapter 5 to study the labour supply decision of households in an *intra*temporal setting.

consumption tomorrow for consumption today, holding utility constant. Where the curve is steep, for example, he is willing to give up a lot of future consumption to increase today's consumption. A horizontal curve indicates reluctance to give up consumption tomorrow for consumption today.

The second aspect of indifference curves, curvature, shows how the willingness to substitute depends on the relative abundance of consumption in the two periods. The more abundant consumption tomorrow is relative to consumption today, so the greater the willingness to swap tomorrow's for today's. Moving along an indifference curve upwards and to the left, Crusoe is less and less willing to give up coconuts today as the consumption of coconuts tomorrow relative to today grows larger and larger.

Box 8.1 provides more details on the phenomenon of intertemporal substitution.

Naturally, Crusoe wants to consume as much as possible in both periods, but he is limited by his intertemporal budget, which was derived in the last chapter. It is represented as the straight line in Figure 8.2. The best that he can do is point R, where the highest possible indifference curve just touches the budget line. A more desirable indifference curve, such as IC_3, is beyond his means as it lies above his budget line. He can afford the utility level corresponding to IC_1 because this curve cuts the budget line, but can do better. The highest utility level Crusoe can reach is associated with IC_2, which is tangent to his budget line. Box 8.1 provides a more detailed interpretation.

 Box 8.1 Indifference Curves, Intertemporal Substitution and Optimal Consumption

Each indifference curve represents combinations of consumption today and tomorrow for which utility or satisfaction is held constant. Moving to the right along a given indifference curve, today's consumption increases while tomorrow's declines. At any particular point, the slope of the indifference curve shows how many units of goods tomorrow we are willing to give up for an additional unit of goods today. The technical term for this willingness to trade goods tomorrow for goods today is the **marginal rate of intertemporal substitution**.

In most cases, the willingness to substitute consumption across time changes when moving along a representative indifference curve. As we move left to right, it becomes flatter and more horizontal, because we are willing to give up increasingly less consumption tomorrow for consumption today. The opposite occurs as we move from right to left. The curvature of the indifference curve captures the sensitivity of the marginal rate of intertemporal substitution to relative consumption. In Figure 8.1, panel (a) describes the normal situation, but it is worth thinking about two opposite extremes. At one end of the spectrum, there can be no substitutability at all. The consumer is better off only if consumption is increased in fixed proportion in both periods. The

indifference curves would look like a series of right angles in panel (b) of Figure 8.1; happiness can only be increased by raising consumption in both periods. At the other extreme, the marginal rate of substitution is constant. The consumer is always willing to substitute the same amount of consumption today for consumption tomorrow, regardless of how much is consumed. Then indifference curves are straight downward-sloping lines, as in panel (c).

Consider Figure 8.2, which characterizes optimal consumption. The key feature of point R in Figure 8.2 is that the marginal rate of substitution is just equal to the slope of the budget line, or $1 + r$. To see why, suppose that Crusoe obeys his budget constraint but has a marginal rate of substitution of 1. He is willing to exchange one coconut today for one tomorrow. By lending 1 today, he gets $(1 + r)$ tomorrow—a good deal for him—and can make himself better off, i.e. move towards R. If he goes too far, the marginal rate of substitution will exceed $(1 + r)$. He then prefers to shift consumption back to the present, increasing his utility by doing so. Only when the marginal rate of substitution is equal to the intertemporal price of consumption has Crusoe exhausted all gains from intertemporal trade.

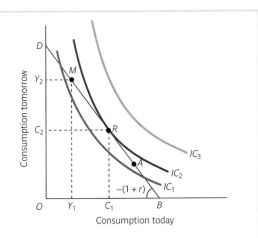

Fig. 8.2 Optimal Consumption

The budget line shows how much can be consumed today and tomorrow for given endowment (represented by point M) and real interest rate (the slope). Optimal consumption is achieved at point R. In this case the consumer borrows today $C_1 - Y_1$ and repays $Y_2 - C_2$ tomorrow. Consumption at R is also possible for an individual with endowment A, who lends today and dissaves tomorrow.

When Crusoe is on his budget line, he spends his total wealth (OB) in the course of the two periods:

(8.1) $$C_1 + \frac{C_2}{1+r} = Y_1 + \frac{Y_2}{1+r} = \Omega.$$

If he can borrow or lend as much as he wants at the going interest rate, his consumption pattern over time depends on the present value of his income—his budget constraint—and not on the particular timing of his income. In Figure 8.2, a 'student Crusoe' (with endowment M) borrows because his current income Y_1 is low relative to his future income Y_2, while a 'professional athlete Crusoe' (endowment point A) with high current and low future income will save. Since both individuals lie on the same budget line, they have the same wealth OB. If both have identical tastes, as described by their indifference curves, saving and borrowing allows them to have identical consumption patterns. Differing borrowing and lending patterns reflects the difference in their endowments. Access to financial markets make this possible.

8.2.2 Implications

The principles developed here have wide-ranging and important implications both at the individual level and for a country as a whole. We examine some of these implications.

Permanent versus temporary changes in income

A first implication is that we can understand how people react to changing economic circumstances. We take up three examples.

Case 1: a temporary increase in income

Imagine that, today, Crusoe's harvest is unusually plentiful, rising to Y'_1 in Figure 8.3, while next period's harvest Y_2 is expected to remain unchanged. For simplicity, the figure represents the case where, initially, consumption was exactly matching income in both periods so that there was no need to borrow or lend (points A and R overlap). The endowment point now shifts from A to A', on the new budget line $B'D'$, which is parallel to the initial line BD since the real

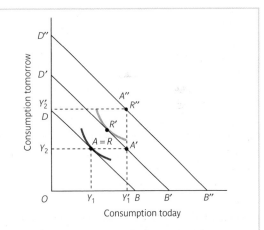

Fig. 8.3 Temporary and Permanent Income Changes

The shift from A to A' describes a temporary increase in income. Consumption rises both today and tomorrow (the household moves from R to R'). Part of today's income windfall is saved to sustain higher spending tomorrow. The shift to point A'' represents a permanent increase in income. It does not require consumption smoothing through saving or borrowing. The best course of action is permanently to increase consumption (to point R'').

interest rate remains unchanged. It is natural to expect that Crusoe will consume more. However, the key insight is that his consumption (point R'') will rise in *both* periods. Consumption today increases less than the windfall, since part of it is saved and spread over time. A temporary increase in income is accompanied by a permanent, but smaller, increase in consumption.

Case 2: a permanent increase in income now and in the future

What if, instead, the increase in income is permanent, in the sense that both Y_1 and Y_2 rise by equal amounts? (Think of a lasting improvement in the harvest outlook.) The new endowment point is A'' and the corresponding budget line is $B''D''$. Optimal consumption moves to point R''. As a first approximation, points A'' and R'' coincide and consumption rises in both periods.[3] Being equally better off in both periods, Crusoe sees no reason to save or borrow. A permanent increase in income is absorbed in a permanent increase in consumption of similar size.

Case 3: an expected future increase in income

Finally, consider the case when income is unchanged today, but is correctly expected to increase tomorrow. If Robinson knows that his future crop will be more plentiful, he will borrow today against his future income to afford a better standard of living right away. Far from reckless behaviour, borrowing makes him better off. In a setting with many periods, forward-looking consumers would try to assess the permanent component of such future shocks and change current behaviour accordingly.

An implication of this reasoning is that only new information about the future should alter existing consumption behaviour. If future incomes are correctly anticipated, they are incorporated into current wealth and current consumption fully reflects this information. The only reason why consumption should change is if unexpected disturbances affect current or future income significantly enough that wealth changes. Since all that is known of the future

is already taken into account in the evaluation of wealth, only true surprises can alter wealth and therefore consumption. Put differently, changes in consumption must be unpredictable. This is known as the **random walk** theory of consumption, because changes in consumption should be random.[4]

Consumption smoothing

The common theme of the three cases is that people dislike variable consumption patterns. When faced with a temporary change in income, rational consumers save or borrow to spread the effects on consumption over time. In bad times, this may take the form of dissaving (spending from accumulated savings) or borrowing (from the bank, from relatives, or using a credit card). In good times, consumers accumulate assets or repay their debts. This phenomenon is known as **consumption smoothing**. It explains why consumption is less variable than GDP, and is in general the most stable component of aggregate demand. Box 8.2 describes an example of consumption smoothing when the shock is perceived as temporary and of consumption change when the shock is perceived as permanent. This being said, it is very difficult to detect permanent from temporary shocks; consumers (and economists) may be misled by their perceptions.

Permanent income and the life cycle[5]

Most households do not expect a constant flow of income over their lifetimes. Typically, young people earn less than older people, as represented in Figure 8.5. The principle of optimal consumption implies that they should borrow when young and repay debts or even save when older in order to smooth the pattern of consumption over time. It is rational for young people to borrow many times their annual income to buy an apartment or house, which they plan to inhabit for a long time and to pay off the loan over the course of their lives. Naturally,

---

[3] This is only an approximation. Impatient consumers may bring forward some of tomorrow's windfall, whereas more patient agents would save some of today's windfall for tomorrow's consumption. The exact answer will depend on the shape and position of their indifference curves.

[4] The random walk theory of consumption was formulated by Robert E. Hall of Stanford University. It is surprisingly difficult to reject this theory empirically.

[5] The permanent income hypothesis was developed by Chicago economist Milton Friedman (1912–2006) and was cited as his main contribution when he was awarded the Nobel Prize in 1976. The life-cycle theory of consumption was also recognized by the Nobel Prize committee as an important contribution of MIT economist Franco Modigliani (1918–2003).

Box 8.2 Germany and Ireland During the Crisis

Both Germany and Ireland went into a deep recession in 2009. Figure 8.4(a) shows that the decline in the output gap was very similar at the outset. While Germany soon recovered, Ireland entered into a deepening and prolonged slump. German consumers had good reason to believe that this was a temporary adverse shock. While consumption growth declined a little—from a low trend anyhow—the movement was limited and short-lived,

see Panel (b) in Figure 8.4. The Irish consumers soon realized that the very rapid growth that they had enjoyed over the previous decade was over. They had overborrowed to participate in a housing boom that ended up in massive bank failures. For them, this was a permanent shock, one that would last years. Consumption fell dramatically. While the growth rate recovered in early 2010, by end 2011 it was still in negative territory.

they must assume what they will continue to earn in the future, and no one can be sure of anything. Nevertheless, mortgage lending is a common fact of everyday life in all modern economies, usually combined with a life or other type of insurance policy.

The principle of **life-cycle consumption** is illustrated in Figure 8.5. To maintain a constant flow of consumption, individuals should spend each year an amount corresponding to their **permanent income**. Permanent income is that income which, if constant, would deliver the same present value of income as the actual expected income path. It is a good measure of sustainable consumption over one's lifetime. In the two-period thinking of this chapter, permanent income Y^P would therefore be defined as

(8.2)
$$Y^P + \frac{Y^P}{1+r} = \Omega = Y_1 + \frac{Y_2}{1+r}.$$

The life-cycle principle can also be applied to a country as a whole. If income is expected to grow, it is optimal for a country to borrow abroad, and thus run current account deficits for a while, and pay back later through current account surpluses. This may explain why the new EU members, who can reasonably expect to catch up with the old members, often run current account deficits. One glaring exception is China, as Box 8.3 points out.

Consumption and the real interest rate

When the real interest rate rises, so do the rewards to saving. Why? Because the price of consumption tomorrow relative to consumption today declines. Does saving always increase and consumption always decline? The question is harder to answer than it first appears.

Figure 8.6 shows that one determinant of consumption today is whether Crusoe is a net borrower (e.g. a student) or a net lender (e.g. a professional athlete). In both panels of the figure, endowments today and tomorrow are held constant, so the budget line rotates around point A. Optimal consumption shifts from point R to point R'. Net lenders (panel b) gain from higher interest rates, moving to a higher indifference curve and consuming more in both periods. The borrower (panel a) faces higher interest costs and is in the opposite situation, as he must devote more resources to service the debt, and his current consumption declines. Increases in interest rates have important redistributive effects between borrowers and lenders: an increase hurts the former and benefits the latter.

In general, the effect of the interest rate on consumption is ambiguous because it works through two channels. First, an increase in the interest rate makes the budget constraint steeper, since it determines the slope of the intertemporal budget constraint. It increases the cost of goods today relative to those tomorrow, making it more attractive to save (consume tomorrow). Second, it reduces the value of wealth Ω, which is the present discounted value of all income. This effect will depend on how much of our wealth stems from future, as opposed to current, income. The more wealth we have today, the more we profit from an increase in interest rates and the more likely this wealth effect will predominate.

8.2.3 Wealth or Income?

An old tradition in macroeconomics, which can be traced back to John Maynard Keynes, links consumption

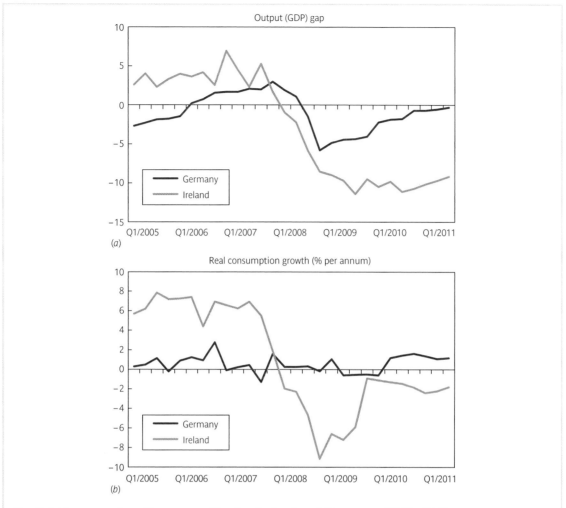

Fig. 8.4 Permanent vs. Temporary Shocks: Ireland and Germany, 2005 – 2011

Panel (*a*) displays the output gap (in per cent of GDP). The initial impact of the crisis is similar in the two countries, but Germany recovers quickly while the shock is deeper in Ireland. Panel (*b*) shows the annual rate of growth of consumption. Ireland enjoyed fast growth during its 'Celtic tiger' years, part of which was based on an unsustainable housing boom. The perception that these boom years have come to an end seems to have pushed consumption into a severe and lasting decline.

Source: OECD, *Economic Outlook*.

spending by households to current income—which we have called disposable income Y^d and defined as GDP less net taxes. Keynes argued that most people simply set aside a fraction of disposable income for saving, and consume the rest.[6] The evidence seems to support this hypothesis. Figure 8.7 shows the evidence

for France, plotting consumption expenditures in each year in the period 1980–2006 against disposable income in the top chart and, in the bottom chart, against a measure of household wealth, which includes liquid financial assets of families as well as the value of fixed assets and real estate. The link between consumption and disposable income is strong, in fact stronger than that between consumption and wealth.

---

[6] This assumption regarding saving and consumption is also central to the Solow growth model studied in Chapter 3.

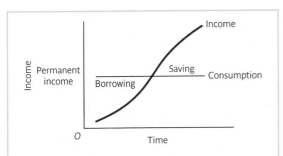

Fig. 8.5 Life-Cycle Consumption

When income is expected to increase over a lifetime, consumption smoothing implies borrowing when young and paying back when older.

This evidence challenges a key implication of the theory developed in the previous sections: that consumption is driven by wealth, not current income, and that households strive to smooth their consumption relative to income. One possible reconciliation is that income and wealth grow in tandem, so that the observed consumption–income relationship may reflect a common dependence on wealth. Yet wealth appears more volatile than disposable income, partly because of fluctuations in share prices on stock markets.

It is likely that households regard short-term stock market gains and losses as temporary and pay attention only to long-term increases in wealth. In addition, private wealth is not well known, in part because people are reluctant to provide information about their assets, in part because expected future income—an important component of wealth—is not measurable and therefore left out.

A second explanation is related to a household's ability to borrow and lend. In our parable, Crusoe can borrow freely at a given interest rate. This might be the case if present and future incomes of individual households—against which borrowing is pledged—were known with certainty to lenders. In real life, banks and other lending intermediaries cannot know the repayment prospects of all individual borrowers with certainty. A common banking practice is to demand collateral—the borrower pledges tangible wealth, such as a house, in case of non-payment. This option is not available to all households. Banks charge higher interest rates to customers who appear riskier and sometimes refuse to lend at any rate, or place ceilings on the amount that can be borrowed. Consumers who cannot obtain credit in spite of future earnings potential are said to be **credit rationed**.

 Box 8.3 Why China Defies the Permanent Income Hypothesis

In the late 1980s, China was a poor country with a GDP per capita about 7% of that of the Netherlands. By the mid-2000s, it had grown to 20%. At the current rate of growth, China is likely to reach Portuguese levels of GDP in 15–20 years, and few doubt that China will eventually close the gap. The permanent income hypothesis suggests that China should run a substantial current account deficit during this catch-up period. In fact, its current account has been steadily increasing, reaching 10% of GDP.

While there are many explanations of the high Chinese saving rate, none of them alone is really convincing. One view is that Chinese citizens cannot borrow against future income because the banking system is rather under-developed. Another is that citizens save so much because there is no system of social security as it is known in Europe, so they need to save for health

expenditures and retirement income. State-owned firms, which are highly profitable because they are sheltered from competition, are also big savers. Yet another is fear that borrowing on international capital markets could bring even greater problems, including loss of government control over the economy that comes with international investment. Most frequently cited is the view that China intentionally keeps its currency undervalued to artificially boost competitiveness, and by doing so makes imports of cheap consumptions goods unattractive. (The precise meaning of undervaluation will be explained more fully in Chapter 15.) At any rate, each of these reasons implies that Chinese households are away from their optimal intertemporal consumption paths and could easily increase their well-being with a few well-placed reforms. Unless there are more reforms, the economy is likely to stay that way.

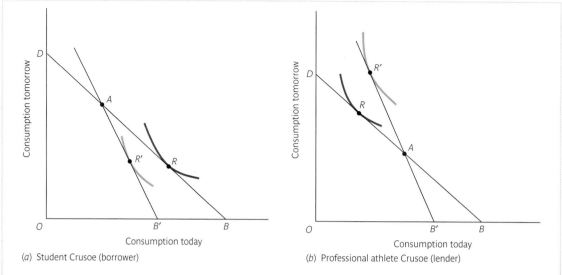

(a) Student Crusoe (borrower)   (b) Professional athlete Crusoe (lender)

Fig. 8.6 The Effect of an Increase in the Interest Rate

As the interest rate increases, the budget line becomes steeper and rotates about the endowment point A. The response of the consumer depends on whether she is a borrower or a lender. The borrower (a) will tend to consume less today because the interest rate at which resources are brought forward has increased. The lender (b) consumes more today, since the same amount of lending can increase the amount of consumption possible tomorrow without reducing today's.

In the presence of credit rationing, spending is governed by current disposable income, not wealth.[7] This is shown in Figure 8.8, which uses Figure 7.10 as its point of departure. Because Robinson Crusoe is prevented from borrowing, his consumption possibilities are limited to the kinked line *CAB*. In particular, he cannot reach the segment *AD* of his intertemporal budget constraint, and his preferred consumption plan *R* is not possible. In that case, the best option for him is point *A*, where he consumes exactly his income in both periods. If a significant proportion of households is rationed in credit markets, disposable income will be the dominating influence on consumption, which will only matter for non-rationed households. Box 8.4 illustrates the importance of national borrowing constraints in the early phase of the process of economic transformation in Eastern Europe. But even in advanced countries, credit rationing affects a substantial proportion of households. It is therefore not surprising to

observe the tight link between consumption and disposable income in Figure 8.7.

8.2.4 The Consumption Function

How can we summarize all we have learned thus far? Consumption is driven primarily by wealth, and wealth is based on current and future incomes of households. By this argument, current income should matter less than future expected income. At the same time, current income may be a good predictor of what is to come. In addition, many people are credit-rationed and cannot borrow even when their expected future income is higher. For them, disposable income is the effective determinant of consumption.

In the end, we can write down the consumption function as a compact way of linking consumption to its two main determinants:

(8.3)
$$C = C(\Omega, Y^d).$$
$$+ \quad +$$

The plus signs underneath the arguments of the function reminds us that consumption increases with both wealth Ω and disposable income Y^d. The

---

[7] Chapter 7 provides a detailed treatment of interest rates and credit rationing.

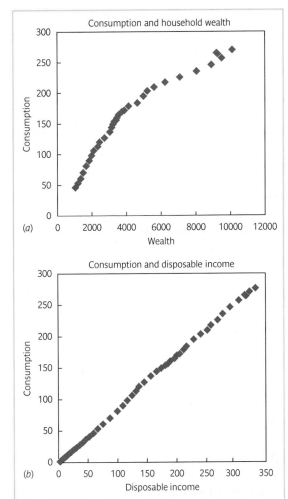

Fig. 8.7 Consumption, Disposable Income, and Wealth in France, 1980–2006

The link between real consumption and net wealth of households is strong (panel (*a*)), but appears less tight than the link between consumption and disposable income (panel (*b*)).

Source: OECD.

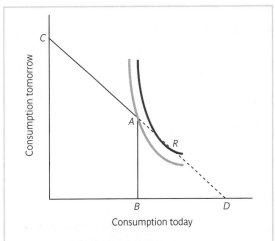

Fig. 8.8 Credit Constraints

If Crusoe cannot borrow, his budget constraint shrinks from *CD* to *CA*. He would like to be at point *R*, however, borrowing today and paying back tomorrow. The best outcome for him under the circumstances is to consume at point *A*, with consumption equal to income both today and tomorrow.

consumption function is a fundamental tool that will be used throughout the rest of this textbook.

What about the interest rate? Section 8.2.2 noted that the real interest rate affects consumption, but that its direct role is ambiguous; this is why we do not include it in (8.3). On the hand, a higher interest rate is bound to reduce consumption indirectly through wealth. So the real interest rate affects consumption after all, but through its effect on wealth.

8.3 Investment

The second component of aggregate demand to be explained is investment, also known as gross domestic capital formation. Investment goods include machine tools, computers, office furniture, land-moving equipment, buses and lorries, and construction of new factory buildings, as well as increases in

Box 8.4 **Current Income and Spending in East Germany and Poland**

The rapid conversion of East Germany (the former German Democratic Republic) and Poland to market-based economies in 1990 provides a unique example of an anticipated increase in permanent income. In both countries, the adoption of market-based institutions implied that income levels would eventually reach those of Western Europe. However, the transition to a market economy was bound to be painful. Some dislocation was inevitable. Income initially fell as inefficient production was shut down and workers had to change occupations and industries. Yet, remember that wealth is defined in (8.1) as the present value of current and future incomes. This is why, despite the fall in initial observable income, wealth increased because future incomes were bound to be much higher than before. The permanent income hypothesis implies that consumption had to rise ahead of income. This could only happen if people are able to collectively borrow abroad, or receive transfers. As part of German unification, the

citizens of the Eastern *Länder* had access to a well-developed domestic financial market. For the former East Germany borrowing 'abroad' meant getting loans from West German banks, or receiving credits or grants from the government. On the other hand, Poland started out with a large external debt, which made it difficult for the government to borrow more, and its citizens and firms certainly did not have access to credit, despite high growth. Figure 8.9 shows the dramatic difference. While GDP fell in East Germany after 1990, private consumption there rose to equal total East German GDP. Public spending and private investment also rose. As a result, the current account deficit—the difference between total spending and income—reached nearly 100% of GDP. In credit-constrained Poland, spending tracked income. In fact, because of its large external debt, Poland had to run a primary surplus. In contrast, East Germany's large external debt was assumed by West Germany.

inventories of goods to be sold at a future date. Software programs used in computers that are purchased by businesses are also considered as investment spending. All these goods have the common trait that they are not intended for consumption; instead they make the production of goods and services possible in the future. The decision to invest is therefore an intertemporal decision.

8.3.1 The Optimal Capital Stock

As in Chapter 7, we will assume that labour input is constant. Accordingly, we set $L = 1$ so it is possible to write the production function using the shorthand $F(K)$ for $F(K,1)$. This represents the amount of output that can be produced by a representative firm, giving output Y available tomorrow when capital K is in place. The production function is depicted in panel (*a*) of Figure 8.10. A related concept, already introduced in Chapter 3, is the **marginal productivity of capital (MPK)**. This is the amount of extra output that can be obtained when an additional unit of capital is installed ($\Delta Y/\Delta K$), and is the slope of the production function.[8]

Because of the principle of declining marginal productivity, the MPK declines as more and more capital is put in place, as is shown in panel (*b*) in Figure 8.10.

The MPK is the return from an additional unit of capital. What about the cost? When he saves, Crusoe chooses between planting resources or lending them in the capital market. In the latter case, he can expect 'tomorrow' to receive the coconut plus interest. Alternatively, he could borrow a coconut, plant it himself, grow the tree, and pay back principal and interest tomorrow. The same is true for any firm. If the investment is funded with resources that could instead be invested in financial assets, the **opportunity cost** of the investment is $(1 + r)$. If the investment is financed by borrowing, the **marginal cost** of investment is $(1 + r)$.[9] In both cases, the cost is the same: it

___

vertical distance which returns us to the production function. The ratio $\Delta Y/\Delta K$ is simply the slope of the line connecting the point of departure and the point of return. For smaller and smaller steps ΔK, this slope ultimately becomes the slope of the curve itself (formally, it is the line tangent to the curve at the initial point).

[9] The careful reader may appreciate the following precision. Presumably, capital can be resold. Here we assume that Crusoe abandons his coconut grove upon rescue. If he could sell it, the expected resale value comes as a deduction from investment cost. Box 8.6 elaborates on this point.

___

[8] To see why, take one point on the curve. An increase ΔK in the stock of capital is represented as a horizontal move from the initial point. How much output ΔY is available? It is measured as the

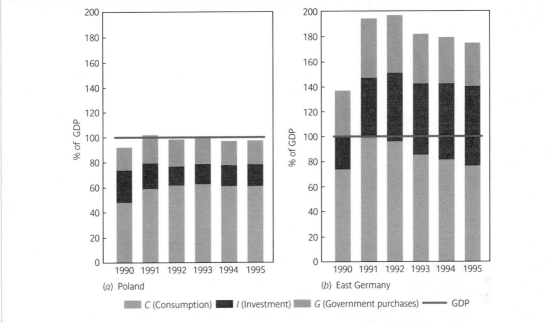

Fig. 8.9 GDP, Domestic Demand, and the Current Account: Poland and East Germany

Spending in East Germany rose after unification as firms, citizens, and authorities were able to borrow against higher expected future income. There is no link between spending and income, because 'foreign' borrowing is almost as large as income. In Poland, which has similar long-run growth prospects, spending follows income because of the impossibility of borrowing large amounts abroad.

Sources: DIW Wochenbericht; World Bank; CSO; DGII.

is shown in panel (*a*) of Figure 8.10 as the ray *OR*. The ray represents the total cost, $(1 + r)K$, of capital installed today and productive tomorrow, the sum of the principal and the interest charged. (The cost of equipment here is unity because it takes one coconut to start a tree.) The marginal cost of capital, or the cost of one incremental unit of productive capacity, is simply $(1 + r)$. It is represented in panel (*b*) by a horizontal line.

The firm's profit in the second period is the difference between what it produces and the cost of production:

(8.4) $\text{profit} = F(K) - K(1 + r).$

In panel (*a*), this is measured as the vertical distance between the curve depicting the production function and the ray *OR*. To maximize profit, the firm chooses the **optimal capital stock** $\overline{K}$ such that the distance between the two schedules is as large as possible.

This occurs where the slope of the production schedule (given by its tangent) is equal to the slope of the cost-of-capital schedule *OR*. Then the marginal productivity of capital (MPK) is equal to the marginal cost, here the opportunity cost equal to $1 + r$:

(8.5)   MPK   = $1 + r.$

marginal	=	marginal
productivity	=	cost of
of capital		capital

In Figure 8.10(*b*), the optimal capital stock $\overline{K}$ corresponds to the intersection of the MPK and marginal cost curves. Box 8.5 provides an extension of this result to the case when capital does not depreciate completely and can be resold after the second period.

If each and every firm behaves optimally, the same principles can be applied to the economy as a whole. Two conclusions follow. First, the optimal capital stock depends positively on the expected effectiveness

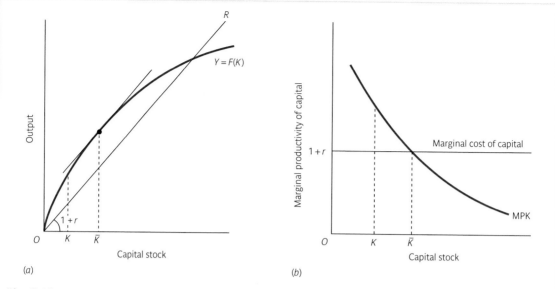

Fig. 8.10 The Optimal Capital Stock

The optimal stock of capital D is achieved when the firm's production function is furthest from the line *OR*, which represents the cost of capital. There the marginal productivity of capital is equal to its marginal cost (MPK = 1 + *r*). Investment is the difference between the desired capital stock D and the previously accumulated capital stock *K*.

 Box 8.5 Optimal Capital Investment: Looking Beyond Two Periods

In the real world, capital investments typically last more than two periods—sometimes many decades. Capturing this important aspect of investment and capital is relatively easy. Suppose that Crusoe, instead of abandoning his capital stock, sells it to Friday, who chooses to stay on the island and continue his economic pursuits there. A 'resale market' changes the investment decision for Crusoe in an important way. As before, the optimal decision means that MPK equals marginal cost, but now the MPK includes the resale value of capital. For simplicity, suppose first that the price of trees is equal to one (coconut). Then the optimal condition is

(8.6)
$$\underset{\substack{\text{marginal} \\ \text{product} \\ \text{of capital}}}{\text{MPK}} + \underset{\substack{\text{resale} \\ \text{value} \\ \text{of capital}}}{1} = \underset{\substack{\text{marginal} \\ \text{cost} \\ \text{of capital.}}}{1+r,}$$

The cost of capital is 1, the same as the value of output by assumption (1 coconut). This condition can be simplified to

(8.7)
$$\text{MPK} = r.$$

When Crusoe can recoup the principal of his investment, the marginal product of capital is set equal to the real interest rate *r*, rather than 1 + *r*. In practice, firms can resell at least some of their equipment at some price, so an investment can be justified by a lower MPK than would be the case were it to be abandoned entirely. Reality will tend to be somewhere between equations (8.7) and (8.6), depending on depreciation, or loss of value of the installed capital over time.

This loss of productive equipment can be quantified by a **rate of depreciation** δ, which we have already seen in our discussion of economic growth in Chapter 3 and of intertemporal resource constraints in Chapter 7.

Box 8.5 Optimal Capital Investment: Looking Beyond Two Periods (*Continued*)

With depreciation, tomorrow's value of a unit of today's capital is no longer 1, but $1 - \delta$. Taking this into account, (8.7) becomes

(**8.8**) $\underset{\substack{\text{marginal} \\ \text{product}}}{\text{MPK}} + \underset{\text{resale value}}{1-\delta} = \underset{\substack{\text{marginal} \\ \text{cost}}}{1+r,}$

which simplifies to

(**8.9**) $\text{MPK} = r + \delta.$

The optimal capital stock is reached when the marginal product of capital is equal to the sum of the interest rate r and the depreciation rate δ. Because depreciation can be thought of as an additional cost of capital, the right-hand side is often called the **user cost of capital**. The original rule for the optimal capital stock (8.5) can be regarded as a special case of complete depreciation ($\delta = 1$).

Fig. 8.11 Technological Progress
Technological progress makes more output possible with the same stock of capital. In panel (*a*) the production schedule shifts upward. In panel (*b*) the MPK schedule moves up to the right to MPK′. The optimal stock of capital is now D′, which is larger than the initial value D.

of the available technology, captured by the marginal productivity of capital. An improvement in technology means that more output can be produced with the same capital stock. In Figure 8.11, the production function in panel (*a*) and the MPK schedule in panel (*b*) both shift upward. The optimal stock of capital increases from $\bar{K}$ to $\bar{K}$.

Second, the optimal capital stock depends negatively on the real interest rate. If the real interest rate increases, the cost schedule *OR* rotates counter-clockwise in Figure 8.11(*a*) and the marginal cost schedule shifts upwards in panel (*b*). The intuition behind this

important result is that, for a given state of technology, higher opportunity costs of capital reduce the amount of capital that can be optimally employed and still be more profitable than simply 'lending' the resources in the financial markets.

8.3.2 Investment and the Real Interest Rate

Investment occurs for two reasons: (1) to bring the capital stock to its desired level, and (2) to make up for capital lost through physical or economic depreciation.[10] In Figure 8.10, we can find the optimal stock of capital $\overline{K}$ and the stock of capital inherited from past investment K—perhaps there were already some coconut trees around when Crusoe came to his island. Ignoring depreciation, optimal investment is simply the difference $\overline{K} - K$. Thus, given the present stock of capital and the rate of depreciation, the determinants of optimal investment are the same as those of the optimal stock of capital. An increase in the real interest rate, which lowers the optimal stock of capital, also lowers optimal investment since the capital stock brought forward from the last period and the rate of depreciation remain unchanged. Accordingly, the investment function could be expressed as

(8.10) $I = I(r)$.

8.3.3 The Accelerator Principle

In Chapter 3, the relative stability of the capital–output ratio was stressed as one of Kaldor's stylized facts about economic growth. It is reasonable to expect that, for the capital stock to reach its optimal level derived in Section 8.3.1, investment would have to move in roughly the same proportion. This idea gives rise to a simple way of thinking about investment. Suppose the optimal capital stock in the second period is proportional to the expected output level: $K = vY$ where v is a constant.[11] If firms invest to keep the capital stock at its optimal level, an increase of GDP from Y_1 to Y_2 requires a change from $K_1 = vY_1$ to $K_2 = vY_2$. Ignoring depreciation, this means an investment of

(8.11) $I_1 = K_2 - K_1 = v(Y_2 - Y_1) = v\Delta Y_2$.

This relationship captures the **accelerator principle**. It is called the accelerator because in order for investment to remain constant, output must increase. Increases in investment are therefore associated with an *acceleration* of output. In practice, the capital–output ratio is between 2 and 3 in most economies. Put differently, annual GDP represents between one-third and one-half of the installed capital stock. GDP movements therefore are associated with much larger swings in investment.[12] A second, central insight of the accelerator principle is the dependence of investment today on expected growth in output *tomorrow*. This provides a convincing reason why investment is more volatile than GDP. It is based on expectations of the future. In the following sections we will develop this idea in greater detail.

8.3.4 Investment and Tobin's q

Why do observers of the economic scene continuously monitor the evolution of the stock markets? Prices of shares often move in erratic ways which may not seem particularly related to the present economic situation, or at least in a way that is obvious. In fact, stock prices are intimately related to macroeconomics. Aggregate economic activity affects stock prices, and stock prices are important determinants of aggregate economic activity. One important linkage is household wealth. When stock prices rise, shareholders become richer and spend more. When the stock market crashes, consumption tends to slow down.

A second connection, which is our focus here, relates stock prices to investment in plant and equipment. Shares in publicly traded companies are titles of ownership. They represent claims on the present and future profits of firms. Profits are the difference between sales and costs. In the aggregate economy, these costs are primarily wages and non-wage labour costs. Share prices can be thought of as the market's best estimate of the value of those present and future profits.

For a number of reasons, the stock market valuation of a firm and its installed capital may well differ from the price of the capital goods, sometimes called the replacement cost of the capital stock. One such reason is the existence of intangible assets which

---

[10] In Chapters 3 and 7 we saw that the change in the capital stock ΔK is equal to $I - \delta K$, where δ is the rate of depreciation, and therefore δK is the amount of capital that is used up each period. This relation can be rewritten as $I = \Delta K + \delta K$, which shows that I—gross investment—must cover both ΔK—the intended net investment—as well as replacing depreciated capital.

[11] This proposition is both empirically and theoretically tenable. The long-run stability of the capital–output ratio was one of Kaldor's stylized facts introduced in Chapter 3. Theoretically, consider a Cobb–Douglas production function with constant employment equal to 1: $Y = AK^\alpha$. Then the MPK is given by $\partial Y/\partial K = \alpha AK^\alpha = \alpha AK^{\alpha-1}/K = \alpha Y/K$. The optimal capital stock is K^* such that MPK $= 1 + r$, so $\alpha Y/K^* = 1 + r$, and $K^* = \alpha Y/(1 + r)$. Setting $v = \alpha/(1 + r)$ implies (8.11).

[12] To account for depreciation, (8.11) is simply changed to $I_1 = v\Delta Y_2 + \delta K_1$. The same conclusions apply.

include such factors as the firm's know-how and its trained labour force, its network of distributors and retailers, its reputation among customers, etc. Another reason is the fact that 'Rome wasn't built in a day'. Establishing a new firm from scratch requires time and resources. These costs are greater, the more rapidly an investment project is undertaken. To summarize this, we use a ratio, called **Tobin's *q***, which is defined as follows:[13]

(8.12)

$$\text{Tobin's } q = \frac{\text{Market value of installed capital}}{\text{replacement cost of installed capital}}.$$

The numerator of Tobin's q is the firm's value as priced by the stock market, the total value of all existing shares. The denominator is the amount that would have to be spent to replace the capital goods incorporated in existing firms.

The ***q*-theory of investment** relates the behaviour of aggregate investment to Tobin's q. When Tobin's q is greater than one, installed capital in the existing firm is more valuable than what it would cost to purchase it new and start a new firm from scratch. For this reason, entrepreneurs (people who start and run businesses) should take the hint and purchase new plant and equipment. Investment is then positive. For example, a Tobin's q of 1.2 would imply that a firm that spends 100 on new investment in plant and equipment increases its market value by 120. Installation and use in production adds a value of 20 to uninstalled equipment. Given the principle of declining marginal productivity, investment reduces the return on the capital over time and therefore reduces Tobin's q. Firms will continue to invest, increasing the capital stock and reducing the marginal product of capital, until Tobin's q has returned to unity.

Alternatively, when q is lower than 1, selling off equipment at replacement cost is profitable and

Fig. 8.12 The *q*-Theory of Investment
When Tobin's q is larger than 1, it pays for firms to invest. When Tobin's q is less than 1, there is no incentive to invest, but rather an incentive to disinvest, or to dismantle or abandon productive capacity.

therefore desirable from the point of view of the firm's shareholders, so net investment should be negative. In the aggregate economy, this can occur only if gross investment is exceeded by depreciation or capital is dismantled, sold, or scrapped. The dependence of investment on Tobin's q is displayed in Figure 8.12.

How is the q-theory related to the previous section, which showed that the interest rate is a key determinant of investment? The stock market values firms by discounting future earnings using the real interest rate. Any increase in the interest rate leads to heavier discounting and therefore to a decline in stock prices, *ceteris paribus*. Thus, the negative effect of the real interest rate on investment is already incorporated into Tobin's q.

But Tobin's q does more than just take the interest rate into account. It also incorporates two other factors in the investment decision. First, gains in productivity of capital raise future income, and thereby increase share prices and q. An excellent example of how this can occur was the massive rise (and later, decline) in stock prices in the wake of the internet and new communications technologies. Second, q incorporates the role of expectations. Investment is almost always a bet on the future. Firms buy and install equipment now to produce output for several years under uncertain conditions. How they will be able to take advantage of the equipment is not known when the investment occurs. Uncertainty ranges from the general economic situation, to competition in domestic

[13] It is named after US economist and Nobel laureate James Tobin (1918–2002), who pointed out in 1969 that investment should be positively related to the ratio of a firm's market valuation to the replacement value of its capital stock. In the meantime, more sophisticated analyses have shown the conditions under which this 'average q' concept—which is readily measured using stock market values and investment good prices—is equal to the marginal concept presented in the text. For our purposes, we will simply assume that these conditions are met.

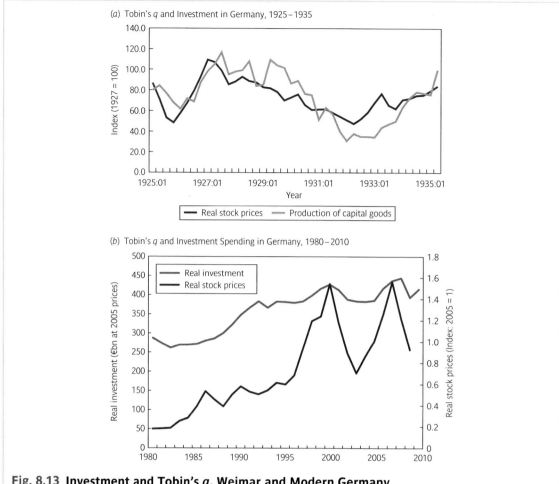

(a) Tobin's q and Investment in Germany, 1925–1935

(b) Tobin's q and Investment Spending in Germany, 1980–2010

Fig. 8.13 Investment and Tobin's *q*, Weimar and Modern Germany

Both in historical and more modern contexts, investment has consistently followed movements of Tobin's *q*, as proxied by a stock price index divided by the consumer price index.

Sources: IMF; Ritschl (2004).

and foreign markets, to the evolution of technology and even political developments. All these aspects are continuously evaluated by the stock markets, which explains why share prices are so volatile: forward-looking markets factor into share prices volatile expectations of many volatile underlying factors. In the end, this explains why investment is the most volatile component of GDP. It was Keynes who linked the high variability of investment to the **animal spirits** of entrepreneurs, i.e. their fickle and volatile expectations of the future profitability of investment.

To see how well Tobin's *q* predicts investment expenditures, let us consider Figure 8.13, which presents data for Germany during 1980–2010 as well from a much earlier period, the late 1920s and early 1930s, which included the Great Depression. The link is evident, with stock prices leading investment with a variable but relatively short lag. Not all companies are traded on stock markets. Many are too small to issue shares, and many larger ones are reluctant to 'go public'. It is often cheaper for firms to draw on their own savings (retained earnings) because profits are usually taxed less when reinvested than when distributed. Some firms prefer to finance investment by borrowing rather than by issuing shares, especially in continental Europe, where bank lending plays an important or even dominant role. Despite these limitations, Tobin's *q* still does a pretty good job measuring the incentive to invest for these firms. It reflects both expected profitability—the numerator—and the real cost of borrowing through the discount factor and the cost of capital—the denominator.

Tobin's q explains the link between the stock market and the state of the economy. The economic function of stock exchanges is to evaluate the future profitability of the large number of listed firms and to place a value today for the whole stream of future earnings from capital ownership. For the macroeconomy as a whole, average stock prices represent the value of the capital stock in place (financial markets also assess the degree of riskiness related to unavoidable uncertainty, and this is factored into share prices—the subject of Chapter 14). Present and especially future economic conditions affect stock prices. Conversely, we should expect stock markets to affect economic conditions since stock prices influence investment through Tobin's q.

8.3.5 The Microeconomic Foundations of Tobin's q[14]

Installation costs

We now have two ways of thinking about the firm's investment decision. The first is that the firm invests to reach its optimal capital stock. The second approach sees investment as taking advantage of the difference between the market value of capital already in place (installed) and its replacement cost—the cost of new capital goods. From either perspective, one might expect firms to seize such opportunities quickly. In practice, however, they do not adjust the capital stock instantaneously to its optimal level. For this reason, q can and will differ systematically from its long-run value—unity—for some time. One reason for this is that firms face installation costs in addition to the direct costs considered so far. It turns out that taking **installation costs** into account allows us to integrate the previous theories.

The idea behind installation costs is simple. With adequate resources, it could have been possible to dig the Eurotunnel in just six months. Doing so, how-

ever, would have been enormously 'costly' in many ways, so it was completed over several years instead. Intuitively, the bigger the investment per unit of time, the more costly it is to install it. Examples of installation costs include the fact that each addition of new equipment in a factory disrupts existing production and that workers must be trained to operate new equipment.

Installation costs explain why Tobin's q is not always equal to unity. In the absence of installation costs, firms would always set capital input to its optimal level, equating marginal productivity and marginal cost as in equation (8.5), rewritten as

$$\text{(8.13)} \qquad \frac{\text{MPK}}{1+r} = 1.$$

MPK/$(1 + r)$ is the present value of the return on investment. It is next period's return on the latest addition of capital discounted back to today.[15] It must be equal to the marginal cost of equipment, which is unity. When installation is costly, however, the cost of investing is not just the price of equipment. It now includes an additional cost, the marginal cost of installing new equipment, φ. It is assumed that φ is an increasing function of the investment undertaken, the faster you do it, the more expensive it is.[16] The optimal investment decision is to invest until the present value of the MPK of new equipment is equal to the augmented marginal cost of equipment:

$$\text{(8.14)} \qquad \frac{\text{MPK}}{1+r} = 1 + \varphi$$

Comparing (8.13) and (8.14), we see that installation costs raise the MPK required to justify the investment. This means that less capital is invested, more precisely that the firm takes small steps to reach the desired long-run capital stock $\overline{K}$, since marginal productivity is higher the lower is the stock of capital. Since installation costs increase with the amount of investment each period, the next round of installation is cheaper, φ is lower, so firms will engage in

---

[14] This section is a more advanced presentation of the q-theory of investment based on installation costs. It is similar to the reasoning used to establish the optimal stock of capital and can be skipped without any loss of continuity. The WebAppendix to this chapter presents a formal analysis.

[15] Remember, there are just two periods, so 'tomorrow' is a shorthand for the indefinite future. Otherwise we would have to discount all future MPKs.

[16] For example, the investment costs associated with a 10% increase in the capital stock could be four times the costs implied by a 5% increase.

Box 8.6   **User Cost of Capital, Tobin's *q*, and the Price of Investment Goods**

In Robinson Crusoe's world, coconuts were used for both consumption and investment. In the real world, investment and consumption goods have different prices. This complicates slightly, but does not invalidate, the main line of reasoning. Let us suppose that a coconut in the ground (investment) is identical to a coconut in the mouth (consumption), but in the second period, the tree can be sold for p^K in terms of the consumption good. Now, profit in units of the consumption good is

(8.16) $$\text{profit} = \frac{F(K)}{1+r} - (1-\delta)p^k K.$$

The optimal stock of capital will obey a modified version of (8.9) in Box 8.5:

$$MPK = (1+r) - (1-\delta)p^k$$

(8.17) $$= [(1+r) - (1-\delta)(1+\pi^k)] \approx r + \delta - \pi^k,$$

where $\pi^K = p^K - 1$ is the rate of price increase for investment goods.[17] The user cost concept of Box 8.5 allows for a changing relative price of investment goods over time. An increase in the real interest rate and depreciation lowers optimal investment, all things being equal. An increase in the rate of change of investment goods

prices *increases* it. Why? By selling his investment, Crusoe reduces the effective cost of using the capital goods in production. It is easy to see that any government policy that increases the resale value of the investment, including tax breaks, will similarly reduce the user cost of capital.

Similar to equation (8.12), a reasonable approximation of Tobin's *q* is

(8.18) $$q = \frac{MPK/(r + \delta - \pi^K)}{1}.$$

The only difference is that the extended version of Tobin's *q* now compares the present discounted value of the marginal product of capital with the value of new capital goods, the price of investment goods, which is equal to 1 in the first period.

Finally, if installation costs φ are paid for a marginal unit of investment, optimal investment must obey

(8.19) $$q = MPK/(r + \delta + \pi^K) = (1 + \varphi).$$

At any point in time, the marginal gain from an additional unit of capital equals the marginal costs of that new capital, which includes the installation costs of investment.

more investment, and so on until φ is driven down to zero and (8.13) holds. That way firms break the path towards $\overline{K}$ into small steps that entail smaller costs.

Installation costs and Tobin's q

The stock market should value the return on an additional unit of investment by the present value of its marginal return, MPK/(1 + r). In the case of Robinson Crusoe, the replacement cost of capital is simply the cost of coconuts (uninstalled equipment) which is 1. Tobin's *q* is therefore[18]

(8.15) $$q = \left(\frac{MPK}{1+r}\right)\Big/ 1.$$

Equation (8.15) establishes the link between the two investment principles. The optimal capital stock of capital is reached when (8.13) is satisfied, that is when Tobin's *q* is equal to 1. When *q* is above 1, the MPK exceeds 1 + *r*, and investment is warranted. When *q* is lower than 1, the MPK is low, given the replacement cost of physical capital. As new capital is put in place, the MPK declines, as does *q*. Investment becomes smaller and installation costs φ decline until they become negligible. At that stage *q* = 1, MPK = 1 + *r*, and the stock of capital is at its optimal level. Installation costs cause firms to move towards the optimal capital stock incrementally. Along the way the return on investment in present value terms

---

[17] The expression $(1 + r) - (1 - \delta)(1 + \pi^K) = r + \delta - \pi^K + \delta\pi^K$ is well approximated by $r + \delta - \pi^K$ for small values of *r*, δ, and π^K.

[18] We cheat a bit here. The definition of Tobin's *q* is based on the market value of firms, while what matters in theory is the *marginal* return on investment. The market value of firms depends on the *average* return on all capital, not just the latest addition. We overlook the difference between these two definitions of average and marginal *q*.

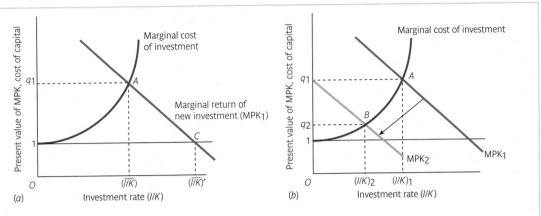

Fig. 8.14 Tobin's *q*

In panel (*a*) profits are maximized at point *A*, where the marginal return of investment in present-value terms is equal to its marginal cost. The marginal cost of capital is 1 (unit of forgone consumption). The optimum rate of investment is (*I/K*)'. Tobin's *q* corresponds to point *A*: it is the ratio of the marginal return on new investment to the cost of new capital. In the absence of installation costs (point *C*), the optimum rate of investment (*I/K*)' brings the capital stock immediately to its optimum level. In panel (*b*) investment starts at point *A* as before. With a higher stock of capital, the MPK then declines as represented by the shift from MPK_1 to MPK_2. With Tobin's *q* still above unity, investment continues but at the lower rate (*I/K*)$_2$. The process continues until *q* is equal to 1, and no further investment is warranted.

exceeds the replacement, or user, cost of capital.[19] Box 8.6 provides more details on both the user cost of capital and its relationship to Tobin's *q*.

The geometry of installation costs

Installation costs have two particular properties. First, they increase with the size of the investment. Big steps are proportionally more expensive than small ones. Second, they are transitory. Once the equipment is in place, the only relevant cost is the interest rate and depreciation—the opportunity cost of resources employed in production. Figure 8.14 modifies panel (*b*) of Figure 8.10 in two ways. First, investment is measured on the horizontal axis as the investment rate *I/K*, which gives a better indication of the intensity of disruptions which give rise to installation costs.[20] Second, on the vertical axis, marginal costs and returns are

expressed in today's present discounted values. The marginal cost of capital in present value is equal to 1, because one unit of capital implies giving up one unit of consumption good today.

The horizontal schedule represents the cost of investment in the absence of installation costs. With installation costs, the cost of investment exceeds the cost of capital. The more equipment is put in place, the higher is the marginal cost. Hence the upward-sloping marginal cost of investment curve. The marginal return on investment is MPK/(1 + *r*). It is downward sloping because of the principle of declining marginal productivity.

Firms invest until the marginal cost equals the marginal return at point *A* in panel (*a*) of Figure 8.14, where the two curves intersect. The value of an additional unit of capital installed—Tobin's *q*—exceeds the replacement cost of capital. Without installation costs, the firm would choose point *C* instead and invest more. It may be surprising that the marginal return is higher with installation costs than without them. Rather than reducing the long-term profitability of investment, installation costs simply induce firms to invest at a slower rate. In the long run, firms achieve the same desired capital stock as in the absence of adjustment costs.

[19] A related approach, pioneered by Professors Finn Kydland of University of California, Santa Barbara and Edward Prescott of University of Arizona, both Nobel Prize laureates, stresses that it takes time to design, acquire, and put in place new equipment. The implications are similar to those of installation costs.

[20] In the absence of depreciation, $I/K = \Delta K/K$. Focusing on the investment rate is justified by the idea that a given amount of investment is more disruptive in a small firm (or economy) than in a large one.

Panel (b) of Figure 8.14 shows how the investment rate moves over time. With q above 1, investment first occurs at rate $(I/K)_1$ corresponding to point A. Each MPK schedule is drawn for a given stock of already installed capital. Moving along the schedule, we find the profitability of further additions to the existing capital stock. Once the capital stock has increased as a result of investment, however, these additions become less productive– a direct result of the principle of declining marginal productivity. So, as further investment accumulates, the MPK schedule shifts downwards in the figure, from MPK_1 to MPK_2.[21] Investment will continue as long as Tobin's q is greater than unity, but will do so at a declining rate, here at rate $(I/K)_2$ corresponding to point B. The process will continue until q is driven back down to 1 and the capital stock has reached its long-run, optimal level.

8.3.6 The Investment Function

The investment function summarizes all the macroeconomic relationships that have been developed until now in a convenient and compact way. First, investment is inversely related to the interest rate because it measures the opportunity cost of the resources invested. Higher interest rates imply lower investment spending. Second, the accelerator mechanism captures the stable long-run relationship between the capital stock and output. Since the rate of proportionality is greater than 1, increases in output lead to magnified increases in investment expenditures. Finally, Tobin's q reflects the fact that some firms finance investment expenditures by issuing shares on the stock market. High stock prices mean that the market places a high value on existing, installed capital, so firms can raise more resources per share issued, and this encourages investment. They provide a central indicator of the market's assessment of the profitability of new investment. Because a higher interest rate discounts future profits more heavily and reduces q. Tobin's q also incorporates some but not all of the effect of real interest rates on investment (for firms that raise money by issuing bonds or borrowing from banks, it is the interest rate alone that represents the cost of investment). These results can be summarized by the following investment function, which will be used in various forms throughout the book:

$$\textbf{(8.20)} \qquad I = I(r, \Delta Y, q).$$
$$\phantom{\textbf{(8.20)} \qquad I = I(} - \; + \; +$$

This function states that investment depends negatively on the real interest rate r, positively on the change in GDP, and positively on Tobin's q.[22] Holding interest rates constant, an increase in Tobin's q increases investment.

! Summary

1 Rational consumers attempt to smooth consumption over time, borrowing in bad years, saving in good ones. Consumption is driven primarily by wealth, the present discounted value of current and future incomes, and initial net asset holdings. Over a life cycle, income typically increases. To smooth out consumption, agents typically borrow when young and pay back later.

2 Individual consumption smoothing means that, in the aggregate, temporary disturbances are met by current account imbalances (national saving or dissaving) to reduce the need to adjust consumption abruptly. In contrast, permanent

---

[21] The observant student will note that for linear marginal product and marginal cost schedules and in the absence of depreciation, the intercept of each successive MPK curve with the vertical axis is determined by the value of q in the preceding period.

[22] In theory, Tobin's q should contain all information necessary about the profitability of investment. Since many firms finance investment with retained earnings or by borrowing, the interest rate also matters directly. In addition, as with households, many firms are rationed on the credit market, so they have to rely upon current income to finance spending on productive equipment. This would rationalize a third term related to the discussion of the accelerator in Section 8.3.3.

disturbances lead to immediate consumption adjustment rather than to borrowing or lending.

3 The world is uncertain and financial markets are imperfect. Uncertainty about future incomes and the inability of banks to assess individual future prospects without error will make it difficult if not impossible for some households to borrow against future expected income. For these households, current disposable income also affects aggregate consumption.

4 The effect of changes in the real interest rate on current consumption is ambiguous. Lenders tend to increase, while borrowers decrease, consumption in response to increases in the interest rate. In the aggregate, however, higher interest rates are likely to reduce consumption by reducing wealth.

5 The consumption function relates aggregate consumption to wealth (positively) and disposable income (positively).

6 The optimal capital stock equates the marginal productivity of capital to the marginal cost of capital. The optimal capital stock increases when the real interest rate declines and when technological gains raise the marginal productivity of capital.

7 Investment over and above capital depreciation increases the capital stock. As is the case with the optimal capital stock, investment is driven by the real interest rate.

8 The accelerator mechanism links investment to changes in output. This is both a mechanical relationship (in the long run the capital-output ratio is constant) as well as a symptom of credit rationing for some firms, which then react sensitively to their own current cash flow.

9 The ratio of the market value of installed capital to the replacement cost of installed capital is called Tobin's q. It is an approximation of the ratio of the present discounted value of the marginal return of investment to the marginal cost of capital. This ratio is equal to unity when the capital stock has reached its optimal level. When Tobin's q is larger than unity, the capital stock is below its optimal level and firms benefit from further investment.

10 The market value of installed capital, the numerator in Tobin's q, is determined in the stock market. In setting this price, stock markets look ahead. The forward-looking nature of Tobin's q mirrors how firms take into account expected future earnings when they make investment decisions.

11 Because of various installation costs, firms do not acquire their optimal capital stock immediately. Rather, they spread investment over time, gradually bringing capital up to the optimal level.

12 The present discounted return to investment exceeds the marginal cost of capital to compensate for installation costs. Investment proceeds until the present value of its return, at the margin, equals the marginal cost of investment, the sum of borrowing and installation costs.

13 The investment function states that aggregate investment depends upon: (1) the real interest rate (negatively); (2) GDP growth (positively); (3) Tobin's q (positively).

⊙ Key Concepts

- **consumption function**
- **investment function**
- **indifference curves**
- **utility**
- **marginal rate of intertemporal substitution**
- **life-cycle consumption**

- **permanent income**
- **random walk**
- **consumption smoothing**
- **credit rationed**
- **marginal productivity of capital (MPK)**
- **opportunity cost**

- ◆ marginal cost of capital
- ◆ optimal capital stock
- ◆ rate of depreciation
- ◆ user cost of capital
- ◆ accelerator principle

- ◆ Tobin's q
- ◆ q-theory of investment
- ◆ animal spirits
- ◆ installation costs

❓ Exercises

1 A household has income of £10,000 today and £50,000 tomorrow.

(a) If the real interest rate is 5%, what is its wealth (i) in terms of today's consumption, (ii) in terms of tomorrow's consumption? Compute the household's permanent income (see Box 8.2).

(b) If today's income unexpectedly increases by £1,000, what is the change in permanent income?

(c) If income goes up by £1,000 permanently (in both periods), what is the effect on permanent income?

(d) Now answer the same questions with a 10% real interest rate.

(e) Suppose the utility of the household is given by $\log(C_1) + \beta\log(C_2)$, where β is a positive constant less than 1. Derive optimal consumption today and tomorrow for (a), (b), (c), and (d).

2 Show, graphically, the effects on current and future consumption of an income windfall gain expected in the future. Now apply this reasoning to the national level. How should a consumer react to a tax cut that is announced to be temporary (in period 1 only)? How would consumers react to an expected future tax cut?

3 Define the permanent income hypothesis. How does it relate to the more general theory of consumption under intertemporal utility maximization?

4 Suppose you expect to live for six decades. Your income is €15,000 in the first, €100,000 in the second, €150,000 in the third, €250,000 in the fourth, €200,000 in the fifth, and €100,000 in the last. What is your permanent income if the interest rate

is 3%? 5%? If you consume your permanent income each year, what does your savings pattern look like? How does your answer change if you decide to bequeath €50,000 to your favourite charity?

5 There is evidence that spending on durable goods drops faster than spending on non-durables during a recession. Can you give some economic reasons why? (Hint: think of durable goods expenditure as a form of saving.)

6 A company is considering expanding its computer equipment today by €50,000. Suppose the interest rate used in discounting future profit is 10%, and suppose that the equipment is scrapped after one period.

(a) If the new investment generates €60,000 of profit, should the company undertake the investment? How does your answer change if the firm only expects to earn €54,000?

(b) Now suppose the equipment can be sold on the resale market for €15,000. How does your answer change? Discuss how the emergence of a more efficient resale market (eBay, etc.) could increase investment.

7 Governments sometimes try to stimulate the economy by offering firms a temporary tax credit. Firms that purchase capital goods before a deadline receive a tax reduction on income made in the next year. Explain why this measure should increase expenditures on investment. Would you expect a permanent or a temporary measure to have more effect?

8 Suppose a firm produces Y_2 output in period 2 using the production function $Y_2 = A\log(K_1)$, where K_1 is the capital in place in period 1. Suppose the firm has no outlays besides K_1, the price of output is given at p_2, and that $(1 - \delta)$ of the capital can be resold for p_2^K per unit. Future outlays and revenues are discounted at rate r.

(a) Write down a mathematical expression for the profits of the firm. How do profits depend on p_2? On p_2^K? On δ? On r? On A? On K_1? Use informal arguments, a spreadsheet, or calculus to explain your answer.

(b) Use calculus to find the optimal stock of capital K_1 as function of p_2, p_2^K, δ, r, and A.

(c) Now suppose the same firm can instead *rent* capital at rate U for one period, after which the capital must be returned to the rental agency. Write down a mathematical expression for the profits of the firm. At what point should the firm be indifferent between renting and 'owning' the capital it uses?

9 Should a temporary increase in taxes to finance a temporary increase in public spending reduce the current account deficit? What about a permanent increase in both taxes and public spending? What is the effect on the current account in an open economy?

10 It is sometimes argued that the Eurozone crisis is related to the mismanaged boom in spending and investment that followed the adoption of the euro. How can you explain this boom and what do you expect the effect to be on the (primary) current account? (Hint: think of the impact on the interest rate, on private wealth and on stock prices.)

11 Over the next 10 or 20 years, Greece, Portugal and many other European countries will have to raise taxes to reduce their public debts. What does this means for consumption, now and over the future?

12 In Ireland, Spain and the UK, housing prices increased considerably over the 2000s, until they fell abruptly starting in 2008. Is there any reason why consumption should be affected?

→ Essay Questions

1 A great deal of debate has arisen in Germany on the financing of the expenditure necessary to improve the much-neglected infrastructure in its new eastern states. One side favours increased taxes, which would fall largely on households. The other side favours an increased budget deficit. Which side is right? How important is it to know whether the spending increase is permanent or temporary?

2 Should wars—temporarily but abnormally high expenditures of the government—depress or raise consumption of households? In formulating your answer, think about all the budget constraints discussed in Chapter 7.

3 Over the past 20 years the price of computers and software—an essential investment good for modern companies—has dropped steadily. At the same time, the rapid rate of technical change has increased the rate of obsolescence of equipment and programs. In addition, the development of new service companies has made it easier to install and employ these new innovations. Explain, carefully, using the concepts you have learned, how these developments should affect the user cost of capital, Tobin's q, and investment.

4 The public debt crisis forces some countries to precipitously cut their budget deficits because governments cannot borrow any more. Most raise taxes on households and firms, which are taxpayers. Some economists argue that this is a self-defeating strategy. What is your view?

5 Booming economies frequently show negative current account balances. International organizations like the International Monetary Fund often must judge whether a current deficit is 'good' or 'bad'. Explain what this might mean or imply. Use your answer to interpret the case of Poland: in the period 2003–2007 Poland grew 5.1% per annum, as compared to 2.4% in the EU. During this period the current account deficit was 2.6% of GDP, declining from an average deficit of 4.6% of GDP in the period 1998–2002.

Money and Monetary Policy 9

The invention of a circulating medium, which supersedes the narrow, cumbrous process of barter, by facilitating transactions of every variety of importance among all sorts of people, is a grand type of advance in civilization.

Chambers *Encyclopedia*, 1870

First of all let me state the simple fact that when you deposit money in a bank, the bank does not put the money into a safe deposit vault. It invests your money in many different forms of credit—bonds, commercial paper, mortgages and many other kinds of loans. In other words, the bank puts your money to work to keep the wheels of industry and of agriculture turning around. A comparatively small part of the money you put into the bank is kept in currency—an amount which in normal times is wholly sufficient to cover the cash needs of the average citizen. In other words the total amount of all the currency in the country is only a comparatively small proportion of the total deposits in all of the banks.

Franklin D. Roosevelt[1]

9.1 Overview

We have already encountered money in Chapter 6, when we established the neutrality principle, but we never really explained what money is, who makes it, how, and for what purpose. This is what the present chapter does. It seems strange to have to explain something that we use every day, yet it is surprising how little most people understand what it is. Seventy-five years ago, in the wake of a national banking panic, US President Roosevelt was forced to explain to nervous American citizens how a bank works and why they shouldn't withdraw their money all at once from their accounts. Then, as now, the system of money and banking is rather complicated, and is in a state of constant change.

Virtually every civilization has used one form of money or another, and money has been at the centre of attention in civilizations since the beginning of recorded history. Money is a form of wealth but it has a number of special qualities. Its return is typically very low—banknotes yield no interest at all—and yet it is perceived as desirable. The reason is that money uniquely facilitates commercial transactions, big and small alike. As a result, it lies at the heart of any economy.

We will start by defining money. We will then look at the supply of money and introduce an important institution with great influence over the supply of money: the central bank. The next step is to study the demand for money. When this is done, we will be equipped to see how demand and supply are equilibrated in the money market, and how that market works. This will take us straight to a detailed study of **monetary policy**, the way the central bank sets the interest rate or other conditions in the money market. Monetary policy affects the daily economic life of everyone in many ways. We will see that the practice of monetary policy has evolved over the years, marked sometimes by great progress, other times by adverse setbacks. In developed countries, the current conventional wisdom argues for a strategy called inflation targeting. Having thus mastered the basics of modern monetary policy, we conclude the chapter with a discussion of why banking is risky, why it crucially matters for the economy, what can be done to avert financial crises, and what to do when they occur.

---

[1] US President Franklin D. Roosevelt, in a national radio address on 12 March 1933, see <http://millercenter.org/scripps/archive/speeches/detail/3298>.

9.2 Money: What is it? Who Makes it?

9.2.1 Definitions of Money

Most of us would agree that banknotes and coins are money. But what about bank account balances? Travellers' cheques? Savings accounts? Other financial instruments? These are all various forms of money, most of which have been invented fairly recently. Once upon a time, gold, silver, and other commodities were used as money in the form of coins, sometimes bulky ingots. Slowly but surely, paper money (banknotes) have edged out these **commodity monies**. Paper money backed by commodity money became the dominant form of money by the end of the nineteenth century. In the beginning of the twentieth century, central banks began issuing paper money and coins that were not backed by any precious metal. Devoid of any intrinsic value, **fiat money**—from the Latin word '*fiat*' meaning 'let it be done'—is legal tender simply because of the government decision. Money changed again with the widespread use of sight deposits (bank accounts that are payable on demand, often called demand deposits or current accounts) or with plastic cards that give more rapid and secure access to money.

A century or so ago, there were doubts whether paper money could ever be as trustworthy as coins made from precious metals. Today, we use it to pay for whatever we want to buy without really wondering about its lack of intrinsic value. As a matter of fact, we use fewer and fewer notes and coins, relying instead on plastic cards and cheques, both of which are debited from our bank accounts, as well as on internet transfers at our home computers or smartphones.

Most of us see little distinction between coins, banknotes, and bank deposits, and treat them as highly substitutable for each other in transactions. This is a rationale for our first definition of money: currency in circulation plus sight deposits. This **monetary aggregate** is denominated as M1:

$$M1 = \text{currency in circulation} + \text{sight bank deposits.}$$

Sight deposits at banks have three main characteristics: (1) they may be converted into cash on demand at the issuing bank, (2) cheques can be written or bank transfers can be made against them, and (3) the interest paid is either nil or very low. They are convenient for everyday purchases, but not very attractive from the point of view of interest. This is why banks often offer other types of accounts that bear higher interest rates, but whose funds cannot be used as easily as normal money—i.e. by writing cheques or stopping at a cash dispenser. Yet such funds can often be conveniently transferred into regular sight deposits—often a phone call, a series of keystrokes on a telephone handset, or an internet connection is enough. Ease of transfer renders these assets very similar to sight deposits in the eyes of their holders. This is why they are included in a broader definition of money, M2:

$$M2 = M1 + \text{time (or savings) deposits at banks}$$
$$\text{with unrestricted access.}$$

An even broader measure includes instruments such as large certificates of deposit, or time deposits with a longer term and possibly restricted access, foreign currency deposits, and deposits with non-bank institutions. The precise meaning of 'larger' and 'longer maturity' depends on national rules and regulations. The distinction is one of degree: these instruments are less liquid, meaning that they are more costly or difficult to convert into cash or current accounts. Thus the definition of M3:

$$M3 = M2 + \text{larger, fixed-term deposits}$$
$$+ \text{accounts at non-bank institutions.}$$

M1 is perfectly liquid, meaning that it can be used for commercial transactions, unlike the other components of M2 and M3, which must generally be converted into M1 for that purpose.

Every country has its own practices and its own definitions of monetary aggregates. While not fully comparable, the examples in Table 9.1—M0 is explained later—show that, in the UK, people use less cash than on the continent and in the USA, but that the other monetary aggregates are proportionally larger—a

Table 9.1 Money in Three Countries, 2011

		Currency	M0	M1	M2	M3
UK	(£ bn)	53.9	60.7	1084.3	2038.8	2278.7
	as % of GDP	3.6	4.0	71.9	135.2	151.1
Euro area	(€ bn)	843.2	1335.3	4785.8	8590.6	9740.3
	as % of GDP	9.0	14.2	50.8	91.2	103.5
USA	($ bn)	1068.5	2647.6	2222.8	9744.3	
	as % of GDP	7.1	17.5	14.7	64.6	
Poland	(Zl bn)	101.8	138.1	468.0	863.8	881.5
	as % of GDP	6.7	9.1	30.7	56.7	57.9

Notes: The USA no longer publishes M3 figures.
Source: IMF, OECD, central banks' bulletins.

sign of more sophisticated retail banking. Indeed, in Poland, the difference between M2 and M3 is small, suggesting that customers do not yet have access to higher-yield bank deposits.

The pace of technological development in banking has revolutionized the definition of money over the past century, yet more change is possibly in store. Many believe we are not far from the limit of this process, a cashless society that the Swedish economist Knut Wicksell once imagined and which is described in Box 9.1. From now on, we will refer to money without being specific about its definition, calling it simply M and thinking of it as:

M = currency in circulation + bank deposits.

9.2.2 The Money Makers: Central and Commercial Banks

Table 9.1 shows that currency (coins and banknotes) is only a small fraction of what we call money, regard-

Box 9.1 The Vision of Wicksell: A Cashless Society

Once upon a time, money was gold or silver, or seashells, or large stones on South Pacific islands. Such commodity money has an intrinsic value, since it is made of goods that can be used for other purposes. These goods are 'wasted' when used as money, and this is one reason why paper and cheap metal have replaced silver or gold. A century ago, the Swedish economist Knut Wicksell (1851–1926) went further. He asked: Why have money at all? He envisioned a central record keeper who would keep a tally of all credits and debits. Whenever an individual worked, his balance would be credited; whenever he spent, the balance would be debited. In principle, it would be possible to run a negative balance, i.e. to borrow from the system. In the end, instead of producing currency, the central bank would

operate and guarantee this record-keeping system and determine the value of the unit of account.

At the time, Wicksell's moneyless society was dismissed as impractical science fiction. A century later, the technical problems of establishing such a 'moneyless society' have been largely solved. Large powerful computers can keep accurate, up-to-date records and investigate the creditworthiness of households and businesses. The year 2003 was a watershed. For the first time, US consumers paid more for goods and services using credit and debit cards than with cheques or cash. A number of experiments are being run to test for payment systems that could eliminate currency completely. Similar increases are expected soon in Europe, especially in France and the UK, where credit and debit cards are commonplace.

less of the definition we use. Bank deposits make up the rest. This part of what we call money is produced by the monetary authorities—the central bank and/or the Treasury—while the bigger part, bank deposits, is created by commercial banks.

Can it be that most of what we routinely consider money is actually created by private institutions? The answer is yes. Most of modern money, often seen as a symbol of statehood, is not directly produced by the government. But then, can banks create money as they wish? Ultimately the answer is no. Banks do create money but under the control and supervision of the central bank. This is what we now examine.

Central banks

The central bank is a public or quasi-public agency with an explicit, exclusive legal mandate to control money and credit conditions.[2] It is also the 'bankers' bank'. Commercial banks—in some countries, the largest ones only—hold their own accounts at the central bank. They can use these accounts to settle payments against other commercial banks, for example, when customers transfer funds from one bank to another. Central banks generally do not take deposits from the private sector, but most serve as their respective government's bank.

Central banks produce two sorts of monies. They issue currency (sometimes, this is done on its behalf by the Treasury) and, as we will see, they also create **bank reserves**, the deposits held by commercial banks at the central bank. The sum of currency in circulation and commercial bank reserves is known as the **monetary base**, sometimes called M0.[3] Table 9.1 shows that M0 is not much larger than the

amount of currency in circulation, implying that the reserves of commercial banks are relatively small. Yet, these reserves are the tool through which central banks control money creation by commercial banks.

Commercial banks

Traditionally, commercial banks collect funds from depositors and make loans to borrowing customers. In effect, they channel money from depositors to borrowers. This is why they are also called **financial intermediaries**. Over recent years, banks have taken on additional functions, like managing portfolios on behalf of their customers, providing insurance, or even trading financial assets on their own account, but we will ignore these activities. Box 9.2 explains how these other activities contributed to the gravity of the financial crisis that started in 2007.

When you deposit money in your bank as a sight deposit, you may think that your money is there, waiting for you to withdraw or spend it whenever you fancy to do so. Reality is very different. Most likely, the money that you have deposited was promptly lent to one of the bank's many customers. For the bank, your deposit is a liability of immediate or short maturity. It is due immediately if it is a sight deposit, or soon, say three months or one year. The bank may lend to people who buy cars or houses, or to firms that buy inventories, raw materials, or wages, which can be paid back over several years. These loans are the bank's assets, and they tend to be of much longer maturity than its liabilities. The practice of taking on short-term liabilities and using them to acquire long-term assets is called **maturity transformation**. It is the *raison d'être* of banks but is a fundamentally risky activity. Banking is inherently risky and this is why banks are regulated.

To see why, it is useful to present a snapshot of the state of a bank's financial operations, its **balance sheet**. The balance sheet is a summary statement of what the bank owns—its assets—and what it owes—its liabilities. Figure 9.1 gives a simplified version of the balance sheet of a typical bank. The balance sheet shows that the primary liability is the deposits of its customers. Additionally, the bank may have borrowed from the central bank. On the asset side, a commercial bank keeps some cash in its vaults or as a deposit with the central bank. It also holds various

---

[2] The Bank of England was a private institution from its founding in 1694 until its nationalization in 1946, much like the Banque de France, founded in 1800 and nationalized in 1945. The Bundesbank was established in 1949 as a successor to the Deutsche Reichsbank founded in 1876. The oldest central bank is the Swedish Riksbank, founded in 1668. Other dates of foundation are: Bank of Japan, 1882; Banca d'Italia, 1893; Austrian National Bank, 1816; Swiss National Bank, 1905. The Federal Reserve of the USA was founded in 1913 and is owned by the member banks, although profits above a statutory maximum are remitted, as in most countries, to the government (Goodhart 1988).

[3] Other expressions used are 'high-powered', 'base money', or 'central bank money'.

Box 9.2 Shadow Banking vs. the Volcker Rule

When the Wall Street investment bank Lehman Brothers collapsed in September 2008, policy-makers were shocked to discover how much banking had changed in two decades following widespread deregulation. In fact, banks had transformed themselves from their traditional role—described in this chapter—into complex, interlocking financial institutions. Alongside traditional deposit-taking and lending activities, banks have become increasingly involved in a variety of risky transactions, including complex trades on their own account ('proprietary trading'). Often banks use, legally or illegally, the deposits of their customers. While such activities are undoubtedly profitable, they can easily go south, leading to large losses for the bank. A bad deal—or even rumours of one—can ruin a financial institution, destroying the deposits of customers who entrusted their money with little or no clue of such risky deals. For this reason, banks are required to hold sufficient capital (that is money invested by bank shareholders) to absorb losses due to these activities. That capital, loosely speaking, is the 'net worth' of a bank in Figure 9.1. The idea is that shareholders are first in line to absorb a bank's losses but, as long as some capital is left, the bank is solvent and the deposits are not threatened.

In good years, profits are distributed to the shareholders in proportion to their ownership stakes in the bank. Their total investment in the bank is, roughly speaking, equal to the bank's capital, its net worth. It stands to reason that the larger the capital base, the less profit that is available for each pound or euro of capital, so shareholders generally prefer that their banks hold less capital. Banks are competing with other financial institutions for owners in the market and usually oblige. Bank capital regulations are designed to make sure that banks have sufficient capital to serve the shock absorber function mentioned here. In earlier times, banks were simply forbidden to engage in risky lending financial dealings.[4]

Current bank regulations, such as Basel I or Basel II, penalise risk—to the extent that bank regulators can detect it. Riskier investments must be 'backed up' by more capital. For example a bank loan to a tourist concern to build a hotel would be riskier than, say buying an AAA-rated government bond. Naturally, banks see capital regulations as a nuisance, and as a rule try to evade them. One trick was to 'hide' very risky investments by creating legal subsidiaries—called Special Purpose Vehicles or SPVs—that held the riskiest assets away from the eyes of bank supervisors, often offshore on some foreign, unregulated island. These SPVs are part of what is called shadow banking. (Hedge funds, discussed later, are another part of shadow banking.) When the crisis hit, many risky SPVs went bankrupt and the banks themselves had to refinance them or absorb their losses. All of sudden, the riskiest assets were visible for all to see.

The crisis of 2007–8 showed that most large banks had massively expanded trading on own accounts and faced equally massive losses. Most developed countries are preparing regulation that limits or forbids shadow banking and proprietary trading. Advising President Obama, Former Federal Reserve Chairman Paul Volcker wrote that 'adding further layers of risk to the inherent risks of essential commercial bank functions doesn't make sense, not when those risks arise from more speculative activities far better suited for other areas of the financial markets' (*New York Times*, 30 January 2010). His proposal, called the **Volker Rule**, was incorporated in US bank regulation, due to take effect in 2012. It explicitly prohibits proprietary trading and other risky activities by commercial banks. Needless to say, banks vigorously resist and lobby against such legislation.

---

securities that can be traded on financial markets. Its main activity, however, is to make loans. These loans are assets since its customers owe them to the bank. The excess of assets over liabilities is the bank's net worth. It shows up as a liability since the bank owes it to its owners, typically shareholders.

[4] In the United States, the Glass–Steagall Act of 1933 was a reaction to pre-Depression abuses, in which banks invested customers' deposits in the stock market, often combined with borrowed funds. This law lasted until 1999, when—after intense pressure by Wall Street financial institutions—the US Congress rescinded it. The abolition of the Glass–Steagall Act added much fuel to the housing boom and ultimately the financial crisis in the United States. Some things never seem to change!

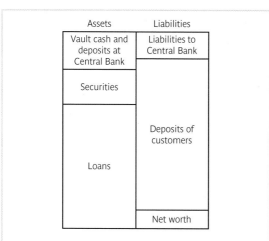

Fig. 9.1 Balance Sheet of a Commercial Bank

To see why maturity transformation can be risky business, imagine that all customers of a bank wanted suddenly to withdraw all the money that they had deposited. Since most of the money has been lent out, it is no longer in the bank (recall the radio address of US President Roosevelt at the beginning of this chapter!). Yet those deposits are means of payment, and represent perfect substitutes for cash; banks are legally obligated to convert these deposits on demand into currency. A mass conversion of deposits to currency at short notice would be impossible. Such **bank runs** or **bank failures** are unlikely events and usually driven by widespread panic: the afflicted bank is unable to meet its obligations and it must close, leaving angry customers pounding at the door.[5] Risk of bank runs is another reason for bank regulation and supervision by governmental authorities. We will encounter some of these regulations later on in this chapter.

9.2.3 Money Creation by Commercial Banks

An even more interesting and less well-understood fact about banks is that they actually *create* money

when they grant loans—when they create credit. To see why, consider the case of Ms A who receives €1,000 in cash from abroad and deposits it in her bank, Bank No. 1.[6] Looking for a profitable use for these funds, Bank No. 1 lends this money as soon as possible to Mr B, another trustworthy customer. Mr B needs the money to buy a sofa. Soon enough, the €1,000, initially deposited by Ms A, will be handed over to the store that sold the sofa to Mr B. The shopkeeper now owns this €1,000. Ms A too owns €1,000. As far as she is concerned, her money is in the bank. In fact, she owns a deposit in her bank which is backed by a loan in the amount of €1,000, but the €1,000 in currency is long gone. Effectively, the €1,000 now has two owners: Ms A and Mr B!

And the story is not over. The sofa storeowner will deposit the money in his own account at Bank No. 2, which will quickly lend it to Ms C, who will spend it to buy a laptop for her business. The computer store will rightfully think that it possesses an additional €1,000—because it does! There is no reason to stop here, of course. The conclusion is that each loan amounts to the creation of new credit and money, and that the process can seemingly go on and on. But it will end.

To see why the process of credit and money creation does in fact stop, imagine that Ms A wants to withdraw her money from the bank, say to take a vacation abroad. Will Bank No. 1 admit to her that the money is gone and will only be back in two years' time? Of course not! A natural part of the banking business is to anticipate this possibility; Bank No. 1 will have planned for it. Note first that someone down the chain is likely to be a Bank No. 1 customer, so that at least some of the initial €1,000 will come back. If Bank No. 1 were the only bank in the country and if people never held currency, the money would always come back. In practice, because there are many other banks and because people keep some money in cash, Bank No. 1 knows that it cannot rely on returning monies to pay back Ms A. But the bank also has many other customers and it knows that they tend to keep a big part of the sums that they deposit on their accounts for a long time. On average,

---

[5] The spectacular failure of Northern Rock bank in the autumn of 2007 in the UK is a recent example of a bank run. Bank runs are rare events in most countries—before that, the last one in the UK took place more than 140 years ago. Bank runs will be examined in more detail in Section 9.5.

[6] The money could also come from under her mattress, or a treasure chest. The important fact is that it represents an injection of cash (currency) from outside the banking system.

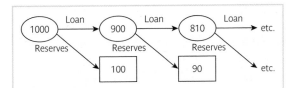

Fig. 9.2 The Money Multiplier

An initial deposit triggers a succession of loans, paid in the form of deposits. When the bank keeps 10% of any deposit as reserves (cash or deposit at the central bank), each loan is 90% of the previous one. Thus the chain of loans and deposits eventually dies out.

Ms A is not expected to withdraw all of the money that she initially deposited.

Precisely for this reason, modern banking is often called a 'fractional reserve banking system'. If the bank figures out that, say, only 10% of the sums deposited will be withdrawn at any point in time, all it needs to do is to keep 10% of its deposits in reserves, and can lend out the rest. In the case of Ms A's deposit, the bank will keep €100 in cash and lend the remaining €900. In that case, the initial amount of money created is only €900. After it is deposited in Bank No. 2, a new loan of €810 (this is €900 less 10%), will be arranged, and the process will go on as shown in Figure 9.2. At each step, the amount of newly created money declines by 10%. After a while, it will have become tiny. This is why the money creation process is not infinite. A little bit of algebra tells us that the initial €1,000 will lead to a succession of loans that add up to €9,000:[7]

$$€900 + €810 + €729 + €656.1 + \ldots = €9,000$$

There is another side to this story. Bank No. 1 received €1,000 and put aside €100, Bank No. 2 received €900 and put aside €90, Bank No. 3 received €729 and put aside €72.9, etc. Jointly, all banks put aside €1,000.[8] In the end, the initial €1,000 has led to a series of loans for a total of €9,000 and to the setting aside of

€1,000. It all worked as if the €1,000 were fully set aside (more cash in the vaults) by the banking system taken together to support the creation of new money for a total of €9,000 (shown in the asset side in Figure 9.1). On the liability side, deposits increased by €10,000 as well: the initial €1,000 deposit and the €9,000 loans which have been credited to customers' accounts.

This chain of money and credit creation is known as the **money multiplier** process. It says that any time new money is injected in the economy—in the example we assumed that the initial €1,000 came from abroad—the result is an increase in money stock which is a multiple of that initial increase. This process explains two fundamental characteristics of modern fiat money systems. First, as we just saw, money is created by private commercial banks as they make loans to customers who want to borrow. Second, as we explain in the next section, central banks can still control the size of the money stock if they wish to.

The new money is created 'at the stroke of a pen'—this old-fashioned expression is better described as a series of keystrokes in the bank's computerized accounting systems. Effectively, the money is 'backed' by trust in the banks—trust in the underlying value of the loans and securities on the asset side of the banks' balance sheets. Money only has value as long as those assets have adequate value.

Deposits, bank liabilities that represent the largest component of money, are guaranteed by bank assets. Cash and securities are generally considered safe. Loans in contrast are as good as the borrowing customers' willingness and ability to repay. They are not fully safe. To cushion against the risk that loans might lose value, banks' owners are required to maintain a minimum amount of capital (net worth) in their balance sheets. These so-called Basel rules impose minimal **capital adequacy** (see Box 9.2). When the value of loans declines on the asset side, the net worth can decline on the liability side without fully disappearing. If it did, the bank would effectively be bankrupt.

9.2.4 Central Bank Control of the Money Supply

In the previous example, commercial banks set aside 10% of any money deposited on their customers'

---

[7] If a proportion p is lent at each step, the sum of all loans made is $1{,}000p + 1{,}000p^2 + 1{,}000p^3 + \cdots = 1{,}000p(1 + p + p^2 + p^3 + \cdots) = 1{,}000p/(1 - p)$. If $p = 0.9$, we find indeed 9,000.

[8] Continuing to denote the proportion that is lent at each step by p, the amounts put aside are $1{,}000(1 - p) + 1{,}000p(1 - p) + 1{,}000p^2(1 - p) + \cdots = 1{,}000(1 - p)(1 + p + p^2 + \cdots) = 1{,}000(1 - p)/(1 - p) = 1{,}000$.

Table 9.2 Reserve Ratio Requirements in Selected Countries

Country	Deposits subject to reserve requirements	Compulsory reserve ratio requirement
Denmark	Short-term (one month) liabilities	15%
	Total liabilities	10%
Czech Republic	Deposits of less than 2 years maturity	2%
Euro area	Deposits up to 2 years maturity	2%*
Hungary	All deposits	5%
Poland	All deposits	3.5%
Sweden	None	
Switzerland	None	
UK	None	
USA	'Transaction accounts' in excess of $44m	10%

(*) The ratio has been temporarily reduced to 1% in December 2011.

accounts. Presumably, they kept it in the form of cash—which often requires an expensive and secure (robber-proof) vault. The more convenient alternative to this is to deposit these amounts with the central bank. Much like households and firms hold sight-deposit accounts at commercial banks, commercial banks also hold—usually if they are large enough—sight-deposit accounts at their central banks. They can draw on these accounts to receive cash. In effect, these are two equivalent forms of commercial bank **reserves**.

$$\text{Commercial bank reserves} = \text{cash held in bank vaults} + \text{bank deposits at the central bank}.$$

Together with the amount of currency in circulation, the bank reserves constitute the monetary base M0:

monetary base M0 = currency in circulation
                 + commercial bank reserves.

The proportion of deposits set aside in the form of bank reserves is called the **reserve ratio**.[9] In the previous discussion, we presented the reserve ratio as a prudential measure taken by banks to be able to pay out requests of withdrawals by customers. In some countries, banks are free to choose their reserve

ratios; in others, the reserve ratio is imposed by the central bank. Table 9.2 provides some examples.

In the previous example, the initial bank deposit by Ms A came from abroad. This happens, of course, much as some domestic currency is sent abroad (we will examine the implications of this in Chapter 11). Most of the time, however, new money is created domestically. The story starts when Mr D requests a loan of, say, €1,000 from his bank. When the bank grants the loan to Mr D, it credits his account with €1,000. As before, money is created by banks hand-in-hand with lending activities. The only hitch is that the new loan, hence the new deposit, immediately raises the amount of reserves that the bank wants or needs to hold. If the reserve ratio is 10%, the bank must find an additional amount of reserves of €100. It may have these extra reserves at hand, but most likely, it will not. Banks have an incentive to lend as much as they can while holding as few reserves as they must. This is where the reserve ratio kicks in. Whether it is imposed by law or simply chosen for prudential purposes, the reserve ratio rr implies that reserves must be at least a fraction of deposits, which can be formally stated as follows:

(9.1)   reserves $\geq rr \times$ deposits.

Since banks have an incentive to hold exactly the amount of reserves that they need, not more, as a

---

[9] In some countries, it is called the liquidity requirement.

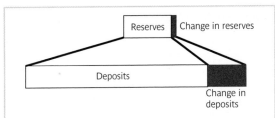

Fig. 9.3 The Reserves – Money Stock Link

When reserves are a constant proportion (*rr*) of deposits (*R = rrD*), deposits cannot grow without an increase in reserves. Conversely, a change in reserves *DR* allows banks to increase their deposits—by granting loans—in much larger amounts. The reserve multiplier is the inverse of the reserve ratio.

first approximation, the inequality can be thought of an equality:

(9.1') $\text{reserves} = rr \times \text{deposits}.$

It is represented in Figure 9.3 as the pyramid linking reserves to existing deposits. But the figure may also be read in reverse: the volume of deposits cannot exceed a multiple of existing reserves. Rearranging (9.1) results in:

(9.2) $\text{deposits} \leq (1/rr) \times \text{reserves}.$

The factor $(1/rr)$ is often called the *reserve multiplier*.[10] Equation (9.2) means that together, commercial banks cannot expand their deposits, i.e. money creation beyond a multiple of existing reserves. If, as in the previous example, $rr = 10\%$, then $1/rr = 100$, which

explains why reserves are rather small, as we noted earlier when looking at Table 9.1. If (9.1) holds as an equality, then (9.2) does as well, and we now have

(9.2') $\text{deposits} = (1/rr) \times \text{reserves}.$

which states that, by choosing the volume of reserves, the central bank can control total bank deposits. Since $M = \text{currency in circulation} + \text{bank deposits}$ and the central bank precisely sets currency in circulation, central banks can control the money supply. How, central banks control reserves in practice is our next topic.

9.2.5 Creation of Bank Reserves by the Central Bank

When you go to your bank and ask for a loan, it may be the case that fresh loanable money in exactly the right amount had just been deposited in cash by some other customer. The bank is also unlikely to tell you that you have to wait until adequate cash deposits have been made by others before a loan is possible (banks *never* do this). In fact, because it knows you and your creditworthiness, it is good business and standard banking practice to lend you money that it does not have! It will simply credit your bank account (which you will open with that bank) by the amount that you asked for—all assuming, of course, that you are willing to pay back principal and interest over some agreed-upon period. In that moment, new money is created. In fact, this is very similar to the money creation process described in Section 9.2.3. Box 9.3 explains why.

 Box 9.3 The Two Equivalent Money Creation Processes

In Section 9.2.3 we showed one way for commercial banks to create money. In this section we showed an apparently different way for banks to create money. It turns out that there is no difference, in fact. In Section 9.2.3, €1,000 coming from abroad was deposited in cash into the banking system and the system went on to create €9,000. All in all, the money supply increased by €10,000: €9,000 of bookkeeping money and €1,000

injected from abroad. With a reserves ratio of 10%, the corresponding bank reserves of €1,000 consisted of the initial €1,000 in cash (remember, currency is part of M0). In the present section, a loan of €10,000, increases the money stock by €10,000. The only difference is that the €1,000 of required reserves does not come from abroad, it is created anew by the central bank.

[10] Since reserves are a (small) fraction of deposits, *rr* is less than one. Then 1/*rr* is (much) larger than one.

The next step is for the bank to set aside the corresponding amount of reserves (*rr* times your loan). One possibility is for your bank to borrow the required reserves from the central bank.[11] If the central bank agrees, it will simply credit the reserve account of your bank and thus create the reserves that are needed. In the end, your bank created money by depositing the amount of your loan into your account and the central bank created reserves by depositing a proportion *rr* of your loan into your bank's account. Easy!

We can further understand the central bank action by looking at its own balance sheet, which is shown in Figure 9.4. The currency of circulation, money created by the central bank, is technically a liability, even though no one expects the central bank to 'reimburse' the money that it creates.[12] Its other liabilities are deposits by its 'customers', the commercial banks, and, sometimes, the government. Its assets include foreign assets—called foreign exchange reserves—loans to banks and securities, and often government bonds or loans to the government. When a commercial bank needs cash, it asks for a central bank loan or it sells securities to the central bank,

Assets	Liabilities
Foreign assets	Currency in circulation
Loans to commercial banks	Deposits by commercial banks
Securities	Deposits by government
	Net worth

Fig. 9.4 Balance Sheet of a Central Bank

both of which appear on the asset side of the central bank balance sheet. In return, the commercial bank receives cash or has its account with the central bank credited, both of which appear on the liability side of the central bank balance sheet. Money creation by the central bank therefore 'lengthens' its balance sheet.

9.3 Short-run Equilibrium in the Money Market

9.3.1 The Money Market

Banks are usually quite busy places. They make loans to customers on a daily basis. At the same frequency, new deposits are taken in and many loans are repaid. For a large bank, deposits and withdrawals are likely to more or less cancel out at the end of the day. If the

day has been good, more loans were made than repaid, the loan portfolio has expanded, and the bank needs additional reserves. On a less active day, total loans outstanding have contracted and the bank holds excess reserves. Good and bad days alternate, so on some days a bank is short on reserves, sometimes it has excess reserves.

This is why, in the example of Section 9.2.5, the normal reaction of your bank will be to try to borrow from another bank which owns some excess reserves that it is willing to part with. It will go to the **money market**, also called the **interbank market** or the **open market**. This is not a physical marketplace, rather it is a network of banks that facilitates the buying

---

[11] We will see in Section 9.3.1 that it is also possible for an individual bank simply to borrow those reserves from some other banks that neither need them nor wish to lend them to customers—so-called excess reserves.

[12] In the days before fiat money, banknotes promised to pay gold or silver when redeemed; now they promise nothing more than another banknote!

(borrowing) and selling (lending) of reserves, i.e. deposits at the central bank (high-powered money). As long as total bank credit remains constant, some banks have excess reserves while others are short. Overall, they just deal among themselves.

Now imagine that, collectively, the commercial banks face a growing demand for loans. They will collectively need more reserves. The central bank will then have to decide whether or not to create these additional reserves (exactly like in Section 9.2.5). However, normally the central bank does not respond face-to-face to a given bank. Instead, it deals with the money market as a whole.

When the central bank creates reserves, it makes a loan to commercial banks through the money market, pretty much like commercial banks provide loans to their customers. It also charges interest for these loans. Similarly, when banks lend reserves to each other, they also charge interest. Money markets vary from country to country, but they typically bring together large banks and financial institutions, such as insurance companies or mortgage lenders, which handle large amounts of cash. In normal times, they all are highly reputable institutions that know each other well, they lend and borrow large amounts, usually without asking for collateral or guarantees. Since 2007, however, times have not been normal; Box 9.4 tells the story.

The interest rate at which they do so is the rate at which large financial institutions can fund themselves. In effect, for them, the **interbank interest rate** is the ultimate cost of financing their needs. This rate is the basis for all interest rates. Indeed, a bank charges its customers the money market rate *plus* a premium that represents their riskiness. The interbank rate is called EONIA (European Overnight Interest Average) in the euro area, the Fed Funds in the US, the Sterling interbank rate in the UK, etc. Figure 9.5 shows that the various rates charged by commercial banks follow the same evolution as in the interbank rate in the euro area.

9.3.2 The Demand for Money

The private sector—households and corporations—needs money to carry out daily transactions. This is the demand for money M. Either it is holding the money already and paying an opportunity cost of foregone interest, or it can be 'bought' at a bank, at the cost of interest paid for it. In order to satisfy this demand, commercial banks create much of what we call money when they grant loans to their customers. As they do so, they need to acquire sufficient reserves to meet their reserve ratio. Thus the public demand for money M translates into the commercial banks' **derived demand** for central bank money M0.

What determines the public's demand for money M? One simple answer is: the amount of transactions, since this is what makes money useful in the first place. We previously discussed this issue in Chapter 6 where we suggested that money demand can be represented as a constant proportion k of nominal GDP PY. This is somewhat simplistic. Suppose that you wish to hold more money (cash and 'money in the bank'). How do you get it? One way is to borrow from your bank and pay the corresponding interest rate. Another way is to sell some assets. In that case, you give up the interest that you can earn on your assets to receive cash, which does not yield interest, or for deposit at the bank, which yields a very low interest. In both cases, the interest rate emerges as the cost of holding money. This is why the demand for money declines when the interest rate increases. Thus, while money demand is a proportion k of nominal GDP, this proportion is not really constant. It becomes smaller when the interest rate increases.

As we saw, different borrowers face different interest rates, depending on how risky they look in the eyes of their banks. On the other hand, Figure 9.5 shows that all these rates move together. For simplicity, we ignore the risk premia and think of a single interest rate, that we denote i. In the end, we represent the demand for money as

(9.3) $$M^d = k(i)PY$$

where $k(i)$ declines when i rises (formally, $k(i)$ is a decreasing function of i). Now the derived demand for M0 by commercial banks is a fraction of the public demand for M, since any new bank loan, which

Box 9.4 Fear, Loathing and Mistrust Among Lenders

The financial crisis began on 9 August 2007 when banks started to mistrust one another. For several months, things had gone wrong in the US mortgage markets where billions of dollars had been lent to people with poor credit ratings. Local mortgage companies originated these so-called sub-prime loans but these claims were packaged together into specially designed assets and sold to many of the world's largest banks (see Box 9.10 for more details). When borrowers could not make their monthly payments, the large banks started to worry. They worried about themselves, of course, but they soon started to suspect that most other large banks were also facing similar serious risk losses. For decades, these banks had been making loans routinely to each other in full trust, without ever considering that one of them could be unable to repay its loans. On that fateful day, suspicion spread like wildfire, heralding the worst financial crisis ever. In a matter of minutes, interbank markets seized up in the USA, in the Eurozone, in the UK and around the world.

Figure 9.6 provides a visual description of tensions on the euro interbank market. The figure displays two interest rates on 3-month interbank loans. Eurepo is the rate at which banks lend to each other but the borrower is required to provide as collateral 'the best possible asset'; these loans are considered as highly safe. Euribor is the rate that applies to loans without collateral, based on trust in the borrower.[13] If the borrower is considered as not fully safe, these loans are perceived as risky and the interest rate is higher. For decades, the two rates were nearly equal because banks fully trusted each other. In August 2007, the two rates abruptly separated. The difference—called spread—narrowed down in the USA during 2010 but not in the euro area. In fact, it even widened during 2011 as the initial financial crisis morphed into a sovereign debt crisis. Until then, government debts were considered as perfectly safe, but that old presumption came to be challenged, starting with Greek debt and spreading to many other euro area countries. Since they hold large amount of 'safe' public bonds, partly to use them on the interbank market, banks worried about each other.

[13] Eurepo stands for euro repo (a contraction of repurchase agreement). Euribor means euro inter bank offer rate.

Fig. 9.5 Interest Rates in the Euro Area, 2007–2011

EONIA is the interbank interest rate in the euro area. The figure also displays the interest charged to corporations for large (more than €1 million) and smaller (less than €1 million) loans and the interest charged for consumer credits, in all cases for a one-year loan. Lenders charge a larger interest rate to borrowers that they perceive as riskier, but all rates tend to closely follow the evolution of EONIA.

Source: ECB, *Monthly Bulletin*, December 2011.

means more bank deposits, must be accompanied by an increase in reserves as indicated by (9.2). It follows that the derived demand for M0 also declines with the interest rate. It is represented by the downward-sloping schedule D in Figure 9.7.

9.3.3 Market Equilibrium

Now imagine that, starting at point A, the nominal GDP increases. This means more transactions and therefore an increase in money demand Md. Households and firms will try to borrow from banks the extra money that they need and, as banks respond by granting loans, their own need for reserves increases. This is captured in Figure 9.7 by

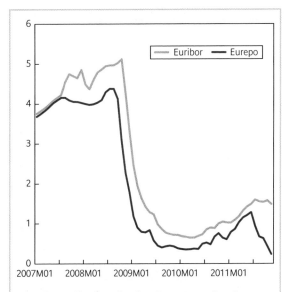

Fig. 9.6 Mistrust in the Euro Interbank Market (3-month interest rates)

Euribor is the interest rate that applies to uncollaterized loans in euros among large banks. Eurepo concerns loans that are guaranteed by 'best quality' collateral. The difference measures the perceived risk that banks assign to dealing with each other.

Source: European Banking Federation, http://www.euribor-ebf.eu/

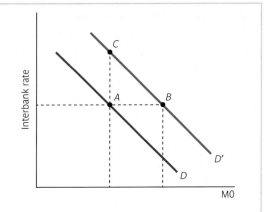

Fig. 9.7 The Money Market

The public's demand for money is negatively related to the interest rate *i*, which represents the cost of borrowing from commercial banks. This demand translates into a derived demand for the monetary base by commercial banks. If the public wants to hold more money, the derived demand schedule shifts to the right from D to D'. The central bank may decide to keep the interest unchanged (point B), or not to respond, in which case the interest rate rises (point C), or it can pick any combination of M0 and the interest rate as long as it lies on the demand schedule.

the rightward shift of the derived demand schedule from D to D'.

How can the central bank respond to the new situation? It has many options, since it is the sole producer of M0. One option is to keep the initial interest rate unchanged. This requires the central bank to provide the additional monetary base M0 needed, moving to point B. Another option is to keep M0 unchanged, which means that we move to point C and the interest rate rises accordingly. In that case, the interest rate rises enough to offset, via a decline in $k(i)$, the impact on money demand Md due to the increase in nominal GDP. In fact, the central bank can pick any point on the new derived demand schedule D'. We return to this choice in Section 9.4.2.

9.3.4 Open Market Operations

As the sole producer of base money, the central bank exercises the dominant influence on the market. Institutional details vary from country to country, but the broad features are similar. Banks on the money market typically lend to each other over very short periods of time, from overnight to two weeks. The central bank monitors the situation closely and ensures that either the interest rate or the quantity of money is in line with its intentions. Nowadays, for reasons developed in Section 9.4.1, most central banks choose to control the interest rate. This is represented in Figure 9.8 by the horizontal money supply schedule S. The schedule makes an important point: a central bank can set any interest rate it chooses, provided it stands ready to provide or withdraw liquidity in any amount

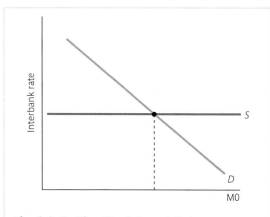

Fig. 9.8 Setting the Interest Rate

In principle, the central bank can achieve any interest rate it chooses by supplying whatever amount of money the private sector wishes to hold at that rate.

needed to meet the derived demand corresponding to this rate.

Central banks typically announce the rate that they would like to see; the position of the supply schedule S in Figure 9.8 is public knowledge. One or two mouse clicks on a central bank's website can reveal the currently chosen interest rate. This rate is called the 'refi' in the euro area, the Federal Funds or target rate in the USA, the Bank Rate in the UK, or the 'repo' rate in Sweden.[14] In order to enforce this rate, each central bank provides its interbank market with the exact amount of reserves that are demanded. To that effect, it carries out **open market operations**, which means it purchases and sells assets using reserves, which are its own liabilities. These open market operations take many different forms. For instance, the European Central Bank (ECB) conducts auctions of reserves every week, complemented with monthly ones (more details are presented in Box 9.5). The National Bank of Hungary also conducts weekly auctions. In the USA, the Federal Reserve Bank of New York intervenes directly on the money market whenever the market rate deviates from the targeted federal funds rate by pur-

chasing or selling US government securities. By doing this, it injects or withdraws reserves from the banking system. Many other central banks, such as those of the Czech Republic, Poland, Sweden, and the UK, also routinely carry out open market operations. When needed, the ECB too intervenes in the market directly (this is called 'fine-tuning operations'). Some banks even intervene by purchasing and selling foreign exchange. All these mechanisms have the same intended effect: to regulate the supply of reserves, or high-powered money, in the money market.

In normal times, as the economy grows, demand for bank credit is rising. Through their liquidity-creating operations—auctions and open market operations—central banks allow bank reserves, and therefore the monetary base M0, to grow along with that demand. This allows commercial banks to step up lending to their customers, which increases M1 and the wider monetary aggregates. But what if a central bank wants to slow down the growth of reserves, for instance because it wants to raise the interbank interest rate? Since central bank loans are of very short duration, commercial banks are continuously repaying their borrowings and borrowing again in a procedure that is called rolling over. If it wants, the central bank can decide not to renew maturing loans, or to renew them only in part.

Any loan is risky, because a bank can never know if it will be repaid. Central banks are not supposed to take risks, so they take extensive precautions. First, they ask borrowing commercial banks to provide collateral—that they deposit an equivalent amount of high-quality assets, for example Treasury bonds, i.e. public debt, or bills issued by large corporations of highest quality. Second, they lend only for a limited period of time, usually a week or ten days. When the period expires, the commercial banks must repay the central bank in exchange for the collateral that they deposited, with no guarantee of being able to borrow again. In contrast to commercial bank lending, central banks take no risk. This is why the interest at which central banks lend is the lowest in the country, as shown in Figure 9.5—low risk means low return.

---

[14] Markets use 'refi' as shorthand for Main Refinancing Rate and 'repo' for Repurchase Operations.

Box 9.5 How the European Central Bank Does It[15]

In order to keep the interbank market rate as close as possible to its target rate, the ECB has set up a complex system for financing commercial banks.

Open market operations: In normal times, the ECB carries out three kinds of open market operations:

- Main refinancing operations, which are weekly auctions for loans with a maturity of one week, is the main channel through which commercial banks obtain reserves. Banks submit competitive bids on rates and quantities and the ECB chooses how much to allocate at which interest rate.

- Longer-term refinancing operations, which take place once a month and serve as a modest complement to the main refinancing operations. The loans have a maturity of three months.

- Fine-tuning and structural operations, which are conducted from time to time to deal with special circumstances, at the ECB's discretion.

Standing facilities: The ECB also maintains two facilities open to eligible individual banks at their request. These facilities set a ceiling and a floor for the overnight money market rate EONIA. Individual banks can either deposit their reserves at the marginal deposit rate (the floor) or borrow from the ECB at the marginal lending rate (ceiling). These facilities are always available but infrequently used under normal conditions.

To signal its intentions, the ECB publicly announces the refi rate at which it will conduct its next main refinancing operations, as well as the floor and ceiling rates. Figure 9.9 shows that the key short-term market rate EONIA normally moves within the tunnel set by the lending and deposit rates, closely following (sometimes even anticipating) the ECB's main rate, the refinancing rate. The ECB can thus exert tight, if not perfect control of the very short-term interest rate.[16]

Crisis management: Box 9.4 explains how interbank markets froze up, first during the financial crisis, and at the outset of the euro area debt crisis. European banks found it increasingly difficult to borrow to meet their needs. Like many other central banks, the ECB has worked hard to keep banks afloat. In particular, it has massively expanded its normally modest long-term refinancing operations. Although central banks normally try to keep reserves in short supply by offering only very short-term loans, the ECB has recently reassured banks by offering liquidity at up to 3-year repayment horizons. Furthermore, the ECB has offered loans in whatever quantity banks were asking for. The result has been massive acquisition of central bank money by the commercial banks. The banks hold poorly remunerated reserves for fear of being shut off from the interbank market.

9.4 Monetary Policy in Practice

9.4.1 Objectives

The neutrality principle, presented in Chapter 6, asserts that, in the long run, the inflation rate is determined by the rate of growth of the money stock. In chapters to come, we will show that inflation does

---

[15] Full details are provided by the ECB on its website at <www.ecb.int>. Each central bank also presents in great detail its own procedures. For a list of all central banks, see <www.centralbanking.co.uk>.

[16] Note that in the wake of the financial crisis, like most other central banks, the ECB slashed its interest rates. Elsewhere, the key rate was brought to near-zero, not in the euro area where the ECB stopped with a refi at 1%. Yet, through its refinancing operations, it saw to it that EONIA be close to the deposit rate set at 0.25%.

Fig. 9.9   ECB Interest Rates (January 1999 – December 2011)

The ECB conducts weekly auctions at the pre-announced main refinancing interest rate. The marginal lending facility and deposit facility rates determine, respectively, a ceiling and a floor for the interbank rate EONIA (Euro OverNight Index Average) that tends to closely follow the refinancing rate.

Source: ECB.

not bring lasting benefit to an economy, and can create much trouble. For that reason, price stability—a low rate of inflation—is socially desirable. Bringing these two fundamental results together, it becomes quite obvious that monetary policy should, first and foremost, be dedicated to achieving price stability. Indeed, with few exceptions, most central banks are delegated the ultimate responsibility of delivering price stability.

On the other hand, money is not neutral in the short run. Chapters 10 and 11 will show that, over a horizon of one to about two to three years, lower interest rates can lead to an expansion of output and employment. Conversely, a tighter monetary policy stance is followed by an output slowdown and a rise in joblessness. This implies that central banks cannot

avoid also being concerned with the level of economic activity. This seriously complicates their job. It is always easier to have only one objective on the radar screen. But what happens if short-run considerations call for a relaxation of monetary policy at a time when inflation is already high and possibly rising, which would call for an increase in the interest rate? Such conflicts of policy objectives greatly complicate the conduct of monetary policy around the world.

Central banks are run by non-elected officials to whom the nation delegates a great deal of power. For this reason, central banks were placed in many countries under the direct control of the finance ministry. So the argument went, this placed an important responsibility in the hands of elected officials, as

Box 9.6 Risk taking at the ECB

Like all central banks, it was ECB's normal procedure to studiously avoid taking risks through its lending procedure. One of its key strategies was to avoid outright purchases of assets from commercial banks in the process of providing liquidity to the markets. The ECB preferred to lend via repurchase agreements, meaning that borrowing banks were always committed to buy back the assets that they were depositing at the ECB, crucially at the same price as they initially had sold them. Even if the value of the asset had fallen during the period it was on the ECB's book, the bank was formally committed to buy it at the original value, so the ECB was immunized against losing money in such trades.

When the prices of public debts of several countries started to fall in 2010, the ECB faced a dilemma: on the one hand, it wanted to keep the bond markets as orderly as possible, which called for purchasing those public bonds whose values were rapidly declining. On the other hand, the ECB was keen not to take the risk of suffering losses in case some countries might end up partially defaulting on their public debts. After intense internal debates and rare public disagreements, the ECB initiated in May 2010 the Securities Markets Programme (SMP), in which it bought—for the first time and in conflict with its original mandate—outright distressed public bonds. The ECB indicated that it would impose a 'haircut' on these purchases, meaning that it would buy them at a discounted price. Still, further value declines could not be ruled out. The amounts purchased under the SMP are thought to be very large— about €400 billion in euro area agreement bonds alone. Sovereign bond defaults could impose significant losses on the ECB.

should be in a democracy. Yet politicians tend to focus more on the short run, i.e. the upcoming elections, while inflation is a long-run consequence of monetary mismanagement. Time and again, subservient central banks have been instructed to pay more attention to the short than to the long run. Often, the result was high inflation, in some cases even runaway inflation (see Box 9.7).

To deal with this conflict, many countries have made their central banks formally independent from ruling governments and given precise tasks. The general thrust of these tasks is strikingly similar. For instance, monetary policy at the Norwegian central bank 'shall be oriented towards low and stable inflation', but 'shall also contribute to stabilizing output and employment'. The long-run objective of low inflation comes first, while the shorter-run objective of stabilizing output and employment comes next. The question is how central banks deliver.

9.4.2 Instruments and Targets

Before delving into more technical aspects of monetary policy, it is useful to summarize some fundamental facts that will guide our thinking about it.

By making bank reserves money more or less abundant, central banks affect interest rates—in the first instance interest rates in the money market. It lowers interest rates by making money more abundant and raises them by making money scarce.

Because it influences the growth of the money supply, monetary policy determines inflation in the long run. It takes something like two to three years for policy to affect inflation.

By affecting the level of interest rates, monetary policy can affect the level of economic activity—output and employment—in the short to medium run. It takes two to three *quarters* for these effects to become noticeable.[17]

Stable inflation, GDP growth, and employment are thus not directly under the control of the central

---

[17] In Chapter 10 the transmission mechanisms of monetary policy will be spelled out in more detail. At this point it is enough to recall from Chapter 8 that an increase in interest rates reduces investment expenditures by increasing the opportunity cost of invested resources and lowering the value of capital already installed. It also reduces consumption indirectly by reducing the present value of wealth.

Box 9.7   Hyperinflation: Historical and Current Episodes

Time and again, a country will fall into the trap of letting the money supply grow at excessive rates for long periods of time. The reason is relatively simple: the government tries to pay for its expenditures by borrowing directly from the central bank in a process that eventually gets out of control.[18] The consequence is always run-away inflation. Hyperinflation was defined as a situation when *monthly* inflation rates exceed 50%, which means an annual rate of price increase of about 8,600%. On average, then, prices rise by some 2% every day.

Many hyperinflations often occur after wars. This was the case in the 1920s in Germany, Greece, and Hungary.

In Germany, prices rose by 29,524% during the month of October 1923. This meant an average *daily* rate of 19%. The situation was so bad that factories would stop production at lunch to pay their workers and give them time to go shopping before prices had risen again and further eroded the purchasing power of their wages. More recently, Serbia broke the world record when, in January 1994, prices rose by 60% *per day*. These episodes destroy the economy and put the basic fabric of society under severe strain, sometimes even leading to civil unrest and war. The most recent episode of hyperinflation can still be observed in Zimbabwe, as already recounted in Box 6.2.[19]

---

bank. Its challenge is to use available instruments to affect these variables. We have already discussed three instruments under the direct control of central banks: (1) the interbank reserve or money market interest rate, (2) the supply of reserves, and (3) the required reserve ratio. Figure 9.7 shows that a central bank cannot control both the money stock and the interest rate. It can only choose a position on the schedule representing the derived demand for reserves. If, as in Figure 9.8, it chooses the interest rate, it must accommodate the demand for reserves corresponding to this interest rate. It could do the opposite and choose the volume of reserves to supply, but then it would have to accept whatever interest rate the money market requires.

Monetary targeting

During much of the 1950s and 1960s, conventional wisdom was that central banks ought to maintain low and stable interest rates. This was thought to be good for investment and growth. As it turned out, with the interest rate set too low, money grew quite rapidly. Unsurprisingly, this policy led to

high inflation rates in the 1970s, as can be seen in Figure 9.10.

As an immediate reaction to the damaging inflation of the 1970s, many central banks targeted the rate of money growth. The strategy of monetary targeting rests on the link between bank reserves and deposits as stated in equation (9.2). Strictly speaking the central bank only controls the money stock indirectly by controlling the monetary base—currency in circulation and bank reserves. As long as equation (9.2) remains stable, a choice of monetary base determines the money supply, allowing the central bank to choose a rate of money growth consistent with the inflation rate that it hopes to deliver in the long run.[20]

---

[18] Since the central bank *creates* money, it is an ideal place for governments to look for cheap finance. Commentators often speak of 'switching on the printing presses'. We will explain more precisely why and how this happens in Chapters 13 and 17.

[19] Speaking in February 2006 on Government-owned television ZBC, President Mugabe not only gave advance warning for the country's hyperinflation episode, but also gave us the reason why they happen: 'Those who say printing money will cause inflation are suggesting that you just fold your hands and say "aah, let the situation continue and let the people starve". The Good Lord up there has given you a brain and the brain must function, not in a stereotyped manner but in a flexible manner … so I will print money today so that people can survive.'

[20] This rate is simply given by equation (6.6) in Chapter 6, which indicates that in the long run, inflation settles at the rate of money growth, after adjustment for the trend growth rate of GDP.

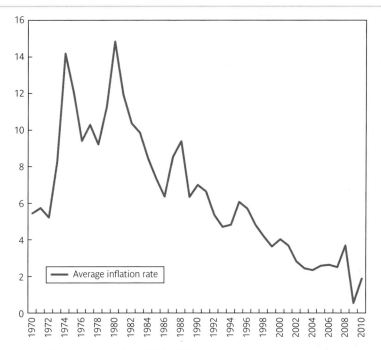

Fig. 9.10 Inflation in OECD Countries, 1969–2010
The figure presents the average inflation rate in the OECD countries. Inflation soared in the 1970s, was reduced over the following two decades and appears to have stabilized at a low level since the late 1990s, with an uptick in 2008 followed by a sharp drop thereafter.
Source: OECD, *Economic Outlook*.

Money growth targeting is widely credited for the successful disinflation of the 1980s. It was also generally abandoned in the 1990s for a number of good reasons. One of them is that it was never clear which monetary stock should be targeted: M0, M1, M2, M3, or some other aggregate? This control became difficult after the financial sector was deregulated because it introduced innovation after innovation that blurred the distinction between these aggregates. Another problem with monetary targeting—which has grown more acute since the onset of the global financial crisis in 2008—has been increasing instability in the derived demand for M0. The money multiplier became highly variable and the money base M0 no longer gave central banks a precise handle on the wider aggregates.

Inflation targeting

The difficulties associated with monetary targeting paved the way for a new strategy, **inflation targeting**. The reasoning behind inflation targeting consists of two observations: (1) It is easier to target interest rates than reserves. Figure 9.7 displays the demand for M0, derived by the overall money demand as specified in (9.3). Let us look directly at the demand for money, represented by the downward-sloping schedule D in Figure 9.11. The central bank, we saw, can decide where to move the economy along this demand schedule, say point A. Under monetary targeting, the central bank determines the corresponding money supply. This is represented in Figure 9.11 by the vertical money supply schedule S^M. If it proves too difficult to control the quantity of money, the central bank can still hit point A by deciding on the interest rate. This is

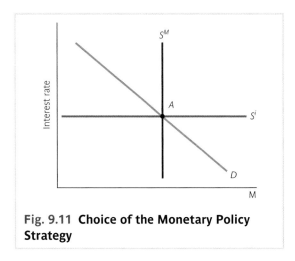

Fig. 9.11 Choice of the Monetary Policy Strategy

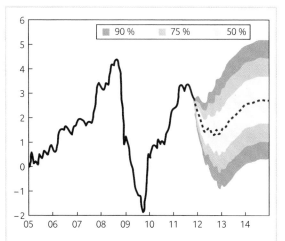

Fig. 9.12 Inflation Forecast by the Swedish Riksbank

The figure, published in December 2011, shows past inflation in Sweden and the Riksbank forecast over the following three years. In order to emphasize that any forecast is uncertain, the Riksbank reports how much trust it puts into its own forecasts. The central, lighter part of the fan indicates that the bank estimates that there is 50% probability that inflation will actually be within this area. The darker and much wider zone corresponds to a 90% probability. The further out you look, the less certain is the forecast.

Source: Monetary Policy Update, Riksbank (December 2011).

represented by the horizontal money supply schedule S^i. In short, if it becomes difficult to control the *quantity* of money precisely enough, it makes sense to control its *price*, the interest rate.

(2) If the money supply is difficult to control, it is better to use the interest rate directly as an instrument for controlling inflation. For reasons that will become clear in Chapters 10 and 12, inflation-targeting central banks determine the future path of inflation as best as they can and set the interest rate accordingly. If the forecasted inflation rate is too high, they raise the interest rate. If future inflation is below target, they cut interest rates. This is why the strategy is better called the inflation *forecast* targeting strategy. Inflation-targeting central banks regularly publish their inflation forecasts. Figure 9.12 shows the example of Swedish central bank, the Riksbank.

Inflation targeting was first implemented by the Bank of New Zealand in the late 1980s. Since then, it has been widely adopted, even though the three largest central banks, the ECB, the Fed, and the Bank of Japan, remain unconvinced, for various reasons.[21]

---

[21] In practice, the major central banks seem to follow the inflation strategy but do not publicly acknowledge it. The ECB, in many ways a successor of the Bundesbank, was renowned for its commitment to money growth targeting. The Fed is hamstrung by the mandate in the Full Employment Act of 1946, a law which requires it to care about both inflation and employment. The Bank of Japan is still trying to exit from a long period of zero inflation and poor growth, which is often referred to as the 'lost decade'.

The natural appeal of inflation targeting is that it is closest to the central bank's mandate, price stability. With a simple, verifiable target, it is easier for the central bank to explain its decisions and to reassure the public that its actions are driven by a clear and transparent commitment to price stability.

What happens if the central bank makes a mistake? When governments do this, they face the consequences at the next election, and they know it. Being independent, central banks do not face any democratic sanction and may become a bit too complacent, if not downright arrogant. There is no perfect solution to this problem. Governments are almost always the ultimate owner, and they can and do reassert control over the central bank from time to time by passing new laws or holding legislative hearings. Box 9.8 shows how the Bank of England is made more accountable, at least in theory.

> ### Box 9.8 The Governor's Letter: How the Bank of England is Made Accountable
>
> The Bank of England adopted the inflation-targeting strategy informally in 1993 and has pursued it formally since 1997, when it received statutory independence from the Treasury. On both dimensions of inflation targeting and monetary independence, the Bank has strongly influenced the practice of central banking. The Bank of England is said to be *instrument-independent*. It is free to set the interest rate as it will, but the inflation target is set by the Chancellor of the Exchequer in an annual 'remit letter' that is made public on the Bank of England's website. The inflation target in the summer of 2008 was 2%.
>
> Of particular interest is the sanction mechanism imposed when inflation deviates from its announced policy. If this deviation amounts to more than 1% on either side of the 2% target rate, the Governor must write an open letter to the Chancellor (the Minister of Finance). This happened for the first time in April 2007 when inflation reached 3.1%. Governor Mervyn King dutifully obliged and wrote the letter. With inflation surging, the Governor sent another letter in June 2008. All in all, by end of 2011, there have been 11 such letters. The letters, and the Chancellor's courteous and sympathetic responses, can be read at <http://www.bankofengland.co.uk/monetarypolicy/framework.htm>. It is currently unclear whether these letters have any real impact on the conduct of monetary policy.

Reserve requirements as a tool of monetary policy

Reserve requirements can be used to affect the money supply. For example, if the required reserve ratio is raised from 5% to 6%, with unchanged supply of reserves, deposits must contract by roughly 20% (the percentage increase from 5 to 6 is $(6 - 5)/5 = 20\%$). This is a drastic move, which not only stops commercial banks from lending, but might even cause them to call in (demand immediate repayment of) some existing loans. Because this move can be very costly and disruptive to banks and their customers, reserve ratios are normally changed only in small increments, and then only in emergency situations. It is more frequently used in countries in which the internal money market is less developed. One example, discussed later in Chapter 11, is China. As Table 9.2 shows, the reserve ratio is purely voluntary in a number of countries.

9.4.3 The Taylor Rule

A simple way of summarizing the way central banks deal with their two tasks is the **Taylor rule**, which will be used extensively in the following chapters.[22] The Taylor rule states that the central bank will raise the interbank market interest rate, denoted by i, when the inflation rate π exceeds its target inflation rate $\bar{\pi}$, and when real GDP Y exceeds its current equilibrium or trend level $\bar{Y}$:[23]

$$\textbf{(9.4)} \qquad i = \bar{i} + a(\pi - \bar{\pi}) + b\frac{Y - \bar{Y}}{\bar{Y}}.$$

The target inflation rate $\bar{\pi}$ is meant to correspond to price stability. The trend GDP level $\bar{Y}$ is defined as the GDP that would be observed if unemployment was at its equilibrium level, as defined in Chapter 5.[24] The per cent difference $(Y - \bar{Y})/\bar{Y}$ between GDP and its trend is called the **output gap**.[25] As a first approximation, we can think of the rule as determining where the supply schedule S is placed in Figure 9.8.

The Taylor rule anchors interest rate policy around a level $\bar{i}$ that is called the **neutral** or **natural rate**. It is the interest rate that the central bank would want to set if both inflation and GDP were stabilized at their desired levels. The coefficients a and b give the

---

[22] This 'rule', which is the result of extensive observation of actual central bank behaviour, is named after John Taylor, an US economist at Stanford University.

[23] The trend level of output corresponds to the long-run sustainable evolution of GDP, as explained in Chapters 3 and 4.

[24] In fact, most central banks do not just look at actual inflation but at forecasts. We ignore this distinction.

[25] Both inflation and output are expressed in percentage deviations, respectively, of the rate of increase of the price level from target, or of output from its trend level.

relative importance attributed to deviations of inflation and output from their targets; for example, in its original formulation, the chosen values were $a = 1.5$ and $b = 0.5$.

These values are used in Figure 9.13 to see how closely the Taylor rule corresponds to observed central bank policy. For each country, the figure compares the actual interest rate and the one predicted by the rule. Given the extreme simplicity of the rule, we would not expect a tight link. Remarkably, the Taylor rule is a reasonable representation of what central banks actually do. We will use it as a tool to represent monetary policy—the way the central bank's interest rate policy reacts to inflation and output. The main differences appear during the crisis in countries where the output gap was negative and unusually large. This would have implied a negative nominal interest rate, which is implausible and unlikely under normal conditions.[26] This is known as the **zero lower bound** and has led some central banks to drive their interest rates to zero, or close to zero.

9.5 Financial Institutions and Monetary Control[27]

We have seen that modern money is not made out of precious metal. In fact it has no intrinsic value at all. It is valuable only for the trust others have in it: if others are willing to accept it as a means of payment, be it for something bought in a store or for one's own hard work. The fact that its value depends on widely shared trust implies that money is a public good—it must be carefully guaranteed and preserved by the government. This is why banks are tightly regulated and supervized. Despite all this precaution, confidence crises arise from time to time.

9.5.1 Bank Regulation and Supervision

Money is created when commercial banks grant loans to their customers, with the hope that principal and interest will be repaid. It is a fundamental and unalterable fact that banks have less information about their customers' creditworthiness than the customers themselves. A loan customer will tend to misrepresent circumstances that would otherwise lead to a refusal of credit. This fundamental **information asymmetry** has wide-ranging implications that affect virtually any financial operation.[28]

One direct implication is that banks routinely make 'bad loans', i.e. loans that are never repaid in full. A bank that makes too many bad loans can go bankrupt, and in this case the depositors—who are not investing, but simply banking—may lose their money. Depositors can thus never be perfectly certain that their money is safe and, because bank deposits are only as safe as the bank itself, the value of money itself is constantly at risk. Just as confidence in banknotes and coins rests on the quality of the central bank that issues them, the confidence in money created by the commercial banks is based on the expectation that those funds are freely and immediately convertible into currency at any time. The history of commercial banking is full of bank failures which turned into bank panics, as worried depositors attempted to withdraw cash from their bank accounts, not only from the failing bank but from all financial institutions—just to be safe.

One bank failure is painful for its depositors, but not lethal for the economy. The greater risk is that the whole banking system could fail as a chain reaction

---

[26] It is implausible, but not impossible: While the central bank cannot give money away, in a crisis situation in which loan contracts are auctioned, bidders may be willing to pay more than €100 for a guarantee of €100 tomorrow—especially when it comes from an especially reliable borrower.

[27] This section presents non-essential material that can be skipped without loss of continuity. Its main interest is to provide background information useful to understand the banking crisis that started in 2007.

[28] Three economists, George Akerlof from Berkeley University, A. Michael Spence from Stanford University, and George Stiglitz, then at Princeton University, were awarded the Nobel Prize in 2001 for having uncovered and analysed the phenomenon of information asymmetry.

Fig. 9.13 Examples of Taylor Rules

The figures compare actual interest rates with those predicted by the Taylor rule (9.4) with a = 1.5 and b = 0.5, and where the neutral interest rate is chosen on the basis of past experience or central bank statements.

Sources: OECD, Economic Outlook; IMF, International Financial Statistics.

takes hold, called contagion, which would bringing healthy banks down along with the bad ones. **Systemic risk**, as the phenomenon is called, arises because banks (and, more generally, financial institutions) hold each other's liabilities. These so-called correspondent balances are the plumbing of the modern economy. They allow banks to deal with each other on the interbank market. Should one bank go bankrupt, its liabilities to other banks become worthless, which can easily lead to more bankruptcies.

A seriously aggravating factor is that bank depositors—households and firms—can easily become suspicious, even if the underlying fear is unfounded. Fearing that trouble in one bank could contaminate the others, they may attempt to withdraw their deposits from all banks. This panic movement is called a **bank run**. But, as already explained in Section 9.2.3, a bank can never pay back all of its deposits immediately, since they have been mostly invested or lent out. This is why bank runs can easily provoke a generalized collapse of the whole banking system. Such bank runs occurred in Argentina and Uruguay in 2002. For the most part, they are contained to an individual bank, such as Northern Rock (2007) in the UK or Countrywide Financial (2007) and IndyMac (2008) in the USA. Sometimes the 'run' does not even originate with retail depositors, but with other banks that withdraw funds from suspect banks or withhold credit from them—the case of IKB Bank in Germany in 2007 is a good example.

To reduce these risks, national governments impose regulations on banks, and international agreements have been worked out to establish norms of good banking practice. Regulations include the supervision of bank accounts and operations, restrictions on asset ownership and banking activities, and the imposition of a number of prudential measures. Most important, banks are generally required to maintain a minimum net worth—the excess of assets over liabilities—in relation to their volume of deposits. As stated already, this is meant to create a buffer in case assets suffer a sudden loss of value.

The purpose of all these regulations is to limit risk-taking by banks, to give monetary authorities advance warning in case of failure, and generally to ensure prudent conduct in the provision of banking services. Bank runs are also less likely when deposits are insured, at least up to some limit. Deposit insurance is now compulsory in most developed countries.

9.5.2 Lending in Last Resort

Systemic bank failures represent one of the worst threats to modern economies. Within days or weeks, a large fraction of the money stock can disappear. This cripples most daily transactions and precipitates countless bankruptcies and plant closures. Unemployment soon explodes and standards of living fall precipitously. GDP declined by 10% or more in the wake of systemic bank collapses in Korea in 1998 and Argentina in 2002, especially hurting the poor who lost their modest savings. Europe and the US in 2009 were spared bank runs and the resulting economic dislocation because central banks and governments acted promptly.

Central banks are not just in charge of price stability. They are also entrusted with the task of preserving financial stability. In normal times, they are asked to limit money growth. In bad times, when bank deposits threaten to vanish, they alone can produce unlimited quantities of money. When they do so, they act as **lenders of last resort**. In principle at least, the central bank is expected to provide failing banks with sufficient monetary base to avoid immediate bankruptcy and reassure depositors that they can continue to normally withdraw money from their deposits. But the lender of last resort function must be handled with great care.

On the one hand, banking systems can be unstable in the face of large, sudden withdrawals, which may be based as much on irrational fears or misinformation as real threats. Supplying liquidity in crises can spare considerable pain and suffering. On the other hand, if banks believe that the central bank will always bail them out when in trouble, they may take on excessive risks. The danger is that crisis alleviation via lending in last resort can in itself become a source of crises. Box 9.9 summarizes the policy dilemma faced by central banks in this regard.

9.5.3 Technological Innovation in Banking and Monetary Control

Banks are constantly devising new ways of satisfying the financial needs of their customers. Many of these

Box 9.9 Bank Runs and Lender of Last Resort: A Double-Edged Sword

When the safety of commercial bank deposits becomes suspicious, their owners attempt to withdraw their funds and convert them into cash. Because they only hold a small proportion of deposits in cash or reserves at the central bank, commercial banks have then no other choice than to close. This does not just infuriate depositors who feel defrauded, it undermines the whole economy. Often bank runs start with one failing bank and quickly spread to the whole banking system. To prevent a financial and economic meltdown, central banks must intervene decisively to prevent contagion, at worst to bail out the whole banking system. Ideally, central banks would provide the bank(s) under pressure with enough cash to pay back all deposits and thus placate depositors' anxieties and put an end to the runs. In practice, there is just not enough paper money available—remember that currency amounts to a small fraction of bank deposits. Usually, therefore, central banks provide commercial banks with emergency cash and instruct them to pay back their customers a fraction of their deposits, in the hope that this will keep the economy going for a while.

Another limit of lending in last resort is moral hazard, another implication of information asymmetry. We have noted that banking is a risky business. One reason why banks limit the risk that they take, and the returns that come along with risk-taking, is that they want to avoid bankruptcy. But if lending in last resort systematically saves them from bankruptcy, banks have less reason to behave prudently, which undermines the banking system and the stability of the currency. The information asymmetry here comes from the fact that central banks do not know how much risk commercial banks take and that, if they expect a bail-out, banks have an interest in taking more risk than they really should.

Central banks are torn between two conflicting aims. On the one hand, they cannot stand by when the banking system collapses. On the other hand, they do not want to encourage risky bank behaviour, if only because excessive risk-taking is bound to result in even more frequent crises. One response is for central banks or supervizing agencies to closely monitor commercial bank practices and, when needed, to require banks to correct the problem. If the instruction is not heeded, the misbehaving bank may lose its licence. A second response is to impose prudential measures, such as increasing required bank capital (issuing shares) in proportion to the amount of risk taken. Following the 2007–8 crisis, a new international agreement—called Basel III because it was agreed among central bankers and regulators who met in Basel—has recommended a new set of norms; few countries have adopted these norms to date. A third response is for central banks to maintain a large degree of uncertainty as to what they would do in case of bank failure. This explains why central banks deny in public that they are ready to carry out lender-of-last-resort operations. They hope that depositors will be encouraged to keep an eye on their banks in good times, and withhold their patronage if there is cause for concern. Finally, lending in last resort is not extended automatically. The accepted procedure is to follow the Bagehot principles (named after Walter Bagehot (1826–1877), a renowned British financial economist of the late nineteenth century):

- Lend only against marketable collateral. This forces banks to hold an adequate amount of safe assets (with low returns) alongside risky loans (with higher returns).
- Lend in large amounts at a higher rate than the market interest rate. Large amounts are meant to stop the bank run, higher rates are meant to make the operation punitively costly.
- Sell or liquidate insolvent banks, with losses to be borne by their owners. The managers and shareholders should bear the cost of imprudent lending as a way of reducing the moral hazard problem.

developments are also prompted by the banks' attempts to escape monetary policy and regulation. In general, a central bank's objective of reining in money growth runs counter to individual banks' interest in increasing profitability. Similarly, banking

regulation may aim to protect customers by limiting the range of banking activities, including risk-taking, but these measures will also reduce bank profitability. Pressed by competition and prompted by continuous technological innovations—in financial instruments,

computer power, and communications systems—
banks constantly innovate by exploiting loopholes
in existing legislation. As a result, monetary control is weakened and banks may become more fragile. This fragility is confirmed by continuing bank
failures and the collapse of prestigious institutions
like Barings of Britain (one of the oldest banks) or
LTCM (Long-Term Capital Management, a firm created and run by several Nobel Prize winners) in the
USA. The sub-prime crisis that started in 2007,
revealed huge gaps in existing regulation, as
explained in Box 9.10.

Box 9.10 The Sub-prime Crisis of 2007 and its Aftermath

The sub-prime crisis involves many of the issues discussed in this chapter. The fact that it occurred in one
of the most developed countries of the world, despite a
wealth of financial experience accumulated over
decades, illustrates the inherent instability of financial
institutions as well as the unending race between regulation and innovation driven by regulation avoidance or
downright evasion.

This complex situation—which we simplify greatly
here—started in the US mortgage market, the market
for long-term home loans. Sub-prime mortgage loans
were granted to low-income customers who are normally too risk-averse to borrow the amount necessary to
buy a house. In addition, typical loan contracts stipulated low initial interest rates that increased automatically after two or three years. This new line of business
proliferated as the result of securitization, which works
as follows. Soon after being granted, the loans—the
right to receive payments from the borrowers—were
sold to other financial institutions. This trick allowed
the original mortgage lender to collect a fee for issuing
the loan while escaping the associated risk of default
since they no longer actually owned the mortgage. It
also allowed the originator to recover the cash and issue
more new loans.

The purchasing institutions collected a large number
of these risky loans and re-sold them in bulk all around
the world. Such 'mortgage-backed securities' changed
hands frequently, going from one country to another.
They ended up being held mostly by large banks. This
construction created another asymmetric information
problem: the ultimate asset-holders—the large banks—
had very limited understanding of the risk that they
were taking on board—they had no information on the
original sub-prime borrowers.

The crisis was triggered by a turnaround in the US
housing market, which had been buoyed up by abundant mortgage lending for many years. House prices
had risen by almost 100% from 1999 to 2006. Just as
the market slowed and house prices started to decline,
sub-prime borrowers had to pay higher adjustable interest rates, and many defaulted. In principle, the house
served as collateral and guaranteed the value of the
loans. But, with declining housing prices, collateral
value became insufficient. In effect, hundreds of thousands of loans had lost value. The first hitch was that no
one could quickly assess the situation, for house prices
kept declining for three years and the securities did not
trade in transparent markets.

The second hitch was that the owners of the sub-
prime mortgages were to a large extent unknown. Most
financial institutions, including commercial banks, had
some hidden here and there in their balance sheets, but
how much exactly? Each commercial bank started to
wonder whether the others had more or less exposure
to the risk. As described in Box 9.4, the interbank markets dried up in many of the most developed countries,
including the USA, the euro area, and the UK. The result
has been a deep recession in 2009, shown in Figure
9.14. Fears that we would enter the decade-long depression of the 1930s did not materialize, partly because
central banks around the world scrambled to provide
liquidity to the money market, injecting hundreds of
billions over days. Governments too acted vigorously,
allowing the budgets to go deep into red numbers. A
couple of years later, however, the rapid rise of public
debts triggered a new crisis in the euro area. At the time
of writing (end of 2011), the euro area is expected to
undergo a second recession in 2012 and, of course, no
one knows where the new crisis will end.

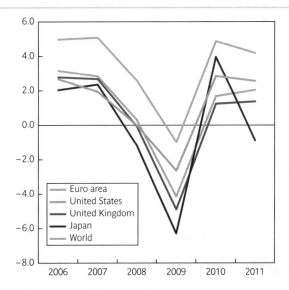

Fig. 9.14 The Great Recession

The figure displays growth rates of GDP. Such deep and broad-based declines have been unseen since the 1930s. The recession hit hard the developed countries but the rest of the world did not escape a sharp dip in its growth rate.

Source: OECD, *Economic Outlook*.

⚠ Summary

1 There are different definitions of money, but broadly speaking it is the sum of currency in circulation and deposits in banks and, possibly, other financial institutions.

2 Most of what we call money and employ in everyday transactions is created by commercial banks at the same time they make loans to customers. The rest of the money supply—currency, banknotes, and coins—is produced by the monetary authorities.

3 For prudential or regulatory reasons, commercial banks hold cash—currency or deposits at the central bank—in proportion to their customers' deposits. This reserve ratio forces commercial banks to acquire more reserves whenever they create more money. The banks' demand for reserves is derived from the public demand for money, i.e. for bank loans.

4 The central bank directly controls the amount of currency in circulation. It controls indirectly the other component of the money stock, bank deposits, by deciding whether to provide commercial banks with bank reserves.

5 Facing the derived demand for the monetary base, central banks can decide on which quantity to supply, or to supply whatever quantity is demanded to achieve a particular interest rate. An additional instrument available to the central bank is the required reserve ratio, when it exists.

6 The neutrality principle indicates that inflation is ultimately driven by money growth. This has led most countries to delegate to their central banks the responsibility of achieving and maintaining price stability. Central banks are usually also expected to care about output growth and employment, which are affected by monetary policy in the shorter run.

7 Combining these two objectives is not always easy, so central banks have developed monetary policy strategies, which have evolved over time. The money growth strategy proved its mettle in bringing inflation down following the faulty low-interest rate strategies of the 1960s and 1970s. With low inflation and rapid changes in banking and finances, the money growth strategy gave way to inflation targeting.

8 The Taylor rule describes monetary policy as setting the interest rate in response to deviations of inflation from its designated target and to the output gap. Despite its simplicity, the Taylor rule offers a reasonable, reliable interpretation of what central banks do.

9 Banking is a risky business, largely due to the information asymmetry problem. Since banks create money and monetary stability is essential to the functioning of the economy, banks are regulated and supervized.

10 Because commercial banks supply money and credit to an economy, their failure cannot be taken lightly. An isolated bank run can increase the risk of generalized contagion. This is why central banks must be ready to act as lender of last resort, providing liquidity while sanctioning bank failure due to imprudent practices.

🔑 Key Concepts

- monetary policy
- commodity money
- fiat money
- monetary aggregates (M0, M1, M2, M3)
- bank reserves
- monetary base
- financial intermediaries
- maturity transformation
- balance sheet
- Volker Rule
- reserves, reserve ratio
- money multiplier
- capital adequacy
- derived demand

- money market, interbank market, open market
- interbank interest rate
- open market operations
- money growth targeting
- inflation targeting
- Taylor rule
- output gap
- neutral interest rate
- information asymmetry
- systemic risk
- bank runs, bank failures
- lender of last resort
- zero lower bound

❓ Exercises

1 Suppose that the long-run growth rate of GDP is 3% and that the reserves ratio is 10%. What should be the money growth target if the central bank wants to achieve an inflation of 2% in the long run? How quickly, then, should it allow reserves to grow?

2 Define and explain the distinction between objectives, targets, and instruments of monetary policy. Give some examples of conflicts between different instruments, and between different targets. Do you think it is necessarily better to have many or fewer instruments and targets?

3 Table 9.1 shows that the size (relative to GDP) of the monetary aggregates varies from country to country. Explain why and how these ratios may reflect the degree of financial development of the country.

4 In some countries the reserves ratio is not set by the central bank, rather it is left to the discretion of commercial banks. Does it matter for the control of the money stock? Does the same problem exist where the central bank controls interest rates instead?

5 Figure 9.11 shows the difference between the money growth and the inflation-targeting strategies. Consider an increase in the demand for money. How will the central bank react under the money growth strategy by keeping S^M unchanged? Under the inflation-targeting strategy if S^i is kept unchanged?

6 Sterilization is a procedure whereby the central bank conducts an open market operation and simultaneously conducts another to prevent it from changing the money supply. Consider the example of a foreign exchange market intervention in which the central bank buys or sells its domestic currency against foreign assets. Using Figure 9.4, show the effect of a sale of domestic currency on the following balance sheet items: foreign assets and currency in circulation. What happens to the money supply? Then explain an open market oper-

ation that can be carried out to sterilize the foreign exchange market intervention.

7 During the financial crisis, some central banks have bought large amounts of 'toxic assets' (packages of sub-prime loans) from desperate banks. Use Figure 9.4 to describe these actions. Now imagine that these assets lose value: how will that be treated in the central bank's balance sheet?

8 Why is deposit insurance a way of reducing the odds of a bank run? What are the limits of this scheme?

9 Consider the Taylor rule (9.4). Assume as in the text that $a = 1.5$ and $b = 0.5$ and that the neutral interest rate is 4%. What interest rate is implied by the rule when inflation is 2% above target while the output gap is zero. What if the output gap is 3%? And − 2%?

10 The target inflation rate in Sweden is 2%. Looking at Figure 9.12, what do you expect the central bank (the Riksbank) to do over the years 2012–2014?

11 Box 9.5 describes the open market operations of the ECB. Explain carefully why the marginal lending facility establishes a ceiling on the market rate and why the marginal deposit facility establishes a floor.

12 Since the beginning of the crisis, the US central bank (the Federal Reserve Bank, often called the Fed) has bought huge amounts of public bonds, in effect multiplying the size of its balance sheet by three. Most of this newly created money is being held by commercial banks in the form of deposits at the Fed. Is it a threat to inflation? (Hint: what happens to the money supply?)

→ Essay Questions

1 The mandate of the Eurosystem sets price stability as its overriding priority. In the USA, the Federal Reserve System is legally committed to pursue both 'stability of the currency' and a 'high level of employment'. Compare and discuss these mandates.

2 One of the tasks of a central bank is to intervene as lender of last resort as described in Box 9.9. One of the trickiest parts is to determine if a bank is insolvent (it cannot recover) or just illiquid (it has no fundamental problem but is running out of cash).

Explain why it matters and how this distinction might be made.

3 Why do central banks need to have targets? Discuss and evaluate the various possible targets.

4 Having purchased vast amounts of public debts, the ECB is worried of suffering large losses in case some governments default. There is a risk that its net worth (see Figure 9.4) could become negative. Yet, some highly reputed central banks, like the Banco Central de Chile and the Bank of Israel—have operated for years with a negative net worth. Is this a problem? Discuss.

5 In April 2007, the Governor of the Bank of England had to write his first letter to the Chancellor of the Exchequer to explain why it missed the inflation target. Read the letter <www.bankofengland.co.uk/monetarypolicy/pdf/cpiletter070417.pdf> and the Chancellor's response <www.hm-treasury.gov.uk/media/7/4/chxresponse_170407.pdf>. What are the Governor's explanations and what do you think of the Chancellor's response?

Macroeconomic Equilibrium in the Short Run

10

The long run is a misleading guide to current affairs. In the long run we are all dead.

J. M. Keynes

10.1 Overview

John Maynard Keynes said a lot in his short life, but this description of the long run is perhaps his best-known pronouncement. On the one hand, it is a normative and controversial judgement that policies should care more about the present than the distant future. But it is also a statement of fact: the economy needs time to reach that long run, and we need to understand what happens in the meantime. This chapter is concerned with the central question of macroeconomics posed in Chapter 1: Why do countries experience business cycles? These recurrent, irregular periods of ups and downs are presented in a stylized way in Figure 10.1. We saw in Chapters 3 and 4 that, in the long run, the GDP appears to increase without limit. This long-run growth is shown by the smoother curve displaying an upward trend. In the short run, however, economic activity fluctuates around that trend, with periods of relatively fast growth followed by periods of slowdown, or even negative growth called **recessions**. This chapter

shows that business cycles can be explained by disturbances, or shocks, that originate in goods and financial markets.

To study the short run behaviour of the economy, we adopt a crucial **Keynesian assumption** that prices are constant. In most countries where inflation is low, it is a reasonable assumption over, say, a couple of years. This is why this chapter is about the short run. The Keynesian assumption is a convenient analytical short cut. Not having to track prices will simplify the analysis a lot. It turns out that it is also a rather accurate description of the short run.

Macroeconomic price flexibility is a reasonable working assumption for the long run. Under price flexibility, the monetary neutrality principle applies, and money and prices behave independently of output. This long-run independence, or **dichotomy**, of the real and monetary dimensions of the economy was stressed in Chapter 6 and serves as an important anchor for analysis. But by adopting the Keynesian assumption, we will upset this dichotomy. Under the condition that prices are constant, rigid or just 'sticky' (i.e. slow-moving), it implies that the nominal and real sides of the economy interact with each other. Macroeconomics therefore incorporates two fundamentally different perspectives. In the long run, prices are fully flexible and neatly separate out nominal and real sides of the economy. In the short run, prices do not move, or move rather slowly, the dichotomy fails and everything becomes more complicated. The working assumption of constant prices will help us explain more easily the complex aspects of the business cycle.

The Keynesian model focuses on two markets: (1) the market for goods and services—which we will henceforth call the goods market, and (2) the money market, which we studied in Chapter 9. In the next

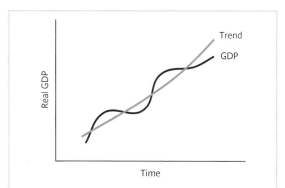

Fig. 10.1 Cyclical Fluctuations

The Keynesian assumption helps explain short-run fluctuations of real GDP around its long-run growth trend.

chapter we will add the foreign exchange market, providing an open economy version of the Keynesian model. Our reasoning follows the **general equilibrium** approach. General equilibrium is the simple requirement that all markets achieve equilibrium *at the same time*, and that these equilibrium conditions are mutually consistent with each other. This is a very powerful method of analysis, which allows us to capture the many interactions that take place among the different markets in one step. Figure 10.2 offers a preview of the full open economy analysis. Through the interest rate, the money market affects the goods market, and thus the level of output. The goods market, in turn, affects the demand for money and thereby the interest rate. Later on, we will also allow the real exchange rate to influence the demand for domestic goods. We will see how interest and exchange rates affect each other, and therefore the goods market.

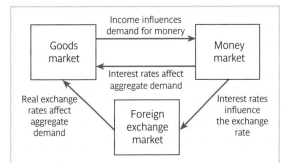

Fig. 10.2 General Macroeconomic Equilibrium

Conditions in domestic money and goods markets affect each other. Interest rates and exchange rates influence the level of aggregate demand, while income affects the demand for money and, for a given money supply, interest rates. General equilibrium occurs when equilibrium conditions in the three markets are consistent with each other.

10.2 Aggregate Demand and the Goods Market

10.2.1 The Market Equilibrium Assumption

We start with the fundamental accounting identity of Chapter 2:

(10.1) $Y = C + I + G + \text{PCA},$

where all variables are measured in real terms, i.e. at constant prices. In Chapter 2, we presented this equation as an identity which described the various categories of spending on domestic goods that make up the GDP. As a definition, this equation is true by construction and we could leave it at that, but here we view it in a different light. We now think of the left-hand side of (10.1) as the **supply** of goods and services by domestic producers, while the right-hand side brings together various components of world **demand** for goods and services produced domestically. These components are given by C, the demand by resident households for consumption goods, investment spending I by firms on capital goods, the public sector's own demand for goods G, and the

primary account PCA. The PCA is the difference between the world's demand for our goods, exports X, and the domestic demand for foreign goods, imports Z.

Viewed this way, (10.1) is no longer a definition or an identity. Rather, it is a market equilibrium condition. We require it to hold not only because national accountants get numbers right, but because we *assume* that the goods market is in equilibrium so that demand equals supply. But how are the two brought into balance?

When we look at particular markets (apples, clothing, computers, machines tools, steel, oil, etc.), we usually think of that good's price as the mechanism which brings demand and supply in line. When looking at the macroeconomic picture, all goods and services that enter GDP, and the average price of these goods is the price level. In the short run, it is convenient and realistic to adopt the Keynesian assumption that prices on average are sticky, i.e. that they move slowly and in a predetermined way. In the language of macroeconomics, the price level is assumed to be exogenous. Later on, in Chapters 12 and 13, we will return to that assumption and allow the general price level to respond endogenously to evolving aggregate demand and supply forces.

To see what a fundamental difference this assumption can make, let us suppose that demand (the right-hand side of (10.1)) is greater than supply (the left-hand side). If prices were flexible, they would rise, as prices tend to do when there is excess demand. Higher prices would lower demand, but would also raise supply. If they are sticky, how can the market return to equilibrium? The Keynesian answer implies that we can now interpret (10.1) as an *explanation* of GDP's movements over time. Demand responds to exogenous forces, while supply responds passively to shifts in demand. For the short run, this is the central and far-reaching implication of the Keynesian assumption.

10.2.2 Determinants of Demand

What, then, are those exogenous forces that shape demand? In order to answer this question, we need to think hard about the behaviour of consumers, firms, and the primary current account (PCA). In doing so, we will return to many of the insights from Chapters 7 and 8: the behaviour and resource constraints of households, enterprises and the government. As a short cut, we consider public spending G and tax receipts T as exogenous; in words, the behaviour of the public sector is independent of economic conditions. To emphasize this assumption, we will frequently write exogenous variables with an upper bar: $\bar{G}$ and $\bar{T}$.

In Chapter 8 we explained the factors which drive private consumption and investment in detail. Now, all we need to do is to synthesize these results in a simple and compact way. We start with consumption, which originates in household behaviour. Measured in real terms, consumption is driven by wealth and disposable income. Wealth, represented by the symbol Ω, is assumed to be exogenous.[1] Disposable income Y^d, income after tax, is the difference between GDP Y and tax payments by the private sector

$\bar{T}$, which is measured net of transfers to households and firms. Our description is summarized by the following **consumption function**:

(10.2) $C = C(\underset{+}{\Omega}, \underset{+}{Y - \bar{T}}).$ (consumption function)

As before, signs underneath the two determinants of consumption indicate the effect of each variable on demand. More wealth and a higher disposable income each raise consumption demand. Note that, while taxes are assumed to be exogenous at this stage, GDP is endogenous, and represents total aggregate income, which is equal to total demand, which we are in the process of explaining.

In Chapter 8 we also studied the demand by firms for investment goods. Although it is a smaller fraction of total demand, it tends to fluctuate the most and is considered by most macroeconomists to be highly relevant for the ups and downs of the business cycle. This demand is represented by the following form of the **investment function**:

(10.3) $I = I(\underset{+}{q}, \underset{-}{r}).$ (investment function)

The investment function states that investment expenditures increase when Tobin's q increases, and declines when the interest r rises. Remember from Chapter 8 that, all other things equal, investment is driven by business expectations or entrepreneurial 'animal spirits'. This is captured by Tobin's q. The interest rate matters for investment for two reasons: (1) because a higher interest rate reduces Tobin's q; (2) because firms borrow from banks to finance investment.[2] When borrowing costs rise, firms invest less.

The interest rate is an important variable in the analysis of this chapter, so it will be useful to make clear which interest rate we are talking about. In Chapters 7 and 8 we studied the *real* interest rate r, which measures the real cost of borrowing or the return to lending. Later, in Chapter 9, we examined the *nominal* interest rate, denoted by i, which is quoted by banks or reported in the financial press. We learned

---

[1] Generally, wealth changes very slowly in response to household savings, so this assumption can be justified for short-run analysis. On the other hand, when asset prices change, wealth can change suddenly. An good example of this is consequence of the recent collapse of housing prices in the United States, Spain, and Ireland. We return to this point later on.

[2] More precisely, firms use the interest rate to evaluate investment projects. This explains not only why Tobin's q falls when interest rates rise, but it also why a firm deciding how to invest its money would invest less in physical equipment when interest rates are higher.

that the nominal interest rate is the cost of holding money, and that includes a component which reflects inflation. Later, when we study inflation in Chapter 13 and afterwards, we will distinguish between the nominal and real interest rate. The Keynesian assumption that prices are sticky implies that inflation is zero or negligible, so we can treat these two rates as the same. For future reference, however, we note that it is the real interest rate r that matters for spending decisions and the nominal interest rate i that is relevant when we look at monetary questions.

Then there is the last term in (10.1), the primary current account (PCA). Recall that the primary current account surplus is defined in Chapter 2 as the difference between exports (X) and imports (Z) of goods and services, measured in terms of domestic output:

(10.4) $$PCA = X - Z.$$

First consider imports. Recall that total domestic spending, also called absorption (A), includes spending on both domestically produced and imported goods and services.[3] Imports are thus a component of absorption: the more we spend, the more we import. This proportion need not be constant, however. In particular, it will depend on the country's competitiveness. In Chapter 6, we saw that competitiveness can be measured by the real exchange rate σ, the relative price of domestic to foreign goods. A real depreciation—a decrease in σ—makes foreign goods relatively more expensive, and therefore discourages imports. Conversely, a real appreciation—an increase in σ—boosts imports, which are now cheaper. These observations are summarized by the **import function**, which says that imports rise with absorption and with the real exchange rate:

(10.5) $$Z = Z(\underset{+}{A},\underset{+}{\sigma}).$$

Turning to exports, we need only recognize that they are the imports of the rest of the world. Accordingly, they behave as our imports, from the foreign perspective. Thus our exports depend on foreign absorption A^* (and its determinants, foreign wealth Ω^*, foreign disposable income Y^{d*}, foreign Tobin's q^*, etc.). If our real exchange depreciates—if σ decreases—our goods

become cheaper in the foreigners' eyes and stimulate our exports. Conversely, a real appreciation—an increase in σ—depresses exports, which have become more costly. We bring these observations together in the form of the **export function**:

(10.6) $$X = X(\underset{+}{A^*},\underset{-}{\sigma}).$$

We combine these results in the form of the **primary current account function**, which is simply the difference between the export and import functions in (10.5) and (10.6):

(10.7) $$PCA = X(\underset{+}{A^*},\underset{-}{\sigma}) - Z(\underset{+}{A},\underset{+}{\sigma})$$

$$= PCA(\underset{-}{A},\underset{+}{A^*},\underset{-}{\sigma}).$$

The PCA function tells us that any factor that boosts one of the components of domestic absorption $A = C + I + G$ (increases in wealth, disposable income, Tobin's q, real growth, public spending or tax cuts, or a decline in the interest rate) will increase imports and reduce the primary current account (increase the primary account deficit). In contrast, anything that boosts foreign spending (increases in foreign wealth, disposable income, Tobin's q, real growth, public spending and tax cuts, or a decline in the foreign interest rate) will increase foreign absorption A^* and therefore our exports, which improves our primary current account. Finally, a real exchange rate appreciation (an increase in σ) leads to a deterioration of the primary account as imports rise and exports fall. Conversely, a real depreciation improves the primary account.

Macroeconomists like to take short-cuts. Because the factors that affect absorption and aggregate demand also affect output—that is the Keynesian assumption—then factors that affect absorption will ultimately affect output. The obvious short-cut is to replace the PCA function in (10.7) with the following version:[4]

(10.8) $$PCA = PCA(\underset{-}{Y},\underset{+}{Y^*},\underset{-}{\sigma}).$$ (primary current account function)

---

[3] Recall that absorption A is defined as $A = C + I + G$.

[4] This is done to avoid carrying along one more variable, absorption. We could keep absorption in our formulation and, in the end, eliminate it. We would just end up where we will soon be. Exercise 11 at the end of this chapter invites you to check this assertion.

In the end, we will work with this primary current account function, which states that the PCA is negatively related to domestic real income, positively to foreign income, and negatively to the real exchange rate. This completes the picture of aggregate demand in an open economy.

10.2.3 Goods Market Equilibrium

The groundwork having been laid, we can proceed to study equilibrium in the goods market. We know how much consumers want to buy, how much firms want to invest in productive equipment, and the government's spending intentions. In addition, we have characterized how much of all that should fall on domestic or foreign goods and the intentions of foreign customers. Adding up the various demand functions according to the national income identity, we obtain the planned or **desired demand function**:

(10.9) $DD = C(\Omega, Y - \overline{T}) + I(r,q) + B + PCA(Y, Y^{*}, \sigma).$
$+ +\phantom{Y - \overline{T}) } -+- +\phantom{Y^{*},} -$

(desired demand function)

Why is this called 'desired' and not actual demand? In short, because a number of the factors that drive aggregate demand—real GDP, the real interest rate, Tobin's q, the real exchange rate—also depend on demand, as we shall see. For instance, real income Y affects demand, but at the same time it represents aggregate supply which, according to the Keynesian assumption, adjusts to demand. So (10.9) describes what aggregate demand would be—what the economy would desire to spend—given particular values of these endogenous variables, not necessarily what it will in fact be. Indeed, we need to ascertain that the values of these endogenous variables are compatible with each other.

While this may seem like a bad case of circular reasoning, it illustrates the fundamentally simultaneous nature of general equilibrium in economics. It simply corresponds to the circular flow diagram presented in Chapter 2. This diagram shows that what is spent must be earned so that the GDP measures both total income and total output. The point of the desired demand DD function is to cut through the circularity. It tells us what demand should be *given GDP*, which is total income. At the same time, GDP also measures output, which is determined by demand

under the Keynesian assumption. A graphical analysis will help us understand this simultaneous determination of demand and output.

We start with a description of how Y (GDP) affects desired demand, ignoring for the time being the other variables shown on the right-hand side of (10.9). We note that Y matters in two ways: first, it affects consumption positively. But, second, it also exerts a negative effect on the primary account, since higher income increases imports. Which effect dominates? Theory and evidence say that it is the consumption effect. The reason is that imports represent a fraction of domestic spending. When an increase in GDP causes consumption to rise, imports too rise but by a (variable, the real exchange rate matters as well) fraction of consumption. In the end, desired demand (also called aggregate demand) rises with the GDP, which is represented in Figure 10.3 by the upward-sloping DD

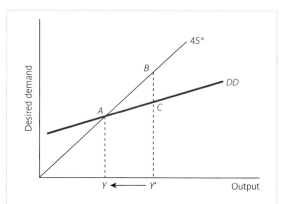

Fig. 10.3 The 45° Diagram

Desired demand DD increases with income (which derives from the sale of output), but less than proportionately, because part of any additional income is typically saved and part of spending falls on imported goods. Equilibrium occurs when demand equals supply, i.e. when firms produce output—measured along the horizontal axis—equal to desired demand—measured along the vertical axis. This happens along the 45° line. Equilibrium occurs at point A, where desired demand and output are equal. The corresponding output level Y is called equilibrium GDP. If output exceeds its equilibrium level, for example Y', supply (point B) exceeds demand (point C) so firms accumulate inventories of unsold goods. Sooner or later, they will cut production and the economy will move towards equilibrium.

schedule (or curve). But demand increases less than the GDP, which explains why the *DD* schedule is flatter than the 45° line. This is formally shown in Box 10.1.

The goods market is in equilibrium when GDP, interpreted as output, is equal to GDP interpreted as spending. Output, the left-hand side of (10.1), is represented by the horizontal axis in Figure 10.3, while desired spending, the right-hand side of (10.1) and described by (10.9), appears on the vertical axis. Market equilibrium requires that both be equal. Graphically, it means that equilibrium must occur along the 45° line. The *DD* schedule describes how much people want to spend, given their income, which they can freely choose. Point *A*, at the intersection of both schedules, represents the situation where desired aggregate demand is met, i.e. is equal to output. This state is called **goods market equilibrium** and the corresponding output level, *Y*, is **equilibrium GDP**.

To grasp the meaning of equilibrium in the goods market, consider the case where GDP is *Y'*, above its equilibrium level *Y*. Output is represented vertically by point *B*, desired demand by point *C*. The fact that *B* is above *C* means that we face a situation of excess supply. Since no one is forced to spend more than they freely choose, firms can only sell the quantity represented by point *C*. In this situation, firms produce more than their customers want to buy. The excess supply, measured by *BC*, is stored aside as inventories of unsold goods. This is a situation that cannot last very long because firms will not produce goods that they cannot sell. Sooner or later, they will reduce their production and the output level will decline. Graphically, production moves from point *B* down and to the left along the 45° line. Less production means less income and desired spending declines. Graphically, desired spending moves from point *C* down and to the left along the *DD* schedule. The process will continue until we reach point *A*. Conversely, starting below equilibrium GDP, we observe a situation of excess demand. Firms satisfy this demand at first by drawing down their previously accumulated inventories but, at some point, they will raise production and the economy will move rightward until point *A* is reached.

Box 10.1 The Slope of the *DD* Schedule

The slope of the *DD* schedule is measured by the increase of desired demand in response to an increase in output. From equation (10.9) we see that GDP, which also measures total income, affects desired demand via consumption and via the primary current account:

$$\Delta DD = \Delta C + \Delta PCA.$$

Let's look at each channel separately. From Chapter 8, we know that consumption increases by less than income because consumers wish to smooth changes in income:

$$\Delta C < \Delta Y.$$

A simple way of describing this result is to introduce the marginal propensity to consume *c*, which captures the response of consumption to a (marginal) change in income: $\Delta C = c\Delta Y$. If $c < 1$, then indeed $\Delta C < \Delta Y$.

Next, consider the PCA, the difference between exports *X* and imports *Z*. Exports do not demand on domestic GDP, while imports rise with spending and therefore with GDP. Overall, therefore, the primary account deteriorates when GDP rises:

$$\Delta PCA = -\Delta Z < 0.$$

Suppose, for simplicity, that imports are a constant fraction *z* of consumption, say $Z = zC$, and that all investment goods are bought from a domestic producer. Thus, we have $\Delta Z = z\Delta C$. The proportion *z* must be less than one. Since it is positive, it implies that $1 - z$ too is positive but also less than one. Putting this altogether, we have

$$\Delta DD = \Delta C - z\Delta C = (1 - z)\Delta C = (1 - z)c\Delta Y.$$

Since both *c* and $1 - z$ are both less than one, it follows that $\Delta DD < \Delta Y$, the slope of the *DD* schedule, $(1 - z)c$, is less than 1, and the *DD* schedule is flatter than the 45° line.

Let's summarize what we have learned about the goods market in the short run. First, GDP returns to its equilibrium level because firms adjust the production level to meet the market's demand. Second, any disequilibrium in the goods market is relatively short-lived. Firms use their inventories as a buffer. They accumulate inventories when demand is unexpectedly weak and they run down inventories when demand outstrips production. This is why firms carefully monitor their inventory levels.

It may appear that some fundamental accounting identity is violated in this description of an economy out of equilibrium. The national accountants solve that problem by treating the accumulation of inventories as final sales. Implicitly, firms sell to themselves the goods that they stock—they 'invest' in extra inventories. For instance, with output at Y', income and GDP exceed the aggregate demand forthcoming by the amount BC, while total GDP is read off point C. Conversely, inventory decumulation is treated as negative sales and subtracted from actual spending—as if firms would disinvest, or buy back from themselves the goods that they sell from existing stock.[5]

10.2.4 The Keynesian Multiplier

The DD schedule captures the effect of GDP on demand, taking as constant all the variables besides GDP. If these variables change, the DD schedule will shift and equilibrium GDP will change. Understanding these effects provides the first explanation of output fluctuations, the purpose of this and subsequent chapters.

For example, public spending on goods has been considered as exogenous thus far and constant. What would happen if it were to increase by $\Delta \bar{G}$, from $\bar{G}$ to $\bar{G}'$? We look at what happens in Figure 10.4, assuming that the economy starts from equilibrium at point A with real GDP level Y. Desired demand has now increased by $\Delta \bar{G}$, at any level of output. As a result, the desired demand schedule shifts upwards by that amount. With output equal to Y, the new situation is

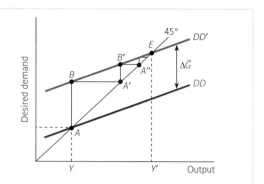

Fig. 10.4 The Multiplier

An exogenous increase in government spending shifts the demand schedule vertically by $\Delta \bar{G}$. Supply rises to meet increased demand, and the economy's equilibrium output ultimately rises to point Y'. The multiplier effect—that the change in output ΔY (given by $Y' - Y$) exceeds the initial impulse $\Delta \bar{G}$—can be understood by following the staircase up from point A. The direct effect, an increase in demand and output, raises GDP to point A'. However, this point is still not equilibrium, because DD lies above the 45° line. Thus, desired demand and output increases again, to point A'', and so on, all the way to point E.

described by point B, where desired demand exceeds output. For a while, producers will make up the difference by drawing down their inventories but, within a few weeks, they will start raising their output to match the new demand. They will continue to do so until equilibrium output is reached at point E and output has risen to Y'.

Let us track down what happens on the way from A to E. At the initial output level Y, desired demand first increases by ΔB. Excess demand $AB = \Delta B$ is eliminated when firms increase production by $BA' = AB$ and the economy moves to point A'. Yet point A' is not a market equilibrium, since it is not on the DD' schedule. At point A' we have neglected to account for the fact that, when output rises from A to A', income does too, raising desired demand to point B'. As firms raise output to eliminate the excess demand AB, more income is generated, which creates more excess demand in the amount $A'B'$. Firms will again raise output by $A'B'$, which takes the economy to A''. And once again, more output means more income and therefore a higher level of desired demand. The staircase

---

[5] More precisely, national accountants treat the accumulation of inventories as an investment: total investment is the sum of desired investment and undesired inventory accumulation:
$$Y = C + I^{\text{desired}} + \Delta(\text{inventories}) + \bar{G} + PCA.$$

Box 10.2 The Multiplier's Algebra

In Box 10.1, we showed that the slope of the DD schedule is $c(1-z)$. So when government spending increases by ΔG, output and therefore incomes first increase by $\Delta \overline{G}$ as well.[6] This so-called first-round effect is the size of the first step in Figure 10.4. Then desired spending increases by $c(1-z)\Delta \overline{G}$, which is the size of the second step. The third step corresponds to an income increase of $c(1-z)\Delta \overline{G}$, so desired spending increases by $c(1-z)[c(1-z)\Delta \overline{G}] = c^2(1-z)^2 \Delta \overline{G}$. Since c and $1-z$ are smaller than 1, c^2 is smaller than c and $(1-z)^2$ is smaller than $(1-z)$. Continuing in the same way, the size of the next step is $c^3(1-z)^3 \Delta \overline{G}$, etc. In the end, the whole income increase is

$$\Delta Y = \Delta \overline{G} + c(1-z)\Delta \overline{G} + c^2(1-z)^2 \Delta \overline{G} + c^3(1-z)^3 \Delta \overline{G}$$

$$+ \ldots + c^n(1-z)^n \Delta \overline{G} + \ldots$$

$$= [1 + c(1-z) + c^2(1-z)^2 + c^3(1-z)^3 + \ldots$$

$$+ c^n(1-z)^n + \ldots]\Delta \overline{G}$$

$$= \frac{1}{1-c(1-z)}\Delta \overline{G}.$$

The last formula is a standard result from algebra (if a is less than one, $1 + a + a^2 + \ldots + a^n + \ldots = \frac{1}{1-a}$). This shows that the multiplier is $\frac{1}{1-c(1-z)}$, which is larger than unity. Note that, if there is no leakage to savings ($c = 1$) and to imports ($z = 0$), the multiplier would be infinite. Needless to say, this case is not of practical relevance.

---

process continues until the economy reaches point E, which is on both the new desired demand schedule and the 45° line.

How do we know that this apparently unending process stops at point E? Note that the first step of the staircase is of size $AB = BA' = \Delta \overline{G}$. The second one, of size $A'B' = B'A''$, is smaller. The graphical reason is that the desired demand schedule DD is flatter than the 45° line, and there are two reasons for this. First, some of the additional income created is saved and not spent. Second, some of the extra spending falls on imports, and imports create income abroad, not at home. Thus while more demand creates an equal increase in supply and therefore income, the extra spending generated by the additional income is smaller. Savings and imports operate as leakages which drain some of the newly created income away from additional spending. This is why each step in the staircase is smaller than the previous one.

Eventually, the steps become minuscule. Box 10.2 gives a formal description of this process.

The other remarkable result is that ΔY, the total increase of output from Y to Y', is a *multiple* of the initial exogenous increase in demand $\Delta \overline{G} = AB = BA'$. This is why the effect is called the **Keynesian demand multiplier**. It is very general: no matter which exogenous change triggers the process, and whether the disturbance is positive or negative, equilibrium output always responds to demand, sometimes by a larger amount.[7]

The multiplier effect corresponds to the fundamental insight provided by the circular flow diagram in Chapter 2. Each individual's spending is someone else's income. By raising incomes, an exogenous increase in demand generates additional desired demand, which means more spending and income, a never-ending process, although at each stage, the effect becomes smaller, and eventually dies out. The circular flow diagram showed where these leakages occur: taxes, savings, and imports each capture a portion of any additional income.[8] These three leakages

---

[6] This embodies an important assumption that the entire first round of spending is spent on goods produced domestically. In many open economies this assumption is implausible, so that some of the first round 'leaks' immediately in the form of imports. In the Exercises at the end of the chapter you are asked to show that the multiplier in this case is $(z/1 - c(1-z))$ which may not be greater than 1.

[7] The overall effect may take several months to complete.
[8] Here, however, taxes are exogenous and constant.

Table 10.1 Government Spending Multipliers

	Government consumption Years after change		Government investment Years after change	
	1	**2**	**1**	**2**
Denmark	0.3	0.7	0.7	1.1
France	0.6	1.0	0.8	1.2
Greece	0.5	0.9	0.8	1.2
Belgium	0.3	0.7	0.7	1.1
Germany	0.4	0.8	0.8	1.2
Italy	0.6	1.0	0.8	1.2
Poland	0.4	0.8	0.8	1.2
Portugal	0.4	0.8	0.8	1.2
Spain	0.5	0.9	0.8	1.2
Turkey	0.6	1.0	0.8	1.2
UK	0.5	0.6	0.8	1.2
USA	0.7	0.8	0.9	1.3

Source: OECD (2009). [OECD, *Economic Outlook Interim Report* Appendix 3.2.p. 138 'high estimates']

represent domestic income not *automatically* re-spent on domestic goods and services.

The word 'automatically' is important. For example, some of the additional taxes collected along the way could be used to support additional public spending but it would be an exogenous decision by the government to raise $\overline{G}$ even more than the initial boost $\Delta \overline{G}$. Similarly, higher savings are available to finance new productive equipment. However, firms must be convinced to invest more. Improved expectations of future profitability captured by Tobin's q, which we treat here as exogenous, would do this. Finally, a rise in imports will generate higher incomes abroad, triggering there another multiplier effect which might well lead to higher foreign GDP Y^* and more exports. All of these effects are plausible but, since we consider $\overline{G}$, T, Ω, and Y^* as exogenous, at this stage we cannot logically treat them as responding automatically in the circular flow of income.

It should be clear, by now, that big leakages reduce the multiplier. We can check this a bit more formally. If a large proportion of any additional income is saved or if a large proportion of any additional spending is imported, the *DD* schedule becomes flat. It is easy

to see from Figure 10.4 that the flatter the *DD* schedule, the smaller is the multiplier effect.[9]

In practice, there is much debate about the size of the multiplier. A part of the debate, presented in Chapter 20, is associated with doubts about, or even rejection of, the Keynesian assumptions. Another part of the debate is related to more technical issues, for example what is assumed to happen to some of the variables that we have ignored in the previous reasoning (tax revenues, Tobin's q, etc.). Finally, the speed at which GDP responds to fiscal policy actions varies, depending on countries and circumstances. The multipliers presented in Table 10.1 show the effect of an increase in public spending over the following two years and should be regarded as very well-informed guesses. Generally, the multiplier is higher in large and relatively closed economies, like the euro area and the USA, because import leakages are small. These estimates, used by the OECD, also tend to indicate that the multiplier is modest in many cases and not always greater than one.

---

[9] Using the result in Box 10.2, it is easy to see that a lower c or higher z decreases the multiplier.

10.2.5 Endogenous and Exogenous Variables

When using this framework, we return to the distinction made in Chapter 1 between endogenous economic variables we are trying to explain, versus those exogenous variables we take as given to the analysis. Whether a variable is treated as endogenous or exogenous is an analytical assumption made for convenience. Indeed, by declaring a variable to be exogenous, we free ourselves from the obligation of explaining its behaviour. Naturally, we would like to explain everything at once, but being careful has its rewards. Treating most variables as exogenous is an effective way to get a handle on complex phenomena of interest. Later, it is possibly to endogenize variables considered exogenous by introducing new theoretical mechanisms, i.e. the behaviour of government spending and taxes to changes in output, unemployment, etc.

A review will be helpful at this stage. The Keynesian assumption implies that the price level P is exogenous. Instruments of government spending and taxation policy, such as government purchases $\bar{G}$ and taxes $\bar{T}$, are assumed to be under direct control of the government and thus are also treated as exogenous—hence the overbar symbol.[10] As in Chapter 8, household wealth Ω is also assumed to be exogenous, as are foreign variables such as foreign GDP (Y^*) and the price level (P^*), since they are also not influenced by domestic changes as long as the economy under consideration is small relative to the 'rest of the world'. The nominal and real exchange rates too are also treated as exogenous, although we will change that in the next chapter. Finally, the interest rate and Tobin's q will be endogenized in the next section.

In the end, the only endogenous variable so far is output Y. Two other variables, consumption and the PCA, were also treated as endogenous in so far as they depend on output. This section has provided the first explanation of business cycles. It shows how output responds to changes in the exogenous variables. Figure 10.4 deals with one example, when the government increases public spending. It is good practice to consider each of the exogenous variables, ask what happens when it changes, and trace graphically the effect of these changes on GDP.

10.3 The Goods Market and the *IS* Curve

In this section, we add the interest rate to our list of endogenous variables. In the spirit of general equilibrium analysis, we are seeking to explain output and the interest rate *jointly*. This objective will be achieved by the end of this chapter. To do so, we will continue to use graphical tools to assist us in our reasoning. The two endogenous variables will appear on the figure, output Y along the horizontal axis and the interest rate i along the vertical axis.

10.3.1 From the 45° Diagram to the *IS* Curve

In Figure 10.3, the DD schedule shows how desired demand varies when output changes, holding everything else (the interest and exchange rates, Tobin's q, public spending and taxes, private wealth, foreign demand) constant. This is the time to remember that Tobin's q is inversely related to the real interest rate r.

When r rises, future profits are more heavily discounted and Tobin's q declines. While expected future profits—animal spirits, as we called them—will be considered exogenous, Tobin's q is now endogenous to the interest rate.

We can now ask: What happens to equilibrium output when the interest rate changes? The answer is given in the first panel of Figure 10.5. The starting point A, where equilibrium is achieved, lies on the desired demand schedule drawn for an interest rate i. Now suppose that the interest rate declines from i to i'. We know that Tobin's q will increase. Looking at the investment function (10.3), we see that investment

---

[10] We treat net taxes as exogenous for simplicity, for the time being. In the WebAppendix to this chapter, more realistically, taxes are allowed to depend positively on income Y. Indeed, in practice, governments usually set tax *rates*, which implies that tax revenues tend to rise with output and income.

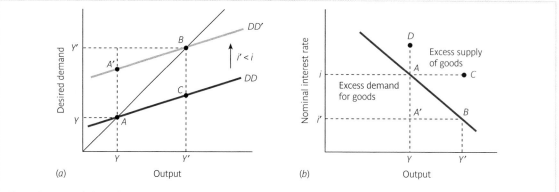

Fig. 10.5 Deriving the *IS* Curve

A reduction in the interest rate from *i* to *i′* leads to an increase in investment spending, which in turn leads to an increase in equilibrium output, as shown in the left-hand side panel. This relation is summarized by the *IS* curve in the right-hand side panel. For a given change in interest rates, the *IS* curve is flatter, the larger is the increase in equilibrium output measured by the horizontal distance between *A′* and *B* in both charts. The length of *A′B* in turn depends on: (1) the sensitivity of demand to interest changes, represented by the size of the vertical shift of *DD*, or *AA′*, in panel (*a*); and (2) the multiplier effect, measured by the horizontal distance *A′B* in the same panel. A steeper desired demand schedule implies greater sensitivity of desired demand to output, larger values of the demand multiplier, and a flatter *IS* curve.

will rise since both of its determinants, the interest rate and Tobin's q, act in the same direction. At each level of income, desired demand is now higher, which means that the *DD* curve shifts upwards. The new equilibrium is now achieved at point *B* (with a multiplier effect), which means that equilibrium output increases from Y to Y′.[11]

This result is summarized in the second panel of Figure 10.5. Points *A* and *B* correspond respectively to the initial (interest rate *i* and GDP Y) and final (*i′* and Y′) situations. Of course, we can repeat the same reasoning for other interest rate levels, to obtain more points like *A* and *B*. They will trace out a negative relationship between the interest rate and equilibrium output depicted by the downward-sloping schedule known as the **IS curve**.[12] For given values of

exogenous variables, the IS curve represents the combinations of nominal interest rate i and real GDP that are consistent with goods market equilibrium.

How do we remember that the IS curve is downward sloping? It is enough to remember two things. First, the IS curve is the response to the question previously asked: What happens to aggregate demand and equilibrium output when the interest rate changes? Second, a higher interest rate reduces private spending on investment, which reduces demand and, *via* the multiplier, equilibrium output.

10.3.2 The Slope of the *IS* Curve and the Multiplier

What makes the IS curve more or less steep? This is not a hugely important issue. Still, we briefly answer the question for the sake of completeness.[13] In Figure 10.5(*b*), the slope of the curve is given by the ratio of *AA′* to *A′B*. *AA′* represents the size of the assumed interest rate reduction, while *A′B* tells us how much equilibrium GDP rises in response to this reduction. Intuitively, the more equilibrium output rises in response to a given reduction of the interest rate, the flatter is the IS curve.

[11] We can add another channel. A rise in q means that stock prices (the price of shares in companies) increases. Since stocks are part of wealth Ω, wealth too increases. This raises private consumption in line with the consumption function (10.2). Thus wealth can be made endogenous as well.

[12] The name of this curve comes from the identity (2.6): $I - S = T - G + PCA$, and was first derived by Nobel Prize laureate Sir John Hicks. For simplicity, he assumed government budget balance ($T = G$) and no foreign trade (PCA = 0), so the identity can be reduced to $I = S$. We draw the IS curve as a line because we do not really know, nor do we need to know, its exact shape. For a derivation of the IS curve using calculus, see the WebAppendix.

[13] The slope of the IS curve is formally derived in the WebAppendix.

In order to understand what determines the size of $A'B$, we turn to panel (a). The first item of interest is the upward shift of the DD schedule. The vertical distance of the shift corresponds to the initial rise in investment spending generated by the lowering of the interest rate. Obviously, the further up the DD schedule shifts, the longer will be $A'B$ and the flatter will be the IS curve. Thus, the responsiveness of investment to an interest rate reduction is the first factor that influences the slope of the IS curve.[14]

Now note that point A' in Figure 10.5(a) does not correspond to equilibrium in the goods market. Demand has risen, but output has not yet responded. By the arguments we have made all along, supply will rise to meet demand, which increases income and demand. This is the multiplier story all over again. So the second factor that determines the length of $A'B$ is the multiplier itself. The larger it is, the longer is $A'B$ and, therefore, the flatter is the IS curve.

Summarizing, the IS curve is flatter (1) the greater the sensitivity of demand to changes in interest rates, as measured by the vertical shift of the desired demand schedule (AA') in panel (a), and (2) the larger the multiplier that translates the initial exogenous change into higher total demand, as measured along $A'B$.

10.3.3 Off the *IS* Curve

More interesting is to understand what happens when the economy is *not* on the IS curve. The short answer is that the IS curve represents the goods market equilibrium condition, so that points off the curve describe conditions of either excess demand or excess supply. But which is which?

Let us start from point A in Figure 10.5(b), on the IS curve, and imagine that output increases while the interest rate remains unchanged—for example, that we move to point C vertically above B. Spending has risen as well but less because of the leakages discussed in Section 10.2.4. In Figure 10.5(a) demand is represented by point C while supply is represented by point B. At point C in panel (b), therefore, there is not enough demand to absorb all of the new output. This is a situation of **excess supply** on the goods market,

and inventories rise. Similarly, moving vertically up from point A to a point like D corresponds to an increase in the interest rate at unchanged output. This also leads to excess supply in the goods market because the higher interest rate reduces aggregate demand.

Thus the IS curve determines two regions: (1) above and to the right we observe excess supply in the goods market—inventories are being accumulated; and (2) below and to the left, we have **excess demand** in the market for goods and services, and inventories are run down. At the boundary of the two regions, the IS curve represents those combinations of GDP and the interest rates which are consistent with goods market equilibrium. We have seen in Section 10.2.2 that the economy can stay temporarily off the IS curve, while firms use their inventories as a buffer stock, but fairly soon they will adjust their output, returning the economy to goods market equilibrium on the IS curve. For example, from point C in Figure 10.5(b), the economy will move to point A as firms cut production after a period of inventory accumulation. Similarly, from point D the economy will move horizontally to the left until it reaches the IS curve. More generally, on the right of the IS curve where there is excess supply, goods market equilibrium requires that the economy shifts to the left so that output is brought down to a level compatible with desired demand. Conversely, starting from a situation of excess demand on the left of the IS curve, the economy will move to the right as firms expand output to meet demand. This is what the Keynesian assumption implies.

10.3.4 A Key Distinction: Movements Along or Shifts of the *IS* Curve

A common pitfall for students is to confuse *shifts* of the IS curve with movements *along* it. This is directly related to the distinction between exogenous and endogenous variables examined in Section 10.2.5. The IS curve describes how the two endogenous variables, the real GDP (Y) and the nominal interest rate (i), are combined to achieve equilibrium in the goods market, *everything else being held constant*. What is 'everything else'? All the variables that we treat as exogenous when we draw the IS schedule. As long as these exogenous variables remain constant, the IS

---

[14] We noted in footnote 11 that consumption is also likely to rise. The more it does, the flatter will the IS curve be.

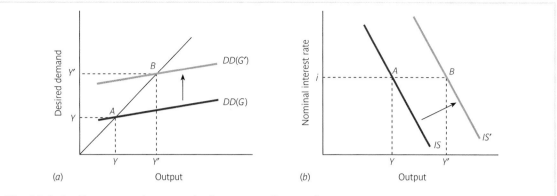

Fig. 10.6 An Exogenous Increase in Aggregate Demand
At unchanged interest rate i, an increase in any of the exogenous components of demand is represented in panel (a) by an upward shift of the aggregate demand schedule. Equilibrium occurs at point B and the new equilibrium output Y' is higher than the initial level Y. Panel (b) shows that the IS curve shifts to the right at the given interest rate.

curve stays in place and we can only move along the curve. Any change in any exogenous variable, however, causes the IS to shift.

In Figure 10.6, an example shows what happens when desired demand increases exogenously, e.g. if

public spending is increased, or the real exchange rate depreciates. In both panels, we start from point A, with output Y and interest rate i. In panel (a), the desired demand schedule shifts upwards. Then the multiplier process gets under way and we eventually

 Box 10.3 **The American Dream, An American Nightmare**

A home or an apartment is an important acquisition for anyone, and as a rule, households hold most of their wealth in their house. Most households purchase houses on credit, a long-term loan called a mortgage. Recent changes in regulation of the way lending is conducted given for house purchases around the world, and especially in the USA, led to new ways to shift income to the present by borrowing more money to purchase the house, and second, to convert additional house value after the purchase (home equity) into cash today by borrowing against it. Effectively, this deregulation made it easier to behave like the consumers with access to credit markets, as described in Chapter 8.

Assuming that households ultimately respect their intertemporal budget constraints and repay their mortgages, these changes can make them better off. Yet in a world of uncertainty it is possible for consumers to borrow too much. Low interest rates in the early 2000s led to excessive borrowing and a run-up of house prices never seen in US history. The first panel of Figure 10.7 shows how dramatic that increase was. It plots a price

index of the average value of houses in key US cities divided by the consumer price index. As an average, it masks the fact that some regions experiencing increased of house prices of 300% and more over the period 1990–2007. Many consumers regarded this increase in wealth as long-lasting and took out loans guaranteed by their new-found wealth to finance additional consumption.

After 2007, house prices dropped dramatically as owners of second and third homes rushed to sell and insolvent borrowers walked away from their loans. As property values declined, the value of wealth declined, so the basis for consumer loans dried up, while banks toughened lending requirements. The result was not only the deepest recession since the 1930s, but also a drop in consumption given income, meaning that households were tightening their belts, more than would have been expected given the recession. This is shown by the second panel which shows the behaviour of consumption around its long-run trend which prevailed from 1970–1995.

end up at point B, where output is Y'. Now remember that the interest rate is exogenous for panel (a). Implicitly, therefore, we have assumed that it has not changed and that is the same at points A and B. Now transcribe this into panel (b). Point B corresponds to the same interest rate i and to the new output level Y'. This point lies on the new curve IS', which shows how the curve has shifted. In the end, the rule is simple: any exogenous change that raises aggregate demand shifts the IS curve to the right, which quite logically means more output. Conversely, when demand exogenously declines, the IS curve shifts to the left.

Which are the relevant exogenous variables? Fiscal policy is a premier source of shifts in the IS curve. The government is a large player in the macroeconomy, and changes in government purchases of goods $\overline{G}$ (e.g. military procurement or road construction) or services (e.g. the number of civil servants or their pay packets) exerts a significant influence on aggregate demand. Similarly, changes in taxation $\overline{T}$ alter disposable income available to households or firms, with knock-on multiplier effects on consumption.

Second, consumption depends on household wealth Ω. Wealth can take many forms, such as land, apartments and houses, financial assets, precious goods such as jewels, Persian rugs, and art, etc. Several of these components can be highly volatile and provoke sharp changes in consumption and thus the position of the IS curve. A classic example is the Great Depression of the 1930s, which followed the crash of stock prices on Wall Street. Many recessions in the past century have been associated with sharp increases of asset prices, increases in consumption spending, and subsequent collapse. The global financial crisis (2008–2009) was driven by a collapse of overvalued house prices in the United States and some other countries. It serves as an excellent example of how a collapse of wealth can affect consumption. Box 10.3 gives details.

Third, changes in expectations of the future can have dramatic effects on investment decisions of businesses. Keynes spoke of 'animal spirits'—business expectations driven by gut feelings or observing others, as opposed to rational calculations. These

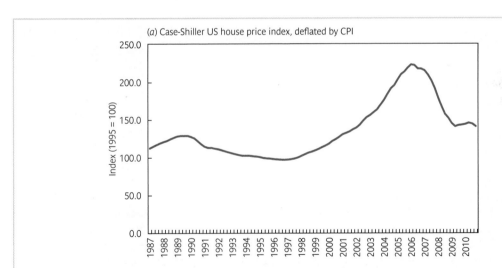

Fig. 10.7 Consumption and House Prices in the USA, 1987–2010

Because dwellings constitute an significant component of household wealth, consumption is strongly influenced by the valuation of apartments and houses. This can be seen in data from the Great Recession in the United States. The upper panel plots the Case–Shiller Home Price Index, which measures the evolution of average housing prices in the USA, divided by the consumer price index. It has been normalized to take the value 100 in 1995. The lower panel shows the deviation of consumption expenditures, in per cent, from a long-term trend. The plot shows not only a dramatic drop in consumption following the collapse of house prices after 2007, but it also shows a rise in the late 1990s, which is likely related to both the steady rise in house prices as well as a stock market boom at that time.

Sources: Standard & Poor/Case–Shiller, *OECD*; authors' calculations.

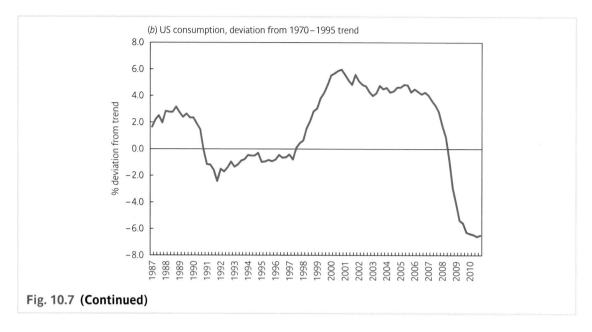

(b) US consumption, deviation from 1970–1995 trend

Fig. 10.7 (Continued)

expectations of the future profitability of investment—correct or not—are captured in Tobin's q. An increase in Tobin's q implies an increase in investment at any level of investment spending, and means that the *IS* curve shifts out at any interest rate. Similarly, a decline in Tobin's q would imply lower investment expenditures at any level of interest rates and an inward shift of the *IS* curve.

Finally, foreign disturbances matter for an open economy. They affect the *IS* curve through the primary current account. The current account is not only a source of leakage, but it also transmits foreign distur-

bances. Indeed, the PCA function (10.8) shows that changes in world activity Y^* can generate export-led expansions or recessions. All other things equal, an increase in Y^* will increase the PCA and cause the *IS* curve to shift rightwards. The same applies to the real exchange rate $\sigma = SP/P^*$, which determines the economy's competitiveness. Any change in either the nominal exchange rate S or in domestic and foreign prices P and P^* will affect the real exchange rate σ and shift the *IS* curve. A real exchange rate depreciation (σ falls) implies a rightward shift of the IS curve; a real exchange rate appreciation moves the *IS* curve leftwards.

10.4 The Money Market, Monetary Policy, and the *TR* Curve

10.4.1 The Taylor Rule and the *TR* Curve

After studying the goods market in Section 10.3, we turn to the money market. There, banks interact with households and firms, and the demand for money is equilibrated with its supply. In the same way as before, we look for levels of real GDP and interest rate which represent equilibrium in the money market. In Chapter 9, we saw that a central factor of the

money market is the conduct of monetary policy by the central bank. Central banks can either try to control the quantity of money in the market, or the level interest rates for short-term lending by banks among themselves. They cannot control both.

Nowadays, central banks conduct monetary policy by setting certain interest rates directly in the money market, and the economy adjusts accordingly.

Effectively, this is the equivalent of a money supply curve. In Chapter 9, we showed that central bank interest rate policy is well-tracked by the **Taylor rule**. The Taylor rule states that the central bank increases the interest rate relative to the 'neutral level' if the inflation rate rises relative to its target rate, or if output rises relative to its trend level. The neutral—sometimes also called natural—interest rate is the one that would be chosen by central bank if inflation and output were both on target. The Taylor rule presented in Section 9.4. stated that the interest rate setting policy of modern central banks can be represented by the following relationship:

$$\textbf{(10.10)} \qquad i = \bar{i} + a\underbrace{(\pi - \bar{\pi})}_{\substack{\text{inflation}\\\text{gap}}} + b\underbrace{\left(\frac{Y - \bar{Y}}{\bar{Y}}\right)}_{\substack{\text{output}\\\text{gap}}}$$

where π is the inflation rate, $\bar{\pi}$ is the central bank's inflation target, and $\bar{Y}$ is trend GDP. Recall that $\bar{i}$ is the neutral—sometimes also called natural—interest rate, which the central bank would choose if inflation and output were both on target ($\pi = \bar{\pi}$ and $Y = \bar{Y}$). The coefficients a and b indicate how responsive the central bank is to inflation and the output gap, respectively.

In the short run, the neutral interest rate $\bar{i}$ is a policy variable of the central bank. It is the anchor of the Taylor rule which summarizes the central bank's monetary stance.[15] For that reason we will also call it the **target interest rate** of the central bank. The Taylor rule will be simplified in this and the next chapter because we make the Keynesian assumption that prices are constant, i.e. that both inflation and its target rate are zero $(\pi = \bar{\pi} = 0)$.[16] Under these assumptions, we can write the Taylor rule in the following simple form:

$$\textbf{(10.11)} \qquad i = \underbrace{\bar{i}}_{\substack{\text{target}\\\text{interest rate}}} + b\underbrace{(Y - \bar{Y})}_{\substack{\text{output}\\\text{gap}}}$$

which says that central bank policy 'leans against the wind': it raises the interest rate whenever output Y

increases relative to potential output and, conversely, cuts rates when Y declines.[17] Monetary policy conducted by the central bank is centred around $\bar{i}$, the nominal interest rate which the central bank would choose if the economy were at its equilibrium or trend level of output.

Just as the *IS* curve shows combinations of interest rate and output consistent with goods market equilibrium, the Taylor rule gives rise to a combinations of output and interest rates which characterize the monetary policy of the central bank. Combined with a demand for money, we can describe the interaction of the Taylor rule and the demand for money as representing money market equilibrium. This will be discussed in more detail later. This set of pairs of interest rates and output consistent with central bank's monetary policy as summarized by its Taylor rule is called the **TR curve**. The TR curve is shown in Figure 10.8. It is upward-sloping because a higher level of GDP, all other things equal, causes the central bank to raise interest rates. A lower level of GDP prompts interest rate cuts by the central bank. When the economy is at its trend level, the

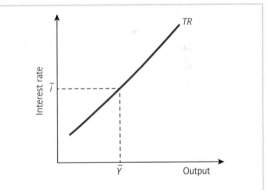

Fig. 10.8 The *TR* Curve
The central bank sets interest rates according to a Taylor rule. Since inflation is treated as exogenous in the short-run analysis, the level of output plays a larger role for the Taylor rule. When output rises relative to its trend level, central banks tend to lean against the wind, i.e. raise interest rates, while they cut interest rates in recessions.

---

[15] In the long run, this will not be the case. Chapter 13 goes into detail on this crucial point.
[16] While Keynesian analysis often assumes inflation equal to zero, this is not necessary for most of the analysis which follows.

[17] To simplify the graphical analysis in this chapter and the next, we will consider only absolute deviations from trend output.

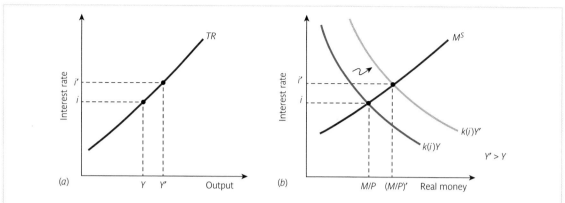

Fig. 10.9 The *TR* Curve and Money Market Equilibrium

When GDP increases, the *TR* curve implies an increase in interest rates as dictated by central bank policy in panel (*a*). At the same time, increased GDP and income lifts the demand for money; in panel (*b*), the demand curve for money has shifted to the right. As a result, the money supply has increased from M/P to (M/P)′. The money market is equilibrium with the central bank supplying the money demanded at the higher level of output and interest rates.

interest rate set by the central bank is equal to its target rate $\bar{i}$.

Because the *TR* curve describes how the central bank behaves, the economy is *always* on it, in contrast to the *IS* curve, where we saw that there can be excess demand and supply of goods. Money market equilibrium is depicted in panels (*a*) and (*b*) of Figure 10.9. Panel (*a*) reminds us that the central bank chooses the interest rate that its Taylor rule dictates, but it must then provide the amount of bank reserves that the market demands at that interest rate.[18] Graphically, demand and supply must be equal when the central bank chooses a point along the money demand curve. This is captured by the right hand panel (*b*) of the figure. In order to steer the interest rate to its chosen level, the central bank must supply the amount of money that corresponds to the chosen interest rate and the level of output associated with it. This supply of money traces out as the M^S curve in panel (*b*).

10.4.2 Slope of the *TR* Schedule

The slope of the *TR* schedule shows how vigorously the central bank reacts to the output gap, raising the interest rate when the output gap is positive and cutting

it when the gap is negative. In fact, this vigour of response is summarized completely by the parameter *b*. To see this, compare different monetary policies symbolized by *TR* curves TR_0, TR_1, and TR_2 in panel (*a*) of Figure 10.10. TR_2 corresponds to the most vigorous interest rate reaction (points B and F), followed by TR_1 (points C and E). TR_0 corresponds to a constant interest rate policy (*b* = 0).

In Figure 10.10, curve TR_2 corresponds to the case when the money supply does not change at all. The central bank refuses to supply any new reserves to the money market. This type of policy is called **monetary targeting**. It implies large fluctuations of interest rates in money market equilibrium in response to swings in GDP, and corresponds to a much steeper *TR* curve. This is drawn as points *B* and *F* in the panels of Figure 10.10.

Even if it is no longer practiced, monetary targeting has a special role in both the theory and practice of macroeconomic policy. In the original analysis of Keynes' ideas, the money supply was fixed by the central bank. Monetary policy was summarized by the *LM* curve, which is still used by many instructors of macroeconomics today. It is discussed in Box 10.4. The general case is represented by the upward-sloping schedule TR_1 in panel (*a*) of Figure 10.10. It says that the central bank adjusts the supply of money as GDP fluctuates.

[18] We saw in Chapter 9 that different central banks employ different 'battle tactics' (open market purchases and sales, rediscounting), but they all have the same overall objective—setting the market interest rate at some target level.

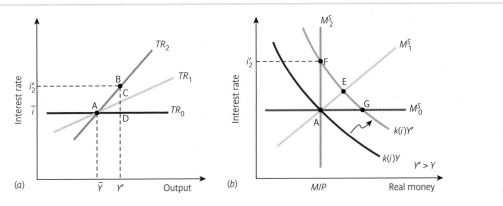

Fig. 10.10 The Slope of the *TR* curve

Different slopes of the *TR* curve correspond to different degrees to which central banks lean against the wind and raise interest rates in light of an economic expansion, or cut them as output declines. As output increases from Y to Y′, different *TR* curves will imply different interest rates. TR_2 depicts the most stringent of monetary policies, involving sharp increases in response to increasing output. TR_1 corresponds to less-sensitive monetary policies, while TR_0 implies that interest rates are held constant. Each *TR* curve implies a different supply of money consistent with the interest rate chosen by the central bank. TR_0 implies the largest increase in the money supply; TR_2 is constructed to imply an unchanged money supply in response to the increase in GDP.

 ## Box 10.4 Twentieth-Century Keynesian Analysis of Money Market Equilibrium: *LM* curve

Keynes wrote the *General Theory* in the depths of the Great Depression. The idea of studying the demand and supply for money as the primary determinants of interest rates—as opposed to the demand and supply for loans on the other side of banks' balance sheets—was revolutionary. Keynes' analysis consisted of a couple of equations, and there was little graphical analysis to help. At the time, it seemed plausible to assume that central banks could exert close control over the money supply. Against this backdrop, in 1937 the eminent contemporary of Keynes, the Oxford economist and Nobel Laureate J.R. Hicks, clothed Keynes' ideas in mathematical garb, summarizing money market equilibrium as the equality of a money supply under the control of the central bank and Keynes' 'liquidity preference'—the demand for money described in Chapter 9. He also developed a graphical framework, which was used for many decades: the *IS–LM* diagram. It is the precursor of the *IS–TR* analysis in this book.

For a constant money supply, this money market equilibrium can be depicted in the same panels of Figure 10.10 used to derive the *TR* curve. Starting from point A, we consider on the right-hand side the intersection of the demand for money, $k(i)Y$, and the supply of money (M/P):

(10.12) $$M/P = k(i)Y.$$

Hicks' thought experiment was to ask if there are other combinations of output and interest rates consistent with money market equilibrium for a given amount of money supply. Put differently, what happens to money market equilibrium if GDP rises from Y to Y′, holding all else constant? The demand for money rises as firms and households need more to carry out increased volume of transactions. As is evident from panel (b), an increase in Y keeping M constant increases the equilibrium interest rate. Indeed, the supply has not changed so the interest rate must rise to fully offset the effect on demand of higher output. From panel (a), this implies a

Box 10.4 **Twentieth-Century Keynesian Analysis of Money Market Equilibrium: *LM* curve** *(Continued)*

second pair of equilibrium combinations of output (GDP) and interest rates which are consistent with money market equilibrium (Y_2' and i_2') which are on the TR_2 curve in panel (*a*). Hicks called this positive relationship between GDP and the interest rate for a given money supply the *LM curve*.[19] The *LM* curve is upward-sloping because when the central bank targets the money supply, rising interest rates are necessary to restore money market equilibrium in the wake of an increase in GDP (i.e. real income and output), which raises the demand for money.

Until the 1990s, the *LM* curve was the standard textbook description of short-run money market equilibrium. Combined with the *IS* curve (also due to Hicks), it

formed the basis of undergraduate education for millions of economics students and analysts. The *IS–LM* asked what happens when the money supply is fixed. Yet the question remained: What will be the central bank's response? The *LM* curve can be thought of as a special case of the *TR* curve in which the central bank chooses the interest rate that maintains a constant money supply, for a given output level. For a time, central banks did try to control the money supply and the *LM* curve was the right way to think about the macroeconomy. Now that most central banks set interest rates directly and behave according to the Taylor rule, the *LM* curve has lost its usefulness as a pedagogical device and will not be used in this textbook.

10.4.3 Monetary Policy: Moving Along or Shifting the *TR* Curve

As with the *IS* curve, it is important to distinguish between movements along or shifts of the *TR* curve. The *TR* curve represents the monetary policy of the central bank, so it only moves *when that policy itself changes*. At this stage of the analysis, the central bank's Taylor rule (10.10) is summarized by two parameters. The first is the slope of *TR* curve, given by *b*. This shows the strength of central bank's reaction of output moving from its trend, and corresponds to the underlying objectives of the central bank in 'leaning against the wind' and preventing swings of output. The second key parameter is the central bank's target interest rate $\bar{i}$. This is the desired level of interest rate at a 'normal' level of output. For reasons explained in more detail in Chapter 13, $\bar{i}$ is also sometimes called the central bank's estimate of the **short-run neutral interest rate**.[20]

Unless $\bar{i}$ changes, the economy moves along the *TR* schedule. Thus, an increase in GDP, holding all else

Fig. 10.11 Shifts of the *TR* curve

If the central bank reduces its target rate from $\bar{i}'$ to $\bar{i}$, the *TR* schedule shifts downwards and to the right. When output equals trend level at $\bar{Y}$, the interest rate was set at $\bar{i}$; now it is set at to $\bar{i}'$. This is an example of expansionary monetary policy. A contractionary policy would correspond to an increase in the target rate to $\bar{i}''$.

---

[19] The name '*LM*' originates from the fact that, along the curve, the demand for liquidity (*L*) equals the money supply (*M*) in equation (10.12). For an explicit derivation of the slope of the *LM* curve using calculus, see the WebAppendix to this chapter.

[20] In Chapter 13 we will see that in the long run, the neutral interest rate must be equal to the sum of the equilibrium real interest rate *r* plus the target rate of inflation. In the short run, central banks can choose the target interest rate to deviate from this long run condition.

constant, will be associated with higher interest rates, while lower GDP will induce the central bank to reduce interest rates. When the values of those parameters do change, the TR curve will change position. One possibility is an increase in b which would cause the TR curve to rotate around the point defined by trend GDP $\bar{Y}$ and the target interest rate $\bar{i}$, as shown in Figure 10.10, say from TR_1 to TR_2. This would imply that the central bank is more concerned about reducing output fluctuations.

A second possibility is that the central bank changes its target interest rate, for instance reducing it from $\bar{i}$ to $\bar{i}'$. This would imply a downward shift of the TR schedule from TR to TR' in Figure 10.11. At any level of output, the central bank will now choose a lower interest rate; as we will see shortly, this means a more expansionary monetary policy. Similarly, the central bank could decide to raise interest rates at any level of output. This would imply an upward and leftward shift of the TR curve.

10.5 Macroeconomic Equilibrium

We are now ready to study the macroeconomy when both goods and money markets are in equilibrium. The resulting framework will provide a useful tool for understanding how output and the interest rate respond to exogenous disturbances. This is an important step forward. Indeed, in Section 10.2, on the basis of an analysis of the goods market, we had developed a way to understand the behaviour of the output gap, our initial interpretation of business cycles. Section 10.3 derived combinations of output and interest rates consistent with a goods market equilibrium under the Keynesian assumption; Section 10.4 did the same for money market equilibrium, given that the central bank's behaviour follows a Taylor rule. We now ask under which conditions *both* goods and money markets are in equilibrium *at the same time*. In effect, we are imposing mutual consistency on the two markets as a condition for macroeconomic general equilibrium. The next step will be to analyse the effects of changes in exogenous influences on output and interest rates.

10.5.1 Macroeconomic Equilibrium in the *IS – TR* Model

For the time being, we ignore the exchange rate and the fact that the economy may be subject to financial flows. This is a good characterization of the equilibrium of the global economy for which the current account is zero, or a large economy subject to controls on movements of financial capital. Deficits and surpluses on the current account (PCA less than or greater than zero) are financed passively by financial markets. In the next chapter, the objective is to show how things change when we consider an economy open to active financial flows.

Using the *IS–TR* apparatus is straightforward. We have seen that the economy cannot stay for long off the *IS* curve and that it is always on its *TR* curve. So, for both goods and money markets to be in equilibrium simultaneously, we require that the economy lies at the intersection of the *IS* and *TR* curves. In Figure 10.12, macroeconomic equilibrium is achieved at that intersection, point A. At this point there is neither excess demand nor supply for goods, nor is there excess demand or supply of money, given the central bank's policy summarized by the Taylor rule.

To help understand this powerful notion of equilibrium, it is useful to remind ourselves what other combinations of output and interest rates would imply. All other points in the diagram which are off the *IS* and *TR* curve represent either disequilibrium in the goods market, an inconsistency of monetary policy with the Taylor rule, or both. All points above the *IS* curve imply an excess demand for goods, while all points below it imply an excess supply of goods. Similarly, all points above the *TR* curve imply that interest rates are above the level consistent with the central bank's monetary policy—the central bank can be expected to take action to reduce them. For all points below the *TR* curve, the central bank can be expected to raise interest rates.

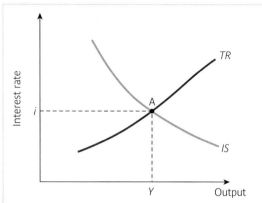

Fig. 10.12 Macroeconomic Equilibrium
Macroeconomic equilibrium occurs when both the
goods and money markets are in equilibrium
simultaneously. This occurs at the intersection of the *IS*
and *TR* curves at point *A*.

10.5.2 Real Shocks: Shifts of the *IS* curve

We can use the *IS–TR* framework to understand the
effects of exogenous disturbances, or **shocks**, to the
macroeconomy. These shocks can originate either in
the real side of the economy or from the monetary
side of the economy. They may originate at home or
abroad. In the *IS–TR* diagram, shocks are captured as
shifts of one curve or another. In this section, we consider shocks to the goods market—shifts of the *IS*
curve. The reasoning applied will be to ask: After the
shock occurs, where is the *new* curve in relation to
the original one?

Consider, for example, the effect of an exogenous
change in government purchases of goods and ser-
vices, $\bar{G}$, say, an increase from $\bar{G}$ to $\bar{G}'$. This corresponds to the type of action taken in the wake of the
Great Recession in 2008–9. For example, the government might increase spending on schools—teachers,
computers, or classrooms.[21] Starting from *IS* in the
first panel (*a*) of Figure 10.13, an exogenous increase
in government spending makes every point previ-

ously consistent with goods market equilibrium now
out of equilibrium. In fact, for every point on the old
IS curve, aggregate demand now exceeds output.
Logically, the exogenous increase in government
spending implies that the new curve should lie to the
right of the old *IS* curve; there is an exogenous
increase in the demand for goods at any level of interest rate, which is met by a greater supply. This shift is
shown as the shift from *IS* to *IS′* in panel a) of Figure
10.13. The new equilibrium occurs at point *B*. An
exogenous increase in demand leads to a higher output and a higher interest rate.

This is an interesting result in its own right, but it
is just as important to understand what is happening
in the background. First, higher demand results in
higher output. After all, the Keynesian hypothesis is
that output responds to demand. But there is more to
the outcome than that. We know that the *IS* curve
rightward shift is larger than the initial boost in
demand because of the multiplier effect. So we know
that the total increase in output results from a succession of impulses running from more demand to
more output, and from more output to more income
and therefore yet more demand.

Second, the interest rate has increased. This is
because the *TR* curve is upward-sloping. By assumption, the position of the *TR* curve has not changed,
because the factors that determine its position
remain changed. Therefore, we move with the *IS*
curve *along* the *TR* curve. As output rises, the monetary authority raises interest rates. Because interest
rates have risen, output rises less than it would have
under a situation of constant interest rates. This
example illustrates how considering the feedback
from the goods market to the money market imposes
consistency on the overall macroeconomic outcome.

Exogenous shifts in components of real aggregate
demand have effects which are qualitatively similar
to shifts to government spending. It is possible to
identify a number of factors behind the *IS* curve
which can be the source of exogenous shifts of aggregate demand, given income. Besides government purchases $\bar{G}$, these include:

◆ taxes (net of transfers) $\bar{T}$

◆ household wealth Ω

◆ Tobin's q

---

[21] We will consider the increase in government spending as $\bar{G}$
irrespective of whether it is government consumption or
investment. Table 10.1 suggests that this aspect may be
relevant in practice.

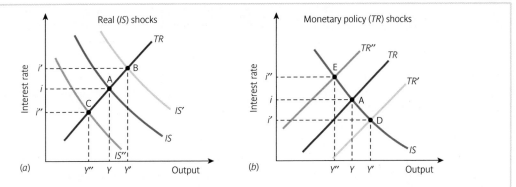

Fig. 10.13 Macroeconomic Shocks

In panel (*a*), starting from point *A*, an exogenous increase in demand shifts the *IS* curve to *IS′*. This takes the economy to point *B* along the *TR* schedule, which shows that the central bank raises the interest rate in response to output expansion. An exogenous decrease in demand shifts the *IS* curve to *IS″*, leading to lower interest rates and output. In panel (*b*), an expansionary monetary shock, an exogenous cut in the target interest rate, moves the *TR* curve to *TR′*, leading to greater output and lower interest rates; a contractionary monetary shock raises interest rates and reduces output.

- the real exchange rate σ

- foreign income Y^*.

To understand the direction of the shift implied by exogenous changes in these variables we merely need to think about the impact they would have on aggregate demand given output (*Y*). An increase in taxes $(\Delta \bar{T} > 0)$ shifts the *IS* curve to the left, since this would reduce aggregate demand at every level of output or interest rates; a tax cut $(\Delta \bar{T} < 0)$ shifts the *IS* curve up and to the right. An exogenous increase in Tobin's *q* $(\Delta q > 0)$ would lift investment expenditures for any level of output and income, shifting the *IS* curve to the right; a drop in Tobin's *q* $(\Delta q < 0)$ shifts the *IS* curve to the left. A rise in the real exchange rate $(\Delta \sigma > 0)$ reduces international competiveness and reduces net exports, depressing aggregate demand and shifts the IS curve to the left, while a decrease $(\Delta \sigma < 0)$ would raise aggregate demand and shift the *IS* to the right. Finally, an exogenous increase in household wealth Ω causes households to increase their consumption at all rates of interest, shifting the *IS* curve to the right, while a decline in wealth causes the *IS* curve to shift to the left. The last event is highly relevant for understanding the impact of the financial crisis on the real economy in all countries, but especially those which were hit by the end of the real

estate bubble of the 2000–2010 decade, as discussed in Box 10.3.

10.5.3 Monetary Policy Shocks: Shifts of the *TR* curve

Now consider another thought experiment. The central bank decreases its target neutral interest rate, an example of an **expansionary monetary policy shock**. This means that at any level of output, the central bank will fix the nominal interest rate at a lower level than before. This policy change is represented as an exogenous decline in the target interest rate from $\bar{i}$ to $\bar{i}'$, with $\bar{i}' < \bar{i}$.

This event is tracked in panel (*b*) of Figure 10.13. Graphically, the TR curve shifts down to TR′, and the economy moves from point *A* to point *D*. The outcome of this expansionary monetary policy is higher output and a lower interest rate. As the central bank provides more liquidity, banks can lend to customers at lower interest rates. Why do bank customers wish to borrow more? Because interest rates are lower. With a lower interest rate, investment spending rises and we move down and to the right along the IS curve. As we do so, the multiplier takes over and consumers start spending more because their incomes rise. Note, however, that the equilibrium interest rate does not decline from $\bar{i}$ to $\bar{i}'$. As output rises from its initial value, the central bank's desired interest rate rises, even after the initial lowering of the target rate. That is the implication of the Taylor rule.

The *TR* curve could also shift upwards. This means a higher rate of interest at every level of GDP. This is called a **contractionary monetary policy shock**. The central bank has decided to raise its target interest rate, exogenously, for any level of output (and at any phase of the business cycle). This policy is captured as an exogenous increase in the target interest rate from $\bar{i}$ to $\bar{i}''$, with $\bar{i}'' > \bar{i}$. In the second panel of Figure 10.13, the *TR* curve shifts up to *TR''*, and the economy comes to rest at point E. The outcome of this contractionary monetary shock is lower output and a higher interest rate. Why? As the cost of lending rises for the banks, they pass these higher rates on to their customers and the level of demand drops. As before, the rise of the interest rate in equilibrium is less than the shock, because the economy moves along a downwardly sloping *IS* curve, leading to lower output and inducing the central bank to moderate its tougher interest rate stance in the end.

10.5.4 A General Approach

We have given a number of examples of how we can use the *IS–TR* model to uncover the impact of exogenous disturbances on output and the interest rate. We could consider much more complex cases involving combinations of the two or more of the disturbances mentioned in the last section. For example, what is the effect of a simultaneous increase in stock prices and in the money supply? What might one predict from an exogenous appreciation of the exchange rate combined with a cut in taxes? It is fairly common for policy-makers to combine or mix policy measures. As we will see in the next few chapters, the net effect of several policy measures or shocks taken together sometimes is qualitatively ambiguous. All the same, there is a well-defined strategy for studying these macroeconomic effects:

◆ First, we ask which curve is affected by the disturbance. This is where the remarks presented in Sections 10.3.4 and 10.4.4 are convenient.

◆ Second, we spot the new equilibrium at the intersection of the new *IS* and *TR* curves.

Finally, we can go beyond the graphical analysis and interpret the results by tracking down the various channels involved in the response of the economy to the disturbance.

The *IS–TR* model can be used to study the effects of any arbitrary demand disturbance coming from the real or the monetary side, in any combination that can be described in terms of the elements of the model. In the chapters that follow, we will do so extensively. The same procedure applies to: (1) identify which schedule is affected by the disturbance, (2) identify the new equilibrium, and (3) understand what this means for the goods and money markets, using both panels in Figure 10.13.

10.5.5 Monetary and Fiscal Policy in the *IS – TR* model

According to the Taylor rule, the central bank does not *decide* to be expansionary or contractionary. It merely reacts to economic conditions according to a behavioural rule. For a given target interest rate, monetary policy is *automatically* expansionary when the output gap is negative. Conversely, it becomes contractionary when the output gap is positive. It is natural then to ask: Why would the central bank shift its own Taylor rule as it did in the previous section? Why would it deliberately increase interest rates unconditionally?

Of course, the central bank can and does change its behaviour. This is because behaviour does not occur in a vacuum. New information comes to light each day that conditions or influences the policy of the central bank. For example, the central bank may learn that an adverse demand shock is about to occur, and decides to cut interest rates—or comes under political pressure to do so. In that case, the *TR* curve would shift downwards. According to (10.10), this is the case when the central bank revises downwards its target interest rate. Similarly, a new forecast of sharply rising future inflation in spite of current moderate inflation could prompt the central bank to raise its short-term target rate. These types of policy changes do in fact occur, and are best thought of as exogenous shifts of the *TR* curve in the *IS–TR* framework.

The image of monetary policy conveyed by this discussion is a rather optimistic one. As a matter of fact, monetary and fiscal policy have served as important

Box 10.5 Monetary Policy under Duress: The Zero Bound

The Taylor rule assumes that central banks can choose any interest rate they please. The global financial crisis showed that central bankers cannot always do so. In particular, the nominal interest rate cannot be reduced to below zero: a negative nominal interest rate would mean that depositors at banks or holders of banknotes would actually *pay* for the privilege—which is impossible without additional restrictions on the rules governing the institution of money.[22] The linear form of the *TR* curve cannot thus literally be true. In fact, equation (10.10) implies that when the output falls below the value $\bar{Y} - \bar{i}/b$, the interest rate i must turn negative; following its own rule, the interest rate desired by the central bank has hit a lower bound. If GDP drops precipitously as it did in 2008–2009, it may be simply impossible for central banks to reduce their interest rates as much as their policy preferences would dictate, possibly because the *IS* curve has shifted so far to the left. Figure 10.14, which plots interest rates in the UK, the Eurozone and the USA in the period 1990–2011,

shows that room for margin using the traditional instrument of interbank interest rates was exhausted by 2010.

Under these conditions central banks may turn to other, more exotic forms of monetary policy. For example, in the depths of the financial crisis, the US Federal Reserve resorted to open market purchases of securities, including Treasury bonds and mortgage-backed securities; in 2010, it explicitly tried to purchase bonds of long maturity in an effort to reduce interest rates. In 2011, the Bank of England considered doing the same. The European Central Bank was spared this fate in the first phase of the financial crisis, but as the second hit, it has also purchased on the open market large quantities of government debt owed by Eurozone countries— those of Greece, Italy, Portugal and Ireland, which were in a state of financial distress. The zero lower bound on nominal interest rates poses a thorny problem for those who were sure that monetary policy contained enough weapons to fight the worst recessions.

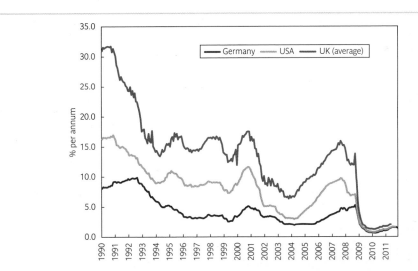

Fig. 10.14 Short-term Interest Rates in the UK, USA, and Germany, 1990–2011

Nominal interest rates fluctuate over the business cycle. Until the Great Recession, however, they maintained an average value across fluctuations of several percentage points. Since late 2009, they have hovered close to zero. Because nominal interest rates cannot be reduced below zero, this limits the effectiveness of monetary policy in severe recessions.

[22] Silvio Gesell, an Austrian monetary economist of the early twentieth century, invented a system of *Schwundgeld* (vanishing money), which actually reduced the value of banknotes over time. Many have tried to implement this idea but it has never caught on, probably because there was always a 'normal' form of money available as an alternative.

means of smoothing the business cycle, and a more detailed discussion of these issues can be found in Chapter 16. All the same, the severity of the Great Recession has challenged policy-makers in fundamental ways and pointed out the limitations of policy, as Box 10.5 illustrates.

❗ Summary

1 General equilibrium occurs when all markets simultaneously clear. In the short run, macroeconomic equilibrium is characterized by equilibrium in two markets: the market for goods and services and the domestic money market, which is governed by monetary policy adopted by the central bank.

2 The Keynesian assumption posits that prices are sticky, which implies that output is driven by demand. When prices are constant, inflation is nil—and expected to remain nil—and the nominal and real interest rates are the same.

3 The consumption function states that private consumption spending depends on disposable income and wealth. The investment function relates investment spending by firms to the cost of obtaining funds, measured by the real interest rate and Tobin's q.

4 The primary current account improves when income and output in the rest of the world expands and the real exchange depreciates, and worsens when the domestic GDP and absorption rise at home.

5 An autonomous increase in demand for domestic goods triggers a multiplier mechanism: more demand means more output, and more output means a higher income and hence a new round of demand increases. The multiplier process is dampened by leakages in the income–demand chain: savings, taxes, and imports.

6 The IS curve represents the GDP levels and interest rates compatible with equilibrium in the market for goods and services. It is downward sloping because a higher interest rate reduces domestic demand and output. The IS curve is flatter the more sensitive demand is to the interest rate, and the larger is the multiplier.

7 The TR curve describes how the central bank sets the interest rate in order to stabilize inflation around its target and output around its trend. It is upward-sloping because the central bank generally raises interest rates when output rises. The short-run position of the TR curve is determined by the central bank's own target interest rate, which is exogenous in the IS–TR framework.

8 Macroeconomic equilibrium is found at the intersection of the IS and TR curves. This allows us to study how GDP and the interest rate respond to exogenous disturbances.

⚙ Key Concepts

- ◆ recessions
- ◆ Keynesian assumption
- ◆ dichotomy
- ◆ general equilibrium
- ◆ supply, demand

- ◆ consumption function, investment function
- ◆ import, export, and PCA functions
- ◆ desired demand function
- ◆ goods market equilibrium
- ◆ equilibrium GDP

- Keynesian demand multiplier
- *IS* curve
- excess supply/demand
- Taylor rule
- *TR* curve

- target interest rate, short-run neutral interest rate
- monetary targeting
- real and monetary shocks
- expansionary/contractionary monetary policy shocks

❓ Exercises

1 Compare two economies, country A and country B. Country A has a higher marginal propensity to consume from disposable income than country B. Which should have a flatter desired demand schedule? Show graphically that the steeper the desired demand schedule, the larger is the Keynesian multiplier.

2 Desired demand (*DD*) is represented by the following simplified function:

$$DD = 5000 + 0.75(Y - T) + \bar{G} - 100i - 1000\sigma.$$

Domestic and foreign price levels have been assumed constant and equal to one. Let $i = 5\%$ throughout. Initially $G = T = 3,000$. σ is the nominal exchange rate and is assumed fixed at one.

(a) Compute the effect on GDP of an increase in T from 3,000 to 3,500. Show your result graphically. What is the value of the (lump-sum) tax multiplier?

(b) Compute the effect on GDP of an increase in G from 3,000 to 3,500. Show your result graphically. What is the value of the government spending multiplier?

(c) Compute the net effect on GDP when both G and T increase by the same amount, from 3,000 to 3,500. Show your result graphically. What is the value of the balanced budget multiplier? Compare your answers and discuss.

3 Using the logic behind Box 10.2, show that if the government increases spending but some of that increased spending falls on imports—and that fraction is the same as the marginal propensity to

import (z), that the multiplier is smaller than $(1/1 - c(1 - z))$ When is the demand multiplier less than 1? Can it be negative?

4 In reality, tax revenues are not exogenous, but move positively with income/GDP. Suppose that $T = \bar{T} + tY$, where t is an exogenous tax rate. Use this tax revenue function to derive the government spending multiplier in the following simple model:

$$C = c_0 + c_1(Y - T)$$

$$I = \bar{I}$$

$$G = \bar{G}$$

$$PCA = PCA_0 - mY$$

5 Compare your answer with that when $t = 0$. Comment on your result. Define the *IS* curve. Why is it downward-sloping? Show how the *IS* divides the *IS–TR* diagram into two regions, such that points off the *IS* curve correspond to market disequilibrium, which can be characterized as excess demand or supply in the goods market.

6 Derive the *IS* curve for the economy in Exercise 4, with $I = \bar{I} - 20i$. Plot it in (Y, i) space.

7 Define the *TR* curve. Why is it upward-sloping? Explain why the economy cannot be off the *TR* curve, by definition. Show how interest rates and output respond to situations in which the economy is away from the crossing of *IS* and *TR* curves.

8 Suppose that the Taylor rule of an economy is $i = 5 + 0.5 (Y - \bar{Y})$, where i is measured in percentage points. Plot the *TR* curve in the *i*, *Y* diagram. What is the effect of an increase in $\bar{i}$ from 5 to 6 on the *TR* curve? Solve for an analytical expression for output (*Y*) and interest rate (*i*) in an equilibrium in an economy with this *TR* curve and the *IS* curve in Exercise 6.

9 The *policy mix* is the combination of fiscal and monetary policy actions. Show graphically how a combination of fiscal and monetary policies could be used to reduce output without changing the (effective) interest rate.

10 Show what happens to the money supply when demand for money increases exogenously, holding the *TR* curve constant. Suppose that, in response to an exogenous decline in the demand for money, the central bank *raises* its target interest rate. What happens to the money supply? Why do you think the central bank might react in this way? Using Figure 10.10, explain why the TR schedule becomes vertical when *b* = ∞. (It may help to reason in the following way: consider the

effect of a larger *b*, and then let *b* become arbitrarily large.)

11 Show the effect on the *TR* schedule of an increase in the sensitivity *b* of the Taylor rule. What is the effect on the interest rate? (Hint: start from a situation where output is at its trend level.)

Consider an increase in demand for goods in the *IS–TR* model. Using the apparatus of Figure 10.12, show graphically what happens to output, the interest rate, and money supply when the *TR* schedule is horizontal. How would you answer the question if the *TR* schedule is upward sloping? Interpret the difference.

This exercise confirms the argument presented in footnote 3. Ignoring foreign absorption, the PCA function is $PCA(A, \sigma)$. Note that absorption is $A = C + I + G$, so with (10.1) we have $Y = A + PCA(A, \sigma)$. Show that this implies $PCA = PCA(Y, \sigma)$. Use the simple representation of the PCA function $PCA = a - bA - c\sigma$ to compute the modified function $PCA(Y, \sigma)$.

→ Essay Questions

1 Military spending is considered to be consumption in the GDP accounts. Explain why sharp increases in military spending in the USA and the UK after the terrorist attacks in 2001 increased GDP in those countries in the short run. Would you expect the effect to be larger in the US or the UK, and why? How does your answer compare with the long-run effects of such spending?

2 Does the Taylor rule summarize everything about monetary policy of a central bank? What do you think determines the slope of the Taylor rule by central banks? Is your answer likely to be constant over time?

3 There are many ways of conducting an expansionary fiscal policy: raising public spending, cutting

income taxes, profit taxes, or VAT. What difference does it make for different groups in the country? In your discussion, as you take a general equilibrium view of the question, look at the two possible exchange rate regimes.

4 The behaviour of inventories is a closely watched indicator of the state of the economy. Discuss under which conditions it is a valid indicator of things to come. In particular, does an increase in inventories signal an economic slowdown or a boom? (Hint: a change in inventories can be either intended or unintended.)

5 'Open economies, because they have low multipliers, are likely to be more stable than large economies.' Discuss.

International Capital Flows and Macroeconomic Equilibrium

11

The immediate cause of profit-oriented capital movements is an interest-rate differential. The main point is to find out how this interest-rate differential can come about.... A more complete theory of capital movements is an indis-

pensable foundation for the study of the international, or more generally the interlocal, aspects of business cycles.

R. Nurkse (1961)

11.1 Overview

Chapter 10 presented the determination of demand and output when the Keynesian assumption holds and aggregate demand determines output in the short run. While the *IS* curve recognizes the existence of trade in goods and services, we ignored international trade in financial assets. Trade in financial assets is important for a number of reasons. First, every current account deficit must be financed by a capital account surplus, meaning that foreigners were willing to purchase assets from residents—where assets include stocks, bonds, real estate, but also bank account balances, short-term loans, and other liquid instruments. The current account deficit would not otherwise be possible. Second, and more important, trade in financial assets can take on a life of its own, driven by international differences in the rate of return on comparable investment opportunities.

Repairing this omission changes the analysis significantly. This chapter presents the small open-economy version of the *IS-TR* model, known as the **Mundell–Fleming model**.[1] This framework is most relevant for studying the behaviour of small, open economies and is particularly relevant in a world in which financial markets are integrated and capital is mobile internationally. It holds special significance for Europe, both within the monetary union and for countries outside of it.

Central to this chapter is the crucial role of the **exchange rate regime**. We consider two possibilities. The first is that the exchange rate be fixed. The central bank commits to maintaining a certain value of the nominal exchange rate, the value of its currency

in terms of other currencies. Second, and alternatively, the central bank may let the exchange rate float freely, leaving its value to be determined by the market. The exchange rate regime turns out to be crucial to the behaviour of the economy. For this reason, the two regimes of fixed and flexible exchange rates are studied separately.

The Mundell–Fleming model is relevant for Europe for several reasons. First, all European economies are open, and most are truly small. Second, for those in the European Monetary Union, the nominal value of the common currency, the euro, is fixed at 1:1 across member countries, without any actively intervening national central banks.[2] The Eurozone is thus one of the most credible of all forms of fixed exchange rate regimes, since the option of changing the exchange rate is ruled out—without leaving the arrangement entirely. Third, many nations within and outside of the European Union have floating exchange rates—Poland, Iceland, Norway, Sweden, and the UK to name a few—and have policy options which differ from countries in the Eurozone.

We start by looking at the implications of financial openness. When there is free trade in financial assets without **capital controls**, a fully financially integrated economy loses the control of its own interest rate. This limits the room for manoeuvre of the central bank and explains why and in which way the exchange regime matters so much. We begin with the stark implications of the fixed exchange rate regime, and then contrast these with the case of a flexible exchange rate regime. Along the way, we

---

[1] It is named after the Nobel Laureate Robert Mundell (1932–) from Columbia University and the Briton J. Marcus Fleming (1911–1976), who worked at the IMF.

[2] As of December 2011, the Eurozone consisted of Austria, Belgium, Cyprus, Estonia, Finland, France, Germany, Greece, Ireland, Italy, Luxembourg, Malta, the Netherlands, Slovenia, Slovakia, Spain, and Portugal.

develop and refine the Mundell–Fleming model. This is a powerful tool for understanding business cycles, the role of macroeconomic policies, and details of the interplay between goods markets, domestic financial markets, and international financial integration.

11.2 The Implications of Being Small

What is a small, open economy, exactly? Small means that the economy has no discernable impact on the rest of the world. Open means that it is profoundly affected by events that take place beyond its borders. Trade openness—sometimes referred to as current account openness—occurs when goods and services can be exchanged with only limited impediments like tariffs, quotas, and various other restraints. Financial openness—sometimes referred to as financial account openness in reference to the balance of payments, see Chapter 2—describes the situation when people can lend and borrow freely. Box 11.1

further explains how openness is defined and measured. Most countries can be seen as small and open. Prominent exceptions are Japan, China, USA, and the European Union taken as whole. These entities are large in absolute size and their trade with the rest of the world is comparatively limited. They can affect conditions elsewhere in the world but their impact is shrinking, as new economic powers emerge in Asia and South America. As a first approximation, the small and open economy assumption may be increasingly applicable to them as well.

Box 11.1 What is Openness?

In Chapter 1, we presented a first definition of openness related to external trade in goods and services, which is related to GDP by exports and imports.[3] Table 11.1 reminds us of how open and how closed some countries are. As in Table 1.2, we present the average of exports and imports as a percentage of GDP. As one might expect, Table 11.1 shows an inverse relationship between economic size and trade openness: the bigger the country, the less it needs foreign markets and suppliers. Even so, the two largest entities, the euro area and the USA, are far from being closed.

The second definition of openness involves financial markets. In Table 11.1 financial openness is measured by how much a country has lent to the rest of the world (its cross-border assets) or how much it has borrowed abroad (its cross-border liabilities), where 'country' refers to households, banks, firms, and the public sector.

The table shows both assets and liabilities. In many cases, assets and liabilities are not very different (in the same way that exports and imports can be large and of the same order of magnitude). Financial openness allows borrowers and lenders to search the world for the best financial deal. Still, some countries, such as the USA, Brazil, or Poland have more external liabilities than assets. They are called net debtor countries.[4] Conversely, Japan and Switzerland are net creditors.

Developed countries tend to be more open than developing countries, both in trade and finance. The globalization process has begun to change this relationship. Poland, Korea, Brazil, China, and India are among the growing number of so-called emerging market countries in the process of becoming fully integrated in to world financial markets.

---

[3] Remember the goods market equilibrium condition states that output Y is equal to $C + I + G + X - Z$.

[4] Remember that 'liabilities' are used in the broad sense to include all inward foreign investment, including not only debt obligations and government borrowings, but also portfolio and foreign direct investments.

Table 11.1 **Measures of Openness and Economic Size**

	Share of world GDP 2009 (%)	Trade openness 2009 (% of GDP)	Financial openness	
			Total assets 2007 (% of GDP)	Total liabilities, 2007 (% of GDP)
Denmark	0.4	46.0	227.1	234.8
Poland	0.6	38.8	35.3	93.4
Sweden	0.7	45.3	253.1	259.1
Belgium	0.7	71.6	523.1	493.7
Switzerland	0.7	46.2	749.2	607.9
Netherlands	1.1	65.6	486.1	486.5
Brazil	2.2	11.1	30.9	71.8
Korea, Dem.Rep.	1.9	47.9	56.6	78.7
China	7.4	24.5	67.5	45.2
United Kingdom	4.2	28.9	456.1	476.5
Germany	5.0	38.4	219.1	193.3
Japan	12.1	12.5	121.8	72.1
European Monetary Union	17.3	35.6	165.0	181.0
United States	28.6	12.6	130.8	147.9

Sources: The World Bank, *World Development Indicators*; Lane and Milesi-Ferretti (2007).

11.3 International Financial Flows

11.3.1 The Interest Parity Condition

We encountered the exchange rate for the first time in Chapter 6. We saw that, in the long run, the nominal exchange rate is driven by the purchasing power parity principle, a consequence of competition in trade in goods and services. From a short-run perspective, trade in financial assets is more important. An alternative parity condition will lie behind the determination of interest rates and nominal exchange rates. This is the **interest rate parity condition**. We will see that even small deviations from this parity condition gives rise to large, sometimes very large, capital flows as investors try to take advantage of international differences in investment opportunities.

Let us consider a typical international investor, for example a large bank, which routinely borrows and lends all over the world. The domestic interest rate is i, while the **international rate of return** is i^*. Note that we describe i^* as a rate of return, not an interest rate because, as we will see later, we must take movements of the exchange rate into account.

Imagine, to start with, that $i < i^*$. One option available to our international investor is to borrow at home, where the interest rate is low, and invest abroad, pocketing the difference.[5] As they do so, they

[5] In order to do this type of financial deal, one needs to have collateral, i.e. assets which can be pledged in case the deal fails. Large international investors have no difficulties doing this.

raise the demand for money at home and i will rise towards i^*. Possibly, i^* will decline towards i because large amounts of money flow into foreign financial markets, although this is only true if the home economy is sufficiently 'large' to affect the rest of the world. This will go on as long as $i < i^*$. Conversely, if $i > i^*$, money will flow from the rest of the world into our high-interest rate country, pushing i down and i^* up. The implication is that neither $i > i^*$ nor $i < i^*$ is possible. The only logical way out is $i = i^*$. This is the interest rate parity condition.

Just as the purchasing power parity condition equates price levels, the interest rate parity condition states that returns on similar assets cannot differ systematically across countries when there is free trade in financial assets—when financial capital is perfectly mobile. In contrast to the purchasing power parity condition, which takes time to assert itself because good prices move slowly, the interest parity condition is a property which applies even in the very short run. It is well known that financial traders—hedge funds, banks, individual investors—are constantly monitoring the whole world, minute by minute, for investment opportunities. When they find one, they can move huge amounts of money instantly and at little cost. As a result, the working assumption is that the interest parity condition is satisfied at all times, and that any deviation is eliminated immediately. Interest rate parity is simply the equilibrium condition for international financial markets.

11.3.2 The *IFM* Line

The interest parity condition is depicted as the horizontal **international financial markets (IFM) line** in Figure 11.1. Here is where the small country assumption comes in. If the economy is small relative to the rest of the world, the foreign rate of return i^* is exogenous. It changes for reasons unrelated to domestic conditions. It follows that it is the domestic interest rate i in the small economy that bears the burden of adjustment whenever the interest rate parity condition is not satisfied. In what follows, we will assume that i^* is constant, unless we explicitly consider a shock, or exogenous change, to its position.

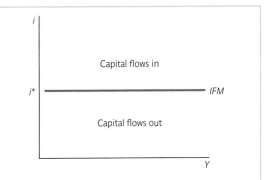

Fig. 11.1 International Financial Market Equilibrium

When capital can move freely across borders, assets of similar quality should yield the same return. Otherwise, unexploited profit opportunities would exist—borrowing would occur where interest rates are low and lending where they are high. This is incompatible with the international market equilibrium. Note that i^* denotes the return on foreign assets converted in the domestic currency. For a small financially open economy, i^* is exogenous.

As with the *IS* or *TR* curves, it is instructive to discuss what happens when the economy is not on the *IFM* line. Above it, the domestic interest rate exceeds the international required rate of return. Capital inflows occur as international investors take advantage of higher returns at home. The inflows, which can be massive, promptly drive the domestic interest rate i down to the world level i^*. Conversely, below the *IFM* line, capital flows out and increasing scarcity drives up the interest rate i back to i^* from below.

11.3.3 Capital Mobility and Financial Account Restrictions

So far, we have assumed that capital is freely mobile. In fact, some countries do impose restrictions on their financial accounts. The most extreme type consists of declaring the national currency inconvertible. It is then legally impossible to convert the currency into foreign ones.[6] More moderate restrictions

---

[6] In this case, black markets usually flourish.

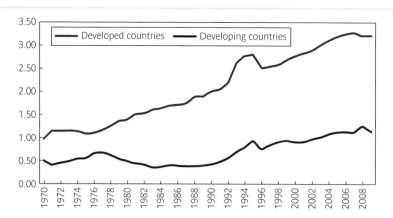

Fig. 11.2 **The Evolution of Financial Account Restrictions**

The figure presents an index of the degree of the ease with which financial assets can be bought and sold internationally, as an unweighted average of developed or developing countries as classified by the IMF in 2011. The higher the value, the fewer the restrictions imposed on capital movements. The value of the index is normalized so the value for advanced economies in 1970 equals 1.0. While developing countries have relaxed capital restrictions over the past few decades, they continue to maintain significantly stricter controls than developed countries.

Source: Chinn and Ito (2008); IMF World Economic Outlook.

limit or forbid some transactions, like investing abroad or the foreign acquisition of categories of domestic assets. Capital controls, as these restrictions are generically called, were quite common until the mid-1970s. Figure 11.2 plots the evolution of financial account restrictions in the last three decades of the twentieth century. It shows that developed countries abandoned capital controls in the 1980s. The same process started a decade later among developing countries, but most continue to maintain restrictions on capital flows.

With capital controls, the interest rate parity need not hold, because the mechanism described in the previous section cannot operate. Legal restrictions prevent traders from taking advantage of the profit opportunities. Of course, the temptation to circumvent the law is strong and indeed capital controls tend to be systematically evaded. As long as they are not fully evaded, however, the interest parity condition is likely to be systematically violated.

Why do countries impose restrictions on capital movements? We have seen how deviations from the interest parity condition can trigger massive capital flows. As we will see, these massive movements of capital can interfere with the central bank's conduct of monetary policy, either because the central bank would like to influence monetary conditions at home, or because it would like to influence the level of the nominal exchange rate. More often than not, countries abandon capital controls because the forces of international financial integration are simply too powerful.

As we proceed to explore the implications of the interest parity condition, it is important to keep in mind that full capital mobility is not a universal feature. The framework presented in this book is well suited to studying developed countries, but it is less helpful for developing economies. Partly because there is a wide variety of capital controls, partly because their effects vary depending on the prevalent conditions, there is no simple equivalent treatment for these countries. If capital controls were watertight, we could simply overlook the interest rate parity condition and work with the macroeconomic equilibrium described in Chapter 10. As a first approximation, this may be the best way to proceed.

11.3.4 Exchange Rate Regimes

Because it draws the attention to capital flows, the IFM line forces us to take explicit account of the exchange rate regime. *In fact, it is difficult if not impossible to predict the consequences of macroeconomic shocks without doing so.* Because of the enormous variety of regimes, it is convenient to consider two polar cases: (1) fixed exchange rates, and (2) fully floating exchange rates.

The International Monetary Fund (IMF) reported in 2008 that 114 of its 198 member countries had adopted one form or another of fixed exchange rates. Under a fixed exchange rate regime, the monetary authorities maintain the value of the exchange rate at a publicly announced parity. This is an official value of the national currency in terms of another currency, usually the dollar or the euro. For instance, Denmark and several countries in Central and Eastern Europe (currently, Bosnia and Herzegovina, Bulgaria, Croatia, Macedonia, Latvia, and Lithuania) peg their currencies to the euro. Most developing countries, including China and several African countries, have adopted fixed exchange rate regimes of various types. Taken to the limit, national sharing of a currency—a monetary union—is the ultimate form of fixed exchange rate regimes. Besides the 17 EU countries of the Eurozone, Andorra, Montenegro and San Marino have also adopted the euro.

The other extreme form of exchange rate policy is to allow the exchange rate to float freely. This means that the central bank takes no direct responsibility for the value of its currency, which is set on foreign exchange markets—markets described in more detail in Chapter 14. The floating rate regime currently applies to the Eurozone, the UK, the USA, and Japan, as well as smaller European economies like the Czech Republic, Switzerland, Hungary, Norway, and Poland. It is studied in Section 11.5.

In between these two polar regimes there are a number of versions of 'managed floating'. Here, the authorities do not commit themselves to a particular parity but nevertheless attempt to prevent large exchange rate fluctuations. This is the case for Romania and Serbia as well as for many Latin American and East Asian countries. This regime is a 'mixed bag' that does not lend itself to a clean-cut analysis. Depending on the weight put to exchange rate stabilization, it can be approximated by either a fixed or a flexible exchange rate regime.

11.3.5 Preview of What Follows

The macroeconomic equilibrium studied in Chapter 10 included two markets: the goods market and the money market. In the meantime, we have added a third: the international financial market. For each of these three markets, we have established those combinations of real GDP and nominal interest rate which are compatible with equilibrium. The IS curve deals with the market for goods and services, the TR curve corresponds to monetary policy and the money market, while the IFM line describes the international financial equilibrium. Each of these curves are drawn 'all other things equal', meaning that they do not shift as long as the exogenous variables associated with that curve remain unchanged.

In the following sections, we extend the Keynesian analysis of the last chapter to include a wide variety of disturbances that small open economies face. The analysis is thus inherently more realistic and relevant than in Chapter 10, yet it builds carefully on that analysis. In studying each particular scenario, it is important to ask and answer the following three questions.

(1) What is the exchange regime? The exchange rate regime is crucial for understanding how the economy reacts, because it leads to the elimination of one of curves in the IS–TR analysis. Under a fixed exchange rate regime, we ignore the TR curve and, under a flexible exchange rate regime, we ignore the IS curve.

(2) Which curve is affected by the disturbance under consideration? An exogenous disturbance affects (at least) one of the three markets and therefore leads to a shift in the corresponding curve.

(3) Where is the new equilibrium and how should it be interpreted? How and why has the economy moved from the initial to the new **general equilibrium**?

11.4 Output and Interest Rate Determination under Fixed Exchange Rates

11.4.1 What is a Fixed Exchange Rate Regime, Exactly?

We saw in Chapter 9 that a central bank that fixes an interest rate must be prepared to supply commercial banks with whatever volume of reserves they demand at that rate. A very similar reasoning applies in the case of a fixed exchange rate. In fact, the central bank will use its assets and liabilities to perform operations in foreign exchange, just as described in Section 9.3.4. Currencies are traded on foreign exchange markets, which are described in Chapter 14. These markets resemble the interbank market. The players are much the same: large banks and other financial institutions. The main difference is that, on the exchange market, domestic money is traded against foreign monies, while it is traded against high-quality short-term domestic assets in the money market.

Imagine that, one morning, the currency appreciates above its declared parity. It is incumbent upon the central bank to weaken its own currency. The way to do so is to sell whatever quantity of the currency is necessary to bring the exchange rate back down again. Similarly, if the value of the currency fell below its parity, the central bank would intervene, purchasing its own currency and selling its holdings of foreign currency. These operations are called **exchange market interventions**.

11.4.2 The Loss of Monetary Policy Autonomy—No *TR* Curve

The similarity with open market interventions goes much further, with a crucially important implication. We have seen in Chapter 9 that a central bank cannot simultaneously choose the money supply and the interest rate. In an open economy with full capital mobility, the message is even more severe: a central bank cannot both choose the exchange rate and its interest rate (i.e. its Taylor rule). Because the central bank cannot choose the interest rate in an open economy with full capital mobility, the *TR* curve has

no meaning! We only use the two other curves, *IS* and *IFM*, to study the behaviour of the economy.

Another way of thinking about the loss of monetary autonomy under a fixed exchange rate regime is that a central bank can only choose one point on the money demand curve presented in Chapter 9 and shown again in Figure 11.3. The central bank faces two constraints: (1) the demand for money, and (2) the foreign rate of return i^* required by the international financial market equilibrium condition.[7]

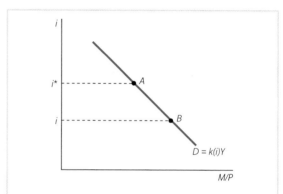

Fig. 11.3 The Money Market Under Fixed Exchange Rates

Starting from point *A*, the central bank decides to lower the interest rate from i^*, the foreign rate of return, to *i*. Money market equilibrium occurs at point *B*. But $i < i^*$ is incompatible with international financial market equilibrium, so capital flows out. In order to support its currency, the central bank must buy it on the foreign exchange market. As a result, the money supply declines and the interest rate rises along *D*. The central bank must continue its interventions as long as $i < i^*$. The only position compatible with international financial market equilibrium is point *A* where $i = i^*$.

---

[7] The money demand curve was described formally in Chapter 9 as k(i)Y, with k′ < 0. Holding income Y constant, an increase in interest rates reduces the demand for real balances; holding the interest rate *i* constant, an increase in income Y increases the demand for real balances.

The only plausible outcome is point A. There is simply no room for manoeuvre.

Imagine that the central bank attempted to lower the interest rate to reach point B in Figure 11.3 with interest rate i. To keep things simple, we ignore any possible impact of this action on output.[8] From Figure 11.1, we know that capital flows out when $i < i^*$. Traders borrow at the low rate i and, in order to invest abroad and obtain the higher return i^*, they sell the domestic currency. This weakens the currency on the foreign exchange market. In order to honour its fixed exchange rate commitment, the central bank must intervene and buy back its currency.

Now remember from Chapter 9 that money is 'money in circulation'. As the central bank sells foreign exchange in the open market, it receives domestic money (its own liabilities) in payment. When it performs this transaction, it withdraws money from circulation, and the money supply declines. In Figure 11.3, we move from point B up and to the left along the money demand curve. Capital outflows will proceed and foreign exchange market interventions continue until $i = i^*$, all the way back to point A. We see that whatever money is supplied on the open market must be promptly removed from the foreign exchange market. This link can be severed, as explained in Box 11.2, but only temporarily. More generally, any attempt by the central bank to change the money supply or the domestic interest rate will be undermined by a commitment to uphold the official exchange rate parity. In Box 11.2 sterilization is examined in more detail as a way to relax the constraint, and Box 11.3 shows how China has tried to deal with this problem.

11.4.3 Demand Shocks—Shifts of the *IS* Curve

How does an exogenous change in the demand for goods affects the level of output and the interest rate, the two endogenous variables in our framework? We examined this question in Chapter 10, but in a context

without international capital mobility. Adding full financial market integration changes the rules of the game significantly.

With a fixed exchange rate and capital freely moving across borders, we know that we only need to consider the *IS* and *IFM* curves. We start from point A in Figure 11.5. To fix ideas, we look at the role of fiscal policy. An expansionary policy, e.g. an increase in public spending or a tax reduction, raises domestic demand. This analysis would apply to similar exogenous increases in aggregate demand, for example if firms became more optimistic and invested more (Tobin's q increases), or if foreign demand for domestic goods were to rise (Y^* increases), which would increase exports and improve the primary current account.

The increase in public spending is captured in Figure 11.5 by a rightward shift of the *IS* curve, from *IS* to *IS'*. The economy moves from point A to point B at the intersection of *IS'* and the *IFM* line. As in Chapter 10, the demand expansion results in an increase in income but now the interest rate remains unchanged, equal to the foreign rate of return i^*.

It might be tempting to conclude that financial openness does not make much of a difference in the context of full capital mobility. This would be completely incorrect! To see why, imagine the situation in the absence of capital flows, e.g. because of watertight capital controls. In this case, we can ignore the *IFM* line, the central bank recovers its ability to carry out an effective monetary policy, and the *TR* curve is relevant again. The new equilibrium occurs at point C. Note that, relative to point B, income has increased less and the interest rate has risen. These two effects are related. The interest rate has increased because the Taylor rule leads the central bank to raise the interest rate to limit output fluctuation (*TR* curve). Relative to point B, output is lower at point C because the higher interest rate adversely affects investment spending. This crowding-out effect reflects the fact that a higher demand reduces, or crowds out, investment spending when it is met by a higher interest rate. In contrast, under full capital mobility the interest rate does not increase—there is no crowding-out effect—and the expansion is stronger.

The loss of **monetary policy autonomy** under a fixed exchange rate regime is a consequence of full capital

---

[8] An exercise at the end of the chapter asks you to verify that the main conclusion stands when we take into account the fact that a lower interest rate should raise output. However, since monetary and financial reactions are much faster than goods market changes, so the simplified presentation is a good approximation to what happens in practice.

Box 11.2 Monetary Side Effects of Foreign Exchange Market Interventions

A foreign exchange market intervention automatically affects the money supply. Foreign exchange purchases by the central bank are paid for with the domestic currency, while sales mean that domestic money—the liability of the central bank called the monetary base (M0)—is withdrawn from circulation. This illustrates how the central bank introduces its liabilities into circulation—either by lending to the banks or the government, called domestic credit, or by purchasing foreign exchange. The monetary base is thus matched by the sum of loans to commercial banks or purchases of **foreign exchange reserves**. This means that

(11.1) $M0 = R + DC,$

where DC represents domestic credit[9] and R measures the foreign exchange reserves owned by the central bank. When a central bank increases the monetary base, it must either increase its holdings of foreign exchange, or increase domestic credit, or both.

When the central bank is pegging the exchange rate, the demand for monetary base is given by the interest rate (which is given be the foreign interest rate i^*). Effectively, it loses control of M0. It is easy to see, then, why an exchange rate intervention (which changes R) is offset by an equal and opposite change in domestic credit, and why an attempt by the central bank to increase its lending to the private banks or the government will be met by a reduction of foreign exchange reserves (the case just described). The latter represents the case of **unsterilized intervention**: in order to prevent its currency from weakening, the central bank buys back its monetary base by selling its foreign exchange. As shown in Table 11.2, this action contracts the money supply, hence the *minus* sign—and reduces the value of reserves by an equivalent amount—another *minus* sign, with no effect on domestic credit—hence the equals sign.

Sterilized intervention occurs when the central bank offsets the foreign exchange market intervention with another operation in the domestic money market.

It re-injects the previously purchased domestic currency by purchasing other assets on the open market, giving financial institutions the very liquidity back which it withdrew when it sold its foreign exchange reserves for its own money. Both M0 and DC increase, hence the *plus* signs in Table 11.2. Combining the two steps (see the bottom row), we see that the central bank has raised its stock of domestic assets DC and reduced its stock of foreign exchange reserves R by the same amount, leaving the money base M0 unchanged. Since the total money supply is a multiple of the base, the sterilized intervention has in fact cut the link between the money stock and the foreign exchange market intervention.

Experience teaches that sterilized interventions can restore only temporarily the ability of the central bank to carry out an independent monetary policy. The central bank will not be able to sustain point B in Figure 11.3. As long as i is below i^*, capital continues to leave the country, and the central bank must continue its interventions to maintain the exchange rate at its parity. This cannot go on forever, though, because the stock of foreign exchange reserves is declining and will be exhausted sooner or later. If the capital flows are large, and they usually are, the reserves can be depleted in a matter of days, sometimes even hours.

The situation is different when i is above i^*. Sterilized interventions by the central bank lead to an accumulation of foreign exchange reserves, which can be purchased with monetary base effectively without limit. Naturally there must be a catch, and there is. In the long run, a swelling monetary base lays the groundwork for inflation. Central banks are forced to invent other tricks to neutralize the impact of the monetization of foreign exchange intervention. Box 11.3 tells the story of China, which has fixed the exchange rate of its currency, the renminbi, with the US dollar since 1995.

While sterilized interventions can give the central bank extra room for manoeuvre, it cannot change the fact that the domestic interest rate is ultimately determined by the foreign rate of return.

---

[9] Domestic credit is a general term describing any form of loan by the central bank to the non-bank sector (private or government). It could take the form of direct lending to the government, the purchase of government debt, or refinancing of commercial lending by private banks.

Box 11.3 Fixed Exchange Rates and the Chinese Dollar Problem

In 1995, China began pegging its currency, the renminbi (sometimes also called yuan), to the US dollar. In doing so, it was able to prevent an appreciation of its own currency from hurting its exports and expanding its imports. Over time, this policy led to a string of large current account surpluses. Then, recognizing its increasing attractiveness, international investors also began to invest in China, resulting in large financial account surpluses. The consequence of this 'double-surplus' on the current account and financial balances can be read from the balance of payments in Chapter 1: the monetary authority, the People's Bank of China was intervening over all those years, accumulating an unprecedented stock of foreign exchange reserves of more than $3 billion ($3 million millions, or $3,000,000,000,000!). Figure 11.4 shows that growth has hardly slowed in the aftermath of the global financial crisis. For an uninformed observer, it might be natural to think that the Chinese are trying to 'buy up the world.' Yet such rapid growth in reserves is a natural product of the process described in Table 11.2.

Unsterilized intervention means that the money supply will grow. This rapid growth of the high-powered money supply (monetary base) leads to rapid growth of the money supply, which in the long run means inflation (see Chapter 6). To prevent this, the People's Bank of China has consistently conducted sterilized interventions; the accumulation of dollar reserves is simply a by-product of this policy. Fortunately, rapid growth of the Chinese economy has meant that money demand absorbed much of this swelling money supply. Nevertheless, the People's Bank has pursued several measures to reduce money growth. First, it raised the reserve requirements to reduce the market multiplier (see Chapter 9). Second, to absorb the liquidity effects of its dollar purchases, it began to issue its own debt, with the effect of reducing DC in (11.1)! In fact, it has even brought DC into negative territory, meaning that the central bank is indebted to the banking sector and not the other way round, as is normally the case.[10] For a long time, the People's Bank of China was even making a profit on its sterilization activity![11] By late 2007, however, US interest rates declined and Chinese rates rose. As a result, the People's Bank of China has begun to lose money—an unusual outcome for a central bank. Given the huge size of its reserves, the losses are significant, probably unsustainable. This may explain why it has started to let its currency appreciate faster.

---

mobility. The only feasible way to recover some leeway is to break the link between i and i^*. This is why some countries resort to capital controls. As discussed in Section 11.3.3, however, capital controls are sometimes helpful, although in a limited fashion.

Table 11.2 Sterilized and Unsterilized Foreign Exchange Market Interventions

	Unsterilized interventions			Sterilized interventions		
	M0	R	DC	M0	R	DC
Step 1	−	−	•=	−	−	•=
Step 2				•+	•=	•+
Overall	−	−	•=	•=	−	•+

11.4.4 International Financial Disturbances—Shifts of the *IFM* line

An international disturbance will usually take the form of a change in the international rate of return i^*. Understanding how a shock to i^* affects a small open economy is an important step to understanding modern macroeconomics, and represents an important example of the interdependence of national economies.

Consider the case when the foreign rate of return rises exogenously from i^* to $i^{*\prime}$, because, say, the monetary conditions around the world are becoming

---

[10] In (10.3), when the value of foreign exchange reserves exceeds the money base (R > M0), we must have DC < 0.

[11] Interest rates were lower in China than in the USA, so the central bank could obtain a higher return on dollar-denominated reserves than it was paying on its yuan-denominated debt to the commercial banks.

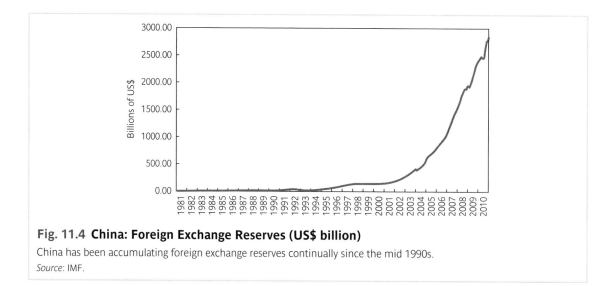

Fig. 11.4 China: Foreign Exchange Reserves (US$ billion)

China has been accumulating foreign exchange reserves continually since the mid 1990s.

Source: IMF.

tighter. The result is the upward shift of the *IFM* line to *IFM'*, as shown in Figure 11.6. At point *A*, the initial point of intersection of the *IS* and *IFM* curves, the interest rate is now too low. Capital flows out and the central bank must intervene on the foreign exchange market and buy back some of its own currency. The money supply declines endogenously and the economy moves to point *B*. Output declines because the higher interest rate reduces aggregate demand.

This example shows that, under a fixed exchange rate regime, the domestic economy is exposed to international financial disturbances. If interest rates rise worldwide, they must rise at home as well, which provokes a recession (*Y* declines). The fixed exchange

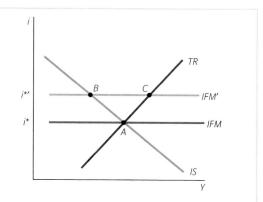

Fig. 11.6 An International Financial Shock

The increase in the rate of return on foreign assets is captured by the shift from *IFM* to *IFM'*. Starting from point *A*, the new general equilibrium occurs at point *B*, where output has declined. Under flexible exchange rates, starting from point *A*, the exchange rate depreciates. The resulting gain in competitiveness increases the demand for domestic goods. The *IS* curve shifts to the right (not shown) until it passes through point *C*, where the new macroeconomic equilibrium occurs.

Fig. 11.5 Demand Shocks Under Fixed Exchange Rates

The demand expansion is shown as shifting the *IS* curve from *IS* to *IS'*. The new equilibrium occurs at point *B* where the goods and international financial markets are in equilibrium. Without capital mobility, the equilibrium would occur at point *C*.

rate regime creates a situation of *international monetary interdependence*, which reflects the loss of monetary policy autonomy. When the financial crisis started in the USA in 2007–8, the world rate of return i^*—largely determined by the United States—fluctuated widely. It first rose as investors panicked and asked for higher returns, then it declined as the Federal Reserve Bank, the US central bank, precipitously cut its own interest rate—one instance when the USA can be seen as a large economy that can pick its interest rate and affect the whole world. Europe was impacted directly by these gyrations.

11.4.5 A Parity Change

Monetary policy is ineffective as long as the central bank remains committed to a specific exchange rate parity. That does not mean that monetary policy cannot be used at all. Most countries that adopt a fixed exchange *regime* allow for adjustments of the exchange rate *level*. These regimes, called 'fixed but adjustable' exchange rates, provide some limited degree of monetary policy effectiveness.

Discrete, occasional changes in the exchange rate level are called **revaluations** or **devaluations**, depending on the direction of the change.[12] A revaluation is an increase in the external value of the currency:

moving from S to S' with $S' > S$. A devaluation would correspond to $S' < S$. For given price levels at home and abroad (the Keynesian assumption), a change in the nominal exchange rate translates directly into a change of the real exchange rate $\sigma = SP/P^*$. Herein lie the real effects of nominal exchange rate changes.

Revaluations and devaluations are conducted by way of an official declaration. The central bank announces the new parity at which it stands ready to buy and sell the domestic currency against foreign exchange. Consider the case of a nominal devaluation, a lowering of the nominal exchange rate S. The devaluation lowers the real exchange rate σ, raises the country's competitiveness, since its goods are now cheaper relative to foreign goods. Exports rise, imports decline, and the primary current account improves. Graphically, the IS curve shifts outwards to IS' in panel (b) of Figure 11.7. Output increases as the economy moves from point A to point B along the IFM line—which does not shift because the small country assumption implies that i^* is exogenous. As would be expected, a devaluation is expansionary. Conversely, a revaluation is contractionary.

What happens in the money and foreign exchange markets? A parity change is not merely a declaration of intent by the central bank; to be effective, intentions

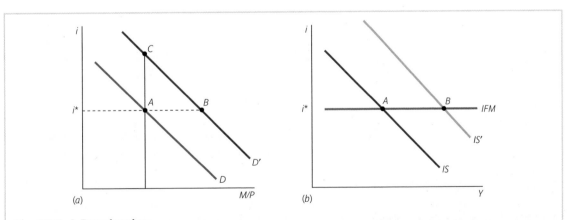

Fig. 11.7 A Devaluation
In panel (b), a devaluation shifts the IS curve out to IS'. The economy moves from point A to point B and output increases. The output expansion raises the demand for money in panel (a), which shows that the central bank must allow the money supply to expand to keep the domestic interest rate i equal to the foreign rate of return i^*.

[12] When the exchange rate floats, its changes are called appreciation or depreciation, see Section 11.5.

must be backed by actions. Indeed, a devaluation must be accompanied by a monetary expansion, a revaluation by a monetary contraction. This is shown in panel (*a*) of Figure 11.8. The increase in output found in panel (*b*) translates into a larger demand for money. In order to make the new parity 'stick', the central bank must supply the additional money demanded at the going interest rate imposed by the international financial market equilibrium condition (point *B*).

Suppose that it didn't follow through with a monetary expansion, and chose to set the interest rate at some other, higher rate ($i > i^*$). For simplicity suppose it simply kept the money supply constant. The domestic interest rate would rise towards point *C*. This would trigger capital inflows, which would force the

central bank to intervene on the foreign exchange market, buying foreign exchange and paying with domestic currency to prevent the **appreciation**. If the intervention is unsterilized, the domestic money supply rises and we end up at point *B*. Whether it is done through open market operations or foreign exchange market operations, the result is the same.

We have seen that, when capital is freely mobile, monetary policy autonomy is lost under fixed exchange rates and that monetary and exchange rate policies are just two sides of the same coin . A more accurate conclusion is that monetary policy can still be carried out, but through **realignments**—devaluations or revaluations—i.e. by changing the exchange rate level without abandoning the regime itself.

11.5 Output and Interest Rate Determination under Flexible Exchange Rates

We now take up the case of a regime of freely floating exchange rates—a description of the situation of the United States, the euro area, the United Kingdom, Sweden, and many Eastern European countries. The central bank explicitly refrains from intervening in foreign exchange markets. Three conclusions follow immediately.

(1) The central bank recovers its ability to conduct monetary policy. It can follow a Taylor rule (represented by the *TR* curve).

(2) By definition, the central bank gives up the exchange rate policy instrument. The value of the exchange rate is determined by market forces.

(3) Given prices' stickiness, a flexible exchange rate implies that the country's external competitiveness is endogenous and so is the position of the *IS* curve. This last result is established in the next section.

11.5.1 Monetary Policy Shocks—Shifts of the *TR* curve

We start by imagining that the central bank pursues a more expansionary monetary policy—in the

terminology of Chapter 10, a monetary policy shock—in a regime of flexible exchange rates. In particular, we study the case when the central bank is willing to set a lower interest rate at any level of output. The *TR* curve shifts downwards, as shown in panel (*b*) of Figure 11.8. There is no other exogenous change, so *IS* and *IFM* remain where they are. Note that the three curves now intersect each other two by two in three different positions: points *A*, *B*, and *C*. Which of these points is sustainable as the equilibrium of the economy?

Look at point *C* at the intersection of the *IS* and *TR'* curves. The interest rate has declined, reflecting the easing of monetary policy, which has led to more spending. Point *C*, however, is below the *IFM* line. With $i < i^*$, capital flows out. This time, however, the central bank does not intervene on the foreign exchange market, and allows the exchange rate to change. Under capital outflow, it will depreciate, as those exiting the currency sell it and buy other currencies. The resulting real **depreciation**, given domestic and foreign prices, in turn, means that the economy becomes more competitive. Exports rise, imports decline, the primary current account improves, and

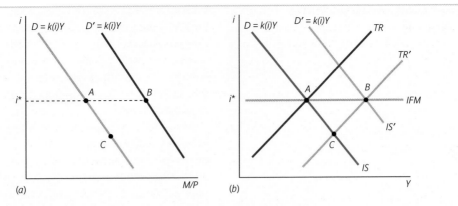

Fig. 11.8 Monetary Policy Shocks Under Flexible Exchange Rates

Starting at point *A* in panel (*b*), the central bank moves the *TR* curve to *TR'*. At point *C*, the lower interest rate triggers capital outflows and the exchange rate depreciates. The resulting gain in competitiveness raises demand for domestic goods and the *IS* curve shifts to the right. It will move all the way to *IS'* and full equilibrium is achieved at point *B*. In panel (*a*), we see that the central bank succeeds at increasing the money supply because money demand shifts outward due to the rise in output found in panel (*b*).

demand for domestic goods increases. Graphically, the *IS* curve starts shifting to the right. How far will it go? As long as $i < i^*$, capital outflows continue, the exchange rate continues to depreciate, and the *IS* curve continues to move rightward. When it reaches the position *IS'*, the three curves now pass through point *B* and all markets are simultaneously in equilibrium. Thus point *B* shows the total effect of the monetary policy change.

We have just seen that, under flexible exchange rates, the *IS* curve moves to meet the intersection of the other two curves. This simply reflects the fact that, being left free to float, the exchange rate is endogenous and its movements affect external competitiveness and demand.

The outcome may be puzzling. Here we have a central bank that adopts a more expansionary policy stance that succeeds in raising output, and yet cannot change the interest rate because it is tied to the world rate of return. How can that be? The answer is that, with capital mobility, monetary policy does not operate through the interest rate, but through the *exchange rate*. The longer answer is told by the money market with the help of panel (*a*) in Figure 11.8. As in panel (*b*), the central bank intends to move down the money demand curve, presumably all the way to

point *C*, and to provide liquidity to the open market along the way. But capital mobility implies that, as soon as the interest rate declines, money flows out. Any additional money created by the central bank immediately leaks abroad in the form of capital outflows. Is the economy stuck at points *A* in both panels? No, because the capital outflows depreciate the exchange rate. The depreciation, in turn, raises demand and output from *Y* to *Y'*. With a higher volume of transactions to finance, money demand shifts out in panel (*a*) as the economy moves from *A* to *B* in panel (*b*).

The central bank ends up increasing the money supply because it manages to raise real aggregate demand through an exchange rate depreciation.[13] Still, as previously noted, it does not succeed in lowering the interest rate. As under a fixed exchange regime, we see that monetary policy and the exchange rate are deeply related. In the end, an expansionary monetary policy in an open economy under exchange flexible rates operates by bringing about an exchange rate depreciation.

---

[13] In practice, given the speed of reaction of financial markets, the economy does not really go through point *C*.

11.5.2 Demand Shocks—Shifts of the *IS* curve

An exogenous increase in aggregate demand is shown as the rightward shift of the *IS* curve from *IS* to *IS'* in Figure 11.9. As in the previous section, the economy cannot be said to be in general equilibrium as the three curves *IS'*, *TR*, and *IFM* no longer pass through a common point of intersection. Consider first point *B*, at the intersection of the *IS* and *TR* curves and off the *IFM* line. With the domestic interest rate exceeding the foreign rate of return, capital flows in and the exchange rate appreciates. As external competitiveness declines, the current account worsens and the *IS* curve starts shifting to the left. This proceeds as long as the interest rate exceeds the foreign rate of return, and until the *IS* curve is back at its initial position and the economy is back at point *A*. The demand shock is simply 'crowded out' by the negative effect of the exchange rate appreciation on aggregate demand *via* the primary current account.

The result applies to any of the exogenous components of real demand we encountered in Chapter 10: expansionary fiscal policies (public spending, taxes), business optimism or pessimism, or foreign demand

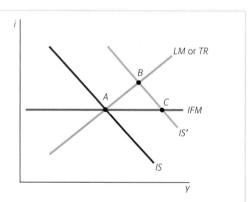

Fig. 11.9 A Demand Shock Under Flexible Exchange Rates

An expansionary demand shock shifts the *IS* curve to the right. At point *B*, however, *i > i** and capital flows in, the exchange rate appreciates, external competitiveness declines, and the *IS* curve shifts back to its initial position. Demand disturbances are eliminated over time.

feeding through exports. The general conclusion, under flexible exchange rates, is that an economy cannot sustainably lift itself up via higher domestic or world demand. In the end, demand impulses are eventually neutralized by exchange rate changes. Output is insulated from both domestic and foreign demand disturbances.

This conclusion also applies to exogenous contractions of demand, but in reverse. Under flexible exchange rates, an exogenous contraction of aggregate demand will give rise to a beneficial depreciation which in the short run will 'crowd in' net exports (by making exports less expensive and imports more expensive).

The position of the *IS* curve depends on the real exchange rate σ. With sticky domestic and foreign prices, the real exchange rate is driven by the nominal exchange rate, which is determined in the foreign exchange market. The exchange rate, therefore, is endogenous, as is the *IS* curve. More precisely, the exchange rate changes in such a way that the *IS* curve shifts to meet the two other curves, *TR* and *IFM*.

Under flexible exchange rates, the macroeconomic equilibrium is determined by the *TR* and *IFM* curves. In the same way that the *TR* curve can be ignored when the exchange rate is fixed—because the money supply is endogenous—the *IS* curve can be more or less ignored when the exchange rate floats because the exchange rate is endogenous. Still, the shift of the *IS* curve, required to meet the two other curves tells us what happens to the exchange rate. It appreciates when the *IS* curve must move to the left and it depreciates in the opposite case.

It may appear puzzling that fiscal policy—a type of demand disturbance—has no effect on output, especially when looking at the Keynesian multipliers presented in Table 10.1. Some of those currencies float freely. This is because the Mundell–Fleming model is a short-cut for describing effects that may take longer to resolve. It takes time for demand disturbances to work through the economy. This also applies to the effects of exchange rates on aggregate demand. Another assumption is that any change in the exchange rate affects external competitiveness one for one. If the former operates faster than the latter, there can be some temporary effect of fiscal policy or demand shocks on output—possibly extending over a few years. Thus, while the Mundell–Fleming gives us the bottom line—that the effects of fiscal policy are undermined by exchange rates—also we have a healthy warning that theory should never be taken literally.

11.5.3 International Financial Disturbances—Shifts of the *IFM* Line

The effect of an increase in returns on foreign assets measured in terms of the home currency (i^*) was described in Figure 11.6 for the case of fixed exchange rates. The same diagram can be used to understand what happens under flexible exchange rates. Graphically, we know that the *IS* curve will move to wherever it needs to go through the intersection of the *TR* and *IFM* curves. As the *IFM* line shifts upwards to *IFM'*, equilibrium moves from point *A* to point *C*. The interest rate must rise to meet the foreign rate of return and the economy expands. While we can ignore the *IS* curve to find the new equilibrium, its movement tells us something important: what happens to the exchange rate? In the present case, the *IS* curve will have to move to the right, which can only happen because the exchange rate depreciates.

It may come as a surprise that an interest rate increase could lead to an output expansion. Again, the reason has to do with the exchange rate. Consider point *A* immediately after the upward shift of the *IFM* line. The domestic interest rate is now below the foreign rate of return. This triggers a capital outflow. Since the central bank does not intervene in the foreign exchange market, the outflow translates into a depreciation of the exchange rate. The country's external competitiveness and current account improve and the *IS* curve shifts to the right until it goes through point *C* (the new *IS* curve is not shown).

The increase in the foreign rate of return may be the consequence of a stricter monetary policy stance in the 'rest of the world'. Think of rest of the world as a large economy that trades with us, a small open economy. As the foreign interest rate i^* rises, foreign GDP declines. At home, in contrast, the GDP rises, as we have just seen. A monetary expansion abroad has the opposite effect: a contraction of aggregate demand at home. This is known as the **beggar-thy-neighbour** effect, because one country's expansionary policy comes at the expense of its neighbours. In

contrast, under fixed exchange rates, the reasoning from Section 11.4 shows that foreign monetary policy has the same qualitative effect on foreign and domestic GDPs.

11.5.4 Is a Large Economy a Closed Economy?

This last discussion brings us to an open issue in macroeconomics: how large can an economy be before the Mundell–Fleming framework loses its validity? A large economy has two main characteristics: (1) its trade represents a small share of GDP, as Table 11.1 shows, and (2) it affects, but is not much affected by, foreign economies. Most large economies (the USA, the EU, Japan) also happen to be well-integrated financially. The key step taken in the Chapter 11 relative to the Chapter 10 was to introduce international capital mobility.

It turns out that the better framework for thinking about a large economy is the one presented in Chapter 10. Trade openness does not change the qualitative results of Chapters 10 and 11, but rather affects the size of the Keynesian multiplier. Financial integration, on the other hand, modifies the analysis because the small-country assumption takes the foreign rate of return i^* as exogenous. Since a large country affects but is not much affected by the foreign rate of return, we could ignore the *IFM* curve, leaving the framework of Chapter 10, the *IS* and *TR* curves.

Can a large, financially open economy really ignore the foreign rate of return i^*? Think of an exemplary large economy around, the United States. When its central bank, the Federal Reserve, changes its interest rate, asset holders all around the world reshuffle their portfolios and, in the event, all interest rates are affected, as Figure 11.10 shows. This would leave the impression that the US and its central bank actually fix i^*, while other countries are financially too small to have a similar impact on the US interest rate. At the same time, even the US—$16 trillion economy in a world with a GDP of roughly $70 trillion, is becoming less central, while foreigners are holding more and more dollar assets. Market expectations of future central bank policy—good or bad—are becoming more and more important in determining i^*—which implies that even the largest economies are subject to the constraints of international capital flows.

Fig. 11.10 Long-Term Interest Rates, 1970 – 2011

The chart displays the evolution of long-term interest rates (usually bonds of 10-year maturity) in the USA and in the other large developed countries. The levels are often quite different, for reasons that will be explained later in Chapter 14. Yet month-to-month fluctuations reveal a high degree of coherence. The chart does not say that US interest rates drive the other rates, only that all rates tend to move together. Available statistical evidence does suggest, however, that US rates are the driving force behind the common movements in interest rates over time.

Source: IMF, International Financial Statistics.

11.6 Fixed or Flexible Rates?

This chapter has shown the importance of the exchange rate regime for determining the reaction of a small open economy to shocks. This is true irrespective of whether these shocks originate in macroeconomic policy decisions or in the behaviour of private economy. It also shows that the exchange rate regime is best understood through the prism of monetary policy. Chapter 10 showed that a central bank can control the interest rate or the money supply, but not both. Now we find that life for the central bank is even more constrained: it can either have its own monetary policy (i.e. managing the interest rate or

the money supply), *or* fix the nominal exchange rate on the other hand, not both. If it chooses to peg the exchange rate, it gives up its ability to conduct an independent monetary policy. It can recover policy independence only by letting the exchange rate float. These important results are summarized in Table 11.3. We now examine what they mean for the choice of an exchange rate regime.

A fixed exchange rate regime represents a commitment to refrain from active use of monetary policy. The *TR* curve becomes irrelevant in that case. The **exchange rate anchor** imposes a tight discipline on

Table 11.3 The Mundell – Fleming Model: a Summary of the Importance of the Exchange Rate Regime

	Exchange rate regime	
	Fixed exchange rates	Flexible exchange rates
Impact of shocks and policy on GDP:		
IS curve shock (animal spirits, real exchange rate, wealth; fiscal policy)	Increase	No effect
TR curve shock (changing target interest rate)	No effect	Increase
IFM line shock (change in foreign rate of return)	Decrease	Increase
Impact on available policy instruments:		
Exogenous monetary policy instrument	Exchange rate	Interest rate
Endogenous monetary policy instrument	Interest rate	Exchange rate

the monetary authorities, but it leaves the economy vulnerable to demand disturbances, both domestic and foreign. Graphically, any exogenous shift of the *IS* curve determines a new equilibrium. In addition, shifts of the *IFM* line pose a significant risk to the sustainability of the fixed exchange rate regime. This requires a large investment in credibility—an issue we will pick up in Chapters 16 and 17. Many countries in Europe in the 1980s (e.g. France and Italy) and in Latin America in the 1990s (e.g.

Box 11.4 Fixing the Swiss Franc

In September 2011, the internet was on fire. Philipp Hildebrand, Governor of the Swiss National Bank, had just announced that the central bank, would fix the Swiss franc/euro exchange rate at a price of SF 1.20/EUR. Since the end of the Bretton Woods fixed exchange rate system (1971), the Swiss had refrained from pegging their exchange rate, preferring to float. The move was a shock to financial markets, since Swiss monetary policy had long focused on control of the money supply and keeping the inflation rate low and stable—despite deep economic integration with the countries of the EU (and now, Eurozone) which surround it.

Why did the course change? As Figure 11.11 shows, the Swiss franc had appreciated sharply over the period—from 1.6 to below 1.2 SF/EUR, or about 25%. An exchange rate surge of this magnitude threatened export businesses while spurring massive imports. It is already common for many Swiss, most who live within 100 km of the border to an EU country, to shop abroad.

Switzerland is not a member of the EU, although it has adopted a version of the Schengen Agreement, which allows for easy frontier crossing. This border shopping had increased dramatically in the years since the financial crisis. Evidently, inflows of capital seeking stability were to blame, including capital flight from southern European countries. These capital inflows had driven up the franc to a point where even the real economy of Switzerland was threatened.

The announcement was credible and effective. But just as the *IS-TR-IFM* analysis predicts, it required the Swiss bank to purchase foreign exchange—€100 billion-worth in the months following the announcement. While this is a dramatic increase, it is considerably less than the previous spell of 'grey intervention' at the onset of the crisis, which the SNB had conducted without any explicitly formulated policy objective. Some of the intervention in late 2011 had been withdrawn in the following months, but not before having a dramatic effect on Swiss money supply.

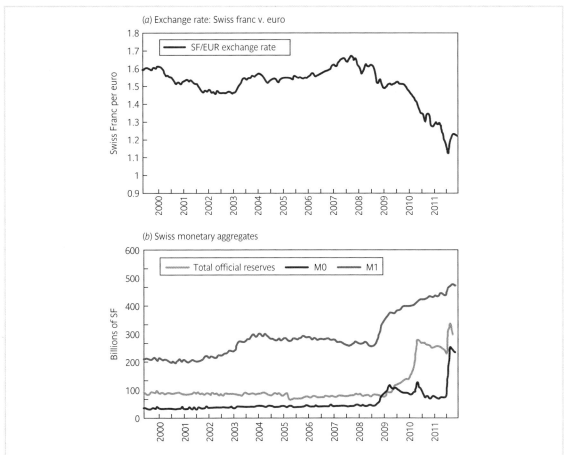

Fig. 11.11 Swiss Franc/Euro Exchange Rate and the Swiss Money Supply, 1999–2011

Switzerland has faced significant capital inflows as a result of the global financial crisis. Since 2009, the Swiss National Bank, the central bank, has acquired significant foreign exchange reserves to slow down the appreciation of the Swiss franc (panel (a)). As a result, total official reserves has risen spectacularly, with significant effect on both high-powered money M0 as well as the broader narrow money measure M1 (panel (b)). It is noteworthy that total official reserves of the central bank exceeds M0, due to foreign central bank holdings of Swiss francs as well as SNB repurchase agreements with those central banks.

Source: Macrobond, Swiss National Bank.

Argentina and Brazil) followed the fixed exchange rate strategy. It can work as long as the declared parity is not challenged by external current or financial account deficits. When this occurs, the exchange regime comes under threat and its credibility as a disciplining device for governments is called into question. This credibility can even be threatened in a monetary union—a question which will be addressed in more detail in Chapter 19.

When the exchange rate floats freely, monetary policy independence is preserved. The *TR* curve

describes how the central bank conducts that policy. The economy as a whole is shielded from real demand disturbances. Graphically, the *IS* curve endogenously shifts to meet the *TR* and *IFM* curves. Yet the exchange rate may widely fluctuate in response to international financial disturbances, upsetting external competitiveness in one direction or another and confronting firms with rapidly changing circumstances. An exchange rate appreciation, for instance, hurts exporters as much as they benefit from a depreciation.

Countries that operate under a freely floating exchange rate regime usually possess sufficient economic and political stability to entrust the central bank with the task of delivering price stability. This is the case of the USA, the euro area, the UK, Sweden, and a few others. Yet it is common for countries to change exchange rate regime in the light of new challenges. Box 11.4 tells the story of Switzerland, which threw in the towel of floating rates after a bruising appreciation after the finan-cial crisis and hitched the Swiss franc to the euro. Other countries have abandoned a fixed exchange rate regime, having been burned by speculative attacks against a previous fixed regime. This is the case, among others, in Argentina, Brazil, Chile, Russia, and many other countries. Other countries let their exchange rate float because inflation is so high that any peg would quickly lead to overvalu-ation and crisis.[14]

ⓘ Summary

1 The Mundell–Fleming model is the logical exten-sion of the *IS–TR* model to an economy which is open for trade in financial assets as well as goods and services. It describes the simultaneous equilib-rium of three markets: (1) the market for goods and services, (2) the domestic money market, and (3) the international financial market.

2 Like the *IS–TR* model of Chapter 10, the Mundell–Fleming model adopts the Keynesian assumption that prices are sticky. Under these circumstances, output is determined by aggregate demand.

3 When a country's financial markets are well inte-grated into world markets, the domestic interest rate is tied to worldwide conditions. Under condi-tions of complete capital mobility, a third equilib-rium condition requires that the domestic interest rate be equal to the world rate of return. This is the interest rate parity condition. This condition does not hold in the case of limited international capi-tal mobility—e.g. because of capital controls. The *IFM* line summarizes the interest rate parity condition.

4 With all three curves, it is possible to study the gen-eral macroeconomic equilibrium, when all three markets are simultaneously in equilibrium.

5 When the exchange rate is fixed, demand distur-bances affect domestic GDP. Committed to uphold the declared exchange rate parity, the central bank cannot however conduct an autonomous monetary policy. The *TR* curve becomes irrelevant and the equilibrium is described by the intersection of the *IS* and *IFM* curves.

6 When the exchange rate is freely floating, the central bank regains monetary policy autonomy, but the exchange rate necessarily becomes end-ogenous. Its movements affects the economy's competitiveness and, therefore, the position of the *IS* curve. The exchange rate movements are such that the *IS* endogenously moves to meet the *TR* and *IFM* curves. The fact that the *IS* curve does not determine the equilibrium outcome means that the economy is shielded from demand disturbances.

7 Monetary and exchange rate policies are just two sides of the same coin: the central bank can peg the exchange rate or it can conduct an autono-mous monetary policy, but it cannot do both at the same time.

8 The choice of an exchange rate regime involves trade-offs. Different countries choose different regimes, and often adapt their regimes depending on the circumstances.

---

[14] Recall that the real exchange rate is defined as *SP/P**. With *S* fixed, if *P* rises faster than *P**, the real exchange rate appreciates. These situations will be addressed in Chapters 13 and 16.

🔑 Key Concepts

- Mundell – Fleming model
- general equilibrium
- exchange rate regime
- interest rate parity condition
- foreign or international rate of return
- international financial markets (*IFM*) line
- exchange market intervention
- foreign exchange reserves

- sterilized and unsterilized interventions
- exchange rate anchor
- capital controls
- monetary policy autonomy
- revaluation, devaluation
- appreciation, depreciation
- realignment
- beggar-thy-neighbour

❓ Exercises

1 Consider a central bank in an economy that has floating exchange rates and sets interest rate according to the Taylor rule. Show graphically what happens when the central bank decides to reduce the target interest rate from $\bar{\imath}$ to $\bar{\imath}'$. State clearly the steps involved.

2 Consider the same central bank in the previous question, but this time under a fixed exchange rate regime. What is the outcome? Trace out the steps of adjustment carefully. What do you conclude about the effect of monetary policy shocks in a fixed exchange rate regime?

3 Show the effect of a demand shock under a fixed exchange rate regime: the economy moves from point A to point B. Explain why point C is not sustainable and why the economy must move to point B.

4 In 2011–12 many southern European countries which use the euro will undertake drastic measures to rein in their budget deficits, in particular tax increases and spending cuts. It is often claimed that such austerity measures are counterproductive, especially in a fixed exchange rate regime. Explain why this is the case. How would your

answer change if these countries had their own currencies and flexible exchange rates?

5 Show the effects of an increase in the foreign rate of return under fixed and flexible exchange rates. What happens to the money supply in each case?

6 In a situation of economic or political instability, a standard reaction of citizens is to exogenously reduce their demand for money. What happens then to the interest rate, income, and the money supply under a fixed exchange rate regime? When the central bank obeys a Taylor rule? Explain also what happens to the nominal exchange rate.

7 Suppose the UK left the European Union, and that this move meant that UK exports to the EU faced the common external tariff. As a result, UK exports drop sharply. (Its imports would also decline, but assume for the sake of the exercise that the decline of exports is larger.) Explain the effect of this exogenous decline in aggregate demand on GDP, interest rates and exchange rate in the UK, given that the central bank lets the pound float. How would your answer change if the UK had a fixed exchange rate with the euro?

8 What is the effect of an exchange rate revaluation in a fixed (but adjustable) exchange rate regime?

9 What is the effect of tax cut under a fixed exchange rate regime? Under a floating exchange rate regime?

10 Figure 11.11 shows that in troubled times, safe-haven currencies like the Swiss franc can rise sharply. Concerned international investors seem willing to accept a lower rate of return than in normal times. Evaluate the impact of becoming a safe-haven small open economy with (1) flexible exchange rates, and (2) fixed exchange rates. What can the central bank do?

11 Consider a small open economy in a monetary union (i.e. a fixed exchange rate regime). Trace through the consequence of a price level decline at home, holding the foreign price level constant.

How would your answer change if foreign prices declined in the same proportion?

12 Do the same question but under a flexible exchange rate regime (so there is no point in talking of devaluation). Answer the question when (1) the central bank keeps the nominal money supply constant and (2) when it follows a Taylor rule. In each case, what happens to the exchange rate?

13 Imagine that the Danish central bank prevents its exchange rate from appreciating by selling 100 million krona on the exchange market and buying euros. Use the balance sheets of the central bank and of commercial banks presented in Chapter 9 to describe carefully this foreign exchange market operation. Use the same balance sheets to describe an operation which sterilizes the effect of the foreign exchange purchase.

→ Essay Questions

1 International financial markets mean that the domestic interest rate is determined abroad. Why does this mean that monetary policy is abandoned, but only in the absence of capital controls? Why are capital controls nevertheless considered a bad idea?

2 As their name suggests, beggar-thy-neighbour policies have a bad reputation. Discuss why this may be the case and what can be done to limit the perceived drawbacks.

3 'Adopting an exchange rate anchor is a mixed blessing.' Comment.

4 Even within a monetary union, it is still possible to have a real depreciation or appreciation, but it involves changes in the price level at home or abroad. Why is this difficult to analyse using the *IS-TR-IFM* framework?

5 Emerging market countries typically have to offer a risk premium when they borrow. This means that their domestic interest rates are higher than those abroad. What is the impact of a sudden loss of trust? Discuss why this could happen. What are the policy options in each case?

Output, Employment, and Inflation 12

When the demand for a commodity or service is high relative to the supply of it we expect the price to rise, the rate of rise being greater, the greater the excess demand. Conversely when the demand is low relatively to the supply we expect the price to fall, the rate of fall being greater, the greater the deficiency of demand. It seems plausible that this principle should operate as one of the factors determining the rate of change of money wage rates, which are the price of labour services.

A. W. Phillips[1]

12.1 Overview

A cup of tea in London that cost 5p in 1965 goes for £1.30 or more in 2011. The baguette in Paris which cost 40 centimes (one centime = one hundredth of the old French franc) in 1965 fetches 13 times more in terms of euros 45 years later. Prices seem to grow relentlessly. Yet inflation is not just about changes in the price of tea in Britain and bread in Paris. Inflation measures the rate of increase of the price level, i.e. the number of units of pounds or euros paid for a bundle of goods. It is easy to see that the inflation rate simultaneously measures the rate at which money loses its value in terms of those goods. The phenomenon does not stop there. When the price level rises, the level of nominal wages tends to rise too. Wages rise partly due to rising productivity, but they also chase prices, which in turn chase wages. And the nominal exchange rate seems to be engaged in the same kind of race. Somehow, all nominal variables seem to leapfrog each other.

Whether very low or excruciatingly high, inflation is a key feature of modern economies. It was not always so. From time immemorial to the middle of the twentieth century, prices were pretty much trendless. Continuing inflation is a relatively new event in the history of humankind, and coincides with the emergence of modern central banks and fiat money. This should not come as a surprise once we remember the monetary neutrality principle. Ultimately, central banks and their ability to create money are the source of inflation.

So far, we have studiously avoided talking about inflation. We alluded to it in Chapter 6 when we established the principle of monetary neutrality, quickly relegating it to the faraway long run. In Chapters 10 and 11, we explicitly ruled it out by adopting the Keynesian assumption that prices are sticky. These were useful steps that allow us now to focus on this central aspect of modern economies. In this chapter, we focus on the 'medium run'. The short run corresponds to the Keynesian view, whereby prices hardly change. The long run is described by the opposite, neoclassical perspective. When enough time has elapsed, all prices are able to adjust and the economy is governed by monetary neutrality, a principle already presented in Chapter 6. In the medium run, prices move but not sufficiently to allow all markets to clear. We start by clarifying these issues.

Then we look at a very simple description of the inflation phenomenon, the **Phillips curve**. We will see that the Philipps curve has been useful for helping us think about the short-run behaviour of inflation. At the same time, it is unstable and seems to vanish at times. So we embark on a detective-like investigation of the puzzle of the 'disappearing Phillips curve'. This leads us to track down the various reasons why prices rise. We start by asking who sets prices (firms do) and why (mostly to cover their production costs). As we study production costs, we return to the wage bargaining process first encountered in Chapter 5, and find that wage negotiators

---

[1] The son of a Kiwi dairy farmer, A. W. Phillips (1914–1975) started out as an apprentice electrician working in an Australian mine, then left for Britain via China and Russia in the late 1930s. After a tour of duty in the Second World War and time spent as a prisoner of war, he studied at the London School of Economics and became a lecturer and later professor there. Phillips is remembered not only for his curve relating unemployment to rates of wage change, but also for the *Moniac*, a complex hydraulic representation of macroeconomy, on display in the Science Museum in London.

worry about prices of goods, for different reasons. We end up facing the apparently circular conclusion that prices drive wages and wages drive prices, in a sort of race between employers—who want high profits—and employees—who want high wages. The outcome of the analysis is an accounting of the factors that add up to a full explanation of inflation. This analysis helps us solve the Phillips curve puzzle. It also allows us to derive the **aggregate supply curve**, which will be teamed up with the aggregate demand curve developed in the next chapter to complete the system of inflation and output determination.

12.2 General Equilibrium with Flexible Prices: The Neoclassical Case

12.2.1 From the Keynesian Short Run to the Neoclassical Long Run

In Chapters 10 and 11, we made extensive use of the Keynesian assumption that prices are sticky. We justified this assumption by asserting that prices move slowly in normal times. In the short run, we said, ignoring inflation is an easy way to make things simple. When thinking about the long run, however, we need to make the diametrically opposite assumption that prices are fully flexible. This is the **neoclassical assumption** against which Keynes rebelled in the 1930s. He well knew the limits of his own assumption, but then famously wrote that 'in the long run, we are all dead'. In a parallel fashion, this section relaxes the Keynesian assumption and presents the view espoused by neoclassical economists ('neoclassicals' for short) writing long before and after Keynes. While some Keynesians and neoclassicals still fight it out, most economists now agree that the Keynesian assumption is acceptable in the short run, and the neoclassical assumption is the right way to think about the long run.[2] This section, therefore, studies the long run, but we also look at how things change over time, from the short to the long run.

In the Keynesian view, the price level is exogenous; output is endogenous and responds one-for-one to demand. In the neoclassical view, it is the price level that is endogenous and plays the equilibrating role in the goods market. It is the price of goods in terms of money. It turns out that, in this case, it is demand that adjusts to supply.

We have already started to examine the neoclassical case in Chapter 6 when we established the monetary neutrality principle. From that chapter, recall the Cambridge equation:

(12.1) $$M = kPY$$

where, for the moment, we treat parameter k as constant.[3] We asked what happens when the money supply increases, say by 10%. In the short run, when prices are sticky, the only way for the money market equilibrium condition (as explained in Chapter 9) to hold is for real GDP to increase by 10%. This is the Keynesian case. If prices are flexible, however, equilibrium can be achieved with a 10% increase in the price level, without any change in real GDP. This is the neoclassical case and its underlying result is monetary neutrality.

If the Keynesian assumption is valid in the short run and the neoclassical assumption characterizes the long run, then it must be the case that an increase in the money supply—which is engineered when central banks cut the interest rate—is followed first by a rise in output that will be eventually dissipated through an increase in the price level. This dynamic adjustment path for output and prices is shown in Figure 12.1.

This can be expressed in terms of rates of change. The inflation rate is the rate of change in the price level, defined as a rate: $\Delta P/P$. Equation (12.1) implies that the price level is given by

(12.1′) $$P = M/(kY).$$

---

[2] This intellectual debate is presented in Chapter 20.

[3] In the analysis of Chapter 9, this would correspond to the case in which the interest rate is constant—as it is in the steady state.

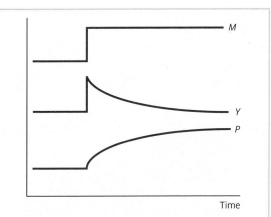

Fig. 12.1 From the Short to the Long Run

A one-off increase in the money supply has short and long effects which are qualitatively very different. The short run corresponds to the Keynesian assumption: prices are sticky and output moves to respond to demand. The neoclassical assumption describes the long run, when prices fully adjust and monetary neutrality implies that output is unaffected.

So for a constant k, the inflation rate, the growth of the money supply $\Delta M/M$, and the growth rate of output $\Delta Y/Y$, the following relationship must hold:

(12.1″) $\qquad \Delta P/P = \Delta M/M - \Delta Y/Y.$

This is the 'rate of change' version of the classical quantity equation. Later, it will help us to think about the long run.

What causes the money supply to increase without bound? This is not an obvious question, since central banks have long abandoned the practice of setting monetary targets and prefer to use their power in money markets to set short-term interest rates. It turns out that this power does not come for free. Setting the interest rate necessarily means that a central bank must be ready to supply all liquidity the economy demands at that interest rate. As a corollary, it must accept the rate of growth in the money supply which results from that interest rate. How the money supply evolves endogenously is explained in more detail in Box 12.1.

 Box 12.1 Where Does the Money Growth Come From?

In Chapter 6, the long-run price level and rate of inflation were related to the money supply and its growth rate. Yet in Chapter 9, we saw that central banks do not set growth rates of monetary aggregates. Rather, monetary policy is executed by setting interbank money market interest rates. In practice, central bank interest rate policy is well-represented by the Taylor rule. It turns out that the Taylor rule automatically implies a long-run rate of money growth. Because it supplies the money demanded given its chosen interest rate, the rate of money growth follows this rate of inflation. In other words: 'Every central bank gets the money growth and inflation rate that it chooses.'

It is easy to see this by re-examining the Taylor rule, which shows how central banks set interest rates:

(B12.1) $\quad i = \bar{i} + a(\pi - \bar{\pi}) \ + \ b\left(\dfrac{Y - \bar{Y}}{\bar{Y}}\right)$

$\qquad\qquad\quad$ inflation $\qquad$ output
$\qquad\qquad\quad$ gap $\qquad\qquad$ gap

In the long run, inflation is equal to target $\pi = \bar{\pi}$ and $Y = \bar{Y}$ so it follows that $i = \bar{i}$. Thus, the condition for equilibrium in the money market is given by

(B12.2) $\qquad M/P = k(i)Y = k(\bar{i})Y = kY.$

In the long run, growth real output $g = \Delta Y/Y$ is given by real factors (the dichotomy assumption) and does not depend on money growth. Since the interest rate is constant, k is constant. Equation (B12.2) is simply another version of (12.1'); the logic of (12.1″) implies that the rate of nominal money growth is equal to the sum of the long run real growth rate and the central bank's inflation rate target:

(B12.3) $\qquad\qquad \mu = g + \bar{\pi}.$

While money growth is neutral, it is not causal for inflation. Instead, the money supply grows endogenously to reflect the underlying trend growth in the economy as well as the choices of the monetary authority.

12.2.2 Supply-Determined Output in the Long Run

Why does price flexibility lead to a situation where demand adjusts to supply? Let us start with the supply side, that is, the long-run output and labour market outcomes studied in Chapters 3 and 5. Figure 12.2(a) displays the production function. Panel (b) shows the demand for labour implied by the marginal productivity of labour—as determined by the position and the slope of the production function, and the supply of labour—as shaped by labour market institutions. The resulting equilibrium at point A in panel (b) indicates how much labour is utilized. The corresponding point A in panel (a) shows how much is produced and supplied. In the classical long run, output equals its trend value $\bar{Y}$ (which is generally growing over time), employment equals $\bar{L}$ and the equilibrium rate of unemployment is $\bar{U}$: These points are labeled as A in both panels of the Figure 12.2. We can also see in panel (b) the equilibrium real wage, the ratio of nominal wages W to the price level P.

It is useful to examine an outcome under the Keynesian assumption, that is when wages and prices are sticky. We studied this situation at length in Chapters 10 and 11. In particular, we look at a situation when demand weakens to $Y < \bar{Y}$. Firms will respond by cutting production and move to point B panel (a) in Figure 12.2. Panel (b), however shows that there is no market equilibrium corresponding to this reduction of production. If wages and prices are sticky, the outcome will be at point B is panel (b).[4] What is remarkable about point B is that it is neither on the labour demand nor on the labour supply schedules. The distance BA measures involuntary unemployment, the extent of disequilibrium seen by employees. Firms too are unhappy since being off the labour demand curve means that profits are not optimized. The paradox is that the real wage is at its 'correct' level, the one corresponding to point A. The following analysis would also hold if the real wage would change to take us to B' (higher than the equilibrium value) or B" (lower than its equilibrium value).

[4] We ignore the possibility that firms hoard rather than dismiss unessential labour. In fact, firms often avoid shedding their employees in a brief recession if they can afford to do so. In this case they would not be 'on their labour demand curve', they would employ more labour than strictly optimal.

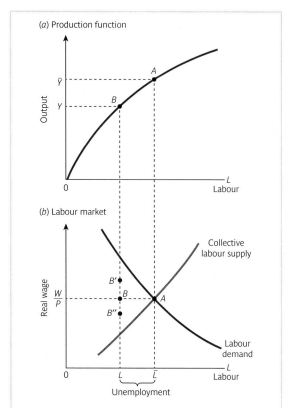

Fig. 12.2 Output and the Labour Market in the Long Run

Long-run output $\bar{Y}$ is produced by firms using long-run labour input $\bar{L}$ (point A in panel (a)) and the equilibrium of labour demand and collective labour demand (point A in panel (b)). Point B depicts a Keynesian situation in which aggregate demand is insufficient and less than trend level of output, even though the real wage is at its long-run level. (Point B' and B" show initial situations in which the real wage is too high or too low, respectively.) From point B, it would be sufficient simply to raise aggregate demand; in the other cases, the real wage must fall or rise via some appropriate combination of nominal wage and price changes. In the neoclassical case, price reductions (by firms) and wage cuts (by employees) will be necessary to restore equilibrium when demand is low. If exchange rates are flexible, a depreciation can help restore demand to long-run equilibrium at point A.

In the long run, the neoclassical principle implies that nominal wages and prices will adjust—rise or fall—until equilibrium is restored in both product and labour markets. This means returning to point A. How will they move? The underlying guiding principle is that prices rise when demand for goods is strong, and fall when it is weak. Similarly, wages rise when demand for labour is strong, and decline when demand for labour is weak. In Figure 12.2, firms facing weak demand would reduce their prices. If the nominal wages (W) remain sticky, real wages (W/P) rise—a falling price level (P) means a higher purchasing power of wages. As we move from B toward B′, involuntary unemployment gets even larger. Over time, as nominal wages become flexible, they would decline.

Are we just going endlessly up and down from B to B′ and back? No, because we must understand what the decline in the price level P means for the demand for goods. The short answer is that a decline in goods prices will encourage more demand and that this will bring the economy back to point A in both panels. How exactly will this come about? Let us go back to the *IS–TR* analysis of the previous chapter. If the exchange rate is flexible, the Taylor rule implies that a declining price level will be met by a demand-enhancing lower interest rate, a nominal and ultimately real depreciation, a process that will continue until demand is restored to its initial value. If the exchange rate is fixed, the decline of the domestic price level also implies a real exchange rate depreciation, which raises foreign

demand. Either way, price and wage flexibility will bring the economy back to point A, with lower price and wage levels but at the initial real wage level.

12.2.3 Implications for the Long Run

If we consider that the neoclassical assumption describes the long run, we can conclude that demand disturbances only have a temporary impact on output and employment. Thus, we start from the Keynesian short run where supply passively adjusts to demand and gradually moves to the long run as prices and wages respond to prevailing conditions. Eventually, the economy is back to full equilibrium or, equivalently, GDP returns to its trend level and equilibrium unemployment (as defined in Chapter 5) prevails again. The supply represents what the economy's resources (physical capital, human capital and the state of technology) can produce and how much income can be earned. This description nicely fits the idea of business cycles represented in Figure 10.1 and the idea that price adjustments gradually substitute for quantity adjustments (see Figure 12.1). The task of the following sections is to examine carefully how prices and wages move in response to temporary disequilibria in the goods and/or labour markets.

12.3 The Phillips Curve: Chimera or a Stylized Fact?

12.3.1 A. W. Phillips' Discovery

The short-run Keynesian assumption and the long-run neoclassical assumptions are fairly easy to deal with: prices either do not change at all, or they fully adjust. The medium run, as represented in Figure 12.1, is considerably messier. Prices do move, but only part of the way in any given period of time. The Keynesian assumption always had the major disadvantage of leaving inflation unexplained by assuming it away. Even die-hard Keynesians conceded at the high point of their influence that they had no clue on how to incorporate inflation in their model. They referred to it as the 'missing equation'. The search for this equation turned up the Phillips

curve, a negative relationship observed to hold between inflation and unemployment, the twin 'bads' of macroeconomics. It is represented in Figure 12.3.

In the late 1950s, A. W. Phillips plotted the annual rate of growth of nominal wages, i.e. wage inflation, against the rate of unemployment in Britain during the period 1861–1957. He found a remarkably robust negative correlation, which was confirmed for a number of other countries.[5] Figure 12.4 plots actual

---

[5] Phillips was not the first to discover the Phillips curve. The American economist Irving Fisher published a paper in the *International Labour Review* of 1926 in which he unearthed a similar relationship in the USA.

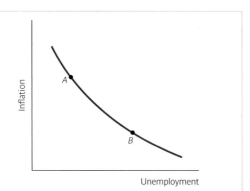

Fig. 12.3 The Phillips Curve in Theory

The Phillips curve implies a negative relationship, or trade-off, between unemployment and inflation: you can get less of one evil only by accepting more of the other. When discovered, it was seen as representing a menu of options from which governments could choose. For example, it could keep unemployment down (point *A*) at the cost of some inflation, or could limit inflation (point *B*) but only by accepting higher unemployment.

Phillips curves—using the rate of price inflation instead of wage inflation—for the UK and the average of 16 advanced economies for the period 1921–1973 (excluding war years). While far less clean than the stylized version (a number of outliers correspond to exceptional events), the actual Phillips curves are consistent with the negative relationship shown in stylized form in Figure 12.3.

The Phillips curve was embraced at the time for two main reasons. First, it provided the missing theoretical relationship that complements and indeed completes the Keynesian *IS–TR* apparatus. Second, even as its durability was increasingly questioned, it remained a practical tool for policy-makers. They can aim at low unemployment but they must accept substantial inflation (point *A* in Figure 12.3), or they may prefer low inflation but at the cost of high unemployment (point *B*), or any intermediate situation. Once they decide, they can use their instruments (monetary and/or fiscal policy) to reach the

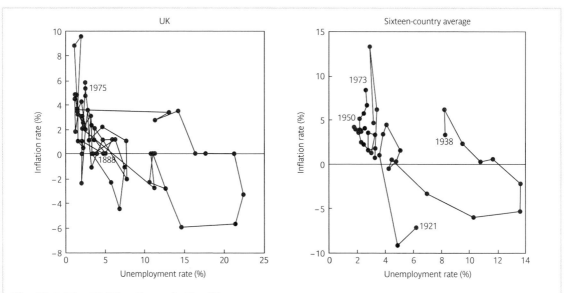

Fig. 12.4 The Phillips Curve in Reality

In reality the Phillips curve was less stable than depicted in Figure 12.3. The two panels depict the evolution of inflation and unemployment in the data for the United Kingdom in the period 1888–1975 and for an average of 16 countries 1921–1973 (excluding 1939–1949). While movements in northwest to southeast directions do dominate the year-to-year movements, there are notable deviations.

Sources: Maddison (1991); Mitchell (1998). Unweighted average of observations for Australia, Austria, Belgium, Canada, Denmark, Finland, France, Germany, Italy, Japan, the Netherlands, Norway, Sweden, Switzerland, the UK, and the USA. For some years, some countries are missing.

chosen point on the Phillips curve.[6] This policy dilemma came to be known as the **Phillips trade-off**.

12.3.2 Okun's Law and a Supply Curve Interpretation

The Phillips curve relates inflation to unemployment. A related relationship between inflation and the output gap will be called the supply curve. The link between the two is another stylized fact, known as **Okun's Law**, which is a negative relationship between output and unemployment.[7] More precisely, Okun's Law links the **unemployment gap**, the distance between actual and equilibrium unemployment as defined in Chapter 5, to the **output gap**, the distance between real GDP and its long-run trend, as illustrated in Figure 10.1. Figure 12.5 plots estimates of the unemployment and output gaps for Germany as an example of how unemployment and output gaps systematically move in opposite directions. The logic is intuitive: when the economy grows fast and output is above trend, demand for labour is strong and unemployment falls below its equilibrium level.

A stylized representation of Okun's Law is displayed in Figure 12.6. Formally, Okun's Law can be represented as follows:

(12.2) $$U_{\text{gap}} = -hY_{\text{gap}},$$

where $U_{\text{gap}} = U - \bar{U}$ and $Y_{\text{gap}} = \dfrac{Y - \bar{Y}}{\bar{Y}}$.

The unemployment gap U_{gap} is defined as the difference between the current unemployment rate U and its equilibrium level $\bar{U}$. Similarly, the output gap is the per cent deviation of real GDP Y from its trend growth path Y.[8] Okun's Law means that when

[6] This view of a trade-off was echoed by Helmut Schmidt, the ex-chancellor of West Germany, who stated in a newspaper interview in 1978 that he would prefer 5% inflation to 5% unemployment. How times have changed!

[7] The law is named after the US economist Arthur Okun (1928–1980). In his research, he showed that a 1% decline of the US unemployment rate was associated with a 3% increase of GDP above trend. Referring to equation (12.2), this implies a value for h of one-third.

[8] Note that the unemployment gap and the output gap are written in different ways. This is a technical detail. In Figure 12.5, both gaps are shown in per cents. Since the unemployment rate is already measured in per cent (of the labour force), its difference from equilibrium unemployment is measured in percentage points. For the output gap to also be in per cent, we compute the difference between GDP and its potential level—both measured in the local currency—as a proportion of potential GDP.

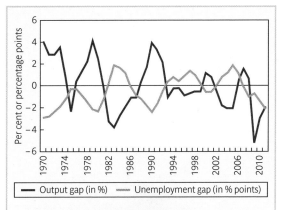

Fig. 12.5 The Output Gap and Unemployment in Germany, 1966–2011

The output gap measures the distance between real GDP and its trend and is computed in per cent of trend GDP. The unemployment gap is the difference between actual and equilibrium GDP, both measured in per cent of the labour force. When business conditions vary, firms adapt the supply of goods and services. To that effect, they adjust their demand for labour. For example, when the economy goes into a recession, firms employ fewer workers and the unemployment rate rises.

Notes: Trend real GDP and equilibrium unemployment are estimated by the OECD.

Source: OECD, Main Economic Indicators.

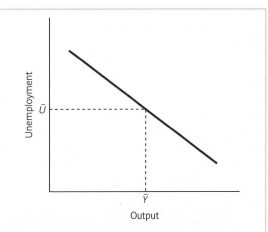

Fig. 12.6 Okun's Law in Theory

Okun's Law implies that, when the economy slows down, unemployment increases; when output rises relative to trend, unemployment declines.

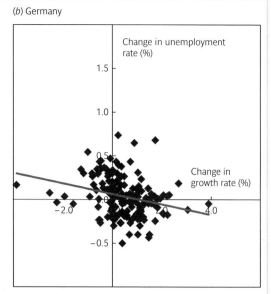

Fig. 12.7 Okun's Law in Reality

Okun's Law is not identical across countries. The two panels show how Okun's Law accounts for changes over time in the unemployment rate (in %) against percentage changes in changes in output, in the USA and Germany. (This is slightly different from the depiction in Figure 12.6.) In the USA, a one per cent increase in output is associated with roughly a one-third percentage point decline in the unemployment rate. In Germany, the response to unemployment change is about a fifth of that in the USA. Okun's Law cannot explain all the variation in unemployment but it does explain a fair amount. It accounts for much more overall variation of unemployment in the USA than it does in Germany.

output is above trend, the output gap is positive and the unemployment gap is negative; when output is below trend as in Figure 12.2., the output gap is negative and the unemployment rate is above trend. The parameter h captures the response of unemployment to GDP fluctuations measured as the output gap.

Figure 12.7 plots changes in the unemployment rate against changes in output for the USA and Germany. The negative relationship is very clear in both countries, but the slope of the Okun relationship is not constant across countries. In Germany, an increase in growth of 1% yields a much lower reduction in unemployment than in the USA. This reflects labour laws that are more protective of workers in Germany. Of course, Okun's Law does not explain all the fluctuations in unemployment, which in reality are affected by many other factors.

When we combine the negative relationship between inflation and the unemployment rate from the Phillips curve with the negative relationship between the unemployment rate and the output gap from

Okun's Law, we obtain the positive relationship between the output gap and inflation shown in Figure 12.8. This relationship is called the **aggregate supply curve**. Section 12.4 provides a complete interpretation of the

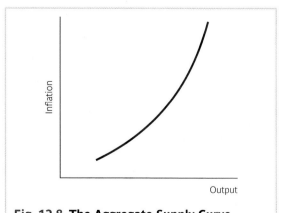

Fig. 12.8 The Aggregate Supply Curve

Combining the Phillips curve and Okun's Law, we obtain the aggregate supply curve. The curve says that inflation rises when output increases.

supply curve, but the intuitive logic that lies behind it is straightforward. The supply curve answers the following question: under which conditions will an increase in aggregate demand lead firms to supply more output and employees to work more to produce that extra output? The short answer is: inflation must increase, to boost wages and profits.

That the aggregate supply curve is upward sloping reminds us of the supply curve in microeconomics. While this similarity is intuitive, it can also be misleading. In microeconomics, the horizontal axis corresponds to the production of a particular good and the vertical represents that good's relative price. Here we deal with *aggregate* output or real GDP on the horizontal axis and the *overall* price index—or here its rate of increase, which is the inflation rate—on the vertical axis. This highlights the difference between micro- and macroeconomics.

12.3.3 **Hard Questions about the Phillips Curve**

Weak foundations

Not long after its discovery, the interpretation of the Phillips curve was perceived as standing on weak theoretical legs. In the late 1960s, Milton Friedman, the Nobel laureate in 1976, and Edmund Phelps of Columbia University,[9] who received the Nobel Prize in 2006, independently attacked the Phillips curve implication of a permanent trade-off between inflation and unemployment or output. They both asked the following question: how could the rate of change of nominal variables, such as wages or prices in pounds or euros, be related to real variables, such as employment, unemployment, and output in the long run? If the monetary neutrality principle is valid in the long run, then rates of change in the price level and other nominal variables should be unrelated to the real economy.[10] In this case, they noted, the Phillips curve should be observed temporarily. Only if workers and firms suffer from **money illusion**—i.e. if they act on increases in their own prices or wages

without taking contemporaneous increases in all other prices into account—will they raise output.

To understand the critique of Friedman and Phelps, it is helpful to think about the long-run behaviour of labour markets and output as presented in Section 12.2. The principle of monetary neutrality asserts that the economy is dichotomized in the long run: the real and nominal sectors of an economy stop influencing each other. If the long run is defined as when output level is on its trend growth path $\bar{Y}$ and unemployment is at its equilibrium rate $\bar{U}$, then the rate of inflation is determined by the rate of money growth, not by the level of output or the unemployment rate. These arguments were presented in detail Box 12.1. Graphically, if unemployment returns to its equilibrium level in the long run, the **long-run aggregate supply curve** and the Phillips curve must be vertical lines, as displayed in Figure 12.9. This conclusion is in agreement with the neoclassical view, developed in Section 12.2, which implies that output is determined by the supply side in the long run.

Wobbly evidence

The critique of Friedman and Phelps was largely ignored in the late 1960s, but it proved to be right on target in the 1970s when, as Figure 12.10 shows, the Phillips curve simply vanished. Quite spectacularly, in the mid-1970s and early 1980s, both inflation and unemployment started to rise, a phenomenon which came to be known as **stagflation**. Stagflation was strictly incompatible with the Phillips curve and its trade-off. A number of consequences followed. Policymakers, now grappling to beat back inflation, became sceptical of 'Keynesian activism'. They started to put greater emphasis on long-run monetary neutrality as a guiding principle for monetary policy. Macroeconomics also underwent a profound transformation, which can be thought of as a massive effort to rehabilitate and reconstruct the Phillips curve.

Over nearly a century, the inverse relationship between inflation and unemployment had seemed relatively robust. Why did it suddenly break down in all countries, and at about the same time? Because it was unlikely to be simply a case of bad luck, the systematic breakdown of the Phillips curve is now much better understood than 3–4 decades ago, and even helped economists better understand the true forces behind it.

---

[9] This is the same Phelps who formulated the golden rule of economic growth in Chapter 3.

[10] In his address to the American Economic Association in 1967 Friedman argued that 'there is always a temporary trade-off between inflation and unemployment, there is no permanent trade-off. The temporary trade-off comes not from inflation *per se*, but from a rising rate of inflation', Friedman (1968: 10).

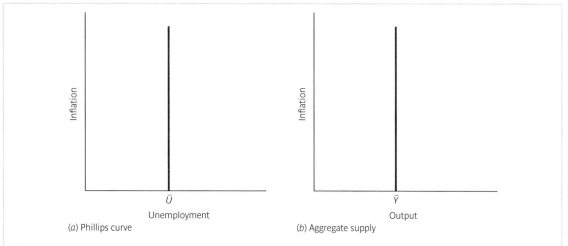

Fig. 12.9 The Long Run

In the long run, unemployment is at its equilibrium rate and output is on its trend growth path. Both the Phillips curve and the aggregate supply curve are vertical. Inflation is determined by the rate of money growth or by the central bank's target rate of inflation, independently of output or unemployment.

The challenge is to explain both the existence of a Phillips curve and its disappearance, as well as the striking similarity between different countries' experiences. Nearly everywhere inflation and unemployment increased sharply, at first around 1973–1974,

and then around 1979–1980, precisely at the time of sharp increases in the price of petroleum, the so-called **oil shocks**. Oil prices increased fourfold in 1973–1974 and then doubled again in 1979–1980. Interestingly, in between the oil shocks, and after the second oil

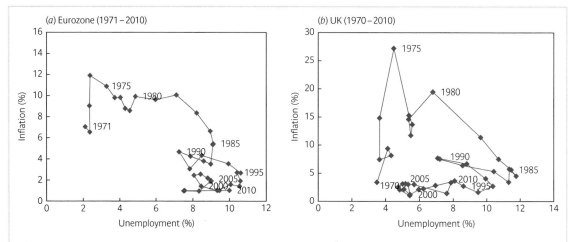

Fig. 12.10 Phillips Curves: Recent Experiences in the Euro Area and the UK

The Phillips curve broke down at the end of the 1960s. In the euro area, the sharp movements of the early and late 1970s coincided with the two oil shocks. Then the great deflation of the 1980s is compatible with the traditional Phillips curve, as are the periods 1990–1994 and 1997–2007. In the UK, the old Phillips curve survives over 1960–1967 until the upward jumps in 1973–1975 and 1979–1981 that coincided with sharp increases in oil prices—the so-called 'oil shocks'. As in the euro area, three different Phillips curves can be identified: during the deflation period of the 1980s, over 1986–1993, and in 1994–2007.

Source: OECD, *Economic Outlook*.

shock, Phillips curves re-emerged, each time further above and to the right of the previous one. Two examples of these episodes are presented in Figure 12.11 and further dissected in the following section.

The weak theoretical foundations of the Phillips curve and its successive mutations over time are two sides of the same coin. Confronted with uncompromising data, economists indeed had to go back to the

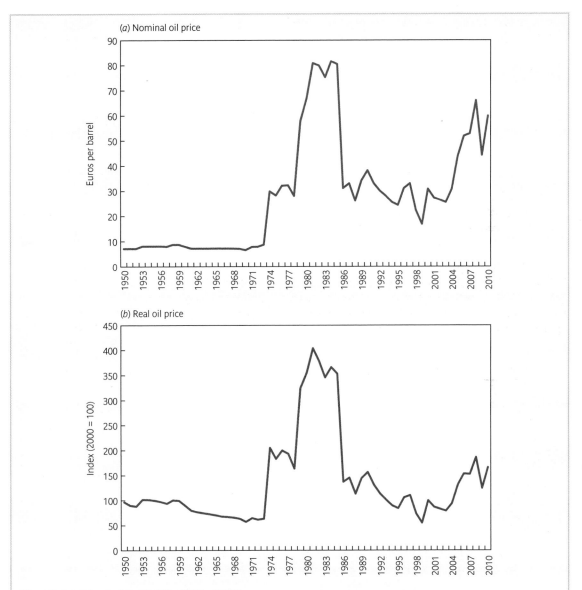

Fig. 12.11 The Price of Oil, 1950–2011

The price of oil is generally quoted in US dollars; in panel (*a*) it has been converted into euros. The first two oil shocks (1973–1974 and 1979–1981) and the two next ones (1999–2001 and 2005–2008) are clearly visible. In 1986, a favourable oil shock occurred—a sharp decline of oil prices. Panel (*b*), which deflates the oil price by the consumer price index, shows that, while oil prices rose sharply in 2007 in euros, in real terms that increase hardly compares in severity with the oil shocks of the 1970s.

Source: British Petroleum, IMF.

drawing board. Yet, as already noted, Friedman and Phelps had already provided the answer to the puzzle even before the puzzle emerged. The next section presents an interpretation of inflation that can account for these facts.

12.4 Accounting for Inflation: The Battle of the Mark-ups

Why do we care about the fate of the Phillips curve in the first place? Recall that it deals with the medium run. In the short run, prices are sticky and we can ignore inflation. In the long run, the Phillips curve is vertical and has nothing to say about inflation. If we want to understand the inflation phenomenon, therefore, we need to understand the time in between. To that end, we will follow a pragmatic, 'divide and conquer' strategy. By breaking inflation into a series of its most important components, we can better account for its immediate sources and will be better equipped to think about it.

12.4.1 Prices and Costs

Price setting

The price level is the average of individual prices, but who sets the prices of goods and services and how?[11] Looking at price tags in stores and price lists in catalogues, you may correctly conclude that producers and retailers decide on the prices of their goods and services. Obviously, each producer prefers higher to lower prices, but their enthusiasm is held in check by the need to attract enough buyers. This is the process that we now study. Box 12.2 recalls a few principles. It explains how competition limits the ability of firms to set prices, and that firms try hard to reduce these same limitations. It describes firms as setting prices as a mark-up above nominal production costs, aiming at a margin consistent with maximizing profits.

Costs

Now that we understand the price mark-up—the relationship of price to cost—it will make sense to look at those production costs, called **average** or **unit costs**, measured in pounds or euros.[12] Unit cost (UC) is simply the total cost of production divided by the number of units produced. It is convenient to break down unit costs into two main categories: labour and non-labour costs:

Unit costs in euros

= total costs in euros/number of units produced

= unit labour costs + unit non-labour costs.

For the economy as a whole, labour costs are the single largest component of unit production costs. Table 12.1 shows that at the macro level, the share of labour costs (wages, benefits, plus contributions to social insurance) ranges from 50% to 70% of value added in developed countries, and is usually higher in labour-intensive services than in capital-intensive industries.[13] For this reason, we will focus on labour costs for the next few sections. We will consider non-labour costs later in Section 12.4.6.

Labour costs and wages

A firm's total labour costs are simply the product of the number of hours worked in the firm (L) and the average gross hourly labour cost (W). Gross hourly labour costs include not only wages and salaries per

---

[11] Chapter 2 presents various ways of measuring the price level.

[12] In theory, the relevant concept is the marginal production cost, the cost of producing another unit of output. In practice, marginal costs are difficult to measure, so we approximate them by unit costs. This is an acceptable approximation under conditions of constant return to scale in all factors.

[13] In interpreting these numbers, it is important to remember the distinction between value added and turnover or total sales, which was stressed in Chapter 1. As a percentage of total sales, wage shares are much lower because total turnover in an economy includes the costs of intermediate goods. The figures reported in Table 12.1 have netted out payments for intermediate inputs produced by other firms.

Box 12.2 When and How Firms Set Prices

Economists speak of perfect competition in goods markets when firms are unable to set prices. A good example is the fruit grower who sells his apples in the town market. With many other sellers around, the farmer cannot set his price very far from some average price for apples of the same variety. If he raises his price just a few cents, he loses all his customers; if he lowers his price, he will sell everything, but regret the forgone profits. Producers of standard products, such as agricultural products or raw materials, have relatively little choice. We say that they have no **market power**.

Yet most firms do have market power, and some firms have a lot of it. In fact, they go to extreme lengths to establish market power because this helps them achieve higher profits. This is called **product differentiation**, which means making each product special and different from the competitors. They do so through design (similar cars always differ in many subtle ways), through advertising and marketing to win consumer loyalty (some people like Volkswagen, others Renault), or product quality and reputation. The pay-off is a higher willingness to pay by their customers, and a greater degree of market power. Firms can charge higher prices above the bare minimum that they need to survive, and still keep a large share of their customers.

Mark-up pricing is a simple description of how firms with market power set prices. Obviously, when setting a price, a firm wants to cover its production costs, and then it tries to do more. The margin over the cost of producing one more good, the marginal cost, is the mark-up. The mark-up depends on the sensitivity of the particular product's demand to price—its demand elasticity. If the market is highly competitive, the demand elasticity is near-infinite, because customers have lots of alternatives: any price increase will drive customers to other sellers. In that case the mark-up is zero and the price is equal to marginal cost. This is the case of perfect competition. If competition is weak, because the firm has been able to differentiate its good and build a 'niche', or because other firms cannot enter the market, the demand elasticity is low and the mark-up will be higher.

Table 12.1 Wage Share of Value Added by Country and Selected Industries, 2009

	Total Economy	Manufacturing	Construction	Finance and Business Services	Basic Metal Industries	Wholesale/ Retail Trade
Belgium	59.1	70.5	54.2	35.2	79.9	62.7
Czech Republic	49.3	52.7	42.6	40.5	56.4	53.5
Denmark	68.3	72.8	84.5	45.3	72.7	81.5
Germany	57.3	78.8	57.1	31.7	n.a.	68.9
Italy	47.7	65.0	43.3	25.5	71.6	43.1
Japan	52.3	56.8	73.5	n.a.	66.8	62.2
Netherlands	58.5	62.9	60.0	51.7	84.2	62.0
Poland (2008)	42.4	49.8	34.6	27.8	n.a.	31.2
Spain	52.8	62.6	52.2	35.3	68.0	49.0
United States	55.4	54.2	70.4	38.7	63.6	57.1

Source: OECD STAN Database

hour, but also paid vacations, direct labour taxes, social security contributions, and other benefits paid by employers on behalf of their workers. (In many European countries, these additional costs can be nearly equal to the net pay received by the worker.) A country's aggregate unit labour cost is computed in the same way. It is the ratio of total labour costs WL, also called the **wage bill**, to total real output, i.e. real GDP Y:

(12.3) $\text{nominal unit labour costs} = \dfrac{\text{wage bill}}{\text{real GDP}} = \dfrac{WL}{Y}$

Nominal unit labour costs must be distinguished from the *real* labour cost of producing a unit of real GDP or, equivalently, the ratio of the nominal wage bill to nominal GDP:

(12.4)

$$\text{real unit labour costs} = \dfrac{\text{nominal unit labour costs}}{\text{nominal GDP}}$$

$$= \dfrac{WL}{PY} = \dfrac{\text{wage bill}}{\text{nominal GDP}}.$$

The real unit labour costs measure the share of GDP (PY) that goes to labour.

12.4.2 The Battle of the Mark-ups: A Simple Story

Prices as mark-up on labour costs

Mark-up pricing means that firms set the price of goods as much as they can above their nominal unit costs. We have agreed to ignore non-labour costs, so we now consider that firms will aim for a price as much above their unit labour costs as it takes to maximize its profits. This can be written as follows:

(12.5) $P = (1+\theta)\dfrac{WL}{Y},$

where $\theta \geq 0$ is the price mark-up. A simple way of thinking of the mark-up is if $\theta = 0.3 = 30/100$, the price is set 30% above nominal unit labour costs.[14]

Wages as a mark-up on prices

Firms mark prices above labour costs, but what determines labour costs and nominal wages? A good start-

ing point is Chapter 5, which notes that wages are set through negotiations between employees and employers. These negotiations deal with two different issues.

First, the employees want to secure as large an income as possible. Yet both wages and salaries as well as employment must originate in value added (GDP) of ongoing firms. Thus, while labour is likely to aim at as large a labour share of output as possible, as we saw in Chapter 5, its efforts are limited by firms' demand for labour.

Second, wage negotiators can only bargain over *nominal* wages. They do not know for sure what tomorrow's price level will be. Typically, wage agreements cover a period of one or more years, and the future evolution of the price level is unknown. Naturally, employees want to protect their nominal wages from inflation. Employers normally agree to incorporate the likely evolution of the price level in wage settlements but worry about overestimating it and paying their workers 'too much'—paying workers too much means making low profits or even losses. This is why the expected evolution of the price level, which is incorporated into the wage agreement, is a central part of negotiations. We denote the resulting expected price level by P^e.

In the end, both sides bargain directly over the nominal wage W and indirectly over the expected labour share WL/P^eY. A simple description of the outcome of the negotiations is that wages are set the unit labour costs as a mark-up γ over the expected price level:

(12.6) $\dfrac{WL}{Y} = (1+\gamma)\overline{s_L}P^e,$

where $\overline{s_L}$ is the 'normal' share that wage negotiators accept as representing an appropriate division of income in normal times, i.e. when the demand for labour is neither too strong nor too weak.[15] The wage mark-up γ shows how the agreed-upon share varies over the cycle. The mark-up can be positive or negative, and it is zero on average. In some years, $\gamma > 0$, and the agreed-upon wage is above its normal level. In other years, $\gamma < 0$ and the wage is lower.

---

[14] Formally, $\theta = \dfrac{P - WL/Y}{WL/Y}.$

[15] Box (12.3) provides a formal explanation.

Putting it all together

We have described prices as a mark-up over unit costs, agreed to ignore all non-labour costs and therefore to focus on unit labour costs, and found that the expected labour share is a mark-up over its normal level. This in turn means that wages are a mark-up over prices. In the end, prices depend on wages and wages depend on expected prices.

Isn't this a bad case of circular reasoning? Quite to the contrary, this description captures the fundamentally conflictual relationship between employers and employees as they divide up the GDP cake. It has earned the title '**battle of the mark-ups**'.[16] The price mark-up, equation (12.1), sets the price level as a mark-up on wages, while the wage mark-up, equation (12.7), sets wages as a mark-up on the (expected) price level. Firms increase profits by reducing labour costs relative to the prices that their products can fetch. Employees increase real wages by pushing them up relative to expected prices.

Note carefully the distinction: *actual* prices depend on wages, while wages depend on *expected* prices. The apparent circularity really links actual prices to expected prices, as can be seen by combining (12.5) and (12.6), resulting in

(12.7) $P = (1 + \theta)(1 + \gamma)\overline{s_L}P^e.$

We see that the circular process has an anchor: P^e, the level of prices expected by wage negotiators to prevail over the course of the contract. We will later find that this expectation is one central determinant of inflation in the medium run.

12.4.3 Productivity and the Labour Share

Before we move on to the next and final step, a clarification may be helpful.[17] We know from Chapter 3 that labour productivity (Y/L) and real wages do tend to grow systematically over time. Productivity does not appear at all in the final outcome of the price- and wage-setting process as represented by equation (12.7). This may be surprising but a bit of reflection shows that it is not.

To see this, recall that equation (12.4) defines real unit labour cost (or the labour share) as WL/PY. When real wages grow at the same rate as labour productivity, real unit labour costs remain constant, as shown formally in Box 12.3. Put differently, when productivity is rising, real wages can increase without raising production costs. This is the base case, which defines the 'normal' labour share $\overline{S_L}$. The battle of the mark-ups studies fluctuations in real unit labour costs that occur when real wages temporarily depart from this principle.

The base case is precisely what we expect to see following the principles developed in Chapter 5 and one of the stylized facts in Chapter 3. Indeed, Figure 1.3 in Chapter 1 showed in that, in four countries over half a century, labour shares fluctuate from year to year, but with little discernible trend. This is just another way of saying that technical progress continuously generates higher incomes, but gross hourly wages (including all employee costs) and hourly productivity track each other pretty well.

12.4.4 Cyclical Behaviour of Mark-ups

Now we turn to the determinants of the two mark-ups. The brief answer is that they tend to move over business cycles. To see which side would 'win' the battle of the mark-ups, we need to separate out the two, distinctly different mark-up decisions.

Start with the price mark-up θ. The price mark-up is like a profit margin—the excess of revenues over variable costs. Firms naturally would like profits to be as large as possible, but have to worry about competition.[18] Competition increases in good times, when there is 'more money in the marketplace'. While firms may try to raise price mark-ups when demand is high, high business volumes increase total profits so much that new firms enter and steal competitors' customers. The effect here is uncertain.

The wage share mark-up γ is the outcome of wage bargaining at the level of collective negotiations, but

---

[16] The battle of the mark-ups approach to understanding inflation has found empirical support in OECD countries in groundbreaking work by researchers at the London School of Economics: Richard Layard, Steven Nickell, and Richard Jackman, among others.

[17] This section may be skipped without loss of continuity.

[18] A natural tendency is for competitors to agree on large mark-ups. Such collusion is usually illegal and competition authorities seek out and prosecute anti-competition agreements.

Box 12.3 **The Wage Mark-Up and the Labour Share**

Equation (12.4) defines the labour share as $\frac{WL}{PY}$. We describe wage negotiators as proceeding in two steps. First, they agree—in a process that can in fact be highly conflictual—on a 'normal' level of this share:

$$\text{Normal share} = \frac{\overline{W}}{\overline{P}}\frac{Y}{L} = \overline{s}_L\frac{Y}{L},$$

where $\overline{W}$ is the corresponding 'normal' real wage. Once this is done, wage negotiators will recognize that the labour market is tight (strong demand because the economy is booming) or weak (in a recession). They then agree—an equally controversial step—on the

expected real wage (W/P^e) as a markup γ on the normal wage, delivering equation (12.6).

What drives the normal labour share? This is a complex social issue. Here we just note that the share remains constant where workers get their appropriate or 'fair' share of productivity gains. To see this, note that the labour share can be rewritten as $\frac{W/P}{Y/L}$. Using the rate of change rule presented in Box 6.3, we see that the percentage increase in the labour share is $\frac{\Delta(W/P)}{W/P} - \frac{\Delta(Y/L)}{Y/L}$. This shows that the labour share is constant when the real wages (W/P) grow at the same rate as labour productivity (Y/L).

---

could also reflect individual outcomes of a more competitive labour market. During boom periods, rising employment generally improves the bargaining position of unions and workers in general, which is reflected in a higher wage mark-up. In addition, firms may offer higher real pay to motivate employees to work harder or longer hours, or even to encourage others to join the labour force.[19] More likely than not, the wage mark-up is—or is likely to be—procyclical.[20]

The battle of the mark-ups, expressed by equation (12.7), shows that the expected price level drives wages via the wage mark-up, and that wages drive labour costs, which drive prices via the price mark-up. Both mark-ups tend to move over the business cycle. It is a well-established fact that, combined together (the *product* $(1 + \theta)(1 + \gamma)$ of the two mark-ups in equation (12.7)) is procyclical. It tends to push the actual price level above its expected level in boom times, and to pull it down in lean years.

This procyclical outcome of the battle of the mark-ups is the foundation of the Phillips curve. We now use (12.7), which describes how the price *level P* is set, to conclude that the inflation rate, the *rate of increase* $\Delta P/P$ of the price level, is driven by two factors: (1) the

combined change of the two mark-ups, and (2) the expected inflation rate. Using the symbol π to stand for the rate of inflation, and π^e to represent the expected rate of inflation, we represent this result as:[21]

(12.8) $\qquad \pi = \Delta(\text{mark-ups}) + \pi^e.$

We are now just two short steps away from reaching the Phillips curve. First, the change in individual mark-ups will be different for different wage-bargaining situations, even at the same stage of the business cycle. Yet only the *average* bargaining situation in the economy is relevant for aggregate inflation—an average of many price changes. It follows that the aggregate mark-up moves with the business cycle. It rises when the real GDP Y moves above its trend $\overline{Y}$, i.e. when the output gap Y_{gap} is positive, and it declines when the gap becomes negative. Alternatively, we can use Okun's Law to describe mark-ups as rising when the unemployment rate U declines below equilibrium $\overline{U}$, i.e. the unemployment gap U_{gap} is negative, and declining in the opposite situation.

---

[19] This reasoning is developed in detail in Chapter 5.

[20] The wage share tends first to fall in an expansion, catching up with a significant lag and continues to rise past the peak of the usual cycle, as can be seen in a Burns–Mitchell diagram.

[21] For the mathematically minded reader: using the results of Box 6.3, (12.7) provides the rates of change of all variables, with the following approximation: $\pi = \frac{\Delta P}{P} = \frac{\Delta \theta}{1+\theta} + \frac{\Delta \gamma}{1+\gamma} + \frac{\Delta S_L}{1+S_L} + \frac{\Delta P^e}{P^e}$. Assuming that the normal labour share is constant, equation (12.8) follows, where $\Delta(\text{mark-ups})$ is formally equal to $\frac{\Delta \theta}{1+\theta} + \frac{\Delta \gamma}{1+\gamma}$.

The second step recognizes that wage bargaining and price setting do not occur all at once, but are staggered over time. It is simply too costly for firms and workers to discuss wages all the time; after all, there's other work that needs to be done! Similarly, firms are not in a position to change their prices every day. Customers expect a certain stability in pricing, and may have even entered contractual agreements to guarantee that stability. As a result, while decisions are taken rationally, they are often based on older information. There is no single expected inflation rate π^e, but rather a complex mix of many expected rates, some relevant for the present, some coming from the past and looking to the future. For the aggregate economy, we can capture this inertial inflation in the economy as $\tilde{\pi}$, which we call the **underlying inflation rate**. As we will see, this is not only a realistic detail, it also turns out to be crucial for understanding the Phillips curve.

We have now reached our final destination. The process captured by equation (12.7) is turned into a relationship between actual and something which resembles expected inflation. Indeed, taking into account the cyclical behaviour of the combined mark-ups, the relationship (12.8) can be written as

(12.9) $\pi = \tilde{\pi} + aY_{gap} = \tilde{\pi} - bU_{gap}$

The first part of the equation is an augmented version of the original Phillips curve. The second is the augmented aggregate supply curve. Both are augmented by consideration of underlying inflation.

The relationship (12.9) offers a simple but very effective accounting of what drives inflation. It asserts that inflation is driven by two main forces:

(1) What people expect or have expected inflation to be, now and in the future.

(2) Cyclical conditions, with wages and prices tending to rise faster in years of rapid economic growth and slowing down in harder times.

The positive parameters a and b simply describe how the mark-ups jointly respond to cyclical fluctuations, represented alternatively by the output and unemployment gaps. They say that a high level of activity leads to higher mark-ups.

12.4.5 More on the Underlying Rate of Inflation

In the last section we introduced a new concept, the underlying rate of inflation.[22] Because this concept is so important, we will spend a little more time discussing it here.

Recall that the expected price level in equation (12.6) is one important component of wage bargaining. It describes how wage negotiators expect the price level to evolve over the course of wage contracts under discussion. In that sense, the underlying inflation rate is forward-looking. In practice, it also includes a backward-looking component for several reasons. First, workers may use past behaviour of inflation to forecast the future. This may be a clever way of learning what the inflation rate is doing, or it may reflect a cheap alternative to hiring some economist to do the job. Second, cost-of-living clauses in labour contracts may actually mandate increases in nominal wages based on past inflation. Third, inflation forecasts are inevitably inaccurate *ex post*, and workers and firms will try to correct their past mistakes—if they can.

Consider the following examples of the last mechanism at work. Suppose a worker's wage contract incorporates a nominal wage increase of 4% in the year to come, reflecting the expectation of 3% inflation plus a 1% gain in labour productivity. After the fact, productivity indeed does rise by 1% but inflation turns out to be 5%! Workers, having lost 1% of purchasing power, will feel 'cheated' of not just 2% inflation forecast error, but also by the fact that their employer made off with 1% productivity. They are likely to try to recover these losses in negotiations for the following year.

Conversely, suppose inflation is only 1% after the year has passed. Then real wages are likely to have risen too fast and profits squeezed. Employers will no doubt use this fact to slow down wage increases in the future. Correcting for past forecast errors is an

---

[22] Sometimes the underlying rate is simply called 'inflationary expectations', relying more on the interpretation that it incorporates the anticipated inflation of firms and workers. Others use the term 'core inflation'—which is sometimes also used to describe the more stable inflation rate for non-food, non-energy items.

integral part of wage negotiations, and indeed this is why the logic of the purely forward-looking price level P^e in (12.8) has to be extended with a combination of forward- and backward-looking considerations. This is what underlying inflation is designed to capture.

Forecast errors are unavoidable. When inflation is reasonably low, the errors are small and the combination of catch-up and forward-looking forecasts encoded in the underlying inflation rate is acceptable. When inflation is substantial, say, around 20% per year, forecast errors can easily be much higher. In periods when inflation is high, it also tends to be more variable, leading to even larger forecast errors. This is why various mechanisms designed to cope with high inflation tend to emerge when the price level is rising fast. For example, explicit or implicit **indexation** clauses can link wages automatically to the evolution of the consumer price index. Another response is to shorten the contract length for wages and prices to shorter periods, like a quarter, or a month. In periods of extremely high inflation, wages and prices may even be reset weekly or daily! Avoiding such situations is why price stability, i.e. low inflation, is so desirable.

12.4.6 Completing the Picture: Supply Shocks

It is now time to look at the non-labour costs of production, studiously ignored until now. These costs correspond to the other factors of production—e.g. capital and land—as well as to intermediate inputs such as unfinished goods, primary commodities, and energy. In general, these costs follow the general trend of final goods prices. Their effect on inflation is then adequately reflected in the underlying inflation rate, adding nothing new to the analysis.

For this reason, these costs can be neglected most of the time. Now and then, however, special circumstances arise when non-labour costs do not behave so innocuously and significantly affect the short-run evolution of inflation, independent of the state of the economy, the market power of workers and firms, or what they have expected inflation to be. These events are treated as exogenous because they happen elsewhere or are special in the sense that they are not explained by the framework that we develop. Because

they affect the costs of production, they are called **supply shocks**.

The leading example of a supply shock is a sharp increase in the price of oil, commonly referred to as an oil shock. Petroleum is a primary energy source and is an especially important raw material for the electrical generation, transport, chemical, and construction sectors. These sectors supply all sectors with inputs, so changes in oil prices have an important impact on production costs across the economy as well as on household budgets. Oil shocks have occurred at various points of time in the 1970s, early 1980s, and mid-2000s. Figure 12.11 gives a historical perspective. Another example of a supply shock is a deep depreciation, which renders imported good prices more expensive when evaluated in the domestic currency. Supply shocks may also be favourable. Oil prices, for instance, fell very fast in late 2008 after having risen considerably in 2007. The strong appreciation cheapens imports and for an open economy can have a significant *negative* impact on the short-term evolution of inflation, even while possibly hurting international competitiveness (raising σ) at the same time.

In the end, we think of non-labour costs as generally following underlying inflation $\tilde{\pi}$, but need to remember that supply shocks can and will occur—the sharp energy price increases seen in 2007–2008 are a clear reminder. To that effect, we allow for an occasional occurrence of a supply shock, a catch-all for exogenous disturbances affecting production costs. We denote this supply shock term by s and extend the aggregate supply curve and Phillips curve (12.9) in an important way:

(12.10) $\pi = \tilde{\pi} + aY_{\text{gap}} + s$ (aggregate supply curve)

(12.11)
$$\underset{\substack{\text{actual}\\\text{inflation}}}{\pi} = \underset{\substack{\text{underlying}\\\text{inflation}}}{\tilde{\pi}} - \underset{\substack{\text{cyclical}\\\text{effect}}}{bU_{\text{gap}}} + \underset{\substack{\text{supply}\\\text{shock}}}{s} \text{ (Phillips curve)}$$

As long as non-labour production costs are in line with the underlying rate of inflation, the supply shock term is zero. Occasionally, in unmistakable circumstances, it can be positive (an adverse supply shock) or negative (a favourable supply shock) or negative. On average it should be nil.

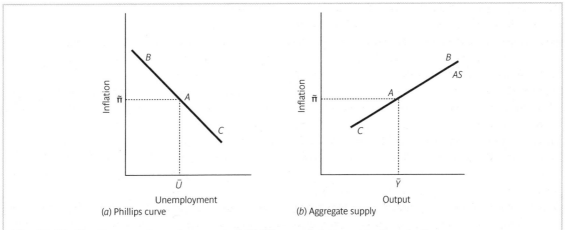

Fig. 12.12 The Expectations-Augmented Phillips and Aggregate Supply Curves

By definition, point A represents the case where actually observed inflation π is at its underlying rate $\tilde{\pi}$ and where unemployment U is at its equilibrium rate $\bar{U}$, and output Y is at its trend value $\bar{Y}$. When unemployment is low and output high, actual inflation is above the underlying inflation rate (point B). When unemployment is higher and output is lower than their respective equilibrium levels, actual inflation is below underlying inflation (point C).

Beyond changes in non-labour costs, two other types of supply shock can be important. First, we assumed that the labour share is constant. A quick glance at Figure 1.2, however, shows that it is approximately trendless, but certainly not constant. Occasionally, it rises or declines, a process that can last several years. Such changes are usually the outcome of deep socio-political events that strengthen or weaken trade unions or employers' associations. We can take care of these events by interpreting changes in the labour share as supply shocks. An exogenous increase of the labour share, for example, adds to labour costs and can be treated as $s > 0$.

Second, supply shocks may also be caused by the government. An increase in certain types of taxes (for example, the value added tax) or prices for regulated utilities can raise the inflation rate even though the underlying rate and labour market conditions remain constant. The variety of taxes borne by firms relate directly to production and affect the final selling price—value added or excise taxes, profit taxes, establishment and property taxes, and so on. Other costs imposed by governments are implicit, but may have a significant impact (e.g. various labour regulations, environmental or consumer protection legislation).

12.5 Inflation, Unemployment, and Output

12.5.1 The Phillips Curve Rehabilitated

The inflation-accounting framework summarized by equation (12.11) effectively solves the puzzle of the Phillips curve. We can explain its persistence over decades, its instability over particular periods of time, and the impression that it shifts now and then. The original Phillips curve claimed that inflation depends only on the level of unemployment. The inflation account shows that cyclical labour market conditions do indeed matter, but so do underlying inflation, equilibrium unemployment, and occasional supply shocks. For a Phillips curve to be visible, these latter factors must be stable so that changes in inflation are mostly driven by cyclical conditions.

When these factors are not stable, the Phillips curve seems to vanish. This is precisely what happened during the 1970s, when price and commodity shocks became a major source of instability (see Figure 12.11). As inflation rose, underlying inflation rose as well and became more variable, reflecting rapidly changing expectations. The Phillips curve's demise reflects the emergence of underlying inflation and supply shocks. In addition, equilibrium unemployment rose in many countries during this period, for reasons explained in Chapter 5. These additional determinants of inflation, above and beyond cyclical factors, have helped to rehabilitate the Phillips curve.

How should we think of the Phillips curve if it proves to be unstable? Much as with the *IS* and *TR* curves, the answer is to keep clearly in mind which variables are endogenous and which ones are taken as exogenous. As long as the exogenous variables remain constant, the curve does not move. When they change, the curve will shift and apparently 'vanish'. This is the way the reconstructed Phillips curve explains the apparent puzzle. The modern Phillips curve is sometimes referred to as the expectations-augmented Phillips curve. This name emphasizes the central role of underlying inflation. Yet, it is more than that; it also recognizes that equilibrium unemployment K may change. It also allows for supply shocks.

Locating the Phillips curve requires a proper understanding of the underlying determinants of inflation. According to (12.10), when supply shocks are zero ($s = 0$) and when actual unemployment equals its equilibrium level ($U = \bar{U}$) and output is on trend ($Y = \bar{Y}$), the unemployment and output gaps are nil and actual inflation equals the underlying inflation rate ($\pi = \tilde{\pi}$). The pair ($\bar{U}, \tilde{\pi}$) serves as an anchor which pins down the position of the Phillips curve at any point in time. Without knowing the equilibrium rate of unemployment $\bar{U}$ and the underlying rate of inflation $\tilde{\pi}$, it is difficult or impossible to pin down the inflation-unemployment trade-off. And because both $\bar{U}$ and $\tilde{\pi}$ may change over time, it essential to understand the determinants of these factors.

This situation corresponds to point *A* in either chart of Figure 12.12. Point *A* uniquely determines the position of the Phillips or aggregate supply curves. The other points on the curves simply follow from allowing the unemployment rate to vary around its equilibrium level, holding underlying inflation constant and setting the supply shock to zero. This is the key intuition from the old Phillips curve that inflation varies with the business cycle. For instance, at point *B* unemployment is below equilibrium and output is above trend, so the demand pressure pushes inflation above its current underlying rate. Conversely, point *C* corresponds to the case where inflation is below its underlying rate because the unemployment rate is above equilibrium and output is below trend. In the left-hand chart of Figure 12.12, this traces out a downward-sloping schedule that resembles the old Phillips curve shown in Figure 12.3. In fact, it is the same but with a crucial difference: its position is determined by point *A*, that is, by the underlying inflation rate and equilibrium unemployment $\bar{U}$.[23]

12.5.2 Underlying Inflation and the Long Run

Underlying inflation captures the rate of inflation agreed upon during wage negotiations, both now and, for some bargaining parties, at points in the past. It has both a backward-looking (it reflects old forecasts of inflation today, as well as efforts to fix past errors of inflation forecasts used in previous contracts) and a forward-looking component (what will inflation be in the future). Somehow, it must be related to the actual rate of inflation. How this is so in the short run is considered in the next chapter. In this section we deal with the long run. We already saw in Section 12.3.3 that the **long-run Phillips curve** is vertical. We now look at how this comes about.

As negotiators consider the amount of inflation to be factored into wage settlements, they strive to guess it accurately. Of course, employees have an incentive to overstate the underlying rate of inflation, but employers have precisely the opposite incentive. If there were no uncertainty and both sides always knew *ex ante* what inflation would be

---

[23] This is why the equilibrium rate of unemployment is sometimes called the NAIRU: the non-accelerating inflation rate of unemployment. At point *B* inflation accelerates above its underlying rate. At point *C* it decelerates. Only at point *A* is inflation stable.

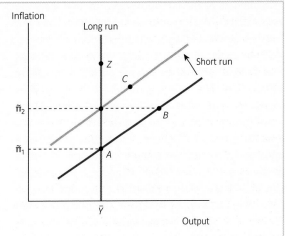

Fig. 12.13 From the Short to the Long Run

For a given underlying rate of inflation, as it moves from point *A* to point *B*, the economy can sustain lower unemployment and higher output but at the cost of higher inflation. This trade-off is not permanent, however. When underlying inflation rises to track higher actual inflation, the short-run Phillips curve shifts up. In the long run when the actual and underlying inflation are equal (for example, point *Z*), there is no longer any trade-off at all.

over the lifetime of the wage contract, underlying and actual inflation would just be equal. Uncertainty therefore means forecasting (or guessing) underlying inflation. More often than not, the guesses are wrong. Yet, the principle of rational expectations from Chapter 7 means that wage negotiators do not make systematic forecast errors. Although forecasts are almost always incorrect, the errors are largely unsystematic and average to zero: in some years inflation is overestimated, in others it is underestimated.

These observations have two important implications. First, there must be a link between actual inflation π and underlying inflation $\tilde{\pi}$. Underlying inflation must track, albeit imperfectly, actual inflation. The backward-looking component implies that underlying inflation *lags* behind actual inflation, but the forward-looking component implies that underlying inflation *leads* actual inflation. The interplay of both components is bound to be rather murky and difficult to detect precisely. As a result, it is far from obvious how to interpret Figure 12.9. There exist statistical techniques to do so, however, and they are routinely used by economists.

The second implication relates to the long run. The rational expectations hypothesis means that actual and underlying inflation cannot remain different in any systematic way. Any discrepancy between π and $\tilde{\pi}$ must be temporary. This fits well with other views of the long run. Obviously, over the years to come, we expect booms and recessions, possibly as consequences of supply shocks, positive and negative. We cannot really guess what the situation will be five or ten years from now. The best bet is the agnostic one, that there will be no shocks and that the economy will not be far from trend, with actual unemployment equal to underlying unemployment. For this reason, it makes sense to *define* the long run as the situation where the economy is back on its trend. This means that the Phillips curve is vertical. From equation (12.10), we know that when $s = 0$ and $U = \bar{U}$, then $\pi = \tilde{\pi}$. In a way, the long run is atemporal; the backward- and forward-looking components of underlying inflation have worked themselves out.

Thus, for the third time, we conclude that the long-run Phillips curve is vertical. We first encountered this result in Section 12.2.2 when we found that long-run price flexibility implies that output is supply determined. Next, in Section 12.3.3, we argued that long-run neutrality—which really follows from long-run price flexibility—implies a vertical Phillips curve. Now, we see that a vertical Phillips curve is also a consequence of the battle of the mark-ups, once we admit that there cannot be any permanent deviation between actual and underlying inflation.

The vertical long-run Phillips curve only tells us that the actual and underlying inflation rates are equal. It leaves entirely open the question of what these rates are. We will see in the next chapter that we need to bring back the demand side of the economy to pin down long-run inflation, actual and underlying. In fact, we already know that. The neutrality principle established in Chapter 6 relates long-run inflation to money growth, i.e. to monetary policy. In Box 12.1, we saw that this principle holds even if central banks set interest rates, because the long neutral interest rate contains the central bank's target inflation rate, and nothing else. We will see that it takes time for underlying and actual inflation to catch up with each other and stabilize at whatever rate monetary policy allows for. Views vary about how quickly this happens, and herein lie some of the most fundamental controversies in macroeconomics, already encountered in Chapter 10 and to be studied further in Chapter 16.

The vertical Phillips curve carries a crucial implication: there cannot be a long-lasting trade-off between unemployment and inflation. Demand policies cannot move the actual unemployment rate permanently away from its equilibrium level. But the equilibrium level can very well shift over time, e.g. as labour markets undergo structural changes. Indeed, one of the implications of Figure 12.10 is that unemployment equilibrium must have shifted over the last decades. It massively increased in the euro area over the 1970s and 1980s—shifting the Phillips curve to the right—and then declined in the late 1990s. In the UK, the decline of the equilibrium unemployment rate started earlier and has been more pronounced—a legacy of Mrs Thatcher's supply-side policies aimed at weakening the bargaining power of unions, lowering unemployment benefits, and reducing the equilibrium unemployment rate.

12.5.3 Aggregate Supply

All of the previous reasoning applies to the aggregate supply curve shown in the right-hand chart in Figure 12.12 since it corresponds—via Okun's Law—to the Phillips curve. Its position is determined by the output

trend and the underlying inflation rate, and it shifts when any of the exogenous variables ($\tilde{\pi}, \overline{Y}$, or s) changes.

The aggregate supply curve conveys two important messages:

(1) In the short run, as GDP fluctuates about its trend growth path, the actual rate of inflation can differ from the underlying rate. In the absence of supply shocks, output and inflation move in the same direction.

(2) In the long run, GDP must return to its growth path, regardless of what the inflation rate is. Real forces determine the growth of real activity and the growth of money supply determines inflation.

The long-run aggregate supply schedule is vertical. It will, however, shift continuously to the right since, as a consequence of long-run economic growth, trend output keeps rising.

12.5.4 Factors that Shift the Phillips and Aggregate Supply Curves

The original position of the Phillips and aggregate supply curves in Figure 12.13 is determined by point A. This point corresponds to the initial underlying inflation rate, to the equilibrium unemployment rate, and trend GDP. Thus, the underlying inflation rate and the equilibrium unemployment rate or trend GDP are taken as exogenous when we draw the curves. The fact that they determine the position of the curve, giving us the location of point A, provides two reasons why the curves can shift. The first is a change in the underlying inflation rate: an increase in underlying inflation shifts the curves up. The second reason is that equilibrium unemployment and trend GDP may change. The supply shock s is the third exogenous variable that shifts the curve.

There is no presumption whatsoever that either underlying inflation or equilibrium unemployment are constant over time. If either changes, point A moves, and so does the whole Phillips curve. This implies that, potentially, there exists an infinity of Phillips curves, corresponding to the infinity of values that the underlying inflation rate or the equilibrium rate of unemployment can take. It just so happened that, over the hundred years surveyed by Phillips, the underlying rate of inflation and the equilibrium rate of unemployment

Table 12.2 Equilibrium Unemployment Rates

	1970	1980	1990	2000	2010
Austria	1.9	2.3	3.6	4.0	4.3
Belgium	2.9	6.3	7.9	8.0	8.2
Denmark	n.a.	5.2	6.7	5.1	4.9
Finland	3.7	3.4	6.2	9.8	7.8
France	n.a.	5.7	8.6	9.0	8.7
Germany	3.3	4.0	6.9	8.0	8.1
Hungary	n.a.	n.a.	n.a.	6.1	7.9
Ireland	n.a.	11.4	14.6	5.8	8.0
Italy	5.3	5.7	9.1	7.6	7.1
Japan	1.6	1.8	2.7	3.8	4.1
Netherlands	2.4	4.4	6.8	4.2	3.7
Norway	1.6	2.2	4.4	4.1	3.4
Portugal	n.a.	7.0	6.3	8.9	8.1
Spain	n.a.	6.4	14.5	12.4	12.6
Sweden	2.7	3.3	5.2	6.6	7.0
Switzerland	n.a.	0.6	1.8	3.3	3.8
United Kingdom	2.7	7.7	8.9	5.2	5.8
United States	5.3	6.6	6.2	7.2	5.3

Source: OECD, *Economic Outlook.*

did not change much, so there seems to have been just one Phillips curve.[24] This changed in the early 1970s when unemployment became much more stable—as the result of active Keynesian policies—while more volatile commodity prices became the dominating factor affecting inflation.

Shifts in the equilibrium unemployment rate occur occasionally. Table 12.2 presents some estimates of the equilibrium unemployment rate obtained by asking what rate would keep the Phillips curve unchanged when the actual and underlying inflation rates are equal and in the absence of a sup-

ply shock.[25] The table shows that the equilibrium rate rose in most countries in the 1970s and then declined in some countries two or three decades later, as the result of labour market reforms. This is one reason for the rightward shift of most Phillips curves in the 1970s, and for the subsequent leftward shift in those countries that managed to bring unemployment down in the 1990s or 2000s. Two examples are presented in Figure 12.10.

Trend output continuously rises as the outcome of long-run growth. To avoid dealing with a curve that constantly moves to the right, in later chapters we will draw the aggregate supply curve with the output gap $(Y - \bar{Y})/\bar{Y}$ on the horizontal axis.

[24] There are good reasons for this. The period corresponds to the time of the gold standard and the Bretton Woods system, both of which constrained inflation from rising too much and kept underlying inflation in check.

[25] This is precisely the NAIRU as explained in footnote 23.

Finally, the supply curve shifts in the presence of supply shocks. If these shocks raise the cost of production, the Phillips and aggregate supply curves shift upwards. If the increase is temporary, the curves will eventually return to their initial positions, unless underlying inflation also increases in the meantime. Oil shocks are a prime example of sudden increases in non-labour costs. The shocks of 1973–1974 and 1980 also played a role in the shifts visible in Figure 12.10.

12.5.5 From the Short to the Long Run

We have salvaged the old Phillips curve by replacing it with two curves: (1) a short-run expectations-augmented Phillips curve, which resembles the old one but can move, and (2) a long-run Phillips curve, which is always vertical. To these two curves correspond, via Okun's Law, a short-run and a long-run aggregate supply curve. These results are brought together in Figure 12.13. In both panels, point A describes the long-run situation where actual and underlying inflation are equal ($\tilde{\pi}_1$), there is no supply shock ($s = 0$), and actual unemployment is at its equilibrium level or output is equal to its trend. Note that point A belongs to both the short- and the long-run curves. As just noted, it represents the long-run situation, but it also determines the position of the particular short-run curve when the underlying inflation rate is $\tilde{\pi}_1$. In other words, the only position on the short-run curve that is sustainable in the long run is point A. Any other position is temporary, as we now illustrate.

To that effect, starting from point A, imagine a demand expansion designed to reduce unemployment and shift the economy to a point like B. The short-run trade-off means less unemployment and more output, but also more inflation. This is because the new inflation π_2 exceeds the underlying rate $\tilde{\pi}_1$, which has been used in previous wage negotiations. Sooner or later, there will be another round of wage negotiations, which will recognize that inflation has increased. Let us assume that they adopt π_2 as the new underlying rate. Graphically, this means that the short-run Phillips and aggregate supply curves shift upwards, passing through point A', which corresponds to the new underlying inflation rate $\tilde{\pi}_2 = \pi_2$.

(The equilibrium rate of unemployment and trend output are assumed constant throughout.) This shift worsens the unemployment–inflation trade-off, since any level of unemployment now requires a higher rate of inflation. If the authorities react by picking point C on the new curves, both unemployment and inflation will rise, while output will decline. Yet point C is not permanently sustainable either, since inflation is now even higher than the newer underlying inflation rate $\tilde{\pi}_2$. So, once again, the curves must eventually shift further up in both panels of Figure 12.13. We can imagine a succession of increasingly desperate policy reactions triggering further shifts in the short-run Phillips and aggregate supply curves, which will eventually drive unemployment and output back to their equilibrium positions at a point like Z on the long-run curve.

The fact that only one point on every Phillips curve is stable led Friedman and Phelps to predict that the historical curves would vanish if the authorities tried to exploit the short-run trade-off, for example by moving from point A to point B. In the end, the economy would end up at point Z in Figure 12.13.

Despite the fact that they are vertical in the long run, Phillips and aggregate supply curves can account for the cyclical behaviour of inflation. Recall from Chapter 1 that the inflation rate tended to be procyclical and lag the GDP slightly. We only need to remember that, like most other curves that we have seen in the past, the Phillips and aggregate supply curves can move when the exogenous variables that determine their positions change. The additional twist is that one of these variables, the underlying inflation rate, is bound to change whenever actual inflation varies for any length of time. This implies that the Phillips and aggregate supply curves are bound to shift whenever we move from the long-run point. From a policy standpoint, it means that the inflation–unemployment trade-off cannot be seen as more than a short-run relationship that may be worse than it initially appears. This last observation calls for caution when pursuing macroeconomic policies. We return to this theme in the next chapter.

❶ Summary

1 The Phillips curve was once considered to be an adequate description of the supply side and the inflation process. Its message was that a permanent trade-off existed between unemployment and inflation. Output could rise to meet an increase in demand but would, in the process, generate a higher rate of inflation.

2 Okun's Law states that the output gap (the deviation of real GDP from its trend) and unemployment (as a deviation from its equilibrium level) systematically move in opposite directions. It translates the downward Phillips curve into an upward aggregate supply curve.

3 From the late 1960s to the late 1980s, Phillips curves around the world vanished. Contrary to the notion of an inflation–unemployment trade-off, inflation and unemployment both rose in the mid-1970s and early 1980s, a phenomenon called stagflation.

4 Accounting for inflation starts with the study of how firms set their prices. The result is mark-up pricing, i.e. setting prices as a mark-up over production costs.

5 Production costs are separated into two broad categories: labour and non-labour costs. Labour costs rise when wages—and related costs—increase faster than labour productivity. They often represent the most important source of cost changes.

6 Nominal wages are also set as a mark-up on the nominal price level.

7 Wages are set through negotiations that acknowledge three main factors: (1) underlying inflation, (2) productivity gains, and (3) the state of the business cycle, which largely reflects the relative bargaining strength of employees and employers. Thus nominal wages are also set as a mark-up on the nominal price level.

8 Wage contracts attempt both to catch up on past inflation and to protect wages from future inflation. Underlying inflation captures both these backward- and forward-looking aspects.

9 Inflation accounting describes the actual rate of inflation as responding to: underlying inflation, demand pressure in the goods and labour markets, and occasional supply shocks.

10 The inflation accounts explain both why a Phillips curve could exist for a century, and then vanish in the light of mounting inflation in the 1960s and early 1970s, to the two oil shocks of 1973–1974 and 1979–1980 and to rising equilibrium unemployment.

11 In the long run, unemployment returns to its equilibrium rate. Equivalently, real GDP cannot permanently deviate from the productive potential of an economy. In the long run, the Phillips curve and aggregate supply schedules are vertical. The economy is dichotomized, growth and real rigidities determine the GDP and unemployment, money growth determines inflation, and there is no trade-off between inflation and unemployment.

12 The Phillips curve describes the supply side and can be transformed into an aggregate supply curve using Okun's Law. The supply curve says that, for increased output to be supplied, inflation increases because production—mainly labour—costs rise faster than anticipated, or than is reflected in underlying inflation.

13 The positions of the Phillips and aggregate supply curves are determined by the underlying rate of inflation and, respectively, equilibrium unemployment rate and trend GDP. Any change in any one of these variables leads to shifts in the short-run curves. Supply shocks, whether positive or negative, also shift the curves.

🔑 Key Concepts

- Phillips curve, Phillips trade-off
- aggregate supply curve
- neoclassical assumption
- wage inflation
- Okun's Law
- output gap, unemployment gap
- money illusion
- long-run Phillips and aggregate supply curves
- stagflation
- oil shock

- mark-up pricing
- market power
- product differentiation
- average or unit costs
- wage bill
- battle of the mark-ups
- underlying inflation rate
- indexation
- supply shocks

❓ Exercises

1 Figure 12.1 describes how *real* GDP and the price level react over time to a one-off increase in the money stock. What happens to *nominal* GDP?

2 Using the *IS–TR* analysis developed in Chapter 11, consider an exogenous decline in demand, for example a reduction in public spending. Show graphically that either exchange rate flexibility or price flexibility is enough to achieve the neoclassical result that output remains constant at its trend level.

3 A Phillips curve is represented by the following relationship: $\pi = \tilde{\pi} - 10(U - \bar{U}) + s$, where s is a supply shock term, on average equal to zero. Draw the Phillips curve when $\bar{U} = 7\%$ and underlying inflation $\tilde{\pi} = 3\%$ and 6%. Okun's Law is $U - \bar{U} = -0.5\dfrac{Y - \bar{Y}}{\bar{Y}}$. Draw the aggregate supply schedule when $\bar{Y} = 10,000$.

4 Using the conditions of the previous exercise, show the impact of supply shocks $s = 5\%$, and $s = -2\%$. Separately show the effect of raising $\bar{Y}$ to 10,200. Why is it argued that improving the performance of the supply side of the economy is good for both inflation and employment?

5 In the 1980s, when inflation in Brazil exceeded 1,000% a year, all prices and wages were indexed week by week. Why was indexation not only popular but generally perceived as vital? If inflation were exactly 1,200% over a year, what is the implied weekly inflation rate (assuming weekly compounding for simplicity). What is the effect of missing the inflation rate by 1% per week over the course of three months?

6 What could be the effect of an increase in value added taxation (VAT) on inflation? Of an increase in corporate profit taxes? Of an increase in personal income taxes? State your assumptions carefully.

7 Using Exercise 3, consider the effect of a reform of labour market institutions which reduces equilibrium unemployment from 7% to 5%. Explain the effect on inflation in the short term and in the long term.

8 Suppose a government underestimates the equilibrium rate of unemployment and attempts to reduce the unemployment rate below the equilibrium rate by stimulating aggregate demand. Show the likely outcome of such a policy using the short- and long-run Phillips curves.

9 The supply curve is given by the following relationship: $\pi = \tilde{\pi} + 0.1(Y - \bar{Y}) + s$. Initially $\pi = \tilde{\pi} = 2\%$, $Y = \bar{Y}$, and $s = 0$. Then the authorities raise output so that $Y - \bar{Y} = 10$ and decide to keep it at this level until inflation reaches the rate of 4%, at which stage they will let the output gap return to zero. Assume that the underlying inflation rate $\tilde{\pi}$ adjusts each period by half of the difference between its previous value and the previously observed inflation rate (for example if we currently have $\pi = 6\%$ and $\tilde{\pi} = 4\%$, then next period the underlying rate will be 5%). There is no supply shock so $s = 0$ throughout. Compute period after period the actual and underlying inflation rate until the economy returns to a long-run equilibrium. What conclusion do you draw?

10 Between 2000 and 2007 the price of oil, quoted in US dollars, increased by 92.4%. Quoted in euros, it 'only' increased by 52.8%. How can you explain the difference? Explain why a 'hard currency' is frequently considered a weapon against imported inflation.

→ Essay Questions

1 Imagine that you are back in the 1960s, when the Phillips curve was believed to be stable. How, do you believe, were politicians arguing about where it is best to be on the curve? What mistake would each side of the debate be likely to make?

2 Why is the battle of the mark-ups important for understanding the origins of inflation? Discuss the significance of each of these assumptions: (1) imperfect or monopolistic competition among firms; (2) labour unions or collective bargaining; (3) constant labour productivity.

3 Why do some economists plead for policy measures that increase the flexibility of wages and prices? What can the counter-arguments be?

4 'That the long-run Phillips curve is vertical means that governments should *never* attempt to reduce unemployment with expansionary policies.' Comment.

5 Under what conditions could a sharp depreciation only temporarily raise inflation?

Aggregate Demand and Aggregate Supply

13

Money influences only monetary variables and not real variables in the long run. The problem is 'how long is long?' The 'Keynesian' answer embodied in the concept of the Phillips curve was 'too long to matter!': the 'monetarist' rejoinder was 'shorter than the Keynesians think!'; extreme rationalism provides the answer 'too short for anything else to matter!'—answers that no one concerned with either the history or the practice of stabilization policy is likely to accept.

Harry G. Johnson[1]

13.1 Overview

This chapter is the watershed of the textbook. It combines the demand side of the economy—the Mundell–Fleming model of Chapter 11—with the supply side—the response of output and inflation consistent with the plans of firms and workers developed in Chapter 12—into a single unified framework. This workhorse of modern macroeconomics is known as the 'AS–AD model'. Until now, aggregate demand was analysed under the assumption that prices are sticky. The task ahead is to deal with inflation.[2] The result will be the downward-sloping curve AD displayed in Figure 13.1: the higher is the inflation rate, all other things equal, the lower is aggregate demand. The upward-sloping aggregate supply curve AS has already been derived in the previous chapter. In a market economy demand equals supply, so the position of the economy is described by the intersection of the AD and AS curves.

In this analysis of aggregate supply, we identified two AS curves: one for the short run and one for the long run. This distinction is fundamental. In the short run, there is a trade-off between output (or unemployment) and inflation. In the long run, the supply curve, shown in Figure 13.1 as LAS, is vertical and the trade-off has disappeared—monetary factors have no impact on real economic variables, e.g. real GDP, unemployment, or the real exchange rate. We will see that a similar conclusion applies to aggregate demand, but it is horizontal in the long run, as displayed in Figure 13.1 as LAD.

Ultimately, the inflation rate is set by exogenous forces: either by inflation in the rest of the world in the case of fixed exchange rates, or by the monetary authority in the case of flexible exchange rates. In the short run, inflation and demand are closely

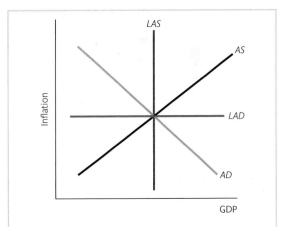

Fig. 13.1 Aggregate Demand and Aggregate Supply, Short Run and Long Run

The complete description of the macroeconomy comes in three steps. In the short run, the AD and AS curves allow us to understand the impact of changes in the exogenous variables. In the long run, the dichotomy principle produces the LAD and LAS curves. The medium run describes how we move from the short to the long run.

---

[1] Harry G. Johnson (1923–1979), a Canadian, was a professor of international trade and monetary economics at the University of Chicago and was known both for his dry wit and a wet whistle. Among his most important contributions to macroeconomics is the monetary approach to the balance of payments, which lies behind our understanding of the workings of monetary policy under fixed exchange rates.

[2] The book has been concerned until now with extremes: Chapter 6 dealt with the flexible price case, while Chapters 10 and 11 assumed constant prices. The real world must be somewhere in between, with price levels and inflation moving but much more slowly than the lightning speed of the neoclassical model.

related, and understanding these interactions and linking the economy's short run to the long run is a key function of the *AD–AS* framework. The chapter concludes with several examples of the *AS–AD* model's usefulness.

As in Chapters 11 and 12, we distinguish sharply between regimes of fixed versus flexible exchange rates under conditions of capital mobility. The reason is that the *AD* curve is derived from the *IS–TR–IFM* framework, which operates very differently according to the exchange rate regime. In particular, monetary policy operates through exchange rates, so that it is lost when the exchange rate is fixed, while fiscal policy is undermined by exchange rate movements when under a flexible rate arrangement. This framework also works differently in the case of a closed economy, without trade and capital movements. In that case, we can simply ignore the IFM line and both fiscal and monetary policies work, exactly as in Chapter 10.[3]

13.2 Aggregate Demand and Supply under Fixed Exchange Rates

We know from Chapter 11 that, when capital is mobile, a country that fixes its exchange rate to another currency loses its ability to pursue an independent monetary policy. The central bank has no choice but to set its own interest rate at the world level. The *TR* curve is irrelevant, so we will ignore it. This means that shifts in aggregate demand will only arise because of shifts in the *IS* or *IFM* curves.

13.2.1 Aggregate Demand in the Long Run

It is always a good idea to start with the long run. We showed in Chapter 6 that **relative purchasing power parity** (henceforth: **PPP**), meaning that the real exchange rate (σ) is constant, is a good rule of thumb for thinking about the long run.[4] With $\sigma = SP/P^*$, the fact that S is fixed and σ is constant in the long run means that the domestic inflation rate (π) must equal the foreign inflation rate (π^*):

$$\sigma = \frac{SP}{P*} = \text{constant and } S \text{ fixed implies } \pi = \pi*.$$

A very simple conclusion follows. *If the nominal exchange rate is constant, in the long run domestic inflation must be equal to foreign inflation.* Put differently, a fixed exchange rate regime rules out permanent differences between domestic and foreign inflation. If they could diverge permanently, the real exchange rate would appreciate or depreciate without limit. For example, if domestic inflation exceeded foreign inflation permanently despite a constant nominal exchange rate, the resulting real appreciation would make the economy increasingly uncompetitive and worsen the current account with no end in sight. *This cannot be a long-run equilibrium.*[5]

This restriction is represented in Figure 13.3(*b*) as the horizontal long-run aggregate demand **(LAD) line**. It is a demand-side restriction, because any permanent deviation would eventually lead to unsustainable current account deficits or surpluses.

Fixing the exchange rate means importing inflation from the country whose currency is used as a peg. The exchange rate becomes an anchor for

---

[3] This issue is discussed in Section 11.5.4.

[4] As stressed in Chapter 6, constancy of the real exchange rate implied by relative PPP should not be confused with absolute PPP or the law of one price. For countries of similar development, such as Germany, the UK, and France, relative PPP is fairly reliable. It tends to break down when comparing countries with significantly different levels of GDP per capita, especially when one is growing much faster than the other over a longer period. These issues are discussed in more detail in Chapter 15.

[5] Within the euro area, exchange rates are fixed in the most extreme way possible: a single currency. In part, the origins of the crisis can be found in persistently different inflation rates, e.g. higher in Greece and Spain than in Germany. In the long run, this is not sustainable.

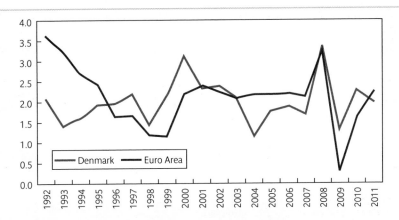

Fig. 13.2 Inflation in Denmark and the Euro Area, 1992–2010

Since the mid-1980s, the Danish central bank has committed to a fixed exchange rate regime. It first pegged the value of the currency, the krone, to the currencies of the European Monetary System (primarily the deutschemark). After 1999 it pegged the krone to the euro. The figure shows that Danish inflation has remained relatively close to inflation in the euro area. Because PPP does not hold in the short run, the relationship does not hold exactly every year. Yet over the period displayed in the figure, average inflation was 2.0% in Denmark, only slightly below the overall euro area rate of 2.1%.

Source: IMF, World Economic Outlook Database.

monetary policy, with a role pretty much like that of inflation in the inflation targeting strategy captured by the Taylor rule. Figure 13.2 shows how this anchor has worked for Denmark, which has fixed its exchange rate since the mid-1980s, first to the deutschmark, and then to the euro.

We know from Chapters 6 and 11 that, when the exchange rate is fixed, it is imported inflation that drives the money supply. Indeed, foreign inflation eventually determines inflation at home. Since economic agents are interested in the real value of money, as explained in Chapter 6, their demand for money grows proportionately to the inflation rate. Under fixed exchange rate, the central bank is committed to satisfy whatever demand for money is forthcoming, and will therefore let the money supply grow along with inflation. When the exchange rate is fixed, it is money growth that adjusts to (foreign) inflation, rather than inflation adjusting to money growth. Box 13.1 formally derives the endogenous growth rate of money under fixed exchange rates.

13.2.2 The Short-Run Aggregate Demand Curve

In the short run, PPP does not hold because prices are sticky. The real exchange rate σ can fluctuate and its

movements directly affect aggregate demand. Our framework for thinking about the short run is the *IS–IFM* framework of Chapter 11, which assumed that the price level was constant. Now we must adapt it to allow for inflation.

To do this, let us ask what happens when the inflation rate changes, all other things being equal. In panel (*a*) of Figure 13.3, we start from general equilibrium at point *A*. We assume that this is a stable equilibrium, at least as long as domestic inflation π is equal to foreign inflation π^*. Now suppose that the domestic rate of inflation rises from π to π'—holding the foreign rate of inflation π^* constant, so $\pi > \pi^*$. In this situation, the real exchange rate will appreciate. Our competitiveness is eroded, the primary current account worsens, and demand for domestic output declines. Graphically, the *IS* curve shifts to the left, say to *IS'*. The new equilibrium occurs at point *A'*, the intersection of the new *IS* curve and the *IFM* line.[6]

Now suppose instead that inflation declines to π'', so $\pi'' < \pi^*$. Competitiveness would improve, the real

[6] Point *A'* is just a snapshot taken during a contractionary process that continues as long as inflation is higher at home than abroad. As long as domestic inflation exceeds the foreign rate, the real exchange rate will continue to appreciate. To keep things simple, we do not elaborate on this aspect.

Box 13.1   The Real Exchange Rate and Money Growth Under a Fixed Exchange Rate Regime

A regime of fixed exchange rates imposes restrictions on domestic inflation and monetary policy and the growth rate of money. This box formally explains these restrictions. It rests on three key concepts developed earlier. The first one is PPP, the second one is the money market equilibrium, both of which are presented in Chapter 6, and the last one is the interest parity condition introduced in Chapter 11.

As recalled in the text, PPP implies that inflation is the same at home and abroad when the nominal exchange rate is fixed. For a small economy, this means that the domestic inflation rate is equal to the foreign rate:

(B13.1) $\pi = \pi^{\star}$.

Next, the demand for money is described as follows in Chapter 11:

$$M/P = k(i)Y$$

Finally, the interest parity condition when the exchange rate is fixed implies that $i = i^{\star}$. Imposing this condition to the money demand equation, we have:

(B13.2) $M/P = k(i^{\star})Y.$

Under a fixed exchange rate regime, the central bank has no choice but to supply all money that is demanded. Equation (B13.2) implies that the money supply is determined by demand and equal to $k(i^{\star})P^{Y}$. Using the arithmetic principle presented in Box 6.3, this means that the nominal money growth rate is:

(B13.3) $\dfrac{\Delta M}{M} = g + \pi,$

where g is the growth rate of GDP.

Using (B13.1) and recognizing that the rest of world target inflation to achieve a long run rate of $\pi^{\star}$, we finally see that the domestic central bank must allow money to expand at the growth rate:

(B13.4) $\dfrac{\Delta M}{M} = g + \pi^{\star},$

Students will recognize the similarities between this result and equation (B12.3) of Box 12.1. This is not a coincidence. Under fixed exchange rates, the role of the target inflation is placed by the foreign rate of inflation, $\pi^{\star}$.

exchange rate would depreciate, and the *IS* curve would shift outwards to *IS″*. The new equilibrium—after a period of one year, say—would be described by point *A″*. Connecting points like *A*, *A′*, and *A″* in panel (*b*) of Figure 13.3, we trace out the **aggregate demand curve** *AD*. The curve is downward-sloping because rising inflation weakens the country's external competitiveness, which reduces domestic and foreign demand for domestic goods. It represents aggregate demand because movements along the curve are induced by shifts of the *IS* curve, the goods market equilibrium condition under the Keynesian assumption that supply passively responds to, and therefore merely equals demand. It is a short-run curve because, as long as domestic inflation differs from foreign inflation, demand continues to change (so that a year later, say, output would have moved further away from *Y* in Figure 13.3, further reducing demand and flattening the demand curve). The long-run demand curve, instead, accepts the implication

from PPP that domestic inflation is equal to foreign inflation. We will see shortly how we move to the long run.

13.2.3 Movements Along versus Shifts of the *AD* Curve

As in previous chapters, it is essential to distinguish between movement along the *AD* curve and shifts of the curve itself. The rule is always the same: the curve shifts when a relevant exogenous variable changes. Since the *AD* curve is nothing more than a summary of the *IS–IFM* framework, the list of endogenous and exogenous variables is similar to those already identified in Chapter 11. The difference, of course, is that the price level and the inflation rate are now endogenous.

This also means that any exogenous variable that shifts the *IS* curve also shifts the *AD* curve. For example, starting from initial inflation rate π, an increase in government spending *G* is represented in Figure 13.3(*a*)

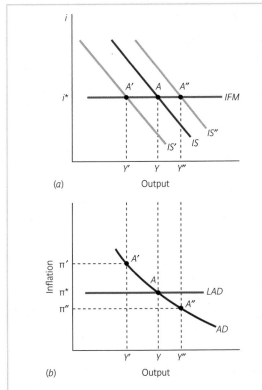

Fig. 13.3 The Aggregate Demand Curve Under Fixed Exchange Rates

Starting from inflation π^* at point A, an increase in the rate of inflation to π' reduces the country's external competitiveness. The IS curve shifts leftward in panel (a). The resulting decrease in demand is reported in panel (b). Conversely, a reduction in inflation to π'' improves competitiveness, shifts the IS curve rightward, and aggregate demand increases. The aggregate demand curve is downward sloping.

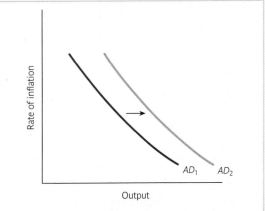

Fig. 13.4 Shifts in the Aggregate Demand Curve

Exogenous changes in demand which shift the IS curve also shift the short-run aggregate demand curve in the same direction. The outward shift shown here could be caused by an increase in government spending (G), reductions in taxes (T), rise in Tobin's q, an increase in foreign GDP (Y^*) or an increase in household wealth (Ω).

Changes in exogenous variables that affect aggregate demand shifts the AD curve, rightwards when aggregate demand rises, leftwards when it declines. Conversely, the AD curve stays in place when these variables remain constant. Any change in other variables implies that we move along the AD curve. Let us now examine how and when this happens.

13.2.4 The Complete System

In Figure 13.5 aggregate demand and supply are brought together. The demand side comes in two parts: (1) the downward-sloping short-run aggregate demand curve AD, and (2) the horizontal long-run LAD line, which reflects the endogeneity of money in fixed exchange rate regimes and the dependence of long-run domestic inflation on the foreign inflation rate. The supply side, derived in Chapter 12, also comes in two parts: (1) an upward-sloping short-run supply curve AS, and (2) the vertical long-run line LAS. The position of the AS curve depends on the underlying inflation rate $\tilde{\pi}$. The supply side in the long run dictates that actual and trend GDP are equal ($Y = \bar{Y}$), which requires that actual and underlying inflation be equal as well ($\pi = \tilde{\pi}$), at that point at which the AS

by a shift from IS to IS''. As long as inflation remains unchanged, in panel (b) the corresponding point is B. The new demand curve which passes through B must lie to the right of the initial curve, as shown in Figure 13.4. This reasoning applies to all exogenous variables studied in Chapter 10: government purchases G, net taxes T, household wealth Ω, Tobin's q ('animal spirits'), and foreign income Y^*. Missing in that list is the real exchange rate, which is now endogenous, because it depends on the evolution of domestic prices—which are no longer fixed—relative to foreign prices.

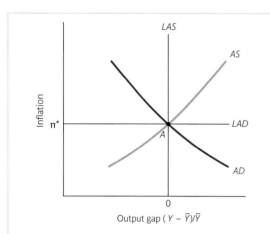

Fig. 13.5 Aggregate Demand and Supply Under Fixed Exchange Rates

In the long run, output is at its trend growth level, the output gap is zero, and the inflation rate is equal to the underlying rate, as well as the foreign inflation rate. The short run is determined by the *AD* and *AS* curves. The figure depicts a situation of long-run equilibrium in which all four curves intersect.

and *LAS* curves intersect. On the demand side, the long-run domestic inflation rate equals to the foreign rate $(\pi = \pi^*)$. In other words, in the long run, the economy stabilizes when the GDP is on trend, inflation is the same as abroad, and the underlying inflation is in line with actual inflation. In Figure 13.5, the two long-run curves intersect at point *A*.

Note that we have changed the horizontal axis from previous chapters. Before, we tracked real GDP *(Y)* along this axis. We now represent the output gap $Y_{gap} = (Y - \bar{Y})/\bar{Y}$. This rescaling is important. We learned in Chapters 3 and 4 that trend GDP $\bar{Y}$ grows over time in most countries. To study the level of GDP would require a continuous rightward shift of the *LAS* line, which would be quite cumbersome and, more importantly, would divert our attention from the focus of this chapter, which is the origin and propagation of business cycles.

Figure 13.5 characterizes a **long-run equilibrium** in which the two short-run curves—the *AS* and *AD* curves—also pass through the long-run equilibrium point *A*. In the following sections, we will study the **short-run equilibrium** as it evolves over time and distinguish it from the long-run position. In doing so,

we explain how the economy moves from the short to the long run.

13.2.5 Fiscal Policy and Demand Disturbances

Short run

We now track down the effects of an exogenous **demand shock**. One common example is a fiscal policy expansion—an increase in government purchases $(\Delta \bar{G} > 0)$ or a reduction in net taxes $(\Delta \bar{T} < 0)$.[7] Initially, at point *A*, the economy is in long-term equilibrium: output *Y* is at its trend level $\bar{Y}$, and actual (π) and underlying $(\tilde{\pi})$ inflation are both equal to the world inflation rate π^*. In the background of the demand-side analysis, the domestic interest rate is equal to the world rate of return $(i = i^*)$, and foreign inflation is equal to foreign central bank's target inflation rate, $\bar{*}$.

The expansionary demand disturbance is depicted in Figure 13.6(*a*) as the rightward shift of the *IS* curve to *IS'*, which moves the *AD* curve to *AD'* in the same direction in panel (*b*). The new curve *AD'* shows the short-run effect of fiscal policy, say after one year. At point *B* output has increased—as would be the case under the Mundell–Fleming framework—but inflation has also risen, which was previously ignored by assumption. The rise in inflation is due to the upward-sloping aggregate supply curve. The combination of a fixed nominal exchange rate $(S = \bar{S})$ and an inflation rate higher than abroad (*P* is increasing faster than *P**) implies that the real exchange rate $\sigma = \bar{S}P/P^*$ appreciates. External competitiveness is eroding and the primary current account is deteriorating. Thus rising inflation reduces the impact of the demand disturbance. This is precisely why the *AD* curve is downward-sloping. Had inflation remained unchanged, when working with the *IS–IFM* fixed-price assumption in Chapter 11, competitiveness would have remained unchanged, and the outcome would have been at point *B'* in both panels, along the *IS'* curve—constant inflation with a larger increase in output. The loss of competitiveness, however, has shifted the curve leftward to *IS"*. The horizontal distance between *B* and *B'* is a measure of the

---

[7] A contractionary fiscal shock would be a tax increase or a cut to government spending.

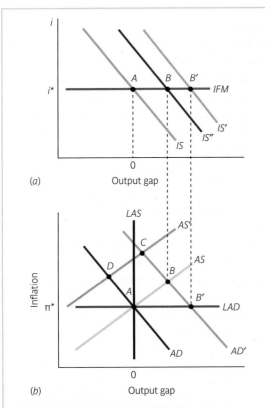

Fig. 13.6   Fiscal Policy Under Fixed Exchange Rates

A fiscal expansion shifts the *IS* and *AD* curves to the right, to *IS'* and *AD'*, respectively. The short-run effect is shown by point *B*, an increase in real GDP accompanied by higher inflation. The increase in inflation reduces external competitiveness and shifts the *IS* curve backward from *IS'* to *IS''*. As underlying inflation catches up with actual inflation, the *AS* curve shifts to *AS'*, which corresponds to a higher underlying inflation rate, equal to the inflation rate prevailing at point *B*. If the government does not change its fiscal policy stance, the new equilibrium occurs at point *C*, where inflation has again increased above the underlying rate, leading to further shifts of the *AS* curve. If the government cancels the fiscal expansion, the aggregate demand curve moves back to *AD*, and the new short-run equilibrium is at point *D*, where actual inflation is now lower than underlying inflation. The *AS* curve starts shifting to the right and will do so until it returns to its initial position and the long-run equilibrium is restored at point *A*.

inflation-induced deterioration of the primary current account.

Long run

The long run is governed by three central restrictions:

- First, the *government budget constraint* rules out permanent fiscal expansions. For the initial shift in aggregate demand to be a long-run expansion, it must occur in *each period*. For fiscal policy to be sustainable and consistent with a steady state, on the other hand, the public debt must be stabilized, as explained in Chapter 7. The fiscal expansion implies that the public debt is rising, which is not sustainable. To reach a new long-run situation, the expansionary policy must eventually be reversed. When this is done, the aggregate demand curve will return to its initial position *AD*.[8]

- Second, output must return to its trend and the economy will stabilize along the *LAS* line. The logic here is that any non-zero output gap implies, by construction, that underlying and actual inflation differ, which is not sustainable indefinitely, either.

- Third, inflation cannot deviate from the foreign inflation rate for very long, if the exchange rate is to remain fixed. Thus, the economy must return to the *LAD* line.

The conclusion is that in the long run, the economy must return to point *A*, exactly where it started. The effect of a fiscal expansion is transitory because a fiscal expansion cannot be permanent if the government's budget constraint is to be satisfied.

The medium run

Summing up so far, in Figure 13.6 we start from point *A*, move to point *B*, and eventually move back to point *A*. The actual path taken by the economy from the

---

[8] In fact, the public debt will have risen in the meantime and must be paid for by a permanently higher primary budget *surplus*. This requires that the *AD* curve shifts back beyond its original position. We overlook this additional complexity. It is acceptable to do so if the fiscal expansion does not last long enough to seriously increase the debt–GDP ratio. In the course of the global financial crisis, this detail appears to have been neglected. We return to this important issue in Chapter 17.

immediate short run at point B to the long run at point A can be reconstructed using the observations just made. We already know that the budget constraint will force the government at some point to reverse gears and either cut spending or raise taxes. When this will happen is a political decision—it could depend on the timing of elections, for instance—and we cannot say much more about it. At any rate, the AD curve must eventually shift back to its initial position.

We can say more about the behaviour of the AS curve. Remember that its position is determined by underlying inflation ($\tilde{\pi}$), which is assumed initially—say, at time $t = 0$—to equal foreign inflation π^*. In Chapter 12, we saw that the underlying inflation has *backward-looking* and *forward-looking* components. The backward-looking component reacts to actual inflation conditions, 'catching up' with current inflation. Now note that at time $t = 1$ when the economy has moved to point B, actual inflation is higher than the initial underlying inflation rate at $t = 0$. Inevitably, wage negotiators—whose appraisal determines the underlying inflation rate when nominal pay increases are agreed—will recognize that the current (time $t = 1$) inflation rate is higher than it used to be assumed. They will naturally agree to push nominal wages faster, in effect raising underlying inflation. Without knowing more about the economy's structure, it is impossible to say where.

For the sake of the argument, suppose underlying inflation is simply equal to the inflation rate in the previous period. Then the AS curve would shift to AS, which intersects the LAS curve at the inflation rate observed at point B. The new (time $t = 2$) short-run curve AS′ cuts the LAS line ($Y = \bar{Y}$) at the underlying inflation rate corresponding to the height of point B. This means that at time $t = 2$, the economy moves from point B to point C, at the intersection of the AD′ and AS′ curves in panel (b). From B to C, inflation further rises, but now, GDP is lower: inflation higher than foreign inflation implies further erosion of external competitiveness and a deeper deterioration of aggregate demand. Behind this is a further leftward shift of the IS curve (not shown) as we move up along AD′. This is an instance of **stagflation**.[9] We are not yet back to the long-run equilibrium, however, if only because fiscal policy is

not yet corrected. At point C, the output gap is still positive and the new current inflation rate exceeds underlying inflation (remember that along AS′, underlying inflation is equal to the inflation observed when the economy was at point B). It is just a matter of time until underlying inflation rises further, pushing the AS curve farther upwards and to the left above AS′. In that case, stagflation continues as the economy moves up along the AD′ curve. Eventually, though, the government will have to reverse the fiscal expansion.

So let's now imagine that the government cancels its fiscal expansion at time $t = 2$ when the economy is at point C. The fiscal policy correction has a contractionary effect and the AD curve moves from AD′ back to AD (assuming a complete policy reversal compatible with the long run). In that case, at time $t = 3$, the economy moves from point C to point D in panel (b). Even though the AD curve is back to its initial position, output is now below trend. The reason is that the AS curve has shifted to AS′ because underlying inflation has increased. The higher inflation hurts external competitiveness. In panel (a), the corresponding IS curve (not shown) is therefore to the left of the initial one (IS) since fiscal policy is back to its initial stance but external competitiveness has been degraded by inflation.

Point D is on the AS′ curve, which corresponds to the underlying rate of inflation at time $t = 2$ at point C. But since point D is below point B, inflation is lower than the underlying rate. The next round of wage negotiations will recognize that inflation is ebbing and underlying inflation will also decline. The AS curve will shift down below AS′ and the economy will move down along the AD curve from point D in the direction of point A. At the intersection of AD and the new AS curve (not shown), which corresponds to an underlying inflation rate equal to the actual rate observed at point D, inflation has again declined below underlying inflation. This prompts a new reappraisal of underlying inflation, a new

---

[9] In Chapter 12 we saw that the instability of inflation was the downfall of the old-fashioned Phillips curve—or its mirror image, the AS curve. By understanding the dynamics of underlying inflation, it is possible to understand why the Phillips curve shifted so much.

Table 13.1 **Tracking Movements in Figure 13.6**

Time	Event	Movement	Equilibrium
0	Initial situation		Point A
1	Expansionary policy	AD shifts to AD'	Point B
2	Underlying inflation catches up with inflation at point B	AS shifts to AS'	Point C
3	Expansionary fiscal policy rescinded/loses impact	Back to initial AD	Point D
4	Underlying inflation catches up with inflation at point D	AS' shifts to the right	Point E (not shown)
5	Underlying inflation catches up with inflation at point E	AS shifts to the right	Point F (not shown)
6	Underlying inflation catches up with inflation at point F, etc.	AS shifts to the right	Point G (not shown)
Long run	Underlying inflation has caught up with actual inflation	Back to initial AS	Point A

downward shift of the AS curve, and a continuing movement along the AD curve. The process will continue until the AS curve has returned to its initial position and the long-run equilibrium is achieved at point A.[10]

To summarize, the acknowledgement of inflation requires that we reason in three steps:

(1) the immediate short run, described by the amended Mundell–Fleming (IS–IFM) framework subsumed in the AD curve and by the short-run AS curve;

(2) the long run, described by the long-run AD and AS curves;

(3) the medium run—the transition from the short to the long run—a drawn-out process driven by successive shifts of the short-run AD and AS curves.

The details of the curves and their movements with reference to Figure 13.6 are summarized in Table 13.1.

Until now, we have emphasized the role of the backward-looking component of underlying infla-

tion. What is the role of the forward-looking component? Anticipating the future evolution of inflation, wage negotiators will reduce the lag between underlying and actual inflation and the AS curve will adjust faster, which will speed up the return to departure point A. We will see in Chapter 16 that this dimension depends strongly on the credibility of the anticipated policy measures which lie behind the anticipations of inflation.

The incorporation of inflation is a crucial amendment of the macroeconomic model. It modifies some of the conclusions that we reached in Chapters 11 and 12. In particular:

◆ First, a demand shock does not just move output, it also changes the inflation rate as we move along the AS curve. Along a given supply curve, an increase in demand raises the inflation rate, while a decline in demand lowers inflation.

◆ Second, bringing inflation into the picture naturally leads us to think beyond the current period. This was already apparent with the Phillips or AS curve because we need to think about the evolution of the underlying inflation rate. On the demand side, we were led to think about the government's budget constraint, which was ignored in Chapter 12 as we strictly focused on the short run. This led us to recognize that fiscal policy is inherently temporary.

---

[10] In fact, the economy will need to move temporarily below point A in panel (b), because a period when inflation is lower at home than abroad is required to bring the real exchange rate back to its original initial level. Only if inflation is below π^* for some period of time is it possible for a real depreciation to occur, competitiveness to be restored and the IS curve to return to its initial position.

♦ Third, a fiscal expansion is partly undermined by the increase in inflation that it generates. The resulting loss of competitiveness—when the nominal exchange rate is fixed—worsens the current account and thus reduces world demand for our goods.

This explains why the countercyclical use of fiscal policy is much less popular than it used to be in the heyday of Keynesianism, before the old Phillips curve was replaced by its rehabilitated version, augmented by forward- and backward-looking elements of expectations of inflation.

13.2.6 Monetary Policy and Realignments

A key lesson from Chapter 11 is that it is impossible to carry out an autonomous monetary policy when the exchange rate is fixed. But we indicated that exchange rate parities can be and are changed, at least on occasion, since most fixed exchange rate regimes are considered 'adjustable'. We now show how exchange rate realignments allow for some limited role of monetary policy.

A devaluation, for instance, means reducing the nominal exchange rate. How is this done in practice? Formally, the central bank simply announces the new parity and follows through with whatever is needed

to make this happen. This means a monetary policy expansion—achieved either on the open market or through foreign exchange market interventions—will be necessary to increase the supply of domestic currency such that its price, the exchange rate, declines as intended. More precisely, more money implies a lower interest rate and capital outflows, which weaken the exchange rate. This in turn raises demand and the interest rate back up to the global return implied by the interest parity condition, the *IFM* line.

For simplicity, the initial situation at point *A* in panel (*a*) of Figure 13.7 is assumed to correspond to a long-run equilibrium, with domestic observed and underlying inflation both equal to foreign inflation. A nominal depreciation translates into a gain in external competitiveness, so that $\sigma = SP/P^*$ declines immediately when *S* is reduced. As a result, the *IS* curve shifts rightward to *IS'*. In the background, the target interest rate is usually cut as already mentioned. Recovering the monetary policy instrument is precisely the role (and some would say the goal) of exchange rate depreciations or appreciations. These are fleeting moments when the central bank can recover monetary room to manoeuvre.

The short run equilibrium is reached at point *B*. In panel (*b*), the demand expansion is shown as the shift of the aggregate demand curve from *AD* to *AD'*, and the corresponding outcome is represented by

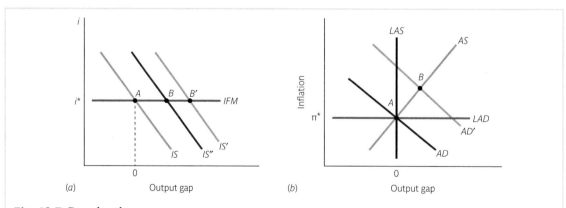

Fig. 13.7 Devaluation

Starting from a long-run equilibrium, a devaluation causes the *IS* curve to shift to *IS'*, but rising inflation undoes some of the real depreciation, so the net effect is a shift to *IS''*, corresponding to point *B* in both panels. Output expands, but not as much in the original Mundell–Fleming model. Ultimately, higher inflation will lead to increasing underlying inflation, which will eventually lead to pressure to devalue again, or a painful period of lower inflation and a negative output gap to restore competitiveness.

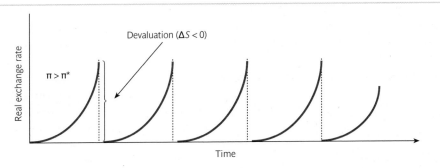

Fig. 13.8 Expansionary Monetary Policy Under a Fixed Exchange Rate Regime
A devaluation causes domestic inflation to rise above the foreign inflation rate. The real exchange rate, initially reduced by the devaluation, starts appreciating again until it returns to its pre-devaluation level. The central bank may devalue the nominal exchange rate again, which immediately depreciates the real exchange rate and triggers a new period of high inflation and real appreciation. In the end, monetary policy results in higher inflation and a chain of successive devaluations.

point B. As is now becoming customary, we find that an output expansion does not come for free, it is accompanied by rising inflation. This, in turn, reverses and undermines partly the expansionary effect of the devaluation, which is captured by the leftward shift of the IS curve from IS' to IS" in panel (a).

Point B does not represent a long-run equilibrium because it is neither on the LAD nor on the LAS curves. It lies on the short-run AS curve with position determined by initial underlying inflation (equal to the world rate of inflation at the outset), but now at point B inflation has risen. As a consequence, underlying inflation increases and the AS curve will shift up. On the other hand, rising inflation means that the domestic price level rises faster than the foreign price level. As a result, the real exchange rate keeps appreciating, the current account deteriorates, and the IS curve further shifts leftwards in panel (a). The economy will return to point A, after a period of inflation above the world level. During the transition back to point A, the inflation differential progressively undoes the real depreciation achieved through

the initial devaluation.[11] At point A, this effect is complete: the competitiveness benefit from the initial depreciation has been entirely offset by the inflation differential with the country to whose currency the domestic currency is pegged.

This is yet another case of long-run monetary neutrality. We knew all along that the long-run equilibrium is at point A, so the question was what would take us there. In the end, if we start from long-run equilibrium, all real variables must return to their initial values, which applies to the output gap and to the real exchange rate. Inflation rate, too, must eventually return to the world level. In the end, devaluations or appreciations only have temporary effects.

Another possibility, however, is for the central bank to devalue again. If it does so, the temporary competitive advantage will again be gradually eroded by the inflation differential, leading to another devaluation, etc. In this limited sense, monetary policy independence is restored under a fixed but adjustable exchange rate regime. Through a succession of devaluations, the central bank can keep pushing temporarily real GDP above trend, but it will have to accept a permanently higher inflation rate. Figure 13.8 illustrates this path of the real exchange rate over time. It will depreciate abruptly at the time of each devaluation, only to appreciate again afterwards. In the end, this strategy merely allows a country to opt for a different inflation rate from the one that prevails in the country to which

---

[11] The careful reader will ask: what gets us back to point A in panel (b)? Here we would need to use the observation in footnote 8: during all the time when $\pi > \pi^*$, the curve AD becomes increasingly flatter, year after year. In the end it will coincide with LAD. In the intervening periods, it will be necessary for $\pi < \pi^*$ for a time, so the real exchange rate can depreciate to its original level.

Box 13.2 Conflict and Coexistence with Different Inflation Rates: France and Germany

France and Germany have long existed side by side with two mutually inconsistent objectives: they have very different views about inflation. Germany, still remembering the devastating hyperinflation of 1922–1923, was committed to low inflation, while France was more interested in using monetary policy to boost short-run growth. Yet as neighbours with deep trade and financial relations, France and Germany were unwilling to allow the exchange rate to fluctuate from day to day according to market forces. Their solution was to peg their exchange rates to each other, first informally in the 1970s, then formally following the launch of the European Monetary System in 1979, and then irrevocably after the adoption of the euro in January 1999. The peg was adjustable and frequent realignments did take place between the currencies, with the franc being regularly devalued vis-à-vis the deutschmark. Figure 13.9 shows the evolution of the real exchange rate between France and Germany during this period. It is the real-life version of Figure 13.8. Occasional depreciations of the franc vis-à-vis the deutschmark appear as sharp declines of the real exchange rate, which are then gradually undone by gradual appreciation, until the next devaluation. The figure also shows that, after a severe crisis in 1993, the real exchange rate stabilized. This reflects France's 'franc fort' policy. In its preparation for monetary union, France gave up monetary policy independence, renounced boom-and-bust devaluation cycles, and gradually managed to achieve an inflation rate virtually identical to Germany's. This can be seen by the fact that the real exchange rate between the two countries has hardly changed at all in since the early 2000s.

Fig. 13.9 The Real Exchange Rate, France vs. Germany, 1975–2011

The nominal exchange rate between the French franc and the German mark was fixed but adjustable during the period 1975–1998. France's greater tolerance for inflation can be seen in recurrent devaluations of the franc vis-à-vis the German currency, the deutschmark. Each devaluation was followed by a real appreciation, until the next devaluation corrected the cumulated exchange rate misalignment. Following German reunification, the situation was reversed: the bilateral French–German exchange rate depreciated (from the French perspective) as German inflation surged in the early to mid-1990s. Since monetary union in 1999, devaluations have been ruled out—meaning that lower inflation in Germany than in France since then has led to a real appreciation of the French–German real exchange rate.

the currency is pegged. Box 13.2 shows how such an arrangement existed between France and Germany for nearly two decades. Of course, if exchange rates become very frequent, the distinction between a fixed but adjustable exchange rate and a floating regime becomes blurred.

13.3 Aggregate Demand and Supply under Flexible Exchange Rates

When exchange rates are flexible, monetary policy and the nominal exchange rates swap roles. Monetary policy is exogenous and under the control of the central bank. The nominal exchange rate, in contrast, is no longer exogenously fixed, but is determined by market forces and is endogenous. The *AD–AS* analysis turns out to be remarkably similar to the fixed exchange rate case—with clear differentiation between short, medium, and long run—but there are fundamental differences. In particular, we will see that the aggregate demand curve is negatively sloped, but for different reasons.

13.3.1 Nominal versus Real Interest Rates: The Fisher Equation

To understand how aggregate demand works when exchange rates are flexible, it is crucial to distinguish between the **nominal interest rate** and the **real interest rate**, which takes inflation into account. So far, we have ignored the distinction between these two rates because we ignored inflation. A simple example explains the issue.

Suppose we borrowed €100 for one year at a nominal interest rate of 5%. At the end of the year, we will have to repay the debt with interest, which will amount to €105 (€100 in principal and €5 in interest). But if inflation is positive, the value of €105 in one year in terms of goods and services will be less than €105 now; prices of goods in terms of euros will be even higher in a year's time. If inflation turns out to be 2%, the real value of €105 tomorrow in terms of today's euros will be about €103.[12] This

means that, valued at today's price level, the real value of our repayment in one year is €103. The real cost of borrowing €100 is therefore €3, which means a real interest rate of 3%. Note that 3% = 5%–2%. More generally, we can state that the real interest rate (r) is defined as the difference between the nominal interest rate (i) and the expected rate of inflation (π^e):

$$(13.7) \qquad r = i - \pi^e$$

real interest rate = nominal interest rate

– expected inflation.

This relationship is called the **Fisher principle** or **Fisher equation**.[13] In the presence of inflation, future repayments are made in money that will be worth less than it is today. This loss of purchasing power of money tomorrow can be seen as a gift to present-day borrowers or, more precisely, it means that the real cost of borrowing is less than the nominal cost, by an amount equal to the inflation rate between today and the future repayment.

The Fisher equation can be written as:

$$(13.8) \qquad i = r + \pi^e.$$

Nominal rates are observed—they are used when specifying terms of loan contracts—but real rates can only be inferred from their definition (13.7). This requires knowing what expected inflation is at the time of the loan contract but expectations are not observable. This is why real interest rates are generally not observable either. Eventually, we will know what inflation will have been during the life of a

---

[12] If the price index is 1 today, it will be 1.02 in one year's time and the real value of €105 tomorrow in terms of goods tomorrow will be 105/1.02≈103.

[13] Named after Irving Fisher, the Yale economist, already referred to in several previous chapters.

contract and can always compute the *ex post* real interest rate—that is, after the fact (see Figure 13.10). However, this *ex post* real interest rate $(i-\pi)$ will differ from the *ex ante* real rate $(i-\pi^e)$, whenever actual inflation differs from what it was expected to be $(\pi \neq \pi^e)$. As a result, someone will be disappointed. If inflation turns out higher than expected, the *ex post* real rate is lower than *ex ante* anticipated, which is

(a)

(b)

Fig. 13.10 Nominal and Real Interest Rates on French Government Debt, 1998–2011

Panel (*a*) shows the nominal and interest rates on French government bonds, called OATs. The rates of interest, or yields, on these bonds are determined by the forces of demand and supply. One type of OAT compensates the owner for inflation, and its yield reflects only the market's assessment of the real returns on financial assets. The other pays in purely nominal terms (in euros). The difference between the nominal and the real interest rates is a measure of the inflation rate expected by market participants, which is shown in panel (*b*). Until the global financial crisis in the fall of 2008, the long-run real interest rate was stable at around 2%, and the implied expected inflation about 2%. Since then, however, real bond yields and the expected inflation rate have both dropped sharply. For a brief time, the markets appear to have expected a deflation—a period of negative inflation—in France.

Source: Agence France-Trésor, Reuters.

good news for the borrower and a source of disappointment for the lender. Conversely, if actual inflation ends up lower than expected, the lender will have earned more than they were asking for.

In Chapter 10, we noted that spending (consumption and investment) is driven by the real interest rate while it is the nominal interest that affects money demand. Indeed, cash bears a zero nominal interest rate—no one gets paid for holding money. So, when comparing return on money with return on other assets, we had to use the nominal rate. The Fisher equation shows that, *ex post*, the real interest rate on money is $r = 0 - \pi = -\pi$, the negative of the inflation rate. This explains why inflation is often called a tax on those who hold money.

13.3.2 Aggregate Demand in the Long Run

In Chapters 9 and 10, the behaviour of central banks was formalized as the Taylor rule:

(13.9) $i = \bar{i} + a\pi_{gap} + bY_{gap}.$

The output gap Y_{gap} is the percentage difference between actual and potential—or trend—GDP, $(Y - \bar{Y})/\bar{Y}$. The inflation gap π_{gap} is equal to $\pi - \bar{\pi}$, and represents how far the current inflation diverges from the central bank's target rate $\bar{\pi}$. Recall that parameters a and b—which are both positive—express the overall monetary policy objectives or 'tastes' of the central bank. A high value of a relative to b would represent an 'inflation-fighting' central bank. In contrast, if b is large relative to a, this would signify that the central bank is more interested in reducing the output gap than keeping inflation close to its target.

The **target or neutral interest rate** $\bar{i}$ is the rate chosen by the central bank when inflation and output are both on target—meaning that both inflation and output gaps equal zero ($\pi = \bar{\pi}$ and $Y = \bar{Y}$). What affects this choice? The Fisher equation gives the answer: the sum of the long-run real interest rate and the target inflation rate. Let's take a careful look at each of these components.

The neutrality principle tells us that the long-run real interest rate $\bar{r}$ is given by the real economy. It is the return available from investments after adjusting for inflation or, according to Chapter 8, the marginal productivity of physical capital. It is driven,

therefore, by technology, the availability of labour and other factors, all of which are beyond the control of the central bank.

This leaves the long-run inflation rate. Since the central bank ultimately controls the inflation rate, it can logically only be the inflation target $\bar{\pi}$ as embedded in the Taylor rule. It follows that the natural interest rate is the nominal rate that corresponds to the economy's real rate plus the inflation target:

(13.10) $\bar{i} = \bar{r} + \bar{\pi}$

A central bank that follows this logic will see to it that inflation rate ultimately returns to its target rate, so $\pi = \bar{\pi}$, while our analysis of the AS curve establishes that, in the long run, the economy will ultimately return to trend, so $Y = \bar{Y}$ and $Y_{gap} = 0$. This means that, by choosing its inflation target, a central bank determines the long-run aggregate demand curve as the horizontal line *LAD* shown in Figure 13.12.

The *LAD* curve resembles the curve obtained in the case of a fixed exchange rate regime, but its rationale is different. When the central bank opts for a fixed exchange rate regime, long-run inflation is driven by foreign inflation; under a flexible exchange rate regime, it is set by the target inflation rate embedded in the Taylor rule.[14] The common feature is that long-run inflation and the position of the *LAD* curve are always determined by the monetary policy strategy. This is an implication of the dichotomy principle.

13.3.3 The Short-Run Aggregate Demand Curve

The similarity between fixed and flexible exchange rate regimes carries over to the short-run aggregate demand curve. Yet the logic behind this curve is fundamentally different under flexible exchange rates. Now, the AD curve is downward-sloping because a higher inflation rate leads the central bank to raise interest rates—to pursue contractionary monetary

---

[14] If the central bank chose to control the money supply instead of following a Taylor rule, the same conclusion would result. The inflation rate in the long run would be given by the chosen rate money growth minus an adjustment for trend growth in the demand for real money balances. Indeed Box 13.1 shows that, in the long run, the inflation rate is the difference between the money growth rate and the GDP growth rate.

policy. To see this, we use again the Mundell–Fleming model, now under flexible exchange rates—the *TR–IFM* framework—remembering that the position of the *IS* curve is endogenous when the exchange rate freely floats.

We need first to adapt the way we use the Taylor rule to a world of variable inflation. In Chapters 10 and 11, the inflation rate was treated as exogenous and set equal to zero for simplicity, so the Taylor rule only involved a relationship between the interest rate and output. With inflation, we must recognize that the interest rate responds both to changes in output and in the inflation rate—that is the thrust of the Taylor rule. This means that inflation is now taken as exogenous in the *TR–IFM* diagram; when it changes, the *TR* curve shifts.

Take *A* in Figure 13.11(*a*) as a starting point, a situation of short- and long-run equilibrium, so that inflation has long been at a level targeted by the central bank. In order to find out the shape of the short-run *AD* curve, we study the effect of changing inflation, 'all else constant', including monetary policy as summarized by the central bank's target inflation rate $\bar{\pi}$ and the neutral interest rate $\bar{i}$.

Suppose the rate of inflation were to rise from π to π'. The Taylor rule states that the central bank reacts by raising the nominal interest rate—by the amount $a(\pi'-\pi)$—for any level of output. This means that the *TR* curve shifts upwards to *TR'* in panel (*a*). The new equilibrium point *A'* shows that the effect of a higher rate of inflation is a decline in output. This reduction is brought about *by a real exchange rate appreciation*, which reduces the demand for goods—the implicit leftward shift of the *IS* curve (not shown).[15] The exchange rate appreciation is a direct effect of monetary policy tightening in the face of higher inflation. The move from *A* to *A'* when inflation rises from π to π' is reported in panel (*b*) to obtain a downward-sloping short-run aggregate demand curve *AD*.

To summarize, the short-run aggregate demand curve is downward-sloping under both fixed and flexible exchange rates, but for different reasons. When the nominal exchange rate is fixed, a higher

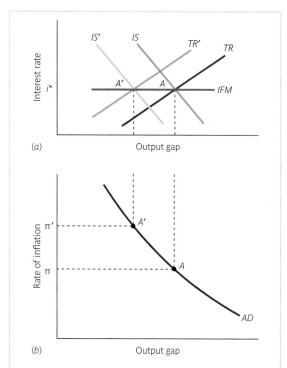

(*a*)   Output gap

(*b*)   Output gap

Fig. 13.11 The Aggregate Demand Curve Under Flexible Exchange Rates

The figure shows the effect of an increase in the rate of inflation on aggregate demand. Starting at point *A* with an inflation rate π, inflation rises to π'. The higher inflation rate at the unchanged target rate of inflation prompts the central bank to raise nominal interest rates, shifting the *TR* curve upward in panel (*a*). Demand is reduced (point *A*), hence the downward-sloping curve in panel (*b*).

inflation rate reduces demand through a loss in external competitiveness. Under flexible rates, higher inflation triggers an interest rate hike by the central bank via the Taylor rule. Competitiveness declines too, but now because the nominal exchange rate *S* appreciates. The common feature is the role of the real exchange rate in both regimes.

13.3.4 Movements Along versus Shifts of the *AD* Curve

The *AD* curve shifts when any of the exogenous variables in the *TR–IFM* model changes. Under flexible exchange rates, the real exchange rate adjusts and the *IS* curve shifts endogenously to meet the intersection

---

[15] At this stage, you may need to return to Section 11.4 of Chapter 11 to remind yourself why the exchange rate appreciates.

of the *TR* and *IFM* curves. This means that factors that affect the *IS* curve only do not have any impact on the *AD* curve. We already saw in Chapter 11 that fiscal policy fails to move the *IS* curve significantly because its effects are offset by the reaction of the exchange rate. This applies to all aggregate demand shocks, including animal spirits and foreign output.[16]

The *AD* curve does shift, however, when either the *TR* or the *IFM* curves do. The *TR* curve represents the monetary policy strategy. The central bank changes its interest rate when the inflation rate changes, but this is what explains the slope of the *AD* curve. Changes in the inflation rate, therefore, takes the economy along the *AD* curve. The remaining reasons why TR shifts would actually move the AD curve are changes in the Taylor rule itself. This includes either changes in the central bank's target inflation rate ($\bar{\pi}$) or in the preferences of the central bank, as represented by parameters a and b in (13.9).[17] For example, a higher target inflation rate would result in an upward shift of the *AD* curve. Changes in parameters a and b, instead affect the slope of the *AD* curve. If the central bank reacts strongly to inflation changes, a higher a for instance, the *AD* curve becomes flatter. This is because an increase in inflation induces a larger increase in the interest rate by the central bank, and with it a stronger real appreciation and a sharper decline in output.

The position of the *IFM* curve remains determined by the foreign rate of return i^*, so changes in this parameter can also affect aggregate demand. As we will see, long run changes require the consent of the central bank or the government more generally, because they ultimately involve the long-run target rate of inflation $\bar{\pi}$. Yet in the short to medium run, i^* can move when international monetary policy becomes tighter (i^* rises) or looser (i^* falls), or when market expectations of future exchange rates change.

This latter possibility will be discussed in detail in Chapter 15.

13.3.5 The Complete System

Figure 13.12 presents the complete system under flexible exchange rates. It includes the now-familiar short- and long-run aggregate supply curves as well as the short- and long-run aggregate demand curves. The figure displays a long-run equilibrium: actual output is equal to trend output—a zero output gap—as required by the supply side, and inflation is equal to target inflation as required by the demand side. The PPP principle also allows us to infer the evolution of the exchange in the long run. The long-run rate of change in the exchange rate compensates for the difference between the domestic and foreign inflation rates: $\Delta S/S = \pi^* - \pi$. If the foreign rate of inflation is below the domestic rate ($\pi^* < \pi$), the exchange rate is depreciating ($\Delta S/S < 0$); if the domestic rate is lower, ($\pi^* > \pi$), it is appreciating ($\Delta S/S > 0$).[18]

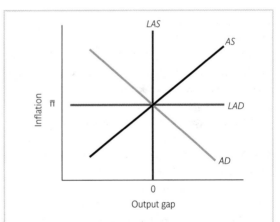

Fig. 13.12 Aggregate Demand and Supply Under Flexible Exchange Rates

In the long run, output is at its trend growth level (the output gap is zero) and the central bank's target inflation rate determines the rate of inflation (the height of the *LAD* curve). The figure depicts long-run equilibrium when the short-run aggregate demand and supply curves pass through the same point as the long-run curves.

---

[16] This is a strong statement, which may be weakened to acknowledge that the deterioration of the primary current account implied by the exchange rate changes (sometimes called 'external crowding out') can often take several months to occur.

[17] The dichotomy principle implies that the real interest rate is determined exclusively by the real economy. Changes in the level of the real interest rate, while it may affect the Taylor rule, are not considered in the analysis which follows.

[18] Short-run movements in the exchange rates can be inferred in a straightforward way from the *TR–IFM* apparatus.

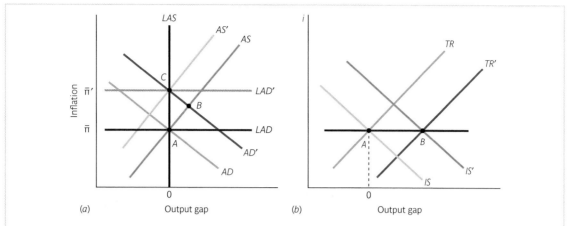

Fig. 13.13 Monetary Policy Under Flexible Exchange Rates

Starting at point *A* in panel (*a*), a monetary policy expansion—here shown as a permanent increase in the central bank's target inflation rate—shifts the *AD* curve rightwards to *AD′*. At the same time, the *LAD* curve also shifts to *LAD′*, reflecting the permanently higher target inflation rate and intersecting the *LAS* curve at point *C*. In the long run, the economy settles at point *C*, with GDP equal to trend output and the increase in inflation equal to the increase in the target inflation rate. Short-run equilibrium occurs at point *B*, where actual inflation exceeds underlying inflation. Thereafter underlying inflation increases to its long-run level and the economy moves from point *B* towards point *C*.

13.3.6 Monetary Policy

Central banks which follow a Taylor rule systematically set the interest rate relative to the natural or long-run target rate when inflation or output depart from their target and trend levels, respectively. In that sense, the rule-based monetary policy does not change, but the rule itself may be changed. It can be the adoption of a new target rate of inflation, or a changing view about the natural real interest rate or the equilibrium trend level of output, or a different sensitivity to the inflation or output gaps (parameters *a* and *b*). Here we consider the case when it raises its inflation target from $\bar{\pi}$ to $\bar{\pi}'$. This means that the neutral interest rate $\bar{i}$, which is the sum of an unchanged real interest rate and the new target rate of inflation $\bar{\pi}'$, will also rise permanently.

Long run

A permanently higher target rate of inflation means that the *LAD* line shifts up to *LAD′* in Figure 13.13(*a*). The dichotomy principle implies that the real side of the economy is left unaffected, so *LAS* is unchanged. In the long run, therefore, the economy will move from point *A* to point *C*. The vertical distance *AC* corresponds to the increase in the target inflation rate.

Short run

The increase in the inflation target implies that the central bank will attempt to reduce the nominal interest rate, producing an exchange rate depreciation and therefore an increase in aggregate demand. This is depicted in Figure 13.13(*a*) by the rightward shift from *AD* to *AD′*. In the background, the increase in $\bar{\pi}$ shifts the *TR* curve down and to the right in panel (*b*) of Figure 13.13. The economy moves from point *A* to point *B* in both panels. Overall, output rises (and unemployment declines) and inflation increases, but by less than the change intended by the central bank.[19]

The medium run

The transition takes the economy in steps from point *B* to point *C* in panel (*a*). At point *B*, where output is above its growth trend level, the actual rate of inflation exceeds the underlying rate. What happens during the transition—and therefore the details of the trajectory—depends on the behaviour

---

[19] We ignore an issue of further complexity. The Fisher principle implies that, eventually, the nominal interest rate must rise, which would shift the *IFM* curve up. Ignoring this aspect does not affect the reasoning.

of the underlying rate of inflation. To the extent that it is backward-looking, underlying inflation is sluggish. Initially, the *AS* curve does not move and the economy moves to point *B*. Over time, underlying inflation begins to track actual inflation, the short-run *AS* curve shifts upwards and the economy moves from *B* towards *C*, along the curve *AD'*. As in the case of a fixed exchange rate regime, along the path from *B* to *C*, actual inflation exceeds underlying inflation. As underlying inflation catches up, actual inflation rises, and output declines along *AD'*. Indeed, the rising inflation rate leads the central bank to tighten its stance according to the Taylor rule. In panel (*b*), this response to inflation is captured by an upward shift of the *TR* curve, as explained in Section 13.3.3. This will go on as long as inflation rises. The *TR* curve must continue to move up until it passes through point *C*, the new long-run equilibrium.

In summary, an expansionary monetary policy—described here as an increase of the inflation rate target—raises output and inflation in the short run. In the long run, the effect falls entirely on higher inflation with no effect on output—the neutrality result is confirmed under flexible exchange rates. In the short run, the backward-looking component of underlying inflation creates the non-neutrality needed for an output effect, while the forward-looking component tends to make neutrality more likely to hold in the shorter run. The role of underlying inflation receives closer scrutiny in Chapter 16.

13.4 How to Use the *AS–AD* Framework

The complete *AS–AD* framework provides macroeconomists with a key tool for studying real-life events and answering important macroeconomic questions. We proceed with three aims: (1) to illustrate the principles developed earlier, (2) to develop familiarity with the framework, and (3) to study and understand historical developments of general interest.

13.4.1 Lags and Time Horizon

We start by briefly providing indications on the duration of the short, medium, and long runs, an issue already discussed in Chapter 1. Here we link this discussion with the *AS–AD* and *IS–TR–IFM* apparatus. The question is: how long does an isolated shock need to work its way through the system? Naturally, the economy isn't served a single shock on a platter, but is constantly subjected to small and large shocks, which move it away from its long run. Despite this fact, an orderly discussion of the short, medium and long run is useful—it gives us a time horizon for understanding the effects of disturbances and more important, policy measures.

The short run corresponds to the Mundell–Fleming model, which is based on the Keynesian assumption of price stickiness. It lasts as long as the short-run *AS* curve remains roughly in place. It takes about one to two years for demand disturbances to affect output, and sometimes up to three years for inflation to react. At this point, inflation triggers changes in the underlying rate of inflation, the *AS* curve starts shifting and we move to the medium run.

The medium run—the transition from the short to the long run—lasts from two to five years. This is when the short-run *AS* curve begins to shift as the backward-looking component of underlying inflation starts catching up with actual inflation. The transition is shorter, the faster underlying inflation catches up. This depends therefore on the relative contributions of its backward- and forward-looking components. As previously noted, if the forward-looking component dominates, the short-run *AS* curve quickly reaches its final position—especially if prices and wages are not sticky. Wage and price **indexation** speeds up the transition. In countries where inflation is very high, formal or informal indexation schemes are usually in place and the long run occurs in the short run! We return to this important issue in the next section.

The long run is defined as the horizon over which the dichotomy asserts itself. This means that we look beyond the business cycle horizon. Although two business cycles are never exactly alike, experience shows that they generally last four to six years.

13.4.2 Supply Shocks

Supply shocks occur when conditions of production change suddenly, with an impact on production costs and the evolution of inflation. Supply shocks come in many different forms, but share the common feature that they invariably create difficulties for policy-makers, who are ill-equipped to face the consequences. This is because traditional demand-side policies are ineffective in dealing with supply shocks. In addition, supply-side policies are complex, slow in generating tangible results, and often politically unappealing.

The simplest example of an adverse supply shock is the sudden loss of human or physical factors of production resulting from natural disasters or wars. This leads immediately to medium- or long-run loss of production potential (think of the Fukushima disaster in Japan, Hurricane Katrina, or earthquakes in Turkey). Supply shocks can be favourable as well, e.g. an acceleration of technological advances. The often-cited information technology revolution (described in Chapter 3) that started in the mid-1990s is a recent example. Previous major episodes include the invention of electric generation and transmission, automobiles, and plastics. The discovery of natural resources or a sustained surge in capital investment (think of the Solow model) are other examples of favourable supply shocks—possibly very persistent ones.

Oil shocks are the most well-known supply shock, with the instances of 1973 and 1979 representing major turning-points in twentieth-century post-war economic history. They marked the end of the rapid growth performance of most European countries, and were followed by markedly higher inflation and unemployment rates. Japan and the USA were also badly affected. After a favourable counter-oil shock in the mid-1990s, oil prices started once again to rise sharply in 2000, again in 2003 in the wake of the Iraq war, quadrupled over the period 2005–2008, then fell again. The *AD–AS* model was developed largely in response to events of the 1970s, just as the *IS–LM* model was a response to the Great Depression.

A short-term policy dilemma

We saw in Chapter 12 that supply shocks shift the aggregate supply curve. The increase in production costs is passed on by firms in the form of price increases at any given level of output. This was represented by the exogenous shock *s* in the aggregate supply equation:

(13.11) $\pi = \tilde{\pi} + a(Y - \bar{Y}) + s.$

When the shock is unfavourable, i.e. when $s > 0$, the short-run aggregate supply curve shifts upwards from *AS* to *AS′*, as shown in Figure 13.14. The move from point *A* to point *B* is the case of stagflation, i.e. declining real growth and rising inflation. If the relative price increase is a one-off event, the *AS* curve will

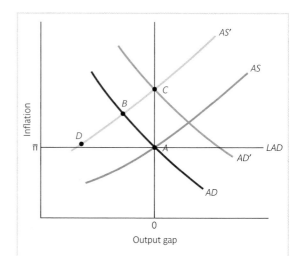

Fig. 13.14 An Adverse Supply Shock

An adverse supply shock shifts the *AS* curve up to *AS′*. The economy will suffer stagflation as it moves from point *A* to point *B*. If the authorities decide to avoid a fall in output and a rise in unemployment, they can adopt expansionary demand-side policies and move the economy towards a long-run equilibrium at point *C*. This would be achieved at the cost of a permanent increase in the central bank's target rate of inflation. If, in contrast, they choose to fight inflation, they can adopt contractionary demand-side policies—a lower target inflation rate—and aim at point *D*. Here the cost is a deep recession.

shift back to its initial position.[20] This is optimistic, however. While the economy is at point B, workers unexpectedly face higher prices. Quite likely, they will demand higher nominal wages and, if they succeed, the backward-looking component of underlying inflation rises. Such second-round effects are the reason why, even after the commodity price increase has been absorbed (when s goes back to zero), the AS curve is unlikely to shift back quickly or completely. The answer will depend on the behaviour of underlying inflation.

Stagflation is a serious policy challenge for governments. One approach is to soften the blow to output and unemployment by adopting an expansionary demand policy (monetary or fiscal, depending on the exchange rate regime). Aiming at point C, and shifting the aggregate demand curve to AD' in Figure 13.14, hastens the return to trend growth but at the cost of higher inflation. Another approach is to prevent inflation from ever rising, so that underlying inflation remains under control. This calls for a prompt *contractionary* policy reaction, shifting the short-run aggregate demand curve back until it goes through a point like D. This reaction deepens the recession but, once the shock has worked itself through (and $s = 0$), the aggregate supply curve moves back to AS and the restrictive demand policy may be lifted to return to point A. The nature of the dilemma should be clear: the authorities can either aim at maintaining output and employment, but at the cost of higher inflation, or they can prevent a sharp inflationary impact, but at the cost of a low output and high unemployment. The reason behind this dilemma is also clear: macroeconomic management policies are demand-side policies and they are ill-adapted to deal with supply shocks.

The exchange rate regime

The reaction of underlying inflation is decisive for determining the outcome of the policy response to a supply shock. Underlying inflation tends to increase because of its backward-looking component, but what about the forward-looking component? The answer ultimately hinges on which long-run equilibrium is expected to be reached. If agents believe that policy-makers are aiming at point D in Figure 13.14, the forward-looking component is likely to support this policy. If wage negotiators are convinced that inflation will be kept under control, they see the jump to point B as strictly temporary and keep underlying inflation at the pre-shock level. Once the shock is over, the aggregate supply curve promptly returns to AS and the economy's trajectory will be from A to B and back to A. If, instead, wage negotiators expect an accommodating policy that aims at point C, underlying inflation will rise and shift the AS curve to AS', even after the shock has passed. The trajectory will be from A to B and beyond, higher and to the left of B along the new AD' curve. However, since the output gap is negative, underlying inflation is above actual inflation, so the AS curve will eventually shift back towards AS', even though the one-off supply shock is over. The economy winds up at point C.

Under flexible exchange rates, it is the central bank that determines the position of the LAD line. By their choice of an inflation target, the monetary authority can choose the long-run inflation rate and decide whether point A or point C will be eventually reached. This is not the case with a fixed exchange rate regime where the position of the LAD line depends on the 'foreign' inflation rate. In the presence of a severe supply shock, a fixed exchange rate regime can be maintained only among like-minded countries which have compatible views of how they will react. In Europe, for instance, the oil shocks of the 1970s and 1980s seriously strained the European Monetary System as different countries adopted different strategies. The adoption of a common currency, which floats freely, means that this decision is now in the hands of the European Central Bank (ECB). Even with a common currency, policy disagreements concerning the correct response to inflation remain. Following the rise of oil prices in 2003–2004, and again in 2007–2008, the ECB has been criticized by some governments as being too tight and by others as being too lax. Since the financial crisis, inflation has been subdued and other concerns have become dominant, but the issues regarding the

---

[20] A supply shock, such as a one-off increase in oil prices, directly affects the price level, not its rate of increase, unless these prices continue to rise. Normally, once they have reached a new higher level, the impact is passed on into higher goods prices. While the level of these prices remains higher, inflation is no longer directly affected by the shock.

management of expectations and credibility will always be waiting in the wings for the next supply shock to arrive.

Lessons from supply shocks

Three general lessons can be drawn. First, an adverse supply shock is bad news. It depresses growth while raising unemployment and inflation at the same time, contradicting the Phillips curve trade-off. Second, traditional demand management policies are not useful for dealing with an adverse supply shock. When the aggregate supply curve moves up and to the left, demand management cannot deal with both inflation and output. Policy-makers must choose between accepting the shock as an increase in inflation or as a drop in output with higher unemployment. The appropriate response should be supply-side policies, aiming at bringing back the aggregate supply curve as soon as possible to its initial position. This is not easy. The best hope is to manage the forward-looking component of underlying inflation and to try to 'disconnect' the backward-looking component. This requires a clear and credible signal from the authorities that they will not accommodate the shock. Third, the exchange regime becomes crucial. A fixed exchange rate can be maintained only among countries that adopt the same policy mix.

13.4.3 Demand Shocks

In principle, exogenous demand shifts are easier for policy-makers to contend with. Most of these shocks are the direct result of macroeconomic policy actions, fiscal or monetary policy depending on the exchange rate regime. Other examples are exogenous events, like the global financial crisis which began with the bankruptcy of the US investment bank Lehman Brothers, and was followed by a freezing-up of credit markets and a worldwide demand slowdown. Another, earlier example of a positive demand shock was German reunification, the source of an unexpected demand surge in central Europe during the first half of the 1990s.

Figure 13.15 shows the consequence of an adverse demand shock as a leftward exogenous shift of the short-run aggregate demand curve from *AD* to *AD'*. The economy moves from point *A* to

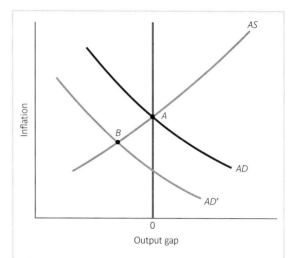

Fig. 13.15 An Adverse Demand Shock

An adverse demand shock is represented by a leftward exogenous shift of the short-run aggregate demand curve. The economy moves from point *A* to point *B*. In principle, the government has instruments at its disposal—monetary or fiscal policy, or both—which could restore the *AD* curve to its original position. This was the standard policy response of the 1960s. While European countries have relied less and less on such policy responses and sat out temporary declines in aggregate demand and output, pressure due to the financial crisis was simply too great, leading to a return to activist policy.

point *B*: inflation declines and output falls below its trend level. In principle, the government has the required instruments at its disposal—monetary or fiscal policy, depending on the exchange rate regime—that could restore the *AD* curve to its original position. In the 1960s, this was the standard policy response. Until the global economic crisis (2008–2009), the use of demand policy was remarkably moderate. Many European countries had reacted to the initial oil shocks with accommodating policies—raising target inflation and allowing a temporary increase to become permanent. After a decade dedicated largely to erasing the scars from those oil shocks by bringing down underlying inflation, most countries were reluctant to give up those achievements again. This meant sticking to inflation targets and preventing monetary policy from becoming excessive again.

The global financial crisis and the ensuing recession—the deepest since the Great Depression of the 1930s—changed all that. A sharp, global reduction in aggregate demand prompted all countries to implement short-term stimulus packages. The idea was to replace or at least supplement aggregate demand lost through postponed or cancelled investment projects or reduced private consumption with government consumption. Even if the multiplier is low—as it is for small open economies—many policy-makers saw little alternative than to ramp up purchases of goods and services by governments to keep aggregate demand from collapsing. The benefits and the costs of fixed versus flexible exchange rates became evident as countries faced different and often difficult choices. Box 13.3 compares the situation of Ireland, a

---

 Box 13.3 Ireland v. Iceland: Vulnerable Islands in a Global Financial Tsunami

Iceland and Ireland are small, wealthy, and very open economies which experienced strong real growth in the 1990s and pursued an aggressive course of international financial integration in the late 1990s and early 2000s. Previously backwater banks in the 1980s rose to become star international players in the early 2000s. In the ten years from 1995 to 2005, demand deposits in Iceland—a country of 320,000 people—grew from $6.8 billion to $65.8 billion! In Ireland growth was similar, from $33.1 billion to $163.5 billion. More frequently than not, these bank deposits belonged to foreign households, foreign firms, or foreign financial institutions. Icelandic banks went as far as to open subsidiaries in the UK and in the Netherlands, offering higher interest rates than the local competition; by all appearances, these banks were running Ponzi schemes (see Box 7.6). The banks eventually collapsed and defaulted on the foreign depositors. In the case of Ireland, the banks financed a housing boom, as in the USA. When housing prices started to decline, many borrowers defaulted because the loans now exceeded the value of their houses. The banks were distressed and some had to be taken over by the state.

The financial crisis was accompanied by a sharp decline in credit and plummeting stock prices (Tobin's q falling), which led to collapses of investment spending and aggregate demand in both countries. At the same time, the IFM curve shot up because the rest of the world sharply raised the interest rate i^* at which it would lend to these countries (Iceland was even shut off from foreign borrowing). In the $AS-AD$ diagram, the AD curve shifted sharply to the left. Table 13.2 shows that both countries experienced similar cumulative declines in real GDP (in Iceland, about 10.4% over 2009–2010; in Ireland, 12.1% in the period 2008–2010). Unemployment skyrocketed and government budget deficits swelled to double-digit percentages of GDP as tax revenues fell in line with incomes.

Despite the remarkable similarity in the nature of the demand shock hitting the two economies, the reaction could not have been more different, highlighting fundamental differences between fixed and flexible exchange rate regimes. Ireland, a member of the Eurozone, had no monetary policy option and had little choice but to bite the bullet. Just as the $IS-TR-IFM$ model predicts, the demand shock hit GDP hard. Second, Ireland had to experience a deflation (falling prices) to adjust to the shock. Initially, fiscal policy was active; the government nationalized and recapitalized one bank after the next, and managed to increase government purchases as well, before engaging in massive budget cuts in 2009–2010 in order to stabilize the public debt. The overall adjustment process was considerably quicker in Iceland, which had freedom to depreciate the currency—from 2007 to 2009 the dollar value of the krona dropped by 50%. Predictably, the recession was over more quickly in Iceland, and its current account, while swinging more wildly than in Ireland, contributed more decisively to the Icelandic recovery. The dark cloud hanging over Iceland is not the ash cloud of it infamous volcanic eruptions, but rather the burst of inflation, which was a necessary side-effect of the devaluation—increasing to over 12% for two years before returning to the 2–3% range. Some economists claim this is a small price to pay for escaping a greater recession. Others see the episode as a blemish on the credibility of the Icelandic economy for years to come.

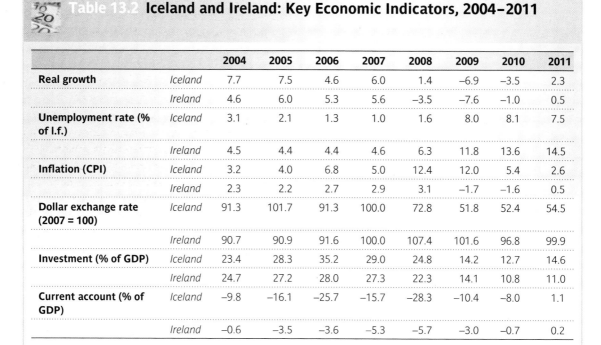

Table 13.2 **Iceland and Ireland: Key Economic Indicators, 2004–2011**

		2004	2005	2006	2007	2008	2009	2010	2011
Real growth	*Iceland*	7.7	7.5	4.6	6.0	1.4	−6.9	−3.5	2.3
	Ireland	4.6	6.0	5.3	5.6	−3.5	−7.6	−1.0	0.5
Unemployment rate (% of l.f.)	*Iceland*	3.1	2.1	1.3	1.0	1.6	8.0	8.1	7.5
	Ireland	4.5	4.4	4.4	4.6	6.3	11.8	13.6	14.5
Inflation (CPI)	*Iceland*	3.2	4.0	6.8	5.0	12.4	12.0	5.4	2.6
	Ireland	2.3	2.2	2.7	2.9	3.1	−1.7	−1.6	0.5
Dollar exchange rate (2007 = 100)	*Iceland*	91.3	101.7	91.3	100.0	72.8	51.8	52.4	54.5
	Ireland	90.7	90.9	91.6	100.0	107.4	101.6	96.8	99.9
Investment (% of GDP)	*Iceland*	23.4	28.3	35.2	29.0	24.8	14.2	12.7	14.6
	Ireland	24.7	27.2	28.0	27.3	22.3	14.1	10.8	11.0
Current account (% of GDP)	*Iceland*	−9.8	−16.1	−25.7	−15.7	−28.3	−10.4	−8.0	1.1
	Ireland	−0.6	−3.5	−3.6	−5.3	−5.7	−3.0	−0.7	0.2

member of the Eurozone, with Iceland, which had its own currency and floating exchange rates during the crisis.

13.4.4 Disinflation

An important policy question faced by many developing countries is how to deal with a high rate of inflation already long in place. We know that high and persistent inflation is the consequence of excessive monetary growth that the central bank has chosen or been forced to choose. The cure must be to slow down money growth, meaning to aggressively implement a lower target inflation rate. Again, how a policy of **disinflation**—a successful reduction in the rate of inflation—is ultimately implemented depends on the exchange rate regime.

Under flexible exchange rates, the central bank can choose its inflation rate target, so the solution to high inflation is technically simple, but often very painful. Figure 13.16 shows why. We start from point A, which we take to be a long-run equilibrium. Thus we assume that the high inflation rate is indeed the central bank's target—we are on some original *LAD* line which is not drawn—and that actual and underlying

inflation are equal—we are on the *LAS* line. If the central bank exogenously reduces the target inflation rate well below the current rate of inflation, the *LAD* curve shifts downward by the reduction of target inflation to *LAD′*. As a consequence it must drastically raise nominal interest rates in the short run.[21] In the *TR–IFM* model (not shown), the *TR* curve shifts to the left, the nominal and real exchange rates appreciate, the current account worsens, and demand declines. This is captured by the leftward shift of the short-run aggregate demand curve from *AD* to *AD′*. The short-run effect of this disinflationary policy corresponds to point B: inflation declines but so does output, and unemployment rises. At point B actual inflation is below underlying inflation so the latter will be revised downwards and, over time, the short-run aggregate supply curve will shift downwards until it reaches the position *AS′*. At point C, a new long-run equilibrium is reached and the disinflation is complete. The cost has been a period of

---

[21] To see this, consider the Taylor rule again and observe that a decrease in $\bar{\pi}$, holding all other things constant, implies an *increase* in the nominal interest rate.

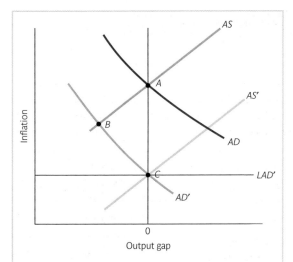

Fig. 13.16 Disinflation

Disinflation moves the economy from point A to point C. Using demand-side policies implies the use of contractionary monetary or fiscal policies which move the aggregate demand curve from AD to AD' and the LAD curve to LAD'. The short-run equilibrium at point B explains why disinflation is usually painful: it requires a period of low output and high unemployment. Long-run equilibrium is achieved at point C when the short-run aggregate supply curve has shifted to AS'. The speed of this shift depends on the time required by underlying inflation to catch up with lower actual inflation.

IS–IMF model (not shown), the IS curve shifts to the left. The resulting decline in aggregate demand is represented by the leftward shift of the short-run aggregate demand curve from AD to AD' in Figure 13.16. Then the logic is the same as under the flexible exchange rate regime. Underlying inflation must decline in light of lower realized inflation rates and the economy will eventually settle at point C on the long-run aggregate demand LAD', which corresponds to the lower foreign inflation rate. Here disinflation also requires a period of negative output gap and high unemployment.

The interesting questions are: how long does it take to move from point B to point C in Figure 13.16? And how much output is lost along the way? The **output cost of disinflation** is lower the faster the AS curve comes down. That, in turn, depends on the speed at which underlying inflation adapts to a declining inflation rate. The backward component slows down the speed at which the AS curve shifts, while the forward-looking component accelerates the adjustment. In periods of disinflation, therefore, it would be helpful to give more weight to the forward-looking component, possibly even shutting down the backward-looking component. The backward-looking component depends on wage- and price-setting institutions, an issue examined in Box 13.4. The forward-looking component is often referred to as the 'psychological' nature of price- and wage-setting, but it can be influenced by policy institutions.

Wage negotiators may have different incentives when formulating their expectations. It is good bargaining tactics for workers to argue that inflation is high, while employers tend to predict declines in the rate of inflation. Jointly, however, employers and employees have an incentive to be as close as possible to target, for errors may be costly in terms of competitiveness and profitability. As they aim at disinflation, policy-makers have a strong interest in convincing wage negotiators that inflation will surely decline, since this will accelerate the downward movement of the AS curve. One solution is to credibly use the exchange rate as an anchor. To do so, the authorities must demonstrate that they will not let the exchange rate depreciate again. This is why a number of countries have adopted **hard pegs**, a variety of fixed exchange rate arrangements that

negative output gap and high unemployment, which may extend over several years as noted in Section 13.4.1.

Under a fixed and adjustable exchange rate regime, high and lasting inflation is only possible if the exchange rate is regularly depreciated, as explained in Section 13.2. Bringing inflation down requires a change in monetary policy. If the fixed exchange rate regime is to be retained, this means doing away with chronic depreciations. In that case, we know that the LAD line is set by the foreign inflation rate, so it is essential to peg the exchange rate to the currency of a country where inflation is suitably low. The peg becomes the anchor that will deliver disinflation. Initially, inflation is higher at home than abroad. If inflation moves slowly, fixing the nominal exchange rate means that the real exchange rate appreciates as long as domestic exceeds foreign inflation. In the

Box 13.4 Wage Negotiations: The Time Dimension

In most European countries and in the USA, wage negotiations are *staggered* over a year or more. One wage negotiation takes the previous one into account, and may even anticipate the next one. Employees do not want to be out-done by their colleagues, and employers do not want the competition to undercut their labour costs. In contrast, in Japan wage negotiations are *synchronized*. They take place every year at roughly the same time, the so-called 'spring offensive' (*shunto*). Each industry opens up bargaining, but closely monitors the state of play elsewhere. When one bargain is struck, it sets the trend and all the others follow quickly. For a time, wage negotiations in Northern Europe were centralized and therefore highly synchronized. Even when they are staggered, some negotiations are *trend-setting*: they result in similar agreements later on and sometimes even trigger readjustments to previously reached ones, thus injecting a dose of synchronization. With wage staggering, aggregate nominal wages (the average of all nominal wages) move slowly, which retards the return to equilibrium unemployment. The *AS* curve will appear flatter. With full synchronization, average nominal wages are stable between negotiations, and then jump. This implies a steeper *AS* curve. The implications for the economy are profound. Either a quick return to the equilibrium unemployment rate if the real wages are set right, or a prolonged departure if they are set incorrectly.

The situation is different in economies where inflation is high and has been so for a long time. There it is common to have mandatory or mutually agreed index-ation schemes for wages. Brazil was particularly advanced in this regard, indexing virtually *all* nominal prices, including house rents, corporate balance sheets, taxes, and public utilities rates. Such indexation schemes can often reduce the staggering considerably, with the same effect as an increase in synchronization of wage-setting.

Although wage indexation removes some of the costs of high inflation to households and firms, it has serious adverse side-effects. First, indexation generally perpetu-ates any real wage gain achieved. This gives an incentive to any group of wage-earners to be the first to bid for higher wages. The result is that all groups rush to be first, as much to protect themselves as to achieve a head start. Second, indexation reduces both public and government support for anti-inflation policies. This is why Germany, after its famous hyperinflation in the 1920s, made indexation illegal. Third, indexation makes disinflation costlier in terms of unemployment. When inflation is on the way up, nominal wages trail behind prices: real wages are reduced and labour demand is robust. When inflation is on the way down, wages indexed on past inflation trail actual inflation: real wages rise, firms' profits are squeezed, and unemploy-ment rises. This is why most European countries with legal or simply widespread indexation clauses elimi-nated them in the 1980s, much against the will of trade unions. Fourth, indexation eliminates downward real wage flexibility as real wages are at least constant unless there is a sharp burst of inflation. The lack of flexibility is a source of unemployment when an adverse supply shock occurs.

---

makes it politically costly or even illegal to devalue.[22] If the exchange rate is not fixed, it is the credibility of the central bank as an inflation-fighter that becomes crucial. This is why a number of countries have given formal independence to their central banks, instructing them to aim at price stability.

Many independent central banks have adopted the **inflation-targeting strategy** as already described, publicly announcing the inflation rate they intend to achieve and explicitly and publicly linking their actions to the target, and staking their credibility on their success in achieving the target.

---

[22] This is the strategy adopted, for example, by Argentina in 2001 and by Bulgaria in 1997. In both cases, it worked, although

Argentina's arrangement collapsed in 2001, for other reasons. By then, however, inflation had turned negative!

! Summary

1 The macroeconomy is analysed as the interplay of aggregate demand and aggregate supply. This framework emphasizes the distinction between the short run and the long run, when output returns to its trend growth path.

2 Under fixed exchange rates, inflation is restricted to be equal to foreign inflation in the long run. Under flexible rates, long-run inflation is determined by the target inflation rate.

3 The short-run aggregate demand curve is downward-sloping. Under fixed exchange rates, an increase in inflation above the foreign rate erodes external competitiveness and reduces demand for domestic goods. Under flexible exchange rates, an increase in the inflation rate relative to the central bank's inflation target prompts an increase in the interest rate. This in turn results in a nominal and real exchange appreciation with a contractionary effect on aggregate demand.

4 Only in the flexible rate regime can the monetary authority determine the long-run inflation rate. Under fixed exchange rates, some monetary independence is possible, but only by repeated devaluations or revaluations.

5 Under fixed exchange rates, fiscal policy can affect aggregate demand and output. The effects of a fiscal policy action are temporary, however. The change in spending or cut in taxes which leads to the shift in the *AD* curve cannot be sustained indefinitely. In the long run, the government's budget constraint prevents a permanently expansionary fiscal policy.

6 A fiscal expansion initially raises the output level at the cost of a higher rate of inflation. Over time, as underlying inflation rises and the unavoidable retrenchment of fiscal policy occurs, demand returns to trend output.

7 Under fixed exchange rates monetary policy is ineffective. This is also the case for fiscal policy under flexible exchange rates.

8 Under flexible exchange rates, a monetary policy expansion—the consequence of an increase in the central bank's target inflation—initially raises output and inflation. Over time, inflation continues to increase, ultimately sowing the seeds of the next recession, as the central bank is forced to raise interest rates and return output back to its trend growth path.

9 An adverse supply shock simultaneously lowers output and raises inflation. Demand management policies are ill-equipped to deal with a supply shock. They may cushion the fall in income at the cost of more inflation, or reduce the inflationary impact at the cost of a deeper fall in output and more unemployment.

10 Disinflation requires a permanent reduction in the target inflation rate when the exchange rate is floating or sticking to the peg under a fixed exchange rate regime. It can be costly in terms of lost output and above-equilibrium unemployment.

11 The faster underlying inflation adjusts, the lower the costs of disinflation. This calls for adopting credible institutions that can convince wage negotiators that the disinflation policy is 'serious'.

⚷ Key Concepts

- purchasing power parity (PPP)
- *LAD* line
- short-run versus long-run equilibrium

- aggregate demand curve
- demand shock, demand disturbance
- stagflation

- ◆ nominal interest rate, real interest rate
- ◆ Fisher principle/equation
- ◆ target/neutral interest rate
- ◆ disinflation

- ◆ output cost of disinflation
- ◆ hard pegs
- ◆ inflation-targeting strategy
- ◆ indexation

❓ Exercises

1 Use the *AD–AS* model to trace out the *short-run* effect under a fixed rate regime of: (1) a one-off increase in taxes; (2) one-off decrease in government spending; (3) a one-off decrease in animal spirits (Tobin's *q*). What are the long-run effects?

2 Use the *AS–AD* model to study the short-, medium-, and long-run effect of a permanent decrease in the inflation target of the central bank. Assume that underlying inflation in the current period is simply equal to inflation which is observed in the previous period. Contrast your answer with the alternative assumption that underlying inflation overshoots inflation in the previous period.

3 Consider the following numerical version of the *AS–AD* model:

AS: $\pi_t = \tilde{\pi}_t + 0.5(Y_t - 5000)/5000 + s$.

AD: $(Y_t - 5000)/5000 = 0.5(i_t - \pi_t)$

Taylor rule: $i_t = \bar{i} + 1.5(\pi_t - \bar{\pi}) + 0.2(Y_t - 5000)/5000$.

Neutral rate: $\bar{i} = r + \bar{\pi}$

Underlying inflation: $\tilde{\pi}_t = \pi_{t-1}$

Assume the real interest rate is equal to 2, the target rate of inflation is 3, and $s = 0$. Use a spreadsheet or other computer program to characterize the steady state as a sequence of values of inflation, output and interest rates which are stable. Then calculate the dynamic evolution of the economy in response to

(1) a permanent increase in the target inflation rate to 5.

(2) a permanent decrease in the target inflation rate to 2.

(3) a supply shock of s = 5 for one period.

(4) a supply shock of s = 5 for four periods.

4 Consider the *AD–AS* model where the economy is not in long-run equilibrium, in particular assume there is a negative output gap (that is, the economy is in a recession). Describe the adjustment under fixed exchange rates if there is no government intervention. Contrast your answer with that under flexible exchange rates.

5 Now consider an economy in a fixed exchange rate regime in which the output gap is positive—a booming economy—and domestic inflation exceeds foreign inflation. Describe the adjustment if there is no intervention.

6 If supply shocks predominate, what can you predict about the correlation between inflation and the output gap? If demand shocks are more important? Under which conditions would you expect to observe a Phillips curve?

7 Use the *AD–AS* and *IS–TR–BP* frameworks to study the short- and long-run effects of an increase in foreign inflation under a fixed exchange rate regime.

8 Under fixed exchange rates, use the *IS–TR–BP* and *AD–AS* models to analyse the effects of a combined tight fiscal policy and expansionary monetary policy.

9 Under flexible exchange rates, use the *IS–TR–BP* and *AD–AS* models to analyse the effects of an expansionary fiscal policy and tight monetary policy.

10 Trace the effects of a favourable supply shock, such as a sudden decline in oil prices using the *AS–AD* framework. Suppose the government wants to take advantage of this event to bring about a permanent decrease in inflation. Under which exchange rate regime is this possible, and how could the government achieve its goal?

11 A government wants to use monetary policy under a flexible exchange rate to keep actual GDP above its trend growth rate for ever. In the *AS–AD* diagram, show graphically the consequences of such a policy.

12 Assume that underlying inflation is entirely forward-looking and that expectations are rational. What are the effects of fiscal policy (under fixed exchange rates) and monetary policy (under flexible exchange rates) on output and inflation? Consider both cases of expansionary or restrictive policies.

13 Central banks that adopt the inflation-targeting strategy usually publish forecasts of future inflation, thus implicitly or explicitly signalling what they plan to do in the future. It is argued that being able to convince the public of their intentions greatly enhances the effectiveness of central bank actions. Use the *AD–AS* framework to explain why this might be the case.

14 Show under what condition does the Taylor rule (13.9) imply that an increase in inflation leads to a higher *ex post* real interest rate, defined as $i - \pi$. Is this a desirable feature of the rule? Why or why not?

➔ Essay Questions

1 'Expansionary demand policies are based on fooling people.' Comment.

2 Why does adding the supply side partly undermine the usefulness of demand management policies?

3 Why are supply-side policies more appealing than demand-side policies. What kind of policies can you imagine which might stimulate the supply side of the economy?

4 'Sluggish expectations are helpful when inflation is rising but troublesome when inflation is declining.' Evaluate this assertion and name possible policy implications.

5 Suppose you are in charge of monetary policy in a developing country and the price of primary commodities (food, oil) rises sharply, as it has in the past year. What will be the consequence of pursuing a flexible exchange rate regime with a fixed target rate of inflation? Are there disadvantages of following a fixed exchange rate regime?

Asset Markets

14

Every great crisis reveals the excessive speculations of many houses which no one before suspected, and which commonly indeed had not begun or had not carried very far those speculations, till they were tempted by the daily rise of price and the surrounding fever.

Walter Bagehot

History demonstrates that participants in financial markets are susceptible to waves of optimism. Excessive optimism sows the seeds of its own reversal in the form of imbalances that tend to grow over time.

Alan Greenspan

14.1 Overview

From Tobin's q to interest and exchange rates, we have encountered many prices which are determined in financial markets. Financial markets profoundly influence the macroeconomy. They affect wealth and spending, the cost of borrowing and investments, and the exchange rate, which lies at the heart of international trade and financial flows. Prices determined in financial markets share a number of unique features. They determine the value of **assets**—the various forms in which wealth is held. They are set in markets which are quite different from goods markets, not only because they are impersonal—transactions are almost never face to face—but also because they can move large sums of money at a moment's notice. We say that asset prices exhibit a high degree of volatility. They often appear driven by the whims of traders whose preoccupation is with very short-term gains, without much apparent concern for the impact of their actions. We often read and hear about speculators who seem to gamble in these markets, casino-style, make a lot of money and occasionally run the economy into the ground. We will examine this possibility, although the story is much more complex.

An especially distinctive feature of assets is that they are durable. They are not consumed, but stored for later use, and later is at the discretion of the owner. Their value is not in today's use, but in tomorrow's resale price. For this reason, they are driven entirely by the future. Almost by definition, the future is uncertain, so assets almost always represent the assumption of risk—the possibility of large or total loss.

In this chapter, we offer a simple, but unified treatment of asset prices and markets as regards their role in the macroeconomy. We start by describing asset markets and explaining some of their key features. They are big because they deal in stocks, not flows. They are fast-moving because profit opportunities are huge, but dissipate in seconds. They put a price tag on uncertainty—a special but unavoidable characteristic of every economy. We then look at the asset prices encountered in many of the earlier chapters: **bond** prices, interest rates, and stocks. We explore why markets sometimes embark on apparently senseless behaviour, producing successive phases of exuberance and bust. We will conclude that this aspect, while sometimes unproductive for the general economy, is a feature of market economies which should be regulated, but cannot be eliminated.

14.2 How Asset Markets Work

14.2.1 Unique Characteristics of Financial Markets

There are many asset markets—money markets, stock markets, bond markets, commodity markets, foreign exchange markets, derivative markets, and more—but they share a number of unique characteristics.

First, unlike goods and services which are bought for consumption and often perishable (fruits and vegetables don't last long, cars and computers become outdated, and services are consumed at the same time they are produced), financial assets are durable. This distinguishing characteristic, plus the fact that they can be held with negligible storage costs, are two reasons why they are a natural vehicle for saving for future consumption—just as Robinson Crusoe did in Chapters 7 and 8. They can be bought now and sold later, either when the time comes to use savings for consumption or when they are exchanged against other assets to cash in profit or avoid a loss.

Second, in contrast with markets which trade in *flows* of goods or services, financial asset markets deal in *stocks*. The volume which can be traded at any point in time can be completely divorced from the creation of new assets, reflecting instead decisions by all asset holders regarding their total holdings. Consider Table 14.1, which displays the total value of **shares** (sometimes called capitalization) listed on five large stock exchanges (New York Stock Exchange, London Stock Exchange, the Deutsche Börse, and Euronext which brings together Amsterdam, Brussels, Paris, and Lisbon) and the total value of trades during one month.[1] The last column reports the average volume of daily transactions during that month as a percentage of the corresponding market capitalization. On any given day, it is usually only a tiny fraction of existing assets that are bought and sold; the rest is simply held.

The paradox of asset markets is that, irrespective of currently trading volumes, the entire stock of tradable assets could be brought to market at once if the owners so desired. Indeed, while normal days are the rule, there can be hectic intervals when market participants become concerned, or even panic, and trading can be multiplied several times over the usual level. This explains the size and potential volatility of financial markets. In early 2012, the capitalization of the London Stock Exchange was about 184% of UK GDP, so it is easy to understand why turmoil in financial markets is bound to affect the economy.[2]

Third, financial markets are typically well-organized trading platforms for standardized assets that can handle large sudden volumes with ease. In earlier times, asset trading occurred in trading halls or exchanges. The action was dominated by shouting, gesticulating traders wading through seas of hastily scribbled papers. Then as now, asset markets were constructed as efficient conduits and processors of information. Today, most markets are computerized, and market participants are linked through telecommunication lines from terminal screens virtually anywhere in the world. The internet has created a single, global market in stocks and other financial instruments, with traders constantly in touch with each other. As Figure 14.1 shows, at any moment in time, 24 hours a day, a financial market is open somewhere in the world, and any individual in the

Table 14.1 Stock Market Capitalization and Trading, March 2011

	Total value of outstanding shares	Capitalization, as per cent of 2010 GDP	Monthly trading volume	Average daily trading/ total value
London	£2,669	184	£211	0.34%
New York	$14,811	101	$1,694	0.50%
Frankfurt	€1,081	43	€125	0.50%
Euronext	€2,265	56	€161	0.31%
Zurich	SFr.1,138	208	SFr.85	0.32%

Source: World Federation of Exchanges. The 'GDP' used to scale Euronext capitalization is the euro value GDP of the Netherlands, Belgium, France, and Portugal.

---

[1] In 2007, the New York Stock Exchange and Euronext merged. The new company NYSE-Euronext still maintains separate US and European trading platforms.

[2] At the time the 5th edition of this book was written (2008), the market capitalization of the London Stock exchange was a mere 125% of GDP.

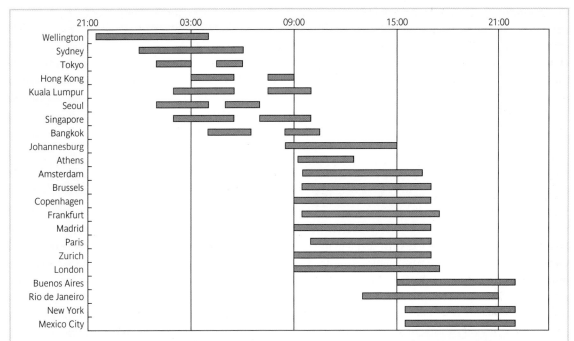

Fig. 14.1 Trading Hours of Stock Markets Around the World, Greenwich Mean Time
Stock markets are located around the world. As the world turns, some market somewhere is open, processing new information and pricing assets accordingly.
Source: Deutsche Börse.

world with access to a telephone or an internet connection may trade on it. This is perfect competition!

14.2.2 Implications: Inherent Potential Instability

These characteristics force us to modify the usual demand and supply analysis in two ways. First, net flows can be misleading. The annual net savings by households represents only the increment to their stock of wealth. Newly created assets—from newly printed money to new shares of a company—are indistinguishable from existing ones and, at any moment, trading can involve both new and old assets. This is why the market for assets is very different from the market for goods. In the goods market, it is demand for and supply of flows that must be balanced. In asset markets, prices move to clear the demand for and supply of the whole stock. Only a small part of the stock is traded because most owners keep what they have; their very inactivity is, in fact, a market decision.

Second, durability means that a key concern of market participants is the future value of each asset that they hold. After all, in contrast to non-durable goods that are promptly consumed, assets are acquired for keeps, not for immediate enjoyment. Two implications follow. First, asset markets are necessarily forward-looking. Market participant decisions are driven by their expectations of what can happen next—in five minutes or in five years. Then, since the future is unknown, financial markets and their participants must deal with constant uncertainty. Unsurprisingly, they are jittery because they know that they do not have complete information about the future. More often than not, they tend to pay close attention to what others are doing. While no one has all the information, it is very likely that someone out there does possess useful information. One of the greatest challenges of trading on the stock markets is inferring what other traders know—or think they know—and of that, what represents the truth. In a matter of minutes, changing expectations, or mere rumours, can radically alter demand and supply, swelling the volume of trade, or drying up markets. Prices, which equate demand and supply on a second-by-second basis, can therefore swing widely. This reasoning applies not just to strictly defined assets (stocks, bonds) but to any durable object that can be (relatively) easily stored and sold—artwork, commodities, or contracts for the future delivery of goods which may not yet exist (such as oil, electricity, wheat, or pork bellies). In fact, all these durable goods are traded on markets (oil in Rotterdam, wheat, cattle and orange juice in Chicago) which closely resemble those for financial assets.

14.3 Functions of Asset Markets

The intense activity associated with asset markets, combined with the often phenomenal profits of market participants, can easily create an impression that financial markets are giant casinos with little economic purpose. This would be a dangerous oversimplification. Asset markets serve essential economic functions, without which we would be significantly worse off for a number of reasons (some of which were already alluded to in Chapters 7 and 8). Markets for financial assets perform three essential economic functions. The first is to bring together borrowers and lenders. The second is to put a price on the future. The third is to create a market for risk by putting a price on uncertainty and enabling participants to control the risk they are exposed to. We now look at these functions in more detail.

14.3.1 Intermediation

Probably the most important function of asset markets, and more generally financial markets, is to provide a meeting place for millions of households and firms who want to shift resources intertemporally—either saving or borrowing—or intratemporally—from one form of asset or liability to another. But most individuals do not deal directly on asset markets. This is not only because the quantities they desire to trade are small, but also because transacting in asset markets requires a great deal of expertise. To avoid these problems, they can act indirectly through **financial intermediaries**. Financial intermediaries channel resources from savers to borrowers and investors.

Like money, financial intermediaries divorce the act of saving (deferred consumption) from the act of investment (the creation of physical productive capacity). As a result, dealings in asset markets tend to resemble wholesale markets involving professional traders, who accept and execute large orders on the basis of mutual trust and charge each other relatively small fees. On foreign exchange markets, an average trade is in the order of €5 million; converting this sum from pounds sterling to euros and back again involves a transaction cost of around 0.05% or about €2,500. Similar fees are charged for large transactions involving stocks or bonds. In return for a fee, intermediaries place orders for several smaller customers at once, or may even 'make a market' by maintaining a large inventory which they can sell from or add to. In this way, intermediaries themselves may become asset-holders.

14.3.2 The Price of Time

The price of the future—or the rewards for waiting—is the interest paid by borrowers, as explained in Chapter 7. By setting interest rates, financial markets price the future. Bonds, which are loan contracts, represent fixed payment streams in the future. The price of these payment streams defines the relevant interest rate. Shares, which represent a form of partial ownership of companies, promise dividend payments over the lifetime of the companies. We will see later how share prices are related to interest rates.

As financial markets bring together borrowers and lenders, they determine the price of time by setting interest rates. Market interest rates are the result of bringing together the demand for assets by lenders with the willingness of borrowers to trade repayment

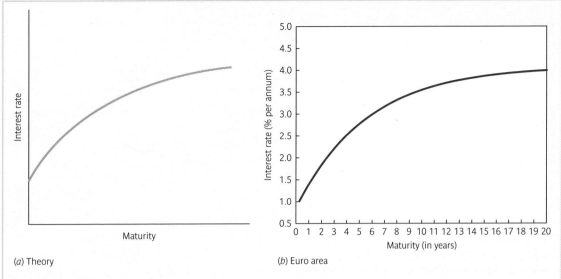

Fig. 14.2 Yield Curves

The yield curve relates interest rates, sometimes called yields, on assets of varying maturity, where the maturities are ranked on the horizontal axis. Panel (*a*) shows a theoretical yield curve: impatience by borrowers and lenders imply the interest rates rise with maturity. Panel (*b*) shows the yield curve observed on 11 May 2011 for high-quality government bonds in euros for maturities that range from 3 months to 20 years.

Source: European Central Bank.

later for cash now. In that sense, market interest rates are tightly linked to the overall impatience of borrowers and lenders.

In Chapter 9, we saw that the central bank determines the short-term nominal interest rate—usually for overnight loans, but sometimes for up to three months—by altering the supply of liquidity to the economy. At very short maturities,[3] the central bank has a monopoly of providing loans, so it can choose any interest rate that it wishes. Since it does so with macroeconomic objectives, very short maturities are unlikely to be related to the cost of time. How, then, can markets price the cost of waiting if the central bank sets the short-term rates?

For the most part, the demand and supply of assets reflect the preferences of borrowers and lenders at different time horizons. The link with the short term is captured by the **yield curve**, which shows how the interest rates vary by maturity. The left-hand chart in

Figure 14.2 shows a theoretical yield curve whose characteristic is that interest rates rise as the maturity increases. One reason is that total uncertainty of the investment often rises as the time horizon lengthens, an issue that is examined in Section 14.3.3. The other reason is the demand for flexibility, or liquidity. For the lender, a longer maturity means that it will take more time to recover the money; it makes sense to ask for a higher interest rate to compensate for being locked in. The borrower is willing to pay such a **maturity premium** because the funds will remain longer at their disposal. Quite naturally, the premium increases with the maturity, all other things being equal.

The right-hand side of Figure 14.2 shows an actual curve, dated 5 May 2011, for the government bond yields (interest rates) in the euro area. It corresponds to very safe bonds, those issued by governments with good reputations as borrowers.[4] The shape of the

---

[3] The maturity of an asset is the time remaining until it is repaid. For example, a bond that will be paid back in one year has a maturity of one year. A share, which will exist as long as the corresponding corporation operates, has no fixed maturity.

[4] Reputation here corresponds to the expectation that the government will indeed pay back its debt on time, according to the original terms of the debt contract, with interest. The yield curve depicted is for governments with the highest rating ('AAA').

Box 14.1 The Term Structure of Interest Rates[5]

Consider a long-term interest rate of L years' maturity. Interest rates are generally quoted in annualized form, i.e. the interest rate paid each year. If the annual interest rate on the long-term loan is i^L, the total return is $(1 + i^L)^L$, because the interest is compounded over L years. Suppose that investors know the one-year interest rate expected to prevail t years from now for sure and it is i_t^e, where the superscript e denotes an expectation, the return from a succession of L annual loans would be given by $(1 + i_1)(1 + i_2^e)...(1 + i_t^e)...(1 + i_L^e)$. The no-profit condition implies that these returns should be equal:

$$(1 + i^L)^L = (1 + i_1)(1 + i_2^e)...(1 + i_t^e)...(1 + i_L^e).$$

As a first approximation, this equality states that the long rate at time t, i_t^L, is an average of expected future short rates:

$$i_t^L = \frac{1}{L}\sum_{i=1}^{L} i_{t+i}^e$$

which is obtained by taking logarithms and using the approximation $\log(1 + x) = x$. In the more general and realistic case when future yields are not known:

$$i_t^L = \frac{1}{L}\sum_{i=1}^{L} i_{t+i}^e + \Psi_t^L$$

where Ψ_t^L denotes the compensation required by investors for additional risk involved in investing in the bond at maturity L (as explained in Section 14.3.4).

yield curve is interesting and reveals a lot about the opinions of investors trading in the market. We already noted that the very short-term interest rates are set by the central bank. Over the years to come, the central bank is likely to change these rates. These expected decisions affect the shape of the yield curve. This is because a two-year loan given today can be arranged in a number of ways: for example, a single loan of two years' maturity, two successive one-year loans 'rolled over' from one year, or a series of 24 one-month loans, etc. Because borrowers and lenders can choose any of these combinations, it stands to reason that they must be roughly comparable if not equivalent: they must impose the same cost to the borrower and the same reward to the lender. If this were not the case—let us suppose that a two-year loan carries a lower interest rate than two successive one-year loans—then no lender would be willing to lend for two years and no borrower would be willing to borrow twice for two successive years. In fact, clever financiers would borrow for two years, lend twice consecutively for one year and make a handsome profit. As many of them rush to take advantage of this opportunity, brisk demand for two-year loans drives the corresponding interest rate up as much as the rising supply of consecutive one-year

loans drives the corresponding interest rates down. In the end, the two strategies will indeed imply the same lending cost and the market will be in equilibrium.[6]

This example illustrates a basic rule of financial markets: obvious profit opportunities are quickly, if not immediately, eliminated by the action of market participants. We will encounter this **no-profit condition**, as it is called, at many places in this chapter. It implies that equivalent financial operations carry the same interest rate or bear the same rate of return. The reasoning applies to all maturities, and carries an implication: long-term interest rates can be seen as averages of the current and expected future short-term rates. Box 14.1 formally shows why this is the case.

The actual yield curve shown in Figure 14.2(b) differs from the theoretical one but not significantly. When the central bank is expected to keep its current

---

[5] This box is for mathematically minded readers.

[6] Naturally, the one-year loan rate at which the investor borrows after one year is unknown from the perspective of today, so the two options are not exactly equivalent. But it is reasonable to expect the two options to be comparable in expectation in any case. Box 14.1 provides more details when they are known with certainty.

short-term rate unchanged for the long term, the slope of the curve then only represents the maturity premium—and later we will see that it also includes the price of risk. But the financial markets certainly do not believe that the central bank will keep the interest rate constant. On 11 May 2011, the very short term rate—for loans over 3 months—bore an interest rate of 1%. Given that the same loan in April 2008 cost almost 3.9% it is unlikely that the financial markets will believe that the current 1% loan rate is a permanent state of affairs. If the central bank is expected to raise the short rate over the coming years, this would be reflected in an even steeper yield curve, as Box 14.1 would predict.

Suppose in contrast that the markets expected rates to fall to levels even lower than 1% and that for a long time—then the term structure of interest rates could be downward sloping. To observe a downward-sloping yield curve seems fairly implausible, until one considers very different economic times—for example in the 1970s and 1980s when short-term interest rates were abnormally high. In other words, while the maturity premium implies that the yield curve is upward-sloping, expectations of declining short-term rates imply that the yield curve is downward-sloping—such a curve is sometimes called 'inverted'. The outcome depends on the relative strengths of these two effects. In Figure 14.2(b) expectations of higher short-term rates reinforce the effect associated with the maturity and possibly risk premium.

14.3.3 Allocation of Risk

Assets are inherently risky because they are held for future sale. Borrowers can default—totally or partially—on bonds, and dividends depend on firms' profitability, and firms can even go bankrupt. Asset-holders generally look for ways to reduce their exposure to potential losses of wealth. This suggests an initial definition of risk: the potential of a wide spectrum of possible outcomes. Some investors are willing to accept some risk in exchange for higher expected returns, but to some degree only, and they wish to protect themselves from catastrophic events, such as a collapse of prices. Not all asset-holders are equally **risk averse**, and their horizons also differ.

This leads us to the second major function of financial markets: to price risk and allocate it to those who are most willing to bear it.

Just as it is possible to purchase insurance to protect against losses involving car accidents, fire, unemployment, and death, it is possible to use asset markets to insure against financial uncertainty. This is done through **diversification**, the holding of a mix of several different assets. Doing so dilutes the impact of any particular bad outcome by mixing a number of risky assets. Box 14.2 explains how diversification works in more detail. In fact, many financial firms offer diversification to their customers by proposing ready-made investment funds (called unit trusts in the United Kingdom), a mix of well-chosen risky assets. They can vary the riskiness of these portfolios and accommodate the different tastes of their customers. 'Funds of funds' have also been proposed to achieve further diversification.

14.3.4 The Price of Risk

Risk can be reduced, but cannot be fully eliminated. Someone must be willing to bear some risk. The way to induce people to bear risk is to compensate them for it. This compensation is called a **risk premium**. It means that the rate of return, or the total payouts of an asset divided by its price, increases with the riskiness of assets. Box 14.3 explains why the willingness to pay for various assets determines the risk premium and why.

Both borrowers and lenders benefit from the existence of financial markets. Taken in isolation, each investment is risky and would have to pay a high yield to attract savers. Financial intermediaries, banks, and other specialized institutions pool these individual risks by offering funds to savers. The borrowers pay lower risk premiums, the lenders bear less risk, and the intermediaries collect a fee. Because diversification tends to be more complete when more assets are involved, the best services tend to be offered by the major financial centres dealing in stocks of companies from all over the world. This is precisely why asset trading tends to concentrate in few places and also why worldwide electronic trading is growing so fast. High stock market trading volumes and concentration are the consequence of the endless search for diversification to the benefit of all,

Box 14.2 Risk Diversification

'Don't put all your eggs in one basket' is folk wisdom. The principle is remarkably simple: if you pool many risky outcomes, the result can be much less risky than any of the outcomes taken individually. Under some conditions, averaging mightily removes variability. To see how this is done, consider the following, simple example with five different assets.

Assets A and B are based on independent flips of a coin. In either case, 'heads' means receiving €100, 'tails' means receiving nothing. On average, if repeated many times, both A and B yield €50. We say that each has an *expected value* of €50.

Asset C mixes assets A and B, and is simply one-half of A plus one-half of B. The expected value of C is also €50.

Asset D also combines A and B in equal proportions, but now the returns to those underlying assets are now decided by a *single* coin flip: 'heads' means A pays €100 and B nothing, while 'tails' means A pays nothing and B delivers €100. By construction, D always pays €50.

Asset E is also based on a equal mix of A and B. Like D it is based on a single flip of a coin but now both yield €100 if the coin turns up 'heads' and both yield nothing if it is 'tails'. Its expected value is €50, since it yields €100 half of the time and €0 in the other half.

All five assets described have an expected return of €50, but they are very different as far as their *variability* is concerned. A and B pay €100 with a probability of 50% and nothing with the same probability. The returns from asset C are less variable. To see this, list the four possible outcomes:

A = heads & B = heads, which pays €100,

A = heads & B = tails and

A = tails & B = heads, either of which pays €50,

and A = tails & B = tails, which pays nothing.

Like assets A and B, asset C offers extreme returns of €100 or nothing, but each with only one chance in four; C further pays out €50 with a probability of 50% with A and B. Asset C is less risky because it diversifies the risks attached to A and B by combining them. Since the returns from A and B are decided by different flips of a coin, they are independent events. In the language of statistics, we say that they are uncorrelated.

Asset D offers even more diversification than C because A and B always move in opposite directions; their payoff is determined by the same coin toss. We say they are perfectly negatively correlated since it is always the case that either A or B pays €100 and the other pays nothing. In this case, diversification has completely eliminated risk. This is a special case of the general proposition that pooling assets is a way to reduce riskiness. This is what diversification is all about.

Asset E is equivalent to owning either asset A or asset B, which in terms of their payoffs are indistinguishable. A single flip of a coin determines that both A and B either yield €100 or nothing. This is a case of perfectly positive correlation. The composite asset E does not reduce risk at all. Perfectly positive correlation prevents risk diversification.

Diversification can reduce risk in investors' portfolios, but it cannot eliminate it (unless the risks are perfectly negatively correlated, which occurs extremely rarely). If much of the risk is macroeconomic (business cycles, policy actions), risk cannot be diversified away. Foreign assets, however, are likely to have different risk characteristics. This creates an incentive to pool markets across national borders, the key reason for the existence of globalized financial markets.

whether they are lenders or borrowers, and whether they are large or small.

The existence of a risk premium is another reason why the yield curve in Figure 14.2 tends to be upward-sloping. We saw in Section 14.3.2 that the maturity premium rises with maturity to reflect the impatience of both borrowers and lenders. Since lending is almost always risky, the interest rate also includes a risk premium. To the extent that, at least in normal times, uncertainty increases as the investment horizon extends deeper into the future, a lender is also likely to ask for a higher premium when they part with their money for a longer time. It follows that the risk premium should also rise with maturity.

Box 14.3 The Price of Risk

Return to the first example of Box 14.2. Investments A and B have the same expected value, €50. How much would you be willing to pay to acquire either investment? Most people are risk-averse, and they would rather get €50 for sure than buy a risky investment with the same expected value. (Those who don't care and would pay €50 are said to be risk neutral; risk lovers would pay even more than €50 for the thrill.) If you are willing to pay, say, €48 for A, the risk premium is €2 or 4% of the risk-free price. If total demand and supply of that asset are equated at €48, then the risk premium represents the market price of risk. Since B has the same characteristics, it should also be priced at €48.

What about investment C? It has the same expected value as A and B, but it is less risky. An investor would be willing to pay more for investment C than for either A or B. If the market price is, say, €49, the risk premium on the new asset is only €1 or 2%. This is how diversification is an efficient way of spreading the risks of individual assets in the market.

Now consider investment D of Box 14.2, when a single flip of a coin produces two investments A and B.

Since this composite investment is riskless, it should sell for €50, with no risk premium. This asset diversifies all the risk away, which benefits both the sellers and the buyers of investments A and B. The last investment E makes A and B perfectly positively correlated, there is no diversification at all. Composite asset E should sell for €48, with the same risk premium as for A and B.

Finally, for a more realistic example, suppose that you pay now, but the coin is flipped only in a year's time. Above and beyond the risky gamble, any investor will expect to receive interest for the time the money was tied up in the investment. Compensation for risk in this case can be expressed as a premium added to the risk-free interest rate available on, say, a government bond. Suppose that, as before, the 'investment' has an expected value of €50 and the market currently prices it at €46 *today*. Suppose, further, that the risk-free rate is 3%. Then the risk premium can then be computed as 5.7% (the total expected rate of return ((€50 − 46)/€46 = 0.08696 = 8.7%) minus the risk-free rate (3%)).

14.4 Asset Prices and Yields

So far, we have looked at assets as paying interest. Being constantly bought and sold, assets have prices attached to each of them. This section explains the important link between prices and yields.

14.4.1 Bonds

Much lending is carried out by banks for their customers. These loans, the banks' assets, are usually not traded, although Box 14.4 will show that this is increasingly the case. Other types of loan are undertaken by large borrowers—governments and large firms—that bypass banks and go directly to the financial markets. In that case, they take the form of bonds, i.e. marketable and tradable forms of debt by the borrower including a contractual schedule of

payments concerning both interest and the principal. Once issued, these bonds are traded, at a price that ultimately determines their **yield**, or rate of return on an asset based on the purchase price of that asset.

Buying a bond gives the holder the right to receive all the interest payments initially promised as well as repayment of the principal—the amount initially borrowed—when the bond reaches maturity. The no-profit condition implies that, at any moment of time, a bond's current price must represent the present value of all the payments to which the bond's owner is entitled. Since these payments will be spread over time, impatience—and risk when there is some—must be taken into account. This gives rise

Table 14.2 Bond Prices and Yields: Some Examples

Description of the payment stream	Price in euros given yield *i*	Yield given price *P*
A. One-year pure discount bond paying 1 euro	$1/(1+i)$	$1/P - 1$
B. Two-year pure discount paying 1 euro in 2nd year	$1/(1+i)^2$	$1/P^{1/2} - 1$
C. Ten-year discount bond paying 1 euro in 10th year	$1/(1+i)^{10}$	$1/P^{1/10} - 1$
D. Consol paying 1 euro per annum, forever	$1/i$	$1/P$

to **discounting**, an evaluation procedure discussed in detail in Chapter 7.

A few examples are presented in Table 14.2. We first look at how the price P depends on the yield i. Bond A is the simplest case of a so-called discount bond of one-year maturity with face value of €10,000, i.e. the bondholder will receive €10,000 in one year. An investor can either buy the bond at price P and receive €10,000 in one year or lend the same amount directly and receive in one year's time the principal P and interest iP (the interest rate i is applied to the total amount lent P), hence a total of $(1 + i)P$. Thus, in both cases, the investor initially spends P. In the case of purchasing the bond they will receive €10,000 in one year, and in the case of the loan they will receive $(1 + i)P$ in one year. The no-profit condition means that both investments should have the same valuation, i.e. the price P must be such that $(1 + i)P = $ €10,000. The price must therefore be $P = $ €10,000$/(1 + i)$. More generally, if V is the face or redemption value, the price of a safe one-year bond must be $P = V/(1 + i)$. This is a general expression of the principle of discounting first introduced in Chapter 7: the present value of a payment stream is simply the equivalent value which, when invested at rate i, produces that payment stream.

Table 14.2 shows a few other examples of more complicated bonds, involving longer maturities or periodic payments over the term of the bond (called coupons). The computations are more complicated too, of course. The last example D is the 'ultimate bond' or **consol**: it exists forever—its maturity is infinite. Such a bond is also called a **perpetuity**. The owner of the consol is entitled to a coupon C, forever; the principal will never be repaid. Someone who pays P for such a consol has the option of giving P to a borrower and asking indefinite payments that

correspond to the prevailing interest rate i, i.e. iP each year. The no-profit condition implies that the two loans be identical so we have $C = iP$. Thus $P = C/i$ must be the price of the consol.[7] We see that the price of a bond is directly related to the interest rate. Roughly, as the consol example shows, a higher interest rate means a lower bond price.

Investors who can buy a bond with face value V at price P naturally want to know what return they will get. All they need to do is to invert the relevant formula. This is done in the last column of Table 14.2. For example, a one-year bond with face value F that sells for price P implies a rate of return $i = (F/P) - 1$. Quite sensibly, the return or yield is larger, the lower is the purchase price relative to the face value.

14.4.2 Stocks

Shares in firms, or stocks as they are also called, are held by households or their intermediaries. For firms, it is an alternative way of raising money. Instead of borrowing, they 'sell a piece of themselves'. Lending to firms is already risky because firms can sometimes go bankrupt. Stocks are even riskier because, in contrast to bonds that regularly serve a predetermined interest, shareholders are paid according to profits and only after firms have covered their costs, including interest on bonds and loans.

---

[7] This result can be shown differently. Receiving C in one year's time is like bond A, so its value today is $C/(1 + i)$. Receiving C in two years' time is worth $C/(1 + i)^2$ today. More generally, receiving C in n years' time is worth $C/(1 + i)^n$ today. So the present discounted value of the consol is $P = C/(1 + i) + C/(1 + i)^2 + \cdots + C/(1 + i)^n + \cdots = C[1/(1 + i)][1 + 1/(1 + i) + \cdots + 1/(1 + i)^n + \cdots]$. The last term is an infinite sum which equals $(1 + i)/i$, so $P = C/i$ the result presented in the main text.

How are stocks valued? Once again, we make use of the no-profit condition. In contrast to what precedes, we will now reason in real terms because we wish to focus on the real value of shares. A share in a company gives rise to the payment of dividends, a portion of profits (in real terms). Let us denote by d_t the dividends paid at the end of period t. The alternative to buying a share is to hold a riskless bond with a real yield r, which we assume constant. The shareholder does not just receive dividends, however. The value of the share that they hold can increase or decrease, which means capital gains when the share price rises, or losses when the share price declines. If q_t is the real share price at the beginning of period t, the rate of return on the company share is the dividend yield, d_t/q_t, plus the anticipated capital gain, $(q_{t+1} - q_t)/q_t$ (a gain if $q_{t+1} > q_t$, a loss if $q_{t+1} < q_t$), valued as a proportion of the share value. For simplicity we will start by treating the future price q_{t+1} as known with certainty and abstract from risk. The no-profit condition implies that both assets have the same yield over period t:

(14.1)
$$r = d_t/q_t + (q_{t+1} - q_t)/q_t$$

yield on safe bond = $\underbrace{\text{dividend yield} + \text{capital gain}}_{\text{total return on shares}}$.

This condition can be transformed into

(14.2)
$$q_t = \frac{d_t + q_{t+1}}{1 + r}.$$

This is nothing but another application of the no-profit condition: today's stock price q_t is equal to the present discounted value of the dividend to be paid at the end of the period plus next period's price q_{t+1}. An important aspect of this result is that today's share price depends entirely on the future: future dividends and the future share price. As already noted in Section 14.2, expectations—q_{t+1} is not known today—of the future price drive today's stock price.

But this is not the end of the story. If q_t depends on q_{t+1}, then q_{t+1} must depend on q_{t+2} in exactly the same way. Of course, the same will apply to q_{t+2}, q_{t+3}, etc., endlessly. In the end, substituting (14.2) for itself in an endless process of telescopic recursion, we find

(14.3)
$$q_t = \sum_{i=0}^{\infty} \left(\frac{1}{1+r}\right)^{i+1} d_{t+i}$$

This formula says that the current price (in real terms) of a share is the present discounted value of future dividends, forever. It shows that the market values a company on the basis of what it is expected to earn, now and in the indefinite future.[8] It also explains why stock prices can rise suddenly when market expectations of future profits rise, e.g. when new technologies are developed. It can also abruptly decline if the markets take a dimmer view of the firm's profitability in the future.

We have noted that shares are very risky. In the previous reasoning, we did not take that aspect into account. Since a share is riskier than a safe asset, its rate of return will have to carry a risk premium. Assuming that this premium is constant, we need to modify (14.1) to state that the expected return on the share is equal to the safe interest rate r plus the risk premium, denoted by ψ:

(14.4)
$$r + \psi = \frac{d_t}{q_t} + \frac{q_{t+1} - q_t}{q_t}$$

Following the same reasoning as before, we find

(14.5)
$$q_t = \sum_{i=0}^{\infty} \left(\frac{1}{1+r+\psi}\right)^{i+1} d_{t+i}$$

We see that the risk premium, like the safe interest rate, *reduces* the share price. Quite logically, the riskier the firm is perceived to be, the lower will its share price be.[9]

14.4.3 More Sophisticated Assets

Bonds, shares, and bank loans are the basic products of financial markets. As you might expect, modern finance has developed a broad spectrum of financial products. As time goes by, these products become

---

[8] What is the relationship between this and Tobin's q used in Chapter 6? Tobin's q is the ratio of the share price (q here) to the replacement cost of installed capital.

[9] The risk premium resembles the value of a consol. This is not a coincidence. The risk premium acts as a permanent drag on the value of the share just as coupons are a permanent source of value for consol holders.

increasingly complex and, indeed, require the talents of sophisticated mathematicians, often referred to as 'quants' (for quantitative types) or even 'rocket scientists'.

These products strive to deal more efficiently with risk, through various means. One obvious approach is diversification, putting together many basic assets just as shown in Box 14.2. Indeed, most investors do not buy individual assets, but shares in **investment funds**, i.e. a collection of assets, assembled by specialized financial institutions. Some funds also offer guarantees such as minimum returns, protection of invested capital, etc. More generally financial institutions are in the business of **securitization**, that is creating new securities out of pools of existing 'underlying' assets, which can be anything that pays to its owners under certain conditions. Often these underlying assets are hard to sell or value individually. In the spirit of the asset C in Box 14.2, securitization creates new, and more marketable mixtures of underlying distinct assets, with the beneficial effect of averaging out or reducing risk to their owners.[10]

Derivatives are complex securities which derive their value from underlying real assets or goods, and which pay under certain circumstances. As such they represent bets on future prices or conditions. The simplest type of derivative is a futures contract, which involves the purchase of goods—such as grain or gold—to be delivered at some future date. Derivatives might also be based on the value of a stock or a stock price index, or allow the holder to sell back certain securities before maturity, or to buy them in the future at some guaranteed price. Traders can thus take positions in the evolution of the price of some underlying good or asset without ever having to take delivery of it.

Many derivatives resemble insurance policies. One type of popular and controversial security which has received much attention in recent years is the **credit default swap**, or CDS. A CDS is a type of derivative security which is based on a particular loan contract,

typically a bond issued by a government, a bank or a company. The CDS is issued by a bank, an insurance company, or a wealthy investor over a specified period of time. The purchaser of the CDS makes stipulated payments every period for the 'protection'. If during this period, the borrower specified in the CDS misses a payment on its debt or defaults—that is, if there is a 'credit event'—the issuer of the CDS is contractually obligated to pay the owner of the CDS a specified amount of money. In some contracts, the missed payment is paid; in others, the entire debt is assumed.

The CDS market has grown by leaps and bounds in the past decade, with outstanding volumes now well into the trillions of dollars. Although it may sound to some to be little different from a punt in a betting shop, the CDS market serves two important functions. First, it provides a tool for transferring risk. Important financial institutions such as banks, pension funds or insurance companies can purchase CDSs to reduce, or hedge, risk on bonds that they hold on their books (own outright). For example, banks holding government debt which looks increasingly risky can purchase a CDS which pays if the country should default. Naturally the risk does not disappear from the economy; in case of a credit event, the issuer of the CDS has assumed it. It must pay the owner of contract—effectively providing insurance against default. A responsible CDS issuer must to be willing to assume more risk, and to set aside money to cover such eventualities.

The second function of the CDS market is to put an explicit price on risk, quite simply the price of the CDS contract. As long as they are traded in competitive and transparent markets, the price should reflect the collective market assessment of the probability that the credit event will occur—high prices imply high default risk, low prices imply low risk. Later in Chapter 17 we will see how CDSs have been used to reveal how much markets mistrust government borrowers in the Eurozone.

Because these financial products can become quite complex, many investors do not fully understand their properties. Sometimes, even the financiers that issue or underwrite them fail to understand fully the risks they are taking. The global financial crisis of

---

[10] Box 14.3 discusses the securitization of housing loans, which is particularly widespread, but the practice has been applied to credit card, automotive and commercial debt.

2008–2009, which was characterized by the issuance of many new types of poorly understood securities, is a case in point. Some of these aspects of the crisis are discussed in Box 14.4.

 Box 14.4 **Mortgage Securitization and the US Financial Crisis of 2008 – 2009**

Traditionally, banks have lent lots of money to households so they can buy the flat or house they live in. These housing loans, called mortgages, were held by banks on their balance sheets and represent an important asset backing for demand deposits that are the largest part of the money supply. While still risky, these loans are 'secured' or guaranteed by the value of the house. If the borrower fails to honour their commitment, the bank takes control of the underlying real asset—a process called foreclosure—and sells it to recover its money.

Starting in the late 1990s, financial innovation in the USA began to allow banks to 'originate' loans for houses without ultimately holding them on their own books. Instead, originators could resell mortgages in bundles to larger financial institutions, and pocket a profit while unloading the risk. The practice of originating and reselling mortgages to large financial institutions is an example of securitization discussed in Section 14.3.2. It represented a drastic departure from traditional banking, which considered housing loans a special commitment to the local community and 'for the long haul'. From an economic point of view, ownership of the mortgage aligned the bank's own interests—in making a profit—with those of the economy as a whole—making good loans and avoiding bad ones.

In the brave new world of securitization, lenders who originate mortgage loans are in business only because larger financial institutions are willing to take these assets off their hands. This was hardly an incentive to act prudently. Many of the loans were of inferior quality.[11] Financial intermediaries sold the bundles of these inferior mortgages to other investors all around the world. This process called securitization is based on the principle of diversification: lending to many persons or many regions should be less risky than lending to a single person, or to a single region. If those mortgage-backed securities were in fact less risky than the simple sum of the individual underlying mortgages, they could fetch a higher value, as explained in Box 14.3. This explains why intermediaries could buy the mortgages at a higher price from the initial lending banks and yet make a profit by immediately reselling the securities.

With hindsight, most analysts now agree that these fancy securities were overvalued—simply because the value of underlying houses that stood behind them was driven by the US real estate boom and thus much more correlated than were they based on individual default risk. By the end of 2006, after many years of rapid growth, house prices started to decline in many parts of the USA. In addition, many sub-prime borrowers faced higher interest rates and realized that the value of their debt—their mortgages—now exceeded the value of their homes. They defaulted on their loans. Foreclosures led to more forced sales of homes in a market in which prices were already falling. Further declines in housing prices triggered more defaults, more foreclosures, and more sales. The mortgage-backed securities were guaranteed by houses whose prices were plummeting, so the value of the securities declined. Many of the world's largest and most prestigious banks lost hundreds of billions of dollars in securities which had high ratings from the industry's most sophisticated and reputed rating agencies. Perhaps due to hubris, perhaps due to ignorance, perhaps due to the hot potato syndrome, bankers were blinded to systematic, macroeconomic risk of the simplest sort—movements in house prices—so mortgaged-backed securities were in fact hardly diversified at all.

---

[11] These loans were called 'sub-prime' because loans were of worse than normal 'prime' quality. Just before the crisis, many loans were made to borrowers whose risk was worse than sub-prime—in banking circles these loans were known as 'NINJA' loans: no income, no job, or assets.

14.5 Information and Market Efficiency

Asset prices reflect the collective judgement of market participants—borrowers and lenders alike. This judgement, in turn, is based on all the information collected by market participants. The information concerns each single asset, its underlying value and future performance—how much it will pay under which circumstances, as in the examples of Box 14.2. It is a hallmark of properly functioning financial markets that participants are engaged in a never-ending search for profit opportunities, either for their customers or for their own accounts. Both the amount of money at stake and the speed at which information moves make it unlikely that opportunities not involving additional risk will be left unexploited for any significant period of time. This is the no-profit condition presented in Section 14.3.2. Markets which satisfy this condition—that publicly available information cannot earn consistently above-average returns—are said to be efficient. The **efficient market hypothesis** maintains that when markets are efficient, prices fully reflect all available information.[12] This observation carries a number of implications that we now examine.

14.5.1 Arbitrage

Arbitrage is an example of the no-profit condition in action. It involves financial trades that do not imply taking on additional risk.[13] It is customary to distinguish three types of arbitrage: (1) yield arbitrage, (2) spatial arbitrage, and (3) triangular arbitrage.

---

[12] The idea of market efficiency is related to the rational expectations hypothesis introduced in Chapter 7. Rational expectations assume that agents do not make systematic forecasting errors. Market efficiency applies this concept to markets and price-setting.

[13] In financial market jargon, this distinction is not always so clear. For example, traders who search for information on corporate takeovers in order to take a position in the stock 'in play' are sometimes called risk arbitrageurs. Technically, this is a contradiction in terms: if a takeover is called off, the 'risk arbitrageur' may be left holding a great deal of stock and may suffer a large loss.

Yield arbitrage concerns two assets which happen to offer different returns. Strictly speaking, it applies to riskless assets, like Treasury bills, but it is sometimes applied to risky assets which bear similar risk (like assets A and B in Box 14.2). Consider the example of two riskless government bonds which offer different rates of interest. Holders of the less attractive bond will sell it and buy instead the one with the superior yield. In fact, the entire stock of the less attractive bond could be put up for sale at once. As the higher-yielding bond becomes more expensive and the lower-yielding bond becomes cheaper, the implied yields converge (the link between yields and prices is explained in Section 14.4). Arbitrage prevents such pricing misalignment from occurring: yield arbitrage imposes identical returns for identical assets.

Spatial arbitrage concerns the same assets traded in different locations. For example, large commercial banks borrow from each other at the interbank interest rate. If the interbank rate in two cities were to diverge, enterprising banks present in both cities would immediately borrow in the cheaper market and lend in the dearer one. With high capital mobility and negligible risk differences, the yields should be virtually identical. This is indeed the case.

Triangular arbitrage applies mostly to foreign exchange markets and is possible when the relative prices of three—or more—currencies are not consistent with each other. If the euro costs one US dollar and one euro costs 8 Danish krone (DKR), then the DKR/\$ rate must be (DKR8/€)/(\$1/€) = 8 DKR/\$. Otherwise limitless profit would be possible by buying the euro where it is cheap and selling it where it is more expensive. Figure 14.3 displays this example.

14.5.2 The Bid–Ask Spread

The risk premium takes another interesting form. To carry out the various operations just described, investors 'go to the market'. There they need to find a counterpart, someone interested in exactly the same

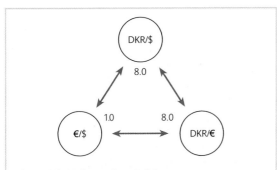

Fig. 14.3 Triangular Arbitrage

When two exchange rates among three currencies are known, the exchange rate between the remaining pair of currencies should be determined by triangular arbitrage. In the absence of transactions costs, any discrepancy between purchasing a currency directly and acquiring it using a third currency is eliminated.

trade, for the same amount, but in reverse. This is extremely unlikely, so the market would be useless were it not for the presence of **market makers**. Market makers are usually large financial institutions that have an interest in keeping the **market liquid** at all times, meaning that trades can be executed quickly and without large swings in price. They stand ready to satisfy any demand, buying or selling any amount—within generous limits—that appears on the market. Each market maker specializes in certain trades, e.g.

the euro–sterling exchange rate or bunds (the debt of the German Government). Of course, as they do so, they provide a service. They also take a risk. For example, the market maker needs to have enough on hand to execute the trade or be willing to purchase the amount needed at an even faster speed. Holding an inventory can be expensive, and value swings are born by the market maker. Quite naturally, the market maker needs to be compensated for both the service and the risk. This takes the form of a **bid–ask spread**.

The bid–ask spread is familiar to anyone who has travelled abroad and has bought foreign currency at an exchange booth. There, as on all foreign exchange markets, exchange rates are quoted in pairs: a lower 'bid' price for those who want to sell the foreign currency, and a higher 'ask' price for buyers. The difference is the market maker's profit—to the extent that trade occurs. The bid–ask spread in wholesale foreign exchange trading is currently quite small—roughly 0.2% on a five-million euro transaction between euros and sterling. Yet it can be much higher for currencies which are inherently risky, or are thinly traded. Box 14.4 gives a nice example of how a bid–ask spread evolved over time for the ostmark, the money of the German Democratic Republic, the communist German country which disappeared from the European map after German unification in 1990.

 Box 14.5 The Short-Lived Market for Ostmarks

Even before the Berlin Wall fell on 9 November 1989, trade in the ostmark (OM), the East German currency, was significant, and quotes for OM in West German deutschmarks were published daily in major West German newspapers. After this historic date, volume increased by an order of magnitude as East Germans tried to convert their savings into harder currency. It was unclear until March 1990 whether monetary unification would occur. This implied automatic conversion of OM currency and bank deposits into DM. The conversion rate of one DM for one OM applying to a part of East Germany's holdings and one for two for the rest—resulting in an average estimated by the Bundesbank at 1.8—was first officially suggested in March. It was then

formalized as part of the state treaty of monetary and economic union between the two German states in May 1990.

Considerable uncertainty characterized this period. Furthermore, before the Berlin Wall opened, the markets were relatively thin and trade was exclusively a Western business. This is reflected in the bid–ask spread which stood at more than 30% in early 1989, as seen in Figure 14.4. As the situation became clearer, trade moved to the streets of East and West Berlin and most banks entered the game. With the decision to establish a monetary union between West and East Germany by July 1990—in effect, replacing OMs with DMs—uncertainty declined, and so did the spread.

Fig. 14.4 Ostmark–DM Rate and Bid–Ask Spreads, August 1989–June 1990

As monetary union approached, the risk involved in holding ostmarks, the currency of the vanishing German Democratic Republic, declined. This is reflected in the bid–ask spread, which fell significantly.

Source: Burda and Gerlach (1993).

14.5.3 Implications of Market Efficiency

The efficient market hypothesis poses something of a paradox: if markets are efficient, we shouldn't have to work very hard to obtain information about those financial assets that are traded—because the market has done it for us already! The current price of bonds, stocks, foreign exchange, and other financial instruments should represent a consensus based on information available to traders in the market. If stock prices decline today, we do not really need to find out

why. The market has already processed the relevant information and drawn the correct implications. As a corollary, it is unlikely that anyone will outperform the market consistently.

Reports of investors systematically beating the markets are more likely a sign of good luck than much else. For every winner we hear about, there are as many losers, who have disappeared from the market either because they ran out of money or because they were sacked by their bosses. Using this line of argument, Nobel laureate Milton Friedman argued that speculation cannot be destabilizing. Those traders who are responsible for pushing asset prices away from their 'fundamental' prices, e.g. such as equation (14.3), are those who buy high and sell low. Prices ultimately return to their fundamental values, so these destabilizing traders should consistently lose money and ultimately exit the market.

14.6 Asset Markets and Macroeconomics

Financial markets are important for the macroeconomy. Ignoring them is a dangerous mistake, as the lead-up to the global financial crisis and the Great Recession has made us painfully aware. In this section we go into more detail of how financial markets affect macroeconomic outcomes.

14.6.1 Financial Markets and the Transmission Channel of Monetary Policy

In Chapter 10, monetary policy was shown to work through the interest rate. Higher rates, we explained, reduces spending by discouraging consumption and investment, and attract capital flows, appreciating the exchange rate and depressing net exports. Lower rates stimulate spending and investment, while causing the exchange rate to depreciate and improving the primary current account. This description is too simple, however. Central banks control the very short-term interest, but borrowing decisions of households and firms typically depend on longer-term interest rates, from maturity ranging from, say, 1 year to 10, 20, or more years. In addition, monetary policy has wide-ranging effects, many of which affect spending and all of which operate through financial markets. This is the issue of the **transmission channels of monetary policy**. There are four main channels of transmission: (1) the interest rate; (2) asset prices; (3) bank credit; and (4) the exchange rate. We now review the first three, leaving the fourth one for the next chapter.

The interest rate channel

We have already looked at the interest rate channel in Section 14.3.2 when we studied the yield curve. Because ordinary people and firms borrow at longer terms than the very short-term rate set by the central bank, monetary policy succeeds in affecting spending decisions to the extent that it moves the longer end of the yield curve. It does so by influencing market expectations of what the short-term interest rate will be in the future.

This is a fairly tricky exercise. Figure 14.5 displays the US yield curve at five points in time: January 2007, 2008, 2009, 2010, and 2011. This spans the period before, during, and after the financial crisis. In 2007 the yield curve was flat, with both short and long interest rates just under 5%. As the economy began to slow down and financial concerns built up during 2007, the Fed reduced—as the Taylor rule would predict—the federal funds rate sharply, leading to a drop in short-term interest rates by more than 150 basis points, which translated into a decline at the longer end, but much smaller. After the financial crisis hit in September 2008 with the failure of Lehman Brothers, the Fed drove its short-term rate to nearly zero and has kept it there. The long end of the yield curve initially declined (January 2009) but then moved up. By January 2010, the very long-term interest rates were back to where they were three years earlier. The Fed seems unable to influence rates of interest at maturities beyond 3–5 years. One interpretation is that the markets expect that things will return to normal within, say, 10 years. Yet, much of the influence of monetary policy in a fairly closed and large economy as the USA is exerted through interest rates of more than 3-year maturity. In effect, the Fed has run into the zero lower bound problem presented in Chapter 13; nominal interest rates cannot be reduced below zero. This is why the US central bank has experimented with 'nonconventional' methods of monetary policy, including large-scale

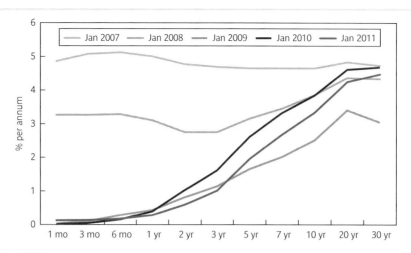

Fig. 14.5 US Yield Curves

Each curve displays the interest rate on high-grade assets (Treasury bonds) at various maturities ranging from the short term (here one month) to the long term (here 20 or 30 years). The successive yield curves from 2007 to 2011 show that monetary policy is not always able to achieve the desired interest rates at longer maturities, especially in periods of deep recession.

Source: Federal Reserve Board.

open market purchases of long-term Treasury debt, a clear effort at flattening the yield curve. Whether this effort is successful is a hotly debated issue.

This example illustrates an important aspect of monetary policy. The ability of a central bank to affect long-term interest rates—those that matter for monetary policy transmission—depends on its ability to convince the markets of its future actions. One reason long-term interest rates in the US have not fallen is because market participants are worried that future interest rates will rise—either due to an increase in inflation, increased money tightness associated with the recovery, or both. Trust and transparency also matter as a success factor for a central bank. This has led some central banks to first issue forecasts of inflation—to give an idea of what they might want to do—and, more recently, to even indicate what interest rates they anticipate to set. This new approach was first adopted by the Reserve Bank of New Zealand, then by the Bank of Norway, the Swedish Riksbank, and the Central Bank of Iceland. In 2011, the Fed itself has indicated that it intends to keep its short-term interest rate near zero for a very long time, at least through most of 2013.

The asset price channel

We have seen in Section 14.4 that the interest rate affects the market value of assets. For example, when the central bank raises the interest rate, stock and bond prices tend to decline, as do housing prices. This reduces private wealth. Households react by increasing their savings in order to restore their wealth to a desired level. This means less consumption. Similarly, declining stock prices lead firms to postpone share issues, thus depriving them from the means to carry out some of their investment projects.

The credit channel

Another possible way for monetary policy to affect the economy is via the availability of credit *independently of its cost*—since the cost of credit is the interest rate channel. As noted in Chapter 9, for regulatory and prudential reasons, commercial banks need to hold liquid assets in proportion to the credit that they grant. A tightening of monetary policy, for example, implies less liquid assets in the banking system and thus leads banks to reduce the credit that households and firms require to carry out spending.

The credit channel can also be narrowed significantly by the behaviour of banks among themselves. If banks become very cautious, they may stop lending their excess reserves to each other. This leads to less lending than would otherwise be forthcoming. This mechanism was important during the financial crisis and has proved problematic in Europe, as the sovereign debt crisis spread and banks began to mistrust each other regarding their exposure to countries with debt problems.

A common theme of these channels—and of the exchange rate channel as well—is that monetary policy works indirectly and that its impact is mediated by the financial markets. Importantly, because financial markets are entirely driven by expectations, changing the short-term interest rate is only the beginning of monetary policy. More important for central banks is the management of market expectations to move long-term rates and asset prices in a direction that supports their intentions. This is why central banks are very preoccupied with their communication strategy.[14]

14.6.2 Market Efficiency or Speculative Manias?

We have now seen that financial markets are crucial for two main reasons. First, they allow borrowers and lenders to achieve their aims at the best possible conditions. Since most investment spending is financed through borrowing—from banks, by issuing bonds and shares—a well-functioning financial market is crucial for economic growth. Second, and in addition, monetary policy works through the financial markets. A well-functioning financial market is essential for the conduct of monetary policy.

This is why it is important for financial markets to be efficient. The next question, then, is whether they really are. Some studies do turn up statistically measurable deviations from market efficiency. For example, if stock prices decline today, there is a tendency for them to revert over time to their previous values.

This could imply that markets overreact to news, and that the markets may not be fully efficient. Yet why doesn't anyone buy these 'oversold' assets when it is profitable to do so? This would restore the price to its fundamental value immediately. The answer may lie in risk aversion, the fact that too few traders are willing to take risky positions long enough for the expected reversion to correct prices to occur. In this case, the deviation from the fundamental value may be consistent with the absence of profit opportunities, *given that the risk involved in correcting it has its own price*: the expected 'profits' are insufficient to compensate for the riskiness of betting against the irrational price. Betting against the market involves considerable risk, and deviations from fundamental values can get worse before they get better.

How and why might asset prices deviate from their fundamental values? It is always tempting to write off asset markets as irrational and prone to fads. But there are often more intellectually satisfying accounts. One appeals to the coexistence of professional traders and inexperienced amateurs. This involves the phenomenon of rational speculative bubbles presented later.

Noise traders

In the first example, only a subset of traders are informed and have access to information about the true underlying value of assets. The remainder are **noise traders** who act on limited and 'noisy' information. These noise traders can be either irrational or simply misinformed, and they behave accordingly. The result is that they systematically lose money to the informed traders. Noise traders arrive continuously on the scene, with new ones replacing those who systematically lose and quit in disgust, so that there are always some of them around. Despite perfectly efficient and rational behaviour on the part of the professionals, stock prices may diverge from their fundamental value for long periods of time.

Bubbles

The second account of deviations from efficiency is the presence of **speculative bubbles**, persistent deviations of asset prices from their fundamental values. To see how bubbles may arise, consider the share valuation example from Section 14.4.2. Let us assume, for simplicity, that the real dividend of the stock is

---

[14] This was not always so. Back in the 1970s, many developed countries severely restricted the financial markets. Central banks were then able to control long-term interest rates directly and even the allocation of credit by commercial banks. This remains the case in many developing countries, in China for instance.

fixed forever at d. Ignoring the risk premium, some computation shows that the share value should be

(14.6)
$$\bar{q} = \sum_{i=0}^{\infty} \left(\frac{1}{1+r} \right)^{i+1} d = \frac{d}{r}.$$

This is called the fundamental value of the share. The puzzling observation is that an infinity of other paths of prices also satisfy the pricing relation (14.2). Consider the case where the stock price is q', higher than $\bar{q}$. This violates (14.6). The dividend is too low to justify such a price. But imagine now that market participants observe $q'_t > \bar{q}$, market participants and believe that the share price will increase next time to q'_{t+1}. Then, using (14.1), we can have

(14.7)
$$q'_t = \frac{d + q'_{t+1}}{1+r},$$

satisfied for the 'right' expected future price q'_{t+1}. Thus, it is possible for the share price to exceed its fundamental value—and violate the condition (14.6)—and yet to satisfy the pricing formula (14.2) from which the fundamental value is derived. This may look a little strange, but actually makes sense. The fundamental value (14.6) assumes that the price remains constant forever because the dividend is assumed constant forever. But, even with a constant dividend, the share price may be expected to rise tomorrow. In fact, if it rises to $q'_{t+1} = (1+r)q'_t - d_t$, that higher price today $q'_t > \bar{q}$ becomes justified as the no-profit condition is not violated—at least for that period. The expected capital gain offsets the 'too low' dividend d. Then, in period $t + 1$, the story will repeat itself. With $q'_{t+1} > \bar{q}$, we need q'_{t+2} to rise again above q'_{t+1}, and so on.

Thus an overvalued share (when its price exceeds its fundamental value) can be justified by subsequent further price increases, on and on. Any price today can thus be validated by its subsequent evolution. This means that, if the price is once above its fundamental value, it could be justified by further price increases. Figure 14.6 plots possible evolutions of the share price over time, for given r and d. Only one initial price does not 'explode', and that price is precisely the fundamental value.

The non-fundamental paths, which are exploding without any apparent fundamental justification, are

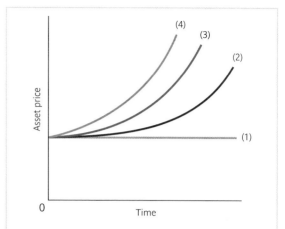

Fig. 14.6 Possible Stock Price Paths
Path (1) is the fundamental value of the asset. The price of the stock is equal to the present value of the dividend d, which is assumed constant, so it satisfies the arbitrage condition. Paths (2), (3), and (4) also satisfy the arbitrage condition, but are explosive bubbles.

self-fulfilling. Without violating any market efficiency condition, prices rise because they are *expected* to. The apparently inexorable growth of the share price is called a speculative bubble. It is a bubble because it keeps growing until it bursts, and speculative because its growth is due to the expectation of future capital gains. A bubble is rational in the sense that it will continue to grow as long as traders believe that the bubble will continue to grow, validate market expectations, and offer the 'normal' return.

There is a catch, however. History shows that bubbles do eventually burst. Why? Because if an asset price were to grow indefinitely, it would eventually exceed the world's wealth, and become too expensive for anyone. And if no one can afford it, its price must decline. In the late 1980s, Japanese real estate had become so expensive that the value of the Emperor's gardens were greater than the entire state of California! Sure enough, not long afterwards the bubble burst, and Tokyo, while expensive, no longer has streets paved with gold. Similarly, in the heat of the real estate bubble in the USA in 2006, house prices had risen to unprecedented heights, more than four times historic averages in some regions.

But the logic of a bubble is that its price must be expected to grow for a very long time, simply because

Box 14.6 **Tulipmania**[15]

History has given us several instances of price behaviour that looks like speculative bubbles. In Holland during the seventeenth century, the price of rare tulip bulbs rose by extraordinary rates within the space of a month, only to collapse thereafter.

The bubble involved tulip bulbs with non-negligible fundamental value because they were of exotic varieties. Yet they became exorbitantly expensive. Figure 14.7 displays the price of tulip bulbs in the first two months of 1637, when they increased by over 3,000%, and then collapsed sharply. For example, the price of the Switser variety is reported to have fallen to one-twentieth of its 2 January 1637 price. In one of the most authoritative accounts of the Tulipmania episode, Charles MacKay (1980) wrote:

The demand for tulips of a rare species increased so much in the year 1636, that regular markets for them were established on the Stock Exchange of Amsterdam, in Rotterdam, Harlem, Leyden, Alkmar, Hoorn, and other towns. Symptoms of gambling now became, for the first time, apparent. The stock-jobbers, ever on the alert for a new speculation, dealt largely in tulips, making use of all the means they so well knew how to employ, to cause fluctuations in prices. At first, as in all these gambling mania, confidence was at its height, and everybody gained. The tulip-jobbers speculated in the rise and fall of the tulip stocks, and made large profits by buying when prices fell, and selling out when they rose. Many individuals grew suddenly rich . . . nobles, citizens, farmers, mechanics, seamen, footmen, maidservants, even chimney-sweeps and old-clothes women, dabbled in tulips. People of all grades converted their property into cash, and invested it in flowers. Houses and lands were offered for sale at ruinously low prices, or assigned in payment of bargains made at the tulip mart. Foreigners became smitten with the same frenzy, and money poured into Holland from all directions. The prices of the necessaries of life rose again by degrees; houses and lands, horses and carriages, and luxuries of every sort, rose in value with them, and for some months Holland seemed the very antechamber of Pluto.[16]

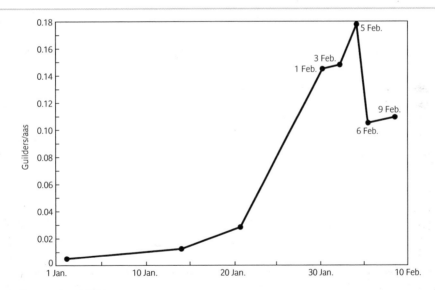

Fig. 14.7 **Tulipmania, 1637**

History has given us several instances of price behaviour that looks like speculative bubbles. In Holland during the seventeenth century, the price of rare tulip bulbs rose by extraordinary rates within the space of a month, only to collapse thereafter.

Source: Garber (1990).

---

[15] Part of this description is taken from Peter Garber's (1990) survey of the Tulipmania boom.

[16] Pluto was the ancient Greek god of wealth.

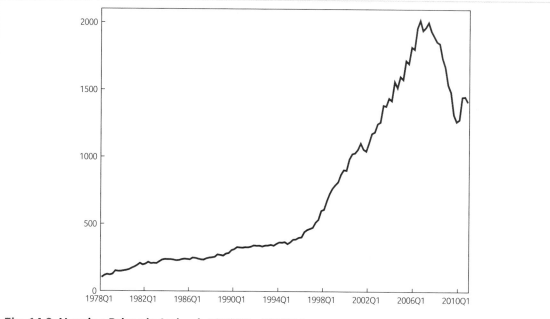

Fig. 14.8 Housing Prices in Ireland, 1978Q1 – 2010Q4

The index is set to be equal to 100 in 1978Q1. From then to 2007Q2, the index rose by roughly twenty-fold. The moderate pace quickened in the mid 1990s and reached a peak in 2007Q2.

Source: Housing Price Statistics, Bank for International Settlements.

no one really knows when the bubble will end and the asset price will return to its fundamental value. In fact, it *cannot* even be the case that the markets know that a bubble will end! Suppose there was a date, call it period *T*, when the bubble would end with certainty and the price simply stabilizes. If it does stabilize, forever, then it must be the case that the price is then at its fundamental value. Now imagine the period just before, *T* − 1. For the bubble to exist at *T* − 1, the price must be expected to rise. Since the price in *T* will be at its fundamental value, in *T* − 1 it must be below the fundamental value. This is a contradiction, however, with the earlier observation that the price of a bubble always lies *above* its fundamental. So the period just before stabilization of the price cannot be *below* the fundamental, it can only be *at* the fundamental. Working backwards, it is easy to see that the same reasoning applies all the way back to the present: there can be no bubble that is anticipated to stabilize! So a bubble can grow for a while, but rational traders know that it *must* end with a bang—literally 'burst'—and they must stand

ever ready to jump. Just as in a game of musical chairs, someone can't move fast enough, and is left standing.[17]

Bubbles may appear bizarre because they have all the features of economic rationality and market inefficiency, save for the end. Box 14.6 reviews a famous historical bubble-like episode that occurred in the seventeenth century in Holland and strangely concerned tulip bulbs. History offers a plethora of suspicious episodes: the run-up of the world's stock markets before the crashes of 1929, 1987, and 1989, the explosion of property prices in the UK, Japan, and Scandinavia in the late 1980s. Pretty much the same thing occurred in the US housing market bubble in 2007, as well as in Spain, the UK, and Ireland in the

---

[17] Usually the informed professionals get the seats first, which highlights an important link between noise trading and bubbles. As the great New York financier Bernard Baruch put it: 'When beggars and shoeshine boys, barbers and beauticians can tell you how to get rich it is time to remind yourself that there is no more dangerous illusion than the belief that one can get something for nothing.'

Fig. 14.9 The Rise and Fall of NASDAQ Stocks, 1996–2003

NASDAQ stands for the National Association of Securities Dealers Automated Quotation (system). It is the US stock exchange that specializes in high-technology companies, especially personal computers, telecommunication, and the internet. After more than quadrupling in value over the period 1997–2000, the NASDAQ index collapsed just as spectacularly by more than 60% from its all-time peak.

Source: <www.bigcharts.com>.

years that followed. Figure 14.8 displays an index of housing prices in Ireland. Prices rose by 360% between 1978 and 1995, and then picked up speed rising by another 450% until the peak in the second quarter of 2007. Since then, houses have on average lost a third of their peak values.

In each of these instances, market participants are convinced that the boom will continue. In each case, the bursting of the bubble is followed by serious economic dislocation. The information technology revo-

lution, which is transforming the way we collect information for both work and leisure is seen by many as a technological 'golden age'. This led to a breathtaking ascent of high-tech stock prices in the late 1990s, many of them representing shares in corporations that were not (yet?) turning out any profit at all. The sharp decline that followed in 2000–2001, is reminiscent of a bubble. Figure 14.9 shows that the NASDAQ index did not recover after the bust.

ⓘ Summary

1 Asset markets are special in several ways: (1) they concern stocks and not flows, (2) they deal with uncertainty, and (3) they are purely forward-looking.

These characteristics imply that financial markets are inherently volatile and, sometimes, even unstable.

2 By putting a price tag on the future and on risk, financial markets allow households and corporations to decide on saving and borrowing without having to gather the whole array of uncertain information that affects their own future. They allow those savers who are most willing to bear risk to do so, at minimum cost.

3 Financial assets are traded with ease by professional intermediaries in large, well-organized markets. While financial intermediaries can be thought of as intervening on financial markets on behalf of their customers, in fact most of the transactions correspond to trade among intermediaries.

4 Bond prices are inversely related to interest rates. The same tends to apply to stock prices, which are also driven by expected dividends. Beyond bonds and shares, there exist an ever-increasing variety of derivatives.

5 The no-profit condition implies that returns among similar assets—similar in terms of risk and maturity—must be equalized.

6 The no-profit condition is a characteristic of efficient financial markets. In the absence of risk-taking, it takes the form of arbitrage.

7 In the presence of uncertainty and undiversifiable risk, the no-profit condition implies that expected returns are equalized up to a risk premium which rewards risk-averse agents for bearing risk.

8 Markets are efficient when they gather all the available information and treat it to the point where prices reflect fully what is known and the risks attached to any single asset. The evidence on market efficiency—at least in its weak form, meaning that it is impossible to profit from publicly available information—is mostly favourable, in spite of phenomena such as speculative bubbles or noise trading.

9 The asset markets play a crucial role in transmitting monetary policy actions to the economy. The three channels are: (1) the interest rate channel, (2) the asset price channel, and (3) the bank credit channel.

10 The forward-looking nature of financial markets can lead to phenomena like rational bubbles which occur when asset prices continuously rise because they are expected by enough of the market to rise further. Bubbles eventually collapse, sometimes imposing large disturbances on the overall economy.

💿 Key Concepts

- assets
- financial intermediaries
- yield curve
- maturity premium
- risk aversion
- diversification
- risk premium
- discounting
- no-profit condition
- yield

- efficient market hypothesis
- arbitrage
- bonds, shares
- market maker
- market liquidity
- bid – ask spread
- investment funds
- derivatives
- securitization
- credit default swaps

- ◆ transmission channels of monetary policy
- ◆ consol, perpetuity
- ◆ noise traders
- ◆ speculative bubbles

❓ Exercises

1 Assets markets are considerably more volatile than goods markets. Asset markets balance stocks while goods markets balance flows. What is the link between these two observations?

2 Why is the bid–ask spread the common way of organizing pricing of financial assets? Give two interpretations of the bid–ask spread.

3 Consider three assets A, B, and C with uncertain outcomes (payoffs) depending on three possible future states of the world.

Payoffs in state 1: A: €100; B: €50; C: €150.

Payoffs in state 2: A: €0; B: €150; C: €100.

Payoffs in state 3: A: €200; B: €100; C: €50.

What mix or in which proportions could you purchase asset A, B, and C to diversify fully (eliminate) risk? Suppose Asset C is no longer available. How does your answer change? How would your answer change if asset C is no longer available and state 3 is no longer possible?

4 Assume that, in the previous exercise, each state has one chance in three to happen. What is the expected return of each of the three assets A, B, and C? If the risk premium is 2% of the expected return, what will be the prices of these assets?

5 The yield curve is said to be inverted when it is downward-sloping. How can you explain this occasional phenomenon?

6 It is often criticized that stock prices, which are often owned by wealthy individuals, rise in recessions. Can you give an explanation for this fact? (Hint: Think of the Taylor rule.)

7 Suppose that a central bank raises its interest rate and therefore reduces the money supply. In case No. 1, the central bank promises to do so temporarily, say for three months, and then revert to the present situation. In case No. 2, it promises to maintain its action for the indefinite future. What does this mean for its impact on the economy? In your answer, examine the situation of the three channels of transmission.

8 Consider the example of a speculative bubble in the text (Section 14.6.2). Now imagine that while, as before, there are two assets, investors no longer have perfect foresight. The private asset can be purchased at variable real price q_t and pays a fixed real dividend d. Now, however, there is a probability s that in the following period $q_{t+1} = 0$ (i.e. the bubble will burst), and a probability $(1 - s)$ that it can be sold at $q_{t+1} > 0$. Investors are risk neutral and equate the rate of return on the government 'safe' asset r with the expected rate of return on the private asset.

(a) Write down the arbitrage condition.

(b) Solve for the 'non-exploding' value of current q_t.

➔ Essay Questions

1 What are the conditions needed for a financial market to be efficient? Are they likely to be met in practice?

2 People have bad opinions of financial markets, seen as a source of illegitimate enrichment for already wealthy people. Discuss this view critically.

3 Financial derivatives have attracted a lot of attention recently, especially since the fiscal and financial crisis. Many advocate the abolition of such instruments. State arguments for and against such a position.

4 'Monetary policy operates through expectations.' What does this imply for central bank communication?

5 Most central banks follow a Taylor rule and strongly resist the idea that they should also react to asset price changes. Evaluate their position.

The Exchange Rate

15

Suppose a man climbs five feet up a sea wall, then climbs down 12 feet. Whether he drowns or not depends upon how high above sea-level he was when he started. The same

problem arises in deciding whether currencies are under- or over-valued.

The Economist, 26 August 1995

15.1 Overview

In one sense, the foreign exchange rate market is just another financial market, a platform for trading one currency against another one. Like other assets, currencies are durable and their value today depends on the values expected to prevail tomorrow. But this market receives special attention in our book, and does so for several reasons. First, the price of foreign currencies, the exchange rate, matters not just for financial transactions, but also for trade; in the short run it determines a country's external competitiveness (as we saw in Chapter 10). Second, monetary authorities often fix, or at least stabilize the exchange rate, and this influences the effectiveness of fiscal and monetary policy (as explained in Chapter 11). To that effect, they intervene on the foreign exchange market. Third, the dynamics of the exchange rate affects the interest rate, an aspect that had been ignored thus far. It is now time to ask more carefully how the exchange rate, both nominal and real, is determined when it is endogenous and not fixed by the monetary authorities.

We start with a description of foreign exchange markets. Present virtually all over the world in the form of computer terminals, they are dominated by one currency, the US dollar, with a growing role for the euro and a handful of lesser vehicle currencies. The amounts traded are staggeringly large. We then think again about the link between interest rates at home and abroad. The link was presented briefly in Chapter 11 but plays a crucial role in the entire textbook. It deserves more attention. In Section 15.2, we show how to make it more precise. The results are two interest rate parity conditions that directly involve the

exchange rate—current and anticipated. Section 15.4 then shows how the analysis presented in Chapter 11 can be modified to take account of this more precise view of international interest rate parity.

Interest rate parity conditions can explain what drives the nominal exchange rate—a volatile asset price subject to both short-run fluctuations and long-term swings. As in previous chapters, we start by separating the short and the long run. The short-run analysis, presented in Section 15.5, is similar to that of Chapter 14, treating the exchange rate as an asset price. Not surprisingly, it is solely driven by financial considerations and market expectations. In stark contrast, the long-run analysis developed in Section 15.6 focuses on the real side of the economy in the form of the national intertemporal budget constraint. The exchange rate is part of a long-run mechanism enabling national economies to repay their long-run obligations, if they have any, or encouraging more spending, should they have positive net international positions. This leads us to the concept of an equilibrium real exchange rate.

In summary, the long-run analysis explains the real exchange rate while the short-run analysis explains the nominal exchange. All that remains is to bridge the two outcomes—to show how the short run is consistent with the long run, which it must be. The result, presented in Section 15.7, is an internally consistent treatment of the exchange rate. The last section ties up some important loose ends involving the implications of principles developed in this chapter, including the regular occurrence of **currency crises**.

15.2 The Foreign Exchange Markets

15.2.1 Main Characteristics

The remarkable thing about the foreign exchange market is that it does not exist in a physical sense, and hasn't for decades. Instead, hundreds and thousands of traders sit in front of computer terminals around the world and round the clock and swap currencies with each other. Furthermore, they do not trade in banknotes, but rather in the liabilities of commercial banks—bank deposits. As financial intermediaries, they act on behalf of their customers, who need currencies for trade or financial transactions. Most often, they do it for their colleagues in the same financial institution, who buy and sell assets denominated in various currencies, or for their own trading accounts when they spot a fleeting deviation from the no-profit condition.

A characteristic of the exchange markets is that they are dominated by a few currencies, called **vehicle currencies**. Until recently, the US dollar was *the* vehicle currency, present in one side of nearly half of all transactions. Table 15.1 shows that its importance has receded somewhat. The euro is the second most important international currency. Other currencies play minor roles although the growing importance of emerging market economies is reflected in the shares of their currencies.

Like other asset markets, the foreign exchange market is designed for wholesale trades involving standardized transactions of large size. This feature reinforces the domination of the vehicle currency and means that most exchanges operate via the US dollar, as Table 15.2 shows. This means that, for instance, a trader who wants to change Polish zlotys into Indian rupees will first change the zlotys into dollars and then the dollars into rupees. This gives rise to triangular arbitrage, as explained in Section 15.2.3.

Table 15.1 Shares of Currencies in Foreign Exchange Market Transactions

	2001	2004	2007	2010
US dollar	44.9	44.0	42.8	42.4
Euro	19.0	18.7	18.5	19.5
Yen	11.8	10.4	8.6	9.6
Sterling	6.5	8.2	7.4	6.4
Australian dollar	2.2	3.0	3.3	3.8
Swiss franc	3.0	3.0	3.4	3.2
Emerging market currencies	3.7	3.9	5.4	6.5

Source: Bank for International Settlements (2011), <www.bis.org/publ/rpfxf10t.htm>

Table 15.2 Shares of Currency Pairs in Foreign Exchange Market Transactions

	2004	2007	2010
US dollar/euro	28	27	28
US dollar/yen	17	13	14
US dollar/sterling	13	12	9
US dollar/Australian dollar	6	6	6
US dollar/Swiss franc	4	5	4
US dollar/Canadian dollar	4	4	5
US dollar/Swedish krona	0	2	1
US dollar/other	13	15	11
Euro/yen	3	3	3
Euro/sterling	2	2	3
Euro/Swiss franc	2	2	2
Euro/other currencies	2	2	3
Other currency pairs	2	3	2

Source: Bank for International Settlements (2011), <www.bis.org/publ/rpfxf10t.htm>

Table 15.3 **Average Daily Foreign Exchange Transaction Volume (US$ billion)**

1992	1995	1998	2001	2004	2007	2010
820	1190	1490	1239	1934	3324	3981

Source: Bank for International Settlements (2011), <www.bis.org/publ/rpfxf10t.htm>

The volume of foreign exchange traded each day is breathtaking. Table 15.3 shows that total transactions on an average day in 2010 amounted to almost 4 *billion* (million million) US dollars. This *daily* turnover represents about one-quarter of *annual* GDP of the USA and more than four times that of the Netherlands. The growth of this market is even more dizzying: since 1992, turnover has increased by almost 400%—an annual compound growth rate of 7.8% per annum, compared with world GDP, which grew in US dollars since 1992 by only 2.6% annually.

15.2.2 Instruments

The basic deal involves immediately changing one currency for another one. The price at which this is done is called the **spot exchange rate**. An alternative is to agree now to do the transaction at some specified date in the future. The corresponding price is the **forward exchange rate**. Current forward contract maturities range from 'tomorrow' to one year. When two traders agree to a forward contract, they commit today to transact at a future date using an exchange rate which may be different from the prevailing spot rate when the future rolls around. The no-profit condition implies that traders will want to avoid consistently paying too much, and so forward and spot markets are intimately linked as shown in detail later. Another important type of deal is a **swap**, a formal agreement by one trader with another to a simultaneous spot and a forward transaction, one long (a purchase) and one short (a sale). An example would be a sale today of €5 million for dollars and a purchase agreed today for €5 million in three months' time. (The purpose of such transactions will be made clear shortly!). In 2007, swaps

represented more than half of all foreign exchange market transactions.

15.2.3 Triangular Arbitrage

Whether we like it or not, the world of foreign exchange trading is on the dollar standard. Because the US dollar is most frequently used on one side of foreign exchange transactions, direct exchange rates between most pairs of currencies are implicitly set by the dollar rate of each currency in the pair. The question is whether these cross rates are mutually consistent. The no-profit condition presented in Chapter 14 implies that this is indeed the case—up to the bid–ask spread, of course. Recall the example illustrated in Figure 14.3. If the exchange rate of the Danish krone (DKK) vis-à-vis the euro is 8—it takes 8 krone to buy 1 euro—and if one euro is worth $1, the krone–US dollar exchange rate must be (DKK 8/€)/($1/€) = 8 DKK/$.

This outcome is an example of triangular arbitrage presented in Chapter 14. Suppose the three exchange rates were not consistent with each other, e.g. that the DKK/$ exchange rate is 7 instead of 8. This means that the krone is overvalued vis-à-vis the dollar, or overvalued vis-à-vis the euro. A trader could immediately use, say, DKK7 million to acquire $1 million (ignoring the bid–ask margins, which would have to be subtracted as a 'transaction cost'), then sell the dollars into euros to acquire €1 million, which they would finally use to buy back DKK via the Euro/DKK rate (8 DKK/€) to obtain an instant profit of (8 − 7)/7 = 14.3%! Note that this operation entails minimum risk, and just a few mouse clicks at the terminal. Indeed, the trader could execute these orders simultaneously. A trading desk at a bank could even use borrowed funds—a so-called leveraged trade—so that the bank's own capital isn't even necessary. Understandably, it would be folly to pass up such a 'money pump', so dozens of other traders will join the fray, forcing the exchange rates to move virtually instantly: massive purchases of the dollar would lift its value, while massive sales of the euro would lead to a depreciation. Such pricing inconsistencies—even much smaller ones—would be self-eliminating, because they offer such large profits.

15.3 The Interest Parity Conditions

In Chapter 11, we noted that full capital mobility implies that domestic and foreign returns must be aligned. This is yet another application of the no-profit condition presented in Chapter 14. We called i the interest rate on domestic bonds and i^* the 'return' on foreign bonds, stressing that it was evaluated in the domestic currency. We now look at what this means in more detail. This will lead to two versions of the condition: (1) covered interest parity, an example of riskless yield arbitrage, and (2) uncovered interest parity, which explicitly accounts for risk.

15.3.1 Covered Interest Rate Parity

The **covered interest rate parity (CIRP)** condition is the result of arbitrage between domestic and foreign currency returns in the absence of risk-taking. Consider the following example. An investor based in the Netherlands can obtain an annual rate of interest i on Dutch government bonds issued in euros and i^* on equally British Treasury bills issued in pounds. Both investments are of very low, and comparable risk, and have a maturity of one year. Yet they are not exactly equivalent because the value of the sterling return in terms of euro may change over the investment period, thereby altering the total return measured in euro for the sterling-denominated investment. Let the sterling price of one euro at the beginning of the year be S_t. (At the end of December 2011, 1 euro cost about 0.83 UK pounds.) This is the spot exchange rate. Selling one euro at the beginning of the year, a Dutch investor would obtain S_t pounds that she can invest in the UK bond to receive $(1 + i^*)S_t$ at the end of the year. This is a completely certain return in pounds sterling, since both the interest i^* and exchange rate S_t are known at the beginning of the year.

When comparing the two investments—the Dutch bond versus the UK bond—the investor will naturally want to convert back into euros the pounds that she earned. The hitch is that she faces foreign exchange rate risk: the exchange rate that will prevail at the end of the year is unknown at the beginning of the year. Financial markets offer the possibility of eliminating the risk by signing a forward contract at the beginning of the year to sell the total value of her end-of-period investment, $(1 + i^*)S_t$ pounds, for a certain euro exchange rate today. The corresponding forward exchange rate, denoted by F_t, is known and agreed upon at the beginning of the year. Thus the investor can be certain that for every pound invested this way, she will receive $(1 + i^*)S_t/F_t$ euros at the end of the year. Because the forward contract eliminates all exchange risk, the foreign investment is said to be **covered** or **hedged**.

For a Dutch investor, the benchmark for judging the attractiveness of the UK bond investment is a Dutch government bond, which yields $(1 + i)$ for every euro invested at the end of the year with no exchange risk. Arbitrage guarantees that the two returns must be equal. The result is the covered interest rate parity (CIRP) condition, which can be formally written as

(15.1) $$(1 + i) = (1 + i^*)S_t/F_t.$$

A useful approximation of the CIRP condition can be found by arguing a bit more loosely.[1] Let the interest rate on Dutch bonds be $i = 3\%$ and for UK Treasury bonds $i^* = 4\%$. Obviously, the UK bills look more attractive, but the investor is no fool. She knows that the 4% are earned in pounds, so she consults the financial page of the newspaper and looks up the forward exchange rate of the pound in terms of euros. Assume that it is equal to the spot rate so that $F_t = S_t$. Then pounds and euros are 'the same' and indeed the pound investment is much more attractive. In fact, it violates the no-profit condition. For the condition to be satisfied, the higher interest earned on UK bills must be offset somehow.

---

[1] Using straightforward mathematics, take logs of both sides of (15.1) to obtain $\log(1 + i) = \log(1 + i^*) - \log(F_t/S_t)$ and recall that as a first approximation: $\log(1 + x) \approx x$. As a result, we can write $\log(1 + i) \approx i$, $\log(1 + i^*) \approx i^*$, and $\log(F/S) = \log(1 + (F - S)/S) \approx (F - S)/S$.

Suppose the forward value of the pound is less than its spot value. This means that the pounds available at the end of the year will be cheaper in terms of euros. This **forward discount** implies a **capital loss** for our investor. For example, if the loss is of 3%, the return from the pound investment will be 4% in interest rate less the 3% capital loss, thus offering a total return of 1% when evaluated in euros. This is less than the 3% offered in euros by the Dutch bond. This, too, is incompatible with the no-profit condition. There might seem to be no profit here, just a loss. Of course, myriads of British investors will have seen that investing in Dutch bonds is more profitable than investing in UK Treasury bills. Given the interest rates, the no-profit condition is satisfied when the capital loss on the UK investment implied by the forward rate exactly offsets the difference in interest rates, i.e. when it is exactly 1%.

More generally, the Dutch investor compares the domestic interest rate i on one hand, and the return on the foreign investment, on the other hand. The return on the foreign investment brings an interest in pounds of i^*, but it must be converted back into euros. If the forward value of the pound in euros is less than its spot value—the pound is at a discount vis-à-vis the euro—our investor suffers a capital loss: her pounds one year ahead are worth less than today. Equivalently, the euro is at a **forward premium** vis-à-vis the pound. Measured as the interest rate in percentage terms, the forward premium of the euro is $(F_t - S_t)/S_t$. Arbitrage requires that both investment strategies yield the same return:

$$(15.2) \qquad i \quad = \quad i^* \quad - \quad \frac{F_t - S_t}{S_t}$$

| interest rate the Netherlands | $=$ | interest rate in the UK | $-$ | forward premium. |

A positive premium means that the forward value of the euro in terms of pounds is higher than its spot value, i.e. that the euro is 'stronger' forward than spot. In that case, the euro interest rate i can be lower than the sterling interest rate i^* and, yet, the two investment strategies bring equal returns.[2]

---

[2] The WebAppendix further develops the concept of the forward premium.

15.3.2 Uncovered Interest Rate Parity

Instead of engaging in a forward contract, our investor can buy sterling at spot rate S_t, invest in UK bills for one year, and wait until the end of the year to buy back euros at the then prevailing spot exchange rate S_{t+1}. As explained before, this investment strategy is risky because no one knows at the beginning of the year what the exchange rate will be by year's end. What appeared to be a good deal may turn out disappointing if the euro appreciates vis-à-vis sterling, leaving the investor with fewer pounds than expected. Of course, the euro can depreciate unexpectedly, and the deal will turn out to be terrific. Leaving the foreign investment **open**, or **uncovered**, or **unhedged**, the investor takes a risk, and this will involve a risk premium, as predicted in Chapter 14.

To examine the new situation, we start by assuming that the investors are risk neutral, meaning that they do not worry about risk. Then the risk premium is zero. The strategy is the same as before, except that the pound investment will not be sold at the end of the year using the forward rate F_t agreed upon earlier, but at the then-prevailing spot exchange rate S_{t+1}. Going through the same reasoning, the expected return in euros from one euro invested in pounds is $(1 + i^*)S_t/S^e_{t+1}$, is the end-of-year exchange rate as expected at the beginning of the year. A one-year investment in euros still yields $(1 + i)$. The no-profit condition for a risk-neutral investor implies that both returns are expected to be equal. This gives the **uncovered interest rate parity (UIRP)** condition, which can be written formally as

$$(15.3) \qquad 1 + i \quad = \quad (1 + i^*)S_t/S^e_{t+1}$$

| euro return from investment in euros | $=$ | expected euro return from investment in pounds, |

which can be approximated as

$$(15.4) \qquad i \quad = \quad i^* \quad - \quad \frac{S^e_{t+1} - S_t}{S_t}$$

| interest rate in euros | $=$ | interest rate in pounds | $-$ | expected appreciation of euro vis-à-vis pound. |

The UIRP asserts that rates of return are equalized across countries once expected exchange rate changes are taken into account. On the left-hand side of (15.4) we have the one-year euro interest rate; on the right-hand side we have the pound interest rate less the expected capital gain or loss from changes in the sterling–euro exchange rate, expressed in percentage terms, for the same one-year maturity. Expectations cannot be observed directly, but the UIRP provides an implicit measure of what the market expects. If interest rates in the euro area are lower than in the UK ($i < i^*$), then the euro must be expected to appreciate, and the expected rate appreciation of the euro is given by the difference in observed interest rates: $(S_{t+1}^e - S_t)/S_t = i^* - i > 0$.

To be indifferent between euro-denominated assets with a lower interest rate than pound-denominated assets, investors must be compensated by an expected capital gain. If euro rates are higher, the UIRP implies that sterling is expected to appreciate vis-à-vis the euro.

15.3.3 Risk Premia

Empirically, the UIRP does not hold most of the time. The interest rate spread between, for example, the euro and the pound does not predict future movements in the exchange rate very well. But this shouldn't be too surprising. Expectations of a depreciation or appreciation would explain the interest rate spread only if investors are risk neutral. If investors instead are risk averse, the UIRP need not hold at all. Risk aversion also plays an important role in connecting interest rates and exchange rates internationally.

The uncovered interest parity condition can be modified to accommodate risk aversion. Our Dutch saver has the choice between remaining safely invested in euro-denominated assets or assuming the risk associated with British assets, i.e. assets denominated in the UK currency.[3] The no-profit condition implies that both investment strategies must be equally desirable, but the British investment must also include a premium that makes up for the risk of choosing foreign-currency assets (from the Dutch investor's perspective, there is a risk of loss when

converting to the home currency). If ψ_t represents the risk premium, the no-profit condition requires

$$(15.5) \qquad i^* - \frac{S_{t+1}^e - S_t}{S_t} \quad = \quad i \quad + \quad \psi_t$$

$$\underset{\substack{\text{euro-return} \\ \text{from investment} \\ \text{in pounds}}}{} = \underset{\substack{\text{euro-return} \\ \text{from investment} \\ \text{in euros}}}{} + \underset{\substack{\text{risk} \\ \text{premium.}}}{}$$

Turning things around, we can *define* the risk premium as the deviation from the uncovered interest rate parity condition, which can vary over time:

$$(15.6) \qquad \psi_t \quad = \quad (i^* - i) \quad - \quad \frac{S_{t+1}^e - S_t}{S_t}$$

$$\underset{\substack{\text{risk} \\ \text{premium}}}{} = \underset{\substack{\text{interest} \\ \text{differential}}}{} - \underset{\substack{\text{expected} \\ \text{appreciation.}}}{}$$

We looked at the situation from the point of view of a Dutch investor who seeks to be compensated for the risk of holding pound-denominated assets. At the same time, British investors will hold euro-denominated assets. They face the same type of exchange risk, but in the reverse direction. All things being equal, they too would require a premium on euro-denominated assets, i.e. a negative ψ. So, euro area-based investors want a positive risk premium, UK investors want it negative. What is the end result? As always, the answer is given by the market. In the end, the risk premium will be such that it exactly balances all these demands and supplies from the UK, euro area, and elsewhere. As these demands and supplies vary, so does the risk premium. In fact, this is known to be volatile and usually small because for any UK investor taking the action described, we are likely to find a euro area-based investor doing the same.

Clearly, the risk premium is a complicated phenomenon whose full treatment is beyond the scope of this textbook.[4] All we need to understand is that the existence of a risk premium ψ_t (which can be positive or negative) means that we should not expect the uncovered parity condition to hold exactly. It will be true up to a—generally volatile—risk premium.

---

[3] The payoff is in pound sterling is risky because the investor lives in a region which does not use the pound as legal tender, so that exchange rate risk is equivalent to nominal price risk, which means consumption risk. For the investor residing in the UK, a euro investment would be risky for the same reason.

[4] Finance theory (the Capital Asset Pricing Model or CAPM) states that in equilibrium, the risk premium is determined by the correlation between the asset's return and the return from the world portfolio.

Box 15.1 **The Real Interest Rate Parity Condition**

This real interest parity condition follows from the UIRP condition, e.g. in the form of (15.4). Rearranged, this means that the interest rate differential is equal to the expected exchange rate appreciation of the domestic currency. But we saw in Chapter 6 that relative purchasing power parity (PPP) equates the inflation differential to the rate of appreciation of the currency in the medium to long term:

(15.7) $\pi_{t+1}^{*} - \pi_{t+1} = (S_{t+1} - S_{t})/S_{t}.$

If forecasts of inflation at home π_{t+1}^{e} and abroad π_{t+1}^{*e} are consistent with PPP, the definition of the real inter-

est rate $r_t = i - \pi_{t+1}^{e}$ and $r_t^{*} = i^{*} - \pi_{t+1}^{*e}$ along with UIRP (15.4) and relative PPP (15.7) imply

(15.8) $r_t = r_t^{*}.$

This relationship is called the **international Fisher equation**. Based on relative PPP, it is a proposition for the medium to long run. As such, it is a useful benchmark for evaluating long-term foreign investment strategies, as it implies that the real rate of interest should be largely the same in all countries and is independent of the evolution of exchange rates.

15.3.4 Real Interest Rate Arbitrage in the Long Run

The UIRP conditions, with and without a risk premium, link nominal interest rates at home and abroad and embody the tight linkages implied by international financial integration. Does the arbitrage argument extend to the *real* interest rate, which is decisive for intertemporal decisions? Intuitively, one might expect an arbitrage opportu-

nity to arise if real interest rates—with similar risk characteristics—differed significantly across countries. As shown in Box 15.1, it turns out that the purchasing power parity condition (PPP) does imply that real interest rates at home and abroad will be equal. While the nominal interest parity condition holds in the short run, PPP only holds in the long run and, therefore, so does the real interest rate parity condition.[5]

15.4 Exchange Rate Determination in the Short Run

15.4.1 The Exchange Rate as an Asset Price

Panel (*a*) of Figure 15.1 presents day-to-day changes of the nominal €/£ exchange rate during 2010. Sharp changes are often followed by movements of similar magnitude in the opposite direction. The variability of nominal exchange rates is often remarkably high, with daily changes of almost ±1% per day commonplace. (A daily change of 1% corresponds to an annual compounded return of more than 3,000%!) As we saw in Chapter 14, this pattern is typical of asset price

movements. In the short run, exchange rates are hard to distinguish from other asset prices. They are forward-looking, driven by market expectations of future values.

On the other hand, longer-term fluctuations seem of a different nature. Panel (*b*) of Figure 15.1 shows quarterly changes of the average exchange rate

---

[5] We discuss purchasing power parity in Chapter 6. The relative version is employed here. The Fisher equation, which relates real and nominal interest rates explicitly, was introduced in Chapter 13.

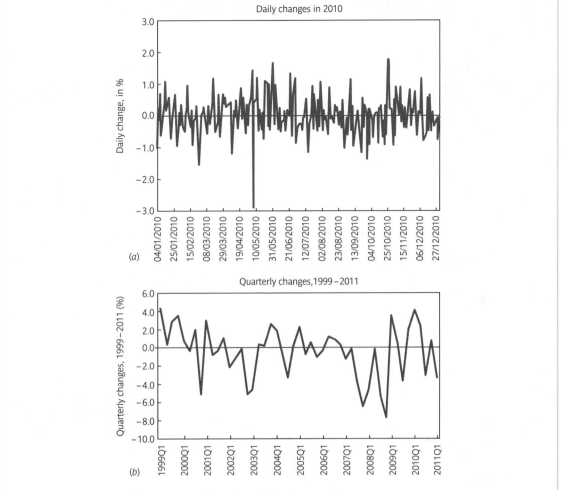

Fig. 15.1 Changes of the Euro/Sterling Pound Exchange Rate

Day-to-day variability of the nominal exchange rate is considerable. Sharp changes in one direction are frequently undone on the following day. In quarterly data, more systematic, and even larger movements become evident as noisy movements are averaged away.

Source: European Central Bank.

since the introduction of the euro in 1999. The movements are larger than in the day-to-day case, but there are fewer changes which are abruptly reversed. Annual exchange rate changes are even less volatile. In Chapter 6 we saw that the real exchange rate is the relative price of domestic and foreign goods. We also have learned in our analysis of macroeconomic fluctuations that prices tend to be sticky. This observation suggests that, in the long run, the exchange rate should look rather like the relative price of goods than the price of an asset. It

should be governed by more than the simple logic of financial markets discussed in Chapter 14 and in Section 15.3.

The exchange rate is a ubiquitous economic variable which has two distinct faces: it is an asset price, but is also a relative price of goods. The economist Michael Mussa recognized this fact in the first few years after the global system of fixed exchange rates collapsed in the 1970s and exchange rates were determined by market forces for the first time. His prescient observations, which are still relevant today,

Box 15.2 **Mussa's Stylized Facts and the Asset Behaviour of Exchange Rates**

In 1979, Michael Mussa, professor at the University of Chicago at the time, assessed the first half-decade of floating exchange rates after the end of the Bretton Woods system.[6] His observations, which remain true today, can be summarized in the following stylized facts:

1. On a daily basis, changes in floating foreign exchange rates are largely unpredictable.

2. On a month-to-month basis, over 90% of exchange rate movements are unexpected, and less than 10% are predictable.

3. Countries with high inflation rates have depreciating currencies, and over the long run the rate of depreciation of the exchange rate between two countries is approximately equal to the difference in national inflation rates.

4. Countries with rapidly expanding money supplies tend to have depreciating exchange rates vis-à-vis

countries with slowly expanding money supplies. Countries with rapidly expanding money demands tend to have appreciating exchange rates vis-à-vis countries with slowly expanding money demands.

5. In the longer run, the excess of domestic over foreign interest rates is roughly equal to the expected rate of appreciation of the foreign currency. On a day-to-day basis, however, the relationship is more tenuous.

6. Actual changes in the spot exchange rate will tend to overshoot any smoothly adjusting measure of the equilibrium real exchange rate.

7. The correlation between month-to-month changes in exchange rates and monthly trade balances is low. On the other hand, in the longer run, countries with persistent trade deficits tend to have depreciating currencies, whereas those with trade surpluses tend to have appreciating currencies.

are summarized in Box 15.2. The exchange rate is so central to the way the macroeconomy functions—it acts as a bridge between the nominal and real sides of the economy. Different patterns over the short and the long run provide the key that we need to understand this bridge. In this section, we look at the exchange rate as a relative asset price, focusing on the short run. Later, in Section 15.6, we think about the exchange rate as the relative price of goods, focusing instead on the long run, as we did with the economy in previous chapters. As we do so, we will see how these two views are consistent with each other.

15.4.2 Implications of the Interest Rate Parity Condition

Thinking of the exchange rate as an asset price leads us back to the interest rate parity conditions. Its volatility suggests that its movements are largely driven by market expectations of the future. Indeed, exchange markets are continuously absorbing and assessing news regarding political conditions,

[6] We discuss the Bretton Woods system in more detail in Chapter 19. For the moment it is sufficient to know that exchange rates during this period (1946–1971) were fixed by an international agreement and were very difficult to change.

releases of economic data, and pronouncements by government ministers, central bankers, bank analysts, prominent businessmen, gurus, etc. After the fact, much of this 'news' will be amended, made more precise, or disavowed, if not actually proved wrong. In the meantime, however, it exerts a powerful influence on the evolution of the exchange rate. This provides an explanation of the pattern shown in Figure 15.1: news—both genuine facts and rumours—move the exchange rate up one moment, and down the next. The importance of 'news' helps us to make sense of Stylized Facts #1 and #2 described in Box 15.2.

The UIRP condition is therefore the right point of departure, since it directly involves the expected future exchange rate. Ignoring the risk premium for the moment, we can start with (15.3) and note that it links the current interest rates i_t and i_t^* at home and abroad, the current exchange rate S_t, and its expected value next period S_{t+1}^e. (We now index the interest rate explicitly in each period using time subscripts.) We can reinterpret the UIRP condition as saying that the current exchange rate S_t depends on the current interest rates i_t and i_t^* and on the exchange rate S_{t+1}^e expected to prevail next period. This logical implication

Fig. 15.2 The UIRP Condition Repeated Over and Over Again
As a financial asset price, the nominal exchange rate is inherently forward-looking. All versions of UIRP impose tight restrictions on the relationship between interest rates at home and abroad, and the current and expected future exchange rate as shown in the upper chain. This relation is recursive, which means it also applies at future dates as well. If traders understand this and apply the no-profit condition, successive applications of the UIRP imply that the current exchange rate is a function not only of current, but future expected future interest rate differentials—plus some longer-run terminal condition as shown in the lower part.

of the UIRP condition is shown in the leftmost blue arrow in the upper part of Figure 15.2.

This way of representing the UIRP condition is interesting because it shows that we can think of the current spot exchange rate S_t as determined by domestic and foreign interest rates and by the market's current *expectation* of next period's exchange rate S_{t+1}^e. Like all asset prices, the nominal exchange rate is *forward-looking*. What happened before is irrelevant—bygones are bygones and the exchange rate is not tied to its past. It is totally free to jump to any level warranted by current or expected future conditions. Especially important is the implication that any increase in S_{t+1}^e raises S_t. In other words, an appreciation anticipated to occur in the future will show up *immediately* in the current exchange rate.

Can we say anything more about S_{t+1}^e? Next period, the situation will be the same. The UIRP condition will still be valid next period, so S_{t+1} will be explained by the interest rates i_{t+1} and i_{t+1}^* at home and abroad, and by expected future exchange rate in period $t+2$, S_{t+2}^e. This is shown in the second blue arrow of Figure 15.2, upper part.

Now we can imagine how the markets reason. Today's exchange rate is explained by the interest rates i_t and i_t^* and by the expected exchange rate S_{t+1}^e. As they try to guess S_{t+1}^e they are naturally led to link it with their expectations of i_{t+1}, i_{t+1}^*, and S_{t+2}^e.[7] This means that today's exchange rate is driven by current and next period's interest rates and by the exchange rate expected to prevail two periods ahead. Naturally, S_{t+2}^e will also be driven by the same factors, which will bring i_{t+2}, i_{t+2}^*, and S_{t+3}^e into the picture. Once we move in this direction, there is no end in sight! The last arrow of Figure 15.2 stops the clock n periods ahead, letting the reader imagine how far away $t + n$ may be. This so-called recursive reasoning is common in macroeconomics, and is made more formal in Box 15.3. It provides equation (15.10), the exact formula suggested in the last row, which will be used in what follows.

As with stock prices, the current exchange rate reflects all current and future interest rates at home and abroad, and its own long-run value. This expression shows just how important expectations of the

---

[7] Note that $i_{t+1}, i_{t+2}, i_{t+3}$, etc. are actually not known as of now, so we really talk about expectations and we should add the '*e*' subscript. To keep notation tidier, we dispense with this precision.

Box 15.3 **Iterating Forward the UIRP Condition**

Start with equation (15.3) and rewrite it so that it now explains the current exchange rate in the current period t:

(15.9)
$$\left(S_t = \frac{1+i_t}{1+i_t^*} S_{t+1}^e. \right)$$

Obviously, the UIRP will also hold in the next period $t + 1$, so we will have

$$S_{t+1} = \frac{1+i_{t+1}}{1+i_{t+1}^*} S_{t+2}^e.$$

This means that, as seen from today's perspective, our best guess of S_{t+1}^e is based on our best guesses of the interest rates in period $t + 1$ and of S_{t+2}:

$$S_{t+1}^e = \frac{1+i_{t+1}^e}{1+i_{t+1}^{*e}} S_{t+2}^e.$$

When this is recognized, we can substitute S_{t+1}^e in (15.9) with the next period version (15.9) and, dropping the superscript 'e' for the interest rates, we find

$$S_t = \frac{(1+i_t)}{(1+i_t^*)} \frac{(1+i_{t+1})}{(1+i_{t+1}^*)} S_{t+2}^e,$$

and, performing the operation n times:

(15.10)
$$S_t = \frac{(1+i_t)}{(1+i_t^*)} \frac{(1+i_{t+1})}{(1+i_{t+1}^*)} \frac{(1+i_{t+2})}{(1+i_{t+2}^*)} \cdots \frac{(1+i_{t+n})}{(1+i_{t+n}^*)} S_{t+n+1}^e.$$

This is the precise formulation of the symbolic link shown in the lower part of Figure 15.2.

future are for the present. Even events far into the future can have a large impact on today's exchange rate. This is why exchange markets—and asset markets in general—are so concerned with information. Even remote future events affect the present.

While not yet providing a complete theory of exchange rate determination, this analysis shows that relative conditions in national money markets are essential for understanding how macroeconomic conditions influence nominal exchange rates. For instance, it shows how the anticipation of future tight monetary policy at home (i is expected to rise) can lead to an appreciation *today* (S increases). This is an observation commonly made when interpreting movements of the nominal exchange rate.

15.4.3 An Apparent Contradiction and its Resolution

We have a remarkably consistent account of the effect of future monetary policy on the current exchange rate. Yet a contradiction seems to lurk in the deep corners of Figure 15.2. Suppose that the interest rate i_t at home rises unexpectedly. According to (15.9), (15.10) or Figure 15.2, the exchange rate S_t should immediately rise, i.e. *appreciate*. Yet, looking at the UIRP

condition (15.4), we see that a higher interest rate at home should be associated with an expected *depreciation* of our currency. How can this be?

Because both conclusions are based on the same UIRP condition, it cannot be a contradiction: both have to be true! But to resolve this paradox, it is important to make clear what is given and what is free to adjust. Given the foreign interest rate, uncovered interest parity links the domestic interest rate i_t to the expected *rate* of appreciation $(S_{t+1}^e - S_t)/S_t$. Turning this relation on its head, the *level* of the exchange rate S_t, is related to the interest rate i_t, given the expected future *level* of the exchange rate, S_{t+1}^e. Similarly, in (15.10) or Figure 15.2, we take as given all future domestic and foreign interest rates and S_{t+n}^e, the expected future exchange rate far off into the future. Thus, there is no real contradiction, only a confusion of future exchange rate levels and rates of appreciation. In the moment when the news arrives, there is a jump adjustment to allow for the UIRP to hold in future periods.

It is possible to show this diagrammatically in Figure 15.3. We have seen that a higher interest rate i_t is accompanied by an expected depreciation over the future according to (15.4), and by a higher exchange rate S_t, according to (15.9) or (15.10). In effect, these

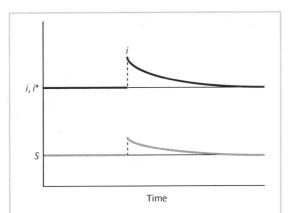

Fig. 15.3 An Increase in the Domestic Interest Rate

When the domestic interest rate (*i*) rises above the world interest rate, uncovered interest rate parity requires an expected exchange rate depreciation. Given an unchanged expected long-run nominal exchange rate, the exchange rate must appreciate now in order to generate that expected depreciation later.

two conclusions must both hold simultaneously. As the domestic interest rate rises i_t above the world rate i^*, the current exchange rate S_t appreciates immediately, but temporarily so. Indeed, if it is expected to depreciate next period or sometimes in the future, we can now have both a current appreciation and a

future expected depreciation. Put differently, the exchange rate must appreciate enough now to be consistent with the expectation of depreciation in the future. These shifts reflect the phenomenon of **exchange rate overshooting**: following a monetary policy relaxation, the exchange rate initially depreciates a lot (this is why we go all the way to *IS'*), then appreciates back but not fully to its initial level (we go back to *IS'*, not *IS*). This is an additional reason why exchange rates apparently 'move too much'. Box 15.4 gives more details.

15.4.4 The Fundamental Determinants of the Nominal Exchange Rate

The 'cumulated' interest parity condition (15.10) states that the exchange rate is determined by present and future interest rates and that it is anchored by its long-run value. The exchange rate **fundamentals**, therefore, are those variables that can affect the current and future domestic and foreign interest rates as well as the long-run exchange rate. Domestic and foreign economic conditions—as captured by the *IS–TR* and *AD–AS* frameworks—drive domestic and foreign interest rates. The fundamentals thus include present and future monetary and fiscal policies at home and abroad. They also include those factors that affect the exchange rate in the long run. We now examine what these are.

 Box 15.4 Interest Rate Parity and Short-Run Open Economy Macroeconomics

In the *IS–TR–IFM* model of the small open economy, the international financial markets integration (*IFM*) line imposed consistency of local money market interest rates with the return available on foreign assets *measured in the local currency*. The UIRP condition (15.4) makes the meaning of this return precise: it is a foreign interest rate *i* less the expected rate of exchange rate appreciation*. As a result, the position of the *IFM* schedule depends on the expected rate of change of the exchange rate. It will shift whenever the exchange rate is expected to change. In the case of a fixed exchange rate regime, nothing changes as long as the chosen exchange rate peg remains credible and is not expected to change. In that case, $S_{t+1}^e = S_t$ and the parity condition confirms that $i = i^*$. When the exchange rate is floating, however, this simplification cannot really be

defended. But it turns out that the key results of Chapter 11 still hold; in fact, the UIRP acts like a magnifying glass, reinforcing the short-run potency of monetary policy under fixed exchange rates. This box sketches this effect graphically; a full treatment can be found in the WebAppendix.

Consider the case of a monetary expansion—the central bank lowers its target interest rate $\bar{i}$.[8] This is shown by the rightward shift of the *TR* schedule in Figure 15.4 where the economy is initially at point *A*. In Chapter 11, we reasoned that at point *B*, the economy is below the *IFM* line: the interest rate is now too low, capital flows out and the exchange rate depreciates. This increases the country's external competitiveness, the current account improves and the *IS* curve shifts to *IS'*. The new equilibrium was at point *C*. Under flexible exchange rates, the *IS*

Box 15.4 Interest Rate Parity and Short-Run Open Economy Macroeconomics (*Continued*)

curve is endogenous and moves to meet the *TR'* and *IFM* schedules. If we now recognize that the exchange rate depreciation is likely to be anticipated, the interest parity condition implies that the domestic interest rate must be higher for investors to be indifferent between investing at home and abroad. As a consequence, the *IFM* line too is endogenous to changes in expected exchange rate changes. In the present case, it shifts up to *IFM'*. Graphically, this implies that the *IS* curve will have to shift until it passes through point *D*, the intersection of *TR'* and *IFM'*. The interest rate parity condition causes monetary policy in the short run to be *more* expansionary than in the original case—*D* lies to the right of *C*. The initial shift from *IS* to *IS'* corresponds to the depreciation caused by capital outflows that reflected the vertical distance from point *B* to the original *IFM* line. The interest parity condition shifts *IFM* to *IFM'*; however, this *increases* the distance from *B* and calls for an even larger depreciation. The expected future depreciation driving the shift from *IFM* to *IFM'* immediately causes an *additional* depreciation over and above the one identified earlier. This extra depreciation further shifts the *IS* schedule from *IS'* to *IS''*. Finally, as we move from *B* to *C* and to *D* along the *TR'* schedule, the central bank, which initially relaxed its policy stance, is induced by expanding output–due to booming exports as following the exchange rate depreciation—to raise the interest rate over and beyond where it initially was.

There is one slight logical problem with Point D, however. It cannot be a resting place, since at any point along *IFM'*, the exchange rate must continue depreciating! This is logically inconsistent with the fact that *i* should be *i** again. In fact, once point *D* is reached, capital outflows stop and the depreciation should also stop. How does that work? Easy: as the expected

depreciation slows, the *IFM* line moves from *IFM'* back down again—again, a consequence of UIRP. The exchange rate depreciation can only stop when the *IFM* line has once again returned to its initial position at point *C*. The conclusion is that, by ignoring the interest rate parity in Chapter 11, we miss the temporary trip from point *B* to point *D* and back. In the background, we also ignore the shift from *IS'* to *IS''* and back.

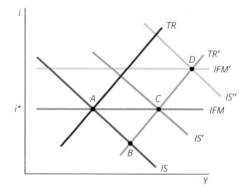

Fig. 15.4 Monetary Policy Under Floating Exchange Rates

Starting at point *A*, a monetary policy expansion is captured by the downward shift of the Taylor rule schedule from *TR* to *TR'*. At point *B*, the lower interest rate triggers capital outflows and the exchange rate depreciates. The *IS* curve shifts to *IS'* to reflect improved external competitiveness. But, if expected, the exchange rate depreciation raises the domestic interest rate according to the UIRP condition and the *IFM* schedule shifts up to *IFM'*, which triggers a further depreciation and the shift from *IS'* to *IS''* until it passes through point *D*.

15.5 The Exchange Rate in the Long Run

15.5.1 The Long Run and the Primary Current Account: A Review

We now turn to the second role of the exchange rate: the relative price of domestic goods in terms of for-

eign goods. This notion is captured by the real exchange rate $\sigma = SP/P^*$. For given prices at home P and abroad P^*, the nominal exchange rate S determines the real exchange rate. For the time being, we take these prices as given as part of the general macroeconomic picture in the short run. Later, we return to this issue in more detail.

The nation's intertemporal budget constraint was introduced in Chapter 7. It states that a nation cannot borrow beyond its means and that accumulated assets can and should be eventually spent. In present-value terms, the country meets its external constraint when the current and future primary current account deficits match the initial net asset position of the country (or the surpluses must at least match the initial debt). In the simplified two-period framework, this statement was written formally as

(15.11) $$PCA_1 + \frac{PCA_2}{1+r} = -F_1,$$

where F_1 is the net external position of the country at the beginning of the period. F_1 is positive when the country was a net lender previously, and negative when the country is a net debtor.

As long as it meets its intertemporal budget constraint, the country is free to choose the pattern of its primary accounts over time. This degree of freedom evaporates in the second and 'last' period. Tomorrow's primary account must match the accumulated net external position. As in Chapter 7, 'tomorrow' is a metaphor for the long-run steady state when, on average, short-run fluctuations simply cancel out. Then the primary current account must be such that, by the end of period 2 (the proverbial 'end of time') the country repays its accumulated debt, or spends its assets, principal, and interest, inherited from period 1:

(15.12) $$PCA_2 = -(1+r)(F_1 + PCA_1) = -F_2,$$

where F_2 is the net external position of the country at the beginning of the second period. A positive asset position ($F_2 > 0$) allows a deficit in the second period, while a position of external indebtedness ($F_2 > 0$) requires a surplus.

15.5.2 The Equilibrium Real Exchange Rate and the Primary Current Account in the Long Run

The requirement that the long-run primary current account is consistent with the country's external budget constraint determines the **equilibrium**, or **long-run, real exchange rate**. The link between the

primary account and the real exchange rate was studied in Chapter 10. There we described the primary current account function, which relates the primary current account surplus to the real exchange rate. In particular, the current account deteriorates when the real exchange appreciates. Other factors, such as current and foreign GDPs, also affect the primary current account, but they are mostly cyclical and therefore irrelevant for the long run. For this reason, we write the primary current account function simply as $PCA(\sigma, \ldots)$. The dots simply remind us of these other factors. The key relationship to remember is that the PCA is a negative function of the real exchange rate σ. The primary current account function is depicted in Figure 15.5 by the downward-sloping schedule. The diagram shows that, everything else held constant, each level of the current account is associated with a particular level of the real exchange rate. If the current account is to be in surplus, the real exchange rate must be rather low to create the export demand and reduce the import demand. Similarly, a current account in deficit will require an appreciated exchange rate, all else given.

Next, we return to the national budget constraint (15.12), which requires that the primary current account be consistent with the solvency. In the two-period parable, this means that in the second period (the long run) the primary current account must be

Fig. 15.5 The Primary Current Account Function

The primary current account function shows the relation between the real exchange rate and the primary account balance. It is downward-sloping because a lower real exchange rate, all other things being equal, leads to an improvement in the primary current account.

equal to the negative of the country's net foreign asset position, plus interest. That net foreign asset position is given by F_2. When F_2 is negative, it means a primary current surplus is necessary to pay off that debt. If F_2 is positive (the country is a net creditor, or has a positive investment position) the country should run down its accumulated assets via a deficit. Since this long-run constraint is independent of the real exchange rate, it is shown as the vertical schedule $-F_2$ in Figure 15.6. For net international creditor countries ($F_2 > 0$) this schedule lies to the left of the zero point, since $-F2 < 0$; they can live beyond their means in the future. Net international debtors will lie to the right of zero; $F_2 < 0$, so $-F2 > 0$ and the schedule $-F_2$ will lie to the right in the figure.

For the budget constraint to be satisfied in period 2, the economy must be at the intersection of the primary current account schedule and this vertical line. At point A, the equilibrium exchange rate can be read

Fig. 15.6 The Equilibrium Real Exchange Rate

Long-run equilibrium requires that the future primary current account be consistent with the net asset position, F_2. To point A corresponds the equilibrium real exchange rate $\bar{\sigma}$. A less favourable net asset position $F'_2 < F_2$ implies a lower primary current account deficit (or a larger current account surplus) in the future. The vertical schedule is shifted to the right. If indebted ($F_2 < 0$), the country must have a greater future primary current account surplus to service the greater external debt and the long-run real exchange rate $\bar{\sigma}'$ must be lower to generate that surplus. If the country is already a net creditor ($F_2 > 0$), a lower level of net foreign assets today implies a lower deficit tomorrow consistent with the national budget constraint.

off the vertical axis. Quite simply, the downward-sloping primary current account schedule shows what real exchange rate level is necessary in the long run for a country to obey its intertemporal budget constraint and honour its international obligations. This is the equilibrium real exchange rate $\bar{\sigma}$.

As it represents a long-run tendency, the equilibrium real exchange rate is unlikely to correspond to the observed real exchange rate at any point in time, if only because it fluctuates widely. When the real exchange rate is above its equilibrium level, we say that it is **overvalued**; in the opposite case it is **undervalued**. In the long run, however, it must return to its equilibrium value to ensure that the budget constraint is not violated. Markets see to it and, eventually, lead the real exchange rate to its long-run equilibrium value.

15.5.3 The Fundamental Determinants of the Real Exchange Rate

The result that the net external position drives the equilibrium real exchange rate is a very powerful one. It means that, eventually, market forces will take the real exchange rate to where it should be. The time required to get there can take several years or longer. The concept of an equilibrium real exchange rate looks beyond such transitory phases to focus on the steady state. Using two metaphors from the nautical world, the real exchange rate is the lighthouse that shows where the real exchange rate is headed, but it is also an anchor which ultimately pins down the real and, as we will see, the nominal exchange rate in the long run.

Graphically, the result that the equilibrium exchange rate is determined by the *PCA* schedule and the initial net foreign asset position is deceptively simple. It is possible, however, to go beyond the curves and ask which variables, known as the fundamental determinants, or fundamentals for short, are responsible for the evolution of the real exchange rate. What follows is a list of the most important fundamentals.

Non-price competitiveness

We start by thinking harder about competitiveness. Competitiveness is a matter of relative prices—i.e. the real exchange rate—but also of many other things. To start with, it matters a great deal how well designed and original are our goods. A bottle of champagne is unique, and can fetch a high price before consumers switch en masse to similar wines, which may be good or even better but do not carry the glamour of the original. Similarly, German cars have a reputation of reliability that gives them the edge, much as British bankers have built up the formidable City of London network or the Italian manufacturers have developed a knack for style and design. When something of this kind happens, the country becomes fundamentally more competitive and, for any level of the real exchange rate, its primary current account improves. Graphically, in Figure 15.7, the *PCA* schedule shifts upward and to the right, to *PCA'*. This gain in non-price competitiveness translates into a higher equilibrium exchange rate $\bar{\sigma}'$. This result can be explained in two ways. First, because they have become more attractive, domestic goods can be sold at a higher relative price. Second, starting at the old equilibrium rate $\bar{\sigma}$, i.e. at unchanged relative price, more goods can now be sold, which will result in a larger primary account current than required by condition (15.12). In the long run, this surplus will have to be eliminated by a real appreciation, which makes our goods more expensive and their goods cheaper.

A good example of a rapid improvement in non-price competitiveness is the transformation process in Central and Eastern Europe. As the Berlin Wall was dismantled in 1989 and the Soviet Bloc crumbled, these countries moved from central planning to the market economy. Starting with antiquated productive

equipment and a dilapidated public infrastructure, they quickly started to catch up with the West. As they climbed up the export quality ladder, their non-price competitiveness quickly improved. Unsurprisingly, their real exchange rates have been continuously appreciating, as the comparison with 'Old Europe' shows in Figure 15.8.

Natural resources

The Netherlands in the 1960s and the UK and Norway in the early 1980s were lucky enough to discover large reserves of gas or oil under the North Sea. In a matter of a few years, they could reduce their import bill or even become net exporters. If we break the primary current account into two components, oil and non-oil, we can write $PCA = PCA^{non-oil} + PCA^{oil}$.

Before the discovery, PCA^{oil} was substantial and negative, such as in oil-importing countries. Afterwards it became nil or even positive. If the primary current account was at its long-run level before the discovery, as PCA^{oil} improved very sizably, it became too strong. The discovery of natural resources has much the same effect as an improvement in non-price competitiveness. This is well captured by the rightward shift of the *PCA* schedule in Figure 15.7. As before, it implies that the equilibrium real exchange rate has appreciated. What happens next is told in Box 15.5.

Net external position

We have seen that the net external investment position is another fundamental determinant of the real exchange rate. All other things being equal, the more positive the external investment position, the more appreciated the equilibrium exchange rate will be. Similarly, indebted countries will require depreciated real equilibrium exchange rates in order to generate the resources for debt service.

To see how the net external position affects the equilibrium real exchange rate, we return to Figure 15.6. Point A describes a situation of long-run equilibrium: when the external debt position is F_2, which is actually a net debt so $-F_2 > 0$, the equilibrium real exchange rate is $\bar{\sigma}$. Now consider the same country, with the same *PCA* schedule, but with a net debt asset position F_2' that is even more negative than F_2. To this debt corresponds a new vertical schedule which lies to the right of the original one, and a new equilibrium real exchange rate $\bar{\sigma}'$ that is lower than $\bar{\sigma}$. We see that the larger the net external debt, the more the real exchange

Fig. 15.7 The Equilibrium Exchange Rate and Non-Price Competitiveness

A gain in non-price competitiveness is captured by the rightward shift of the *PCA* schedule to *PCA'*. The equilibrium real exchange rate rises from $\bar{\sigma}$ to $\bar{\sigma}'$.

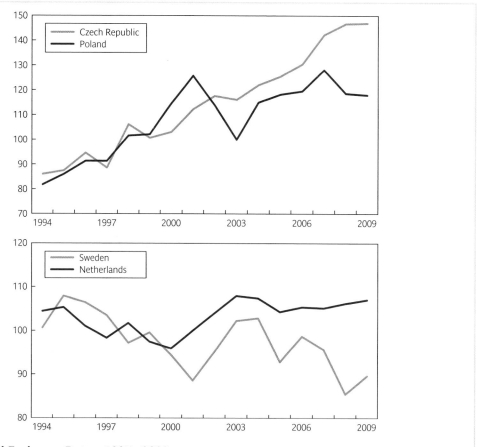

Fig. 15.8 Real Exchange Rates, 1995 – 2009
Countries that experience continuous catch-up growth tend to improve their non-price competitiveness. Their equilibrium real exchange rates appreciate and, normally, so do their actual real exchange rates. In contrast, developed countries tend to have more stable real exchange rates over the long term. This tendency is borne out in comparisons of the Czech Republic and Poland, on the one hand, and Sweden and the Netherlands on the other.
Source: IMF, *International Financial Statistics*.

rate must depreciate in the long run. Conversely, an improvement in the net external position will be associated with a real exchange appreciation.

The net external position of a country is a legacy of its history and evolves slowly. It may also take many years for the actual exchange rate to respond to changes in its equilibrium value. When the exchange rate is **misaligned**, meaning that it is not at its equilibrium level, its net external position must be changing. Indeed, we know that when the current account is in surplus, the country lends to the rest of the world, and it borrows when the current account is in deficit. In the long run, the real exchange rate is at

its equilibrium level and we have $PCA = -F_2$ so that the current account is $CA = PCA + (1 + r)F_2 = 0$. Figure 15.5 shows that if the exchange rate were overvalued, so that $\sigma > \bar{\sigma}$, relative to point A, we would be up and to the left along the PCA schedule. This would imply $PCA < -F_2$ and therefore a current account deficit. A net borrower, it lives beyond its means. Conversely, if $\sigma > \bar{\sigma}$, the exchange rate is undervalued and the country's net asset position improves as it runs a current account surplus.

This might seem worrisome. Could debts spiral out of control? If the exchange rate is allowed to play its corrective role, the answer is no. But examples abound

Box 15.5 The Norwegian Cure to the Dutch Disease

When oil was discovered in the UK's North Sea in the mid-1970s, the sterling real exchange rate soon appreciated by more than 30%. Ironically, the result was a shift away from 'traditional' industry (other traded goods besides oil) towards services, with massive plant closures and unemployment as industrial workers could not be immediately absorbed by the oil industry or the service sector. This striking process of de-industrialization—needed to eliminate the non-oil current account surplus—is called the Dutch disease, ever since it was first diagnosed in the 1960s when gas was discovered in the Netherlands' side of the North Sea.[9] The Dutch disease explains why resource-rich countries typically find it more difficult to develop and maintain an industrial sector. The problem can be seen today in contemporary Russia. This should not be a source of long-term concern though: why produce industrial goods when Mother Nature provides easy exports? In the short run, however, the adjustment can be painful.

In order to avoid this curse, Norway established the Government Petroleum Fund in 1990 (renamed Government Pension Fund—Global in 2006). As described by the Ministry of Finance:

Central government's net cash flow from petroleum operations is transferred in its entirety to the Government Pension Fund Global via the state budget, whereas the guidelines stipulate that only the expected real return on the Fund should be returned to the budget for general spending purposes. In this way the Fund serves as a long-term savings vehicle to let the Norwegian Government accumulate financial assets to help cope with future expenditures associated with the ageing of the population. . . . At the end of 2005 the Fund amounted to close to NOK 1400 billion or 99 per cent of mainland GDP (i.e. excluding petroleum activities). Projections indicate that the Fund will grow to 180 per cent of mainland GDP at the end of 2010. Given the present guidelines for fiscal policy, the Fund is expected to reach a level of around 250 per cent of mainland GDP in the years after 2030, before starting to gradually decline.[10]

Importantly, all the Fund's resources must be invested abroad. This provision saves Norway from the Dutch disease. Since much of oil income does not enter Norway, there is no pressure on the exchange rate to appreciate. As a result, the account is in perennial surplus. This would make no sense in the long run, but for Norway the long run is when oil reserves will be exhausted. In the meantime, keeping the current account in surplus prevents de-industrialization. Norway's central bank sums up the situation well: 'The Petroleum Fund makes it possible . . . to avoid abrupt shifts in the industry structure, such as we have seen in many other countries with substantial revenues from natural resources, and contributes to sustainable business and industry in the long term.'[11]

---

of countries such as Indonesia and Nigeria, which were made fabulously wealthy by oil discoveries, but then squandered their wealth and even became highly indebted as a result. More recently, countries in southern Europe have seen their current accounts deficits grow without a corrective depreciation. Box 15.6 looks at the case of Sweden to provide an interpretation of Figure 15.8, and of the future of the US dollar.

15.5.4 How to Think About the Equilibrium Real Exchange Rate?

In practice, disturbances large enough to produce significant changes in the equilibrium real exchange rate are rather rare events. When considering countries of comparable level of economic development, it is a good rule of thumb to view the equilibrium real exchange rate as stable or even constant. This implies relative PPP, which we already encountered in Chapter 6, and possibly even the absolute version of PPP, which is much stronger and says that price levels across countries are comparable. While we stress that PPP is a powerful rule of thumb, one must be always on the watch for the possibility that a major change is under way. We have just seen the main fundamentals that determine the equilibrium

[9] The WebAppendix presents the phenomenon in more formal detail.

[10] 'The Norwegian Petroleum Sector and the Government Pension Fund—Global' by Secretary General Tore Eriksen, Ministry of Finance <www.regjeringen.no>.

[11] Norges Bank <www.norges-bank.no>.

Box 15.6 Indebted and Depreciated: The Cases of Sweden and the USA

Figure 15.8 shows that Sweden's equilibrium exchange rate depreciated in the 1990s. A plausible interpretation is the deterioration of its net external position visible in Figure 15.9. In the early 1990s, partly due to an overvalued exchange rate, Sweden suffered a deep financial crisis. When the krona depreciated and became undervalued, foreign liabilities, which exceeded foreign assets by some 20% of GDP, became large when evaluated in the domestic currency, hence a precipitous decline in the net external position. The exchange rate eventually recovered from its undervalued level but not to its previous value. Since then, the external position has improved, which suggests that the krona's equilibrium real exchange rate has risen. This is consistent with recent strong economic performance of the Swedish economy.

Figure 15.9 also depicts a gradual deterioration of the US external position over the past decades. In the mid-

1980s, the USA switched from being a net lender to being a net debtor, and the trend has accelerated in recent years. This has prompted many observers to conclude that the equilibrium level of the dollar has fallen and to predict that the actual exchange rate would soon. For many years, the dollar defied these predictions. Since 2003, the dollar has started its much-awaited correction. Many people are surprised, or upset, with the continuing weakness of the dollar, because it boosts US competitiveness at the expense of its trading partners. The same people also lament the USA's large external debt and continuing current account deficits. But how else can the USA stabilize its net external debt without improving its current account? And what better way to do this than with a significant real depreciation of the dollar?

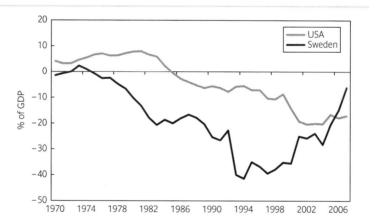

Fig. 15.9 Net External Positions of Sweden and the USA, 1970–2007 (% of GDP)

The net external position, here measured as a percentage of GDP, subtracts the estimates of liabilities to foreign residents owed by both public and private sectors from the sum of assets held by domestic against foreign residents. The paths taken by Sweden and the USA reflect the very different paths their economies have taken over the past two decades. *Source*: Lane and Milesi-Ferretti (2007).

real exchange rate, so we now know why it may change.

An important case in point is the catch-up process that poorer countries experience during a successful take-off growth phase. We observed in Figure 15.8 that the real exchange rates of the

Central and East European countries appreciated steadily since they embarked on their transformation process that began in the early 1990s. This is an excellent example of a general phenomenon known as the **Balassa–Samuelson effect**. It is described in Box 15.7.

Box 15.7 The Balassa–Samuelson Effect[12]

Experienced travellers invariably notice that wealthier countries are systematically more expensive than poorer ones. This is not merely a perception, but a hard fact (see Table 15.4). To see why, consider a poor country. Obviously most wages are much lower than in a rich country, but they will grow when and if the country catches up with the richer country. This will happen when it accumulates capital, imports advanced technology, and generally becomes more productive. As this happens, we expect standards of living, and therefore local wages, to grow. Now work backwards in time from when catch-up will have occurred and wages will have caught up with those of the most advanced economies. For this to happen, wages must grow faster during the catching-up period. Since wages make up production costs, the same reasoning applies to price levels. To grow faster in poor rather than in rich countries and eventually converge to the same levels, prices must start from a lower base.

When the problem is considered in more detail, there are several mechanisms for price levels in richer countries to be higher than in poorer ones. Wages in non-traded goods and services tend to follow those that are traded, while the latter depends on labour productivity. Poor countries tend to have lower productivity in traded goods, which translates into lower wages in both sectors and via costs, into lower prices. Another explanation derives from the sheer fact that non-traded goods need not follow the law of one price, so in countries with high concentration of wealth, non-traded goods tend to be more expensive. It is for this reason that the famous Big Mac burger cost $8.31 in oil-rich Norway, but only $4.93 in the euro area and $4.07 in the United States, and only $2.35 in Thailand!

This phenomenon is documented more systematically in Table 15.4, which shows price levels and GDP per capita in a sample of countries around the world, as measured in 2009. For ease of comparison, both prices and GDP are indexed relative to the USA. For example, in 2009, Argentine GDP per capita was only about 30% of US levels, and prices in the same currency were 46% lower. In rich Norway, GDP per person was 24% higher, and the price level was 56% higher than in the USA. The association between income and price levels is unmistakable, although not perfect.

15.6 From the Long to the Short Run

15.6.1 The Equilibrium Real Exchange Rate as an Anchor

We now reconcile the present short-run 'financial market' and the long-run or 'relative price of goods' views of the exchange rate. Each perspective is rooted in its own compelling logic. The short-run view was encoded in Figure 15.3 or equation (15.10). Both link the current nominal exchange rate to the expected future exchange rate far into the future, with a bridge being the intervening expected future rates of interest at home and abroad. Of course, no one knows what the future will be, but markets that set the exchange rate nevertheless have to make a guess. Between now and the distant future, many things will happen. There will be expansions and recessions, current account surpluses and deficits, and much more. Yet, a good bet is that, in the long run, the relative-price-of-goods view will prevail because a country cannot forever escape its budget constraint, and just as important, the real exchange rate will play a role in enforcing that budget constraint. Over- and under-valuations do occur, but not forever.

---

[12] The Balassa–Samuelson effect is named after Bela Balassa (1928–1991), a Hungarian-born economist at Johns Hopkins University, also known as a gourmet and author of a confidential restaurant guide, and after Paul Samuelson (1915–2009), the 1970 Nobel laureate from MIT. A formal derivation is available in the WebAppendix.

Table 15.4 **GDP per Capita and Price Levels, 2009 (USA = 100)**

	GDP per Capita	Price Level		GDP per Capita	Price Level
Europe			**South America**		
Austria	90.0	113.3	Argentina	29.8	54.4
Belarus	30.4	46.7	Bolivia	9.3	42.0
Belgium	84.6	117.7	Brazil	23.1	98.3
Croatia	37.3	85.6	Chile	30.0	76.0
Czech Republic	56.0	79.1	Peru	18.1	56.4
Denmark	81.9	155.8	Venezuela	21.6	121.8
Finland	76.2	131.9			
France	75.4	120.1	**Asia**		
Germany	79.4	112.8	Bangladesh	3.3	36.8
Greece	66.2	100.0	China	17.8	48.9
Hungary	39.5	76.9	India	7.9	32.2
Ireland	78.7	134.9	Indonesia	9.6	57.8
Italy	67.7	113.6	Israel	62.4	98.1
Luxembourg	204.7	104.1	Japan	76.8	122.1
Norway	123.9	156.4	Korea	58.5	70.7
Poland	40.3	66.8	Pakistan	5.4	35.1
Portugal	49.0	98.0	Saudi Arabia	53.7	59.5
Russia	34.4	62.3	Singapore	112.3	65.5
Slovak Republic	47.0	79.5	Sri Lanka	9.7	46.6
Spain	67.8	102.7			
Sweden	86.2	114.1	**Africa**		
Switzerland	97.3	146.1	Central African Republic	1.6	59.2
Turkey	23.9	76.5	Chad	3.2	47.4
United Kingdom	81.1	97.9	Congo, Dom. Rep.	0.5	59.0
			Côte d'Ivoire	3.3	77.8
North America and Oceania			Egypt	11.5	46.1
Canada	87.7	108.5	Ethiopia	1.9	38.0
Mexico	28.3	62.4	Kenya	3.1	57.2
United States	100.0	100.0	Nigeria	5.2	55.9
Australia	104.3	117.6	South Africa	19.0	67.9

Source: Penn World Tables 7.0, < http://pwt.econ.upenn.edu/php_site/pwt_index.php>

Returning to Figure 15.2 or equation (15.10), we can now think of the very long-run nominal exchange rate S_{t+n}^e expected far into the future with its long-run level. As n gets larger, we are getting closer to expectations of the long-run nominal exchange rate $\bar{S}$. This long-run concept—which will never be observed but is in the back of all our minds—is the anchor which pins down the nominal exchange rate, not only in the long run, but also in the short run. This is the missing link between the short- and long-run views of the exchange rate. In the next section, we show how to bridge the gap between a short-term volatile asset price and the long-run one, given by monetary and real conditions over periods of ten years or more.

15.6.2 The Bridge to the Long Run: the Parity Conditions

If the day-to-day exchange rate S_t and the long run $\bar{S}$ are to be consistent with each other, the latter must represent a succession of internally consistent versions of the former. Moreover, in this connection, we need to convert a long equilibrium *real* exchange rate $\bar{\sigma}$, to a long-run *nominal* exchange rate $\bar{S}$, as it enters Figure 15.2 or equation (15.10). How do we bridge these gaps?

Actually we already know the answer! The real determinants of $\bar{\sigma}$, the long-run (or equilibrium) real exchange rate, were discussed in Section 15.5. If we think of $\bar{\sigma}$ as the 'doubly-deflated' long-run nominal exchange rate, then $\bar{\sigma} = \bar{S}\bar{P}/\bar{P}^*$. The price levels $\bar{P}$ and $\bar{P}^*$ are those which prevail at home and abroad, respectively, in the long run. These price levels will be the result of cumulated inflation between now and then. By relative PPP, the nominal long-run price ratio $\bar{P}/\bar{P}^*$ will be a function of cumulative relative inflation differentials between the two countries. Chapters 6 and 12 inform us how to think about inflation in the long run, so we know how to think of $\bar{P}$ and $\bar{P}^*$. It only remains to use the definition of the real exchange rate to pin down the long-run nominal exchange rate, which can be rearranged as $\bar{S} = \bar{\sigma}\bar{P}^*/\bar{P}$.

Thus, the long equilibrium *nominal* exchange rate is driven by the long equilibrium *real* exchange rate and by the long-run price levels at home and abroad. Anything that raises the long equilibrium real exchange rate also raises the long equilibrium nominal exchange rate, holding the evolution of domestic and foreign inflation constant. Given a long equilibrium real exchange rate, the long equilibrium nominal exchange rate is higher, the higher is the foreign price level (due to higher cumulative inflation) and the lower is the domestic price level (due to lower cumulative inflation).

The bridge between short and long run helps us understand Stylized Facts #3 and #4 in Box 15.2. Higher domestic inflation relative to foreign inflation, will drive $\bar{P}$ higher relative to $\bar{P}^*$—and lead to a more depreciated $\bar{S}$. This has direct consequences for the *current* nominal exchange rate S_t (Stylized Fact #3). Recalling that inflation and money growth go hand in hand in the long run, we can now understand Stylized Fact #4 as well.

The last step is to replace S^e_{t+n} with $\bar{S}$ in (15.10). The result is:

$$(15.13) \quad S_t = \frac{(1+i_t)\,(1+i_{t+1})\,(1+i_{t+2})}{(1+i^*_t)\,(1+i^*_{t+1})\,(1+i^*_{t+2})} \cdots \frac{(1+i_{t+n})}{(1+i^*_{t+n})} \bar{\sigma} \frac{\bar{P}^*}{\bar{P}}.$$

We have now completed the link between the current nominal exchange rate and its long-run value. Indeed, this expression indicates that the current nominal exchange S_t depends on three sets of fundamentals.

(1) The path of future domestic and foreign interest rates—therefore all relevant economic conditions affecting the interest rate (as captured by the *IS–TR* framework): monetary and fiscal policies, foreign demand, etc.

(2) The real exchange rate $\bar{\sigma}$ that is required to meet the nation's intertemporal budget constraint—therefore the foreign debt and the country's competitive position.

(3) The level of prices $\bar{P}$ and $\bar{P}^*$ at home and abroad far into the future—therefore present and future inflation, both at home and abroad.

The list of fundamentals is long because of the ubiquitous role of the exchange rate in the relative price of goods and assets. In light of this, it is easy to understand why exchange markets react to a very broad range of indicators. Yet, the link between the budget constraint and the current exchange rate is also long—it passes through the real equilibrium exchange rate $\bar{\sigma}$, and then the corresponding long-run spot rate $\bar{S}$ — and partly clouded by the long string of domestic and foreign interest rates that appear in (15.13). This was the central point of Stylized Fact #7.

15.6.3 Implications for Open Economy Macroeconomics in the Short and the Long Run

Perfect capital mobility and the conditions of interest and relative purchasing power parity impose restrictions on both the long-run as well as immediate short-run determination of the exchange rate. We saw in Box 15.3 how price rigidity and UIRP combine to make exchange rates more volatile. The medium run is too complex for an intermediate-level macro textbook, but we can sketch the general results here. It is worth stressing that our chief analytic frameworks in macroeconomics, the *IS–TR–IFM* (for the short run, Keynesian perspective) and the *AS–AD* (for the medium- to long-run analysis) models, give the right answers.

Box 15.3. already examined in detail the consequences of UIRP for the short-run behaviour of the exchange rate. But the fixed-price assumption, the linchpin of the *IS–TR* analysis, can only hold for a few quarters. A permanent increase in target inflation from $\bar{\pi}$ to $\bar{\pi}'$ will ultimately lead to a rise in actual inflation, which will undo the initial effect of the depreciation, as domestic inflation rises relative to foreign inflation. From the perspective of the *AS–AD* analysis, output must return to its original level (output gap returns to zero) so the real exchange rate cannot be permanently depreciated relative to its initial level—this is a consequence of the neutrality assumption . As a result, the nominal exchange rate is forced not only to 'move too much' in the short run, but it is also forced to obey PPP in the long run, meaning the long-run rate of depreciation will have increased by $\bar{\pi}' - \bar{\pi}$.

15.7 Exchange Rate Volatility and Currency Crises

15.7.1 Volatility and Predictability

It is useful to return to Figure 15.1 at the beginning of the chapter. The volatility of the exchange rate in the short run visible in panel (*a*) is a direct consequence of (15.13). The spot exchange rate responds to expectations of the very large number of events that may potentially affect all future interest rates and the long-run spot rate $\bar{S}$. As expectations are constantly changing, the exchange rate reacts. Much of these expectations are very noisy. Over time, much of this noise will cancel or dissipate, as panel (*b*) illustrates. As the comparison between Stylized Facts #1 and #2 indicates, gradually the long-run fundamentals that drive $\bar{S}$ come to dominate. This still leaves much room for uncertainty and correspondingly large fluctuations. Exchange rate movements largely reflect the uncertainty that we face when thinking ahead.

Stylized Fact #1 makes another point. An implication of (15.13) is that the current spot exchange rate reflects what we think we now know about the future. What makes tomorrow or next year different from now? The answer is the arrival of new information. This means that the exchange rate changes between one period and the next as a result of new information, which is unpredictable by definition—if we could predict the arrival of new information, it wouldn't be new information anymore! This is why exchange rate movements are largely unpredictable.

The unpredictability of short-run fluctuations is sometimes cited as a proof that economists do not really understand the exchange rate. The preceding observation explains why this argument is wrong. Quite to the contrary, understanding what drives the exchange rate implies that it must be unpredictable! Those who make predictions must implicitly claim that they know things that the market does not know. This may be the case now and then, but it is very unlikely that it is systematically true.[13]

---

[13] This argument holds for all asset prices determined in weakly efficient markets.

Fig. 15.10 Korea's Exchange Rate (index 100 = 2005 average)

The exchange rate is measured as US$ per Korean won. In two months at the end of 1997, the won lost half of its value. In a similar fashion, the financial crisis 2008–2009 hit Korea, an exporting economy, hard. But in the meantime growth has returned.

Source: IMF.

15.7.2 Currency Crises[14]

A particular form of volatility is a currency crisis. One example, among many, is the crisis that affected Southeast Asia in the late 1990s. Figure 15.10 shows the evolution of Korea's exchange rate. Korea was then one among several East Asian 'dragons' that had been growing at close to 10% per annum over more than a decade. It was hailed as a success story, which led to the country's joining the OECD, the club of developed countries. Despite this success, the Korean currency, the won, collapsed in 1997 and the economy plunged into a deep recession. While it has recovered, its growth still pales in comparison to its spectacular growth performance in the first half of the 1990s. In fact, Korea has become a mature OECD economy with world-class corporations. Yet, a decade later, the won again lost some 40% of its value in the weeks that followed the Wall Street crisis of September 2008.

---

[14] This is a brief presentation of the currency crisis phenomenon. A more extensive analysis can be found in Chapter 19.

This example illustrates the fact that currency crises occur frequently and not just in badly managed countries. Most often, though, they are the consequence of the authorities' efforts at maintaining an overvalued exchange rate. The most typical case involves a fixed exchange rate regime combined with rapid domestic inflation. In Chapter 11, this was shown to be an untenable situation. For a given level of the equilibrium real exchange rate $\bar{\sigma}$, the corresponding equilibrium nominal exchange rate $\bar{S} = \bar{\sigma}\bar{P}^*/\bar{P}$ will decline as the price level increases. If the central bank continues to intervene heavily in the foreign exchange market to keep the actual nominal exchange rate S fixed, the currency becomes increasingly overvalued. As selling pressure mounts, foreign exchange reserves quickly decline and, eventually, the central bank must throw in the towel. A brutal adjustment follows.

The case of Korea is more interesting. Prior to the 1997 Asian crisis, there was no serious inflation and the current account was approximately balanced, suggesting at face value that the exchange rate was not overvalued. Yet, several countries in the region had overvalued currencies. This was the case, in particular, of Thailand, which faced a currency crisis in June 1997. At that stage, the markets started to wonder whether neighbouring countries were not in a similar situation. The collapse of Korea's currency is an instance of a **self-fulfilling crisis**.

The interpretation of crises follows directly from Figure 15.2 or equation (15.10). This relationship implies that today's exchange rate S_t is driven by its expected value in the future, S_{t+n}^e. If markets expect S_{t+n}^e to fall, Figure 15.2 predicts that the current rate will fall *immediately*. When the nominal exchange rate is kept fixed at an overvalued level, it is enough for markets to expect a depreciation at some point in the future for the depreciation to occur now. This means that crises can be triggered by abrupt changes in expectations of faraway outcomes.

And this is exactly what happens when the exchange rate is overvalued. As long as the central bank continues to defend the fixed parity S^{fix} which is overvalued relative to the long run (i.e. $S^{fi} > \bar{S}$), the market may continue to believe that $S_{t+n}^e = S^{fix}$. When the stock of reserves becomes depleted, the market knows that the central bank cannot maintain the fixed parity S_{fix} and that the exchange rate will have to be devalued to its equilibrium level. In that instant, the expectation switches to $S_{t+n}^e = \bar{S}$. This expectation can be based on a simple extrapolation of how long the reserves will last, or may even anticipate that the market may clean out the central bank sooner than that.

Furthermore, a crisis can even be self-fulfilling. In such a situation, the trigger is a change of view about the equilibrium exchange rates $\bar{S}$. This change of view can be brutal because it is panic-driven. Even a small probability of a depreciation implies potentially large losses from holding assets denominated in the currency in question. Even if most market participants do not believe that a depreciation is in the making, a rumour that it could is sufficient to convince them to sell their assets denominated in that currency as a precaution. Large sales—a capital outflow—can depress the exchange rate and can even validate the expectation that the currency might be devalued. This leads to more panic sales and eventually to a full-blown crisis.

Such crises were common in the time of the European Monetary System, the fixed-exchange rate system which was the predecessor to the European Monetary Union. We discuss this system more in Chapter 19. The 2008 currency crisis in Korea is another example of a self-fulfilling crisis. At that time, like a decade earlier, the Korean macroeconomy (inflation, external balance) was healthy but many firms and some households had borrowed in dollars and euros to spend or invest in wons. This created a vulnerability: should the won depreciate sharply, Korean borrowers would find difficult, often impossible to honour their debts. This would lead to widespread bankruptcies and further defaults on foreign borrowings. At a time of exacerbated market anxiety, investors in Korea panicked and sold their holdings in wons, which produced the vicious circle that they had initially feared.

The main conclusion is that volatility and crises are part and parcel of foreign exchange markets, in fact of all financial markets. Exchange rates and asset prices are driven by expectations which can shift rapidly. Self-fulfilling crises happen when expectations, whether justified or not, are ratified *ex post* by the panic that they generate. Volatility and misalignment of the exchange rate is, however, not merely a problem of an asset market as we have seen: it also affects the functioning of the macroeconomy and the well-being of millions of households and firms.

⚠ Summary

1 Foreign exchange markets are a worldwide network of traders who constantly swap currencies and assets denominated in different currencies. They deal in large amounts and promptly arbitrage away any potential source of profit. This ensures consistency among all bilateral cross-rates.

2 The no-profit condition, a characteristic of efficient financial markets, ensures that the covered interest parity condition is satisfied. When capital is internationally mobile, a higher domestic interest rate is matched by a forward exchange rate premium.

3 In the presence of risk, the no-profit condition leads to an uncovered interest parity condition. When capital is internationally mobile, an expected exchange rate depreciation should be compensated by a higher domestic interest rate, and conversely, up to a risk premium.

4 If both uncovered interest parity and purchasing power parity conditions hold, real interest rates are equalized worldwide. Since PPP holds at best in the long run, real interest rate equalization is only a long-run proposition.

5 Exchange rates are forward-looking variables. An implication of the uncovered interest parity

condition is that today's exchange rate is driven by today's interest rates and by the expected exchange rate next period.

6 Today's exchange rate is linked to present and future interest rates at home and abroad, and to a long-run spot nominal exchange rate. The link takes the form of a chain of present and future uncovered interest parity conditions. It is in the nature of an asset market that all that is currently known about the future is reflected in today's value of the exchange rate. Changes in the exchange rate occur primarily because new information arrives, including revisions of expectations about the future.

7 In the long run, the real exchange rate must ultimately be consistent with the country's intertemporal budget constraint. The constraint means that past international borrowing must be repaid by eventual current account surpluses. Conversely, past international lending allows a country to eventually dissave through current account deficits. This is what defines the equilibrium real exchange rate.

8 The equilibrium real exchange rate appreciates when the net external position improves or when the economy becomes more competitive for reasons like the discovery of natural resources or gains in non-price competitiveness.

9 Purchasing power parity occurs in the long run when there is no change in the country's net external position (when the current account is balanced on average) or non-price competitiveness. Economies that catch up by improving their productivity see their equilibrium real exchange rates appreciate. The resulting Balassa–Samuelson effect is a key reason for PPP not to hold.

10 The long- and short-run views of the exchange rate are not inconsistent. Real factors that drive the long-run real exchange rate are present in today's nominal exchange rate via the exchange rate expected in the long run. Thus the long-run exchange rate is the *anchor* that guides the path of future expected exchange rates and relates it to the current value.

11 The fundamental determinants of the exchange rate include all the variables that affect the equilibrium real exchange rate and the domestic and foreign interest rates that link the current exchange rate to its long-run equilibrium level. Domestic and foreign inflation, which determine the link between the equilibrium real exchange rate and its nominal level, are also among the fundamentals.

12 The forward-looking aspect of the exchange rate explains its volatility and even the occasional occurrence of currency crises.

Key Concepts

- vehicle currencies
- spot and forward exchange rates, swaps
- covered interest rate parity (CIRP)
- uncovered interest rate parity (UIRP)
- hedged, covered
- open position (uncovered, unhedged)
- forward premium/discount
- capital gains and losses
- exchange rate overshooting

- international Fisher equation
- equilibrium, or long-run, real exchange rate
- fundamentals
- undervalued, overvalued
- misaligned
- Balassa – Samuelson effect
- currency crises
- self-fulfilling crises

❷ Exercises

1 Suppose that you could buy and sell US dollars for $1.25/EUR and pounds for 0.75 £/EUR, but that at the same time the dollar–pound rate was 1.65 $/£.

(a) What strategy would you pursue to take advantage of this 'money pump'? What would be the likely effect of the market's recognition of its existence?

(b) Question (a) ignores the existence of a bid–ask spread. How would your answer change if the bid–ask spreads were: $1.24–1.26/EUR, 0.74–0.76 £/EUR, and 1.64-1.66 $/£?

2 The interest rate in Austria is 3% while it is 10% in Hungary. What does this imply for the forward premium/discount of the forint, the Hungarian currency, vis-à-vis the euro (which is used in Austria)?

3 Consider the same interest rates as in the previous question. What would you do if you were 100% sure that the forint/euro exchange rate would remain constant, perhaps because there was a fixed exchange rate regime? Would this necessarily be a violation of the no-profit condition? Explain.

4 Suppose the Polish currency, the zloty (PLN), is trading at 0.225 Euro/PLN, and market participants anticipated that Poland would fix its exchange rate to the Euro in one year at a rate 0.25 Euro/PLN. What do you think will happen to the exchange rate today? How would it help to know interest rates in Poland and in the Eurozone?

5 For decades, interest rates in Switzerland have been lower (by 1–2%) than in Germany while the exchange rate between the Swiss franc and the deutschmark first and now the euro has remained stable. What does this mean for the interest rate parity condition? How could you explain this phenomenon?

6 Within the euro area, interest rates on government bonds have become quite different recently. For instance, on 21 December 2011, interest rates on 10-year government bonds were: 3.35% in Germany, 8.23% in Ireland, 12.99% in Portugal, 6.74% in Italy and 31.29% in Greece. Interpret these numbers. Is a no-profit condition being violated?

7 Since 1970, Australia's current account has almost always been in deficit, sometimes large ones. The real exchange rate has lost very little, some 10%. Is it surprising? How can this be explained?

8 Figure 15.11 shows that Korea's nominal exchange rate has considerably appreciated since the 1997–1998 crisis described in Section 15.8.2. What are possible explanations for this appreciation?

Fig 15.11

9 'The equilibrium real exchange rate remains constant when the actual real exchange rate remains durably close to its equilibrium level.' What is the logic of such an assertion? Is this always true?

10 Facing market pressure for an appreciation of the Swiss franc, the Swiss central bank lowered its interest rate. Why?

→ Essay Questions

1 'The advantage of a fixed exchange rate regime is to greatly reduce exchange rate uncertainty.' Comment.

2 True or false: 'Financial institutions tend to be for flexible exchange rates, while firms in manufacturing and traded output in general tend to be in favour of fixed exchange rates.'

3 'The fact that currency crises can be self-fulfilling is greatly disturbing because it suggests that any country can see its money hugely devalued, for no good reason.' In commenting on this statement, carefully draw the difference between self-fulfilling and other types of crises.

4 Equations like (15.10) suggest that the market must look at horizons so far out that they seem to make little sense. Use the logic of the yield curve, presented and explained in Chapter 14, to explain the similarity between the two logics and provide an interpretation of how the markets think about the very long run.

5 Concern has been raised that the discovery and extraction of oil in Kazakhstan and other central Asian countries might have adverse affects on their economies. What might be the reasons for these concerns? What affects would you predict the discoveries to have on the real exchange rate and the long-term current accounts of these countries?

PART IV

Macroeconomic Policy in a Global Economy

What can a government, or several governments acting together, do to influence and improve upon macroeconomic outcomes? Having worked through two-thirds of this book, the answer to that question might seem obvious to many readers, but the right answers are in fact never always clear. While governments are obviously always 'larger' than individual economic agents, it is important to ask: Can they really always influence their environment in predictable ways? Should they? Will they? The global economic and financial crisis of 2008–2009 represented the sharpest decline of economic activity since the Great Depression. It also posed the greatest challenge to policy-makers in the past half-century. While a global reaction did follow, there remains much dispute about the direction, nature and even the necessity of policy response. In particular, the evolution of the world economy and its intertwinement is a new development which did not at all characterize the world in the 1930s. New situations demand new innovative responses, not old recipes. This is why we study macroeconomics—to give us a dynamic, adaptable set of ideas for dealing with new challenges. At the same time we cannot forget the valuable lessons of history—for as the Spanish philosopher George Santayana warned: 'Those who cannot remember the past are condemned to repeat it.'

The following four chapters deal with different aspects of these questions. Chapter 16 is concerned with the potential for aggregate demand management policies, i.e. government actions which steer the economy's path by moving the *AD* curve. In Chapter 17, particular aspects and issues of fiscal and monetary policies are taken up in detail, regarding the stability, credibility, and political and economic sustainability of such policies. Since moving only one of the two curves may not be appropriate in all situations faced by policy-makers, it is important to discuss supply-side policy as well. In Chapter 18, we confront the issues already raised in Chapter 4: how can countries improve their standards of living and possibly their rates of growth in a sustainable way? Finally, Chapter 19 examines the scope of policy and policy coordination in the international financial arena. For citizens of the world, this question has achieved enormous importance through the globalization of capital markets but, more urgently, in light of the recent banking and credit crises.

For Europeans it has raised questions of existential nature—what does it mean to be a European? Can national boundaries and centuries of cultural and social history be eradicated in a decade of monetary union? Is this a desirable way of sustainably increasing wealth and prosperity? Most importantly, are Europeans willing to voluntarily give up some element of their national economic sovereignty to guarantee the survival of their common currency?

Demand Management Policies

16

Policymakers are unable to predict with great confidence even how (or how quickly) their own actions are likely to affect the economy. In short, if making monetary policy is like driving a car, then the car is one that has an unreliable speedometer, a foggy windshield, and a tendency to respond unpredictably and with a delay to the accelerator or the brake.

Ben Bernanke, Governor of the Federal Reserve of the United States

16.1 Overview

Writing in 1930, John Maynard Keynes yearned for the day when economists 'could manage to get themselves thought of as humble, competent people on a level with dentists.' Since Keynes and the Great Depression, policy-makers have hoped that macroeconomic management of the business cycle would be no more complicated than getting a tooth filled. In this chapter, we explore the theoretical possibility of demand management policy, and address a number of factors that limit what macroeconomic policy can achieve. In the 1970s, attempts to manage the macroeconomy ended with high levels of inflation, unemployment, and public indebtedness. The painful medicine administered in the early 1980s to combat those problems left a bitter taste and little stomach for experimentation with policy activism.

Yet while confidence in governments' ability to smooth out aggregate fluctuations has waned for several decades, it is hard to deny that governments can affect demand, and well-timed aggregate demand policy can put an economy back on track or prevent a catastrophe. No better evidence for this was policy response to the 'Great Recession' brought about the global financial crisis 2008–2009. Regardless of political affiliation or policy view, there was widespread consensus among serious economists that the collapse of aggregate demand associated with the crisis was a threat to global stability and that it required some sort of policy response. Differences of opinion focused on issues of extent and emphasis.

The age-old controversy between **neoclassical** and **Keynesian** economists has evolved a lot since 1936, when Keynes launched his celebrated attack on the economic orthodoxy of his time. Over the decades, waves of new arguments have been brought forward

by each side of the debate, only to be undermined by new counter-arguments from the other side. Yet despite ever-increasing sophistication, the same familiar themes continue to dominate the discussion. First, how quickly do goods and labour markets adjust to shocks? Second, how do agents form expectations and how quickly are these embedded in their decisions? Third, given that inflation is usually a short-run by-product of demand policy, what are its costs to households, businesses, and society as a whole? These questions comprise the first section of this chapter.

The next section deals with the fundamentally random nature of the business cycle and the feasibility of demand management policy. Even if the thorny issues of scope and credibility of managing demand are resolved, economists must admit that they are not gods. Despite their ability to make pronouncements on television and advise governments, economists are not oracles either. The prevalence of random influences in the economic system at any point in time will prevent them from predicting future outcomes with perfect precision, even if they have the correct model in hand. This fundamental uncertainty—shocks as we have called them—cannot be forecast, by definition. Few people anticipated the oil shocks in the 1970s, and no one foretold the fall of communism and the Iron Curtain in the late 1980s, the development of the internet, terrorist attacks in 2001, or the current banking and sovereign debt crises. These events have all proven to be portentous in the economic sense, heralding large adjustments of the economy, but were wholly unanticipated by economic actors.

Finally, the chapter concludes by asking about the nature of the business cycle. Are the shocks which set an economy in motion primarily real, or do they come from the monetary or financial economy? Do they originate in demand or supply? While it is not easy to settle this, it is possible to assess particular episodes, much like a doctor diagnoses a patient with many contradictory symptoms. Economic policy, like medicine, is often as much an art as it is a science.

16.2 Demand Management: What are the Issues?

16.2.1 Equilibrium or Disequilibrium: That is the Question

Since the publication of *The General Theory* in 1936, a fierce debate has raged between the Keynesians, who had embraced the Keynes' way of thinking about the macroeconomic short run, and those who tend to defend the classical framework of flexible prices and rely on the inherent self-corrective nature of the economic system. The latter group, known as the neoclassicals, stressed the role of money and monetary developments while de-emphasizing the usefulness of fiscal policy. Whereas early debates centred on arcane issues such as the slopes of curves, the contemporary debate revolves to a large extent around the question of nominal price rigidity. While there is near-universal consensus that prices and wages are sticky, disagreement persists about the extent of that stickiness and its relevance for shaping the evolution of output.

The debate is neatly illustrated in Figure 16.1. Starting from point A, an expansionary demand policy (an increase in the target rate of inflation under flexible exchange rates, or increased spending and/or tax cuts under fixed exchange rates) takes the economy first to point B. Under flexible exchange rates, the output effect is dissipated and the economy ultimately comes to rest at point C, where the effect is entirely absorbed by a permanently higher rate of inflation and exchange rate depreciation. Under fixed rates, the economy returns to A; only if the world simultaneously chooses a higher inflation rate consistent with C will the long-run inflation rate be higher. Regardless of the regime, the central question for the usefulness of demand policy depends on how much time the economy spends at B.

The path taken from B to C depends on the speed at which the short-run AS curve shifts. This in turn depends on how the underlying inflation rate reacts to actual inflation. As discussed at length in Chapters 12 and 13, the underlying rate of inflation reflects the forward-looking expectations of wage- and price-setters, who are free to set prices at the present, the expectations of future inflation embedded in wages and prices set in earlier periods but not free to

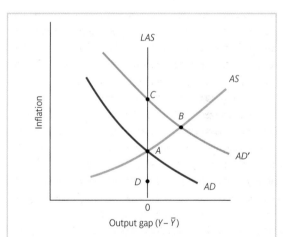

Fig. 16.1 The Neoclassical Case

An aggregate demand expansion—an increase in the target inflation rate under flexible exchange rates or expansionary fiscal policy under fixed exchange rates—moves the economy from point A to point B in the short run. In the case that a higher target inflation rate has been chosen, the economy lands at point C in the long run. If deviations from trend $\bar{y}$ are short-lived, the move is actually from point A to point C, which is not really helpful. It is more desirable to aim at point D, where inflation is low.

change, and elements of contracts which are simply based on past inflation, such as wage and price indexation. Quick adjustment means a fast move from *A* to *C*, in which case policy only creates inflation, at best with a temporary boost to GDP. If the economy spends most of the time on its long-run aggregate supply schedule (or curve) *LAS* anyway, it follows that a superior solution is simply to aim at point *D*, where inflation is low. In this view, the move from *A* to *D* is very rapid and low inflation can be achieved at little or no output cost. This is the neoclassical perspective.

Keynesians tend to see the economy as appending a lot of time away from its *LAS* schedule, usually below it. As a result, they frequently endorse **activist demand policies** aimed at returning it to its long-run potential. They are interested in avoiding situations like the one corresponding to point *A* in Figure 16.2, where output is below its trend level, and unemployment is above its equilibrium level. By construction, actual inflation is below its underlying rate at point *A*. Over time, the underlying inflation will decline and the short-run *AS* curve will shift downwards until point *C* is reached. In the Keynesian view, this adjustment may take a very long time, during which unemployment is high and output is forgone. This

means frustration among the unemployed, and inefficiency as productive resources remain under-utilized. The preferred solution for Keynesians is to pursue an expansionary policy, shifting the aggregate demand schedule out to *AD'* and bringing the economy quickly to point *B*.

The disagreement boils down to a simple question: can the economy stay away from the vertical aggregate *LAS* schedule for a long time? Put differently, how quickly does the short-run *AS* shift to bring the economy to rest on the vertical long run aggregate supply curve? Neoclassicals argue that these shifts occur too fast for policy to make much difference and, moreover, policy is unnecessary if GDP is never far from its growth trend. They assert that the forward-looking component of underlying inflation dominates the backward-looking component. Keynesians disagree. It is remarkable that so sharp a divergence about the desirability of policy actions arises from an apparently narrow dispute concerning what seems to be a point of detail. Indeed, it is possible to agree completely about the analysis of demand and supply—as presented in Chapter 13 and recalled here—and yet disagree on every aspect of economic policy simply because there is some doubt about the speed at which the *AS* curve shifts.

16.2.2 Persistence of Expectations and Underlying Inflation

The speed at which the *AS* curve shifts depends on the relative importance of the forward-looking component of underlying inflation. This raises the question of whether this component ultimately correctly anticipates developments that will determine the future inflation rate. For some time, Keynesians argued that people learn slowly about events and therefore adjust their expectations very gradually. Put differently, the forward-looking component of underlying inflation was thought to be driven by the past and not to contain information that fundamentally differs from the backward-looking component.

Neoclassical economists achieved a great victory when they argued that the only consistent way of thinking about expectations is to treat them as rational. The **rational expectations** hypothesis discussed in Chapter 7 posits that people do not make systematic errors. They may occasionally underestimate

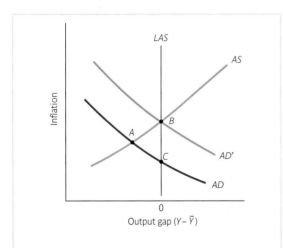

Fig. 16.2 The Keynesian Case
When the economy is below trend at point *A*, waiting for prices to adjust to reach point *C* may take a long time. An expansion of aggregate demand can return the economy to full employment at point *B*.

future inflation, and then overestimate it, but on average they get it right. If they do, and if the forward-looking component of underlying inflation dominates, then the *AS* curve will move fast. Two implications follow. First, on average, the economy will always be close to, if not exactly spot on, the *LAS* schedule. Second, the only departures from the *LAS* schedule will be the result of random expectation errors, which does not provide much room for policy to play a useful role. Indeed, in that case policy must rely entirely on surprises and errors. If surprises can be engineered now and then, they cannot be systematic, simply because there is no such thing as a systematic surprise. As for expectation errors, they can only be exploited by policy-makers if they know better than the public at large. If that is the case, one obvious and democratic solution would be for the government to share that knowledge with the general public.

The rational expectation hypothesis is intellectually compelling, not because it sees people as cold and heartless automatons, but rather because it rules out systematic (and possibly downright stupid!) mistakes on the part of economic agents. For instance, it is hard to accept that workers and firms would consistently underestimate inflation when it is rising systematically, because so much is at stake. In every country in the world, banks and economic consultants produce and sell forecasts to firms, trade unions, the media, and even the government. Their services are valued if they are right, or at least not systematically wrong. And, as they all compete for the same customers, it is reasonable to expect that those that are systematically wrong would eventually go out of business.

Modern Keynesians are usually willing to concede this point, but with two responses. First, they note that underlying inflation consists not only of expected inflation. Even if all agents perfectly anticipate the future, they may have signed nominal contracts in the past that lock them into prices and nominal wage increases, which were in turn based on rationally expected inflation in those earlier periods. Thus, when inflation deviates from these older expectations, there will be some interval of time when agents can do little or nothing about their errors. During that interval, which can be long-lasting, the economy deviates from trend output. Second, the speed at which the short-run *AS* curve moves depends on the speed at which actual inflation—i.e. prices—reacts to expected inflation. Once again, price stickiness is at the heart of the debate.

This discussion is far from simply academic. The question of how long economies can deviate from their long-run potential is a central practical issue for reform and stabilization programmes, such as those proposed and administered by the International Monetary Fund. For many decades the problem of high inflation plagued developing countries. It is often difficult to establish a credible anchor for agents' expectations. Put differently, when inflation has been more than 10–20% per year for many years, underlying inflation tends to reflect stubborn expectations that the central bank and the government can do no better. In such cases, a fixed exchange regime, a so-called hard-peg, may convince the population that the government means things different. The most extreme version of this idea is to join a monetary union, and many southern European countries had less than stellar reputations before joining the European Monetary Union. Box 16.1 describes the failure and success of Argentina und Bulgaria, which chose such an exchange rate anchor to pin down inflationary expectations and break the back of the forward-looking component of underlying inflation, even at the cost of giving up monetary authority, a price of fixed exchange rates stressed in Chapter 11.

16.2.3 The Costs of Inflation

Figure 16.2 depicts an important drawback to the Keynesian policy response of demand management. It is accompanied by higher inflation. Unless contractionary policy is pursued with the same vigour as expansionary policy, demand management policies can easily take on an inflation bias. Some politicians argue that this is an acceptable price to pay. Couldn't lower joblessness and higher output outweigh the inconvenience of permanently higher inflation? The cost of inflation is another source of disagreement between Keynesians and neoclassicals. Inflation is certainly undesirable, yet it is surprisingly difficult to identify and quantify those costs. Later we present a list of potential reasons why inflation bothers economists and possibly reduces people's well-being.

Income and wealth redistribution

Inflation has important redistributive effects—it shifts income and wealth from some groups of the population to others. To start with, inflation often distorts relative prices. When prices rise rapidly, even small differences in rates of increase of particular goods or of wages can lead to dramatic relative price changes. If labour unions are powerful, real wages will tend to stay ahead, which hurts firms' profitability, eventually deterring investment and harming growth. Those on fixed incomes and with limited political clout, such as pensioners or dole recipients, do not keep up. Real exchange rates tend to swing widely when inflation is high. This shifts income between local and foreign producers, and between the local producers of traded and non-traded goods since exchange rates exert strong influence on traded good prices but leave non-traded good prices relatively unaffected. Box 16.2 presents a spectacular example.

In addition, inflation redistributes wealth. When inflation comes as a surprise, it changes the value of nominal assets such as money, conventional government and corporate bonds, and bank accounts. In contrast, real assets—such as housing and land, durable goods, foreign exchange, and precious metals—tend to maintain their value in the face of changing inflation. Nominal assets tend to factor a certain rate of inflation into the agreed nominal rate of return, which can be associated with the underlying rate of inflation. When actual inflation lies significantly above the underlying or expected level, real interest rates can become negative, and wealth is redistributed from lenders to borrowers. Hyperinflations, in particular, can leave a legacy that survives many generations: 85 years after the terrible hyperinflation of the early 1920s, Germans still consider inflation as an absolute evil.

 Box 16.1 **The Exchange Rate Anchor: Argentina and Bulgaria**

The exchange rate anchor can represent potent medicine in economic policy, but it can be tricky to administer. It can work beautifully, but it can backfire if taken for too long and with inappropriate supporting measures.

Argentina offers an example of a success story that ended very badly. Throughout its modern history, Argentina has been crippled by high and ever-rising inflation rates, up to 10,000% in 1990. Powerful vested interests, acting in the background, ensured that the central bank could not or would not impose the required discipline. In early 1991, the Menem Government passed the 'Convertibility Law', which tied the peso to the US dollar at a remarkably visible rate of 1:1. Figure 16.3 (*a*) shows that inflation quickly declined. By 1993, it was about the same as in the USA, and stayed that way for the rest of the decade.

The Argentine cure, however, was directed too much at the symptoms and not enough at the root causes of the inflation disease. In the late 1990s, individual provincial governments began to run large budget deficits

that in the aggregate were translated into current account deficits.[1] Mounting losses of foreign exchange reserves alarmed international investors. Soon capital outflows added to the loss of reserves. In late 2001, facing acute economic and political instability, the government resigned. Its successor immediately abolished the Convertibility Law. The exchange rate promptly lost two-thirds of its value, output fell by more than 10%, and inflation was on the rise again.

Bulgaria presents more of a success story, driven by an intense desire to enter the European Union. Plagued by acute political instability, Bulgaria found it difficult to emerge from central planning in the early 1990s. Inflation soared and the currency collapsed. By 1997, its value was less than one-hundredth of what it used to be in 1991. A year later, the exchange rate was pegged to the deutschmark—and later to the euro. Inflation promptly declined, as Figure 16.3 (*b*) shows. Despite considerable difficulties posed by the recent financial crisis, Bulgaria remains committed to a fixed exchange rate regime.

[1] The link between fiscal and external deficits is clear from the accounting identity (2.7): PCA=(S–I)+(T–G). The link between deficits and debt is discussed in Chapter 7.

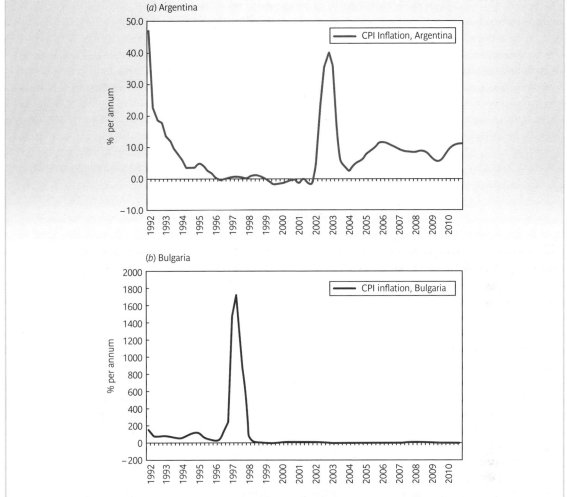

Fig. 16.3 Exchange Rate Anchors in Argentina and Bulgaria, 1992–2010

In Argentina, the exchange rate vis-à-vis the dollar was fixed at the one-for-one parity in 1991. The resulting constraint on monetary policy led to a massive decline in the inflation rate, which even turned negative for several years. When the peg was abandoned in late 2001, the exchange rate collapsed and, soon afterwards, inflation jumped. After a period of punishing inflation, Bulgaria fixed its exchange rate in 1998. As panel (b) shows, inflation promptly disappeared.

Source: IMF, International Statistics

Uncertainty and the value of price signals

In a market economy, prices play a central role as signals. They tell producers what and how to produce, consumers what and how to consume, whether to save, etc. In particular, the relevant signal is the relative price of one particular good measured in terms of another—not the price of goods in terms of pounds, euros, or dollars. Understanding these relative price signals is crucial to the efficiency of a market economy. It is here that high inflation can inflict great damage on the ability of market economies to function. This is because high rates of inflation usually are associated with more variability of inflation. The more variable inflation is, the less confidence firms and households have that nominal price movements they observe represent changes in real economic opportunities. Firms and households under-react to true relative price signals, because it is difficult to rec-

Box 16.2 **Switzerland: The Safe Haven**

As the financial crisis hit the world, panicked investors looked for safe havens where they could park their wealth. Despite the near-failure of its largest bank, Switzerland continues to represent a haven of stability and security. Figure 16.4 shows that the Swiss franc started to appreciate vis-à-vis the euro in late 2008. By September 2011, when the Swiss National Bank decided to peg the exchange rate, the franc had appreciated by more than 40%. As a result, foreign imported goods became cheaper—yet by much less than 40%, as discussed later—which forced domestic competing firms to also cut prices. By contrast, non-traded goods prices are sheltered from foreign competition. The figure shows that while housing rents—houses are the ultimate non-traded good—kept increasing along the previous trend, the overall price index abruptly stabilized and even started to decline. Producers of traded goods complained bitterly, while firms producing non-traded goods and services did not feel any pressure at all. The real winners probably were foreign firms exporting to Switzerland that were able to maintain Swiss franc prices unchanged, pocketing much of the 40% price increase in their own currencies. As already described in Chapter 11, the Swiss central bank came under heavy pressure to prevent any further appreciation by adopting a one-sided peg (the franc is free to depreciate but cannot go below 1.20 franc per euro).

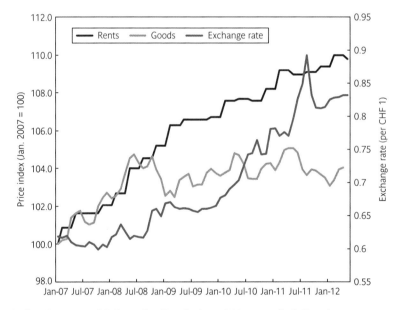

Fig. 16.4 The Swiss Franc and Prices for Traded and Non-traded Goods

Sources: Swiss National Bank and Swiss Federal Statistical Office.

ognize those signals when all nominal prices are changing and do so in a highly variable manner—they find it hard to distinguish movements in the price level from changes in relative prices.

Convincing evidence for such distortionary effects of inflation can be found in Figure 16.5. Panel (a) documents the positive link between inflation level and variability. Panels (b) and (c) show that

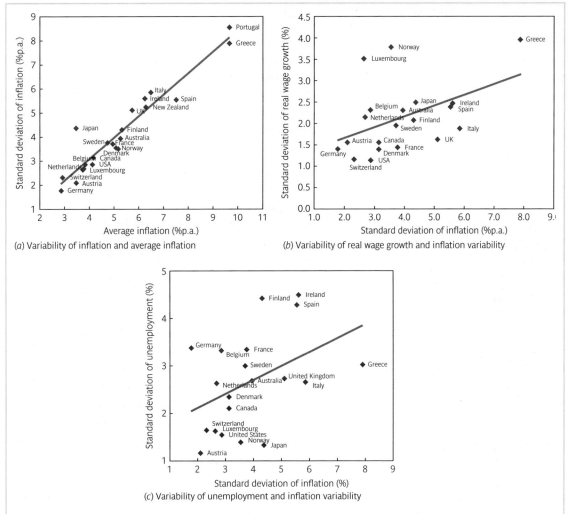

Fig. 16.5 Variability of Inflation, Real Wages, and Unemployment: OECD Countries, 1960–2010

For the past 50 years, higher average rates of inflation in the OECD economies have been strongly associated with more volatile inflation rates (correlation coefficient: 0.95). More variability of inflation rates is in turn accompanied by more volatile real wage growth (correlation = 0.46) and more volatile unemployment rates (correlation = 0.43), but these linkages are weaker.

Sources: IMF; OECD, *Economic Outlook*; Bureau of Labor Statistics.

more variable inflation is positively associated with more variable real wages and unemployment. Nominal fluctuations have real effects. When the efficient functioning of the price mechanism is attenuated, overall productivity declines, eventually resulting in lower growth and higher unemployment. Indexation—the contractual linking of individual prices or wages to the overall rate of inflation—can worsen matters because it tends to freeze relative prices and to lock in real rigidities. This further dulls the reaction of economic agents to relative price signals.

Box 16.3 Optimal Inflation

The late Milton Friedman argued that the optimal rate of inflation should be negative—a **deflation**, a period in which the price level falls steadily. More precisely, Friedman argued that the optimal inflation rate should equal the negative of the real interest rate. By the Fisher principle, the nominal interest rate should be set to zero.[2] Friedman's radical argument rested on a principle that production of a good should be expanded as long as the marginal benefit, i.e. what consumers and firms are willing to pay for it, exceeds the marginal cost. This principle can be readily applied to money produced by a central bank. For the public, the price of money is the opportunity cost of holding it, and in Chapter 9 showed that this is the nominal interest rate. The cost of creating money turns out to be virtually nil (the production of even a €100 banknote only costs the central bank or minting company a few cents). In theory, the state can make its citizens better off by providing them with the public good of money, which costs virtually nothing to make, at no cost. Naturally, if it did so, interest rates would have to be very low. As the argument goes, they should be zero.[3]

In principle, Friedman was right. Money is expensive to hold, especially if you own a lot of it. Its cost is most evident when inflation and nominal interest rates are very high. In such episodes, the demand for money all but vanishes, and people spend a lot of energy to avoid using it. Yet for a number of good reasons, Friedman's prescription has never been taken up in practice. To start with, deflation means that goods and services will be cheaper tomorrow than today—why buy anything now when prices will be lower next year? This pattern has been visible in Japan recently, as it suffered a prolonged slump for the decade of the 1990s. Second, it is hard to distinguish low inflation from price increases that represent quality improvements, which definitely should not be forced to be zero! Finally, it is a fact of life that almost all goods and services are taxed, so why should money be treated any differently? Inflation is a tax on money holdings, and has a role to play alongside all other taxes. In fact, in many countries where tax collection is weak, because of the costs of setting up a non-corrupt administration, inflation is one of the very best sources of tax revenues that can be tapped. For these countries, it may even be efficient to have significant inflation. In contrast, tax collection in developed economies, is less of a problem.

As already noted in Chapter 9, many central banks around the world have adopted **inflation targeting**, meaning that they publicly state and commit to some inflation rate as an objective of policy. The underlying presumption is that inflation is acceptable when people stop worrying about it. Table 16.1 presents their targets for 2003. Typically, these central banks aim at inflation rates around 2%. This is also the inflation rate which the European Central Bank associates with 'price stability'.

The value of money

While indexation may hurt the efficiency of the price system, it is often seen as one way to prevent income and wealth redistribution due to inflation.

---

[2] The real interest rate should equal the marginal product of capital less depreciation, as was presented in Box 8.6 in Chapter 8. The real interest rate r is the nominal interest rate i less the inflation rate π, i.e. $r = i - \pi$. When $i = 0$, it follows that $r = -\pi$.

[3] Friedman did *not* advocate handing out money on every street corner! To the contrary, he argued that as monopoly provider of money, the central bank should simply hold down the opportunity costs of holding money—and the way to do this is to reduce inflation *below* zero, and drive the nominal interest rate to zero. In the long run, this actually means being quite stingy with monetary growth!

This is because richer and better educated individuals are better equipped to protect their wealth, while the poor often have no obvious mechanism to prevent their real wages and social transfers from eroding. If all nominal values—all prices and wages, but also nominal interest rates, asset prices and the exchange rate—are indexed, the losers are simply those who hold money, which, by definition, is not indexed. The losses suffered when the value of money declines steadily—more frequent trips to the bank—may seem trivial. Yet examples of hyperinflation in history show that the consequences can be highly disruptive. Box 16.3 describes these costs and explains the concept of an ideal or 'optimal' rate of inflation.

Table 16.1 Inflation Targets Set by Inflation-Targeting Central Banks in 2011

	Australia	Brazil	Canada	Chile	Colombia	Czech Republic	Hungary
Inflation target	2 – 3%	4.5% ± 2%	2% ± 1%	3% ± 1%	3% ± 1%	2% ± 1%	3%

	Iceland	Israel	Rep. of Korea	Mexico	New Zealand	Norway	Peru
Inflation target	2.5 ± 1.5%	1 – 3 %	3 ± 1%	3%	1 – 3%	2.5%	2% ± 1%

	Philippines	Poland	South Africa	Sweden	Switzerland	Thailand	United Kingdom
Inflation target	4% ± 1%	2.5% ± 1%	3 – 6%	2%	less than 2%	0.5% – 3%	2% ± 1%

Source: National central banks.

16.3 Feasible Demand Management Policy

16.3.1 Frisch, Slutsky, and the Modern View of the Business Cycle

An important aspect of demand management policy is that it be *feasible*—that the central bank or the finance ministry can actually execute it, and do a good job at it. An important controversy between Keynesians and neoclassicals concerns the ability of governments to conduct policy effectively. The most important reason for scepticism is the nature of the cycle itself.

Economists' initial optimism about demand management policy was driven by a belief that the economy was more or less **deterministic**, meaning that the present depends mechanically on the economic history of the past. Business cycles do in fact exhibit important regularities and seem to follow an internal logic. Throughout the history of economic thought, economists have sought mechanisms by which each cycle sows the seeds of its successor, so that cycles go on reproducing themselves, just like the rising and falling of the tides. This would be the case if the economic system constantly generated forces that successively speeded it up and then slowed it down. It turns out that it is quite possible to

imagine how this can come about. And it would be easy to imagine how a dose of demand policy, properly administered, could cancel the wave to produce a flat growth path.

This optimistic view was badly shaken by the discovery that cycles can be generated from purely random, or stochastic, factors. This **stochastic view of business cycles** can be traced to the work in the late 1920s and early 1930s by the Russian Eugen Slutsky (1880–1948) and the Norwegian Ragnar Frisch (1895–1973).[4] To understand this important discovery, consider an economy which starts away from its steady-state equilibrium path but returns to it over time—for example, the growth model of Chapter 3. The question to ask here is: how did it get off that path in the first place? Slutsky and Frisch reasoned that economies are constantly subject to random disturbances, or shocks. These might come from demand (e.g. alternating optimistic and pessimistic entrepreneurial

---

[4] Ragnar Frisch received the first Nobel Prize in Economics in 1969. Eugen Slutsky, who perhaps deserves more credit than he received, was a researcher at the Conjuncture Institute in Moscow during Stalin's dictatorship and was unable to publish this discovery until eight years later, when his work was finally translated into English.

animal spirits or the consumer mood, or policy actions) or supply (e.g. exceptionally bad or good crops and natural disasters; important inventions or discoveries like the steel furnace, railways, electricity, or computers, as well as minor ones; social unrest). The list of potential shocks is endless. Like drops of rain generating ripples on a lake, these shocks constantly buffet the economy, moving it away from its previous position.

These shocks, often referred to as impulses, change the demand or supply conditions in the economy. Once randomly disturbed, the economy embarks on a deterministic adjustment described in the previous section, until the occurrence of the next shock. The **impulse-propagation mechanism** transforms, or cumulates, these random impulses into irregular cyclical oscillations. Even though the response to individual shock is damped, old oscillations are constantly being supplemented by new ones corresponding to more recent shocks. In the vision of the business cycle shown in Figure 16.6, it is sufficient to accept the view that an economy is regularly buffeted by endless series of shocks, and never really settles down to its stationary state. The rest of this chapter follows on this lead, which is the cornerstone of modern business cycle theory.

How likely is it that purely random impulses working their way through the economy actually generate the kind of behaviour corresponding to our earlier stylized facts? Can shocks which continuously move the economy away from its steady state and followed by its internal dynamic actually explain business cycles? Box 16.4 recalls how this question received an affirmative answer at the dawn of the computer era. Figure 16.7 shows how the *AS–AD* model can transform random shocks into realistic cycles. In panel (*a*), 200 purely random shocks drawn over time are plotted.[5] Such observations—truly random impulses—could represent a succession of unforeseeable events, large or small. Panel (*b*) shows what happens when these shocks are 'filtered' by the propagation mechanism implied by a version of the *AS–AD* model described more precisely in Box 16.5. The result is a

Fig. 16.6 The Impulse-Propagation Mechanism

Random shocks hit the economic system, which produces business cycles. The cycles result from the averaging or cumulation of these random disturbances over time.

succession of artificial business cycles which resemble those of, say, the UK data presented in Figure 1.5. Although the impulses themselves are not cyclical at all, the transformed variable exhibits irregular, periodic movements which resemble realistic business cycles.

The impulse-propagation mechanism is now the dominant way of thinking about business cycles, because it accords well with the stylized facts. Box 16.5 explains in detail how the *AS–AD* model provides a natural framework for thinking about how cycles arise. Since they are random, the shocks typically generate cycles of different sizes and magnitudes. If many of these impulses are related to permanent technological innovations, not only will they trigger cycles, but in the long run they will also cumulate into a process of long-run growth. This is consistent with the observation that in the long run, the growth process (the accumulation of positive shocks) dwarfs business cycles (the reaction to individual productivity and other shocks).

16.3.2 Uncertainty, Policy Lags, and the Friedman Critique of Demand Policy

For policy, fundamental uncertainty behind the business cycle is bad news. It necessarily implies that governments will never be able to completely iron out the cycle. The mere fact that markets fail to adjust to shocks quickly due to nominal rigidities does not imply that governments can offset them effectively. The same uncertainty or incomplete information that prevents markets from making the best possible use of available resources may also hamper government actions. Furthermore, private actors in the economic system such as firms and wage negotiators

---

[5] Such a random variable which is identically and independently distributed is often called white noise. White noise has the property that current and past values contain no information helpful in forecasting future values.

Box 16.4 Computers, Scientists, and Business Cycles

Although the path-breaking work of Slutsky and Frisch on random events and cycles took place in the 1930s, hard evidence that random influences can generate cyclical behaviour resembling actual economies was not forthcoming until the late 1950s, when computers became widely available to researchers. Frank Adelman, a nuclear physicist, and his wife Irma, an economist, studied an economic model developed by Lawrence Klein, the 1980 Nobel laureate from the University of Pennsylvania, and Arthur Goldberger of the University of Wisconsin. (This model consisted of 25 equations summarizing the most important macroeconomic relationships in the US economy.) First, the Adelmans found that the Klein–Goldberger model could not generate a cycle on its own because the fluctuations died down after a few years. Yet, when continually perturbed by random shocks, it produced data that had the same statistical properties as actual US business cycles. They concluded that:

Ever since the path breaking article of Frisch on the propagation of business cycles, the possibility that the cyclical movements observed in a capitalistic society are actually due to random shocks has been seriously considered by business cycle theories. The results we have found in this study tend to support this possibility ... The agreement between the data obtained by imposing uncorrelated perturbation upon a model which is otherwise non-oscillatory in character is certainly con-

sistent with the hypothesis that the economic fluctuations experienced in modern, highly developed societies are indeed due to random impulses. (Adelman and Adelman, 1959: 620.)

The Adelmans simulated, or solved, their model 100 years into the future on an IBM 650 and were proud that 'computations for one year could be made during an operating time of about one minute'. Now that simulations take seconds or less on a laptop, this approach has become routine. Much effort has gone into improving and enlarging models and the algorithms used for simulations. More recently, Robert E. Lucas of the University of Chicago and 1995 Nobel Prize laureate in economic sciences, made this research strategy explicit:

Our task as I see it ... is to write a FORTRAN [a programming language] program that will accept specific economic policy rules as 'input' and will generate as 'output' statistics describing the operating characteristics of time series we care about, which are predicted to result from these policies. (Lucas, 1980: 709–10.)

In the last decade, the economics profession has taken Lucas's challenge to heart. Rather than isolated policy interventions, central banks and finance ministries are more likely to evaluate the macroeconomic effects of policy *rules*—Taylor rules for monetary policy, and tax and stabilization rules for fiscal policy, for example.

have a strong incentive to discover their mistakes promptly and take corrective action. It is not obvious that governments face the same incentives or, even if they do, that they can react as quickly.

Indeed, macroeconomic economic policy must contend with a number of lags. First, a **recognition lag** hinders policy-makers' ability to intervene effectively. This is simply the time needed to discover that some policy intervention is required. As the previous section suggests, there is good reason to believe that fundamental uncertainty will always be present, and governments will be just as surprised as private agents. Next, governments need time to formulate policy. This is called the **decision lag**, and is usually

associated with the details of parliamentary democracies. Depending on the government structure, this can be coupled with an **implementation lag**, as ministries must originate, and parliaments must pass, legislation. Even if implemented quickly, policies need time to produce their effects. This is especially true of monetary policy. It can take several quarters before the easing of money market conditions and depreciating exchange rates have an impact on real activity. To make matters even worse, the duration of this **effectiveness lag** is quite variable, ranging from a few months up to two or three years.

How should governments react to the long and variable lags in economic policymaking? One possible

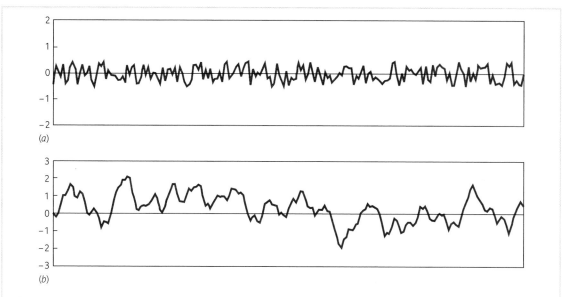

(a)

(b)

Fig. 16.7 Impulses and Propagations: An Example

Panel (a) depicts 200 observations of a random variable, ε_t. Panel (b) displays data from panel (a) after they were transformed, or 'filtered', by the formula $Y_t = 1.3\,Y_{t-1} - 0.4\,Y_{t-2} + \varepsilon_t$, starting from a given Y_0 and Y_{-1}. This 'filter' has the ability to mimic a true data series, working only with purely stochastic influences. It is the solution to one particular version of the $AS-AD$ model studied throughout this book.

 Box 16.5 **Impulse-Propagation Mechanisms in the $AS-AD$ Model**

Chapter 13 showed how the $AS-AD$ model can help us understand the determinants of output and inflation in the short and long run. It can also be used to study business cycles. The point of departure is to identify the shocks as factors that shift either the AS or AD curves. **Demand shocks** shift the AD schedule, while **supply shocks** affect the position of the AS curve. Both demand and supply shocks can be positive or negative. Positive shocks, for example, move the relevant schedule rightwards; negative shocks shift them to the left. Lags in economic relationships are the central source of dynamics in the $AS-AD$ framework. Lags exist for various reasons: slow responses of demand to income and of supply to demand imply that the AD schedule reacts gradually to demand disturbances. Consumers smooth spending relative to income, and adjustment costs may

slow the response of investment to new opportunities. The supply side may also be a source of **persistence**, if underlying inflation catches up only gradually with past inflation.

As an example, consider a permanent increase in the target inflation rate of the central bank operating in a system of flexible exchange rates.[6] Assume that underlying inflation is equal to last period's inflation and start with an economy already in a stationary state at point A. (This is a simplifying assumption which abstracts from other cycles already underway that would interfere with the one under study.) The cycle triggered by this disturbance is tracked in Figure 16.8. The increase in the target inflation rate leads to a reduction in the nominal interest rate and an increase in aggregate demand. This takes the economy to point B in panel (a), with an

---

[6] A formal analysis is provided in the WebAppendix to this chapter. While such a shock is not commonplace, it is useful to help focus ideas. A similar shock worth discussing is a

permanent increase in the *foreign* inflation rate under fixed exchange rates.

increase in both output and inflation. Owing to demand lags, the initial shift of the AD curve to AD' represents only an initial, partial response. For a time, the AD schedule will continue to move rightwards towards AD". Indeed, the lagged response of output means that the longer-run shift of the AD curve always exceeds that of the short run and that, as output rises, the AD curve keeps moving to the right.

The AS curve will also shift upwards, as underlying inflation gradually catches up with the actual inflation rate. Over time, the economy moves towards point C.

With actual output in excess of its trend level, inflation catches up and eventually overtakes the target inflation rate.[7] This implies that the real money stock declines and with it output. Declining output means that the AD curve begins to move leftwards. Actual inflation then starts to decline, followed by underlying inflation and a downward shift of the AS schedule (not shown). Pursuing this reasoning, it appears that the adjustment will be characterized by the 'loops' shown in panel (b), with alternating periods of output above and below equilibrium level—i.e. business cycles.[8]

Fig. 16.8 The Propagation Framework in the AS–AD Model

In this example, the initial impulse is a permanent increase in target inflation by the central bank. In panel (a), from its initial stationary equilibrium at point A, the economy first moves to point B, as the AD curve begins to respond to the monetary impulse. Gradually, underlying inflation increases in response to actual inflation, and the AS curve, whose position depends on underlying inflation, slides to AS'. Further lagged responses of demand to money growth result in gradual shifts of the AD curve towards AD", bringing the economy to point C. Further movement in underlying inflation towards actual inflation moves the AS schedule towards AS" (point D). Because output has begun to decline, the AD curve begins a descent. As inflation declines, underlying inflation follows and the AS curve also moves downwards. The economy follows a loop of the kind exhibited in panel (b).

reaction is to do nothing at all! This is what Milton Friedman argued in the 1950s. According to the **Friedman critique**, ill-timed policy interventions may actually worsen the cycle. Under the best of circumstances, there is no guarantee that policies will be implemented in time, or achieve the stated objectives. If the government has no information advantage over the private sector, it might even do more harm than good. The best policy that governments can pursue is a steady hand, rather than making matters worse by adding uncertainty.

Figure 16.9 illustrates the point. The blue line represents the path of output subjected to business cycle

[7] How do we know this? As long as money growth exceeds inflation, the real money stock M/P expands. When the interest rate is stable, the demand for money $M/P = k(i)Y$ grows at the same growth rate as trend output. For M/P to return to its trend, however, inflation must exceed money growth for some time.

[8] The example was chosen because a single impulse induces a cyclical reaction which resembles a cycle. More generally, this property is not a necessary condition for stochastic shocks to generate cyclical behaviour.

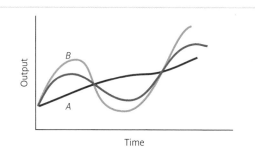

Fig. 16.9 Lags and Demand Management Policy

The blue line shows the business cycle arising from fluctuations in aggregate demand in the private sector. A demand management policy correctly implemented would smooth out the fluctuations (curve A). If there are significant effectiveness lags, the government may need to enact these measures well in advance of the turning points in the cycle. If instead the government reacts passively, it may simply reinforce the cycle (curve B).

fluctuations that would arise if the economy were just left to itself. A perfectly thought-out and implemented policy would begin to stimulate the economy just when it is nearing a peak so that, given the various lags described, its effects come into play just at the time it is needed. Similarly, it would turn restrictive just when the trough is passed, so as to moderate the strength of the upturn. Ideally, the outcome would be curve A. Now add uncertainty about the recognition, decision, implementation, and effectiveness lags. In the worst case, we face the risk of causing outcome B. The stimulus planned for the downturn affects the economy exactly when it is coming out of the recession, while restraint comes into play just when the economy has peaked. Here, policy makes things worse!

At the same time, the problem may not always be as severe as Friedman's critique makes it out to be. Returning to Keynes' metaphor, we might say that if the dentist is called early enough and allowed to act decisively, he may prevent the most serious of toothaches. He might also be able to prescribe some medicine which may act automatically and take some of the pain and swelling the next time a molar must be pulled. For example, ministries can prepare tax cuts or increases in advance, in order to cut down on the

implementation and effectiveness lags. Governments can be given greater budgetary authority to reduce the time associated with the decision lag. The adoption of **automatic stabilizers** is an effective way for legislators and policy-makers to get around the machinations of politics. Automatic stabilizers, which are discussed in more detail in Chapter 17, slow an economy down in a boom phase and stimulate it in recessions. The most important aspect is the automatic part. They need little or no political decisions and can thus evade the political wrangling that may impart a decision lag on an otherwise well-informed government.

In order to conduct monetary policy more effectively and independently, central banks have also entered the forecasting business, either generating their own 'in-house' predictions or employing outside consultants to help. In practice, national policy-makers use the many indicators of business conditions discussed in Box 16.6. For example, real stock prices and real money balances are relatively reliable leading indicators, and anticipate downturns by roughly four to six quarters. The yield curve, capacity utilization, changes in inventory stocks, investment spending plans, and real exchange rates can sometimes prove useful in the forecasting game, offering somewhat less lead time. The very fact that the lead time of these indicators is frequently less than a year suggests that keeping ahead of the cycle is difficult.

16.3.3 Politics and Political Constraints on Demand Management Policy

So far, governments have been described as well-meaning entities which care about the nation's welfare. Alternatively, we could see governments as distinct economic agents run by politicians who care about getting elected and staying in power. Policy then becomes endogenous to both economic and political circumstances, and, reciprocally, economic circumstances are partly shaped by policy actions. The loop is closed and provides interesting, if not always encouraging, insights into the role and function of demand management policies. Demand management policies may not be employed to stabilize the economy, even if they are effective. What's more, their abuse by politically motivated governments can even be a *source* of business cycles.

If governments care about remaining in office as long as possible, it is natural to expect them to use macroeconomic policies to boost their re-election prospects. Incumbent governments will try to make sure that the economy is booming and employment is high on election day. Naturally, this might soon be followed by inflation, so governments will often tighten their policies after being re-elected. Panel (a) of Figure 16.11 shows the prediction from this view of **electoral business cycles**.

A different view is that, when in power, a political party pursues a partisan agenda. This agenda can be motivated by ideology or by the coalition of interests that back the party. The **partisan business cycle** view predicts that changes of party in power result in policy changes that generate their own cycles. It is customary to describe left-leaning governments as being Keynesian and right-leaning governments as being neoclassical. Then, if a left-leaning government replaces a right-leaning government, we should expect to see GDP growth initially increase and unemployment decrease, at the expense of rising inflation and deficits, which will require a contractionary correction, followed by yet another expansion, etc. This pattern is shown in panel (b) of Figure 16.11. The opposite political shift, from left to right,

Box 16.6 Leading and Lagging Indicators

Central banks and ministries are in the business of forecasting GDP. National budgets depend on tax revenues, and tax revenues depend on economic activity. Not only do governments need to get ahead of the curve when making policy, they also need to communicate overall economic trends to the public. In Chapter 1 we learned that many variables move together over the cycle, or are coincident (e.g. consumption, investment, and interest rates). Yet if one variable systematically leads or lags another, contemporaneous correlation may be small or nil, an important link may exist. These links can help policy-makers anticipate turning points in the cycle and reduce the bite of the Friedman critique. The Burns–Mitchell diagrams in Figure 16.10 display the cyclical behaviour of a number of frequently tracked macroeconomic variables, averaged over eight OECD economies.[9] Recall that the horizontal axis of the Burns–Mitchell diagram indicates the number of quarters before (–) or after (+) the peak of the reference cycle for GDP. The vertical axis generally displays the value of an index which takes a value of 1.0 on average over the reference cycle (in some cases we display percentage deviation from an average value). The diagrams show average tendencies, and not perfect regularities. Evidently, some variables tend systematically to peak ahead of, and others systematically to trail behind, output. For example, stock prices, real money balances, the primary current account, the real exchange rate, vacancies, and inventory investment are all examples of leading indicators. They tend to predict the emergence of recessions and expansions. Variables which attract the most attention in the press such as employment, unemployment, and inflation tend to be lagging indicators. Investment, short-term interest rates, and capacity utilization are examples of coincident indicators, although in some countries they provide a quarter or two's advance warning of a downturn.

Our knowledge of the macroeconomy can account for these regularities, and you are asked to do so in the exercises at the end of this chapter. Financial variables are useful leading indicators because they are forward-looking. Share prices generally decline three to four quarters in advance of a downturn. Since real stock prices are a measure of Tobin's q, financial markets anticipate the next phase of the cycle and, for example, expect poorer profitability during the downturn phase. The real money supply starts to decline six months to a year in advance of the onset of a recession. The real exchange rate appears—on average—to depreciate sharply five to six quarters before the onset of a recession. It even appears to overshoot, and starts to appreciate, just before the business cycle peak is reached.

[9] Burns–Mitchell diagrams are used as a descriptive device to summarize the average behaviour of variables over a 'representative cycle'. They are described in detail in Chapter 1.

The eight economies considered are the UK, Spain, Canada, France, Germany, Italy, Japan, and the USA.

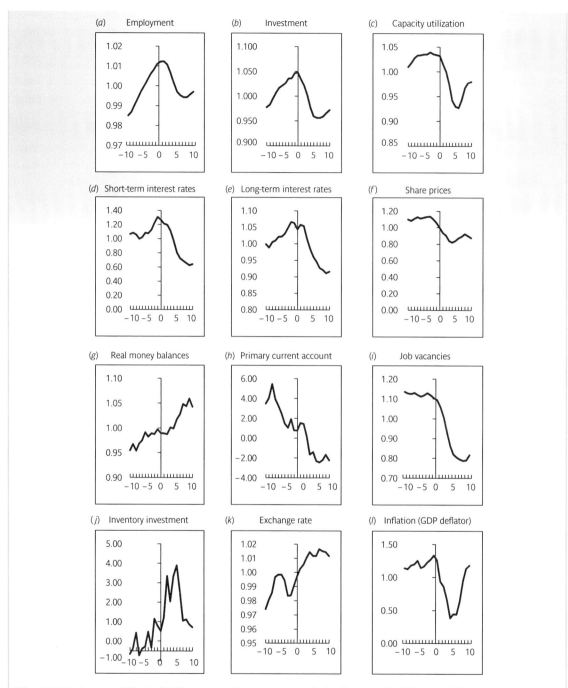

Fig. 16.10 Burns – Mitchell Diagrams, Macroeconomic Indicators in Eight OECD Economies, 1970 – 2010

Burns–Mitchell diagrams display the average behaviour of key macroeconomic variables centred around the peak or a trough of well-defined business cycles across several countries. Here the zero point corresponds to a cyclical peak. For more detailed explanations of the Burns – Mitchell diagram, see Chapter 1.

Sources: OECD; IMF; authors' calculations.

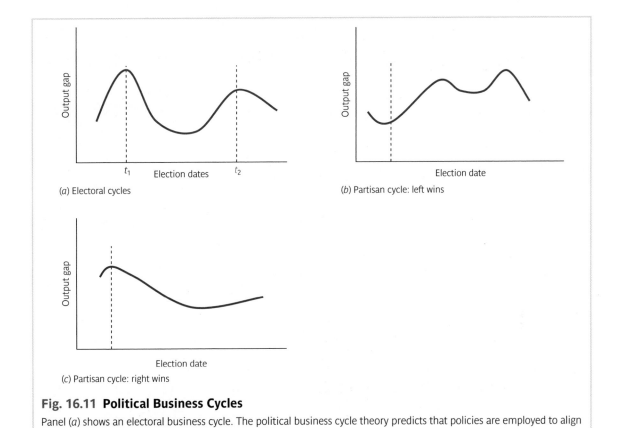

(a) Electoral cycles

(b) Partisan cycle: left wins

(c) Partisan cycle: right wins

Fig. 16.11 Political Business Cycles

Panel (a) shows an electoral business cycle. The political business cycle theory predicts that policies are employed to align the peak of the cycle with election dates. Elections are then followed by austerity-oriented policies. Panel (b) shows the effect of a change from a right-wing to a left-wing government; the opposite change is shown in panel (c).

is expected to generate policies that focus more on price stability and are less activist, as shown in panel (c). The interesting innovation of the partisan business cycle hypothesis is that by the very nature of the election process, the economy *must* be subject to a shock after every election! Rational workers and firms will prepare for an election by expecting some 'average' of the parties contending for public office. By construction, they will be wrong *ex post*. This shock, combined with the propagation mechanism already discussed, can give rise to business cycles.

The existence of **political business cycles** is not firmly established, and there are good theoretical and empirical reasons to be sceptical. The general view that governments can manipulate their macroeconomic instruments to achieve political gain on election day runs sharply against the forward-looking view of rational expectations adopted in this

book. Citizens who care about the future should see through government attempts to manipulate voters' sympathies. They should understand, for instance, that a boom designed to arrive on election day will be followed by restrictive policies soon afterwards. Not only should they not be impressed, but also they could be expected to vote against a government that actually destabilizes the macroeconomy.

Similarly, the idea that partisan governments use macroeconomic policy to favour interest groups is not as straightforward as it may seem. Presumably, voters span the whole spectrum of opinions, as shown symbolically in Figure 16.12. To be elected, a party must gather support from all the voters who share most of its views *plus* the '**median voter**' in the centre. This median voter, who holds the key to electoral success, does not hold right- or left-wing views, so why should there be a shift in policies? The only

Fig. 16.12 **Partisan Politics**

Voters' views are spread over the range of ideologies and political preferences. To be elected, a party needs to win a majority, which means its own supporters *plus* the median voter.

reason is that the median voter is first seduced, only to be cheated upon later. This would explain both partisan policy swings and the rejection of governments which have served the interests of its constituencies at the cost of incurring the median voter's wrath. The other possibility is to form coalitions of left- and right-wing parties that shun the centrist electorate. In that case, the equilibrium of the extremes could still deliver policy stability.

In practice, it is probably an oversimplification to presume that left-leaning governments are always Keynesian while right-leaning governments are neo-classical. When supply-side shocks were dominant, the pendulum shifted towards the neoclassical view. The late 1990s, a period of rising popularity of the neoclassical views, witnessed the emergence of the 'third way' among left-leaning parties in a number of countries (New Labour in the UK, Schröder in Germany, Clinton in the USA, etc.), while right-leaning parties have adopted the 'compassionate Conservative' image championed by Bush and Chirac. Since 2008, all major political parties in the OECD economies have endorsed some form of fiscal and monetary stimulus for the economy. Given the magnitude of the global economic demand shock that was associated with the Great Recession, this is not surprising.

16.4 Sources of Business Cycle Fluctuations and the Future of Demand Management Policies

16.4.1 Demand or Supply Shocks?

The analysis of Section 16.3 and the example in Box 16.5 showed how the *AS–AD* framework can account for business cycles. The next step is to isolate the nature of those cycles, as predicted by the *AS–AD* framework, and to identify the component that demand management policy might be used to counteract. Only when the policy-makers are convinced that they face a demand shock can it make sense to pursue activist demand policy.

It is natural to start with the distinction between demand and supply shocks. The standard case studied in the previous section—a permanent increase in the central bank's target inflation under flexible exchange rates—is one example of a long-run demand shock. Using similar reasoning, one can see that a cut in taxes, an increase in government spending, or an attack of animal spirits or exuberant consumers would cause a short-run surge in demand. In particular, demand shocks are characterized by rising output

relative to trend and increasing inflation, while supply shocks see output and inflation moving in opposite directions. Is the theory's prediction, that demand shocks lead to loops of the type depicted in Figure 16.8, borne out by the facts?

The case of German unification, as seen from the perspective of West Germany, represents a readily identified demand shock.[10] While output in the East was collapsing, consumption, investment, and government spending by East German residents was rising rapidly. Consumers who had been repressed for several decades and anticipated an increase in their future incomes met West German banks eager to attract new customers, especially as none of them was indebted. This also applied to local governments, which loaded up on new infrastructure and equipment. Most of this spending went to West German firms, which were poised to satisfy this extra demand.

---

[10] For East Germany, it was more likely a mixture of negative demand and supply shocks.

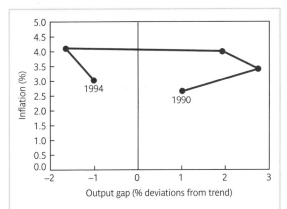

Fig. 16.13 A Demand Shock: The Effect of German Unification on West Germany, 1990 – 1994

German economic and monetary unification occurred in 1990. Spending by former East German households, firms, and governmental authorities increased dramatically, and most of this demand fell on West German producers. The figure traces out the effect on West German GDP—measured as a deviation from its trend—and rate of inflation.

Sources: OECD, *National Accounts*; OECD, *Main Economic Indicators*.

Figure 16.13 shows that the outcome was indeed a counterclockwise loop, with an initially positive co-movement of output and inflation. The initial demand surge was accommodated little significant inflationary pressure. After two years of expansion, the signs of overheating became more and more evident: increasing nominal wage demands by unions, high rates of capacity utilization, etc. In the end, the Bundesbank (the German central bank at the time) refused to tolerate further inflation and money growth, and sharply raised interest rates. Inflation declined, but at the cost of a recession.

The second example traces an economy's reaction to a supply shock, the first oil price increase in 1973–1974. Panel (*a*) of Figure 16.14 shows the theory. The *AS* curve shifts up to *AS'* because the cost of a major input, energy, abruptly rises. Without any policy reaction, the shock moves the economy from point *A* to point *B*. Thereafter, once the initial burst of cost increases is absorbed, the *AS* curve moves back to its initial position—but only gradually so, since underlying inflation is on the rise, trailing actual inflation.

Similarly, with a reduced GDP, the *AD* curve also moves down, so that the return is shown as the curved trajectory from *B* to *A*. If, instead, the authorities decide to fight the inflationary implication of the oil shock and tighten up demand, the *AD* curve shifts leftwards to *AD'* and the economy moves from *B* to *C* and will return to point *A* via point *D*, for example.

Panels (*b*) and (*c*) give two examples of reactions to the oil shock. Panel (*b*) shows that the Swiss National Bank adopted an explicitly anti-inflationary strategy. After the shock, inflation increased and output continued to grow as it completed the expansion phase started a few years before. But then, restrictive demand policies, implemented through a reduction of the target inflation rate, provoked a sharp recession followed by a gradual decline in inflation—the overall cycle matching trajectory *ABCD* in panel (*a*). In contrast, authorities in the UK did not fight inflation, which was already high at the time: panel (*b*) depicts a loop similar to the *ABA* trajectory in panel (*a*).

To think about cycles using *AS–AD* analysis—and how to deal with them—it is crucial to know which types of shock predominate. When supply shocks are prevalent, demand policy will not be particularly useful since restoring output will be at the cost of much higher inflation. In the face of a large demand shock, a missed chance to employ demand policy may be costly. Identification of shocks is a tricky business, and economists employ both sophisticated statistical methods as well as historical comparisons to help pin down the facts.

16.4.2 The Real Business Cycle Challenge

Many, if not most, of the shocks that hit modern economies are real in nature. This should be not terribly surprising, since it is not the job of central banks to subject the economy to arbitrary shocks but rather to create stable, predictable monetary conditions. A number of researchers have used this as an argument to ignore the monetary and financial side of the economy when explaining the business cycle. While this **real business cycle (RBC) theory** represents a minority of macroeconomists, it is a group which has nevertheless contributed in

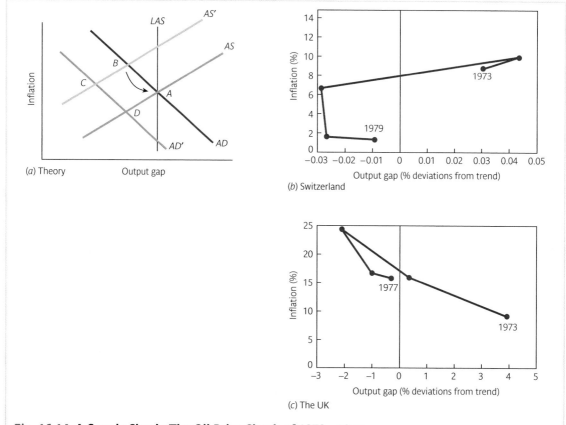

Fig. 16.14 A Supply Shock: The Oil Price Shock of 1973 – 1974

An adverse supply shock is captured by an upward jump of the *AS* schedule to *AS'*. Once oil prices stabilize, the *AS* curve gradually comes back down. A country intent on fighting inflation, like Switzerland shown in panel (*b*), also curbs demand, bringing the *AD* schedule down to *AD'*. The UK, shown in panel (*c*), does not exhibit the same aversion to inflation, so its cycle more closely resembled the trajectory from *A* to *B* and back to *A* in panel (*a*).

Source: OECD, *Main Economic Indicators*.

important ways to the way that macroeconomists think.[11]

In the *AS–AD* framework, business cycles are propagated in part because prices are sticky. Prices adjust slowly to shocks, and during that time, shifts in nominal demand have real effects, as shown in Chapters 10 and 11. Does this mean that business cycles are impossible when prices are perfectly flexible? Real business cycle theory argues that fluctuations can be seen, to a

first approximation, as a market-clearing, equilibrium phenomenon. The approach is provocative. In an economy with completely flexible prices, the only shocks that affect the real economy are supply shocks—those which shift the *LAS* schedule right and left. To the extent that monetary and fiscal policies do not affect the *LAS* line, they are irrelevant. At the same time, if the economy is always on its long-run supply schedule, the propagation mechanism found in the *AS–AD* model is shut down. Real GDP simply moves randomly in response to random supply shocks. So it would seem that such an economy would be free from cyclical tendencies. Yet this is not the case.

---

[11] In 2004, the Norwegian Finn Kydland (1943–) a Norwegian, and the American Edward Prescott (1940–) were awarded the Nobel Prize in economics for their work in this and related areas.

The hallmark of RBC theory is its emphasis on propagation mechanisms which have nothing to do with price stickiness and dynamics of underlying inflation. It starts by focusing on supply shocks related to the production technology. The main source of impulses is new discoveries, inventions, product innovations, or process improvements. These shocks alter the productivity of factors of production, change the environment of economic agents, and cause them to change their behaviour. In the RBC framework, shifts in the aggregate production function—which correspond to shifts in total factor productivity—are called **technological shocks**. They are the sole exogenous impulses that disturb the economy.[12]

The RBC theory asserts that the *LAS* curve is the only one of interest. But how does the RBC approach translate the shock to technology into a cycle? RBC stresses two main channels. The propagation mechanisms which lie behind the RBC approach can be found in the parable of Robinson Crusoe in Chapters 7 and 8.[13] The first involves the accumulation and decumulation of physical capital. An increase in marginal productivity of capital provides an incentive to invest. The build-up of capital takes time, and contributes to a higher output level along the way. Since the technology shock is temporary, its passing will mark a decline in the productivity of capital, triggering a process of disinvestment and a fall in productive capacity back to the initial level. The second propagation mechanism involves the response of labour supply in the short run to what is a temporary opportunity. The result is a flexible-price business cycle.

Figure 16.15 illustrates the initial impact of a favourable temporary productivity shock. In the first instance, it raises the marginal productivity of both capital and labour. In the short run, the stock of capital is constant, so the rate of return on capital must

Fig. 16.15 A Productivity Shock

A productivity shock raises the marginal productivity of capital and labour. In the short run, the stock of capital is unchanged and the real interest rises. When aggregate labour supply is inelastic ($L^{S(\text{INELASTIC})}$), the labour supply curve is vertical so the effect on productivity gain is to raise the real wage rate without any change in employment. When aggregate labour supply is elastic ($L^{S(\text{ELASTIC})}$), the response is a small changes in wages with larger fluctuations in employment.

rise as in panel (*a*); real interest rates rise.[14] Output rises up since the same amounts of capital and labour are now more productive. On the demand side, wealth rises because both wage and profits are higher, so consumption also increases.

The second propagation mechanism is related to the other factor of production, labour. One feature of the second panel of Figure 16.15 is unappealing: if labour supply is inelastic, there is no change in

---

[12] In the sticky price interpretation of the business cycle, fluctuations in the Solow residual—which is highly correlated with real GDP—are endogenous and are one of several manifestations of a normal business cycle.

[13] In fact, the RBC approach is frequently associated with more advanced versions of the growth theory presented in Chapter 3.

[14] If the same shock affects the whole world, the world real interest rate is likely to rise. If it affects only one country, the real interest rate can still rise temporarily even if the nominal interest rate cannot change when the exchange rate is fixed. Expected inflation would then absorb the difference.

employment over the cycle. This contradicts the aggregate evidence (the Burns–Mitchell diagrams of Figure 16.10) that employment and unemployment fluctuate a lot. To make productivity shocks consistent with large changes in labour supply, we need a good reason for the aggregate elasticity of labour supply to be so high. The primary determinant of the slope of labour supply, as emphasized in Chapter 5, is the leisure–consumption choice: each period a worker decides whether to work, earn money, and consume—or to enjoy leisure. Our conclusion, backed by empirical evidence, was that the supply of labour is inelastic at the household level. A flat aggregate labour supply curve would only result from the aggregation of different households (see Figure 5.4).[15]

Instead, the RBC approach accounted for the high elasticity of labour supply by studying the behaviour of a representative household choosing between leisure today and leisure tomorrow. Just as Crusoe chooses when to consume over time, the RBC approach stresses the possibility of taking less leisure—working harder—in those periods when its price is high—when wages are high and rising. To the extent that the shock depicted in Figure 16.15 is a short-lived event, Crusoe will be more likely to substitute leisure for work. A favourable temporary productivity shock raises today's wage and the real interest rate. This in turn has two effects. First, a higher wage and a higher real interest rate today make work effort worth more today relative to tomorrow. The substitution effect means that Crusoe works harder today. Second, and in contrast, the income effect implies that Crusoe works less today and tomorrow, since more leisure can be afforded in both periods at the same work effort. If the substitution effect dominates the income effect, the labour supply schedule in panel (b) of Figure 16.15 is elastic and significantly more labour is supplied. GDP rises over and above the direct productivity effect of the productivity shock. In later periods, after the boom subsides, workers 'cash in' and work less. As labour supply is reduced,

GDP decreases. All of that occurs without assuming any wage or price rigidity.

16.4.3 The Failure of the Real Business Cycle Approach

The RBC view represents an extreme version of the *AS–AD* model which sees no role for nominal variables or aggregate demand. Initially, the advent of the RBC theory was an exciting development because it forced researchers to explain business cycle facts without appealing to wage and price stickiness, which themselves are hard to explain. Yet in the end, the RBC agenda has failed to convince the majority of the profession, to a large extent because the theory cannot account for important features of the data. In this section, we review some of these limitations:

◆ **Equilibrium and Optimality**. While the *AS–AD*, or sticky price, account of business cycles relies on disequilibrium in markets—prices do not adjust immediately to changing demand and supply conditions—the RBC theory views the rising and falling tides of economic conditions as an equilibrium response to productivity shocks. It studiously avoids the terms 'demand' and 'supply' since technology shocks affect both, and economic agents are fully aware of this. One important conclusion of the RBC approach—and one that is disturbing for many economists—is that it is impossible to use demand management policies to improve matters in the macroeconomy. A striking implication of the RBC theory is that it is not even desirable to smooth out the business cycle. This is because households and firms are doing the best they can, given changing constraints, so there is nothing to lament. Deep recessions, for example, are seen as the economy's best response to severe adverse productivity shocks. From the RBC perspective, the Great Recession observed throughout the world and in the USA in particular represents the outcome of severe technological regress. For some reason, this regress did not occur in Australia, Brazil, and China and was much less persistent in Germany and Japan. This makes the RBC account difficult to accept without significant embellishments which deviate from the original idea.

---

[15] In principle, a flat collective bargaining curve would achieve the same result, but the RBC approach has generally avoided considering these forms of market imperfections. Instead, they have preferred to focus on the fixed costs of going to work and the lumpiness of individuals' decisions to take a job.

Fig. 16.16 The Solow Residual and GDP, UK 1971 – 2010 (% per annum)

Growth in total factor productivity, as measured by the Solow residual, is strongly correlated with output. To some extent, the movements in total factor productivity growth appear to be random. Yet persistent periods of negative total factor productivity growth are difficult to reconcile with the notion of technological progress.

Sources: OECD; authors' calculations.

◆ **Technology shocks and total factor productivity**. Another problem with the RBC approach is the measurement of the sole driving force in the business cycle: technology shocks. These are usually measured as the Solow residual of Chapter 3, i.e. growth in total factor productivity (TFP) on a quarter-by-quarter basis. An example of TFP growth calculated for the UK over the past four decades is plotted in Figure 16.16. The extreme volatility and cyclical behaviour of TFP growth is suspect. It is known that neither labour nor capital hired by firms is always fully employed. Because dismissal costs are sizeable and human capital in their workers often firm-specific, firms avoid firing employees immediately in downturns. While production is reduced, workers perform tasks unrelated to production, such as maintenance, building improvements, painting, and cleaning. Later, during an expansion phase, a reserve of labour is available which can be tapped. The same argument applies to the utilization of the capital stock, which is not constant over the cycle (see Figure 16.10). The stylized fact of procyclical total factor productivity is likely due to a faulty measure of inputs: labour in recessions is employed, but not in productive activities—we say it is hoarded—and it is gradually put back to more directly productive use in the upturn that follows. Similarly, capital is used less intensively in downturns, leading to underestimation of its productivity in these periods. It is hard to rule out that the procyclical behaviour of the Solow residual largely reflects similar behaviour of the utilization of hoarded production factors.

◆ **The irrelevance of policy**. Another difficulty with RBC theory is its denial of any role for monetary policy in the business cycle. This view calls into question the existence of central banks and monetary policy because the *AS* curve is always vertical and money is neutral—even in the short run. We saw in Figure 16.8, however, that the *real* money stock is procyclical, and in fact is a leading indicator.[16] In that case, an increase in real aggregate demand is accompanied—or even led—by an increase in demand for money that is passively supplied by the central bank. In recent years, new generations of models stressing the instability of the real demand side—some using techniques pioneered by RBC theorists—have had some successes in reconciling the *AS–AD* model with these facts.

Ultimately, the crux of the debate is about the relevance of wage and price rigidity in the macroeconomic system. Ignoring it or pretending that it is absent is hardly a substitute for proving that it is irrelevant. Evidence indicates that prices—measured as aggregate indices—do appear to be rigid in the short run. It is this element of realism that is lacking in the RBC theory of macroeconomic fluctuations, despite its intellectual rigour. While realism is not essential for a good macroeconomic model, price stickiness has such wide-reaching implications that it would appear essential to include it, or at least to explain why it is unimportant.

These shortcomings of the RBC model have limited its acceptance by a wide spectrum of the economics profession. At the same time, the development of the RBC approach provided researchers with a number of new ideas and methods for understanding how shocks are transmitted, and the newest macro models at central banks and other research centres have incorporated many of them into orthodox thinking.

16.4.4 The Great Recession and Demand Management: New Challenges or Old Dilemmas?

The message of this chapter may seem pessimistic—that aggregate demand management is inherently problematic and can backfire. Yet in practice policy-makers are frequently called to decisive action in the light of large exogenous shocks. After the ter-

rorist attacks on 11 September 2001, much of the world faced an immediate crisis: fear of the unknown, a meltdown of financial markets, a collapse of confidence and animal spirits. The consequences for aggregate demand were foreseeable and dire. The reaction of the USA was swift. A massive increase in government spending on security and military gave a boost to demand. Most importantly, the Governor of the Federal Reserve System, Alan Greenspan, ordered the Fed to intervene massively and to provide liquidity to the banking system; the Federal Funds Rate was reduced several times in succession. There is little doubt that the surge in military and national security expenditures in 2002 helped accelerate the recovery of the US economy in 2003.

Perhaps the greatest challenge to demand management policy was posed by the global financial crisis and the Great Recession which ensued around the world (2008–2009). The initial reaction to the financial crisis was cooperation among central banks across the globe to provide liquidity to banks, to maintain orderly trading conditions, and to help banks take over other banks which had suffered large losses on securitized mortgage investments. In 2009, the US government nationalized two mortgage finance firms, Fannie Mae and Freddie Mac, as well as American International Group (AIG), which had issued excessive amounts of credit default swaps (CDS) described in Chapter 14 and had not set aside sufficient reserves to cover the growing number of defaults. Decisively and in a remarkably non-partisan manner—a tax rebate was enacted in 2008 to stimulate demand, and the new Obama administration passed the American Recovery and Reinvestment Act of 2009, a stimulus package of almost $800 billion of tax cuts, infrastructure spending, and aid to US states.

In Europe, aggregate demand management faces more fundamental limitations. While the ECB has come under increasing pressure to follow the Fed's lead, it was committed to fighting inflation. More importantly, the representative European country—to the extent it uses the euro—has no access at all to monetary policy, and even if it could set it, would have to use it on the entire euro area. Second, even though fiscal policy is effective under fixed exchange rates, most individual European countries are too small and too open to have a fiscal policy that has any sort of meaningful multiplier.

---

[16] RBC proponents aren't disturbed by this. They see money and credit demand as passive, expanding with the economy but without any causal effect on real variables. Their argument is supported by the coincident and strongly procyclical behaviour of interest rates in Figure 16.8. In the *IS–TR* framework, a money supply impulse is expected to work on output via declining interest rates. *Only* if shifts to the underlying *IS* curve predominate—if most impulses come from the real demand side (spending, fiscal policy, the current account)—and if monetary policy works with a lag, is procyclical money and interest rates consistent with a sticky price model.

Despite these hurdles, the ECB followed the Fed's lead and cut the central bank refinancing rate from 3.75% in October 2008 to 1% by mid-2009. Already in November 2008, the European Commission agreed to a coordinated set of national stimulus measures designed to support aggregate demand. Similar measures were enacted in other parts of the world, including Australia, Brazil, China, and India. Despite this considerable intervention, the effects were rather modest, especially for those countries struggling with the deepest recessions. Few had illusions about the government spending multiplier, yet values estimated by economists rarely exceeded 1 and were small for open economies. While some economic commentators were calling for even more stimulus packages in 2010, an uneasy feeling about the risks of pursuing the wrong kind of demand policy was growing. Box 16.7 discusses what seems to be different about the current recession for some advanced economies. It also explores some of the less conventional elements of policy which have been tried out, as well as some old insights from the past.

Box 16.7   This Time It's Different? Unconventional Policies for Unconventional Times

As a result of a freeze-up in world financial markets on the heels of the Lehman Brothers bankruptcy in October 2008, real GDP in 2009 plummeted by 3.5% in the USA, by 5.1% in Germany, by 4.9% in the UK, and 6.3% in Japan. World output, which had been growing by 4.1% per annum from 1999 to 2008, fell by 0.7% in 2009, the first fall in more than three decades. The recession clearly hit the advanced nations of the world differently. While the Asian economies and northern Continental Europe were growing again by 2010, growth in Ireland, Spain, the UK, and the US was anaemic. After the financial crisis, many households, firms and financial institutions found themselves underwater—their debt much larger than the market value of their assets. We say that they had too little equity or net worth (the difference between the value of all assets and all liabilities). In the USA, up to a third of homeowners lived in houses which were worth less than the mortgage loan with which the house was financed.

Under such conditions, standard fiscal policy may not work at all. The underlying problem is that too much borrowing occurred to buy overpriced assets. The traditional monetary policy response, a reduction of policy interest rates, may not prove very useful either. Households which are determined to restore their balance sheets—increasing their equity—will not be interested in more borrowing, even at very low interest rates. Banks may, if only to take the proceeds and buy treasury debt, pocketing the profits. Firms prefer to hoard their cash than to invest it. Figure 16.17(a) shows that in the period 2009–2011, net borrowing of the private sector was *negative*—for the first time since the end of the Second World War. Simultaneously, private households in the US were tightening their belts as they have never done since the Second World War. At the writing of this book, many US Americans, as well as many Britons, Irish, and Spaniards continue to hold back on consumption, despite near-zero interest rates. In doing so, assets prices are depressed, exacerbating the situation. Irving Fisher, writing in the 1930s, made the same observation, writing that

'...the liquidation defeats itself. While it diminishes the number of dollars owed, it may not do so as fast, as it increases the value of each dollar owed. Then, the very effort of individuals to lessen their burden of debts increases it, because of the mass effect of the stampede to liquidate in swelling each dollar owed.' (Fisher 1930, p.344.)

To deal with this situation, central banks have experimented in earnest with unconventional policies. One is open market operations in longer-term debt. Usually central banks buy and sell government securities or lend at the short end of the maturity spectrum. In 'Operation Twist', the Fed began purchasing longer-term government debt while simultaneously selling shorter maturities. In December 2011 and early 2012, the ECB extended up to €1,000 billion in loans to the banking sector at very favourable terms for three-years maturity, a sharp deviation from the usual policy of short-term refinancing. As a result, the balance sheets of the Fed, the Bank of England, and the ECB as well as many other central banks around the world are growing rapidly. Some believe that this policy is the ultimate weapon against the deflationary retirement of debt—and is sowing the seeds of a longer period of sustained inflation.

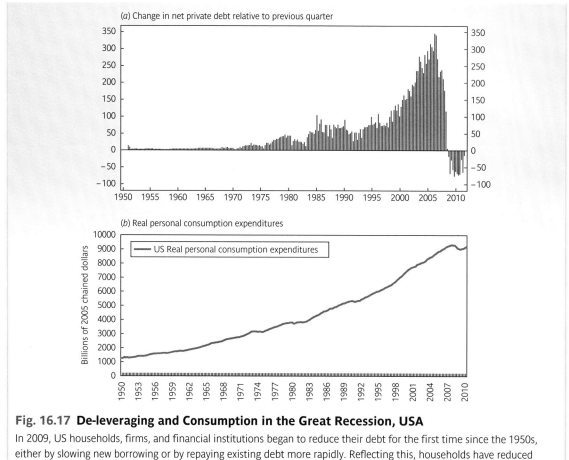

Fig. 16.17 De-leveraging and Consumption in the Great Recession, USA

In 2009, US households, firms, and financial institutions began to reduce their debt for the first time since the 1950s, either by slowing new borrowing or by repaying existing debt more rapidly. Reflecting this, households have reduced consumption spending sharply.

Source: Federal Reserve Flow of Funds Accounts, US Bureau of Economic Analysis

More critically for Europe, the depth and persistence of the recession conveyed the impression that some countries might not recover quickly. Their fiscal situation deteriorated more rapidly than usual, not only because revenues declined with GDP, but because interest rates applied for refinancing old debts and new borrowing were rising. Countries of southern Europe, which had been running risky fiscal policies for more than a decade, were facing swelling budget deficits in an increasingly skittish government debt market. In the next chapter, we describe how slowing of growth and a groundswell of pessimism can lead to such a critical situation.

⚠ Summary

1 While it is theoretically possible for demand management policies to smooth out business cycle fluctuations, recent experience and economic principles suggest a more measured approach.

2 A justification for demand management arises when markets do not clear rapidly, leading to low levels of output and employment over a longer period of time. Neoclassicals and Keynesians mostly disagree on the *degree* to which prices and markets can achieve continuously efficient allocation of resources and optimal satisfaction of individual needs.

3 Neoclassicals argue that market-clearing is a good first-order approximation, and that markets are closer to perfection than governments. Keynesians generally believe that markets suffer from a host of imperfections and that economies can suffer from persistent underutilization of resources.

4 One reason that output may remain below equilibrium output for some time is the speed at which inflationary expectations can be validated and adjusted. Even if economic agents have rational expectations, they may have taken decisions at an earlier date and locked in outdated expectations. This will affect macroeconomic variables today.

5 Uncertainty plays an important role in the debate. For Keynesians, private decisions are taken with imperfect knowledge of future conditions. This results in wrong pricing and resource allocation decisions. For neoclassicals, uncertainty means that policy mistakes are more likely to make matters worse than to improve them.

6 The modern conception of the business cycle is the culmination of many small and large random influences. These shocks are difficult, if not impossible, to forecast. It is thus hard to imagine a government that would be able to offset all these shocks, especially given the recognition, decision, implementation, and effectiveness lags associated with policy.

7 One way around this problem is to make judicious use of leading indicators. Another is to make extensive use of automatic stabilizers which reduce recognition and decision lags.

8 Real-life policy-makers do not always have the best intentions, caring more about being re-elected instead. This may lead some governments to employ demand management policies in a politically opportunistic way.

9 Political business cycles may take the form of expansionary policies being introduced just before elections, to be followed by corrective, contractionary policies after elections. Partisan business cycles may result from the alternation of governments that defend the interests of their constituencies.

10 The real business cycle is an attempt to understand the business cycle as a purely real phenomenon without reference to the financial or monetary sector. While this approach has the attraction of being a self-contained and logical construct, the fact that it fails to address the real or apparent rigidity of wages and prices has limited its acceptance.

11 Demand management policies are no longer as attractive as they were in earlier times. This is partly because economies are more open today, both real and financially. Yet in times of acute crisis, demand management policy can have effects and should be considered.

🔑 Key Concepts

- neoclassicals, neoclassical economists
- Keynesians, Keynesian economists
- activist demand policies
- rational expectations
- deflation
- inflation-targeting strategy
- deterministic, stochastic view of business cycles

- impulse-propagation mechanism
- demand shocks, supply shocks (or disturbances)
- persistence
- recognition, decision, implementation, and effectiveness lags
- Friedman critique
- automatic stabilizers

- ◆ **electoral business cycles**
- ◆ **partisan business cycles**
- ◆ **political business cycles**

- ◆ **median voter**
- ◆ **real business cycle theory**
- ◆ **technological shocks**

❷ Exercises

1 Explain the motivation for Keynesian activist demand policy using a diagram. Explain the neo-classical rejection of that type of policy.

2 Why is the behaviour of underlying inflation so critical to evaluating the effectiveness of policy? What determines this behaviour? How does the exchange rate regime (fixed or flexible) affect your answer?

3 How important is the slope of the *AS* curve for evaluating the effectiveness of demand policy? What underlying characteristics of the economy might contribute to a steeper *AS* curve?

4 What are the costs of inflation? Are there any benefits of inflation? If so, what are they?

5 Flip a coin 50 times, writing down +1 for heads, −1 for tails (you may use a spreadsheet program if you like). Call this variable ε_t. Now create a new variable, defined as $y_t = \frac{1}{4}\varepsilon_{t-1} + \frac{1}{2}\varepsilon_t + \frac{1}{4}\varepsilon_{t+1}$, so the new variable is a weighted average of present, past, and future lagged values. (You will not be able to compute the first and the last values of *y*.) Plot both time series and comment on them. How do your results change if you use $y_t = \frac{3}{4}\varepsilon_t + \frac{1}{4}\varepsilon_{t-1}$ instead?

6 Now repeat your experiment, using a normally distributed random variable for ε_t instead of the

coin flip (you will definitely need a spreadsheet for this). Plot your results. How do they compare to those of the previous problem?

7 Define the Friedman critique of activist macro-economic policy. What is an essential element for it to be true? What could be done by governments to avoid it?

8 Name some leading, some lagging, and some coincident indicators. Explain the behaviour of these variables, using the *IS–TR–IFM* and *AS–AD* frameworks.

9 Why might the slope of the yield curve (long-term rate minus short rate) be a good predictor of the business cycle? How might it depend on the Taylor rule in force? How would it depend on the exchange rate regime? Draw what you think a Burns-Mitchell diagram might look like and explain why.

10 Suppose there is a sharp rise in oil prices, much like in the 1970s under a regime of flexible exchange rates. Suppose that in the first instance, central bank policy does not adjust the inflation target. Explain the consequences, using the *AS–AD* model. Given this outcome, is there an argument for demand management policy, and if so, what kind of policy? What would be the argument against it?

➲ Essay Questions

1 'Aggregate demand policy is based on exploiting misperceptions of the private sector in order to increase GDP.' Discuss.

2 Can activist demand management policies affect equilibrium unemployment?

3 State and critique the Friedman rule for optimal inflation. How might the accuracy of inflation measures affect your support for this rule?

4 Recent bail-out packages for the Greek economy have imposed fiscal austerity measures (spending cuts and tax increases) on this country, which has traditionally run large budget deficits. Explain why the *IS–TR* model as well as the *AS–AD* predict that these austerity measures will lead to larger reductions in income and inflation than under a system of flexible exchange rates. Do you think underlying inflation will react more or less strongly to the measure? How should this affect the adjustment process?

5 Critique the RBC explanation of the business cycle. Many proponents have expanded the range of shocks understood as 'technology' to include regulation, taxation, terms of trade, and rule of law. Do you think this is a useful way of explaining the Great Recession?

Fiscal Policy, Debt, and Seigniorage

17

Chancellor: In my old age I have been freed from pain.
Listen and look at this portentous bill
Which has made welfare out of all our ill:
'Be it known to all men who may so require;
This note is worth a thousand crowns entire.
Which has its guarantee and counterfoil
In untold wealth beneath imperial soil.
And this is hereby a substitute approved
Until such time as the treasure can be moved.'
Emperor: And do my people think it negotiable?
Do army and court take it for pay in full?
Strange though I think it, I must ratify it.
Steward: To collect those fluttering notes, one couldn't try it;

Once issued, they are scattered in a flash.
The Exchanges stand wide open for the queue
Where every bill is honoured and changed for cash—
Silver and gold—at a discount it is true.
And then to butcher, baker, pub it goes,
Half the world only seems to think of stuffing;
While the other half in brand new clothes goes puffing.
The clothier cuts the cloth, the tailor sews.
Long live the Emperor! Makes the cellars gush
In a cooking, roasting, platter-clattering crush.

Goethe's *Faust*

17.1 Overview

Governments play an important role in our economic lives. Especially in Europe, they are big, and have been growing bigger for most of the post-war period. Table 17.1 shows that governments in the European Union spend close to half of GDP, leaving the other half to the private sector. What do they spend their money on? A large part, about one-third of GDP, consists of transfers and subsidies to individuals (health and unemployment insurance, poverty alleviation). Transfers represent income redistribution from the haves to the have-nots, from the lucky ones to the needy ones, expressing a sense of solidarity among citizens and a rejection of excessive inequalities. Governments are also big consumers, constructing roads, purchasing buildings and the services of public employees, and much more. Of course, to pay for all that, they collect taxes—again about a half of GDP.

Governments are not known to be particularly strict in managing their budgets. In fact they have turned out to be big borrowers. Budget deficits are frequent, and most governments are heavily indebted to the private sector and foreigners. While European countries have consolidated their budgets in recent years, on average public debt still represents nearly three-quarters of a year's GDP, and in several countries, including Belgium, Greece, Ireland, Italy, and Japan, the gross stock of public debt represents more than a full year of national output. Is this debt fundamentally bad? Or is there a more optimistic view that debt can and should be used to smooth government tax policies when expenditures are temporarily high?

We begin by looking at the economic functions of governments and how they fulfil their tasks. Do governments have an economic role to play at all? This question has been debated since time immemorial

Table 17.1 General Government Spending and Finances: Eurozone, USA, and Japan, 2010

	Eurozone	USA	Japan
Total spending (% of GDP)	50.5	42.3	40.7
Public consumption			
as % of GDP	21.6	17.0	20.1
as % of private consumption	37.5	24.1	34.2
Budget surplus (% of GDP)	−6.0	−0.6	−8.1
Gross debt (% of GDP)	92.4	93.6	199.7

Source: OECD.

between right, left, and centre, between partisans of laissez-faire and interventionists. In this chapter we focus on two economic functions of governments: the microeconomic function, which includes the provision of **public goods** and services and income redistribution, and the macroeconomic function, which aims at stabilizing aggregate activity.

Governments frequently run budget deficits. Like households, if they spend more than they earn, they must then borrow and accumulate debt. This process is inherently explosive, since more debt means more debt service, hence the need to borrow even more. To get this process under control, governments must run a primary surplus in the future, just as we learned from Crusoe in Chapter 7. But governments also have a unique feature: they can

also borrow from their central banks. When central banks lend to governments, in effect they create money that is used to pay for public spending, just as Mephistopheles did in Goethe's *Faust*. This unique privilege, based on their monopoly right to create legal tender, is called **seigniorage**. Seigniorage provides relief to the government when in need to borrow, but if abused it ultimately means fast money growth and inflation. Finally, government can simply refuse to pay back their debt as originally arranged or default, partially or totally, on its debt. In contrast to private agents, governments can default with impunity, in effect confiscating the wealth of its creditors. Fortunately, this most radical solution is only made use of in times of national emergency.

17.2 **Fiscal Policy and Economic Welfare**

17.2.1 **Provision of Public Goods and Services**[1]

Governments 'produce' goods and services, mostly for collective consumption. Why are they involved in such an activity? The two main reasons are that some goods are fundamentally public goods while others are produced under increasing returns.

The particularity of public goods is that they cannot be appropriated for individual consumption. Once they are available for one, they are available for all. This applies, for example, to law and order, defence, public gardens, or foreign affairs. In addition, some public goods exhibit a special characteristic: their use by one person actually *benefits* others. This is called an (positive) **externality**. A good example is education. All of society benefits from mass literacy. For example literate workers, who are in short supply in some poor countries, interact more effectively, which raises their productivity. Indeed, there is considerable evidence that economic growth is powerfully enhanced by the population's education level,

which we called **human capital** in Chapter 4. The generic feature of collective goods is that they cannot be appropriated by anyone—think of law and order, for instance—and therefore cannot be sold. For this reason, private producers would not produce them, and if they are needed, governments must step in.

Furthermore, the existence of externalities implies that individuals would only buy what they need personally, overlooking the benefits to others. In general, they would buy less than is desirable for society as a whole. For example, if no one else knows how to write and read, my own incentive to learn how do to so is close to nil. This is why basic education is not only public and free, but also compulsory. Police protection is another example. Security could be privately organized, but safe streets are good for everyone, whether they pay for them or not. In practice, only better-off, homogeneous neighbourhoods could afford to set up public safety on their own. Society has an incentive to combat lawlessness on a wider scale than do individuals interested only in protecting their own safety.

A similar reasoning applies to the case of goods produced under increasing returns. One example is

[1] Chapters 4 and 18 discuss the characteristics of public goods and their role in economic growth.

the usage of streets: the cost of paving and maintaining a road is roughly the same whether there are few or many users. Streets could be private and their use charged to users. This would undoubtedly relieve traffic congestion in cities, but perhaps too much. Each of us could react to street tolls by reducing our movements to the point where the cost per remaining user would lead to the curtailment of street provision in some areas, in the end hurting everyone.

While there is a strong justification for *some* government consumption, there are no clear-cut borders between goods and services that can be provided only publicly and those that could be provided privately. One key role of democracy is to choose those borders, and adapt them from time to time as economic and social factors dictate. The absence of unequivocal criteria for deciding what should be publicly provided explains why there is much national soul-searching on the issue. In many countries, debates resurface constantly concerning such cases as education (private schools and universities exist alongside public education), social security (health and retirement insurance are increasingly provided privately), and utilities (highways are built and run by private companies; electricity and telephone networks are privately owned and operated).

17.2.2 Redistributive Goals: Equity versus Efficiency

A fundamental result from microeconomics is that **productive efficiency**—the optimal use of available productive resources—is achieved when each factor of production is paid its marginal productivity. This may result in a very unequal distribution of income and wealth. Indeed, we observe the coexistence of much individual wealth alongside grinding poverty. While this outcome may be efficient from a productive point of view, an altogether different logic emphasizes that human beings have similar basic needs that should be met under all circumstances. Equity or fairness is often seen as a requirement for society to be cohesive and stable. Yet equity and efficiency often work against each other. There is a fundamental **equity–efficiency trade-off**.

Governments can and do reduce inequalities. Progressive income taxes reduce the differences in post-tax incomes. Taxes levied on the better-off pay for transfers to the worse-off. In fact, a significant part of public spending is dedicated to income redistribution. Table 17.2 shows the size of transfers, both as a share of GDP and as a proportion of total government outlays (spending). In some countries, this is the single largest item in the government budget. Not surprisingly, different countries deal differently with the equity–efficiency trade-off. Austria and Sweden seem to place more weight on equity than Japan or the USA, for example.

There is a trade-off, however. Income redistribution for the sake of equity has disincentive effects. Highly paid—and presumably highly productive—people may reduce their work effort in response to

Table 17.2 Government Transfers, Various Countries, 1960 and 2010

	% of GDP		% of government outlays	
	1960	2010	1960	2010
Austria	14.8	31.0	51.8	59.1
Belgium	12.7	32.7	44.8	61.7
Denmark	7.6	38.2	35.1	65.4
Finland	9.0	34.3	41.6	62.3
France	16.3	35.7	53.5	63.0
Germany	14.1	29.9	50.2	62.6
Greece	5.3	28.1	30.6	56.0
Ireland	9.6	28.7	38.7	43.0
Italy	11.2	31.6	45.4	62.9
Japan	4.5	24.8	34.5	60.5
Netherlands	8.6	28.8	n.a.	56.3
Portugal	3.7	29.2	24.5	56.8
Spain	2.9	27.8	23.1	60.8
Sweden	8.6	34.9	32.2	65.9
UK	9.0	29.7	30.7	58.7
USA	6.0	30.9	24.4	52.2

Sources: European Economy; OECD, *Economic Outlook*.

heavy taxation, or may even move abroad. On the other hand, those who receive transfers from the state may find it pointless to work hard for little net reward.

17.3 Macroeconomic Stabilization

Providing public services and redistributing income does not imply that total government spending systematically exceeds revenues. The government could perform its microeconomic functions without running budget imbalances; it only needs to raise enough tax revenue to meet its expenses. As Table 17.3 shows, however, significant surpluses and deficits are the rule rather than the exception, especially in the last year of the table. Do the deficits and surpluses of governments indicate bad planning or irresponsibility? Not necessarily. The second function of public budgets is to stabilize aggregate income and spending, which stabilizes employment at the same time.[2] To achieve these goals, governments should dissave in bad years and save in good years, just as many people do. Public imbalances cannot always be explained by appealing to this motive, however, as we will see.

Table 17.3 Government Budget Balances, Various Countries, 1975–2010 (% of GDP)

	1975	1980	1985	1990	1995	2000	2005	2010	Average 1970–2010
Austria	−2.4	−2.0	−3.0	−2.5	−5.9	−1.9	−1.8	−4.6	−3.0
Belgium	−6.4	−10.2	−9.9	−6.7	−4.5	−0.1	−2.8	−4.2	−5.6
Denmark	−2.4	−3.5	−2.1	−1.3	−2.9	2.2	5.0	−2.9	−1.0
Finland	5.1	3.8	3.5	5.4	−6.2	6.8	2.5	−2.8	2.3
France	−1.9	−0.1	−3.0	−2.4	−5.5	−1.5	−3.0	−7.0	−3.0
Germany	−5.6	−2.9	−1.1	−1.9	−9.7	1.3	−3.3	−3.3	−3.3
Greece	−2.6	−2.3	−10.4	−14.0	−9.1	−3.7	−5.3	−10.4	−7.2
Ireland	−11.2	−11.2	−10.8	−2.8	−2.1	4.8	1.6	−32.4	−8.0
Italy	−10.3	−7.0	−12.4	−11.4	−7.4	−0.9	−4.4	−4.5	−7.3
Japan	−2.0	−3.2	−0.6	2.1	−4.7	−7.6	−6.7	−8.1	−3.9
Netherlands	−3.4	−4.2	−3.7	−5.3	−9.2	2.0	−0.3	−5.3	−3.7
Norway	3.0	5.4	9.7	2.2	3.2	15.4	15.1	10.5	8.1
Spain	−0.2	−3.0	−7.3	−4.1	−6.5	−1.0	1.0	−9.2	−3.8
Sweden	5.1	−5.8	−3.7	3.4	−7.3	3.6	1.9	−0.3	−0.4
UK	−5.2	−3.7	−3.3	−1.8	−5.8	3.7	−3.3	−10.3	−3.7
USA	−5.2	−2.6	−5.0	−4.2	−3.3	1.5	−3.3	−10.6	−4.1

Source: OECD, *Economic Outlook.*

[2] The link between output and unemployment is given by Okun's Law, which was presented in Chapter 12.

17.3.1 Consumption and Tax Smoothing

In Chapter 8 we learned that people generally dislike fluctuations in their consumption levels. As a result, they tend to borrow in bad years to sustain a level of consumption they are accustomed to, and in good years they pay down on their debts and, if possible, even save for the rainy day. The citizens' desire for **consumption smoothing** applies to their consumption of public goods and services as well, and it is the responsibility of governments—and a determinant of their electoral success—to provide a steady flow of public goods and services. To do so, like individuals, governments have to borrow and save, depending on the economic situation. This is more important because government income is very sensitive to cyclical fluctuations. Tax revenues fall when peoples' incomes decline, simply because taxes are usually set as a percentage of income. Because taxes reduce individuals' incomes and, therefore, their private consumption possibilities, it makes little sense to increase them in bad times. **Tax smoothing** is the natural fiscal counterpart to consumption smoothing of households.

This principle has a central implication for the conduct of fiscal policy. If a series of bad years reduces the country's income, which is also the tax base, the government's best course of action is not to try to balance the budget. In the interests of its citizens, it should maintain a steady flow of public goods and services, and finance the revenue shortfalls by borrowing.[3] Conversely, a few particularly good years, during which taxable income rises, should not be used to raise government consumption, but to increase savings. Acting on behalf of the public at large, a government should behave like any economic agent, meeting temporary income disturbances by saving or borrowing, within the limits of its budget constraint. Box 17.1 applies the principle of tax smoothing to the controversial case of Germany's unification.

Budget deficits are financed by public borrowing, which increases the stock of public debt already in existence. Figure 17.1 shows how public debt (as a

---

 Box 17.1 Tax Smoothing after German Reunification

When he endorsed swift reunification early in 1990, Chancellor Helmut Kohl promised that there would be no new taxes for West Germans. Yet the former East Germany entered the Federal Republic with precious little dowry, a hugely inefficient productive sector, a large external debt (mostly to West Germany), poor infrastructure, and considerable environmental liabilities. In the eastern states, output fell by about 50%, unemployment—official and unofficial—rose to about 30%, and state-owned enterprises needed cash to stay afloat until they could be sold. From a budgetary viewpoint, the new eastern states required massive public spending but could not contribute much to financing. The pressure on the federal budget is apparent in Table 17.4 and continued well into the next decade. At the same time, and for many years, Germany's current account surplus of 5% of GDP melted to a deficit of 2%,

showing that the world also helped finance German unification. Yet this evolution is best regarded as temporary. Within a decade or two the eastern provinces will have very good prospects of catching up with the West, and Germany's current account has already moved into surplus again.

In the face of a temporary shock, tax smoothing calls for accumulating public debt and limiting tax increases, possibly borrowing abroad as well through current account deficits. Yet as the full costs of reunification are still being tallied, many have begun to question how much of the obligations of the eastern states are temporary. Kohl's successors, Schröder and Merkel, have come under increasing public pressure to stem the rise of the national debt and close the current account deficit, even if there are good economic reasons to put up with it.

---

[3] Public sector borrowing can be done domestically or abroad. A country with a temporary fall in income must either borrow or reduce its absorption. As a first approximation, it does not matter whether it is the private or the public sector that borrows abroad. Chapter 15 has already discussed the international ramifications of intertemporal imbalances for the real exchange rate.

Table 17.4 **Fiscal Implication of German Reunification (% of GDP)**

	1989	1990	1991	1992	1993	1994	1995	2000	2005	2008
Government expenditures	43.1	43.6	46.1	47.3	48.3	47.9	48.3	45.1	47.0	43.7
Budget balance	0.1	− 1.9	− 3.1	− 2.5	− 3.0	− 2.3	− 3.2	1.3	− 3.4	0.1
Gross public debt	39.8	40.4	41.1	40.9	46.3	46.6	55.7	60.4	71.1	64.6
Current account	4.6	3.0	− 1.3	− 1.1	− 1.0	− 1.4	− 1.2	− 1.8	4.6	6.0

Source: OECD, *Economic Outlook*.

percentage of output) has evolved in selected countries. Debt rises, sometimes spectacularly, during wars and declines afterwards. Wars are periods of unusually high public expenditure, yet they are rarely expected to last very long. The tax-smoothing principle seems to have been applied here (even if some countries eventually defaulted on part of their debt). Similarly, the oil shocks of the 1970s were met in many countries by debt accumulation.

17.3.2 Output and Employment Stabilization

A cyclical downturn means that personal incomes decline temporarily. The laissez-faire view is that, facing a temporary income fluctuation, individuals should borrow and/or save to smooth their consumption pattern, with government playing no particular role. This prescription would be correct if all individuals could indeed borrow during a recession. Credit rationing, however, changes the situation.[4] Individuals who cannot borrow, or cannot borrow as much as they need, are unable to smooth out their consumption. Not only are they hurt, but their declining demand deepens the slowdown through the demand multiplier effect. This effect is illustrated in Figure 17.2 where, starting from long-run equilibrium at point A, a recession occurs, which is captured by the leftward shift of the aggregate demand curve from AD to AD′. Under fixed exchange rates, the government can use fiscal policy to stop

this process. To keep the curve in its AD position and prevent the move from point A to point B, it either increases its own spending or provides tax relief. In effect, the government borrows on behalf of its citizens who cannot get credit or can only do so at prohibitively high interest rates. Conversely, a demand boom provides the government with the opportunity to run a budget surplus and pay back the debt accumulated during previous downturns. Both examples of the government leaning against the wind of the business cycle are called **countercyclical fiscal policies**.

The fact that unemployment rises during recessions provides another rationale for countercyclical fiscal policies. The mere increase in unemployment is not a justification for active fiscal policies. If unemployment rises because its equilibrium level has permanently increased, the economy will eventually settle along its long-run aggregate supply schedule and demand management is bound to fail. Attempts to use fiscal expansions to keep unemployment below equilibrium will only lead to more public debt. However, short-run fluctuations in unemployment around its equilibrium rate occur because price and wage rigidities prevent an optimal utilization of available resources. Countercyclical fiscal policy may be a corrective device to keep unemployment close to its equilibrium level, and output near its trend growth path. Sustaining aggregate demand with public spending when private demand weakens, or directly boosting private demand with tax relief, has the potential to limit the size of business cycles.

---

[4] We explain the mechanism of credit rationing and its importance for consumption in Chapters 7 and 8.

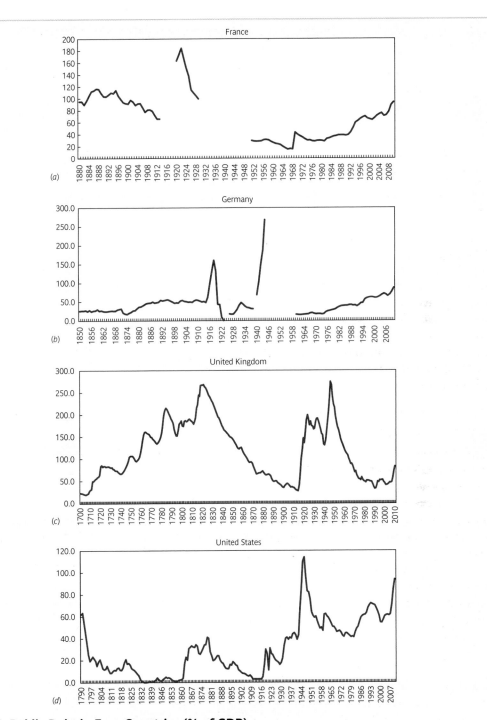

Fig. 17.1 Public Debt in Four Countries (% of GDP)

The UK had a debt-to-GDP ratio of over 100% in 1855, a legacy of the Napoleonic wars. During the First World War the British debt rose to about 200%, and during the Second World War to 300%. The war efforts are also visible for the USA (including the Civil War).

Sources: OECD, Economic Outlook; IMF, <http://pages.stern.nyu.edu/~rsylla/>.

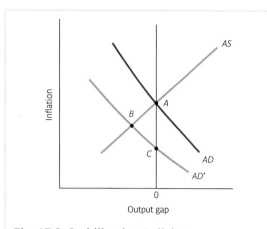

Fig. 17.2 Stabilization Policies

When demand exogenously falls, the economy moves from point *A* to point *B*. In the absence of stabilization policy, the economy will eventually move to point *C*. Fiscal policy can be used to speed up a return to trend output at point *A*, or even to prevent the *AD* schedule from shifting.

17.3.3 Automatic Stabilizers

We have argued that there are good reasons for governments to use their budget to smooth income and consumption. Interestingly, when a government refrains from using discretion to vary public spending and tax revenues, its budget automatically leans against the wind. Public budgets tend to go into surplus during upturns and into deficits during recessions. To see why, it is necessary to separate spending from revenues. While public consumption is less sensitive to cyclical fluctuations, transfers and tax revenues are fundamentally determined by economic conditions. Many transfers, such as unemployment benefits and welfare payment, are tightly linked to the state of the economy. Similarly, when incomes and spending rise, tax collection automatically increases. Conversely, during economic slowdowns, tax collection decreases. The reason is that nearly all taxes are set as *rates* applied to incomes or spending. In the end, given the budgetary process described in Box 17.2, public spending is little—if at all—affected by business cycles. This means that the budget balance is

---

 Box 17.2 **The Budgetary Process**

All democracies follow roughly the same budgetary process. Once a year, the government presents a budget to its parliament, which then debates on—and sometimes amends—each item before voting on it. One part of the budget concerns spending by the various ministries or departments; the other part concerns tax revenue. The parliament approves tax rates, literally hundreds of them, from VAT to income, from petrol to corporate profits or property. While spending authorizations are set in amounts (say, euros) and are therefore immune to changes unless the law is amended, tax receipts in euros are uncertain, depending upon how much is to be taxed at the set rates. This is why parliament cannot decide exactly what the deficit or surplus will be. Instead, it is presented with a forecast of GDP, which underlies a forecast of tax receipts and the associated deficit or surplus. It is well understood that economic conditions will settle the matter as the fiscal year goes on. In general, most governments have a tendency to forecast high growth, large tax receipts, and small deficits, since such forecasts

are not binding and make the authorities look good, at least for a while. It takes an unusually good year to have a better budgetary outcome than announced, while a moderate slowdown may easily result in large 'unexpected' slippages.

The financial crisis wreaked havoc on budget forecasting efforts. Table 17.5 presents forecasts of budget balances for the year 2010. These are the forecasts produced by the OECD twice a year. At the outset of the crisis, estimates of budget outcomes were fairly optimistic. Not surprisingly because of the crisis, the actual deficits turned out to be larger than expected, but the range of inaccuracy is large and changing over time. Italy's budget only worsened by 1.5% of GDP, while it deteriorated by three times that much in the Netherlands—from a comfortable surplus position. The worst mistake was made for Spain, which had fairly sound government finances at the beginning of the crisis, but because of massive bank bailouts saw a budget deterioration of 5.8% of GDP.

Table 17.5 Expected and Realized Government Budgets in 2010 (% of GDP)

Forecast time	Dec 2008	June 2009	Dec 2009	Dec 2010	Actual
France	−3.9	−7.9	−8.6	−7.4	−7.0
Germany	−1.0	−6.2	−5.3	−4.0	−3.3
Italy	−3.1	−5.8	−5.4	−5.0	−4.5
The Netherlands	−0.9	−7.0	−5.9	−5.8	−5.3
Spain	−3.8	−9.6	−8.5	−9.2	−9.2

Source: OECD, *Economic Outlook*.

therefore automatically procyclical—moving from surplus in booms to deficits in recessions. This is confirmed in the case of Netherlands in Figure 17.3.[5] It is possible to avoid cyclical budget fluctuations only if the government raises taxes in recessions and cuts them in booms—which would probably add to the volatility of the business cycle.

To summarize, we have seen that, when an economy slows down, the budget deficit will normally increase, or its surplus shrinks or even moves into deficit. This automatic lowering of taxes acts like an implicit fiscal expansion. Conversely, a better-than-expected economic performance reduces the budget deficit or increases the surplus because of enhanced tax income for the government, a contractionary fiscal policy of sorts. In the end, we see that exogenous shifts in private demand are automatically cushioned—but not completely offset—by budgetary shifts. These are the so-called **automatic stabilizers**. They work in the absence of any policy action. Simply by enacting the budget, as approved by the parliament, the government finds itself conducting a countercyclical fiscal policy, dampening both recessions and expansions.

17.3.4 How to Interpret Budget Figures

With automatic stabilizers in place, the budget is partly endogenous. Policy choices plan a surplus or a deficit, but economic conditions determine the outcome. This is why raw budget figures do not always

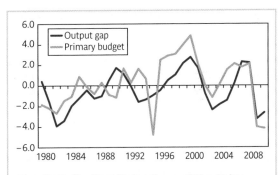

Fig. 17.3 Cyclical Behaviour of the Primary Budget in the Netherlands, 1980–2010

When the economy enters a slowdown (the output gap declines), tax receipts fall and transfers rise usually with a lag of a year or two. The primary budget—the government budget balance excluding service of the public debt (which is largely acyclical)—moves in the same direction as the output gap. It is procyclical.

Source: OECD, *Economic Outlook*.

fully reveal the government's intentions and can be misleading. Table 17.3 shows that most countries underwent budget deficits in 1975 and 1980. These years coincided with the post-oil-shock recessions and the associated deterioration of public finances. Norway, an oil-exporting country, provides a neat counter-example: it underwent a boom and tax revenues were further boosted by oil taxes. In a similar context, it has proved difficult for governments in southern Europe to demonstrate credibly that they are trying to reduce their structural budget deficits, because cuts in spending and increases in taxes tend to depress the economy, which in turn depresses taxes and mask the long-run impact of the cuts.

---

[5] The budget balance is $T - G - TR$, where G is public spending on goods and services, TR are transfers, and T are tax revenues. G is not cyclical, TR is procyclical, and T is countercyclical. Net taxes are $T - TR$, and are countercyclical (if T is countercyclical, $-T$ is procyclical).

The endogeneity of government budgets means that it is not straightforward to determine whether the stance of fiscal policy is tight or easy. A growing deficit may signal an explicit government decision to respond to a cyclical downturn, but it may also reflect the automatic worsening of the budget as the economy slows down. This is bothersome, not just for observers and analysts, but for the government as well. How can it know that its response is appropriate if it does not even know what its effect on the budget is?

Any budget law—which authorizes a given level of spending and sets all tax rates—includes an estimate of the expected balance, explicitly based on a forecast of GDP for the corresponding year. In Figure 17.4 the schedule FP (for fiscal policy) corresponds to such a budget law, i.e. spending and tax rates are taken as exogenous. The positive slope represents the working of the automatic stabilizer. Given the amount of spending and the tax rates approved by the parliament in the budget law, an increase in the output gap—when GDP exceeds its trend or potential level—improves the budget balance because tax revenues increase. Conversely, the budget surplus deteriorates when the output gap declines. For instance, if the budget law assumes that the economy will be on

trend during the corresponding fiscal year, it predicts the budget surplus indicated by point A. If the actual growth outcome is not as good as expected, point A' shows that the budget will end up in deficit.

What if the government decides to react to the budget deterioration by increasing spending or cutting taxes? This discretionary action is captured by a shift of the budget schedule, which moves to FP'. This schedule lies everywhere below FP, simply because the higher spending level or lower tax rates imply that, for any output gap, the new budget surplus will be lower than the previous one. What, then, does this fiscal expansion mean for the budget balance? If the economy does not respond to the fiscal boost during the fiscal year and the output gap remains the same as the one corresponding to point A', the budget deficit will widen, as shown at point B'. If, on the contrary, the fiscal expansion manages to limit the slowdown, the budget will be described by a point on the FP' schedule, somewhere up and to the right of point B'. For example, if the fiscal expansion succeeds in keeping GDP on trend, the new situation is described by point B.

The figure reveals why it is difficult to interpret budget figures. Suppose, for instance, that last year's situation is described by point A and that, in the present year, the outcome corresponds to point B'. We observe a sizeable worsening of the budget balance. Is it due to a fiscal expansion or to an economic slowdown? Both, in fact, but how do we know the role of each contributing factor? This is the question that we need to deal with.

The procedure is to ask what the budget balance would be if real GDP were on its trend path. The corresponding budget balance, which is constructed to be free of cyclical effects, is called the **cyclically adjusted** (or sometimes structural) **budget**. Figure 17.4 considers two budget laws, represented by the schedules FP and FP'. The corresponding cyclically adjusted budgets are represented by points A and B, respectively. The distance AB is a measure of the fiscal relaxation corresponding to the shift from FP to FP'. In general, actual budget outcomes are not equal to the cyclically adjusted budget because the GDP is not at its trend level. Looking at the budget law represented by FP, it is easy to see that a positive output gap implies an actual budget surplus larger than the cyclically adjusted surplus: compare points A and A''.

Cyclically adjusted budgets are routinely calculated and discussed. For example, the original European

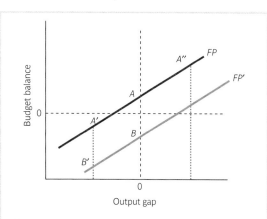

Fig. 17.4 Endogenous and Exogenous Components of Budgets

The line FP describes how the actual budget responds to cyclical fluctuations of output about its trend for a given fiscal policy stance. The move from line FP to line FP' describes a more expansionary policy stance. The cyclically adjusted budget is measured assuming a zero output gap. For fiscal policy stance FP it is given by point A, and for FP' by point B.

Stability and Growth Pact, designed to impose fiscal discipline within the monetary union, considered only actual (i.e. realized) budget outcomes. But since then, emphasis in policy discussions has been shifted increasingly to cyclically adjusted balances. The stark difference between the two budget measures can be seen in Figure 17.5, which displays changes in fiscal balance between 2008 and 2010 for 20 OECD countries. All countries had budgets deteriorate due to bad economic conditions. The blue diagonal divides outcomes into those for which the official government budget surplus deteriorated more than the cyclically adjusted balance (to the left) or less (to the right). Of all 20 OECD countries, only Greece and Italy tightened their fiscal policies on a cyclically adjusted basis over the period 2008–2010. The figure shows clearly that despite the sharp increase in budget deficits during crisis, these numbers overstate the expansionary policy of most OECD governments.

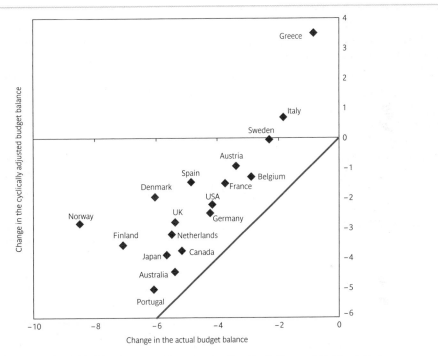

Fig. 17.5 Changes from 2008 to 2010 in Actual and Cyclically Adjusted Budget Balances, 20 OECD countries (% of GDP)

The horizontal axis shows the change of the actual measured budget balance, while the vertical axis displays the change in the cyclically adjusted budget balance over the period of the global recession 2008–2010. By construction, these two measures are equal when the output gap has not changed. This case corresponds to the diagonal shown as the blue line (it looks a bit strange because there is no first quadrant since country experienced a budget surplus). Points located above the diagonal correspond to a recession — a negative change in the output gap — where the structurally adjusted balance deteriorates more than the actual balance. Conversely points below the diagonal correspond to a positive change in the output gap. The figure confirms that all countries went into recession. Points along the horizontal axis capture a neutral fiscal policy stance, when the cyclically adjusted balance is unchanged and fiscal policy is reduced to the effects of the automatic stabilizers. Above the horizontal axis, fiscal policy is *contractionary*, and it is *expansionary* when the country is shown under the horizontal axis. We see that most countries adopted countercyclical fiscal policies, as pledged by the second G20 Summit in London on April 2009. Two countries with serious debt problems, Italy and Greece, undertook discretionary fiscal contractions. In fact, a fiscal contraction was requested from Greece as a condition for the loan received from the other Euro Area countries and the IMF. Fiscal policy was most expansionary in Portugal, which had also to apply for support in early 2011.

Source: OECD, *Economic Outlook*.

17.4 Deficit Finance: Public Debt and Seigniorage

According to Table 17.6, public indebtedness in almost every OECD country is large and growing.[6] Government debt grew especially during the 1970s, with this growth slowing down for some during the 1980s but accelerating for others. Since the financial crisis, government debt is once again on the rise. Yet there is good news. The intertemporal budget constraint does prevent the permanent accumulation of public debt, just as Chapter 7 foretold. At some point, budget deficits must be closed and turned into primary surpluses. Figure 7.8 showed how this rule had

Table 17.6 Gross Public Debt, Various Countries, 1970–2010 (% of GDP)

	1970	1980	1990	2000	2010
Austria	18.5	35.8	57.2	69.4	72.3
Belgium	61.9	74.5	125.8	113.4	96.7
Denmark	n.a.	43.7	66.4	57.1	43.6
Finland	n.a.	13.6	16.3	52.3	48.4
France	40.0	29.7	38.6	65.2	81.6
Germany	17.5	30.2	40.4	60.4	83.4
Greece	18.8	22.8	79.6	114.9	142.8
Ireland	n.a.	69.5	93.3	37.8	96.2
Italy	55.1	86.6	97.3	121.6	119.1
Japan	12.0	55.0	68.6	136.7	199.7
Netherlands	65.5	59.1	87.8	63.9	62.7
Norway	41.7	39.7	29.4	34.1	49.5
Spain	n.a.	19.9	47.7	66.5	60.1
Sweden	29.1	47.2	46.7	65.7	39.8
UK	80.9	55.9	32.9	45.6	80.0
USA	46.3	41.7	63.0	55.2	93.6

Source: OECD, *Economic Outlook*.

worked for several 'problem cases'. Nevertheless, strategies for pursuing **debt stabilization** are a central concern, especially in the context of the European Monetary Union.

Table 17.6 shows that despite the debt crisis brewing since 2008, considerable progress has been made in many countries over the longer haul. Spectacular successes—in the sense of stopping exploding debt paths and even reducing high levels of debt—can be observed in Belgium, Denmark, Ireland, the Netherlands, Spain, and Sweden. Despite the troubles endemic to southern Europe at the moment, these countries made significant progress, in order to fulfill the conditions for adopting the euro.[7] Since the crisis, much of this progress was overturned, a result of the recession and countercyclical fiscal policies as much as structural deficits and most importantly, rising rates of interest for the issuance of new debt.

This section examines the debt stabilization issue. It allows us to understand the forces that lie behind the debt accumulation process, the challenge of stopping this unsustainable evolution, and what happens if it is not done.

17.4.1 The Public Debt with No Growth and No Inflation

Let us start with the easiest case, where the central bank does not finance public deficits and we can ignore the role of seigniorage. It also makes things easier if we assume that inflation is nil because then we do not need to worry about the distinction between nominal and real variables. The government budget deficit is the sum of the primary deficit—the excess of purchases G over net tax receipts T—and of debt service—here a single (real) rate of interest r times the existing debt stock B. In the absence of asset sales (privatizations), foreign aid grants, or

---

[6] The table presents gross debt. Net debt figures, which take state assets into account, are considered unreliable because of the difficulty involved in valuation of state assets.

[7] Chapter 19 provides more details on requirements imposed by the EU and the European central bank for countries adopting the euro, of which the most important involve fiscal policy.

default, this deficit will equal the net borrowing requirement of the country—the net issue of new debt. In the absence of monetary financing (borrowing from the central bank), the government issues new debt ΔB held by the public. This can be formalized as

$$(17.1) \qquad \underset{\substack{\text{debt} \\ \text{accumulation}}}{\Delta B} = \underset{\substack{\text{primary budget} \\ \text{deficit}}}{G - T} + \underset{\substack{\text{debt} \\ \text{service}}}{rB.}$$

$$\underbrace{}_{\substack{\text{total budget} \\ \text{deficit}}}$$

If the overall budget is in deficit—technically, 'the public sector borrowing requirement' is positive—the government must borrow, which means an increase ($\Delta B > 0$) in the public debt B. If it is in surplus, the government can retire some of its existing debt or accumulate assets ($\Delta B < 0$).[8]

Looking at public budgets in this way shows that the debt accumulation process can easily become explosive. The reason is that the debt feeds and grows on itself; the higher the current stock of debt B, the higher is debt service rB, and therefore the larger the deficit and the need to accumulate more debt. Even when the primary budget is balanced ($G - T = 0$), the overall budget is in deficit and the debt continues to grow. In this case, the government keeps borrowing to pay interest on the existing debt, which means more indebtedness. Without any further effort to control it, debt will accumulate at rate r.[9] This feature of indebtedness is general and applies to any debt, be it public or private, domestic (i.e. held by domestic residents), or external.

To halt the accumulation of its debt, the government must run a permanent primary surplus large enough to service the existing debt without having to incur more borrowing. Formally, we ask what

must happen for $\Delta B = 0$ in (17.1). It is easy to verify that this implies

$$(17.2) \qquad T - G = rB$$

primary budget surplus = debt service.

Stabilizing the absolute level of debt can be a formidable task. The longer the government puts off the day of reckoning, the larger the debt becomes, and the larger is the surplus ultimately required to stabilize it. This observation is illustrated in Table 17.7, which presents net debt levels and primary budget balances (as a ratio to GDP) for a sample of countries. At the moment, our attention is focused on the third column of this table, which shows the primary surplus required if the government wanted to stabilize the net debt at its 2010 level, assuming a real interest rate of 5%. Of the countries shown, none of the countries were close to fulfilling this objective. Clearly, the public finances of these countries were hard-hit by lost tax revenues and policy response associated with the deep recession. The numbers for Ireland are *not* a typo! In 2010, the banking crisis forced Ireland's government to recapitalize its banks and incur a series of large one-off expenses.

In any event, moving the structural (cyclically neutral) fiscal balance by 3–5% is painful, if not politically impossible. Fortunately, the situation need not be so dire. The following sections show that the stabilization of the absolute level of debt is excessively stringent because it ignores both growth in GDP and the possibility of monetary finance and inflation.

17.4.2 The Public Debt with Growth and No Inflation

It is misleading to compare the absolute size of the government debt of the USA with that of France and Sweden, or Belgium. A country's ability to service debt (to repay it with interest) is fundamentally related to its economic size, since a given tax rate applied to a larger economy produces more revenues. This is precisely why all the data in Table 17.7 were presented as ratios to GDP, and why the stabilization of the debt/GDP ratio is a more reasonable objective than the stabilization of the debt level itself.

This distinction matters even more because GDPs tend to grow secularly over time. Box 17.3 shows

---

[8] Note that B represents the net public debt, which is the government's gross debt less its assets. The reason is that the government should normally receive interest or income from its asset holdings, which tends to reduce the overall budget deficit, exactly in the way debt service tends to increase the deficit.

[9] The tendency for the debt to grow at the rate of interest r can be seen by looking at (17.1) when the primary budget is balanced: then, $\Delta B = rB$ or $\Delta B/B = r$, which is the growth rate of the public debt.

Table 17.7 **Net Government Indebtedness and Primary Budget Balances, 2010 (% of GDP)**

| | Net debt in 2010 | Primary budget surplus in 2010 | Required primary surplus* | |
			to stabilize the absolute debt stock	to stabilize the debt/GDP ratio
Belgium	80.8	−0.9	4.0	2.0
Germany	50.1	−1.3	2.5	1.3
Ireland	59.9	−30.0	3.0	1.5
Italy	99.1	−0.3	5.0	2.5
Netherlands	34.6	−4.1	1.7	0.9

*Required surplus assuming a 5% real interest rate and a 2.5% real GDP growth rate.
Source: OECD, *Economic Outlook*.

Box 17.3 **Debt – Deficit Arithmetic**

Growth, no inflation

In order to study the evolution of the debt–GDP ratio (B/Y), recall that it grows at a rate equal to the difference in the growth rates of numerator and denominator. Using the equation for budget accounting (17.1), we see that the numerator grows at rate $(G - T)/B + r$, while the denominator grows at rate g of GDP (since we are considering longer periods of time, here we use the trend GDP growth rate). Subtract the latter from the former, multiplying by (B/Y), and rearranging yields

(17.3) $$\Delta\left(\frac{B}{Y}\right) = \frac{G - T}{Y} + (r - g)\frac{B}{Y}.$$

In absolute terms, the debt–GDP ratio increases with the budget deficit (as a share of GDP) and debt service on the debt–GDP ratio adjusted for GDP growth rate (g). As long as the real interest rate exceeds the growth rate, the debt process is explosive. Yet it will grow at the rate $r - g$, which is lower than r as suggested by (17.1). For a given ratio of the primary deficit to GDP, more debt means more deficit and greater borrowing requirements. The primary budget surplus required to stabilize the debt–GDP ratio sets the left-hand side of (17.3) equal to zero:

(17.4) $$\Delta\left(\frac{B}{Y}\right) = 0 \text{ when} \frac{T - G}{Y} = (r - g)\frac{B}{Y}.$$

If the rate of interest r is below the GDP growth rate g, the debt–GDP ratio can be stabilized while running a budget deficit. In theory, fast-growing countries can outgrow their deficits.

Growth inflation and seigniorage finance

When inflation is positive, the role of money and money creation in government finance has to be accounted for. The WebAppendix shows how budgetary accounts are modified to recognize that the deficit can be financed by both new debt issue and seigniorage finance—loans made by the central bank to the government to cover the deficit. These loans are equivalent to the creation of additional monetary base, M0:

(17.5) $$\Delta\left(\frac{B}{Y}\right) + \frac{\Delta M0/P}{Y} = \frac{G - T}{Y} + (r - g)\frac{B}{Y}.$$

Stabilizing the debt–GDP ratio now requires an even smaller primary budget surplus, or can even be achieved with a primary deficit if enough monetary base is created:

(17.6) $$\Delta\left(\frac{B}{Y}\right) = 0 \text{ when} \frac{T - G}{Y} = (r - g)\frac{B}{Y} - \frac{\Delta M0/P}{Y}.$$

Finally, in Chapter 12 we derived the long-run relationship between inflation, monetary growth, and output:

$\pi = \mu - g$. But $\Delta(M0/P)$ is equal to $(\mu - \pi)M0/P$. The stabilization condition for debt then becomes

$$(17.7) \Delta\left(\frac{B}{Y}\right) = 0 \text{ when } \frac{T-G}{Y} = (r-g)\frac{B}{Y} - (\pi+g)\frac{M0/P}{Y}.$$

In the long run, the use of seigniorage to relax the government budget constraint is only possible if the economy (and the demand for real money) is growing.

formally how the debt accounts change when we look at debt–GDP ratios. Beyond the arithmetic details, the logic is easy to understand. When we look at the evolution of the debt–GDP ratio, we can think of a 'race' between the numerator—the level of debt—and the denominator—GDP. The faster the real GDP grows, the less the ratio increases. The level of debt itself may increase while declining as a ratio to GDP; all it takes is for the GDP to rise faster than the debt stock.[10] By the same token, in a growing economy, were the absolute stock of the debt to remain stable, as in the case studied in the previous section (see equation (17.2)), the debt-to-GDP ratio simply would vanish over time. If the real debt grows at the rate r and the GDP at the rate g, the debt-to-GDP ratio rises at the rate $(r - g)$.

This means that when the GDP growth rate exceeds the real interest rate, a balanced primary budget is sufficient for the debt–GDP ratio to shrink. When the real interest rate exceeds the economy's growth rate, however, the debt process is explosive. Yet, the primary surplus required to stabilize the *ratio* of the debt to GDP is significantly smaller than the primary surplus required to stabilize the *level* of the debt. This is precisely because GDP growth helps contain the increase in the debt–GDP ratio. The last column in Table 17.7 drives this point home. Assuming a 5% real interest rate and a 2.5% real GDP growth rate, we see that in 2010 all countries listed in the table need much less of an adjustment to stabilize their debt–GDP ratios (the only exception being Ireland, for the exceptional reasons already stated).

These results help us understand why debt increased so dramatically in the 1970s and 1980s.

Over the 1960s and early 1970s, real GDP growth exceeded the real interest rate in most countries. For example, real interest rates in the UK during the period 1960–1980 averaged 0.9% while real growth was 2.4%. Under such conditions, budget deficits need not imply a growing debt–GDP ratio. The debt accumulation process was not explosive, at least relative to GDP, a fact that probably encouraged complacency about deficits and debt. In contrast, over the period 1980–1995, UK real growth hardly changed (2.4%), while real interest rates averaged 4.7%! The debt process became explosive and required prompt and vigorous action. Several countries failed to adjust quickly enough.

It is now easier to understand how problems faced by the southern European countries in servicing government debt have been aggravated by a real growth slowdown over the decade before the crisis. Table 17.8 displays average growth rates for these countries. Clearly, long term growth (g) has declined in the past 10–20 years. This is a cause of concern not only for social and economic reasons, but also because it can endanger the stability of already-high levels of government indebtedness. For this reason, stabilization programs of the IMF and the European Commission also insist on measures which enhance long-term growth, even while fiscal austerity slows down or even throttle short-term prospects.

17.4.3 The General Case: Inflationary Finance When the Economy is Growing

Inflationary finance represents an alternative way of relaxing the budgetary stringency required for debt stabilization. Simply put, the government exploits its monopoly right to create money in the narrow sense (monetary base) and uses that money to pay its bills. Technically, the government borrows directly from the central bank, or forces it to purchase existing debt and to hold that debt on its own balance sheet

---

[10] The rate of growth of the debt-to-GDP ratio B/Y is

$\frac{\Delta(B/Y)}{(B/Y)} = \frac{\Delta B}{B} - \frac{\Delta Y}{Y}$ a formula that we have encountered in

many contexts, for the first time in Chapter 6. The debt–GDP ratio declines when the real debt grows at a lower rate than the real GDP.

Table 17.8 Economic Growth in Southern Europe, 1980–2010

	1981–1985	1986–1990	1991–1995	1996–2000	2001–2005	2006–2010
Greece	0.2	1.3	1.3	3.5	4.0	0.8
Italy	1.7	3.1	1.3	1.9	0.9	−0.3
Portugal	1.5	6.2	1.9	4.2	0.8	0.5
Spain	1.3	4.7	1.7	4.1	3.3	0.9
Euro Area	n.a.	n.a.	1.4	2.7	1.5	0.8
EU	1.5	3.1	1.5	2.9	2.0	1.0

Source: IMF.

(see Chapter 9). When the borrowed money is spent, it becomes an addition to monetary base, the foundation for money creation by the banking system, and, in the long run for a higher price level.

Producing monetary base is virtually costless: a stroke of a pen—more precisely keying in a few zeros in the computer—or activating the printing press. Since the national government uses the money it creates at face value to acquire real resources, it (or the central bank, which is owned by the government) makes a comfortable profit. The revenue from this lucrative activity is called seigniorage.[11] Seigniorage remains the main source of profit for central banks. As public institutions, central banks are usually required to turn over most of their profits to their governments. Although seigniorage can represent a substantial source of government revenue in times of high inflation, it has rarely done so in recent years.

Naturally, the greater use of seigniorage results in faster money growth (via the money multiplier effect) and, eventually, higher inflation. Formally, the role of seigniorage can be seen when the budget account (17.1) is modified to recognize that any increase in the

nominal monetary base $\Delta M0$ provides real resources to the government. The last part of Box 17.3 provides the mathematical details. Since the real value of seigniorage is $\Delta(M0/P)$, the account is rewritten as

$$\text{(17.8)}\quad \underset{\substack{\text{new} \\ \text{debt}}}{\Delta B/P} + \underset{\text{seigniorage}}{\Delta M0/P} = \underset{\substack{\text{primary} \\ \text{deficit}}}{G - T/P} + \underset{\substack{\text{interest} \\ \text{payments}}}{B/P.}$$

Now that prices are not constant anymore, we define B, G, T, and r in real terms.

Seigniorage is a cheap source of financing for the government. It severs the link that makes the debt process explosive because little or no interest is paid on the monetary base. But the explosiveness is simply transferred elsewhere—into inflation. All hyperinflationary episodes can be linked to a government's attempt to break away from its budget constraint. For the same reason, hyperinflations ultimately end when governments close their deficits, or when central banks stop financing them.

Yet inflation, especially when it is unanticipated, can *help* the government solve its financing problems, via the second mechanism of inflationary finance, the **inflation tax**. The inflation tax simply means that inflation which arises from monetary growth erodes the real value of obligations the government has issued in its own currency. Most important in this regard is the public debt, which primarily takes the form of non-indexed, nominal bonds, but also includes money issued by the central bank. Because the nominal face value of the debt remains unchanged, its real value is eroded, and debt-holders

---

[11] The origins of this expression can be traced back to the Middle Ages, when local lords had the monopoly over coinage. Often, they abused this power to reduce—debase—the gold content of coins minted in their domains. In a similar fashion, governments exploit the monopoly power of the central bank in creating the medium of exchange to acquire valuable resources from the private sector. Modern seigniorage is just another form of taxation. The authorities exchange money, which is costless to produce, against goods and services. It is as if these goods and services were simply confiscated.

suffer a real capital loss. The inflation tax is just the mirror image of this loss: the reduction of the real value of the debt is a gain for the government.

Seigniorage and the inflation tax go hand in hand. Seigniorage leads to money growth and therefore to inflation and debt relief via the inflation tax. Naturally, the inflation tax applies only to debt issued in local currencies. In addition, the inflation tax works only if inflation is unexpected. The reason

is that, when debt-holders anticipate inflation, they demand a nominal interest rate which compensates them for the expected erosion of the principal. This is the Fisher principle of Chapter 13. The nominal interest rate rises in line with expected inflation, leaving the real interest rate unchanged. In that case, the bondholders do not lose, nor do governments gain from inflation—except for the inflation tax on money balances, which do not bear interest.

17.5 How to Stabilize the Public Debt

What are the options open to a government that wants to stabilize an exploding debt–GDP ratio? This is the central question which dogs not only Europe in the second decade of the twenty-first century but also the USA and Japan. Three ways involve short-term approaches, while two additional ones are long-run and require a fair amount of patience. In the short-run, three and only three ways are available to stabilize the debt–GDP ratio: (1) fiscal stringency—reducing the deficit and achieving the required primary surplus by reducing public spending, raising taxes, or both; (2) inflationary finance—the monetization of deficits and use of the inflation tax; and (3) outright default on some or all of the existing debt. All three amount to different forms of taxation: standard taxation in the first case, taxing those who happen to hold nominal assets (money, and nominal bonds) in the second case, and taxing those who own Treasury debt in the last case. In the medium to long run there are two additional options: (4) reducing the rate of interest and (5) raising the long-run rate of growth, or at least achieving the attainable rate of growth determined by factors spelled out in Chapters 3 and 4. In what follows we spell out these options.

17.5.1 Cutting the Deficit

Deficit reduction is the virtuous road to debt stabilization. Politically, though, it is also the hardest to implement. Cuts in public spending elicit significant resistance from those directly affected, e.g. government employees who will fight for their jobs, or

public construction contractors that want to keep their businesses going. Raising taxes is notoriously unpopular with everyone. Another possibility is the privatization of state enterprises, the proceeds of which can be used to pay down debt and reduce interest burdens.

As difficult as it is, deficit reduction as a medium-term policy had been successfully implemented in a number of European countries. As Table 17.9 shows, at the beginning of the millennium, all countries were models of fiscal discipline with zero or even positive primary surpluses; countries with some of the most serious debt problems of previous decades—Belgium, Ireland, and Italy—had actually turned their primary budgets around. (Recall that the primary deficit is the total deficit less interest payments, which for heavily indebted countries is difficult to reduce.) This consolidation is attributable largely to the adoption of the monetary union, as explained in Box 17.4. The problem arises when budget cuts and privatizations are implemented in bad times, i.e. the middle of a deep recession. Such cuts can be highly counterproductive and make the situation worse.

17.5.2 Seigniorage and the Inflation Tax

In the end, monetary finance of fiscal deficits is just another form of taxation, like excise, income, or consumption taxes. It operates by reducing the value of the money base (the central bank's liability) and of

Table 17.9 Primary Budget Balances for Selected European Countries, 1995–2010

	1995	2000	2005	2006	2007	2008	2009	2010
Belgium	3.9	6.2	1.2	3.9	3.3	2.2	−2.6	−1.3
France	−2.5	1.1	−0.6	−0.1	−0.4	−0.8	−5.5	−5.5
Germany	−6.7	4.0	−1.0	0.8	2.7	2.5	−0.7	−1.1
Greece	4.6	3.6	−0.7	−1.5	−1.9	−4.5	−10.1	−3.2
Ireland	2.5	6.3	2.1	3.2	0.3	−6.9	−13.0	−29.7
Italy	3.3	5.2	0.1	1.1	3.3	2.2	−1.0	−0.3
Portugal	−0.4	−0.5	−3.7	−1.5	−0.1	−0.1	−6.6	−4.6
Spain	−1.7	2.0	2.5	3.3	3.0	−3.1	−9.9	−7.8

Source: OECD.

 Box 17.4 Euro Area and the Stability and Growth Pact

When a country has its own currency, it can use seigniorage to finance at least part of its deficits. Once it has fixed its exchange rate or joined a monetary union, it loses this source of financing, just as it loses its ability to determine the domestic inflation rate.[12] The consequences for national fiscal policies are profound. First, the debt stabilization requirement becomes more stringent, as a comparison of (17.1) and (17.7) shows. Second, default is the only option for a government unwilling to face the facts of the intertemporal budget constraint and run primary surpluses. The spectre of default was a great concern for the founding fathers of the European Monetary Union. Europe continues to consist of sovereign countries with their own individual histories and traditions. Sanctions for bad fiscal behaviour available to that other large monetary union, the USA, are non-existent.

For this reason, admission to the monetary union was restricted to countries that fulfilled criteria of prudent budgetary behaviour.[13] Also, once a member, each country was subjected to the Excessive Deficit Procedure. This procedure is defined by the Stability and Growth Pact. In brief, the pact sets upper limits on annual consolidated budget deficits of 3% of GDP. Should a country exceed this limit, it is given an initial 'early warning' and must then take prompt corrective action. Failure to correct the situation exposes the country to a fine. For the reasons presented in Section 17.3.3, during the 2000–2003 slowdown many countries exceeded the 3% limit. In late 2003, the fine procedure should have been triggered against France and Germany, but politics took over and the pact was 'suspended', a decision that subsequently was ruled illegal by the European Court of Justice. While the Stability and Growth Pact has not been adhered to, it has still restrained most governments, as can be seen in Figure 17.5.

The Euro-crisis has renewed discussion of the usefulness of the Stability and Growth Pact, which has now effectively been abandoned. If an individual country in

[12] Seigniorage still takes place at the level of the European Monetary Union. Indeed, the European Central Bank (ECB) is required to turn over its profits to participating countries. But the decision on how fast to let the money base grow, and how much seigniorage to collect, no longer lies with national governments, but solely with the ECB. By virtue of its founding statutes, the ECB is formally independent and required to aim at price stability. It is legally prohibited from financing the government budgets. For a detailed account of the fiscal policy restraints facing countries wishing to join the European monetary union, see Baldwin and Wyplosz (2005).

[13] More details on the so-called 'Maastricht Criteria'—which resulted from the Maastricht Treaty (1992)—can be found in Chapter 19.

a monetary union does not obey its intertemporal budget constraint, it forces the union to pick up the bill—unless the union dissociates itself from the sinner country, or violates the budget constraint for the whole union. Remarkably, these implications were not carefully thought through when the Treaty was signed and the monetary union was founded. It is the ongoing task of the European Monetary Union to add the political infrastructure to ensure that—at least in the long run—there is some Eurozone-wide system of political and economic accountability for budgetary policy. Otherwise the monetary union may not survive in its current form.

the public debt (the Treasury's liability). Inflationary finance is simply a tax on money and bondholders.[14]

This result can be seen in a different way. In the budget accounts, (17.1) for example, it is the real interest rate that matters. For the inflation tax to work, the real interest rate must fall, otherwise the real cost of servicing the debt remains unchanged. When inflation rises unexpectedly and quickly enough, nominal interest rates on long-maturity assets cannot be modified as they are contractually fixed for the whole life of the asset. This explains why *ex post* real interest rates are just the mirror image of inflation.

To a fiscally undisciplined government, the inflation tax may seem like an easy way to escape its debt obligations. It is not as painless as it looks, though. When inflation rises, buyers of new bond issues will demand higher nominal interest rates to avoid getting 'burned'. In addition, suspicious lenders will be less and less willing to agree to long-term loans. As the maturity of the debt shortens, the government must constantly issue new bonds to pay back its maturing debt, and it must then pay the new higher nominal interest rate. If the debt accumulation process remains unstable, the government will be forced to create more money, leading to more inflation, which will soon lead to higher nominal interest rates, calling for yet another increase in inflation, and so on.

This is precisely how many hyperinflations get started. A surprise inflation tax wipes out the value of nominal assets and eliminates the real public debt, but leaves a hyperinflation in its wake. As the recent episodes of Bolivia, Serbia, or Zimbabwe show, hyperinflations take a terrible toll on the economic and social structure of a country, and stopping a

hyperinflation can be very costly too. This is why it is an option only used under extreme political situations. It is no surprise that most hyperinflation episodes occur during wars (Congo and Serbia in the 1990s) or in their aftermath (Germany, Greece, Hungary after the First World War), or in troubled times (several Eastern European countries at the time of the collapse of the communist regimes) when the government is too weak to enforce fiscal discipline.

17.5.3 Default

The most brutal way for a government to stabilize the debt in the short run is simply to default, i.e. to repudiate it. Except for post-war or post-revolution periods—when the blame can be put on exceptional circumstances or previous regimes—governments rarely resort to this approach, and do so only under severe stress. Outright default is always perceived as a major breach of confidence and leaves long-lasting scars on the reputation of governments. As Box 17.5 shows, default was used in Italy's Fascist era to reduce high interest rates, which reflected lenders' doubts that stringent budgetary policies would last. Defaults can also be seen as a form of specific taxation that affects bondholders, much as inflation does. Indeed, partial default is exactly equivalent to a tax on bond income. If, for example, a government reduces the value of its debt by half, this is the same as imposing a 50% tax on interest and repayment of the principal.

The issue of default has different implications when the debt is owned by foreigners. Thus far, it was implicitly assumed that the public debt was held by residents. In that case, debt accumulation or stabilization amounts to a redistribution of income across generations, between those who are taxed now and those who will be taxed in the future. When debt is owned by foreigners, the situation is different. As Chapters 7 and 15 have shown, honouring external

---

[14] More generally, unanticipated inflation redistributes wealth from borrowers to lenders when the assets are nominal, i.e. set in money terms and not indexed to a price level.

Box 17.5 **Mussolini and the Public Debt**[15]

Italy emerged from the First World War with a large debt and a sizeable budget deficit. Between 1923 and 1926, having eliminated all political opposition, Mussolini re-established near budget balance and brought the debt–GDP ratio down by reducing spending and raising taxes (Table 17.10). Yet, concerned that the debt was too short in maturity, and therefore vulnerable to market conditions, in November 1926 the government imposed a mandatory conversion of debt of less than seven-year maturity into fixed-rate (5%) longer-term bonds. In 1934, these bonds were again forcibly converted into 25-year loans bearing a 3.5% interest. The first conversion is estimated to have resulted in a partial default of 20%, the second one in a loss of 30%. After these moves, the government found it very hard to undertake new borrowing. It was forced to cease issuing short-term debt in 1927 and paid a premium estimated at 2–3% on borrowing from banks.

Table 17.10 Public Finances in Italy, 1918–1928

	1918	1922	1924	1926	1928
Tax revenues as % of public spending	23	46	90	100	90
Debt–GNP (%)	70.3	74.8	65.1	49.7	53.8

Source: Alesina (1988).

debt implies transferring resources to the rest of the world. This requires running a primary current account surplus, i.e. spending less than is earned after interest payments. The temptation to default and stop the outflow of resources can be large, especially when the stock of debt is already large. On the other hand, a country which has defaulted cannot borrow abroad for a long time often 10 years or more. During that period of 'international pariah status', the country will find it difficult or impossible to run a current account deficit. Comparing the two situations, honouring the debt requires a current account surplus, possibly for decades, while defaulting only requires a balanced current account, usually for a few years. This explains why sovereign nations are sometimes more willing to default on the external than on the domestic debt when the going gets rough.

17.5.4 Interest Rate Relief

One mechanism often overlooked for stabilizing an explosive debt situation is a reduction of the interest rate at which countries borrow, either at home or abroad. This is not a trivial exercise, since interest rates are determined in capital markets in which many players are active, all of which have a view about the debt and whether it will be serviced on time. As was already shown in Box 17.5, sometimes the rates at which the public is willing to lend to government is dominated by a risk premium (Chapter 15) or even the expectation of outright default. If this expectation is stubborn, it may be impossible for a country to borrow at an interest rate at which it can be reasonably expected to service its debt.

To see this, suppose that a country had a debt–GDP ratio of 100%, long-term growth was 3%, and the real market interest rate for debt was 4%. According to our formula (17.2) a primary budget surplus of 1% of GDP is necessary to keep debt–GDP constant at 100%. But now suppose the markets are risk-neutral, but expect the government to default with a high probability in the coming years. Suppose that investors in the bond markets now demand a higher rate, say 6% per annum, from the government in question. This higher rate is meant to compensate bondholders (lenders) for outcomes in which no payments are made at all (default). At that higher rate, of course, stabilization of the debt/GDP ratio is only possible if the primary current account is 3% of GDP, much higher than before and rendering the probability of default even higher, and so on. There is a distinct

---

[15] This box draws on Alesina (1988).

Box 17.6 Interest Rates Unhinged: The Great European Sovereign Debt Crisis

The Great Recession 2008–2009 inflicted many forms of collateral damage on Europe's economies—in the first instance, a collapse in export demand, a freezing-up of financial markets, a sharp recession and a rise in unemployment. One of the more surprising casualties of the worldwide turndown was the credibility of many European countries as sovereign borrowers. The drop in GDP led to sharp declines in revenues and opened gaping holes in budgets. Pessimism regarding future growth, given the rise of emerging economies in the rest of the world, gave the feeling that the 'Emperor had no clothes'—that debt service, believed by all for decades to be a sure thing, was in fact highly contingent. Credit rating agencies, which should know more about the risk of default of borrowers than anyone else, had given all Eurozone countries very high to highest ratings in the years when the monetary union began. Many countries were now perceived to be in danger of default.

It all began when large financial institutions began to sell off their Greek government bonds in the late fall of 2009. They did this because the new Greek government admitted a few weeks earlier that the budget deficit was in fact twice as large as reported in the official statistics. PIMCO, one of the largest bond funds in the world with more than $1.3 trillion of bonds under management, began to sell their holdings of Greek debt. Greece's budget problems had been known for decades (see Table 17.3), yet investors were convinced when the euro was introduced that no euro-using country would ever

default—in a clinch, the Eurozone would take care of it. Other investors, seeing PIMCO selling, began to sell too.

Like a contagious disease, investors fled to the door, selling not only Greek bonds, but those of other troubled Euro countries as well. Because PIMCO also sold their debt holdings of other problem countries, prices of Portuguese, Spanish, and even Italian bonds fell, raising their interest rates. Figure 17.6 shows how it all began in December 2009 and spread like wildfire. The situation was compounded as the price of insuring such debt—using credit default swaps (CDS) described in Chapter 14—began to rise, as perceived probability of default rose. Credit rating agencies, long on the sidelines, saw rising bond yields and CDS prices as a bad sign, and proceeded to downgrade the governments involved, in a series of small steps. As the governments initiated painful budget cuts, the economic situation deteriorated even further, and bond downgrades continued.[16] Under these conditions it is difficult if not impossible for countries to borrow fresh money—even if they are on a clear and credible trajectory of improvement. It is for this reason that two stop-gap bailout arrangements at lower interest rates were arranged for Greece in 2010 and then for Ireland and Portugal in 2011. The principle of the European Financial Stability Fund is to provide lending to countries unable to borrow at reasonable market interest rates. At the same time, countries are expected to follow through with reform programmes designed to free them from below-market interest rates and enable them to access debt markets normally again.

possibility that the refinancing of government debt 'becomes unhinged'—a situation in which interest rates are high because lenders expect with high probability that default will occur, and because the expected default will occur, interest rates are high. This is an example of self-fulfilling prophesy, similar to non-fundamental asset pricing discussed in Chapter 14. Box 17.6 describes the present situation for many countries of the Eurozone; a glance back at Figure 7.10 hints that why self-fulfilling prophesies are hard to rule out.

Financial markets need to be convinced that their money is well-invested, yet how is it possible to come

from under the cloud of a massive debt overhang? One solution to the problem is for the country to borrow at concessionary rates until credibility is reestablished. But who will make loans at those rates? The International Monetary Fund played such a role in the recent crisis. Alternatively, it may be possible to arrange bilateral loans to tide a country over until the situation improves. In the years to come, the solution

[16] The bond rating agencies, most of which are based in the USA, have come under considerable criticism for giving Greece, Portugal, and Ireland high credit scores when the euro was launched. They seemed to have forgotten the hard lessons of Chapter 11!

for Eurozone countries in trouble is likely to be a European Financial Mechanism which assures that runaway situations are dealt with decisively.

17.5.5 Long-run Economic Growth

The last possible way to get the debt–GDP ratio down is to raise the denominator, GDP, in a sustainable way—this means raising the long-term economic growth

rate (g). This solution is difficult to conjure up in the short run, but the experience of several European countries in the years 1980–2000—Denmark, Germany, Ireland, Netherlands, and Sweden—suggest that it is not out of the question. It does require perseverance and sacrifice. In the next chapter we will explore some of these supply-side policies. They do not offer instant cures, but a prospect of longer-term sustainability.

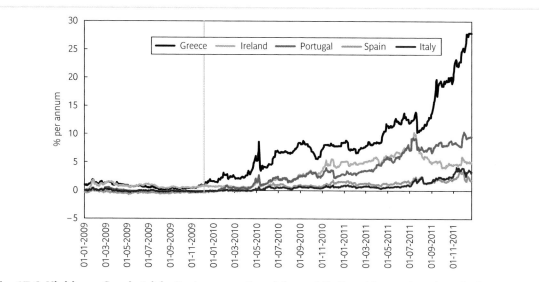

Fig. 17.6 Yields on Greek, Irish, Portuguese, Spanish, and Italian 10-year bonds, relative to Germany, 2009 – 2011 (% per annum)

The curves depict the difference between market yield on a 10-year bond in each of the five countries and that of Germany. In December 2009 (the red line), yields of Greek bonds began to rise, followed by Portugal and Ireland, then Spain and Italy. While some relief for Ireland, Spain, and Italy occurred in the fall of 2011, the situation for Greece and Portugal has further deteriorated.

Source: OECD

❶ Summary

1 One fundamental purpose of fiscal policy is to provide public goods and services. The boundary between what has to be produced publicly and what can be produced privately is not clear-cut.

2 A second function of fiscal policy is the redistribution of income and the alleviation of inequities that may be generated by the market mechanism. Doing so, however, may lead to inefficiencies.

3 A third function is to use the budget to offset temporary or cyclical fluctuations. This is done by running deficits in bad years (financed by borrowing) and surpluses in good years (to repay previous borrowing).

4 Countercyclical fiscal policy has three main benefits: (1) tax smoothing, (2) private consumption smoothing, and (3) private income maintenance.

5 The fact that some households sometimes cannot borrow provides a justification for fiscal policy to step in and support private consumption smoothing.

6 If prices and wages are not fully flexible, fiscal policy can be used to stabilize demand, either directly through government spending, or indirectly through taxation by reducing fluctuations in private sector incomes.

7 When they vote on the budgets, parliaments set public spending levels and tax rates. During a recession (respectively, an expansion) tax receipts decline (respectively, an increase) leading to a deficit (respectively, a surplus). As a result, the budget acts as an automatic stabilizer.

8 The operation of automatic stabilizers makes it difficult to interpret changes in the budget. The cyclically adjusted budget balance provides a way of disentangling the endogenous response to cyclical fluctuations from exogenous discretionary government actions.

9 Indebtedness is an inherently explosive process. When the primary budget is balanced and the debt is positive, borrowing is necessary just to service existing debt. The real debt accumulates at a rate given by the real interest rate.

10 To stabilize the level of the real debt, in the absence of real economic growth or monetary finance, the government must run a primary budget surplus equal to the interest charge. The longer it waits, the larger will be the debt and the interest burden that it faces, and the larger the required primary budget surplus.

11 In a growing economy, stabilizing the ratio of debt to GDP is a less stringent condition than stabilizing the absolute debt level. The required primary surplus is proportional to the difference between the real interest rate and the real GDP growth rate. Not only is this smaller than the real interest rate, it may well be negative, thus allowing permanent primary deficits.

12 Inflationary finance reduces the debt burden for two reasons. First, seigniorage provides resources directly to the government, virtually free of charge. As money growth eventually leads to inflation, the real value of nominal debt declines. Second, the inflation tax reduces the real value of nominal government debt which is not indexed. The inflation tax can be collected, however, only if inflation is unexpected. Otherwise the nominal interest rate rises, which protects lenders.

13 In addition to lowering the deficit—through spending cuts or tax increases—or resorting to money finance, debt can be stabilized by default. This drastic form of taxation has severe consequences for a government's reputation.

14 As long as the public debt is held by residents, debt stabilization or reduction implies income redistribution within the country. When part of the public debt is held by non-residents, stabilization requires a net transfer by residents to the rest of the world. A default redistributes wealth in the opposite direction.

15 Debt stabilization is also possible in the medium to long term by achieving a reduction in interest rates at which government debt is refinanced. This requires investing in credibility and removing fears of default. Increasing economic growth, or at least reaching the potential level of output, can also help stabilize the debt–GDP ratio, but requires a great deal of patience.

🔑 Key Concepts

- **public goods**
- **seigniorage**

- **externalities**
- **human capital**

- ◆ **productive efficiency**
- ◆ **equity – efficiency trade-off**
- ◆ **consumption smoothing**
- ◆ **tax smoothing**
- ◆ **countercyclical fiscal policy**

- ◆ **automatic stabilizers**
- ◆ **cyclically adjusted budgets**
- ◆ **debt stabilization**
- ◆ **inflation tax**

❓ Exercises

1 Are bank notes and coins part of the public debt? Should they be? Why or why not?

2 A country's budget law sets public spending at €30,000 million and the tax rate applied to income is 25%. Last year's GDP was €100,000 million and the forecast is that it will grow by 3%. What is this year's budget surplus (or deficit) set by the law? What will happen to the balance if the economy does not grow at all? If there is a deep recession, a decline of output of 3%?

3 A country growing at a rate of 2% has a debt–GDP ratio of 100%. What is the primary budget surplus that keeps this ratio constant when the real interest rate is 2%? When it is 6%?

4 Suppose the debt–GDP ratio is 150%, growth is 3% per annum, and the real interest rate is 5%.

  (a) What is the primary government budget surplus (as a percentage of GDP) that can stabilize the debt–GDP ratio?

  (b) How does your answer change if interest rates rises to 4%? If growth falls to 2%?

5 The demand for (real) central bank money, the source of seigniorage, declines with the rate of inflation. Suppose, as an example, that this demand (in billions of euros) is given as follows:

Π	0%	1%	2%	5%	10%	20%	25%	50%
$M0/P$	1,000	905	819	607	368	135	82	7

Seigniorage is a tax applied to this demand, whose rate is just the rate of inflation. Compute seigniorage as a function of the inflation rate. (Hint: an inflation rate of 5% corresponds to a tax rate equal to 0.05.) Which inflation rate maximizes seigniorage?

6 Figure 17.5 determines four quadrants (ignoring the diagonal). Characterize and comment on the situation in each quadrant.

7 The budget balance is −300 and GDP is 20,000. Potential GDP, however, is 20,600. Compute the structurally adjusted budget using the following information:

  - ◆ public consumption is not cyclical;
  - ◆ transfers operate as follows: $TR = 13,000 − 0.5^*Y$;
  - ◆ taxes are: $T = 2,000 + 0.3^*Y$.

8 Consider a country where the public debt stands at 60% of GDP. The real interest rate is 3% and the trend growth rate is 2%. In the absence of seigniorage, what is the primary budget required to stabilize the debt level? The debt–GDP ratio?

9 Why does a primary surplus in excess of what is found in (17.2) imply that the public debt will eventually disappear? Why does a primary surplus in excess of what is found in (17.4) imply that the public debt will eventually disappear as a fraction of GDP?

⊖ Essay Questions

1 Make a list of all public services that you can think of. In each case, examine whether they can be privately provided.

2 'The national debt is a great scam, because it will never be repaid.' 'The national debt is irrelevant because we owe it to ourselves.' Comment on these two popular characterizations of government indebtedness.

3 Critics of the Stability and Growth Pact argue that it prevents the operation of automatic stabilizers during cyclical downturns. The proponents respond that the way to deal with the pact is to run structurally adjusted surpluses. Explain and comment.

4 Between 2006 and 2010 the Irish public gross debt rose from 37.8 to 96.2% of GDP. Collect data on Irish budgets and growth during this period to explain this remarkable evolution (possible sources: OECD *Economic Outlook* database, Ireland's Finance Ministry's website: < www.finance.gov.ie>).

5 Debt stabilization is controversial. One view is that it requires running balanced budgets, irrespective of the possible cyclical implications. Another view is that it is far better to use fiscal policy to support rapid growth. Evaluate these arguments.

Policies for the Long Run

18

Economic growth—meaning a rising standard of living for a clear majority of citizens—more often than not fosters greater opportunity, tolerance of diversity, social mobility, commitment to fairness and dedication to democracy . . . But when living standards stagnate or decline, most societ-ies make little if any progress toward any of these goals, and in all too many instances they plainly retrogress.

Benjamin Friedman

18.1 Overview

In Chapter 16, we explored the role of demand management in macroeconomic policy, and Chapter 17 highlighted the usefulness and limitations of fiscal policy in the toolbox of demand management. Demand-induced recessions are costly in terms of unemployment and lost output; recovery can be accelerated by well-chosen activist policies. Yet some argue that no policy at all is better than a misguided activist one. Since the economy returns to its long-run path anyway, they would claim, demand policy does more harm than good. Despite this critique, it turns out that many governments do make use of demand policy, and virtually all of them did so, to varying degrees, in the global recession of 2008–2009.

An alternative or even a complementary policy to demand-side management is to increase the productive potential of an economy, irrespective of the state of aggregate demand. Policy measures which raise the long-run or potential GDP ($\bar{Y}$) are known as **supply-side policies**. This is shown in Figure 18.1, which plots the level of output Y itself on the horizontal axis rather than its deviation from potential output ($Y_{GAP} = (Y - \bar{Y})/\bar{Y}$). Successful supply-side policies raise potential GDP from $\bar{Y}$ to $\bar{Y}'$ faster than if it were left to the normal process of economic growth. The attractiveness of such policies is that they bypass the uncomfortable trade-off between output and inflation. In the short run, more output and lower inflation are possible as the economy moves from A to A'.[1] At the same time, bad supply-sided policies can

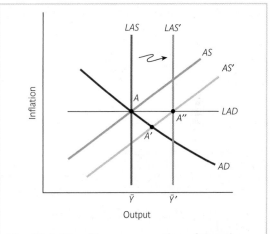

Fig. 18.1 The Macroeconomics of Supply-Side Policies

Supply-side policies aim at mobilizing productive resources to increase equilibrium output. Sustainable shifts in the aggregate supply curve yield both more output and less inflation in the short run (point A'). In the longer run, inflation returns to its previous level (as indicated by the long-run aggregate demand schedule) but output is permanently higher.

reduce $\bar{Y}$, causing higher inflation in the short run and higher unemployment and lower output in the long run.

This chapter surveys a broad spectrum of supply-side policies and assesses their effectiveness. These policies can target labour, product, or financial markets. They may also involve fine-tuning existing government interventions such as taxation or subsidies, or involve changing regulations of product and labour markets. Some reforms require as little as the

[1] Note that the short-run effect of the shift is a reduction in the rate of inflation, as both short-run AS and long-run LAS curves shift rightwards. After the adjustment is complete, inflation will return to its previous level, the target inflation rate set by the central bank (point A'') (see Chapter 13).

streamlining of bureaucratic rules, the uniform application of law, or the elimination of corruption. Others work directly on improving incentives to save, work, and produce. They can increase general efficiency, possibly by requiring less competitive, inefficient industries to shrink, freeing resources for other, more valuable uses. An important warning regarding supply-side policies is that they do not produce immediate results, often requiring five to ten years—sometimes even longer.

We examine three broad approaches to increasing the economy's long-run productive potential. First, good supply-side policy should aim to make product, labour, and financial markets as efficient as possible; and when markets fail that test, government intervention can improve matters. This was also the message of Chapters 4 and 17. Second, given that governments are already interfering in the market place for both good and bad reasons, they should strive to minimize the negative impact of their interventions. One example is regulation; another is taxation; yet another is subsidy policy. Third, unemployment remains a deep concern for Europe, where on average 10% of the labour force is out of work. Yet, in the last 15 years, many countries have made significant inroads against high long-term unemployment problem, including the UK, the Netherlands, Denmark, Finland, Germany, Ireland, and Sweden. Even in the course of the recent cyclical downturn, these countries have proved that unemployment need not be a curse. Even if the political resistance is strong to such reforms, all of Europe can share in these successes. As the quote at the beginning of the chapter suggests, economic growth helps societies sustain their dynamism, maintain social cohesion, and improve standards of living for all of their members.

18.2 Market Efficiency and the Theory of Supply-Side Policy

18.2.1 The Benchmark of Efficiency: Perfect Competition

Adam Smith (1723–1790), perhaps the most famous economist of all time, claimed in his book *The Wealth of Nations* that efficient resource allocation was best left to the market system. One of the greatest achievements of modern economics has been to confirm that, under ideal conditions, market economies can achieve optimal employment of resources.[2] What are those ideal conditions? Most importantly, markets must 'work', meaning that prices must be free to adjust. There must be sufficient competition so that new firms can offer similar or identical products and eliminate excessive profits due to their monopoly position. Externalities identified in Chapter 4 and 17

must be absent. Information should be equally available to all agents. Not surprisingly, these ideal conditions are unlikely to be met in practice. If not, government intervention can improve the allocation of resources and possibly achieve a greater level of output, and ultimately well-being, in the economy.

An important example is the labour market, studied in Chapter 5. Consider Figure 5.7, which shows equilibrium in an ideal labour market. Firms' demand for labour is given by the downward-sloping marginal product of labour curve (MPL). Firms hire labour to the point at which its marginal productivity equals the real wage. Similarly, workers supply hours of labour up to the point at which the utility loss of foregone leisure time is greater than the gain from goods earned from working—the real wage. The market-clearing equilibrium point *A* can be seen as an ideal state. Increasing employment beyond point *A* in Figure 5.7 reduces the MPL below what workers are willing to work for. Reducing employment below

---

[2] In the 1950s, Nobel laureates Kenneth Arrow of Stanford and Gerard Debreu of Berkeley showed how Adam Smith's intuition could be rigorously established. They identified the conditions under which a market economy delivers the socially optimal allocation of resources.

A would raise the MPL above the real wage which would be sufficient to motivate labourers to give up their free time. Put another way, if wages are above the market-clearing level, firms would restrict employment and workers would increase their supply, resulting in involuntary unemployment. If real wages are too low, firms demand more man-hours than workers are willing to supply.

What pushes the real wage towards its equilibrium, **market-clearing** level *w* at point *A*? The answer is competition. In an idealized perfectly flexible market for labour, a lower wage than *w* will not attract as many workers as firms want to employ. Competition among firms will lead some to improve their wage offer. As they succeed in luring workers from their previous jobs, other firms will have to respond with yet a higher wage offer. Competition will bid up wages until they reach the market-clearing level. Conversely, imagine that the wage exceeds *w*. Some will not find a job, or will not be able to work as many hours as they wish. Forces of competition will trigger a decline in the wage as unemployed workers underbid those who have jobs, eventually driving wages to point *A*.

That point *A* represents an ideal state is a general principle: for an economy to achieve the optimum allocation of resources, the market must clear. In fact, *all* markets must clear. Either all prices are right and all productive resources are fully employed, or none of them is, and underutilization and inefficiency spread throughout the economy. Economists tend to be split into two camps on this issue. Some are convinced that markets are naturally efficient, so there is no need for governments to interfere. This is the **laissez-faire** view. Others believe that few markets meet the high standards set forth by Adam Smith. The existence of **market failures**, when and where they can be identified, provides a justification for government intervention. Note, however, how cautiously this statement is worded. Interventions are only justified if two conditions are met. First, they should be limited to clearly identified market failures. Second, they should be targeted directly at the market failure to avoid creating additional distortions of their own. In the sections that follow, we identify several generic market failures and discuss the associated range of possible interventions.

18.2.2 Imperfect Competition and Economic Rents

When several firms compete with each other in the same market, they are under constant pressure to adapt the price and design of their product to the desires of the consumer—otherwise they will lose sales and be forced to exit the market. They will try to operate as efficiently as possible, and in doing so perform the function society wants them to: allocate available resources to their most efficient uses. And that is exactly what Adam Smith predicted.

Competition, however, can be painful. Every economic agent wants protection from competition. Firms strive to acquire a leading position in the market at the expense of their rivals, thereby earning above-average profits aptly called **economic rents**. How do they do this? Firms normally strive to establish market power, or even market dominance or monopoly status, by exploiting increasing returns to scale or by differentiating their products. When production exhibits increasing returns to scale, larger firms can squeeze out smaller firms by producing more, and thus reducing their costs. Eventually only a few firms survive and then dominate the market (think of the market for automobiles). Firms sometimes restrict competition by preventing others from entering their markets. Most means of maintaining dominance in a market are prohibited; threats against competitors and extortion are illegal. Yet it is standard practice for producers to spend significant amounts of money creating brand names and convincing consumers that their products are fundamentally different or unique. Customers who enjoy consuming products that are different—or merely believe that they are—will be willing to pay more for them. Firms use clever marketing to obtain and defend this monopoly power, and can justify the large sums of money spent on product advertising by the resulting profits. Product differentiation thrives on individuals' desire for variety in the market place. It is indisputable that the consumer would prefer variety to monotony, and the quest by firms to innovate and produce variety is spurred by competition.

Measures which increase competition and thereby economic output are generally referred to as **competition policy**. Competition policy can take a number

Box 18.1 EU Competition Policy and National Preferences

Economists love competition because it generally leads to more efficient outcomes. This enthusiasm is rarely shared by firms operating in non-competitive markets, where large profits may be at stake. Policy-makers and consumers may be lukewarm to competition-enhancing measures. Especially in the European Union, where cultures and traditions are defined by national boundaries, reservations abound that unbridled competition might weaken or destroy national identities. It is sometimes difficult indeed to distinguish between respect for consumer preferences for variety and restraint of trade. The latter means less competition, less efficiency, lower output, and fewer jobs without any real gain to consumers.

Examples of this dilemma facing the EU abound. In a highly publicized case involving beer quality in the late 1980s, Germany was taken to the European Court of Justice, which has the final say in matters of EU competition policy. Since 1516, German brewers had produced the golden beverage according to the *Reinheitsgebot* ('beer purity law'), which restricted the content of beer to four ingredients (water, yeast, malted barley, and hops). Such strict regulation of beer quality did not exist elsewhere in Europe. This law was used to exclude 'impure' foreign beer which did not meet the exacting standards of the *Reinheitsgebot*. The European Court of Justice found that beer brewed using rice and other ingredients should be permitted, while allowing German brewers to market their beer as conforming to the previous regime. Many years later and despite the new import rules, national tastes prevail; most German beer drinkers continue to drink German beer. Similarly, Italians now must have a choice between *grano duro* pasta and those made with other wheat varieties. French cheese consumers can try Danish *blø* if they wish. In theory, the consumer is better off.

Still, the *Reinheitsgebot* case raises a number of interesting questions. Should the EU forbid the import of beef from the USA, which may be treated with hormones or antibiotics? Should genetically modified plants be allowed? Should imports of foreign 'culture'—in particular, audio and video recordings—be limited? Should a minimum price of books in bookstores be guaranteed, as in France, Germany, or Austria? Such regulations are usually justified using non-economic arguments. The question remains whether these truly outweigh their economic costs.

of forms. In many countries, monopolies are regulated or supervized closely. Firms are seldom allowed to acquire excessive shares of their markets. Collusion in the form of cartels and price-fixing schemes are illegal. More recently, governments have also limited the ability of firms to dominate their input and output markets. One famous case in Europe involved the Microsoft Corporation and the market power created by its operating system and internet browser programs. Similarly, the UK Government separated electricity generation from electricity distribution as well as train service from rail ownership with the intent of creating more competition. The EU Commission has moved in this direction at the Community level with respect to energy transmission networks. More generally, as European integration proceeds and the relevant market expands to the level of the EU, anti-monopoly powers are being transferred to Brussels. Some interesting cases of EU competition policy are discussed in Box 18.1.

Firms are not the only economic agents which try to avoid competition. Labour markets are frequently characterized by non-competitive behaviour. First, labour supply is intimately linked with the human condition, and competition among workers for jobs is often considered inappropriate, in bad taste, or even unethical. Second, wages are often set in bilateral negotiations, and trade unions are seen as protecting interests of employed workers in a vulnerable situation. An alternative perspective sees trade unions as monopolists with high real wages in mind.[3] With high real wages, labour demand is low and equilibrium unemployment high. If a majority of trade union members accept this trade-off, they will press for an outcome that is not efficient. In a similar way, firms like to control or even reduce competition on labour costs, and are frequently organized in employers' associations. In Europe, these associations

[3] The analysis of trade unions is developed in Chapter 5.

frequently take decisions that are also binding for members, and may be followed by non-members (usually smaller firms). If labour and management set wages in collective bargaining without considering the interest of non-member workers, typically the unemployed, and of non-member firms, the level of competition is reduced, and the economy is less efficient. This subject will be taken up again in Section 18.4.

Competition in labour markets is not limited to labour unions and management. A number of practices by professional associations—of lawyers, doctors, and architects, for example—also restrict the supply of labour and raise wages. Limitations on international immigration can be interpreted as the ultimate restriction of competition for labour. Because so many political and sociological issues are associated with immigration, it would be premature to advocate open borders for everyone on purely economic grounds. Yet

it remains true that immigration is efficient, usually increasing GDP enough to compensate those in the receiving country who are made worse off. Box 18.2 gives more details.

18.2.3 Market Failures and Overall Market Efficiency

The goal of supply-side policy is to improve the functioning of markets and thereby create efficiency gains. Greater efficiency is like a free lunch—in theory, it can be redistributed to other members of society without making anyone worse off, as discussed in the context of immigration in Box 18.2. In general, this means intervening in markets which do not function properly. While Chapters 16 and 17 dealt with temporary interventions to speed up the elimination of demand shortfalls, the problem here concerns failures of markets to achieve efficient outcomes. Solutions to these market failures call for

---

 Box 18.2 The Supply-Side Economics of Immigration

Because labour is so abundant relative to capital in developing countries, many, many people there are very, very poor. In India, for example, GDP amounts to about €4 per day. Yet many Indians are highly educated and would readily migrate to Europe where the hourly wage might average €20–25 per *hour* or even more. Even those without exceptional skills but who are able-bodied and willing to work could compete with the less skilled. Almost on a weekly basis, we hear of Kurds, Chinese, Vietnamese, and Indians who are caught trying to cross EU borders. Most of these people are not seeking political asylum as much as economic betterment. One can hardly blame them for wanting to move. Is it economically efficient to keep these people out?

The analysis of Chapter 5 suggests that it is not, and Figure 18.2 shows why. Two labour supply curves are drawn, one corresponding to that of the natives only, without the immigrants. The second curve to the right is the sum of the natives *plus* the newly arrived migrants. For the moment, the labour demand curve is assumed unchanged by migration. It is equal to the marginal product of labour. For a given wage level, the area under the curve and above that wage represents total profits

earned by firms in the economy. In Figure 18.2, profits are thus AWB before the migrants arrive. After they arrive, the aggregate labour supply curve shifts outwards, wages decline from W to W' and employment rises from L to L'. Total GDP rises by the amount $BLL'D$, the sum of the additional marginal products of the newly employed. Without migration, this increase in GDP would not have occurred.

So if immigration is economically efficient, why all the fuss? First, the distribution of the increase in GDP is not shared by all: profits rise by $WBDW'$ and the migrants earn $CDL'L''$, but wages of native workers have in fact declined from $WBLO$ to $W'CL'O$. Only if the demand for labour shifts out—which may occur if there is new investment by natives, or if the immigrants themselves bring capital with them—would the outcome be different. Second, immigrants place extra demands on infrastructure and the social safety net which they have not helped to pay for. Finally, although economists like to emphasize the efficiency of immigration, other sociological aspects may be more important: humankind's complex tribal, if sometimes crude and primordial, instincts.

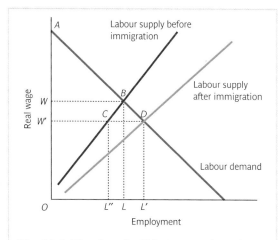

Fig. 18.2 The Supply-Side Economics of Immigration

The consequence of immigration is to shift total labour supply outward. In the new equilibrium, wages decline from *W* to *W'* and employment increases from *L* to *L'*. While GDP rises unambiguously by *BLL'D*, this gain is not evenly spread: the income of capital increases from *AWB* to *AW'D*, migrants now earn *CDL'L"*, while the income of natives declines from *WBLO* to *W'CL"O*.

permanent new policies or reforms which ultimately raise equilibrium output. But many of these failures simply cannot be eliminated; they are in the nature of things. Supply-side policies may help by reducing the extent and the impact of these failures. We start by looking at the origins of 'natural' market failures, which we group in four general categories:

* externalities
* public goods
* increasing returns
* information asymmetries.

Externalities

As discussed already in Chapters 4 and 17, an externality occurs when someone's action inevitably affects others. Pollution is a good example of a **negative externality**: when a firm dumps its waste in a river, those who live or work downstream suffer and have to expend resources to purify the water that they drink. Market incentives are for producers of negative externalities to generate too much of these for the social optimum. In contrast, **positive externalities** provide others with a better outcome. A general conclusion is that not enough is produced when activities generate a positive externality. Putting flowers in your windows costs money, while passers-by enjoy looking at them at no cost. Since you bear the costs of putting flowers on your balcony, you balance the price and the benefits (your pleasure). While putting out even more flowers might further raise society's pleasure, it is unreasonable to expect individuals to behave in the public interest (although they sometimes do).

The market alone apparently cannot redress the externality problem. If, however, **property rights** are well-defined, and it is not too costly to enforce these rights, it can.[4] If, for example, the law specifies that everyone has a right to clean water, it is the polluting firm that will have to spend resources to clean up the water. In facing this situation, the firm will adopt cleaner production processes. Alternatively, it will offer to indemnify those who live downstream to prevent them from taking the case to court (where it would probably lose anyway). Conversely, the law could convey rights to pollute to firms. Then the costs would be shifted to the people who live downstream, who would pay for cleaning the water, or offer money to the firm for it to reduce its disposal or adopt other production processes. While the second solution may seem unfair (and it probably is), it is no less efficient than the first. The general point is that, once property rights have been assigned, the market is more likely to deliver the best possible outcome, given the presumption that nature makes it impossible to produce without creating waste.

Externalities can also be transmitted via market prices. For example, the efforts of countries to develop biofuels may lead to higher prices around the world for grain and other agricultural products, which may in turn lead to malnutrition in poor countries. These **pecuniary externalities** are properly addressed by changing the distribution of wealth and income. But other, inherently **non-pecuniary externalities** are more challenging. Assigning property rights and creating a market is often not enough to solve the problem. An example is training and education. Better

---

[4] This result is known as Coase Theorem, named after Ronald Coase, a US economist who received the Nobel Prize for his work on the importance of property rights in a market economy.

trained people share their knowledge with co-workers and their own children. Thus their knowledge has a value for society at large and, if they are not compensated, they will not accumulate as much human capital as is optimal from the standpoint of the economy, even if the firm invests more in workers out of motives of pure profit maximization. For this reason, society has an interest in stepping in, and subsidizing education. In Chapter 4 we saw how externalities involving education, law and order, and health can influence long-run growth. We look at the policy implications in Section 18.5.

Public goods

Public goods, such as parks, clean air, or information, are special. They are non-rival, meaning that consumption by one does not make them less available to others, and they are non-excludable, meaning that, when they are available, everyone can use them freely. As a consequence, no one can be charged for using them, and they must be provided by the state. Law and order is an externality, but it is also a public good that can and must be provided by a functioning government. In societies which have become 'failed states', law and order are absent, private justice and local warlords take over, economic activity collapses, and poverty spreads. This has been the case in countries torn by civil wars, such as Liberia, the Ivory Coast, or Somalia.

Increasing returns

Some industries are characterized by increasing returns to scale. While important for the macroeconomy, we ignored the possibility of increasing returns at the aggregate level because it usually applies to particular markets. A good example is railways. A railway that just serves two cities will only be used by people living in or going to these two cities. If it includes a vast network, the link between the same two cities will be used by many more people, many of whom will only pass through these two cities. The larger the network, the more valuable is each of its sections, and the larger the profits to be earned from each section. Left to the market, competition can easily lead to a **natural monopoly**, with just one company owning the entire network. But we know that, once it has established itself, a monopoly will tend to

charge monopoly prices, resulting in the socially inefficient under-utilization of its product. There is a need for the state to intervene, in this case by granting monopoly rights to a company—which can be public—in exchange for a regulation which will prevent monopolistic pricing. Recent discussions concerning the divestiture of European power transmission networks and the privatization of the German railways reflect these concerns.

Information asymmetries

It is a simple observation that we know more about ourselves than others. This information asymmetry plays a pervasive role in all sorts of markets. Traders often hide information that may reduce the price they can get for their products. Two examples: used car salesmen and traders in financial markets. Both have little incentive to tell the truth in their businesses. In the first case, the market can easily dry up, even if the salesmen really do tell all they know about the cars they sell. In the second, traders make profit by reacting faster to new information, so they will naturally tend to hide they what they know and what they are up to. Moreover, one trader's move, if badly interpreted by the others, can trigger a stampede. Such herd behaviour seems to lie at the root of financial crises. In both cases, information is a fact of nature, with serious economic implications for the functioning of markets. The state can play a constructive role by prescribing what information must be provided by sellers of used cars or by forcing financial firms to disclose much information that they would prefer to keep for themselves.

Even die-hard free market advocates recognize that markets are subject to failures, that these failures may have serious implications for economic performance, and that only the state can solve most of the associated difficulties. Should the state intervene and solve all market failures? Here economists often disagree. Some, e.g. the public choice school led by Nobel Prize winners Friedrich Hayek and James Buchanan, maintain that the government, when it intervenes, does more harm than good. Others view state intervention as unavoidable, especially in modern societies where economic interactions can be quite complex and thus serve as conduits for the diffusion

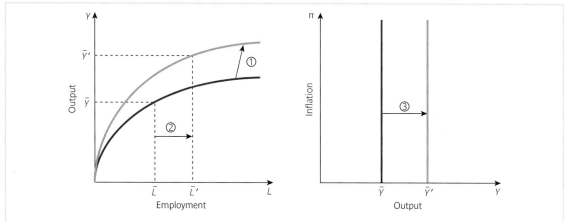

Fig. 18.3 The Impact of Supply-Side Policies

Beneficial supply-side policies are depicted as an increase in the long-run level of output in panel (*b*). As shown in panel (*a*), this increase can result from 1) a shift in the production function due to an increase in total factor productivity or an increase in equilibrium inputs of other production factors while labour input is held constant, or 2) as an increase in labour input, holding the production function and other inputs constant. The outcome 3) is a shift from *Y* to *Y′* in panel (*b*).

of adverse effects of market failures. It is fair to say that no country completely refrains from intervening in the marketplace, for the right or wrong reasons. We look at supply-side policies directed at labour markets in Section 18.4, and at goods markets in Section 18.5. Many market failures not only affect the level of output, but also growth rate. In Chapter 4 we considered the potential for those policies mainly directed at enhancing growth. Similarly, Chapter 14 addressed policies that deal with financial market failures.

In the following sections, policies are discussed which have the objective of rooting out market failures, improving the functioning of markets by increasing competition or the availability of useful information to market participants, or simply making government intervention less costly from the economy's perspective. All are examples of good supply-side policy. They have the common feature of shifting out the vertical *LAS* curve in Figure 18.3 to the right, from $\bar{Y}$ to $\bar{Y}′$. This can occur either as (1) a one-off improvement in total factor productivity which increases output, holding productive inputs constant, or (2) by increasing the supply of productive factors, holding the level of technology and the position of the production function constant. Bad supply-side policy has the opposite effect, reducing output produced by the same volume of factor inputs, or by inducing households and firms to withdraw productive factors from market uses.

18.3 Product Market Policies

18.3.1 Dealing with Externalities

The basic principle is to internalize externalities. This means making those that create an externality bear its costs or the benefits. In the pollution example, this is achieved by making clean water a right. We have illustrated this principle with a few important examples which have recently received prominent attention.

Human capital accumulation

The first example, also mentioned in Section 18.2.3, is investment in **human capital**. It is one of the most crucial factors of economic development. Human capital is acquired at school, of course, but also at work. It may be best to spread training over a lifetime to allow people to update their depreciating capital and learn about newly acquired knowledge. The knowledge of an individual person benefits society in a myriad of ways. It helps co-workers, of course, but better-educated people can make better decisions in everyday life—including taking better care of themselves and their children, or voting as informed citizens. An individual's return from human capital is believed to be significantly smaller for the individual than for society. If they invest with only their individual return in mind, they will underinvest regarding what is justified by the broader social return. For this reason, societies have an interest in encouraging people to invest in more human capital than they would on their own. Free and compulsory education was the first response to this externality. Subsidizing traineeships in firms or continuing education further the same goal. In addition, unemployed people tend to see their human capital depreciate. This provides an additional justification for active labour market policies described in Section 18.5.1.

Law and order

Law and order has all the characteristics of a market failure: it is an externality, it is subject to increasing returns to scale, and it is a public good. It is an externality since everyone benefits from others being honest. Investment in physical and human capital is threatened when crime robs people and firms of their assets, and will be less attractive in the absence of law and order. It is subject to increasing returns to scale, since commonly accepted and enforced law works better than when everyone sets their own rules and practises self-enforcement. Private protection, the spontaneous market response to the absence of law and order, is inefficient. It also accentuates the effect of inequality, as rich people can better defend themselves than poor people. Law and order is also a public good since it is non-excludable and non-rival. Thus, on all three grounds, leaving law and order to the market results in a massive failure. Indeed, from time immemorial, one of the key attributes of any political power has always been the provision of law and order.

Health

Health is obviously a private 'good'. Everyone wants to be healthy. It is also a source of externality. People with poor health do not work well and are often absent; this reduces the productivity of their colleagues. Chronically ill people can lose their jobs and become destitute, relying on society's generosity, or resorting to criminal activity to survive. Sicknesses can also be contagious, a vivid example of externality. Health can be provided privately, as it is in many countries. Private health programmes generate inequalities, and most people think that it is unacceptable that the rich receive better treatment than the poor. But, in addition, because of the externalities that it generates, privately provided health is likely to be inefficient, as everyone will only spend up to the point where their (marginal) benefit equals marginal cost and not consider the positive effects their health have on others. This is why most countries have established systems of social security and enforce compulsory medical examinations and vaccination. A healthy society is a rich society. Causality runs from wealth to health, but it also runs in the opposite direction.

18.3.2 Dealing with Malfunctioning Markets

The solution to market failures is not always to produce public goods and services. In fact, it is increasingly being recognized that private producers tend to be more cost-efficient than publicly owned ones, provided that they are adequately regulated. In this section, we look at monopolies and review some prominent examples of the **privatization** process and of how regulation operates.

Monopolies

Markets characterized by increasing returns tend to evolve to a situation where a very few firms buy out or eliminate the others. When only one firm survives, it is a monopoly. Once it has achieved that position, its incentive is to charge high prices, and possibly to stop innovating, and let the quality of its goods decline. When just two or three dominate, they have incentives to agree among themselves to raise prices and lower competition in terms of quality and innovation. This is called collusion. Thus, in the presence of increasing returns, markets evolve spontaneously to a situation where competition is insufficient to match the principles of market efficiency. Examples of industries prone to increasing returns include automobile and aeroplane production, transport, and telecommunications.

One response is to regulate these industries. Governments step in and either break down the monopolies (e.g. the ongoing deregulation in the electricity, telecommunication, and airline industries), or prevent mergers, and actively fight against collusion. Because competition increasingly takes place at the world level, such anti-trust and anti-collusion policies are often conducted at the supranational level. In Europe, the European Commission has been granted wide authority in that area. For instance, it has blocked several mergers between international giants and imposed pro-competition conditions on others.

Privatization

In many countries, the other response to market failures, especially the existence of natural monopolies, has been to set up state-owned companies that would not seek to exploit their monopolistic power. This has been the case of railways, electricity generation and distribution, water distribution, telecommunications, etc. Since the early 1980s, European policy-makers have looked more critically at the performance of state monopolies. The prices that they charged were regulated, and based on their costs. But who was minding the costs? Suspicion grew that, in the absence of competition, these firms were not producing at the lowest possible cost. Monopolistic rents were not captured in the form of private profits, but in the form of slack production, poor service quality, technological backwardness, and sometimes comfortable salaries, and other advantages. The contrast between Europe and the USA, which relied to a much lesser extent on publicly owned companies, had become glaring.

The response was a wave of privatization, which is still underway. Once a company had become private, it was interested in expanding across borders. The presence of state-owned monopolies in some countries prevented the entry of foreign competitors, while allowing the national company to expand abroad. Clearly, this was an unfair situation. This is why the Single Act of 1992 has given the European Commission the right to force national governments to privatize most of their state-owned monopolies and to open their markets to foreign competition. One example of successful supply-side reform in Europe is a sequence of privatizations and deregulation in the telecommunications industry described in detail in Box 18.3. This process has freed a dynamic force for economic growth and job creation. Twenty years down the road, the process is still far from complete, a testimony of how entrenched the interests are.

Regulation

Regulation is often the best response when markets are not well-behaved. Financial markets are essential for economic growth, since banks and financial intermediaries collect savings to finance investment by firms and public deficits. Yet financial markets are often viewed with suspicion, partly because of markets' tendencies to undergo violent crises, a manifestation of the asymmetric information problem. As a result, they are regulated. In principle, banks are not allowed to take excessive risk with the deposits of their customers, who cannot effectively monitor their banks and stand to lose part of their savings if the bank collapses. Financial traders are restricted in the amount of their business which they can fund with borrowed money, putting a legal ceiling on the risk that they can take, in an effort to limit the occurrence of financial crises.

That regulation affects nearly every aspect of economic life does not only show how widespread market failures are, but also highlights the tendency of the state to do too much. Asymmetric information explains why food labels, airline services, or driving licences are regulated. Yet the regulation of store closing times in many parts of Europe, taxis in Greece, pharmacies in Germany, or chimney-sweeping in Switzerland might really be a case of favouring private interests at the expense of the public good.

Subsidies and industrial policy

For a variety of non-economic reasons, many countries operate elaborate systems of subsidies which

Box 18.3 Telecommunications: Successful Supply-Side Policy

In the early 1990s a number of European countries, led by the UK and later by Germany, began to privatize and deregulate their telecommunications industries. These had been the domain of the national postal systems, which had introduced new technologies slowly and charged high prices for services which cost little at the margin to produce. In effect, the Europeans were doing little more than recognizing the successes of the USA in the early 1980s after the break-up of the monopoly ATT (American Telephone and Telegraph) and the resulting deregulation of long-distance telephone services. The Europeans went farther than the Americans, however. By agreeing on a pan-European standard for wireless technologies and wireless application protocols, they created a common market for an activity which obviously involves massive external effects. They also intensified direct competition with local telecom service provision—which remains a local monopoly in most countries.

The deregulation of telecoms in Europe has led to visible positive supply-side economic effects. The telecom industry has not only been a source of value added and income growth for Europeans, but has also generated hundreds of thousands of new jobs. Most importantly, consumers have benefited. In Germany, the overall price index fell by 27% for telecom services, by 65% for long distance, and by 63% for mobile phone use between 1995 and 2007. Naturally, much of these price declines was due to technological improvements and associated cost reductions. Yet it is hard to imagine price declines like these offered voluntarily by a monopolist, be they public or private. While prices were falling all around Europe, the relative price declines in long-distance service and portable telephone services is closely associated with deregulation in the UK in the late 1990s. More recently, the public auction of third-generation mobile communication radio frequencies heralds the combination of these technologies with the internet, and promises the introduction of new products and services that the old national postal services could never have offered.

---

shield certain firms and industries from the discipline of the market. Table 18.1 displays the evidence for some OECD countries. Subsidized firms can sustain losses for a long time and avoid adjusting to changing economic conditions. In doing so, they keep resources, capital, and labour employed, but do so inefficiently and prevent those resources from being used elsewhere. They do not face the full cost of their operations (part of the costs are charged to taxpayers), or else the factors of production are paid more than their true marginal productivity.[5] In fact, they may even keep factor prices artificially high and hurt other businesses that are not subsidized.

[5] For example, after the oil shocks of the 1970s, a reduced world demand for tankers and the emergence of Asian competition (Japan, Korea) combined to create major difficulties for European shipyards. The UK, Germany, France, and many other countries reacted by subsidizing their shipbuilding companies. In the end, the costs became too large and the situation too hopeless for the subsidies to be maintained. While the subsidies did save jobs for a few years, they did so in a very inefficient way.

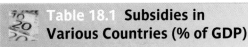

Table 18.1 Subsidies in Various Countries (% of GDP)

	1975	1990	2009
Belgium	3.0	1.7	1.8
France	2.0	1.8	1.4
Germany	1.7	1.7	1.0
Italy	2.6	1.8	0.8
Netherlands	1.4	2.3	1.3
Spain	0.6	1.0	1.0
Sweden	2.4	3.6	1.6
USA	0.3	0.5	0.4

Source: OECD, *Economic Outlook*.

Public ownership of firms is another, more subtle form of subsidization. Unlike private firms, state-owned enterprises (SOEs) rarely face demanding shareholders and are almost never shut down. When they lose money, they generally receive public resources.

This may come either as an explicit subsidy from the government to cover the loss, or as a loan to the company at interest rates unavailable to other firms. SOEs operate in virtually every major industry in Western Europe.

Most countries regard certain economic activities as indispensable for strategic or political reasons. These include defence-related industries, such as steel, energy, high technology, aircraft, and shipbuilding. As many of these activities exhibit increasing returns to scale, governments often try to guarantee that the firms are large enough. This is often the underlying logic behind **industrial policies**. Industrial policies amount to official backing of national corporations or whole industries. This takes the form of subsidies, public orders, and trade policies. **Trade policies** include tariffs on foreign goods, quotas on imports, export credits financed at concessionary rates, and procurement policies whereby domestically produced goods are chosen over cheaper foreign ones, not to mention 'buy domestic goods' campaigns.

The ultimate effect of these policies is to raise prices above competitive levels. Consumers or tax-payers make up the difference. Once again, the principle that prices reflect efficient production costs is violated. Supply-side considerations have led to a reassessment of strategic requirements. The European Single Act of 1992 bans most trade policies already mentioned for intra-European trade. Yet industrial and trade policies survive, often conducted at the EU rather than national level, with such celebrated examples as Airbus, Ariane, and Volkswagen. More recently, private European banks have complained that state savings banks and their parent entities enjoy hidden subsidies in the form of government guarantees. EU competition authorities have demanded that these be privatized or at least set on an equal footing, singling out the German *Sparkassen* and the *Landesbanken*. These institutions respond that they represent the only means of achieving blanket availability of banking services in remote, rural areas, and provide financing for projects that private banks generally shun. As the issue of state aids becomes increasingly political, it assumes the aspects of national preferences discussed in Box 18.1.

18.4 Taxation as the Price of Intervention

18.4.1 The Necessity of Taxation

Public goods are special because they are naturally non-rival and non-excludable. Being non-excludable, public goods cannot be charged to their users. A toll booth can be installed at a bridge's entrance, but what price should its owner charge? Non-rivalry means that the marginal cost of usage is very low; from the perspective of social welfare the price ought to be low, too. But the costs of providing public goods can be high (a bridge is very expensive to build!), so how can the producer be compensated? In addition, a bridge is a natural monopoly if it is the only one in the vicinity. If the owner charges a high price and makes large profits, market competition will lead to a proliferation of bridges, all probably next to each other, which also seems like an inefficient outcome. It is difficult for markets to cope with such failures

because they require some sort of grand plan, which decentralized markets, by their very nature, cannot (and should not!). Most often, public goods are provided collectively (free bridges), or their provision is regulated (privately built bridges are generally subject to strict regulations, including pricing and quality of service).

Public goods are pervasive: transportation and amenities, but also justice and police, passports, national defence and security, and diplomacy, etc. In each case, there is a market solution, but it is inefficient, as not enough of the good in question—and possible none at all—would be privately provided. And in each case, the insufficient provision of the public goods would greatly impair economic activity, possibly leading to the breakdown of other, properly functioning markets. This is why the provision of public goods is a fundamental supply-side policy. The more efficient the provision, the more productive the economy will be. At the same time, efficiency means that public goods are produced at the lowest possible cost—which also involves issues of public procurement policy. Building bridges, roads, and other forms of infrastructure involves large sums of money, and corruption or the bias for local or national producers can represent a significant efficiency loss.

18.4.2 The Effect of Taxation on Efficiency

Once a society has agreed to let government perform certain public functions, public resources need to be raised in order to pay for them. This is done through taxation of final goods and services, factors of production, and other activities. As a rule, taxation distorts markets by driving a wedge between the cost of producing goods and services and the price paid by the consumers. This violates a fundamental principle of economic efficiency, which states that the marginal benefit of the good or service involved should be set equal to the marginal cost of supplying it. When this principle is violated, there is a loss of welfare to both consumers and producers, which can be quantified. This **deadweight loss of taxation** is described in more detail in Box 18.4.

In order to provide public goods, the government needs to raise taxes and accept the associated distortions. Still, it should do so in the least inefficient way. The **Ramsey principle of public finance** states that this is best achieved, first, by spreading taxes as widely as possible over different goods and services and, second, by taxing most heavily those goods with the most inelastic (i.e. steepest) demands and supplies. While the Ramsey principle sounds like a good idea, implementing it is politically contentious. Each producer stands to be hurt when a tax is applied to its production—because the producer surplus is reduced, as Box 18.3 shows—and therefore lobbies hard to obtain as low taxes as possible. Consumers,

---

 Box 18.4 **The Deadweight Loss from Taxation**

Why are taxes a source of market distortion? Figure 18.4 shows the general case of an *ad valorem* tax, which is a percentage of the value of the activity. Under perfect competition, the demand curve summarizes the marginal willingness of the market to pay for the good, while the supply curve describes the marginal cost of producing it (both measured in euros). At point *E*, where the two curves intersect, the marginal consumer is willing to pay exactly what the marginal producer requires to produce it. Perfect competition achieves the social best. Taxes alter this situation; the price paid by the buyer now differs from the after-tax price received by the seller. The new supply curve *S′* shows that the producer receives only a fraction of the market price. At the new market equilibrium point *D*, the price is higher and the amount consumed and produced is lower. Both consumers and producers are worse off.

What are the losses to an economy from **distortionary taxation**? Figure 18.4 gives us a graphical answer. Because of the tax, consumers cannot enjoy the lower price *OG* and pay higher price *OA* instead, purchasing only *AD* instead of *GE*. The area traced out by *ADEG* represents the consumer surplus, or consumers' willingness to pay above the market-clearing price, that is lost due to the tax. At the same time, the lower price (net of tax) to producing firms means that firms will lose profits on goods they would have sold, produced at cost lower than the no-tax price. The existence of these profits is due to the fact that the supply curve is upward-sloping. This second area *BCEG* is known as producer surplus. This consumer and producer surplus are not lost entirely. Despite the price rise, purchases of *AD* will still occur. The tax income from an *ad valorem* tax is given by the rectangle *ABCD*. This leaves the two triangles, *DEF* and *CFE*, which represent lost consumer and producer surplus, or deadweight loss to society. These losses can be quantified. Economic consultants frequently estimate deadweight losses as the cost of taxation when considering different policy options.

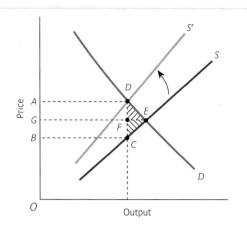

Fig. 18.4 **The Effect of Taxation**

Taxes drive a wedge between the price faced by the buyer and the price charged by the seller. Here a sales tax (e.g. VAT) shifts the supply curve upward. The new equilibrium occurs at point *D*, with less output, a higher buying price (distance *OA*), and a lower selling price (*OB*) than at the tax-free equilibrium point *E*. Tax revenue for the government is measured by area *ABCD*, the quantity sold times the tax rate (the difference between the two prices). Consumers, who could buy quantity *GE* at price *OG*, suffer a 'welfare loss' measured by the area *ADEG*. Similarly, producers suffer a loss represented by the area *GECB*. Of these two losses—area *ADECB*—the government receives *ABCD*. What is left, the triangles *DEF* and *EFC*, represent, respectively, lost consumer and producer surpluses—deadweight losses—arising from the tax.

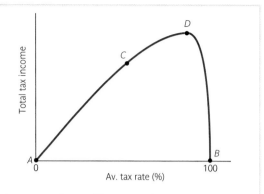

Fig. 18.5 **The Laffer Curve in Theory**

When the tax rate is 0% there is no tax revenue at all (point *A*). As the average tax rate approaches 100%, tax income is also likely to be zero (point *B*). Intermediate tax rates generate positive tax income, e.g. at point *C*. By continuity, the Laffer curve implies a hump-shaped relationship between tax income and average tax rates. Tax revenues are the highest at point *D*.

on the other hand, tend to be spread out and difficult to organize politically. As a result, tax reforms bring a diverse coalition of private interests that often succeed as the silent majority that stands to benefit from them remains inactive. Finally, the principle contains some distasteful implications—the highest rates should apply to necessities such as lodging, food, fuel, and clothing, while luxury goods with high demand elasticities should face low taxes. All the same, the Ramsey principle is often applied in practice—most of all because the tax base declines the least when the elasticity of supply is the lowest.

18.4.3 **Adverse Effects of Taxation on the Tax Base**

By definition, non-distortionary taxes do not affect economic behaviour, because the tax is independent

of economic decisions. An example would be lump-sum taxes levied on individuals without any reference to incomes, wealth, or spending, or taxes levied unexpectedly on past incomes and wealth so that it is too late to react. For this reason, non-distortionary taxes are appealing to governments. In practice, retro-active taxation is considered unfair precisely because it takes people by surprise. Lump-sum taxes are also unpopular, as UK Prime Minister Thatcher's fateful experience with the poll tax in 1990 showed. She tried to implement it and was promptly voted out of office. As a result, nearly all taxes are distortionary.

Because distortionary taxes move the economy away from its first-best equilibrium, it is likely to reduce the tax base on which the tax is paid. In fact, it is conceivable that raising tax rates actually results in *lower* tax revenues, if the tax base shrinks faster than the tax rate increases.[6] This effect is sometimes called the **Laffer curve** and is depicted in Figure 18.5.[7] More precisely, the Laffer curve describes a theoretical

---

[6] A recent European example was an increase in the cigarette tax in Germany, which was followed by a decrease in cigarette tax revenues. Taxes make up 80–85% of the retail price of cigarettes.

[7] Economist Arthur Laffer, then from Chicago, is reported to have been influential in persuading US President Ronald Reagan to cut taxes in the early 1980s.

relationship between *total* government tax revenues on the vertical axis and the *average* tax rate (the ratio of tax receipts to GDP) on the horizontal axis. The tax rate ranges from 0 to 100%. At a 0% rate, tax revenue is nil (point *A*). When the tax rate reaches 100%, no one is likely to work or produce at all so tax receipts are also nil (point *B*). At intermediate tax rates, tax receipts are positive, as at point *C*. The hump-shape of the curve indicates that the tax rate distorts the economy so much that beyond some tax rate, taxable income falls faster than the tax rate increases. The threshold point *D* corresponds to the average tax rate for which tax receipts are at a maximum. Any rate of taxation to the right of point *D* is inefficient because the same tax income can be raised with a lower tax rate, i.e. less distortion.

The Laffer curve was not taken seriously for policy purposes when it was first proposed. This is because its most important detail is unknown: the location of point *D*. In the early 1980s, Laffer claimed that the USA had passed this point. When the USA did cut tax rates, tax revenue actually declined. In recent years, however, economists have begun to pay more attention to the Laffer curve. Figure 18.6 plots Laffer curves that result from inserting labour taxation in a model of the long run which marries economic growth (Chapter 3) with labour markets (Chapter 5). In this model, taxes do affect equilibrium labour supply and output. For an individual, the incentives to work and pay taxes at very high tax rates are very low. As a result, rational individuals will work fewer hours and take more (untaxed) leisure.

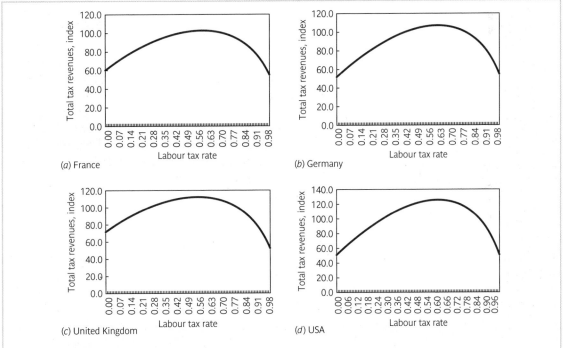

Fig. 18.6 Laffer Curves in Reality?

Raising labour taxation beyond a critical rate reduces the return to work and total labour tax revenues. Economists cannot vary taxes in a country as a controlled experiment to discover this critical rate —but they can isolate it in models which have been 'calibrated' to match features of real economies. The figures plot total long-run tax revenues (measured as an index of average tax revenues in the period 1995–2010) as a function of the labour tax rate in one such model. While the critical tax rate is estimated to be high—around 55–65% in the countries shown—it is not very far above tax rates displaced in Table 18.4. The model which generated these curves does not include more elaborate forms of tax evasion, such as tax shifting, capital flight, and the underground economy.

Source: Trabandt and Uhlig (2012).

In reality, well-paid individuals often expend significant resources to avoid or evade taxes in countries where they are high. In countries with pervasive underground economies, the tax base may be especially sensitive to tax rates. Professor Martin Feldstein of Harvard University has estimated the effects of declared taxable income in response to a US tax reform in 1986. He found that those taxpayers whose tax rates were the highest before the tax cuts experienced the sharpest rise in their contribution to total tax revenues afterwards. The sensitivity of these taxpayers' declared income was the highest, suggesting a significant dead-weight loss as a result of taxation. Combined with the Ramsey principle, these findings raise disturbing questions. Should tax rates for the most productive individuals be the lowest? While this may be efficient, it would seem to be distasteful for most—it seems inconsistent with a widely held ethical principle that resources should be redistributed 'from each according to his ability, to each according to his need'. Yet the logic of efficiency must be addressed, and will continue to pose a major puzzle for social policy.

18.5 Labour Market Policy

Section 18.2 established that markets can fail and require government action. This is doubly true for labour markets. Besides the obvious human dimension—that individuals and their well-being are associated with labour supply, wages, and unemployment—it turns out that a number of aspects of labour markets make them fundamentally different from markets for other goods and services, even under ideal conditions. In this section, we will explore a number of these differences. To the extent that policy-makers recognize and want to correct failures of labour markets or improve badly-conceived regulation, they can design policies which can increase the employment rate—the fraction of working age individuals in work—or reduce the equilibrium rate of unemployment—the fraction of the labour force in work in the long run. Both measures lead to a higher level of equilibrium output.

18.5.1 Heterogeneity and Imperfect Information

One of the most striking facts about labour markets is the degree of turnover, or the rate of flow between the states of the labour force shown in Figure 5.14. Chapter 5 noted that annual inflow into and outflows out of unemployment are frequently larger than the stocks of unemployment at any given point in time. The high rate of in- and outflow points to two important aspects of labour markets: (1) heterogeneity of labour, and (2) incomplete information about its quality.

First, neither workers and the labour hours they supply nor their workplaces are identical. We say that workers and jobs are heterogeneous. A trivial example of heterogeneity lies behind the turnover noted in Table 5.7, which is concentrated among young, female, and unskilled workers. High turnover is frequently a transient phenomenon in the life cycle. It is more characteristic of newcomers to the labour market, and reflects a complicated process of 'picking and choosing'. Even in high labour turnover countries like the UK or USA, it turns out that most workers stay at a given job for a very long time.

Second, because workers and jobs can be so heterogeneous, information is likely to be incomplete. Even with the help of modern technology, such as the internet, it is still impossible to know about all jobs on offer at any point in time. It may be necessary to search harder to find the most attractive jobs. Some employers do not actively advertise job openings and may open a position only after meeting an acceptable candidate. Workers must decide either to accept a job or reject it, searching further without knowing what may lie ahead. Most likely, they will have had some employment experience in the past, which guides their expectations concerning pay and work conditions, yet offers they can expect in the future may not always correspond to patterns in the past.

For example, it is a fact that computer operators—workers who once programmed and serviced large mainframe computers—were highly trained and well-paid professionals in the 1970s and 1980s. As personal computer and local networking technologies became dominant, the demand for computer operators shrank dramatically. Those who lost their jobs may have had difficulties finding new ones at a similar pay level to that in the past. Similarly, a job and the employer who is deciding how to fill it have particular needs and expectations which may not be met by every applicant. In times of tight labour markets it may not be very easy for employers to find their dream candidate.

It is for this reason that unemployment must be interpreted carefully. To the extent that the unemployed are really 'unemployed resources', they represent a lost opportunity and a reason that trend GDP is lower than it could be—a fundamental inefficiency. Indeed, Chapter 5 gave a number of reasons why workers ready to work at current wages are unable to do so. Yet unemployment also contains an element of efficiency. Workers who lose their jobs due to lay-off or plant closure frequently possess industry- or firm-specific human capital which would be wasted or underutilized if they were to accept the first new job opportunity that came along. A crude indicator of the 'efficiency' of **job matching** in a given labour market is the extent to which job openings—called vacancies—and job-seeking, unemployed workers coexist at the same time in a labour market. Because job requirements and worker qualifications are often specific, one can speak of a job-matching process. Forcing jobs and workers together indiscriminately would certainly not be efficient.

The extent of mismatch in the labour market is summarized by the **Beveridge curves** of Figure 18.7. Named to honour the work of British economist William Beveridge in the 1940s, Beveridge curves display unemployment and vacancy rates in an economy over time. Movements in the north-west and south-east directions are associated with the business cycle: firms offer fewer jobs and unemployment is higher in recessions, while the vacancy rate rises and the unemployment rate declines in economic expansions. The *position* of the Beveridge curve, on the other hand, indicates the longer-run efficiency of

job-matching in labour markets. The coincidence of a large number of vacancies with high unemployment—a Beveridge curve far away from the origin—indicates either that workers are badly informed, unable to take up the offers for lack of mobility or adequate skills, or unwilling to change and adapt.

In the mid-1970s, the Beveridge curve seemed to shift away from the origin, suggesting increasingly inefficient or mismatched labour markets—in fact, a rise in the equilibrium rate of unemployment. In the USA, this shift was of temporary duration. It has been much longer-lasting in the UK, while in Germany, the return to the earlier position has been even slower. In contrast, the Great Recession has been associated with a worsening of the Beveridge curve in the USA shifting outwards, while the trade-off in the UK and especially Germany has shifted inwards.

Shifting the Beveridge curve towards the origin—put differently, reducing the unemployment rate at any level of vacancies—can be good supply-side policy. For policy-makers, it means implementing measures which improve the job-matching process. One is to improve information on job openings by increasing the number and effectiveness of job agencies. Advances in networking technology have made it possible for the unemployed seeking work to know about job offers all over a country—as long as they are posted. In the years 2003–2004, Germany embarked on a comprehensive reform of its national employment agency, making data on jobs and training positions available nationwide. Second, the adaptability of workers' skills may be enhanced via job retraining programmes. This means giving workers whose skills are unwanted or obsolete new ones which are in demand. Another possibility is to increase workers' and firms' geographical mobility, e.g. by making the housing market more efficient or providing subsidies to firms in search of new locations. In recent years, countries have begun to make more use of **active labour market policies**. This is nothing but the creative and flexible use of all of the measures already mentioned and more—as opposed to the passive policy of simply paying out unemployment benefits. Especially in the past twenty years, the Nordic countries have combined 'European' solidarity with the unemployed in the form of generous unemployment benefits with activation policies designed to keep the

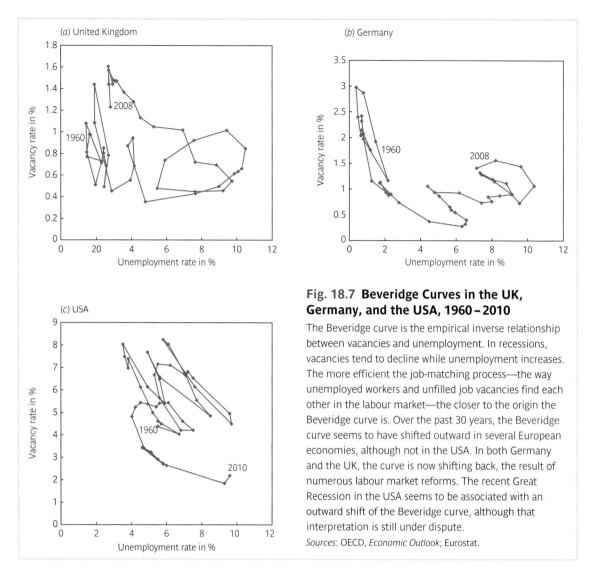

Fig. 18.7 Beveridge Curves in the UK, Germany, and the USA, 1960–2010

The Beveridge curve is the empirical inverse relationship between vacancies and unemployment. In recessions, vacancies tend to decline while unemployment increases. The more efficient the job-matching process—the way unemployed workers and unfilled job vacancies find each other in the labour market—the closer to the origin the Beveridge curve is. Over the past 30 years, the Beveridge curve seems to have shifted outward in several European economies, although not in the USA. In both Germany and the UK, the curve is now shifting back, the result of numerous labour market reforms. The recent Great Recession in the USA seems to be associated with an outward shift of the Beveridge curve, although that interpretation is still under dispute.

Sources: OECD, *Economic Outlook*; Eurostat.

unemployed in touch with the labour market. Despite a number of adverse shocks in the past decade, the Nordic countries continue to boast the world's lowest long-term unemployment rates. Table 18.2 shows the variety of approaches currently employed in the OECD.

18.5.2 Imperfect Contracts and Labour Market Regulations

Because of their social and political aspects, labour markets are often heavily regulated. Regulations cover a wide range of aspects: paid holidays, the length of working days and weeks, safety standards, works councils, union representation, and other fac-

ets of the employment relationship. These regulations often have efficiency costs and sometimes seem only marginally motivated by good economic arguments. The columns of Table 18.3 report the relative severity of the most common types of labour market regulation in OECD Europe.

Imperfect mobility and regulation

One situation of possible exploitation relates to worker mobility. Mobility of demanders and suppliers is a central mechanism for correcting imbalances in a perfectly competitive market. If they feel they are getting a bad deal, they simply move elsewhere. In labour

Table 18.2 Expenditures on Labour Market Programmes, 2009 (% of GDP)

	Denmark	Finland	Norway	Sweden	France	Germany	UK
Active measures:							
Training	0.30	0.43	0.26	0.06	0.36	0.35	0.02
Employment incentives	0.19	0.13	0.03	0.37	0.10	0.11	0.01
Supported employment and rehabilitation	0.68	0.09	0.17	0.22	0.07	0.04	0.01
Direct job creation	0.00	0.08	0.04	0.00	0.15	0.06	0.00
Start-up incentives	0.00	0.02	0.00	0.01	0.04	0.07	0.00
Total active measures	1.17	0.75	0.50	0.66	0.72	0.63	0.04
Passive measures:							
Out-of-work income maintenance and support	1.29	1.49	0.50	0.72	1.40	1.47	0.33
Early retirement	0.44	0.41	0.00	0.00	0.02	0.06	0.00
Total passive measures	1.73	1.90	0.50	0.72	1.42	1.53	0.33
Administration	0.45	0.17	0.11	0.46	0.26	0.37	0.29
Total expenditures	3.35	2.82	1.11	1.84	2.40	2.53	0.66
Overall unemployment rate	6.1	8.4	3.2	8.5	9.1	7.8	7.8
Long-term unemployment rate[a]	0.6	1.4	0.2	1.1	3.2	3.5	1.9

[a] Percentage of labour force which is unemployed with current duration of at least six months.
Source: OECD, *Employment Outlook*.

markets, things may not be so simple. The suppliers of labour are human beings. Mobility means changing jobs, an industry, occupation, or residential location, and people by their very nature tend to be immobile. Furthermore, they may even *value* their 'immobility', preferring to take a pay cut or even risk unemployment to stay put rather than to move to a faraway place or accept a radically new occupation. This is one reason that, even in the UK with its highly dynamic labour markets, differences in unemployment rates between North and South, between Scotland and the Midlands, and between London and the entire country have persisted for decades.

An unscrupulous firm might try to exploit the immobility of its workers by cutting wages after the employment relationship has begun. In perfect market situations, the worker would simply leave the firm, and look for work elsewhere. In doing so, mobil-

ity costs must be incurred. In advanced economies these costs may be rather significant, especially for those low-wage workers. Minimum wages can be seen as a response to such local market power by employers. Another response is to extend union contracts to uncovered workers and firms in the sector.[8] Similar arguments are often invoked to justify workweek and work-time regulations, job protection, and rules concerning job safety. Naturally, minimum wages have a number of disadvantages as well, mostly related to the closing down of labour markets for young workers and those with little skill or training; these were discussed in Chapter 5.

[8] Minimum wages are also justified with arguments related to equity and income distribution. For example, if the elasticity of labour demand is thought to be low at low wages, then raising the minimum wage does little harm while increasing the income of the lowest-income working families.

Table 18.3 Measures of Employment Protection, 2008

	Protection of permanent workers against individual dismissal	Regulation of temporary forms of employment	Specific requirements for collective dismissal	Aggregate index
Eurozone				
Austria	2.2	2.3	3.3	2.4
Belgium	1.9	2.7	4.1	2.6
Finland	2.4	2.2	2.4	2.3
France	2.6	3.8	2.1	3.0
Germany	2.9	2.0	3.8	2.6
Greece	2.3	3.5	3.3	3.0
Ireland	1.7	0.7	2.4	1.4
Italy	1.7	2.5	4.9	2.6
The Netherlands	2.7	1.4	3.0	2.2
Portugal	3.5	2.5	1.9	2.8
Spain	2.4	3.8	3.1	3.1
Average Eurozone	2.4	2.5	3.1	2.6
Other EU				
Denmark	1.5	1.8	3.1	1.9
Sweden	2.7	0.7	3.8	2.1
United Kingdom	1.2	0.3	2.9	1.1
Average Other EU	1.8	0.9	3.2	1.7
Other OECD				
Norway	2.2	3.0	2.9	2.6
Switzerland	1.2	1.5	3.9	1.8
United States	0.6	0.3	2.9	0.8
Average Other EU	1.3	1.6	3.2	1.8

Source: OECD (<www.oecd.org> OECD Indicators on Employment Protection).

Regulation of dismissal

A related argument has been invoked for regulations of dismissal 'without cause' or for 'economic reasons', i.e. not due to malfeasance or misbehaviour on the part of the worker. Lay-offs for reasons related to the business cycle are associated with uncertainty and economic dislocation. In many European countries, prior notice of termination of employment must be given to workers—during which time the employee remains on the payroll and represents a cost to the firm. 'Social plans' are often required for large-scale redundancies, in which the exact list of employees is decided using criteria like age, family status, and re-employability. Severance payments are often legally mandated for workers dismissed for economic reasons. While common in EU countries, job protection is by no means the norm in the OECD. The USA and the UK are examples of countries where 'employment at will' contracts prevail.

While severance regulations make it difficult for firms to reduce employment in the short run, they also increase the effective cost of labour to firms. They make firms more reluctant to hire in good times, precisely because they worry about consequences in bad times. Firms will tend to use the 'intensive' margin more often (overtime, conversion of part-time into full-time) before hiring new workers. Table 18.3 reports a ranking of the degree of 'job protection' provisions offered in a number of industrial countries. It is noteworthy that countries in which youth unemployment rates are high tend to have the most restrictive dismissal laws. Surveys consistently reveal that workers in those countries in which dismissal laws are the most liberal—the USA, the UK, and Denmark—feel the *least* insecure about their job. This perception, which is hardly intuitive, must be to do with the perception workers have about the ease of finding a new job, should their firm go out of business or move abroad.

As the economy becomes increasingly subject to global influences and technological advances, the nature of employment relationships has changed fundamentally. Employment is less likely to involve a lifetime relationship, and is increasingly likely at some point to be 'restructured' or reoriented towards fully new areas of activity. Severance rules of the type described are likely to inhibit the growth of new firms as well as the expansion of existing ones. As the pressures for more flexible employment grow, firms have become increasingly creative in finding ways to undo the intended effects of the legislation. For example, they may chain together several short-term contracts for the same employee, or hire workers from temporary help agencies, shifting the burden to others. In the end, it may be worth considering market solutions in which workers accept to work under 'employment at will' for a wage premium. This would allow firms to pay for additional flexibility while preserving employment protection.

18.5.3 Social Policies Incentives and Taxation

The social safety net

The social safety net refers to the system of transfers and benefits designed to help the disadvantaged and vulnerable in society. These include unemployment benefits, social welfare, old-age pensions, early retirement, health insurance, and disability payments. A large gap divides European countries, which transfer 20–30% of their national income to individuals or firms, from the USA, Japan, and Switzerland, which transfer only 10–15%. This might lead a casual observer to conclude that high European unemployment is a product of the 'social welfare state', which puts too much weight on solidarity at the cost of productivity and economic efficiency. Yet it is overly hasty to claim that Europeans have erred too far in the direction of social protection, in comparison to the rest of the OECD. To some extent, the high level of transfers observed in Europe are a *response* to high unemployment, which may have other underlying causes. At the same time, these transfers—in the form of unemployment benefits, welfare, and premature retirement and disability pensions—take the pressure off workers and firms to adjust to a changing world economy. The greatest danger is that the safety net becomes a trap, leading to long-term unemployment.

It is useful to use the tools developed in Chapter 5 to help think about the adverse effects of the safety net on incentives. The social systems of most countries share two institutional features. First, poor or unemployed people receive transfers—income maintenance programmes or unemployment benefits—from the state. Second, income taxes are progressive: the rate of taxation increases as income rises. Taking up a job not only means receiving a salary, but also paying taxes if the salary is high enough, and losing eligibility for income maintenance programmes. It is conceivable, then, that people can be financially worse off by taking a job, not to mention incurring a loss of leisure, and possibly some activity in the underground economy. Implicitly, these people face an effective marginal tax rate—considering the overall effect of work on their income—in excess of 100%. Box 18.5 shows how safety net programmes may lead to a **welfare trap**, inducing people to remain unemployed or stay out of the labour force, thereby reducing the productive potential of the economy. Recent experience of 'work-to-welfare' in the UK and the USA indicates that the incentive aspect is important for bringing workers on social assistance back to work.

Box 18.5 Crusoe Caught in the Safety Net

In Figure 18.8, Crusoe is faced with a budget constraint which is no longer strictly linear. When not working at all in the market ($\ell = \bar{\ell}$), he receives an unconditional transfer of T from the government—unemployment benefits, welfare, or other payments associated with the social safety net. In this particular social security system, Crusoe must give up his benefits, coconut for coconut, by exactly the amount of his additional income—an effective marginal tax rate of 100%. This is representative of the current situation in many European countries. Since Crusoe loses a euro of benefit for every euro he earns in work, the budget line is flat up to the point at which Crusoe receives T, whether he works or not. Crusoe values leisure, so it is hard to see why he would accept part-time work in this regime. Unless the after-tax wage is high enough, Crusoe is unlikely to work.

Figure 18.8 also shows the impact of reducing the effective marginal tax rate from 100% to some lower rate which is nevertheless higher than that for someone already in work and not receiving welfare payments,

holding T constant. As the tax rate declines, the budget line for the household becomes steeper. At some point Crusoe can make himself even better off than he was at A, by choosing point B. In doing so his income is added to the tax base and contributes to higher GDP. The effect can be intensified if the carrot (the lower effective marginal tax rate) is combined with a stick (lowering T), although this type of reform is politically difficult to implement.

In Germany, the Hartz labour market reforms (implemented after 2004) adopted several of the principles discussed in this chapter. One measure reduced the effective marginal tax rate on work by exempting some earnings from counting against social benefit. Effectively, this becomes a top-up provision. Another measure implemented benefit cuts ('sanctions') for those who consistently turn down job offers. Job centres were reorganized and on the basis of a modernized database were better able to 'activate' the unemployed with credible job offers.

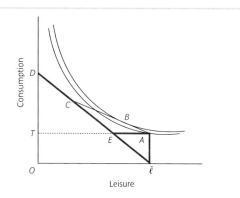

Fig. 18.8 Incentives and the Social Safety Net

In a social welfare system with benefit T for those out of work but with 100% marginal tax rate, the individual depicted in this figure chooses not to work (point A), because starting at zero, small increases in labour supply yield no gain in net income. The budget constraint is $\bar{\ell}AED$. If the individual is allowed to keep some additional income (changing the budget constraint to $\bar{\ell}ACD$), they can improve their well-being by working (point B). The most important problem with lowering the effective marginal tax rate to unemployment benefit and welfare recipients is the cost to the state, which can be considerable.

Labour taxation

Because labour is so essential to economic activity, it is natural to expect governments to tax it. Perhaps because the Ramsey principle of public finance (Section 18.4.2) is so compelling, labour is one of the most highly taxed 'commodities'. As Box 18.6 explains, labour is subject not only to income taxes paid by households, but also to a number of social security contributions by both employees and employers. It is also natural to expect that labour taxation might influence the demand for labour. Higher taxes raise the real cost of labour faced by firms, leading to lower employment in the sector that pays the tax.[9] Table 18.4 shows the rate of taxation on labour in various countries in its various guises. Despite high unemployment, efforts have been rather slow in Europe to reduce the tax burden placed on the labour market. France, for example,

---

[9] This qualification is important. If some type of labour is untaxed, demand for that type of labour will rise when labour taxes increase, increasing employment and wages. The obvious example is the underground economy, which always thrives when taxes are high. Another is self-employment, a status in which workers must provide for their own health and pension outside the state social security system.

Box 18.6 **Taxes and the Labour Market in Europe**

Labour taxes can be grouped into three classes: (1) income taxes, (2) social insurance charges paid by employers, and (3) social security contributions paid by the employees. All three can be added up, as they either reduce the workers' net receipts and thus affect the supply of labour, or increase the cost of labour and reduce demand (governments prefer to call the last two 'contributions'—dedicated to government funds for unemployment benefits, national health insurance, retirement and pension benefits, disability insurance, solidarity with various causes, including low-cost housing and special retraining programmes, etc). Let τ_P be the employer's wage tax rate, let W be the wage of the employee before income taxes and employee social security contributions, let τ_W be the tax rate of contribution of the employee, and let τ_P be the personal income tax rate. The worker's take-home pay after taxes is $W_{take\text{-}home} = (1 - \tau_W)(1 - \tau_P)W$, while the cost of labour to the firm is given by $W_{labour\ costs} = (1+\tau_F)W$. As a result, the effective labour cost is equal to the take-home pay multiplied by the factor $\dfrac{1+\tau_F}{(1-\tau_W)(1-\tau_P)}$ which is often

called the **labour tax wedge**. Holding $W_{take\text{-}home}$ constant, increases in the tax wedge increase labour costs and reduce the demand for labour. In addition to all this, workers also pay income tax on their take-home salary, which may be progressive, meaning that it increases at the margin as taxable income itself rises.

Whether high labour taxation leads to high unemployment or not depends on how the supply of labour or the collective bargaining system reacts. Equilibrium unemployment rate remains unchanged only if wages after taxes fall by exactly the amount of tax—i.e. if workers shoulder the entire burden. But the collective labour supply curve will not be vertical in general. Households may find it attractive at high taxes to work less, work in the underground economy, or take overtime pay in the form of a holiday (leisure), as is often done in Scandinavia. It is thus likely that such high taxes make hiring labour unattractive, and that a reduction of such taxes could increase employment. The problem for governments is how to replace the revenue that is lost.

has exempted or reduced social security contributions by low-wage workers.

Yet, the net effect of high taxes on employment depends on the elasticity of labour demand and supply. If collective labour supply is relatively inelastic—perhaps reflecting the inelastic labour supply of households—the burden of the tax will fall primarily on wages, and employment will be relatively unaffected. In Europe, however, wages are set in collective bargaining, leading, in all likelihood, to a flatter collective labour supply curve. Under these conditions,

high labour taxes reduces employment significantly, and is likely to be associated with a large loss of **consumer and producer surplus**.[10] In the very long run, the elasticity of labour demand is likely to be high, since firms may simply move to other locations where labour costs are lower. Not surprisingly, the integration of European economies is driving a de facto harmonization of taxation across national boundaries, with or without explicit government coordination. This pattern is readily recognized in Table 18.4.

18.6 Supply-Side Policy in Practice

18.6.1 Waiting for Godot? The long and variable lags of supply-side policy

Supply-side policy is like an investment. It involves big sacrifices today, with gains only at some future date, often at a future date which is highly uncertain

and dependent on decisions taken by future policy-makers. For this reason, supply-side policies are a

---

[10] Chapter 5 provides more details on the collective labour supply curve. Producer and consumer surplus are defined and discussed in Box 18.3.

Table 18.4 Labour Taxation in 2010 (in %)

Country	Total tax wedge	of which: Personal income tax	Social security contributions Employee	Social security contributions Employer	Top marginal personal income tax rate
Euro area					
Austria	48	11	14	23	42.7
Belgium	55	22	11	23	45.3
Finland	42	18	6	18	48.2
France	49	10	10	30	37.6
Germany	49	16	17	16	47.6
Greece	37	2	13	22	37.8
Ireland	29	13	7	10	47.0
Italy	47	15	7	24	40.2
Luxembourg	34	13	11	10	34.7
Netherlands	38	15	14	10	50.1
Portugal	38	10	9	19	40.8
Spain	40	12	5	23	43.0
Other EU					
Denmark	39	28	11	0	48.1
Sweden	43	14	5	24	56.5
UK	33	15	8	10	50.0
Switzerland	21	9	6	6	36.4
Czech Rep.	42	9	8	25	20.1
Hungary	46	11	13	22	40.6
Poland	34	6	15	13	23.7
Other OECD					
Australia	26	20	0	6	46.5
Canada	30	13	7	10	46.4
Japan	30	6	12	12	47.2
New Zealand	17	17	0	0	35.5
Norway	37	19	7	11	40.0
United States	30	14	7	9	41.7

Source: OECD Centre for Tax Policy and Adminstration (2010). Columns may not add due to rounding.

hard sell—politically speaking. As with demand-management policies, supply-side reforms require time to show their beneficial effects—usually much more time than it takes for a tax cut to stimulate demand. Even the most gifted politicians will find this difficult to endorse, since the likelihood that they will be around to enjoy the credit for implementing those policies is small indeed. While Wim Kok, Ronald Reagan, and Margaret Thatcher were able to reap some of the benefits of their supply-side policies, the same cannot be said of Jimmy Carter, Leszek Balcerowicz, or Gerhard Schröder, all of whom implemented bold reforms and were either punished or ignored for them.[11]

Consider the types of policies discussed in the last three sections. The failure of labour markets to clear due to excessive real wages cannot be corrected overnight, but rather only in small concerted steps over many many years, especially if a currency depreciation is impossible (as it is within the euro area), whereas the overvaluation may have taken a decade or two to evolve. Similarly, deregulation and privatization take a long time to bear fruit. Deregulation must be well-planned to prevent exploitation of temporary market dominance, and must also allow entry of new firms, including foreign ones. It takes several years before a wave of new firms arrives, increasing competition and forcing relative price reductions and quality improvements. Privatization is the most difficult of supply-side policies to implement, since simply transferring the assets from public to private hands is a politically unacceptable gift and will always yield sour grapes in the future, either by the government vis-à-vis the winners who made fortunes from the assets, or the losers who 'paid too much' for them.

If this weren't enough to discourage policy-makers, the time dimension is compounded by the overall credibility of announced policies. The sacrifices demanded of households at the outset of reform are often significant. The policy change itself may not be irrevocable, so economic agents may be not expect reforms to be long-lasting or permanent. Most obviously, a new government could be elected at a future date which has different preferences and priorities and simply reverse the policy. It is even possible that the *same* government may change its mind after the private sector has acted on its announcement! This so-called **time consistency problem** was first identified by Nobel Prize Laureates Finn Kydland and Edward Prescott, and is concerned with the incentives of those who announce a policy to actually follow through with that policy after others have reacted to the announcement. Time inconsistency is a very general phenomenon, which applies to many fields besides economics. A son will promise to drive carefully if lent his parents' car; a person in prison always pledges not to engage in unlawful activity if released early; politicians promise the moon if elected. All of these promises are time-inconsistent. The risk is that only time-consistent solutions, which are less desirable for all involved, are adopted: no son is lent a car; no inmate is released early; and politicians are never trusted. Under such conditions it is hardly surprising that the private sector needs convincing of the permanence of supply-side reforms.

18.6.2 The Political Economy of Supply-Side Reforms

Supply-side reforms are difficult to enact because there are always losers. These losers are often few in number and have lots to lose. The winners are more diffuse, numerous and thus harder to organize. The political difficulty of implementing supply-side policies is best illustrated by the example of labour market reforms. While unemployment is generally regarded as a curse of modern market economies, joblessness in Europe has been high for almost three decades. In addition, it was seen in Figure 1.1 that, in contrast to the USA, European unemployment has risen steadily over successive business cycles. Unemployment represents underutilized labour resources. If this underutilization is not the conscious choice of households, it is involuntary and represents a supply-side problem. As the leading quote at the beginning of this chapter indicated, an important challenge for the nations of Europe is to address this issue, perhaps using the ideas and concepts developed here.

Suppose there is agreement—among policy-makers, at least—that labour markets should be reformed. How should a country go about it? Several problems

---

[11] Wim Kok was a Dutch union leader and prime minister, who helped engineer the Wassenaar Accord in 1982 between labour, management, and the government in the Netherlands, described in more detail in Section 18.6.2. US President Ronald Reagan permanently cut and simplified personal income taxes in the USA in the 1980s. UK Prime Minister Margaret Thatcher deregulated and reformed UK labour markets, significantly restricting the influence of labour unions. US President Jimmy Carter deregulated the airlines, railroad, trucking, and brewing industries. Polish Finance and Deputy Prime Minister Lezek Balcerowicz imposed 'shock therapy' on Poland after the fall of communism and the dismantling of central economic planning. German Premier Gerhard Schröder introduced the Agenda 2010 and the Hartz reforms of German labour market law, which tightened eligibility and duration requirements for the receipt of unemployment benefits.

arise with simply 'deregulating'. Consider the example of abolishing job protection. First, many companies that had wanted to reduce employment under the old regime will certainly take advantage of deregulation, and lay-offs are likely to increase in the short run. In most European countries, the political consequences of such a move are severe enough to make reform unthinkable. Second, the issue of time consistency already discussed in Section 18.6.1 arises. Suppose a firm that would like to hire more employees expands its employment in response to deregulation. At this point, a government that is fishing for political support might re-impose the dismissal regulations, 'trapping' the firms at higher employment levels. Firms will anticipate this, with the sad result that no new workers will be hired, despite deregulation! Governments must pre-commit to a 'no-reregulate' regime before employers are convinced.

It is also true that an overwhelming majority (90–95%) of workers are employed, so that their domination over the unemployed might even be regarded as democratic, and is generally mitigated by unemployment benefits. Governments often cannot reform labour market institutions because their interventions are often regarded as interference in the collective bargaining process. One noteworthy approach followed by Spain was the expansion of the use of temporary contracts for workers, with some restrictions.[12] Such contracts allow firms to hire workers without restrictions on a limited-time basis. By some accounts, as much as four-fifths of all new hires in Spain since the late 1980s has been under such temporary contracts. This response suggests that firms are willing to hire more workers when job security obligations are absent. Second, young people were the primary beneficiary of such reforms, which has helped relieve an acute youth unemployment problem. Finally, increasing the relative number of workers who have jobs with less protection increased the consensus for broader reforms which followed. By increasing the power of the outsiders, labour market reform became more acceptable.

The political economy of labour markets may be the most important element determining the suc-

cess or failure of reforms. Efforts to increase the attractiveness of part-time work are often blocked by unions, which see their bargaining power diluted by new employees who are unlikely to be members. Work-sharing proposals which increase the cost of labour are resisted fiercely by employer associations. Recent successful reforms in France have shown that management and labour often put many different elements on the negotiating table, trading reduced working time and relief on labour charges for flexibility, wage moderation, and reform of the unemployment benefits system.

18.6.3 Feasible Supply-Side Policy: Peanuts or Big Payoffs?

Let us assume that the supply-side reforms are credible, actually believed by economic agents and acted upon as intended. Five to ten years after the reform was enacted the obvious question arises: was it at all worth the effort? Another difficult aspect of supply-side policies is that the gains are uncertain. Because the sum of millions of individuals' behaviour will ultimately determine the outcome, it is difficult to know how trend output will react.

It is natural to suspect that the gains from supply-side policies are of secondary order. After all, we have talked a lot about about deregulating individual sectors of the economy, reforming the tax system or altering the equilibrium of labour relations. Rather than presenting a complex model used by economists to answer these questions, we present two examples of clearly identified and successful policies in Europe in the past twenty-five years: the Netherlands and Ireland. As our examples will show, the gains can be substantial.

The Netherlands

Plagued by the 'good fortune' of natural gas discoveries in the 1970s, the Netherlands was the mother of the Dutch disease: increasingly valuable natural resources led to overvaluation of the currency, the guilder, which put much manufacturing industry out of business. Most important was the unemployment rate, which almost reached 12% in 1983. A generous social system was proving unsustainable at those rates of unemployment. A stagnant employment rate in the light of increasing demand by women for access to market work put politicians under pressure to find

---

[12] For example, firms were not allowed to 'roll over' the same worker in a series of short-term contracts. Employers have devised numerous loopholes to deal with this restriction.

solutions. Female labour force participation rate in the Netherlands was among the lowest in the EU.

The solution to the Netherlands' problems began with the Wassenaar Accord of 1982, a long-term agreement between labour, management, and the government which moderated real wage growth in the public and private sector in exchange for better treatment of part-time employment and government tax reductions. While not officially part of the agreement, the government followed up with tax breaks for part-time jobs as well as cuts in public sector employment and wages. Most importantly, tax rates on labour were reduced, blunting the net impact of real wage moderation on households' incomes. Real labour costs in the Netherlands grew much more slowly than in neighbouring EU economies in the 1990s, more closely resembling the USA than neighbouring Germany! In the years that followed, other reforms were enacted: the system of unemployment benefits was reformed and the employment agencies reformed to provide more carrot-and-stick incentives for the unemployed to return to work. The benefit was strong growth in employment, especially part-time employment of women, and a drop in unemployment.

The Wassenaar Accord was supply-side policy primarily targeted at increasing potential employment and reducing the unemployment rate. But as Figure 18.9 shows, this policy also had beneficial effects for GDP per capita in this country in the longer run, as the production would predict from an increase in labour input per capita.

Ireland

With its anaemic growth rates, high budget deficits, and unemployment reaching a staggering 18% in the late 1980s, Ireland was called the 'sick man of Europe' by the late German-American economist Rudi Dornbusch.[13] Emigration continued to bleed the economy of its most talented young people to the USA, the UK and continental Europe. Starting in

[13] Rudiger Dornbusch (1942–2002) was professor at Rochester, Chicago and MIT, advisor to Latin American countries and the author of a best-selling macroeconomics textbook (one that sold considerably more copies than the one you are reading!). He is best-known as the father of the overshooting model of nominal exchange rate adjustment under sticky prices which was sketched in Chapter 15, the model which married the long run of purchasing power parity with uncovered interest rate parity.

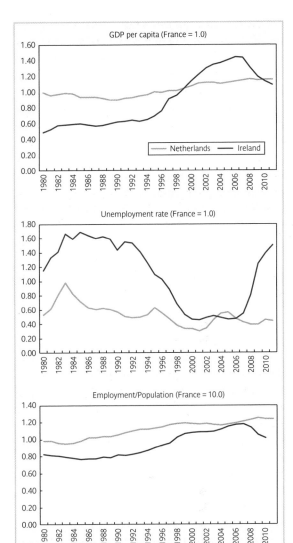

Fig. 18.9 Two Successful Supply-Side Reforms: the Netherlands and Ireland

The three panels show the economic performance of the Netherlands and Ireland relative to France along three dimensions: GDP per capita, unemployment rate, and employment-to-population ratio. The crucial years are 1983 for the Netherlands and 1987 for Ireland. As the charts show, benefits come, but with considerable delay, and often due to a cumulation of additional actions taken after the initial reforms were accepted. These benefits are more concentrated on the employment front in the Netherlands, as opposed to economic growth in Ireland.

Sources: IMF.

late 1987, a programme of fiscal consolidation and wage restraint was implemented with the agreement of the collective bargaining parties. More important, the social partners (labour unions and employers) agreed to a series of centrally bargained 'Social Partnership' agreements stipulating modest increases in money wages. The climate between labour and management improved. In a development similar to that in the Netherlands, the government responded by reducing taxes in the early phase of the reform programme.

In the early 1990s, Ireland cut corporate taxes and introduced incentives for foreign investors to locate in the country. It increased spending on education and infrastructure. Active labour market policies were implemented to help people into gainful employment again. The economy's product markets were deregulated and bureaucracy streamlined to increase attractiveness to foreign businesses considering investing in Ireland.

Figure 18.9 shows that it is hardly an exaggeration to speak of an Irish economic miracle. In the period from 1992–2007, the Irish economy grew at an almost Asian real rate of 6.3% per annum. After 15 years of extraordinary growth, Ireland managed to raise its GDP per capita above that of the UK and France—with the reminder, of course that GDP is not GNI, and that some of Ireland's value added represented income to many UK, US, French, and German capital owners who had built factories and office buildings and contributed to its economic success. In addition—the most convincing sign of all—the population of Ireland stopped shrinking for the first time in decades, rising from 3.55 to 4.34 million, or 23%, during the same period. Hundreds of thousands of expatriate Irish in the USA, the UK and elsewhere returned home to make this miracle happen.

Since 2007 Ireland has been the focus of the world's attention for another, less favourable reason. It was one of the epicentres of the financial crisis, suffering a collapse and near-complete nationalization of its banking system. After 2001, the financial sector began to swell out of proportion, not only due to the enormous growth in the property market but also because of dubious offshore investment projects. The collapse of the Irish property market and world demand for Irish exports took their toll on GDP, which plummeted by 10.1% in the years 2007–2010. Yet the bust which followed the boom will hardly reverse one of the great economic success stories of the last century: over the years 1989–2007, the Irish economy grew by more than 190%! The lion's share of this increase represents sustainable potential output and thus permanent increases in Irish standards of living.

The Irish episode also showed that financial market excesses can ruin a party—as the boom comes to an end, financial markets often play on in a game of double-or-nothing. Lax supervision by Irish banking authorities was the real culprit which laid the grounds for the economic crash after 2007. Good banking regulation is also good supply-side policy.

Summary

The cases of the Netherlands and Ireland demonstrate that the supply-side policy can have long run effects on an economy's long-run potential productive capacity. Performance measures in Figure 18.9, which are based on a benchmark EU country, France, also show how long it can take for the reforms to have a noticeable effect. The political willpower to stay the course in such situations may be difficult to sustain.

Ten years after the introduction of the euro, it has become evident that the member countries' economies were not developing in a synchronized way—some were lagging behind others, leading to current account imbalances and exchange rate misalignments which can cause problems in a monetary union.[14] Supply-side policies represent one important dimension of present and future attempts to bring the slow-growing parts of the Eurozone back into the growth club. The fact that they are painful does not make them undesirable per se, but can make them more difficult to enact. Box 18.7 presents Greece as an example of the difficulty with enacting supply-side policies.

---

[14] In the next chapter we will see a synchronized or harmonized evolution; this is a key feature of properly functioning monetary unions.

Box 18.7   Supply-side Reforms: A Solution to Greece's Problems?

Europe's sovereign debt crisis began in Greece, so it is natural to focus attention on this country's efforts to solve it. At the end of 2011, the Greek public debt/GDP ratio exceeded 165%. From the analysis of Chapter 17 it is easy to see that any sustainable solution to Greece's debt crisis must involve a combination of large and painful primary government budget surpluses for some time, lower borrowing interest rates (r), higher economic growth (g) and/or debt relief (some would say default). While the solution promoted by the 'Troika'—the IMF, the ECB, and the European Commission—has stressed all of these elements, the long-run growth option has received the least attention. Yet this is the most sustainable approach, given that Greek GDP per capita is still only two-thirds of either France or Germany, indicating potential for further growth in that country. Increasing GDP and expanding the tax base in Greece has received the least attention—perhaps because it is the riskiest option and requires the most time to bear fruit.

Greece's problem vividly illustrates the dilemma of supply-side policy: the most sustainable solutions to the debt problem involve the largest upfront costs—many of them unfairly borne by the weakest and most vulnerable—with payoffs coming in 3–5 years at the earliest. The Greek economy has grown under potential, especially since the late 1990s. It has suffered from an overvalued currency and excessive growth in the non-tradable goods sector (see Chapter 17). It is an excellent example of potential gains to supply-side reforms—and why they are so difficult to implement. Cuts in inefficient government employment could free up labour to do more productive things. Small but well-organized interest groups make it difficult to implement these reforms. Privatization of the large airports, the state postal bank, casinos, mining, and other transport industries are consistently resisted by powerful labour unions. The pictures of violent demonstrations in Athens in 2010 made headlines around the world.

Strengthening the rule of law may be one of the cheapest of supply-side reforms. Greece has a reputation for Byzantine government regulations. Investors complain bitterly about corruption and unfair enforcement of tax laws. According to the World Bank's annual 'Doing Business around the World' survey of 183 countries,[15] Greece ranked 100th in 2011, just ahead of Papau New Guinea, Paraguay, and Pakistan, and just behind Guatemala, Vietnam, and Yemen. (For the record: Denmark ranked 5th, the UK 7th, Ireland 10th, Germany 19th, France 29th, Portugal 30th, Spain 44th and Italy 87th.) A significant part of capital flight from Greece in recent years has been to Bulgaria, which was placed 59th in the global line-up.

⚠ Summary

1 Supply-side policies are appealing because, in contrast to demand-side policies, they do not imply a short-run trade-off between unemployment and inflation. They increase output permanently at any given level of inflation and economic growth, and may even increase the rate of growth itself. At the same time, they often take considerable time to take effect and require a longer-term perspective that goes beyond the planning horizons of most politicians.

2 One principle underlying supply-side policies is that markets do not function perfectly. By removing market imperfections, the economy's overall output and productivity can be enhanced.

---

[15] See <www.doingbusiness.org/rankings>. The ranking measures the ease in which businesses can be started, taxes can be paid, contracts can be enforced, building permits can be obtained, property can be registered, credit can be arranged, and bankruptcies are resolved.

3 There are three main sources of market failures: (1) externalities, (2) increasing returns to scale, and (3) asymmetric information.

4 Externalities occur when someone's economic activity has an effect, positive or negative, on others. Positive externalities imply that one does not recognize the benefits to society of one's actions, and will undertake less than is socially desirable. Negative externalities imply that one does not recognize the costs to society of one's economic actions, and will undertake too much of them. Pecuniary externalities are solved once property rights are ascertained. Non-pecuniary externalities call for government interventions.

5 Increasing returns lead to monopolies. Some monopolies are natural, inherent to the task itself. The solution used to be state ownership. Increasingly, state monopolies are privatized and government interventions take the form of regulations.

6 Asymmetric information occurs when one's actions are not known to others. It may lead to inefficient outcomes. Regulation can be designed to alleviate this problem.

7 Public goods that are non-rival and non-excludable tend not be privately provided. Governments can and should step in, and provide these goods which can be highly productive.

8 Taxation is necessary to pay for the operation of government. It is also a source of inefficiency because it drives a wedge between the price paid by the consumer and the price received by the producer, reducing demand and supply.

9 Because the operation of governments requires resources with alternative uses in the private sector, supply-side considerations call for limiting public spending to the production of goods and services that cannot be produced by the private sector. There is much debate on the correct size of government.

10 Governments often subsidize firms and industries. Although the objective of subsidies is to protect firms, they remove the incentive to compete, and ultimately cost jobs. State ownership has similar effects. In some cases, good supply-side policy may imply reductions in subsidies to firms and the privatization of state enterprises.

11 High structural unemployment is a supply-side problem. It arises as a result of labour market distortions, some of which are due to private agents and others to interventions of government. Eliminating structural unemployment is possible by better management of labour taxation, severance regulations, labour relations, and the social safety net. Active labour market policies can help prevent the emergence of long-term unemployment.

12 Supply-side reforms are like social investments which involve high costs up front for gains which are not realized for many years. The immediate gains to policy-makers are not obvious and for that reason these reforms are often postponed or avoided. Evidence suggests that the payoff of good supply-side policies can be substantial.

13 If households and firms understand the political economy of supply-side reforms, it is less likely that they will believe that announced policies will actually be adopted. In addition, the incentive for policy-makers to change their plans after the fact further reduces the credibility of announced reforms and thus reduces the effectiveness of such reforms.

14 Labour market reforms are highly politicized and controversial. Because beneficiaries of reform are often in the minority—for example the unemployed—their interests may be difficult to protect. Broad-based reforms almost always require give and take of the involved parties. Whether conflictual or consensual, reforms require time—as long as a decade—to have a measurable effect.

☾ Key Concepts

- supply-side policies
- market-clearing
- laissez-faire
- market failures
- economic rents
- competition policy
- positive and negative externalities
- property rights
- pecuniary and non-pecuniary externalities
- natural monopoly
- human capital
- privatization
- industrial policies

- trade policies
- deadweight loss of taxation
- Ramsey principle of public finance
- distortionary taxation
- consumer and producer surplus
- Laffer curve
- job matching
- Beveridge curve
- active labour market policies
- welfare trap
- labour tax wedge
- time consistency problem

❓ Exercises

1 Why are supply-side policies both more promising and more difficult to implement than demand-side policies?

2 Why is cutting taxes on capital a supply-side policy? Why is it so controversial, especially in Europe?

3 According to the Ramsey principle of public finance (see Box 18.4), on which would you levy higher taxes, jewellery or petrol? Labour income or capital income?

4 It is often alleged that the Laffer curve is more likely to be relevant in countries with a large underground economy. Explain. How might the underground economy contribute to the 'unemployment trap' described in Box 18.5?

5 Chapter 15 discussed the 'Dutch disease', the reaction of the real exchange rate to an increase in domestic wealth associated with a resource discovery. In the case of Britain and Norway, both countries enjoyed the benefits of the North Sea oil discoveries of the 1970s. Norway subsidized its exporting industries as a response, while Britain used the resources to help balance the budget and therefore pay for transfers and government spending. Why might a subsidy be good supply-side economics in this case?

6 It is sometimes claimed that overtime working contributes to the unemployment problem. In particular, hiring and firing costs make it more attractive to pay current workers to work more (the intensive margin) than to hire more workers (the extensive margin). Furthermore, tax provisions may shield overtime income from normal labour taxation. How might reform of overtime working be difficult under these conditions? Can you think of reform measures that might encourage fewer overtime hours?

7 What is an unemployment trap? How does it work?

8 Show diagramatically how a leftward shift of the collective labour supply curve can lead to a long-run decline in output.

9 What is the difference between active and passive labour market policies?

10 Trace through the macroeconomic effects, in the short and long run, of a policy that reduces equilibrium output (for example, an increase in labour taxation). Under what conditions could this lead to a permanent increase in the rate of inflation? (Hint: use the *AD–AS* framework developed in Chapter 13).

➲ Essay Questions

1 A cut in income taxes in Europe would have significant supply-side effects.' Comment.

2 Why do some countries find it easier to carry out supply-side reforms than others?

3 How would you try to convince workers that they would globally benefit from lower employment protection?

4 Taxes are distortionary but they are used to finance public goods. How would you appraise a proposal for severely cutting public services in order to reduce tax distortions?

5 Define economic rent. Identify an economic rent that you find particularly objectionable and propose ways to eliminate it.

The Architecture of the International Monetary System

19

When we understand that Lombard Street is subject to severe alternations of opposite causes, we should cease to be surprised at its seeming cycles. We should cease too, to be surprised at the sudden panics. During the period of reaction and adversity, just even at the last instant of prosperity, the whole structure is delicate. The peculiar essence of our banking system is an unprecedented trust between man and man: and when that trust is much weakened by hidden causes, a small accident may greatly hurt it, and a great accident for a moment may almost destroy it.

Walter Bagehot (1873)

19.1 Overview

If history has taught us anything, it is that currency and banking crises keep recurring, despite the best efforts of some politicians to ban them. In the years 2007–2012, the financial crisis started as a mortgage banking crisis in in the USA, spread to Wall Street and other money centres, then caused a collapse of global credit and the greatest economic slowdown since the 1930s. More relevant for this book, it spread to Europe and strikes at the heart of the common currency project in ways that economists did not predict. It has made clear the dominant role of international financial markets in determining the intertemporal budget constraints of nations, and by doing so has an enormous say in determining what is nation and what is not. Ultimately, the global economic and financial crisis threatens to throw the project of European integration in all its dimensions off course, with the concomitant threats to well-being, not only for the Eurozone, but also for the United Kingdom, the United States and the rising stars of the still developing world.

For this reason the international community had always been ready for emergency action. This is not the first global crisis. The **International Monetary Fund (IMF)**, in particular, was set up after the Second World Wart to provide emergency funds to lessen the burden of hard-hit countries and to try and prevent contagion—but in a time of fixed exchange rates. After the end of the Bretton Woods System, it has served as an international watchdog, providing objective surveillance of countries for international private and public lenders. With the European sovereign crisis, the IMF has assumed a central role alongside European authorities. Yet, its actions, and those of other international institutions, are often criticized. Could not the crisis have been prevented? Was the international response adequate? Over the last decade, there have been frequent calls to overhaul the international financial system, but very little has happened.

It may well be that financial crises are inherent to financial markets; this certainly seems to be the opinion of William Bagehot, writing in the late nineteenth century. It was once said that international finance has progressed in the same way international air travel has: there is more and more of it, it is terribly important but often superfluous, and if there is an accident, it is nasty and a lot of people get hurt. Similarly, the international monetary world has become a dangerous place. It is also constantly changing. Emerging economies that were once dirt-poor are catching up with the developed world. They have joined the bandwagon of globalization and expect to be treated like equals. Many of the questions on the table are age-old: What exchange rate regime to adopt? Should capital movements be restrained? How to balance the relationship between the developed North and the poor South? What role for international financial institutions like the IMF and the World Bank? In this chapter, we revisit these old questions, as well as the European question: How much sovereignty must a country give up in order to participate in this brave new world?

Section 19.2 provides a brief overview of the history of the international monetary system that will help us to understand the current situation. Section 19.3 describes the role and structure of the IMF, the linchpin of the present system, in some detail. The crises of the 1990s are presented and interpreted in Section 19.4, paving the way for the enduring question of the appropriate exchange rate regime. The last section provides a cautious assessment of a situation in Europe and elsewhere, which is still evolving, but lies at the centre of the European question: what does it mean to be a sovereign nation in a world of globalized trade and most importantly highly integrated financial arrangements?

19.2 History of Monetary Arrangements

19.2.1 The Gold Standard and How It Worked

For centuries, both domestic and international trade was conducted using gold and silver. Metallic monies were used for thousands of years because, as explained in Chapter 9, they were easily recognizable and acceptable by others. Because they were scarce, precious metals were a reasonably stable store of value: they were not easily subject to manipulation, and were a reliable medium of exchange. National currencies as we know them today did not exist. Progressively throughout the nineteenth century, banknotes began circulating alongside gold and silver. These notes were a promise to pay the bearer in precious metal. They were as good as the name of the issuer, mostly his honesty in not issuing more notes than he had precious metal. Initially at least, the notes were issued by private bankers, who often failed to exercise adequate self-discipline. Even if they did, banknotes were not always fully backed by metallic reserves, which led to occasional banking crises. This is one reason why central banks were created, and why they displaced private banks as issuers of paper money. Central banks were formally required to hold close to 100% gold or silver to back their issues of banknotes. These notes were convertible into gold, coins, or bullion at the holder's request, and conversion was indeed routine. With close to 100% backing, banknotes simply represented a more convenient way of holding gold or silver.

This arrangement, known as the **gold standard**, was ultimately formalized internationally and lasted from 1879 to 1914, less than 40 years (see Box 19.1), collapsing one month before the outbreak of the First World War. The gold standard era is sometimes nostalgically associated with the fast growth and rapid industrialization of the time, and is regarded as a great economic success story. This 'success', in turn, is often attributed to the gold standard's automatic adjustment mechanism. In fact, the gold standard had many problems, and adjustment mechanisms were by no means as automatic as is often believed. But it remains a benchmark and, in many respects, new developments, such as monetary unions and currency boards (studied in Section 19.5.3), attempt to re-create some of its most desirable features. So it is well worth a long, hard look.

Domestic operation of the gold standard

In principle, the gold standard was a simple affair. Money was gold, or paper 'backed' by gold. This meant that the gold was literally redeemable on demand. The demand for that money was stable, driven by the need to carry out everyday transactions. Supply too was quite stable. Because the stocks of coinage were so large, even large gold discoveries and the resulting flows of newly coined gold or silver amounted to small monetary shocks. The role of the monetary authorities was merely to establish and guarantee the gold content of their own currencies, the gold exchange rate.

International operation of the gold standard
Fixed exchange rates

By arbitrage, pegging a currency's value to gold was sufficient to determine all exchange rates vis-à-vis other currencies pegged to gold. For instance, if the Dutch guilder was set at the price of 50 per ounce of pure gold (the usual weight reference) and sterling was set at £25 per ounce, the guilder was worth £0.5. If the market exchange rate were to decline to £0.4 (a depreciation of the guilder relative to sterling), it

Box 19.1 **Bimetallism and Gresham's Law**

It was only at the end of the nineteenth century that gold became the premier international medium of exchange. For centuries, silver and gold had competed against each other. **Bimetallism**, as the system was called, established a fixed parity between gold and silver, and coins in both metals were usually accepted for all transactions, both nationally and internationally. The relative value of gold and silver was set by international agreements, which were occasionally called into question as new discoveries of either metal threatened to upset the parity. Troubled times then followed with the operation of **Gresham's law**. This principle states that the currency (metal) that is more valuable (in non-monetary markets) than its official rate stops circulating: 'bad money chases out good'.[1]

Partly because silver became more plentiful, bimetallism ceased to exist in Europe in the 1870s. The last major countries to defend bimetallism formed the Latin Monetary Union in 1865, setting a parity of 15.5 ounces of silver for 1 ounce of gold. This union consisted of Belgium, France, Italy, and Switzerland (for this reason all, save Italy, adopted the 'franc' as the name of their national money). In the USA, where a central monetary authority was absent, bimetallism survived for a longer time. The final blow occurred when the newly created German state switched to gold and unloaded large amounts of silver on the free market. The risk of complete gold loss in a world under a gold standard forced the remaining countries to abandon bimetallism entirely.

would make sense to purchase gold in the Netherlands with guilders, ship it to the UK, sell it to the Bank of England in exchange for sterling, and convert sterling into guilders. For every 100 guilders tendered in the Netherlands for gold, the transaction would yield 2 ounces of gold, sold in the UK to acquire £50. Selling these sterling balances against guilders at the 0.4 exchange rate would yield 125 guilders, a 25% profit! Such a prospect was sure to trigger large sales of sterling and large purchases of guilders in the exchange markets, promptly appreciating the guilder's value back to its only sustainable sterling value, £0.5. To be sure, the example ignores transaction costs, especially the cost of transporting the gold across the sea. Once these are accounted for, the exchange rate can deviate somewhat from the gold-implied parity, leaving a **band of fluctuation** within which it is not worth undertaking the buying, selling, and shipping. These bands were known as 'gold points', and are similar to exchange rate intervention bands employed in modern fixed exchange rate

systems. They implied margins of fluctuation of about 1%. This is another application of the no-profit condition explored in Chapter 15.

The Hume Mechanism

In the absence of advanced capital markets and international financial institutions, flows of gold between nations served as the primary means of financing payment imbalances. This adjustment was identified more than two and a half centuries ago by David Hume, the Scottish economist and philosopher who first described it. The **Hume mechanism** (sometimes called 'gold-specie mechanism') is still highly relevant for understanding the origins, evolution, and resolution of balance of payments imbalances.

The Hume mechanism works like this. A country which ran a trade deficit would automatically lose gold to its trading partners. The metal was often physically shipped abroad to pay for the excess of imports over exports.[2] The exported gold coins were

[1] Living in the sixteenth century, Sir Thomas Gresham had been in charge of royal finances, then became a foreign exchange trader in Antwerp until he created the Royal Exchange, better known today as the London Stock Exchange. It is sometimes argued that the gold standard in the UK was an artefact of Isaac Newton's decision in 1717 to undervalue silver in terms of gold. Within little time, Sir Isaac had only gold on his hands.

[2] Considering the high shipping, insurance, and security costs involved, this was a very expensive way of settling international payments. To save on these costs, some central banks, such as the Federal Reserve Bank of New York, offered (and still offer) custodial services for gold owned by other central banks. In the late 1990s, the New York Fed was the guardian of about 270 million troy ounces of monetary gold, or about one-third the holdings of all central banks. At current market prices this gold is between 400 and 500 billion dollars.

then minted and coined in the currency of the surplus country. Thus, a trade deficit implied a shrinking money supply, a surplus meant an expanding money supply. This had three consequences. First, the reduction of the money supply led to tighter monetary conditions and higher interest rates in the deficit country, which encouraged capital inflows. In this way, capital account surpluses could finance trade deficits. Second, higher interest rates tended to slow down economic activity, which reduced imports at given exchange rates (think of the primary account (*PCA*) function introduced in Chapter 10).[3] Third, the contraction of the money supply associated with gold outflow would reduce the domestic price level directly. Hume saw this effect through simple monetarist lenses (lower gold supply meant lower prices in the long run) but an economic slowdown will also lead to deflation, as rising unemployment weakens workers' bargaining power and firms' markups decline. These price declines (or lower inflation) would improve the deficit country's competitiveness and restore trade balance.

In the export surplus country, the process works in the opposite direction: balance of payment surpluses led to gold inflows, which expands the money supply and depresses interest rates. An economic expansion results, leading to higher prices, which reduces the surplus directly (growing economies will import more) and indirectly (as the real exchange rate appreciates and competitiveness is eroded).

The Hume mechanism is a symmetric adjustment process, which under the gold standard works silently and automatically. It can only be interrupted or interfered with if governments intervene. We will later see that within fixed exchange rate regimes, the Hume mechanism is weakened if imbalances are not allowed to give rise to corrective mechanisms. One assessment of the current problems of monetary union is the failure for the Hume mechanism to function properly.

The main benefits of the gold standard

The world has never seen, and probably never will see, a true pure gold standard. Still, some observers regret the passing of the gold standard. Why? First, the Hume mechanism had the virtue of credibility. Under a gold standard, monetary policy is entirely determined by the stock of gold. In principle, it is out of the politicians' hands. Second, with the money supply naturally constrained by the availability of a rare resource, inflation is not likely to emerge on any significant scale, and it didn't. This is documented in Table 19.1. Third, there is no need for a particular country to be at the centre of the world monetary system, avoiding competition and conflict regarding which country that should be. As we will later see, the last century of monetary relations has been dogged by this issue, even long after gold had left centre stage.

The gold standard certainly produced a stable price level. People were able to base their expectations on a fairly predictable stable evolution of the value of goods in terms of money—in Chapter 16 we saw the advantages of low inflation rates. In the theory of economic policy, the Hume mechanism and the gold standard illustrate the advantages of *rules* over *discretion*. When expectations are being formed, private agents try hard to guess the intentions of policy-makers. In Chapter 12 we saw that workers and firms want to estimate the path of inflation. They also need to estimate the path of central bank policy. Often they base their expectations on past behaviour. If the central bank has misbehaved in the past, these expectations will be pessimistic. Thus even if the central bank has good intentions, a bad outcome is possible: agents expect high inflation,

[3] In the time of the gold standard, there was no monetary authority (central bank) to set interest rates in some regular way like the Taylor rule. The money supply simply interacted with money demand to produce market-clearing interest rates, just as described in Chapter 9.

Table 19.1 Inflation Rates in Five Countries, 1900–1913 (annual average rate of increase in GDP deflator, %)

France	Japan	USA	Germany	UK
0.9	2.8	1.3	1.3	0.9

Source: Maddison (1995).

which the central bank may then feel compelled to validate with an expansionary monetary policy, usually to avoid a recession. The gold standard, by implementing automatic rules, made it easy for economic agents to reckon with the economic policy. By removing policy-makers' discretion to adjust policy, rules can lead to a more credible environment for economic agents.

Limits of automatism

Despite these appealing aspects, the gold standard had several limitations. Sterling was the main currency, backed by the most developed financial centre, London. Britain had been on the gold standard longer than other countries, since 1819 when the Bank of England received its key statutes (Peel's Act). Furthermore, as the largest creditor country, Britain provided the rest of the world with sterling balances which often ended up as reserve currency held by other central banks.[4] Three consequences followed from Britain's dominant, or hegemonic, position. First, the Bank of England was able to set the interest rate for the rest of the world, but naturally concerned with British economic conditions. Second, the demand for sterling as a reserve currency allowed Britain to finance long-running balance of payments deficits, paid with sterling-denominated liabilities of the Bank of England. In doing so, Britain could evade the automaticity of the Hume mechanism: its money supply did not decline when it ran deficits with the rest of the world, because gold was not shipped to cover its deficits. Third, the widespread acceptability of sterling balances allowed the Bank of England to maintain a ratio of reserves to deposits—known as 'the Proportion'—well below 100%. At the height of the gold standard late in the nineteenth century, the Proportion fluctuated between 30% and 50%. To the extent that its gold stock was shielded from the vagaries of the balance of payments and since the Proportion could vary, the Bank of England possessed considerable freedom to set its interest rate.

Britain was not the only country that tinkered with Hume's mechanism. Some countries actually imposed limits on gold exports and imports, as well as on minting and coinage. Many central banks accumulated sizeable reserves of foreign currencies, first and foremost in pounds sterling. Thus, the assumed link between metal and money supply was less than fully automatic. Furthermore, the gold reserves of the Bank of England eventually fell below the value of the Bank's liabilities towards other central banks, leading to an 'overhang' of unbacked British debt. Many scholars consider it a miracle that the overhang never threatened the credibility of external sterling liabilities; others see it as testimony to the power of credibility and trust in monetary systems.

The limits of a metallic standard

The automatic mechanism that is often considered to be the central advantage of the gold standard does not come for free. It can have significant cost in terms of economic instability. While the gold standard years were characterized by low inflation, they also exhibited greater output variability. As already described, there is a trade-off between rules and discretion. If respected, the rules of the gold standard are very strict: the money supply is determined solely by the balance of payments, so macroeconomic adjustments must entirely be dealt with through wage and price changes. If wages and prices adjust slowly in a recession—that is a central message of Chapters 12 and 13—this adjustment process may take a long time. In the meantime, the economy 'goes through the wringer' of unemployment and recession. Despite the credibility of the Hume mechanism, the gold standard has severe costs in some situations.

Another problem is that the overall gold stock—and thus the money supply—depends on natural discoveries. Economic growth, on the other side, requires a continuously expanding demand for real balances. If gold discoveries do not match the demand needs, increases in the real money supply can occur only if the price level declines—i.e. the price of gold must rise.[5] Figure 19.1 shows that the gold supply has increased regularly, with periods of scarcity coming on the footsteps of great discoveries in California, Alaska, and South Africa, as well as

---

[4] During the 40 years preceding the First World War, some 20% of British savings were invested abroad.

[5] Higher gold prices will also discourage its use as jewellery or increase the use of substitutes in industry, thus freeing up some extra gold for monetary purposes. These effects are relatively modest, however.

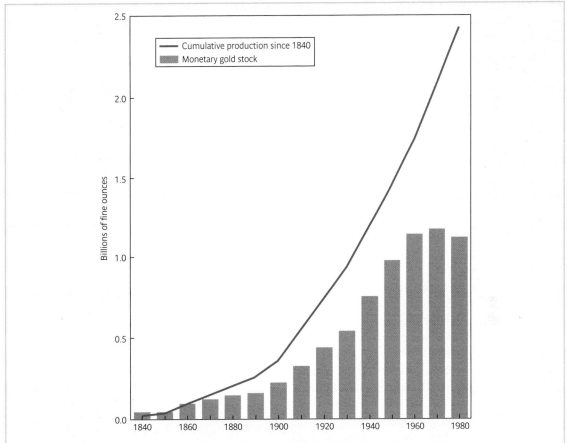

Fig. 19.1 Monetary Gold Stock and Cumulative Gold Production, 1840 – 1980

Although gold production has continued over time, its rate of increase has tapered off. At the same time, the demand for gold for industrial purposes has increased over the past 100 years. Perhaps not coincidentally, gold stocks held by central banks have remained flat for several decades.

Source: Cooper (1982).

technological advances in mining and mineral processing. As these shocks were largely random, the money supply and the price level were hardly stable, even if the average inflation rate was low.

19.2.2 The Inter-War Period

Inter-war monetary arrangements can be conveniently grouped into three sub-periods. The first sub-period ranges from the end of the First World War to the return to the gold standard in 1926. The gold standard was then maintained until 1931, and was then followed by a period of managed float marked by competitive devaluations and a collapse of world trade as a consequence of the Great Depression.

The free float period (1919 – 1926)

In 1919 two countries, the UK and the USA, dominated the world monetary scene. During the First World War, the USA remained on the gold standard, but the UK had suspended the mechanism and allowed the pound to depreciate by about 30%. Under the leadership of a young Chancellor of the Exchequer, Winston Churchill, Britain made the fateful decision to return to the gold standard at the pre-war parity. With strongly deflationary policies in place, the pound was brought back to its pre-war parity in 1925, but remained overvalued due to persistent inflation since 1914. Germany and a number of other Central European countries returned to the gold standard only after experiencing and vanquishing their celebrated hyperinflations. France devalued the franc immediately after the war but underwent rapid inflation in the years 1922–1926. Its return to the gold standard in 1926 after the Poincaré stabilization marked the return to the pre-war situation, albeit at a devalued parity. In doing so, France was able to avoid much of the macroeconomic distress suffered by the UK, just as the Mundell–Fleming framework would predict.

Ephemeral gold standard (1927–1931)

The newly restored gold standard was a poor shadow of its predecessor. It had two competing centres, London and New York. Many currencies were badly misaligned: some were overvalued, like sterling; others were undervalued, like the French franc. Gold holdings became an ever smaller part of foreign exchange reserves as most central banks were accumulating dollar and pound balances. Free convertibility between banknotes and gold was suspended, and most central banks actively discouraged or prohibited the circulation of gold coins.[6] The Hume mechanism was often circumvented by sterilization operations. The only remaining principles of the system were the principles of currency convertibility[7] and fixed exchange rates.

When the Great Depression hit after 1929, the gold standard was already weak. With its overvalued currency, Britain was particularly vulnerable. Its gold reserves shrank quickly while France, with an undervalued currency, was accumulating gold and selling off its sterling balances. Soon Britain's official liabilities exceeded its gold reserves and it had to suspend convertibility in September 1931 and let sterling float. The gold standard was over.

The managed float (1931–1939)

Britain allowed the pound to depreciate sharply to about \$3.3/£, and a number of countries holding large sterling balances followed suit (Table 19.2). Formerly overvalued currencies became undervalued. At a time when all countries were struggling against the Great Depression, these devaluations were a tempting means of gaining a competitive trade advantage at the expense of other countries. A gold bloc, including France, Belgium, the Netherlands, Italy, Switzerland, and Poland, was established to resist the temptation of retaliatory depreciations. The situation worsened seriously in 1933 when the USA, the remaining centre of the gold standard, imposed an embargo on gold exports, introduced exchange controls, and depreciated the dollar from \$20.67 to \$35 per ounce of pure gold. The *coup de grâce* was the dissolution of the gold bloc following the devaluation of the Belgian franc in 1935. 'Beggar-thy-neighbour' policies (competitive devaluations) followed, but were self-defeating since each country attempted to devalue vis-à-vis all the others. The next step was a 'tariff war': each country raised its tariffs to restrict imports, thus encouraging the substitution of domestically produced products. Imports declined but so did exports, as other nations followed suit. While the aim of boosting output failed, international trade collapsed, as shown in Figure 19.2.[8]

19.2.3 The Bretton Woods System of Fixed Exchange Rates

The principles

Preparations for a new monetary order were laid at the **Bretton Woods conference** of July 1944, convened by the Allied nations before the end of the Second World War.[9] The conference led to the creation of the International Monetary Fund (IMF), as well as the International Bank for Reconstruction and Development (known nowadays as the World Bank) and the General Agreement on Tariffs and Trade, the precursor to the World Trade Organization. The new world monetary order was conceived to prevent a repeat of

---

[6] In some cases, e.g. Britain, convertibility was possible only for large denominations, since the Bank of England restricted its conversion to bullion (as opposed to coins). The system is sometimes referred to as the 'gold bullion standard'.

[7] A currency is convertible when holders, both private and official, may exchange it without restriction. Convertibility does not necessarily imply a fixed exchange rate, since a floating rate system also allows participants to freely purchase and sell foreign exchange.

[8] Remember: $Y = C + I + G + X - Z$: *ceteris paribus*, reducing Z raises Y, but if X falls by the same amount, there is no net gain.

[9] Named after a small ski resort in the US state of New Hampshire. The conference considered two plans published in 1943, prepared for the USA by Treasury Secretary Harry White, and for the UK by John Maynard Keynes. The White plan eventually prevailed.

Table 19.2 Beggar-thy-Neighbour Depreciations, Various Countries, 1931–1938 (value of currencies as percentage of 1929 gold parity)

	1931	1932	1933	1934	1935	1936	1937	1938
Belgium	100.1	100.2	100.1	99.9	78.6	72.0	71.7	71.8
Denmark	93.5	70.3	55.8	50.0	48.5	49.0	48.6	48.1
France	100.1	100.3	100.0	100.0	100.0	92.4	61.0	43.4
Germany	99.2	99.7	99.6	98.6	100.3	100.1	99.7	99.6
Italy	98.9	97.4	99.0	97.0	93.0	82.0	59.0	59.0
Norway	93.5	67.2	62.7	56.3	54.5	55.2	54.7	54.1
The Netherlands	100.1	100.3	100.1	100.0	100.0	94.9	80.9	88.8
Switzerland	100.6	100.6	100.2	100.1	100.0	92.6	70.2	70.0
UK	93.2	72.0	68.1	61.8	59.8	60.5	60.0	59.3
USA	100.0	100.0	80.7	59.6	59.4	59.2	59.1	59.1

Source: League of Nations, Statistical Bulletins.

the competitive devaluations and unilateral trade restrictions, which could threaten a post-war economic recovery.

◆ Exchange rates were to be fixed; realignments required prior IMF approval.

◆ The IMF could provide loans as an alternative to devaluation for countries facing balance of payments difficulties.

◆ The dollar was the centre of the system. All countries officially declared a fixed parity, called a par or central value, vis-à-vis the US dollar, which itself pegged to gold directly. Currencies were allowed to deviate by no more than 1% from the par value.

◆ Exchange controls and tariffs were allowed only as temporary measures for the immediate post-war period. In the event, full currency convertibility was only achieved in Europe in 1958, and a number of developing countries still have non-convertible currencies and capital controls.

Gold and the dollar

Officially, all currencies were defined in terms of gold. Yet, at the end of the Second World War, the USA held about 70% of all gold reserves and was the only country credible enough to set a gold parity. With the US Marshall Plan providing European

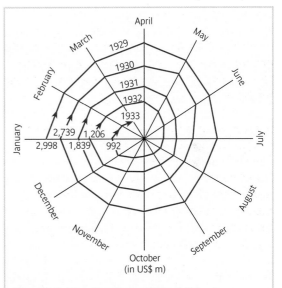

Fig. 19.2 The Decline of World Trade During the Great Depression

During the period 1929–1933, the enormous increases in world trade that had been accomplished in the previous three decades were wiped out by a spiral of protectionist measures. This famous illustration by Professor Charles Kindleberger of MIT, taken from a 1934 publication of the League of Nations, shows just how quickly trade wars can get out of hand.

Source: Kindleberger (1973).

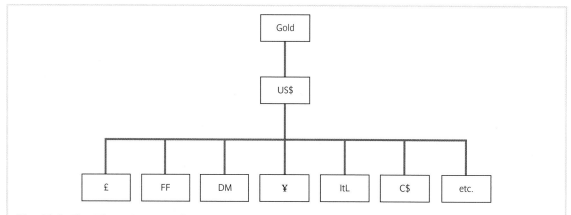

Fig. 19.3 The Three Layers of Bretton Woods

The three layers of the Bretton Woods system consisted of gold, the US dollar, and the other participating currencies. The USA declared a gold parity for the dollar, thereby pegging to gold. Intervention took place mostly in dollars, but implicit was the understanding that gold stood behind the dollars.

countries with dollar balances, the most obvious approach for them was to declare a parity vis-à-vis the US currency.[10] The outcome was a de facto three-tier system, represented in Figure 19.3. Gold remained the fundamental standard of value, but for all currencies this was mediated by the dollar, hence the name **gold exchange standard** given to the Bretton Woods system. The system thus relied on the ability of the USA to maintain the declared parity of $35 per ounce of gold.

The International Monetary Fund

For a long while, the Bretton Woods system worked rather well. After a rash of post-war parity adjustments—including an unauthorized devaluation of the French franc in 1948—exchange rate stability prevailed. Trade expanded quickly and was easily financed by dollar balances, provided initially by the Marshall Plan, then by US trade deficits and the resulting capital flows.[11] The IMF became the respected watchdog of the fixed exchange rate system. It developed an elaborate system of loans to

countries suffering balance of payments difficulties. Its resources were provided by member-country deposits, 25% in gold or US dollars—depending on the country's gold stock—and 75% in the country's own currency. The size of a country's deposit, based on its size in international trade, determines its **quota**. Quotas determine each member country's voting weight and its borrowing rights, and are set anew every five years.

Devaluations were in principle restricted to cases of 'fundamental disequilibria', i.e. balance of payments deficits not of a temporary (cyclical) nature. In order to help member nations avoid devaluation, the IMF made, and still makes, resources available for immediate lending—called 'purchase agreements' when effected and 'repurchase' when reimbursed. Each member country is eligible for immediate lending up to its quota. Beyond that, lending becomes conditional. The IMF requests a formal agreement on specific policy steps and results designed to solve the 'non-fundamental' part of external disequilibria. This **conditionality** has become the central source of power of the IMF, and has survived the collapse of the Bretton Woods system.

The Triffin paradox and the collapse of the Bretton Woods system

As economies grew and international trade developed, more 'international money' was needed. Since

[10] The Marshall Plan was a massive aid programme for post-war Western Europe and Japan funded by the USA.

[11] This was the first sign that the Hume mechanism might run into trouble: the USA provided the 'gold' (dollars) by running balance of payments deficits with the rest of the world, that is, by exporting dollars in return for goods, services, and investment positions.

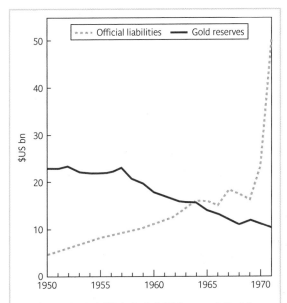

Fig. 19.4 US Official Liabilities and Gold Reserves, 1950–1970

As long as foreigners were willing to hold dollars, the USA could finance its large balance of payments deficits by increases in foreign holdings of official assets (dollars held by central banks). Yet the gold reserve of the USA declined over the entire period shown, as foreign central banks occasionally tendered their dollars for gold. Sometime in 1964, the stock of external official claims against the US gold exceeded the dollar's gold backing. At that moment, the credibility of the gold exchange standard was called into question.

Sources: Dam (1982); IMF.

the US dollar was the international money, more dollars would have to be made available to the world economy. For internationally held dollar balances to grow, the USA must run balance of payments deficits, just as Britain did during the days of the gold standard. Inevitably, US official liabilities abroad had to outgrow the country's gold reserves. Figure 19.4 shows that this happened in 1964. Yet at this point, the USA could no longer guarantee the gold value of the US dollar. This is the **Triffin paradox**,[12] a fatal weakness of the gold exchange standard.

A conjunction of economic and political events brought the situation to a climax. The Vietnam War

and ambitious domestic social programmes (President Johnson's 'Great Society') led to increased public spending in the USA, which accelerated growth and inflation, and deepened the current account deficit. At the same time, countries critical of the Bretton Woods arrangement began to protest loudly. French President de Gaulle publicly complained about the '*privilège exorbitant*', which allowed the USA to use seigniorage to finance its political activities (the Vietnam War) and economic power (the acquisition of European corporations by US companies at the time). In a dramatic gesture, France began to swap dollars for gold in the mid-1960s, increasing its precious metal stock from $3.7 to $5.2 billion between 1964 and 1966.

The markets took notice. Anticipating an increase in the price of gold, they sought to buy it while it was still cheap. The response of the monetary authorities was to form the Gold Pool (Belgium, Italy, the Netherlands, Switzerland, West Germany, the UK, and the USA, with France inactive after 1967), an agreement to sell gold to maintain the $35/ounce parity. As the drain on official gold holdings accelerated, the Pool pulled out of the gold market and declared that they would henceforth trade gold only among themselves—they would neither sell to nor buy from private parties—at the official price. The market price of gold rose substantially higher than the official parities. Tensions within the Gold Pool grew until President Nixon's historic decision to suspend the gold parity of the US dollar on 15 August 1971.

From the Smithsonian Agreement to Jamaica

The severing of the gold–dollar link destroyed a key component of the Bretton Woods arrangement, but the gold crisis was not the sole factor in its demise. Inflation had been rising in most countries in the late 1960s, but at increasingly different rates (Figure 19.5). This led to misalignments which challenged exchange rate parities unchanged since the late 1940s.[13] Speculative capital movements followed. Britain and Italy came under IMF conditionality in 1969. The pound was devalued in 1967, followed by the French franc in 1969, while the deutschmark was

---

[12] It is named after the late Belgian economist Robert Triffin who identified the 'fundamental flaw' of the Bretton Woods system.

[13] The French franc was devalued in 1958; the deutschmark and Dutch guilder were revalued in 1961.

Fig. 19.5 Inflation Rates: USA, UK, Germany, and Italy, 1960–1976

Inflation rates during the Bretton Woods era moved closely together, which is characteristic of a fixed exchange rate regime. As soon as the system collapsed in 1971, inflation rates diverged sharply.
Source: IMF.

revalued. The delinking of the dollar from gold opened the Pandora's box for further realignments. The credibility of the exchange rate system was severely damaged.

The last major effort to save the sinking ship was an agreement reached in December 1971 during a conference at the Smithsonian Institution in Washington, DC. The dollar was devalued vis-à-vis gold to $38 per ounce, yet remained inconvertible into gold, even among central banks. Some currencies were revalued, others devalued. The margins of fluctuations were enlarged from 1% to 2.25% around par value, while the European countries maintained a reduced (half) margin. This was the 'snake' arrangement. By the end of 1972, the pound was floating, soon to be followed by the Swiss franc, the Italian lira, and the Japanese yen. In March 1973, the remaining 'snake' members decided to float jointly vis-à-vis all other currencies, including the dollar, within a wider 2.25% margin. France left, then re-entered, as did Italy; then both left again. Sweden and Norway joined informally. By 1975 the principle of fixed exchange rates was more or less dead, at least for the convertible currencies of the industrialized countries. In January

1976, the Jamaica agreement made official the new role of the IMF. From then on, it would be in charge of overseeing a world monetary system of increasingly flexible exchange rates.

19.2.4 The European Monetary System and the European Monetary Union

For Europe, the Bretton Woods system had offered a convenient, if indirect, way of pegging their currencies to each other. This arrangement had deepened economic ties within the Common Market, consisting of the member countries of the European Community (EC).[14] The demise of the gold exchange standard posed a problem with both economic and political implications. The response was the establishment of the European Monetary System (EMS), which began operation in March 1979. All nine European Community (EC) members at the time formally joined the EMS, but the UK deferred participating in the **Exchange Rate Mechanism (ERM)**, the system of fixed exchange rates, until October 1990. With

---

[14] The European Community is the predecessor of the European Union. The name change was officially decided in Maastricht in 1991.

the exception of Sweden, all newer EC (henceforth EU) members (Greece, Spain, Portugal, Austria, and Finland) subsequently joined the ERM. After violent **speculative attacks** on the ERM parities in September 1992, Italy and the UK left the ERM; Italy rejoined in 1997. The ERM disappeared formally with the launch in 1999 of the **European Monetary Union** (EMU) (we discuss this further in Section 19.5.4). A new EMS-II was established. The modified ERM serves as a gateway to EMU for new EU members and a possible arrangement for EU member countries, such as Denmark, that do not wish to adopt the euro but nevertheless fix their exchange rates to it. As of January 2012, 17 of the 25 EU member countries had adopted the euro.

Key features of the EMS

Three original features characterized the first version of the ERM.

Bilateral parities

Exchange rates were fixed but adjustable. In theory, no currency had special hegemonic status, like the US dollar under Bretton Woods. Fixity was defined as an official central **parity** between any pair of member currencies: a central rate, and a band of fluctuation initially set at ±2.25%, which was expanded to ±15% in August 1993, following a major exchange rate crisis.[15]

Consensus decisions

A country could not alter its parity within the system unilaterally. Realignments had to be agreed upon by every member. Despite the apparent restrictiveness of this rule, realignments are not infrequent.

Mutual support

In order to defend the parities, member central banks were allowed to borrow virtually unlimited amounts from each other at very short notice. Prompt repayment was required—normally within 45 days—but revolving credits were possible.

[15] Technically, the ERM parities were defined vis-à-vis the ECU, the forerunner to the euro, which was simply a basket of currencies of all EMS members. Bilateral parities were derived as cross rates implied by the central ECU parities. A special ±6% band was employed temporarily by Italy, the UK, Portugal, Spain, and Greece.

In practice, the German mark emerged as the central currency. The Bundesbank intervened mostly in US dollars, whereas the other members used EMS currencies more frequently. Germany appeared to manage its exchange rate vis-à-vis the US dollar, leaving it to the other central banks to manage theirs vis-à-vis the deutschmark. This German hegemony in the old EMS is still the subject of heated discussions in central bank boardrooms, yet it is beyond debate that in any currency fixed exchange arrangement with N currencies that an extra degree of freedom exists after all bilateral rates are determined. The logic of this '$N-1$ problem' is spelled out in Box 19.2. Which member or set of members of a monetary union captures the Nth degree of freedom is open. Some would connect it with the largest or dominant economy, others with the most conservative monetary policy, i.e. the one that accumulates reserves over time.

The four phases of the EMS

During the first phase, from its establishment until the mid-1980s, the ERM operated as a fairly loose system which tolerated member countries' diverse tastes for inflation. Realignments were frequent and undramatic, aimed at correcting deviations from purchasing power parity (PPP) resulting from persistent differences in inflation rates between participating countries.

The second phase, from the mid-1980s to 1992, was marked by the gradual emergence of the deutschmark as the system's anchor currency. Realignments were successfully avoided from January 1987 to September 1992. All countries tried to emulate the mark's strong currency status and identified low inflation as the main objective of monetary policy. During this period, the EMS came to be perceived as a major success: the absence of any realignment for nearly six years was attributed to adroit policy coordination. Emboldened by success, the authorities proceeded to prepare a shift to a single currency. The result was the Maastricht Treaty adopted by EU heads of state late in 1991.

This period of tranquillity and optimism came to an abrupt end in the summer of 1992. During the subsequent third phase of crisis and turbulence, continuous upheaval rocked the ERM ship, and it nearly

Box 19.2 The N − 1 Problem

Take N countries with N currencies. There are $N − 1$ independent bilateral exchange rates, as Figure 19.6 illustrates. All the other bilateral rates can be retrieved from these $N − 1$ rates via triangular arbitrage. Now link these currencies together, either in a monetary union or just a system of fixed exchange rates. As $N − 1$ independent bilateral exchange rates are fixed, it follows that $N − 1$ central banks lose their independence, and the Nth remains free of policy constraints. In the Bretton Woods system, all central banks were pegged to the US dollar, leaving the Fed with the task of pegging the dollar to gold. In the EMS, no Nth country was designated, but the Bundesbank captured the Nth degree of freedom. In a monetary union, such as EMU, all N central banks lose their policy-making autonomy and a new central bank is created to manage the new currency.

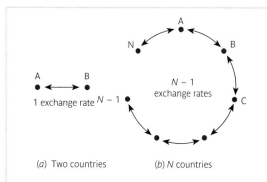

(a) Two countries   (b) N countries

Fig. 19.6 The N − 1 Problem

Two countries which decide to fix their exchange rate lose one degree of freedom. When N countries form a fixed exchange rate system, they commit to $N − 1$ exchange rates, or $N − 1$ degrees of freedom (all the bilateral exchange rates can be calculated from just the $N − 1$ rates shown in panel (b): all the missing arrows can be drawn).

sank. Not only did several realignments occur in quick succession, but two currencies—the British pound and the Swedish krona—actually left the ERM to float on their own. Roughly a year later, in August 1993, the margins of fluctuation were widened to ±15%, and the fixed exchange rate system hardly differed from free floating.

The fourth and last phase of the EMS, which represented two decades of European monetary history, an 'ERM without teeth', was hastily designed in the wake of speculative attacks. With 15% wide bands, the situation was stabilized, allowing an orderly transition to EMU.

The impossible trilogy

With hindsight it is easy to understand why the ERM was under duress. The globalization of international financial markets brought near-perfect capital mobility along with it, allowing investors and speculators to swap billions of short-term assets at the push of a button. A central bank which commits to fixing an exchange rate becomes the ultimate market maker in the money market, and is obliged to accommodate all transactions that the market does not at the set parity. This commitment, as was made clear in Chapter 9, is inconsistent with an independent monetary policy.

The coexistence of fixed exchange regimes and capital controls is thus more than coincidental. Capital controls enable countries participating in fixed exchange rate arrangements to preserve some monetary autonomy. The countries that use capital controls tend to have higher inflation. Indeed, controls may be essential to organize orderly realignments in the face of market attacks.

These policy conflicts and dilemmas are summarized neatly as the **impossible trilogy**. This principle states that the following three aspects of a monetary system are jointly incompatible:

(1) full capital mobility;

(2) fixed exchange rates;

(3) monetary policy independence.

Taken in pairs, however, these features are feasible and have been observed throughout monetary history, and even today. The impossible trilogy is a direct implication of the Mundell–Fleming (*IS–TR-IFM*) framework under fixed exchange rates: if capital is fully mobile, then the interest rate is given exogenously by the foreign rate i^*, and the money supply is endogenous, changing as a result of net capital inflow.

This principle offers a powerful framework for reviewing the EMS experience. The early EMS was able to survive because of the presence of capital controls. During the first phase, it allowed for the coexistence of fixed exchange rates and some degree of monetary independence in the form of different inflation rates compensated for by periodic realignments. The second phase was an attempt to adopt the same monetary policy everywhere under German leadership. As long as economic conditions did not call for different policies, this was a relatively costless way to cope with the impossible trilogy. It is during that period that capital controls were dismantled. However, the shock of German unification and a worldwide recession in the early 1990s raised the benefits of monetary policy independence, and changed all that. The crises that followed correspond to the travails that go with ignoring the impossible trilogy. The solutions adopted—free floating in Italy and the UK, wide bands elsewhere—correspond to the abandonment of the fixed exchange rate.

Once capital controls are removed, the choice boils down to one of two extremes: either a single monetary authority or a free float. The experience of 1992–1993 shows that the temptation of monetary independence plays havoc with a fixed exchange rate arrangement. Politically, it was probably unavoidable that countries relinquishing monetary independence in a system of fixed exchange rates would challenge the Bundesbank's leadership, just as France challenged the American *privilège exorbitant* three decades previous. It is not surprising that the countries that pledged to abandon capital controls in the mid-1980s—Belgium, France, Italy, and Spain—soon thereafter proposed the creation of a European Monetary Union. Nor is it surprising that the Bundesbank initially expressed doubts about the urgency of taking a step which amounted to sharing its undisputed control over European monetary policy.

19.3 The International Monetary Fund

The influence of the IMF is probably stronger today than in the heyday of the Bretton Woods system, if only because it is now in charge of a system that is less internally inconsistent than before. In the post-Bretton Woods 'system', each country is free to choose its own exchange rate regime, and there is no agreed-upon international currency. Gold has long been 'demonetized', meaning that it is no longer a reference, and many countries have since sold large parts of their gold stocks.

19.3.1 IMF Assistance and Conditionality

Countries continue occasionally to face balance of payment problems, although they are somewhat different from those of the Bretton Woods era. In principle, countries are now free to depreciate their currencies in response to adverse shocks, and over the longer haul such policies can bring the current account back to levels consistent with an intertemporal budget constraint. Frequently, though, the authorities prevent their exchange rate from adjusting to shocks by intervening in the foreign exchange markets, sometimes with borrowed foreign exchange. Eventually they may exhaust their foreign exchange reserves. What can they do then? An obvious answer is to treat the causes, and not the symptoms of the crisis. Taking remedial action, usually moving away from undisciplined monetary and fiscal policies, requires time, however, and the house is burning. The solution is to call the IMF, the international firefighter.

When called upon in an emergency, the IMF proceeds in three steps:

(1) It assesses the situation and makes recommendations to the authorities.

(2) Conditionality follows: an emergency loan is extended to the troubled country, which in return commits to a number of policy actions.

(3) As the loan is disbursed, typically in several instalments, the IMF monitors the implementation of the agreement and may suspend further disbursements if the country in question is violating its commitments.

In an average year, some 10–20 standby loans are arranged.[16] The average volume of loans outstanding represents about 12% of world exports. In 2008, 185 countries were members of the Fund.

It is important to stress that the Fund's assistance is not a gift, but a loan, generally with a maturity of 1–4 years. The interest rate charged is slightly above the market rate to discourage using the Fund as a cheap source of money. Most private financial institutions deal only with sovereign borrowers in good standing with the IMF, so the Fund usually has a great deal of leverage over borrowing countries, which are generally excluded from the private capital market. This explains, of course, why countries in trouble turn to the IMF and are also willing to accept the conditions that it requests. Despite popular beliefs to the contrary, most countries actually pay back their loans. The reason is that the IMF has priority over all other creditors, and not repaying the IMF means being excluded from all other sources of international financing. Only a handful of 'pariah' countries have defaulted on IMF loans. They will have to pay back when and if they want to re-enter the international financial arena. Most eventually do.

Most recently, the IMF has been called upon to advise and assist Greece, which in 2010 was the first of a number of Eurozone countries to experience a severe sovereign debt crisis and was the first to receive an assistance or 'bailout' programme. As a member of the European Monetary Union, Greece has no independent monetary policy and was confronted by much the same dilemma faced by troubled countries in the Bretton Woods system in the late 1960s. As explained in Chapter 17, Greece's situation was rapidly deteriorating with fires on several fronts:

(1) a sharp rise in market interest rates to finance chronic Greek budget deficits, which had fallen into primary deficits for many years;

(2) a balance of payments crisis (large current and capital account deficits) similar to those experienced in the 1960s by the UK and Italy in the late 1960s, in which a decade of higher inflation had cumulated to a large misalignment of the real exchange rate;

(3) sluggish potential growth, which was shown in Chapter 17 to increase the primary budget surplus needed to keep the government on a solvent path.

The IMF was invited by the European Commission and the European Central Bank to provide active consultation on implementing a conditionality programme.

19.3.2 Special Drawing Rights

Despite having lost the official status it enjoyed in the Bretton Woods system, the US dollar remains the de facto means of payment for international trade and the foreign exchange reserve of choice at central banks. Although it is sometimes asked whether the euro might challenge or replace the US dollar, the more interesting question is: why should the international means of payment be any particular country's currency? In the late 1960s, many countries lobbied for the creation of a new world currency, reviving an old idea which had been defeated at the Bretton Woods conference in 1946.[17] If the IMF could be transformed into the world central bank, it was thought, it could issue its own currency for all central banks to settle their payments, borrow from each other, and intervene on exchange markets. Unsurprisingly, the USA, the Fund's largest shareholder—with a veto right—objected.

With the objective of increasing and stabilizing the supply of international liquidity, it was decided at the Rio Conference in 1967 to create the **special drawing right (SDR)**. SDRs can be seen as a line of credit allocated by the IMF to each country in proportion to its quota (previously defined). Each member country can draw on its line of credit to obtain convertible currencies from the Fund. At the time of its

---

[16] Standby loans are made in emergency cases. The IMF offers a large menu of lending facilities tailored after particular needs. They can be seen at the IMF website: <www.imf.org>.

[17] The 'Keynes Plan' envisioned the creation of an international reserve currency, the bancor, which would play the role gold did in the old gold standard era, but which would be supplied by an international agency, i.e. not the USA.

conception, the SDR was valued at the rate of SDR 35 per ounce of gold, thus making it worth exactly US$1. The SDRs were not, however, backed by gold or dollars. Just like money created by banks, SDRs are valued simply because they are accepted.[18]

After gold convertibility was suspended, the SDR's value was redefined as a basket of four currencies.[19] SDRs yield an interest rate—the weighted average of interest available on the four underlying currencies. Symbolically, the SDR is the IMF's unit of account. As a basket, it is less volatile than any of its components, which has made it convenient for other purposes. Some countries peg their exchange rate to the SDR. Private debt issues have been denominated in SDRs, although technically they are just a basket of the constituent currencies. Some 9 billion SDRs were initially created in 1970, and more were subsequently added, the last time in 1981, to a cumulative total of 21.4 billion. A new allocation was decided in 1997.

19.3.3 Surveillance

The IMF is not just a firefighter. It is also a safety inspector. It continuously monitors the macroeconomic scene in each member country in order to detect possible risks to its currency and to keep abreast of the local situation, should an emergency arise. Surveillance takes several forms:

- Annual visits and evaluations (called Article IV consultations). The IMF's economic assessments and recommendations, once highly confidential, are now posted on the Fund's website (each country has the right to refuse the release of this information, but that is considered a bad signal).

- Twice a year, the IMF publishes the *World Economic Outlook*, which outlines its views of the situation in member countries.

- For countries in difficult situations, the IMF conducts 'enhanced surveillance', which means more frequent evaluations and recommendations.

- For countries that have borrowed from the Fund, the so-called programme countries, the monitoring is more or less permanent, based on agreed-upon targets for policies and outcomes.

- Each government knows that its policies are monitored and that the conclusions are presented to the Executive Board of the Fund. Box 19.3 explains how decisions are made. Surveillance is justified as a preventive means of avoiding disruptive, 'beggar-thy-neighbour' policies that wrecked the world economy during the inter-war period. When countries pursue economic policies that are criticized by the IMF, this disapproval is noticed by the outside world and usually results in internal and external political and financial pressure, which can go far in correcting aberrant policies.

 Box 19.3 How the IMF is Managed

The ultimate authority is exercised by the IMF's Board of Governors which meets, in principle, once a year. The governors are the finance ministers or central bank governors of all member countries. Quotas are distributed according to a formula that involves GDP, current account transactions, foreign exchange reserves, and a measure of volatility of international transactions. Voting rights are proportional to quotas plus a fixed number of 'basic votes' designed to increase the rights of the smaller countries. Table 19.3 displays the quotas and voting rights of the top twenty countries. The most important decisions require 85% of the votes, which gives the USA de facto veto power.

In practice, the Board of Governors delegates managing authority to the Executive Board, which consists of 24 Executive Directors. They reside at the IMF's

---

[18] Hence the following quote by the economist Fritz Machlup: 'Now the forward-looking experts of the Fund and the negotiating governments have proved that their reputation for backwardness in economic thinking had been undeserved. All that matters for the acceptability of anything as a medium of exchange is the expectation that others will accept it. . . . Money needs takers, not backers.' (Quoted by Dam, 1989: 152.)

[19] The four currencies, and their weights in the basket, are the US dollar (44%), the euro (34%), the yen (11%), and the pound (11%), reflecting their international use. The weights are revised every five years.

Box 19.3 **How the IMF is Managed (*Continued*)**

headquarters in Washington and meet nearly every day. The largest-quota countries (the USA, the UK, Germany, France, Japan, China, Russia, and Saudi Arabia) have one executive director each, while the other executive directors represent several countries, grouped along regional lines. The Executive Directors select the Managing Director to run the professional staff.[20] All decisions are taken by the Board of Executive Directors, which cast votes in the name of each country according to its quota. In this way the Executive Directors represent the interests of their countries, while the staff and the Managing Director represent the institution.

19.4 Currency Crises

19.4.1 Booms and Busts

Over the 1990s, the world has become globalized, meaning, among other things, that trade and financial integration has accelerated. Long-standing trade barriers were brought down as many countries (especially in Latin America and Asia), which had long protected themselves from international competition, shifted gears and have become fierce competitors themselves. They also opened up their financial accounts, establishing full currency convertibility and allowing almost complete capital mobility. These liberalization moves were first met by successes. Growth picked up, often led by exports and fed by very sizeable capital inflows.

Then something very ugly happened in many emerging market economies. Capital flows reversed themselves, first slowly, then in a panic rush for the exit. The authorities scrambled to defend their currencies, quickly exhausted initially plentiful reserves, and then threw in the towel. The result was a string of massive depreciations (some of the order of 50%). Indebted local firms and banks which had borrowed in foreign currency, mostly dollars, saw their debts double overnight, making them effectively bankrupt. Domestic and foreign speculators sold the shares of indebted companies on the local stock markets and parked the proceeds in foreign exchange, doubling the pressure on the beleaguered countries.

[20] A long-standing gentlemen's agreement that the IMF's Managing Director is from Europe while the President of the World Bank is from the USA has recently been challenged and criticized by developing countries.

 Table 19.3 **IMF Quotas and Votes in 2012 (as of 1 Jan)**

	Quotas		Votes
	SDR millions	% of total	% of total
1 United States	42,122.4	17.10	16.76
2 Japan	15,628.5	6.57	6.24
3 Germany	14,565.5	6.12	5.81
4 France	10,738.5	4.51	4.29
5 United Kingdom	10,738.5	4.51	4.29
6 China	9,525.0	4.00	3.81
7 Italy	7,882.3	3.31	3.16
8 Saudi Arabia	6,985.5	2.94	2.80
9 Canada	6,369.2	2.68	2.56
10 Russia	5,945.4	2.50	2.39
11 India	5,821.5	2.45	2.34
12 Netherlands	5,162.4	2.17	2.08
13 Belgium	4,605.2	1.94	1.86
14 Brazil	4,250.5	1.79	1.72
15 Spain	4,023.4	1.69	1.63
16 Mexico	3,625.7	1.52	1.47
17 Switzerland	3,458.5	1.45	1.40
18 Korea	3,366.4	1.41	1.37
19 Australia	3,236.4	1.36	1.31
20 Venezuela	2,659.1	1.12	1.09

Source: IMF <www.imf.org/external/np/sec/memdir/members.htm>

Many economies simply folded, plunging millions of bewildered people into unemployment and poverty.

A similar chain of events also occurred in Europe. Trade and financial liberalization was mandated by the Single Market and led EU countries to integrate one with another. Ireland benefited immensely from this integration and, more generally, for a host of the supply-side policies presented in Chapter 18. As elsewhere, mistakes were made and were easy to overlook in an economy growing at such spectacular rates. Figure 19.7 shows how Irish GDP per capita suddenly accelerated in the 1990s. Relatively poor Ireland overtook France—and most other EU countries as well—and then the miracle came to an abrupt end in 2008. As a Eurozone country, Ireland did not suffer from a currency crisis but it was hit by all the indignities seen elsewhere: a banking crisis and a sovereign debt crisis.

Such **boom-and-bust cycles** are nothing terribly new. They have been observed in Chile in 1982, in Mexico in 1986 and again in 1995, in Thailand in 1997, from where it spread to Korea, Indonesia, and the Philippines, then on to Russia and Brazil in 1998. It had also happened, in a milder way, in the UK in 1991, in Finland and Sweden in 1992–1993, and in the USA, Spain, and the UK in 2007.

Boom-and-bust cycles share a number of common features. The boom starts with liberalization. It attracts foreign investment which feeds growth. Growth becomes too rapid to be sustainable, and soon inflationary pressures arise. The authorities, on the other hand, are so pleased that they overlook the growing overvaluation of the exchange rate—who wants to spoil the party with a devaluation? These easy years are usually characterized by unbounded optimism and laxity, and considerable risk-taking. Domestic banks have little trouble obtaining funds from abroad in foreign currencies and lend them on freely in domestic currency. Governments too often borrow abroad in foreign currency, getting better interest rates and betting on the continuation of the miracle. The IMF is either as optimistic as the local authorities, or is a voice in the wilderness as its danger warnings go unheeded. International investors marvel at their successes, but keep a critical eye on the situation.

Then something happens. The current account deficit deepens too much, or some miracle country elsewhere in the world stumbles. Then the investors move out faster than they came, accompanied, if not preceded, by local investors. The crisis erupts and output falls, often deeply. As Figure 19.8 illustrates,

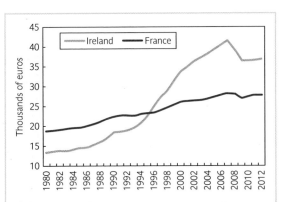

Fig. 19.7 GDP per Capita in Ireland and France 1980–2011

Ireland enjoyed fast and accelerated growth for three decades. Rising optimism and poorly supervised banks fed a housing boom, which sustained and amplified growth. When the tide turned in 2007, Ireland went into a massive crisis.

Sources: AMECO, European Commission.

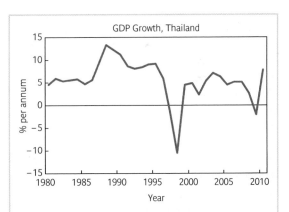

Fig. 19.8 GDP Growth in Thailand

Growth picked up speed, and momentum was carried by massive capital inflows in the 1990s. When these flows reversed direction in 1997, the currency collapsed and the economy went into a tailspin. Despite the severe crisis in 1997–1998, growth recovered in Thailand by the end of the 1990s and remained strong until the global financial crisis in 2008–2009.

Sources: World Bank and Bank of Thailand.

growth eventually returns, and often surprisingly quickly. Yet the confidence of citizens in free markets has been badly shaken, governments have fallen, things may never be the same again. What is remarkable is that things can get so bad after having been so good.

Why do crises occur, then? Crises are like automobile accidents: they seem to happen randomly and unexpectedly, but this is generally not the case. A first class of explanations maintains that dangerous drivers are more likely to have more accidents. Not only can we see the accidents coming, but we can do something to prevent them, either by sending bad drivers to school or by increasing the penalties for hazardous practices. Not all crises can be easily explained by fundamental factors. Many occur for no apparent reason. Self-fulfilling crises occur merely because they are *expected* to occur. While countries with impeccable drivers may be reasonably immune to such accidents, most others are not and can be hit, sometimes as part of a contagious process. We look at these two major interpretations, focusing on currency crises.[21] These crises occur most visibly in countries that operate a fixed exchange rate system, although brutal depreciations also occur in countries that allow their exchange rates to float.

19.4.2 Crises Driven by Fundamentals

Very often currency crises are the unavoidable outcome of policies that are inconsistent with a fixed exchange rate regime. We already know from Chapter 11 that, with perfect capital mobility, monetary policy must be fully dedicated to the fixed exchange rate if that is the chosen regime. Not all governments recognize this point, however. They let the domestic money supply grow too fast, often because this looks like an easy way to finance a budget deficit. We know what happens next: interest rates decline and capital flows out. If the flow is not too large, because of limitations to capital mobility or because real-life markets are a bit more hesitant than theory claims, the authorities believe that they can have the cake and eat it too. They expand money domestically further,

buy it back on the foreign exchange markets to keep up the peg, and sterilize to keep things going.

Recall from Chapter 9 that the asset side of the monetary base is the sum of the central bank's foreign exchange reserves and domestic credit ($M = R + D$). The policy mistake is for the central bank to intervene on the open market to increase the amount of domestic credit that it offers to commercial banks. While domestic credit rises, what happens to demand? It is driven by the private sector's preferences, by the demand for money:

(19.1) $$M = R + D = k(i)PY$$

We can reason assuming that output is constant because it moves little over the weeks or days that lead up to a crisis. For the same reason, we assume that the price level is constant and indexed it as $P=1$. In this short horizon, therefore, money demand is only driven by the interest rate. What then drives the interest rate? We know that, if capital is freely mobile, it must satisfy the interest parity condition presented in Chapter 15. This condition states that the domestic interest rate is equal to the foreign rate less the expected rate of currency appreciation. Formally, it is written as

(19.2) $$i = i^* - \Delta S/S$$

As long as markets believe that the fixed exchange rate will be upheld, if only for just another day, the expected change in the exchange rate ($\Delta S/S$) is nil, and the domestic interest rate i is equal to the foreign rate i^*. This implies that the demand for money stays constant. But how can the money supply stay constant when the monetary authority is increasing domestic credit at the same time?

The intuitive answer is that when money supply runs ahead of money demand, financial institutions sell the domestic currency on the foreign exchange market, which tends to depreciate the exchange rate. Since the rate is fixed, the central bank is compelled to buy back that currency from the selling financial institutions, and does so by selling its foreign exchange reserves. Formally, in (19.1) with demand $k(i)PY$ constant, the supply remains constant, with R declining exactly by the amount that D is increasing. Effectively, financial institutions are selling the

---

[21] We ignore banking and debt crises, although the process is similar.

excess money supply on foreign exchange markets, which puts pressure on the exchange rate, forcing the central bank to intervene to reabsorb the money base that it created in the first place. This looks silly, and it is: it is certainly inconsistent with a Taylor rule. A fundamental crisis, by definition, would be caused by a policy mistake or an adverse shock.[22]

For a while, foreign exchange reserves can be run down gradually. Yet this process cannot continue forever: one day the reserve stock is bound to be depleted. A reasonable central bank would stop its attempt at monetary expansion before it is too late, but here we study what happens if the central bank carries on its misguided policies. Once reserves are exhausted, the fixed exchange rate system must be abandoned for lack of ammunition. But market traders will not wait idly by until the exchange rate collapses. Indeed, the message of Chapter 15 is that they will *anticipate* this event. They understand that once the fixed exchange regime is abandoned, the exchange rate will depreciate. In (19.2) ΔS becomes negative and the interest rate i must increase. This reduces the demand for money and leads to further sales of the domestic currency, which forces the central bank to accelerate the depletion of its foreign exchange reserves. The crisis is the outcome of this cascade of sales of the domestic currency and worsening expectations.

This simple story captures the essence of an exchange crisis. Two aspects are quite striking. First, while it might appear that it is the attack that causes the collapse of the exchange rate regime, nothing could be further from the truth. The exchange rate regime was doomed long before the crisis, its day of reckoning only being delayed by the existence of a large enough stock of foreign exchange reserves. The attack merely determines the timing of the collapse. Second, no one is surprised. All was quiet before the storm, but it was deceiving. Everyone saw it coming and was just waiting for the right time to act. The crisis was fully anticipated. In real life, of course,

there is some uncertainty and things are not quite so clean. Box 19.4 recounts the story of Iceland.

The reasoning so far has emphasized financial causes of crises. Looking at (19.1), however, we can recognize that monetary policy laxity can lead to inflation, as predicted by the *AS–AD* model. When the exchange rate is fixed, high inflation translates into a real appreciation and a loss of competitiveness. Since deflation is long and painful, the most likely way to restore external competitiveness is a nominal exchange rate devaluation. Governments often refuse to devalue their currencies, mostly because they fear a loss of face and adverse political consequences. The markets will watch the deterioration of the current account and a slow erosion of foreign exchange reserves. At some point, they will conclude that the devaluation is overdue. The result will be large-scale sales of the domestic currency and an accelerated depletion of reserves, leading to a full-scale crisis.

19.4.3 Non-fundamental Crises

In contrast with crises that are the outcome of policies that are fundamentally incompatible with a stable exchange rate—one might say, crises that are well-deserved—some currency crises can be self-fulfilling. This term suggests that some crises occur because they are *expected to occur*. The reasoning may sound circular, and it is. A simple variant of the previous example illustrates starkly how crises can be self-fulfilling. The central bank is now assumed to keep domestic credit D constant. The exchange rate peg is credible, as it should be—no one expects the exchange rate to change and the interest rate parity conditions indicate that the interest rate is constant. The demand for money is therefore also constant, as is the stock of foreign exchange reserves. The situation appears perfectly stable and could have gone on forever, were it not for a sudden loss of confidence in the domestic currency, for reasons that are soon to be discussed. If such an exogenous loss of confidence occurs, domestic money is sold and the central bank is forced to spend its foreign exchange reserves to uphold the exchange rate peg. The more it sells its reserves, the weaker it looks and the faster capital flows out as expected depreciation rises, and so does the interest rate, which further reduces the demand for money.

---

[22] Such a policy is inconsistent with adherence to a fixed exchange rate regime, and might otherwise be explained by political meddling. More plausibly, an unexpected recession might reduce sharply the demand for money, leading to a run on the foreign exchange reserves corresponding to the excess money supply at the new level of GDP.

Box 19.4 **Icelandic Aftershocks after the Financial Earthquake**

In the early 2000s, commercial banks in Iceland expanded their activities at amazing speed, both domestically and internationally. Credit boomed and the central bank was as enthusiastic as commercial bank managers about the newly found Eldorado. For a while, as is usual with booms, growth accelerated and foreign exchange reserves grew as the banks repatriated profits earned abroad and foreign investors rushed to receive a share of the pie. But the US financial crisis brutally reminded investors that banks are highly fragile and that prudence is an essential virtue of safe banking. Capital exited as quickly as it came. Even though the Icelandic krona was not pegged, the central bank rushed to slow its free falls, just as it was pouring cash into banks that were facing massive withdrawals. Eventually, the central bank realized that its quickly depleting foreign exchange reserves were insufficient and it had to accept a deep depreciation of the exchange rate. Iceland asked the IMF for emergency support and quickly let its banks be nationalized and restructured. Credit to banks was curtailed and reserves were once again built up over time.

Fig. 19.9 Fundamental Crisis in Iceland in 2008
The evolution of domestic credit and reserves in the months preceding the 2008 currency and financial crisis conforms well with the theory of crises. Easy money (a rising volume of credit) made a crisis inevitable.
Source: IMF.

A natural reaction to this line of reasoning would be to think that any country can be subject to a non-fundamental crisis. Indeed, countries seem to have the same role as commercial banks do in a modern fractional-reserve banking system—as long as there is confidence a particular bank is sound, there won't be a run on it. Here two questions that need to be answered. The first one is: why have the markets lost confidence in the first place? We return to this question shortly. The second question is: does the central bank have the will to fight, or is it rather likely to give up? This is matter of determination and resources.

Central banks typically react to a **self-fulfilling attack** by declaring their firm intention to dig in and fight to the death. But are they willing and able to do so? The central bank must be willing to accept a high and rising interest rate, high enough to reverse the tide of capital outflow. In the meantime, high interest rates depress consumption and investment spending, which can lead to a recession. The central bank must be able to afford the cost of an exchange rate defence, which can be high in both economic and political terms. It must have sufficient reserves to mount the defence. A large stockpile, alongside unflinching central bank determination to resist, may turn sentiment around. If the stockpile is small, it can be enlarged by borrowing from the IMF or other central banks. Box 19.5 explains how East Asian countries have attempted to organize themselves to resist speculative attacks on their exchange rates. Finally, capital outflows can be restricted with controls. The objective is to slow the speed at which reserves are depleted. Box 19.5 also touches upon this issue.

Not all countries, however, stand to fear a self-fulfilling attack. A currency crisis occurs when 'the market' fears that a currency could be depreciated—similarly banking and debt crises reflect a fear that banks will fail or debts will be defaulted upon. However, as explained in Chapter 14, 'the market' brings together a large number of traders who compete fiercely against each other, mainly by taking opposite bets. A speculative attack requires that a large number of traders take a similar view. For that to be the case,

there must pre-exist some **vulnerability** that makes a depreciation plausible. Vulnerabilities are not fundamental weaknesses that make a crisis unavoidable. They are conditions that will make a central bank defence either impossible or too costly.

There are two broad categories of vulnerabilities. The first involves macroeconomic factors. A good example is high unemployment. A restrictive monetary policy response will worsen an already bad situation, to the point where the markets calculate that the central bank will prefer to let the exchange rate go. Another example might be a stock market perceived to be a speculative bubble at risk of crashing. A sharp increase in the interest rate would prick the bubble (see Chapter 14) and could tip the whole market into an uncontrolled free-fall. Examples of crises associated with macroeconomic vulnerabilities include Sweden in 1992, Mexico in 1995, and Argentina in 2001.

Box 19.5 Two South-East Asian Crises and their Aftermath: 1997–1998 and 2007–2008

In June 1997, pressure started to build on the baht, the Thai currency. On 2 July, the Bank of Thailand abandoned its peg, which was followed by an immediate 20% depreciation. Speculation moved promptly to the Philippines peso and the Malaysian ringitt. The peso floated (within bands) on 11 July, and the ringitt followed on 14 July. Next in the eye of the storm, the Indonesian rupiah too was left to float on 14 August. By mid-October, bowing to months of pressure, Vietnam widened the band of fluctuation of the dong, and the Taiwan dollar was devalued. Brazil and Argentina started to feel the pressure at the end of October, while the Bank of Korea started to intervene heavily in defence of the won. When it had to give up on 17 November, the won promptly fell by 10%, which triggered a new wave of attacks against the other currencies in the region (Figure 19.10). Stability finally returned when Korea reached an agreement with the IMF on 3 December, involving the largest loan ever. A conspicuous exception was Indonesia, where a political crisis was under way. The ringitt continued to collapse until President Suharto resigned in late May 1998. By then the ringitt had shed 75% of its initial value.

In 2007–2008, another crisis hit, and many countries from East Asia (Thailand, Indonesia, the Philippines, Malaysia, Korea) faced intense speculative pressure. The crisis started in Thailand, which faced a fundamental crisis. It then spread to other countries in the region, a contagion process that had a strong self-fulfilling flavour. Thailand, Indonesia, the Philippines, and Korea asked the IMF for help. The conditions imposed by the IMF were seen as humiliating and all countries of the region were determined never again to have to borrow from the IMF. To that effect, the Chiang Mai Initiative, named after the city in Thailand it was signed in, organized a system of mutual conditional loans among a dozen of countries. They also undertook to accumulate large stocks of reserves. Under attack in 1998, Malaysia decided not to ask the IMF for help. Instead, it imposed strict capital controls. Since then, the East Asian countries have further developed their cooperation in exchange reserve pooling. Within the G20 Korea is also actively promoting agreements among the world's large central banks for automatic loans.

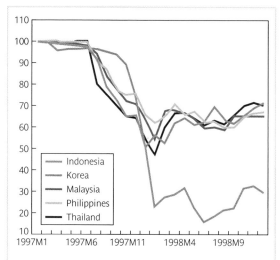

Fig. 19.10 Currency in Crisis (index 100 = January 1997)

The Thai currency was the first to fall in June 1997. The other Asian currencies soon followed, a spectacular case of contagion. When the dust settled, most currencies had lost one-third of their initial value, the Indonesia ringitt being down by 70%.

Source: IMF.

The second category concerns 'balance sheet weaknesses', i.e. a lack of net worth in household, business, or government sectors. This often occurs when the banks, firms, or the government have borrowed money in foreign currency. A depreciation would increase the domestic value of these liabilities and make the debtors insolvent. In that sense, the crisis is self-fulfilling: they are not insolvent in the current situation but a depreciation can bankrupt them. The East Asian crises of 1997–1998, described in Box 19.5, provide examples of this type of crisis. Another example is the case of a highly indebted government. With debt service already high, a sharp increase in the interest rate raises debt service, increases the overall budget deficit, and sends the debt even higher, possibly to levels deemed unsustainable.

The upshot is that self-fulfilling attacks can occur, but only if some underlying vulnerabilities already exist. The vulnerability is not lethal, as in fundamental crises, but when combined with an attack, it makes the cost of a defence of the exchange regime unacceptably high. The existence of a vulnerability is not a guarantee that an attack will occur; it may or it may not, and if it does, it will succeed. An important aspect of non-fundamental crises is the contagion phenomenon. Contagion occurs, when a crisis in one country spreads to others, causing crises there which under a continuation of the status quo would not have occurred. A good illustration is offered by the Asian crisis of 1997–1998, which is described in more detail in Box 19.5.

19.5 The Choice of an Exchange Rate Regime

Ever since the end of the gold standard, policy-makers and economists have debated the merits of fixed versus flexible exchange rates. The choice of exchange rate regime was always perceived to be between fixed-but-adjustable exchange rates of the Bretton Woods system type, or more or less freely floating rates. Fashions have come and gone, from Bretton Woods to Jamaica. Nowadays the pendulum seems to have swung back to a revival of pseudo-gold standard arrangements (monetary unions, currency boards, dollarization) which rely largely on the Hume mechanism. Prompted by the globalization phenomenon and recent crises, the debate has also raised the old question of the desirability of capital liberalization. In this section we review the old debate and move on to the more recent ideas.

19.5.1 An Old Debate: Fixed versus Flexible Exchange Rates

The case for flexible exchange rates

Arguments for flexible exchange rates take two forms: either they praise the virtues of flexible rates, or criticize the limitations of fixed rates. Overall, they can be boiled down to the view that it is better to leave the exchange rate to the markets than to the authorities. On the pro-flexible side:

(1) Exchange rate changes are frequently needed to compensate for inflation differentials (the PPP principle). Fixed exchange rates can only be adjusted sporadically, which leaves long periods when they are misaligned. In addition, such realignments are easily predictable and lead to speculative attacks.

(2) Exchange rate changes are also needed to cope with shocks which alter external competitiveness, e.g. changing energy prices, the emergence of new competitors, etc. With a fixed exchange rate regime, either all prices have to adjust, or the exchange rate must be changed. With wage and price rigidity as a fact of life, the first solution can be protracted and painful, possibly requiring pressure on wages and prices to be brought about by the Phillips curve mechanism, i.e. unemployment.[23]

The most common arguments against fixed exchange rates go like this:

(1) We do not know with much precision what the equilibrium value of the exchange rate should be. Policy mistakes are likely to arise from ignorance, or from misguided political motivations.

(2) Fixed exchange rates are vulnerable to crises. As noted in Section 19.4.4, only those countries with impeccable credentials (no vulnerability, a highly credible central bank) may consider themselves immune to speculative attacks. All the others may be subject to a crisis, first, second, or third generation, with devastating consequences.

The list of cases of exchange rate mismanagement is impressive. It starts with Britain's painful return to an obviously overvalued pre-First World War gold

parity in 1925, to the dollar overvaluation that preceded the collapse of the Bretton Woods system, to numerous cases where thriving black markets indicate that the official parity is off the mark. More recent cases include the decisions of Italy and the UK to leave the European fixed exchange rate mechanism, the Asian crisis, and several crises in Latin America.

The case for fixed exchange rates

This is really a case against flexible rates, and against the view that markets do a better job than the authorities. The case is built on the observation that flexible exchange rates tend to fluctuate widely, too widely to be explained by inflation differentials or real disturbances. Two explanations are usually offered, which are not mutually exclusive:

(1) Overshooting implies that the exchange rate tends to move away from its equilibrium level.

(2) Exchange markets deal with considerable uncertainty with large payoffs when betting right, and large losses when wrong. This leads markets to move in fits and starts, imparting additional uncertainty and instability to the economy.

For good or bad reasons, most European countries have demonstrated a keen attachment to exchange rate stability since 1945. The fear has always been that exchange rate volatility would hurt intra-European trade and threaten the Common Market. The decision to create a monetary union may be seen as the last step in continuous efforts at keeping intra-European exchange rates stable.

19.5.2 The New Debate: Financial Liberalization

Capital controls: The pros and the cons

The process of financial integration, which began in the 1980s and accelerated in the 1990s, has become controversial, if only because it has been linked to the wave of currency crises in the emerging markets. One after another, developed and then developing countries have dismantled capital controls which were put in place at the end of the Second World War, and sometimes long before. The restrictions can take a variety of forms: (1) outright prohibitions of export or

---

[23] In a famous metaphor, a key proponent of flexible rates, Chicago economist and Nobel Prize laureate Milton Friedman noted that the shift to summer time can be achieved by having everyone adapt behaviour and do the same things an hour earlier, or by moving the clock ahead by one hour. The latter is much easier, he argued, than changing the habits of millions of people. Changing the exchange rate is easier than changing millions of prices.

import of money and other financial instruments, (2) limits on such transfers, (3) dual exchange markets (one fixed, for commercial transactions, one flexible for financial transactions), and, more recently, (4) the Tobin tax which is described in Box 19.6. While capital controls are highly controversial, the principles involved are quite straightforward.

Critics of capital controls argue that restrictions to the free movement of capital prevent savers from

getting the best available returns, and prevent firms from borrowing on the best possible terms. Saving and investment both suffer, with adverse effects on long-term growth. They further observe that, by isolating its domestic financial markets, a government can 'milk' them to finance its own budget deficits at costs lower than the international capital market would offer. Furthermore, when capital controls are effective, national interest rates cease to reflect the

---

 Box 19.6 **The Tobin Tax**

Back in 1972, James Tobin, a Yale economist and Nobel Prize laureate, proposed to 'throw sand in the wheels of international finance'. He identified two main objectives, reducing exchange rate volatility and preserving the autonomy of macroeconomic policy (see the main text for the argument), and concluded that restraining capital movements was a worthy effort. The proposal was not well received. As Tobin recalls, 'It did not make much of a ripple. In fact, one might say that it sank . . . I realize that I am opposed by a powerful tide. A widespread orthodoxy holds that financial markets know best, that the discipline they exert on central banks and governments is salubrious' (Tobin 1996).

Tobin claimed that capital movements ought to be slowed down. He was certainly not in favour of the market-unfriendly, administrative restrictions in use at the time. His starting point was the observation that the vast majority of foreign transactions involve round trips of seven days or less, speculative money which serves no productive investment or saving purpose, but rather to enforce the 'no-profit condition'. He argued that a single flat tax on every foreign exchange market transaction of very small magnitude would deter the unproductive short-term trips without much affecting long-term capital movements which underlie productive foreign investment. This is because the longer the holding period, the

less relevant the transaction tax becomes. Investors compute profits and losses from any transaction in annualized terms. For example, a small tax of 0.1% per transaction implies a total cost of 0.2% for a round trip (invest, earn your profit, and bring it back). If the round trip takes a year, it means an annualized cost of 0.2%. If the round trip is quicker, say half a year, the annualized value of the tax about doubles (the law of compounding applies, so it is a bit more but negligibly so). As the horizon shortens, the annualized tax becomes very high, e.g. 10.9% on a week-long trip. As Table 19.4 shows, for very long-term investments the tax becomes negligible.

Recently, the Tobin tax has undergone a revival among both economists and opponents to globalization. One of the motives is the tax revenue that its proponents expect, by some calculations, $300 billion annually with a 0.1% tax. Being an international tax, it could be used for international purposes: the UN and its agencies, relief funds, NGOs, etc. For the same reasons that the Laffer curve exists, there is widespread scepticism that a Tobin tax would yield such revenues, because the markets are likely to react, first by reorganizing themselves to minimize transaction volumes, and second by migrating to safe havens—in the limit, a ship in international waters, stuffed with trading terminals and computer servers.

Table 19.4 **The Impact of a 0.1% Tobin Tax and the Holding Period of Investments**

Holding period of investment	1 day	2 days	1 week	1 month	6 months	1 year	5 years
Implicit tax (annualized basis)	55.2%	24.6%	10.9%	2.4%	0.4%	0.2%	0.04%

local economic situation. Since high and rising interest rates signal a worsening situation, they tend to discipline imprudent governments. Shutting down the signal offers relief to governments, but at the cost of a worsening situation in the future, possibly leading to a crisis on the way.

Those in favour of capital controls present three main arguments. First, following on an argument initially spelled out by Keynes, they claim that financial markets are unstable, prone to fads and panics. The result is volatility that is unjustified by underlying economic fundamentals, and is costly to firms and households.

Second, following on the Mundell–Fleming result that full capital mobility prevents the use of monetary policy under fixed exchange rates, and makes fiscal policy impotent under flexible rates, they argue that restricting capital mobility restores the option of using demand management instruments. When applied to monetary policy, this principle is the impossible trilogy already discussed in Section 19.2.4.

Third, saving is a source of growth if it is invested in productive uses such as plants, machinery, schooling and training, etc. The proponents of capital controls note that the bulk of international capital movements are of a very short-term nature, even aimed at intra-day trading opportunities, rather than long-term investment in human or physical capital.

The link with exchange rate regimes

The macroeconomic policy independence argument has a direct bearing on the debate on the choice of an exchange rate regime. The main weakness of fixed exchange rate regimes under full capital mobility is that in most cases they require the abandonment of an independent monetary policy. It requires some discipline for central bankers to give up any hope of influencing local monetary conditions, and few central banks have lived up to the requirement.[24] As a result, fixed exchange rate regimes are prone to speculative crises and have shown rather limited survival ability.

---

[24] One excellent example is the central bank of the Netherlands after the mid-1980s, which almost dogmatically tracked German monetary policy until monetary union was implemented.

The argument can be turned on its head, however. A direct implication of the impossible trilogy principle is that fixed exchange rate regimes are more likely to survive when capital controls are in place. A good example is Europe's EMS. It operated reasonably well in the 1980s until capital controls were removed by 1990. The system was badly shaken shortly thereafter in 1992. Thus the choice is not just between fixed and flexible exchange rates, but also involves the capital mobility regime. Countries which value exchange rate stability should not rule out restrictions on capital movements altogether. Similarly, countries which favour full capital mobility should not stick to a fixed exchange rate regime for too long. The question of fixed versus flexible exchange rates has become central to the accession process of transition countries, and it is reviewed in Box 19.7.

However, if full capital mobility is considered an inexorable evolution of economic relations, the fixed exchange rate option may be going the way of the hula hoop and bell-bottomed pants. The impossible trilogy means that monetary policy autonomy must be sacrificed, but few countries are prepared for such a step that may be difficult to defend on the domestic political front. Furthermore, the phenomenon of second-generation crises suggests that it may take years, possibly decades, before the central bank has achieved a level of credibility which eliminates vulnerabilities. In the meantime, the threat of currency crises looms large. The **hollowing-out hypothesis** maintains that the choice of exchange rate regimes is no longer between floating rates and soft pegs—the traditional fixed-and-adjustable exchange rates—but between floating rates and hard pegs (regimes described in the next section). Critics of the hollowing-out hypothesis argue that soft pegs are still feasible, provided bands of fluctuations are large enough or the peg is allowed to vary (e.g. crawling pegs) to account for changing economic conditions.

Optimal sequencing

Back in the early 1950s, nearly all countries operated in strictly controlled environments. Many prices were fixed, some goods were even rationed, commercial banks were heavily regulated, and financial markets were limited or non-existent. External controls regu-

Box 19.7 Exchange Rate Regimes in the New EU Member Countries

The ten countries that joined the European Union (EU) in 2004 and the two countries that joined in 2007 are committed to adopt the euro as their own currencies as soon as possible. Meanwhile, they are pledged to join the ERM (see Section 19.2.4), i.e. to peg their currencies to the euro. As Table 19.5 shows, seven of them promptly joined the ERM, and five of them have since adopted the euro. The two remaining countries are the Baltic states, which have expressed their desire to join the euro area. Lithuania actually applied in 2007 but entry was refused because it did not fulfil all the required conditions. Yet, Lithuania and Estonia have rigidly fixed their exchange rate to the deutschmark first, and the euro next, for more than a decade. Their currency board arrangements (described later) make them de facto members of the euro area. Bulgaria is also trying to hitch its monetary fate to the euro, adopting a similar currency board regime.

The three larger new EU members, the Czech Republic, Hungary, and Poland, have not yet joined the ERM, and allow their exchange rates to float more or less. With current inflation rates often much higher than in the euro area and occasional budgetary problems, their chances of being admitted to the monetary union are rather slim in the near term.

Some older EU members have not adopted the euro. Two of them, Denmark and the UK, have been given an 'opt-out' clause, which gives them their right to do so. Denmark decided to join the ERM when the euro was launched in 1999, even though it is not pledged to it either. While Sweden does not have an opt-out clause, it behaves as if it does. Sweden and the UK, therefore, operate a fully floating exchange rate regime and have no plan to change policy. There are occasional discussions in Denmark regarding euro area membership, which would have to be approved by a referendum.

 Table 19.5 Situation of Recent EU Members and Non-Euro Area Members

	EU membership	ERM membership	Euro adoption
Bulgaria	2007	No	No
Cyprus	2004	2005	2008
Czech Republic	2004	No	No
Denmark	1973	1999	Opt-out
Estonia	2004	2004	2011
Hungary	2004	No	No
Latvia	2004	2005	No
Lithuania	2004	2004	No
Malta	2004	2005	2008
Poland	2004	No	No
Romania	2007	No	No
Slovakia	2004	2005	2009
Slovenia	2004	2004	2008
Sweden	1995	No	No
UK	1973	Opt-out	Opt-out

lated exports and imports, tariffs were heavy, and capital flows were essentially forbidden. What a difference a half-century can make! Liberalization seems an inescapable trend, and basic economic principles support this trend. On the other hand, liberalization has not always been an easy journey. The Asian crisis once more showed that there can be serious setbacks on the way.

Is there a better way of liberalizing? The response is to adopt a proper **sequencing** of liberalization. McKinnon[25] has proposed an optimal order of sequencing. It is based on two main ideas. First, liberalization should start with the restrictions that are costliest in terms of economic efficiency. Second, some steps need to be taken before others to avoid inconsistencies. The first step should be the creation of well-functioning domestic goods markets: free prices and abolish rationing. It makes little sense to have free external trade if domestic trade is heavily constrained. The second step should be the gradual liberalization of international trade, starting with administrative measures (quotas on exports and imports), moving on to eliminating export tariffs,

---

[25] Ronald McKinnon, a Stanford economist, has also contributed to the theory of optimum currency areas.

and then finally reducing import tariffs to avoid shocks to domestic producers.

Soon after the first step, the domestic financial sector should be liberalized, under competitive conditions. Banks should be allowed to set interest rates freely on deposits and loans, to open branches as they see fit, and to choose the range of services that they offer their customers. Bank regulation and supervision should be developed in parallel to ensure the soundness of the banking system.

Domestic financial markets come next. Bonds and stock markets are allowed to compete with the banking system to both collect savings and finance borrowing by firms and public entities. Here again, regulation and supervision must proceed in parallel to guarantee a proper functioning of naturally unstable markets. Finally, external financial liberalization follows. The Asian crisis well illustrates the risks of full capital mobility when the domestic financial sector is not functioning properly. Furthermore, the exchange regime must be appropriately adapted to changing circumstances, as rigidly fixed exchange rates are unlikely to survive capital mobility when full capital mobility is established.

19.5.3 Currency Boards and Dollarization

The menu of exchange rate regimes has recently been enlarged. A number of countries have adopted new arrangements which were once regarded as curiosities. These 'hard pegs' differ from the soft pegs by the fact that they do not allow margins of fluctuations and that they rule out realignments (devaluations or revaluations). Hume's mechanism has made a comeback by eliminating discretionary monetary policy entirely and reducing central banks to the role of passive *bureaux de change*. Three varieties of hard pegs have been observed which are worth noting: (1) dollarization and euroization, and (2) currency boards.

Dollarization and euroization

Dollarization is the unilateral adoption by a country of the US dollar as sole legal tender, which can be thought of as a one-sided monetary union with the USA. It can involve the link to another currency, e.g. the euro. It is as close to the gold standard as a monetary system can be, without having gold itself circulate. It functions in the same way, including Hume's mechanism. It is another variety of hard pegs.

A number of countries never had their own currency. Panama and Liberia have had dollarized economies since their independence. Ecuador and El Salvador adopted the dollar in 2000 and 2001, respectively. Argentina flirted with the idea in 1999. In order to bring its hyperinflation to a halt, Zimbabwe effectively adopted the dollar in 2009. Kosovo has euroized. One reason for dollarizing is the perception that a foreign central bank will do a better job at enforcing price stability than an indigenous one. Another reason is a proven inability to come to grips with inflation, as in the case of Ecuador. If trade links with the country whose currency is adopted are intensive, it seems like a good idea. It remains, however, that the domestic interest rate is driven by completely foreign economic conditions, which may be awkward.

Currency boards

Currency boards used to be the arrangement of choice in the British Empire. They have made a comeback, starting with Hong Kong in 1983, followed by Argentina in 1991, Estonia in 1992, Lithuania in 1994, and Bulgaria and Bosnia-Herzegovina in 1997. Currency boards resemble dollarization, except that the local currency is maintained. There are three key features of a currency board:

(1) A fixed exchange rate is established vis-à-vis an anchor currency. The local currency is fully convertible in unlimited amounts into the anchor currency at that rate.

(2) The local currency is fully backed by reserves. This is required to ensure full and unlimited convertibility.

(3) Currency boards often hold reserves of 105% or 110% of their liabilities, a precaution since most money is produced by commercial banks which are not restricted to 100% backing. In practice, it means that the high-powered money supply is entirely driven by the balance of payments via Hume's mechanism. Monetary authorities are completely passive.

With the exception of Hong Kong, currency boards have usually been adopted by countries that have long suffered high inflation and felt that there was no political will to establish a full-blown independent central bank dedicated to price stability. One transition country, Estonia, started off with a currency board, and its success at avoiding inflation has inspired Lithuania and Bulgaria.

It might seem strange for independent countries to give up control over their monetary policy. Yet it is the logical consequence of the impossible trinity: with full capital mobility, fixed exchange rates imply the loss of monetary policy autonomy. Even with a currency board, however, the threat of crises remains. After ten years of using a dollar-based currency board, Argentina gave up and let its currency float, with painful consequences. The only way to eliminate that threat is to eliminate the currencies themselves. Since there is no real policy autonomy to lose, the system can only be strengthened. While this speaks for a monetary union, giving up monetary or exchange rate policy completely has its own consequences and costs, to be outlined in 19.5.4.

19.5.4 Monetary Unions

A monetary union involves the *irrevocable* fixing of exchange rates and the abandonment of margins of fluctuation among a number of countries. In fact, it means that individual currencies are no longer distinguishable; a common currency is used. The immediate implication is that individual central banks lose any remaining autonomy, although one central bank is needed to manage the common currency. This is a special case of the **N –1 problem** spelled out earlier in Box 19.2. The union's central bank manages the overall money supply. Interest rates are the same across the union since money can flow freely. National money supplies are then determined via the Hume mechanism.[26] In principle, if a country in the monetary union runs a balance of payments surplus, money should flow in, the national money supply rises, and interest rates fall. A deficit results in a loss of money, a rise in interest rates, and an associated contraction. So goes the theory, at least.

There is a well-developed theory of **optimum currency areas** which spells out criteria for creating a monetary union. A region constitutes an optimum currency area when its use of a common currency implies no loss of welfare.[27] The best way of thinking about it is to ask what is lost when the exchange rate instrument is abandoned. This becomes problematic when the union is buffeted by asymmetric shocks, i.e. shocks which hurt some members but not the others. It is precisely under these conditions—and when wages and prices are sticky – when the exchange rate is useful. Adjustment to asymmetric shocks must take place through prices, which can be very painful.

The theory of optimal currency areas looks for criteria which makes such adjustment unnecessary. Robert Mundell proposed two main criteria:

(1) *Factor mobility*. Consider the case when an adverse shock, e.g. a loss of competitiveness, hits a country. The country soon goes into a recession, and laments the loss of its exchange rate, which could have been handy to restore its external competitiveness. If, however, its factors of production could move out to more fortunate members of the monetary union, the pain would be spread out, and the common central bank could use the common external exchange rate to adjust optimally. If capital or labour, or both, are mobile, there would be little cost in unemployment of factors, and the loss of internal (within the union) exchange rates would be trivial.

(2) *Absence of asymmetric shocks*. Most of the shocks concern the world demand for and supply (competitiveness) of locally produced goods. If the members of the union produce a similar menu of goods, then the likelihood of asymmetric shocks diminishes. The same applies if the member countries produce a very diversified menu of

---

[26] The mechanism described here is somewhat more general than Hume's in the following sense: an expansion of the local money supply is not predicated on a trade surplus, but could also be achieved with a capital account surplus (an excess of private capital flows).

[27] The seminal work on optimum currency areas is by Robert Mundell, the same economist who shaped the Mundell–Fleming framework presented in Chapter 11.

goods. In that case a particular shock is likely to be of little import.

Practical examples abound which call for a common currency. No one would doubt that London should use the same money as the rest of England, or that Paris should use the same currency as the rest of France. Large, open cities meet the conditions for a currency area hands down. First, national capitals are the epicentres of labour and capital in a country, and mobility—especially of young people—into cities is very high. Second, the shocks, both positive and negative, which hit these capitals certainly have strong correlation with the rest of the country. At the same time, the sceptic might ask: what about Scotland or Northern Ireland in the UK, or Catalonia in Spain, or the new federal states of Germany? Here a single currency has been used, sometimes begrudgingly, for some time; but this was not always the case.

Obviously economic actors can be conditioned to make do with a common currency, with behaviour and economic structures adapting accordingly. The symmetry of shocks between Belgium, the Netherlands, and Germany has increased significantly since the 1960s, so that these countries are as fit for a monetary union now as the German states were in the 1960s. Sometimes politics are more important than economics. As Box 19.8 shows, this was true for the first, unsuccessful European monetary union—under Charlemagne in the ninth century—as it is for the present one.

19.5.5 The European Monetary Union

We conclude this chapter with a quick sketch of the European Monetary Union or Eurozone. This unique arrangement, in which sovereign states share a common central bank and a common money, has existed

---

 Box 19.8 Charlemagne's European Monetary Union

One of the most interesting attempts to use monetary union as an instrument of political union was by the first Carolingian king, Charlemagne. In his quest to unify Europe, Charlemagne was not loathe to employ the sword, but understood the importance of a single, harmonized currency for the promotion of commerce and trade. At the Council of Frankfurt in 794—which was ostensibly about religious matters—a supposed minor detail was also on the table. Charlemagne, who was fascinated by economic affairs, saw the advantage of a common *standard* for coinage in the conquered territories of Spain and Southern and Central Europe. Even if the conversion of precious metal into coins was decentralized, it would be advantageous to use a single definition and metal content for those coins. Charlemagne seemed to understand that the gold standard could have deflationary consequences; because it was so rare, trade using gold was impractical for all but the most valuable transactions.

So the gold *sou* was replaced by the silver *livre carolinienne* (which eventually became the pound!). It was worth 240 denarii, possibly inspired by the success of the Islamic

dinar. Common currency, with common minting standards, enlarged the trading area and reduced transactions costs. Furthermore, the new currency was legal tender:

Everywhere, in every city and every trading place, the new denarii are also to be legal tender and to be accepted by everybody. And if they bear the monogram of our name and are of pure silver and full weight, should anyone reject, in any place, in any transaction of purchase or sale, he is to pay 15 soldi [roughly the price of a cart load of wheat]. (Article 5 of the protocol of the Council of Frankfurt.)

After Charlemagne died, his realm was partitioned among his sons and the political union of Europe soon dissolved into the Middle Ages. Obviously, monetary union was not a sufficient condition for the political unification of Europe, but it did sustain the economy of the Carolingian empire for a number of centuries. Later, the Edict of Pitres in 864 (during the reign of Charles the Bald) would tighten the grip on seigniorage rights, significantly restricting the number of authorized coinage sites. Perhaps the wisdom of Charlemagne was undermined by the greed of his grandson?

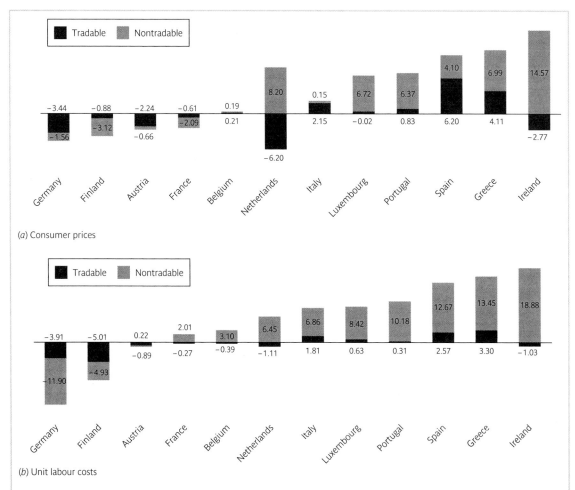

(a) Consumer prices

(b) Unit labour costs

Fig. 19.11 Cumulative Price Level and Unit Labour Cost Changes Relative to Eurozone-12 Average, 1999–2010

This figure cumulates changes in the price level (panel (a)) and unit labour costs, the ratio of wages to nominal productivity (panel (b)) for twelve Eurozone countries that were in the monetary union from the beginning. For each country, pink bars represent the contribution of tradable goods sectors to the total change in unit labour costs; orange bars show the contribution of nontradable sectors. The sum of the two bars represents the total deviation of unit labor costs from the average development in the Eurozone-12 group over the period. Evidently, the lion's share of the misalignment originates in nontraded output.
Source: Brede (2011).

since 1999; euro coins and banknotes have circulated in the 'euro area' since 2002. The Eurozone is an increasingly important component of the global financial architecture. Starting with 11 members, it had grown by 2012 to 17 countries with a population of more than 332 million—more inhabitants than the USA. The role of the euro in international payments is well-established and will probably grow over time.

Many economists were, and still are, doubtful that a common money will advance the cause of European integration. This is because, at the outset, Europe didn't seem to meet the necessary conditions for a

Box 19.9 The Euro-Crisis: Fundamental or Non-fundamental?

The European Monetary Union crisis started in late 2009 with a sharp rise in yields on government debt of Greece, spreading to other southern European countries, Portugal and Italy, that were seen at the time as fiscally sound. It also spread to Ireland and Spain, two countries with solid public finances that were hit by the bursting of private real estate bubbles. Facing severe difficulties in the banking sector, the Irish and Spanish governments were led to recapitalize the banks and to guarantee depositors, which opened up gaping holes in their budgets.

One interpretation of the Euro-crisis—a crisis of banks, government deficits and public debt—is that it is fundamental. In the European Monetary Union, nations of the Eurozone are sovereign, and the Stability and Growth Pact, designed to impose fiscal discipline, obviously failed. Furthermore, the Maastricht Treaty did not explicitly provide for intervention at the EU level in case governments find themselves unable to borrow on financial markets at a reasonable interest rate. In addition, since the advent of monetary union in 1999, some countries (Greece, Portugal, Ireland) have run large persistent current account deficits while others (Germany, Netherlands, Finland) ran surpluses (Table 19.6). In principle, these imbalances should be self-correcting, in line with the Hume mechanism described in Section 19.2. Figure 19.11 shows, the extent to which prices and labour costs—especially for non-traded goods—have deviated across countries since the beginning of the monetary union.

Another, equally plausible interpretation of the crisis is that it is non-fundamental, like the speculative attacks described in Section 19.4.3. Such an attack requires a vulnerability; in this case it was long-lasting budget deficits and quickly mounting public debts. If the financial markets conclude that several Eurozone countries lack the political will to stabilize their debt/GDP ratios, they come to expect defaults and require higher bond yields. These higher interest rate costs, in turn, require higher primary surpluses to fulfil the conditions for solvency, which raises the probability of defaults and therefore calls for further increases in bond yields. The markets began to ask whether the financially healthier countries of Europe would be willing to provide money needed to avoid defaults. This made the crisis a collective one. In this view, in order to convince the markets that the non-fundamental expectations are simply wrong, a sufficiently strong backstop is needed—either a greatly expanded European Financial Stability Fund, or the European Central Bank, taking seriously its role as a lender of last resort.

monetary union put forth by Mundell.[28] By most accounts, Europe is still far from achieving the status of an integrated single economic region such as the states of the USA, or the provinces of Canada, or Mexico, or Brazil. The recent Euro-crisis, which is primarily a fiscal crisis with first-order ramifications for monetary and financial stability, has sharpened this critique. The European Monetary Union faces significant challenges to its existence in the years to come. Box 19.9 summarizes some of the most salient of these challenges, including those that can only be settled in the political arena.

Yet ever since the founding of the Economic Community in 1957, Europeans have believed that increasing integration was the secret to securing lasting peace and preventing future armed conflict. Ironically, Europe has a chronic history of wars over the past two millennia, many of which coincided with or were followed by monetary unions. In particular, monetary union frequently coincided with the rise of new nation-states. Box 19.8 gave one example of an early attempt to institute a monetary union in Europe. It failed, yet it shared many of the motives of the euro—to create the fundamental conditions for greater peace and prosperity. It highlights how economic, political, and social progress in Europe was rough sailing at the outset. In times of growing globalization and international turbulence, the 'European project' may finally reach smoother waters as the continent comes to political and social terms with itself.

---

[28] The influential economist Martin Feldstein stated in a widely-publicized article in 1997 that European Monetary Union could even lead to civil unrest and war.

Table 19.6 **Eurozone Current Account Surpluses (as % of GDP)**

	1980 – 1995	1996 – 2000	2001 – 2005	2006 – 2010
Austria	−1.0	−1.8	1.6	3.4
Belgium	1.5	5.5	3.3	0.5
Cyprus	−5.2	−2.7	−4.1	−10.2
Estonia	−4.6	−7.6	−9.7	−6.8
Finland	−1.5	5.7	6.2	3.3
France	−0.2	2.2	0.8	−1.3
Germany	1.0	−1.0	2.7	6.3
Greece	−3.1	−4.5	−6.7	−12.3
Ireland	−2.4	1.5	−1.1	−3.4
Italy	−0.8	1.6	−0.9	−2.7
Luxembourg	11.7	10.8	10.2	8.1
Malta	−11.0	−7.9	−3.8	−7.5
Netherlands	4.4	4.1	5.2	6.6
Portugal	−2.4	−7.2	−8.8	−10.9
Slovakia	−2.1	−7.1	−7.7	−5.3
Slovenia	2.1	−1.4	−0.8	−3.2
Spain	−1.3	−1.7	−4.7	−7.7

Source: IMF World Economic Outlook Database.

❶ Summary

1 International monetary arrangements initially arose from the need to provide international trade with an easy means of settling cross-border payments. For centuries, both domestic and international trade was carried out using gold and silver. The gold standard in its pure form lasted less than 40 years, from 1879 to 1914.

2 Taken literally, the gold standard implied a rigid monetary rule and a fixed exchange rate regime. By the Hume mechanism, a trade deficit caused a shrinking money supply, while a surplus meant an expanding money supply. Both act to equilibrate trade imbalances.

3 The evolution of the monetary system after the First World War can be seen as a series of ad hoc responses to international crises and system inadequacies. In particular, the Bretton Woods system was designed to avoid the competitive devaluations of the inter-war period by establishing a system of fixed exchange rates based on the US dollar's link to gold. This 'gold exchange standard' was not a gold standard in the strict sense.

4 The collapse of the Bretton Woods system was due to the internal inconsistencies of a system that required increasing amounts of international reserves to be provided by the USA, which were, in theory, convertible into gold. Large US balance of payment deficits in the late 1960s created an overhang of official external dollar liabilities which far exceeded the USA's gold assets.

5 The IMF fulfils two main roles: (1) it exercises surveillance over member countries on a routine basis, and (2) it provides emergency assistance to countries which face balance of payments difficulties. Its loans are conditional on the adoption and implementation of programmes designed to cope with the source of payment imbalances.

6 Currency crises can be divided into two types. (1) First-generation crises occur when domestic policies are incompatible with the exchange rate peg. They are usually anticipated. (2) Second generation crises are self-fulfilling. They afflict central banks which appear vulnerable or uncommitted to an exchange rate target, or which have not acquired sufficient credibility.

7 Currency crises seem to be contagious for three reasons: (1) first-generation contagion through loss of competitiveness; (2) second-generation contagion when markets discover similar vulnerabilities or lack of central bank commitment; and (3) investors' contagion when losses in one country prompt international players to withdraw from other countries which suddenly appear risky.

8 Capital liberalization brings about long-term benefits. But financial markets are prone to bouts of instability which may result in currency crises. In addition, full capital mobility severely restricts the ability to carry out macroeconomic policies (Mundell–Fleming).

9 The choice of an exchange rate regime involves various trade-offs. In the end, small, open economies may favour some degree of exchange rate stability, while larger countries may prefer to integrate themselves in the world economy at fluctuating real exchange rates.

10 The widespread shift to capital account liberalization has had the effect of sharpening the choice between floating and fixed exchange rates. Soft pegs are increasingly seen as dangerous, hence the fashion for hard pegs: monetary unions, currency boards, and dollarization.

11 The European Monetary Union faces challenges which have to do not only with fiscal and current account imbalances, but also with its very architecture. It presumes that the member countries in fact meet the criteria for a viable currency area. Like the Bretton Woods system before it, imbalances can develop that can be eliminated only via the Hume mechanism, or the intervention of a central authority. This central authority has yet to be established.

🔑 Key Concepts

- **International Monetary Fund (IMF)**
- **gold standard**
- **bimetallism**
- **Gresham's law**
- **band of fluctuation**
- **Hume mechanism**
- **Bretton Woods conference**
- **gold exchange standard**

- **quota**
- **conditionality**
- **Triffin paradox**
- **Exchange Rate Mechanism (ERM)**
- **speculative attacks**
- **central parity; parity**
- **European Monetary Union (EMU)**
- **impossible trilogy**

- ◆ special drawing rights (SDRs)
- ◆ boom-and-bust cycles
- ◆ speculative attacks
- ◆ self-fulfilling attacks
- ◆ vulnerabilities

- ◆ hollowing-out hypothesis
- ◆ sequencing
- ◆ $N - 1$ problem
- ◆ optimum currency area

❓ Exercises

1 Why can't beggar-thy-neighbour policies work? What is the difference with tariff wars?

2 Does the Hume mechanism work within a monetary union?

3 'Currency crises cannot be foreseen, markets attack as soon as they expect a crisis.' Comment. In your answer, you may distinguish between first-generation and self-fulfilling crises.

4 Draw the implications of the $N - 1$ problem for the international monetary system and for regional exchange rate arrangements like the EMS.

5 Can self-fulfilling crises also affect the banking system?

6 'The developing countries cannot borrow in their own currencies. This puts them at permanent risk of a currency crisis.' Explain and comment.

➲ Essay Questions

1 The poorer countries regularly propose that the IMF issue more SDRs and that they be distributed mostly to the poorer countries to support their development. The richer countries refuse, contending that this would be inflationary. Discuss.

2 It has been said that the Bretton Woods system was doomed from its start. Explain why. Could its demise have been avoided? How?

3 Is a return to the gold standard feasible? Desirable?

4 The choice of an exchange rate regime is difficult. The European Monetary Union combines fixed exchange rates among its members with a floating exchange rate vis-à-vis the rest of the world. Does it square the circle?

5 Quotas and voting rights at the IMF have been changed in April 2008. The decision is presented in <www.imf.org>. How would you evaluate this change?

Epilogue 20

The ideas of economists and political philosophers, both when they are right and when they are wrong, are more powerful than is commonly understood. Indeed the world is ruled by little else. Practical men, who believe themselves to be quite exempt from any intellectual influences, are usually the slaves of some defunct economist.

J. M. Keynes

Throughout this book, we have emphasized the usefulness of macroeconomics as a tool for understanding and improving the way the world works. To this aim, we have presented a unified treatment of the field, and have downplayed the historical evolution of ideas over the years as well as important controversies, past and present, which have accompanied these ideas. Focusing on controversies can be fascinating, but it can also cloud the extent of agreement and common understanding, leaving the unsatisfactory impression that macroeconomics is too conflict-ridden to be of any practical use. Once the basic framework is well understood, it is both interesting and illuminating to track the field's intellectual history. In this concluding chapter we present a highly compressed survey of the major steps of the field's development, the key players, and the policy debates. Its emphasis is on the European scene.[1]

20.1 **The Keynesian Revolution**

John Maynard Keynes, 1883 – 1946

The birth of macroeconomics is conventionally associated with the publication in 1936 of Keynes' *The General Theory of Employment, Interest and Money*. Its influence has been phenomenal. Some even claim that it changed more lives in the twentieth century than any other single work. Many factors explain this success.

The book came out towards the end of the Great Depression and can be seen as the response of economic research to challenges of the time. To contemporaries who had witnessed the rapid rise of mass unemployment, the classical laissez-faire view looked factually wrong and almost immoral. Others had already moved in the same direction, but Keynes brought together many apparently disparate themes. The idea that prices do not necessarily clear at full employment had been put forward by the British economist Robert Malthus (1766–1834). Knut

Wicksell (1851–1926) and his successors, who came to be known as the 'Stockholm School', had gone quite a long way towards what was to become the *IS* curve. Other economists—including Hjalmar Schacht, who single-handedly vanquished the German hyperinflation in 1923 and later went on to become Hitler's Finance Minister—had long advocated deficit spending on public works during the Great Depression. But Keynes' attack was unique in many ways. *The General Theory* proposed a wholly new concept of equilibrium, even though it took decades to fully decipher what it really meant. It was a combination of scholarly analysis, strident criticism, and practical policy recommendations that appealed to both theoreticians and policy-makers. Keynes did not just aim at fellow researchers. He frequently descended the ivory tower of academia to promote his ideas in the media, where his reputation as a brilliant and provocative polemicist was well established.

The truth is that Keynes was a man of many talents and, by 1936, of great experience as well. As a young economist during the First World War, he had worked

[1] In preparing this chapter, we have benefited from very useful comments and suggestions from Charles Bean, Irwin Collier, Barry Eichengreen, Hans Genberg, Francesco Giavazzi, Guido Tabellini, and Jürgen von Hagen.

in the UK Treasury, which he represented at the Versailles Peace Conference, until he resigned in a rather undiplomatic fashion. In *The Economic Consequences of the Peace*, he criticized the harsh reparations imposed on Germany, maintaining that it would be destabilized by the economic burden of the Treaty. His analysis turned out to be prophetic, and established his reputation among policy-makers. The book also strained Keynes' relations with British government circles until the Second World War. His strident criticism of Chancellor Winston Churchill's decision to return the pound to its pre-war parity did not help in this regard. Maynard, as his friends called him, was also a charismatic intellectual leader. He assembled a group of brilliant economists at Cambridge University who went on to dominate the profession in Britain and beyond.

One important message of the Keynesian revolution was that fiscal policy can be used to fight recessions, in particular when monetary policy is ineffective—either because expansionary monetary policy no longer lowers the nominal interest rate or when investment spending is depressed by bad 'animal spirits'. Deficit spending, as it was then called, was taken on board in many countries after the war, in effect becoming conventional wisdom. German-speaking countries too have been influenced by Keynesian ideas, but scepticism there has been present and, to this day, a large segment of the policy-making and academic establishments see them as dangerous. German reluctance towards Keynesianism is linked to the role that deficit finance had in the hyperinflation of 1922–1923. This mistrust of Keynesian policies has found its way, in a subdued form, in the monetary union's Stability and Growth Pact and in the statements of the European Central Bank (ECB), in which fiscal deficits tend to be seen as a source of concern rather than as a potential means of output stabilization. In most of Europe, though, Keynesian ideas are still alive, although their limits—described in Chapters 16 and 17—are generally well recognized.

Keynes' theory was not fully worked out. *The General Theory* is difficult to read, frequently lacks precision and can sometimes be downright confusing. It fell upon Keynes' disciples to dot the i's. Most of the effort was conducted in his native Britain and in the USA, with some important contributions from other countries, including that of the Polish economist Michal Kalecki (1899–1970), who had anticipated many of Keynes' ideas and went on to try to merge Keynesian and Marxist schools of thought.

Beyond clarifying Keynes' views, one task that his disciples had to grapple with was to reconcile the Keynesian construction with generally accepted theories. It soon emerged, indeed, that the attack on the 'classics', as Keynes labelled established neoclassical economics, was not at all general and rested on the assumption that the price level is constant. This assumption was acceptable in situations of low employment, like the Great Depression, but was seriously at odds with post-war economic conditions, characterized by full employment and, later on, rising inflation. The necessary reconciliation effort, the neoclassical synthesis introduced in Chapter 12, was carried out mostly in the USA, with Nobel Prize laureate Paul Samuelson (1915– 2009) and his MIT colleagues at the forefront, but also by Keynes' colleague in Cambridge, John Hicks (1904–1989), and by Don Patinkin from Hebrew University in Jerusalem (1922–1995).

European macroeconomists were not particularly productive during this period, with a few notable exceptions. Some Swedish economists, under the leadership of Assar Lindbeck (1930–), and their Norwegian colleagues developed a small open economy version of the Keynesian model. Nobel laureates Jan Tinbergen, from the Netherlands, and James Meade (1907–1995), a student of Keynes' in Cambridge, also made major contributions in extending Keynes' framework to the small open economy case. The most innovative construction in the Keynesian tradition was the Mundell–Fleming model presented in Chapter 11. Its architects were Marcus Fleming (1911–1976), a British economist working in the International Monetary Fund, and Nobel laureate Robert Mundell (1932–), who was undoubtedly inspired by the smallness and openness of his native Canada and of Switzerland, where he lived for a time.

An important implication of Keynesian economics was that countries as a whole could be a research subject. Today, it is hard to believe that pre-Keynesian economics was mostly preoccupied with sectors and firms, and had little to say about questions such as growth or employment.[2] In fact, aggregate data, like GDP, the unemployment rate, or the consumer price index, were sporadically collected and seldom the subject of great research interest. The rise of Keynesian economics prompted a vigorous effort at developing the relevant concepts and assembling the data. This effort started in the late 1930s at a time when most of the leading economists were either in the USA or in Great Britain. Unsurprisingly, therefore, the main contributions were developed in these two countries, with early pioneers such as Simon Kuznets (1901–1985) from Columbia University and Richard Stone (1913–1991), a Keynes student from Cambridge, both of whom were eventually awarded the Nobel Prize for their work. Once data was available, and with the advent of the first computers, economists have undertaken to build large-scale models that were meant to mimic the economy. Following early work by Italian-born Nobel laureate Franco Modigliani, these large models have become standard fares in most finance ministries, international organizations, and economic forecasting companies, where they are routinely used to produce forecasts and simulate the effects of policy decisions. Despite the subsequent decline of Keynesian economics, these models continue to exert great influence on day-to-day decisions made by governments, banks, and businesses.

The neoclassical synthesis shows that the Keynesian equilibrium is a special case, which applies when prices are sticky. Obviously, the next task was to explain how prices move, when they eventually do. This led to a search for what was known as the 'missing equation'. This equation was discovered as an empirical regularity by A. W. Phillips (1914–1975) at the London School of Economics, whose work is extensively discussed in Chapter 12. This discovery prompted the next question: What is the theory behind the Phillips curve? Work on this question, mostly in the USA, was well under way just when the curve started to vanish. The disappearance of the Phillips curve, correctly anticipated by Friedman in the late 1960s, paved the way for the rise of the monetarists, a rival school of thought committed to exposing what was seen as fundamental flaws in Keynesian economics.

20.2 **The Monetarist Revolution**

**Milton Friedman,
1912–2006**

Source: Copyright Hulton-Deutsch Collection/Corbis.

By the late 1940s, the Keynesian school had established a strong foothold in the USA, where most of macroeconomic research was conducted, but it never enjoyed total supremacy. The University of Chicago, in particular, remained the bastion of the classical economics that Keynes had sought to upend. Keynesian ideas certainly attracted attention at Chicago. In the 1940s, Chicago economist Lloyd Metzler published an influential attempt to characterize Keynes' ideas formally. But the Chicago academic tradition must have seen a fundamental threat in Keynesian macroeconomics. It is thus not surprising that the 'Chicago School' led an intellectual attack against the Keynesians. Eventually, it was as successful as Keynes' own attack against the classics. Part of the success of the Chicago School is due to Milton Friedman, whose many talents matched those of Keynes himself.

Friedman combined extraordinary intellectual vigour, leadership, charisma, government experience, and communication skills. Like Keynes, he

---

[2] An important exception was the work of Gottfried Haberler (1900–1995), who in 1937 published an important compendium of contemporary business cycle theories—with the important exception of Keynes', which Haberler later strongly criticized.

spent the war years at the Treasury, the US Treasury in his case, where he contributed to the war effort. Like Keynes, he assembled a group of young economists, who regularly met in the 'Workshop in Money and Banking' and went on to rewrite macroeconomics. Like Keynes, he devoted much time and effort to popularize his ideas, writing a regular column in the US magazine *Newsweek* and becoming a popular guest on television shows. And, like Keynes, he did not shy from contacts with politicians, providing advice to unsuccessful presidential candidate Barry Goldwater, as well as to the considerably more successful President Ronald Reagan and to Prime Minister Margaret Thatcher. Many of his Chicago associates became known as the 'Chicago boys'. They achieved considerable—and still controversial—influence in South America and elsewhere.

Friedman pursued several ideas, all of which undermined the key building blocks of Keynesian economics. First, he was an unabashed defender of free markets, which Keynes saw as chronically prone to failures. This led him to actively promote the view, long-advocated by the Austrian-born economist Friedrich von Hayek (1899–1992), that governments are a threat to freedom, and not just in economic matters.[3] Friedman and his colleagues resuscitated the influence of the laissez-faire school, which had been shattered after the Great Depression.

Second, Friedman confronted Keynes' view that fiscal policy is a useful tool for macroeconomic stabilization and that monetary policy is useless. The label 'monetarist', widely applied to the Chicago School, comes from this aspect of Friedman's work.[4] His *A Monetary History of the United States, 1867–1960*, written in 1963 jointly with Anna J. Schwartz (1915–), is generally regarded as a masterpiece that fundamentally changed the way we look at monetary policy. At the empirical level, this book attributes the Great Depression to bad monetary policy, in contrast with Keynes, who tended to blame procyclical fiscal policies. At the theoretical level, the book re-established the classic 'quantity equation' $MV = PY$, where V is the velocity of money. This equation, which was dismissed by the LM equation, brings home the neutrality of money: if velocity V and Y are taken as exogenous, the price level P is directly driven by money. In the classical view, Y is at full employment and V is constant, whereas in the Keynesian view Y is highly variable, P is constant, and V depends on the interest rate.[5] Monetary neutrality, an old wisdom of classical economics discarded during the Keynesian heydays, returned and has not left us ever since. Its implications are profound and lie at the core of the theory and practice of central banking, as explained in Chapter 9.

Third, in a careful study of consumption patterns in the USA, *A Theory of the Consumption Function*, a book published in 1956, Friedman argued that the Keynesian function $C = C(Y)$ had little theoretical foundation and questionable empirical validity. Instead, he put forward the permanent income hypothesis, which relates consumption to permanent income, or wealth. This effectively reinvented the intertemporal analysis presented in Chapters 7 and 8, and previously explored by US economist Irving Fisher (1867–1947) of Yale University. The important consequence of this work was to weaken the significance of the Keynesian multiplier and the view that fiscal policy can be a tool for output stabilization. Later on, the Keynesians restored some of the clout of the old consumption function by arguing that many consumers are credit rationed, as explained in Chapter 8.

Finally, in what may have been his greatest triumph, Friedman explained why the Phillips curve, then still considered as the missing equation linking the short

---

[3] Friedrich von Hayek (1899–1992), another Nobel Prize winner, was a prominent product of the Austrian School, which was disbanded in the late 1930s when the Nazis took over. Hayek moved first to the London School of Economics and in 1950 to Chicago, where he was a colleague of Milton Friedman.

[4] In a true gesture of modesty, Friedman is known to have given credit to Henry Simons (1889–1946) for founding the Chicago School.

[5] The debate was really about which assumption one is willing to make. There is no incompatibility between the quantity and TR equations: the demand for money $M/P = k(i)Y$ implies that $V = 1/k(i)$. Inserting a Taylor rule for i yields an expression for velocity. But this must be considered along with the IS equation to explain the interest rate, and with the AS curve to explain inflation, while the quantity equation was originally meant to be sufficient for understanding the price level and inflation. The quantity equation is also known as the 'Cambridge equation', in deference to pre-Keynes Cambridge.

and long run, would vanish as soon as the authorities attempted to exploit the output–inflation trade-off. Not only did he restore the importance of expectations–and thus established the expectations-augmented Phillips curve–but he restated the long-run neutrality proposition–and thus invented the long-run vertical aggregate supply schedule. His work was published in 1968, and the Phillips curve went awry thereafter, in the early 1970s. Not only were the Keynesians proven wrong, they were once more 'missing an equation'. Monetarism became the new accepted wisdom, in academic circles first, and then among policy-makers. It is important to note, however, that Nobel laureate Edmund Phelps (1933–), from New York's Columbia University, who had reached the same result as Friedman and at roughly the same time, regarded himself as a Keynesian. Phelps essentially foreshadows the eclectic future of modern macroeconomics, as presented in this book, which accepts the expectations-augmented Phillips curve as the missing equation, even if it means that there is no lasting trade-off between output and inflation.

In general, Europe was slow to recognize the power of the monetarists' attack, and did not contribute much to the research effort. In the UK, the academic establishment was dominated by Keynesians, most of whom refused to acknowledge that a major battle had been lost. The election of Mrs Thatcher changed all that. She brought in Milton Friedman as an adviser, proclaiming that her government would follow the master's precepts, including rolling back government, pushing for wage stability by destroying the trade unions' grip on labour markets and, of course, a strict application of the monetary neutrality principle. She had been converted to monetarism by two close advisers working in a think tank that she had created, the Centre for Policy Studies: Alan Walters (1926–2009), a British economist then working at Johns Hopkins University in the USA, and Patrick Minford (1943–), who had resisted Keynesian influence in his bastion at Liverpool University. When, early on during her first term, the scope of Thatcher's policy intentions became clear, 364 academic economists signed a manifesto that promised disaster if these policies were implemented. Two decades later, most of the signatories agree that 'we all are Thatcherites now'.

Elsewhere in Europe, the evolution was gradual, mostly the result of generation changes, as freshly graduated macroeconomists started to popularize either monetarist ideas or less orthodox versions of Keynesian economics. Still, in some countries, such as France, Keynesian ideas remain to this day the dominant reference in policy-making circles. In the 1970s, two French economists, Edmond Malinvaud (1923–), who served for two decades as Head of the National Statistical Institute, and Jean-Pascal Benassy (1948–) of the Centre National de la Recherche Scientifique, had already developed a disequilibrium interpretation of the Keynesian model. The particular feature of this interpretation, which has now been abandoned, is that it assumes that there can be lasting excess demand or supply in goods and labour markets.

In German-speaking countries, as mentioned earlier, Keynesian ideas never quite displaced the classical view, so there was little need for a monetarist counter-revolution. Economists and policy-makers saw the movement as a vindication of their own views, even though monetarism is considerably more subtle than classical economics. During the years of Keynesian domination, the flame of classical economics was carefully maintained at the annual Konstanz seminar, which was initially created by two early monetarists, the Swiss economist Karl Brunner (1916–1989), who worked at Rochester University, and Alan Meltzer (1928–) from Carnegie Mellon University in Pittsburgh.[6] The Konstanz Seminar still meets every year.

The Chicago school also contributed much to our understanding of the open economies. Much of Mundell's work was produced when he was in Chicago, where he also trained a generation of international macroeconomists who developed the 'monetary approach to the exchange rate'. This approach shapes much of Chapter 15, including the stylized facts proposed by Michael Mussa (1944–2012) and the overshooting hypothesis of German-born Rudiger Dornbusch (1942–2002), both students of Mundell. Many other Chicago economists—including Mundell himself—worked at the IMF, where they forged the Fund's doctrine and produced important work under the leadership of Dutch economist Jacques J. Polak (1914–2010).

[6] The tradition at Konstanz is to display a flag that bears '$MV = PY$'.

Yet, Friedman's ideas have not always been widely accepted. One of his other major contributions is the intellectual defence of freely flexible exchange rates, as noted in Chapter 19. He gathered ammunition for this position when he was in Paris in 1950, working at the US governmental agency which administered the Marshall Plan. At the time, he concluded that the European Common Market could not work with fixed exchange rates and he considered the European Monetary Union as a mistake. This view receives much support in the UK.

20.3 The Rational Expectations Revolution

Robert Lucas Jr, 1937 –

Source: The Nobel Foundation.

Thomas Sargent, 1943 –

Source: New York University.

The attack on Keynesian economics was by no means over yet. Another blow came with the rational expectations revolution. The expectations-augmented Phillips curve of Friedman and Phelps had left an important question unanswered: What drives expectations? Most economists thought that inflation expectations gradually caught up with actually observed inflation, i.e. they were only taking account of what Chapter 12 defines as the backward-looking component of underlying inflation. Although Phelps had made some headway in introducing the forward-looking component, the next major step was achieved in Chicago again where Nobel Prize laureate Robert E. Lucas Jr, a student of Friedman, spearheaded the rational expectations revolution.[7] Rational expectations are presented in Chapter 7 and this idea permeates much of this textbook. Lucas and his colleagues[8] argued that if the forward-looking component dominates and if expectations are not systematically biased, the Phillips curve is always vertical, in the short as well as in the long run. As a result, they asserted, systematic policy cannot work. In particular, monetary policy affects output and employment only to the extent that it creates inflationary surprises. Since creating short-lived surprises is hardly a basis for macroeconomic policy, the circle was closed. Friedman's contribution meant that fiscal policy is not helpful but that monetary policy is a powerful instrument, although one whose effects are eventually dissipated in inflation. The rational expectations revolution's message was that macroeconomic policies should not be used on and off with complete discretion. Instead, policy should obey rules and aim at establishing credibility for adhering to the rules.[9] This was not a complete vindication of the classic laissez-faire approach, but an indictment of Keynesian policy activism.

The view that 'only unanticipated money matters' was never very popular with policy-makers. One could say that it is hardly surprising that central banks explicitly reject the view that their role is limited to creating surprises. Yet, empirical evidence failed to support this view, paving the way for the New Keynesian macroeconomics.

[7] Lucas was not the first to formulate this view. It was first advanced by a number of American economists from Carnegie Mellon University—they inspired Lucas, who spent several years there before taking up a chair in Chicago—John Muth (1930–2005), Ed Prescott (1944–), and Finn Kydland (1943–).

[8] In particular Thomas Sargent (1943–) and Neil Wallace (1939–).

[9] The preference of rules over discretion was first expressed by Milton Friedman in an essay written in the 1950s.

20.4 The Microfoundations of Macroeconomics

Finn Kydland, 1943 –

Source: Carnegie Mellon University.

Edward Prescott, 1940 –

Source: Federal Reserve Bank of Minneapolis.

Because of its compelling logic, the rational expectations hypothesis attracted immense interest and opened the way for further innovations in other directions. Clearly, if it is appropriate to assume that expectations are rational, then why shouldn't all other economic decisions be rational as well? Researchers at 'freshwater universities' in the USA—

Chicago, Minnesota, Rochester, Carnegie-Mellon, and University of Pennsylvania—have established the microeconomic foundations of the consumption, investment, and primary account functions studied in Part II of this book. European economists from all countries—many after a sojourn in those US universities—are deeply involved in this research programme.

Insisting on the rigorous discipline of microeconomic foundations may be intellectually attractive, yet business cycles remain a fact of life that must be explained. This led neoclassical economists to the Real Business Cycles (RBC) research programme discussed in Chapter 16. The aim of this effort is to show that models with flexible prices and fully rational agents—in brief, the Robinson Crusoe parable developed in Part II—can reproduce the key features of actual business cycles. The 'RBC school', inspired by the American Ed Prescott from Arizona University and Norwegian-born Finn Kydland from Carnegie Mellon University, has a significant following in Europe. These researchers received the Nobel Prize for their work in 2004.

20.5 New Keynesian Macroeconomics: The Latest Synthesis

Michael Woodford, 1955 –

Source: Photo courtesy of Michael Woodford.

John Taylor, 1946 –

Source: <www.stanford.edu>.

Despite its intellectual attractiveness, the RBC approach was not a great empirical success. Many of

the most important stylized facts of the business cycle remain unaccounted for. Price stickiness simply appears to be a fact.[10] This opened up an opportunity for the New Keynesians, who were already at work on their own response to the rational expectations revolution. Their main aim has been to show that price stickiness is not incompatible with microeconomic foundations and full rationality. New Keynesians have thus been able to produce a new synthesis, which fully rests on rational behaviour but delivers the traditional Keynesian results. Much of this work has been carried out at traditionally Keynesian 'saltwater universities' in the USA (Harvard, MIT, Yale, Princeton, Berkeley),[11] with some important contributions from Michael Woodford, now at Columbia University in New York. In Europe, Jordi Gali, from Pompeu Fabra University in Barcelona, has further developed the microfoundations of the expectations-augmented Phillips curve.

The synthesis starts with RBC microeconomic foundations—complete with rational expectations—and adds price stickiness. The result turns out to be very similar to the *AS–AD* presented in Chapter 13. It contains an *IS* curve, which incorporates the aspect that next period's demand affects that of the current period—and reflects the idea that households strive to smooth their consumption. Second, it also includes a Phillips curve that is almost identical to the one initially proposed by Friedman and Phelps. It allows both for rational expectations of price setters, but admits that some agents do not change prices very often, or do not have the information or the wherewithal to do so. Most importantly, the new Keynesian Phillips curve implies that 'anticipated money matters', so that monetary policy can systematically affect output. Third, it also includes the Taylor rule, named after John Taylor from Stanford University, which is seen as the deliberate and systematic response of monetary policy to fluctuations in inflation and output.

The New Keynesian framework has been wholeheartedly embraced by policy-makers who now read the same books as economists. Importantly, the new *IS* curve and the old-new Phillips curve attract attention to the crucial role of expectations, which has led central banks around the world to become more transparent about their own forecasts and intentions. From the policy perspective, the view that fiscal and monetary policies can play a role as tools for output and employment stabilization is now generally accepted. So too is the recognition that the role of expectations requires much more prudence and care than the traditional Keynesians dared to admit, as explained in Chapters 16 and 17.

20.6 Institutional and Political Economics

Since the rational expectations revolution in the early 1970s, macroeconomics has managed to avoid further paradigmatic earthquakes. A number of innovations have occurred at the frontier between economics and political science. This ongoing research programme starts from the obvious observation that

Friedrich August von Hayek, 1889–1992

Source: Copyright Bettmann/Corbis.

James Buchanan, 1919–

Source: Photo courtesy of James Buchanan.

[10] This is hardly news! Milton Friedman and Anna Schwarz wrote extensively on long and variable lags with which monetary changes affect the price level. Even the old Scot David Hume (1711–1776) was fascinated by the fact that gold inflows in seventeenth-century Spain had so little short-run influence on the price level.

[11] Saltwater universities are located on the East and West coasts of the USA, while freshwater universities are inland, often close to the Great Lakes.

policy actions are not taken in a vacuum, but by policy-makers, who are real-life politicians and keenly sensitive to public opinion as they seek re-election and power. In doing so, they need to calculate what will be the effects of their actions on the economy—the traditional macroeconomic question—and their voters' reactions.

Once these questions are asked, it becomes clear that political systems matter a lot. We need to look at the respective influences of government and parliament, at the degree of independence of the central bank, and at the electoral rules. Here, the variety of institutions across Europe offers a unique source of observation. It comes as no surprise that European economists—some of whom are based in the USA—have often played a leading role in this area of research.

The roots of this new approach are both old and interesting as it has brought together some very different traditions. German-language economists in the tradition of the Historical and Austrian schools have long explored these issues and their *Ordnungspolitik* (this term is hard to translate but formally means 'policy of establishing or maintaining order' or, more precisely, the institutional framework for economic activity) remains very influential in this part of Europe. However, with few exceptions,[12] these approaches have not exerted much international influence, partly for language reasons, and partly because they rejected the formalization of their ideas. The same questions were explored independently by US-based economists of the 'Public Choice School', including Nobel Prize laureates James Buchanan (1919–) and Douglass North (1920–). Most economists associated with the public choice research programme consider themselves more aligned with the laissez-faire view.[13] Coming from a radically different perspective, New-Keynesian economists began to study

why governments make policy mistakes, rather than simply criticizing them, as do laissez-faire economists. They stress that sometimes policy-makers pursue bad policies because they have distorted incentives. Since incentives are determined by institutions, to improve policy-makers' incentives, institutional reforms may be needed. Important contributions have been made by Alberto Alesina, an Italian economist at Harvard, Torsten Persson (1954–) from Stockholm University, and Guido Tabellini (1956–) from Bocconi University, among others. Finally, a few French microeconomists—brought together at Toulouse University by Jean Tirole (1953–) and Jean-Jacques Laffont (1947–2004)—have explored the question of incentives and decision-making under uncertainty. Their results are gradually percolating into macroeconomics, where they allow the study of the interaction between policy-makers and the private sector.

This work indicates that the kinds of differences that oppose laissez-faire advocates and interventionists are too blunt when stated as 'the government should stay out of economics' versus 'governments must take responsibility for economic welfare'. There are some tasks that some governments can usefully perform and others cannot, and tasks of general interest that are better left to the markets. For example, fiscal policy may play a stabilizing role, but governments tend to suffer from a deficit bias, especially in political regimes where decisions are made by divided parliaments. Equally important is the realization that some economic policies cannot be improved unless the political institutions are first reformed. A good example is that central bank independence is generally a precondition for good monetary policy. Employment and growth are two further examples of the important innovations brought by this fundamental intuition.

---

[12] Prominent examples are Bruno Frey (1941–) of Zurich and Roland Vaubel (1948–) of Mannheim University.

[13] Many members of the Public Choice School are part of the Mont-Pélerin Society, a group created by Friedrich von Hayek in Mont-Pélerin near Lausanne, Switzerland.

20.7 Labour Markets

**Richard Layard,
1934–**

Source: British Academy.

**Stephen Nickell,
1944–**

Source: Bank of England.

One of Europe's sad distinguishing features is the high rate of unemployment which has prevailed since the mid-1970s. In a number of reassuring cases, however, some—mostly smaller—European countries have been able to roll back unemployment. As Chapters 5 and 18 emphasize, the problem lies in labour market structures, institutions, and policies. Here again, comparison and analysis of the diversity of situations in Europe has offered a wealth of lessons about the nature of unemployment and the ways to deal with it. European economists have made significant progress, if only to develop a genuine understanding of their own labour markets, which differ profoundly from those in the USA.

Much of the pioneering effort has been conducted at the London School of Economics' Centre for Labour Economics, led by Richard Layard (1934–) and Steve Nickell (1944–). Other important early contributors are Edmond Malinvaud (1923–) from France, Jacques Drèze (1929–) from the University Louvain-la-Neuve in Belgium, Herbert Giersch (1921–2010) from the University of Kiel in Germany, and Assar Lindbeck (already mentioned), who, together with Dennis Snower (1950–) from the University of London, developed the insider–outsider theory. According to this theory, labour representatives defend the interests of the employed workers—the insiders—at the expense of those who are not employed—the outsiders. The overwhelming evidence is that labour market rigidities lie at the root of Europe's unemployment problem. This assessment is not much disputed today but was initially rejected by Keynesian economists, who blamed instead restrictive demand management policies. One way of simplifying the debate is whether the problem lies with a high equilibrium unemployment rate (the case of rigidities) or whether actual unemployment is kept above its equilibrium rate. Interestingly, monetarists always took the view that the equilibrium unemployment rate had risen. The diagnosis that structural problems are at the root of the unemployment problem in Europe is hardly disputed, except by a handful of die-hard Keynesians. In fact, it has been accepted by many governments.

This conclusion has triggered a search for appropriate solutions. Structural problems call for structural reforms, and reforms are always controversial. In the area of labour markets, the controversies are laden with emotional political and social undertones; in some countries deep ideological battles have resurfaced. The reason is simple, and is reminiscent of the problem of dynamic efficiency discussed in Chapter 3. To get to where we want to go, up-front sacrifices are necessary. Real wage moderation, cuts in unemployment benefits, reform of job protection, and the deregulation of product markets may well hurt many individuals today, even if later ultimately leading to future increases in employment and GDP. Finding out how to convince and compensate the losers in reforms is the magic formula which smaller European economies seemed to have found. Several European economists are actively investigating conditions under which politically difficult economic reforms can be adopted. What has to be done is now subject to much agreement, with important detailed work carried out by the economic staff of the OECD and IMF. Some countries have implemented many of these measures, and unemployment has indeed declined, sometimes significantly. In other countries, governments have been too sensitive to even acknowledge the need for action.

20.8 Search and Matching

Peter Diamond, 1940 –

Source: The Nobel Foundation.

Dale Mortensen, 1939 –

Source: The Nobel Foundation.

Christopher Pissarides, 1948 –

Source: The Nobel Foundation.

Unemployment is such a big issue in macroeconomics that it has perspective—how you look at it determines how you think about it. Chapters 5 and 18 established that unemployment is a supply-side problem in the long run, and those more interested in the long run see labour market institutions and preferences as playing the predominant role. Yet throughout our book, unemployment has also been seen as a short-run topic of first-order political and social importance—determined by the ups and downs of the business cycle. Those who are more interested in the short-run perspective stress that sudden declines in aggregate demand lead firms to reduce employment, reduce hires, and increase unemployment.

Yet unemployment is so complex that it takes on yet another, different dimension when viewed from the 'bathtub' or dynamic perspective of inflows and outflows, as stressed in Chapter 5 (Section 5.4). The enormous turnover of workers and jobs despite large, stable stocks of unemployment signals that the uniqueness of each worker and job—and the uniqueness of their coming together, or matching—makes search worthwhile. Reshuffling the personnel deck can actually be productive for an economy. Research shows that even people who have jobs are often on the lookout, even if they are choosier or even deny it entirely. In addition to the fundamental insight that workers and employers search purposefully, Peter Diamond of MIT also recognized that searchers who do 'find one another' in such markets have something special—an economic rent or surplus—that cannot be costlessly recreated without renewed time-intensive search. As a result of this rent, wage determination takes on the role of allocator of surplus, and has no obvious value as it does in neoclassical economic theory, except that it must leave the match at least as attractive to both parties as the option of abandoning the match and resuming search.

Since workers and firms are constantly on the lookout, it is of great importance to understand their behaviour. Offers usually come randomly, but not all at once. The longer and more intensively we search, the more likely we will receive offers. Dale Mortensen (along with John McCall, a pioneer in operations research) stressed that optimal search behaviour of workers and firms under such conditions generally takes the form of a stopping rule or *reservation wage*—a critical value of the offered wage (or more generally, a critical level of satisfactory workplace attributes) below which the offer is rejected as unsatisfactory. This reservation wage will depend on many factors, including unemployment benefits, impatience, and the shape of the distribution of wage offers.

If all that were not complex enough, markets with search frictions are fraught with externalities. Students looking for an apartment in Berlin often have to wait for hours in line for a chance to inspect the premises and compete with hundreds of other candidates. Residents of Paris who work a little late have great difficulty finding a parking space, if only because many people have the same work habits. Clubs in London often organize 'ladies' nights' to make their premises more attractive to certain male visitors (and also to female ones!). Christopher Pissarides of the London School of Economics was interested in the implications of the fact that the probability of an unemployed person making contact with *any* job offer depends crucially on the number of unemployed already in the market relative to available open positions. *Ceteris paribus*, every newly

unemployed person depresses the chances for success of all those already in the unemployed pool, and increases the probability that a vacancy already posted will be filled. This fact, combined with wage determination as a surplus allocation device, can explain why wages depend on 'labour market tightness', yet may not decline automatically in the presence of high unemployment.

The deep insights of markets with search and matching frictions are not limited to the study of unemployment. Markets for financial intermediation (especially banking), for lawyers and architects, for marriage or partners, for apartments and houses, and even the 'market' for parking spaces can be thought of matching markets—even if the price of a parking space is zero! A serious branch of monetary economics considers the use of money as a solution to a matching problem. Combined with powerful mathematical methods to study optimal dynamic decisions under uncertainty, search and matching theory has contributed to the design and implementation of labour market reforms in modern developed economies.

20.9 Growth and Development

Robert Solow, 1924 –

Source: The Nobel Foundation.

Paul Romer, 1955 –

Source: Hoover Institution.

Much as our understanding of labour markets has greatly benefited from institutional economics, one of the most important—and more vexing—issues

Robert Barro, 1944 –

Source: Hoover Institution.

involving the wealth and poverty of nations has also been profoundly rethought. As explained in Chapters 3 and 4, research on the neoclassical growth model[14] conducted at MIT by Nobel Prize laureate Robert Solow, had two key implications: (1) capital is more

[14] This theory is called neoclassical because it relies on standard microeconomic principles, much like neoclassical macroeconomics. But Bob Solow, as he is generally called, has been a leading and enthusiastic proponent of Keynesian economics.

productive where it is scarce, and (2) the key source of sustained growth is unexplained—or exogenous—technological progress. Both implications were deeply unsatisfactory, and both have motivated important innovations to conventional growth theory.

As noted in Chapter 4, Robert E. Lucas Jr challenged economists to explain why capital doesn't flow from rich to poor countries. Poor countries are characterized by low capital intensity and, in theory, must have a much higher marginal productivity of capital than rich countries. One important solution to his puzzle is that high productivity may be high in theory, but in fact is significantly reduced by the prevalence of poor institutions that allow corruption, instability, and war to discourage investment.

However, if technological change is exogenous, it is not possible to explain why institutions matter. In the mid-1980s, Paul Romer (1955–) from Stanford University showed how technological progress could be treated as endogenous. As explained in Chapter 4, the crucial step was to recognize that knowledge does not suffer from decreasing returns. This established a link with Lucas' question: education is an investment in human capital, and it is deterred by poor institutions exactly as investment in physical capital. This discovery allowed many others to explore the process

of growth and economic development. Much empirical evidence has since been produced by Robert Barro (1944–) at Harvard University, in collaboration with Spanish-born Xavier Sala-i-Martin (1963–) from Columbia University, with important contributions by many others, including French-born Philippe Aghion (1956–) from Harvard University.

The result of this research has been a thorough reappraisal of underdevelopment and of policies that try to deal with extreme poverty in many parts of the world. The emphasis has shifted from earlier recommendations by the rich countries to 'do as we do' to try to encourage the establishment of better institutions that would provide political leaders in the poor countries with the incentives to adopt pro-growth policies. This literature has also profoundly affected the international financial institutions, in particular the World Bank and the regional development banks. The results are slow in coming but some important successes have been achieved. The same message also concerns the rich countries, especially Europe, which stopped catching up with the USA in the mid-1980s. The message is that reforms are needed to make the political system interested in supporting agents of change rather than established economic interests.

20.10 Conclusions

Because economists are not free from their own prejudices, it is crucial that they focus as much as possible on developing rigorous theories and conduct dispassionate evaluations of their policy implications. By and large, this is what they have done. Controversies abound, but over time intellectual exchange and the search for unifying truths have brought economists closer together in an ever-increasing degree of agreement. For example, Patrick Minford was harshly criticized in the 1980s when he argued that high unemployment benefits discouraged unemployed workers from looking for new jobs. His former Keynesian critics have now accepted the view that unemployment benefits need to be struc-

tured in a way that reduces the potentially adverse effects on work incentives. In contrast to much of the public debate, professional macroeconomists see their field as an intellectual challenge to solve pressing problems, and not as an ideological exercise.

Macroeconomics was born in Europe as a revolt against classical economists in the wake of the Great Depression. Much of the ensuing research was carried out in the USA. These developments clarified the limits of Keynesian economics and eventually allowed a field to emerge. It is not yet fully unified but controversies are now well understood and circumscribed. Prompted by problems of low growth and high unemployment, European economists have made important contributions that make macroeconomics a lively field with its own flavour. Although there is no such thing as European macroeconomics, a number of macroeconomic issues in Europe merit more attention than they receive in the USA. These range from the role of regulations, taxes, and transfers in labour markets to the functioning of monetary unions. More than anything else, Europe consists of 'small and open' independent countries, and this fact sets it apart from the highly integrated states of the USA. If the last two decades of our textbook is any evidence, it is these differences which make macroeconomics in Europe so special.

→ Essay Question

1 Make your list of future Nobel Prize winners, and explain why you chose them.

📖 References

Adelman, I. and Adelman, F. (1959), 'The Dynamic Properties of the Klein–Goldberger Model', *Econometrica*, 27.

Alesina, A. (1988), 'The End of Large Public Debts', in F. Giavazzi and L. Spaventa (eds), *High Public Debt: The Italian Experience*, Cambridge University Press.

Baldwin, R. and Wyplosz, C. (2005), *The Economics of European Integration*, McGraw Hill.

Bank for International Settlements (2007), 'Foreign Exchange and Derivatives Market Activity in 2007', *Triennial Central Bank Survey*, December.

Barro, R. J. and Sala-i-Martin, X. (1991), 'Convergence across States and Regions', *Brookings Papers on Economic Activity*, 1.

— (2004), *Economic Growth*, 2nd edn, MIT Press.

Bloom, D., Canning, D., Graham, B., and Sevilla, J. (2000), 'Out of Poverty: On the Feasibility of Halving Global Poverty by 2015', CAERE Discussion Paper No. 52, Harvard Institute for International Development.

Bruyn-Hundt, M. (1996), *The Economics of Unpaid Work*, Thesis Publishers.

Burda, M. and Gerlach, S. (1993), 'Exchange Rate Dynamics and Currency Unification: The Ostmark–DM Rate', *Empirical Economics*, 18.

Burns, A. and Mitchell, W. (1946), *Measuring Business Cycles*. New York: National Bureau of Economic Research.

Chinn, Menzie D. and Hiro Ito (2008). 'A New Measure of Financial Openness'. *Journal of Comparative Policy Analysis*, 10(3), 309–322.

Collier, P. and Gunning, J. W. (1999), 'Why Has Africa Grown Slowly?', *Journal of Economic Perspectives*, 13(3).

Cooper, R. (1982), 'The Gold Standard: Historical Facts and Future Prospects', *Brookings Papers on Economic Activity*, 1.

Dam, K. W. (1982), *The Rules of the Game*, University of Chicago Press.

— (1989), *The Rules of the Game*, University of Chicago Press.

DeLong, J. B. (1997), 'What Do We Really Know about Economic Growth?', <www.j-bradford-delong.net>.

Easterly, W. (1999), 'On Good Politicians and Bad Policies: Social Cohesion, Institutions and Growth', The World Bank.

Fisher, I. (1930), *Theory of Interest*, Pickering Masters Series.

Fracasso, A., Genberg, H., and Wyplosz, C. (2003), 'How Do Central Banks Write?', *Geneva Report on the World Economy*, Special Report 2, CEPR, London.

Friedman, M. (1968), 'The Role of Monetary Policy', *American Economic Review*, 58.

Garber, P. (1990), 'Famous First Bubbles', *Journal of Economic Perspectives*, 4(2).

Goodhart, C. (1988), *The Evolution of Central Banks*, MIT Press.

Gordon, R. (2000), 'Does the "New Economy" Measure up to the Great Inventions of the Past?', NBER Working Paper 7833, August.

Hall, R. and Jones, C. (1999), 'Why do some Countries Produce so Much More Output per Worker than Others?', *The Quarterly Journal of Economics*, 114.

Harding, D. and Pagan, A. (2001), 'Dissecting the Cycle: A Methodological Investigation', *Journal of Monetary Economics*, 49(2).

Henry, J., Hernández de Cos, P., and Momigliano, S. (2004), 'The Short-Term Impact of Government Budgets on Prices: Evidence from Macroeconometric Models', Working Paper No. 396, ECB.

Heston, A., Summers, R., and Aten, B. (2006), *Penn World Table Version 6.2*, Center for International

Comparisons of Production, Income and Prices at the University of Pennsylvania, September.

—— (2011), *Penn World Table Version 7.0*, Center for International Comparisons of Production, Income and Prices at the University of Pennsylvania, May.

Hume, D. (1752), *Of Money*.

Keynes, J. M. (1936), *The General Theory of Employment, Interest and Money,* London: Macmillan.

Kindleberger, C. (1973), *The World in Depression*, University of California Press.

Kose, A. and Prasad, E. (2004), 'Liberalizing Capital', *Finance & Development*, September, p. 51.

Kuhn, T. S. (1982), *The Structure of Scientific Revolutions*, University of Chicago Press.

Lane, P. and Milesi-Ferretti, G. (2007), 'The external wealth of nations mark II: Revised and extended estimates of foreign assets and liabilities, 1970–2004', *Journal of International Economics,* 73, 223–250, plus update <www.philiplane.org/EWN.html>.

Lucas, R. E., Jr (1980), 'Methods and Problems in Business Cycle Theory', *Journal of Money, Credit and Banking*, 12.

—— (1990), 'Why Doesn't Capital Flow from Rich to Poor Countries?', *American Economic Review*, 80(2).

Maddison, A. (1991), *Dynamic Forces in Capitalist Development*, Oxford University Press.

—— (1995), *Monitoring the World Economy 1820–1992*, OECD Development Centre.

—— (2006), *The World Economy: Volume 1: A Millennial Perspective*, OECD Development Centre Studies, Paris.

—— (2007), 'Historical Statistics for the World Economy: 1–2003 AD' in *Contours of the World Economy 1–2030 AD: Essays in Macro-Economic History*, Oxford University Press.

Mackay, C. (1980), *Extraordinary Popular Delusions and the Madness of Crowds*, New York: Harmony Books. With a foreword by Andrew Tobias. First published 1841.

Marx, K. (1867), *Capital*, Foreword to Volume I.

Mitchell, B. (1978), *European Historical Statistics*, Columbia University Press.

—— (1983), *International Historical Statistics*, Macmillan.

—— (1998), *International Historical Statistics*, Macmillan.

Mitchell, W. (1951), *What Happens During Business Cycles*, New York: National Bureau of Economic Research.

Ndulu, B. and O'Connell, S. (1999), 'Governance and Growth in Sub-Saharan Africa', *Journal of Economic Perspectives*, 13(3).

Nurkse, R. (1961), *Equilibrium and Growth in the World Economy*, Harvard University Press.

Riksbank, *Monetary Policy Update*, December 2007.

Ritschl, A. (2004), 'News from Tobin's q: Capital Markets were Efficient in 1929', Working Paper, HU.

Schneider, F. and Enste, D. (2000), 'Shadow Economies: Size, Causes, and Consequences', *Journal of Economic Literature*, 38.

Smith, A. (1776), *The Wealth of Nations.*

Tobin, J. (1996), 'Prologue', in M. ul Haq, I. Kaul, and I. Grunberg (eds), *The Tobin Tax*, Oxford University Press.

Trabandt, M. and H. Uhlig (2012), 'How Do Laffer Curves Differ Across Countries?', in A. Alesina and F. Giavazzi (eds.), *Fiscal Policy after the Financial Crisis*, The University of Chicago Press.

Wyplosz, C. (1999), 'Macroeconomic Lessons from Ten Years of Transition', in B. Pleskovic and J. E. Stiglitz (eds), *Annual World Bank Conference on Development Economics*, The World Bank.

🔑 Glossary

This glossary presents brief definitions of the key concepts listed at the end of each chapter. Numbers refer to the corresponding chapter(s).

absolute purchasing power parity (6): theory asserting that price levels are equalized across countries once they are converted into a common currency

absorption (2): total national (private and public) spending on goods and services

accelerator principle (8): the positive effect of an increase in GDP on the rate of investment

accounting identities (2): relationships linking macroeconomic magnitudes to each other by definition

active labour market policies (18): programmes involving direct job creation, job security, retraining, relocation of families from distressed regions, or special programmes to get young people started in the job market

activist policies (16): government policies which try to improve market outcomes by correcting market dysfunctions

aggregate demand (1): the sum of planned consumption, investment, government purchases of goods and services, plus net export of goods and services (the primary current account)

aggregate demand curve (13): downward-sloping curve relating aggregate demand negatively to the rate of inflation

aggregate production function (3): a relationship linking total output to employed resources such as capital, labour, and other factors of production

aggregate supply (12): total volume of goods and services brought to market by producers at a given price level

aggregate supply curve (12): upward-sloping curve linking inflation to aggregate output supplied by firms

animal spirits (8): term referring to entrepreneurs' optimism and willingness to undertake risky investment projects

appreciation (exchange rate) (6, 11): a market-determined increase in the value of a currency (less of that currency must be relinquished to buy one unit of foreign currency); *see:* **depreciation; revaluation**

arbitrage (6, 14): the simultaneous purchase and sale of assets of identical characteristics to earn a profit without risk-taking: spatial arbitrage responds to diverging asset prices across different market locations, yield arbitrage responds to differing asset returns, and triangular arbitrage to three asset prices that are not mutually consistent

assets (14): forms in which households, firms, or governments are able to hold wealth, such as stocks and bonds, bank deposits, cash, or real estate

autarky (7): the state in which a country operates when it does not trade with the rest of the world

automatic stabilizer (16, 17): the economic mechanism that automatically cushions the impact of exogenous changes in aggregate demand, via the effect of income on saving decisions

average or unit costs (12): production costs per unit of output

balance of current transfers (2): payments which are not associated with commercial or financial transactions. An example is the remittance of guest workers to their home countries. When a Polish plumber living in London sends money to relatives living in Warsaw, this counts as a surplus to the Polish balance of transfers and as a deficit to the UK's. Another example is development or emergency aid offered by one country to another

balance of goods and services (2): includes merchandise trade as well as trade in intermediate inputs, goods repair, goods held in ports, and non-monetary gold. The balance of trade in services incorporates a wide and growing variety of invisibles such as transport and travel, communication, insurance, financial and other services. It also includes royalties and licence fees

balance of international income (2): the net income of a nation which originates abroad: wages and salaries paid for work by individuals in countries different from their place of residence and profits or interest income received by residents *less* profits and interest served to foreign residents

balance of payments (2, 11): a summary of all real and financial transactions of a country with the rest of the world

balance sheet (9): a statement of the financial position of a firm or other entity at a particular point in time, indicating its assets, liabilities, and net worth

Balassa – Samuelson effect (15): the observation that price levels in richer nations are systematically higher than in poor ones; attributed to higher non-traded goods price inflation in fast-growing countries

band of fluctuation (19): the range in which the central bank is ready to allow market price of foreign exchange (usually a single currency) to fluctuate without intervening directly in the market

bank reserves (9): the central bank liabilities (cash or central bank deposits) that commercial banks choose or are required to hold to meet demands of depositors and/or the requirements of regulators

bank run/bank failure (9): a situation in which a large number of bank customers attempt to withdraw their deposits at the same time, leading to difficulties paying those depositors in conversion of other, less liquid assets, sometimes even inducing bankruptcy

battle of the mark-ups (12): the interpretation of the wage- and price-setting mechanism whereby firms set prices as high as possible over costs, including wages, while employees try to have wages grow faster than the inflation rate

beggar-thy-neighbour (11): policies, especially exchange rate policies, designed to divert domestic demand away from foreign goods and towards domestically produced goods

Beveridge curve (18): downward-sloping curve relating the unemployment rate to the vacancy rate; the position of this curve measures the efficiency of the job-matching process

bid – ask spread (14): in the foreign exchange market, the bid is the price at which one can sell foreign exchange; the ask is the price at which one can buy it on the market. The spread is the difference—usually quoted as a percentage— between the two prices

bimetallism (19): the use of both gold and silver as a commodity money standard

bond (14): a standardized borrowing instrument issued by large firms or governments with clearly stipulated conditions of payment of principal and interest by the borrower, with prices set in financial markets

boom-and-bust cycles (19): period of expanding/ contracting aggregate economic activity

Bretton Woods Conference (19): meeting held in 1944 and attended by officials from 45 nations to shape a new international money order after the Second World War

British terms (6): one of two ways of quoting the exchange rate, here in units of the foreign currency per one unit of domestic currency (e.g. US$1.52 for $1 for UK residents); *see also* **European terms**

budget line (7): the line expressing the resource constraint of households in consuming today and tomorrow, the slope is the negative of the gross interest rate.

Burns – Mitchell diagram (1): a diagram displaying the behaviour of macroeconomic variables over the typical business cycle as a deviation from their values at the cyclical peak

business cycles (1): succession of periods of rapid growth and slowdown or decline in which output fluctuates around its long-run trend

Cambridge equation (**6**): the simplest formulation of the demand for money, expressing it as a constant (*k*) times nominal GDP (*PY*): $M = kPY$

capacity utilization (rate) (**1**): the proportion of installed equipment currently employed; higher rates occur during booms, lower rates correspond to recessions

capital (**1**): one of the factors of production; usually refers to plant, equipment, inventories, and structures

capital account (**2**): component of the balance of payments accounts that records financial transactions with the rest of the world

capital accumulation (**3**): the increase of the stock of capital, sometimes called net investment or net formation of capital. It differs from gross investment, which also includes the capital put in place to replace depreciated equipment

capital adequacy (**9**): requirement that banks hold capital in a minimum (e.g. 9%) proportion of their liabilities

capital controls (**11**): restrictions on the movement of assets into and out of a country

capital gain/loss (**15**): refers to the gain or loss that is realized upon sale of an asset relative to its acquisition price

capital – labour ratio (**3**): the ratio of the stock of capital to the use of labour

capital widening (**3**): the fact that growth in labour input (population, labour force participation) make new investment necessary, merely to keep the capital–labour ratio at its current level and to prevent it from being diluted

capital-widening line (**3**): the straight line in the diagram of the Solow model with population growth, which shows the investment per capita needed to maintain a constant per capita capital stock per unit per capita (in efficiency units)

circular flow (**2**): the fact that each final sale of a good or service represents income to factors of production employed to produce it; similarly, income to factors of production is either spent or saved, while savings are used to finance final purchases of goods by others

classical dichotomy (**6, 10**): the situation pertaining when equilibrium values of nominal variables can be determined independently of real variables; the real side of economic activity (growth, unemployment, etc.) is affected only by technology and tastes

collective labour supply curve (**5**): the link between the amount of man-hours that workers supply collectively (via wage negotiations or through their unions) and the real wage

commodity money (**9**): forms of money that have intrinsic value in other uses, or derive their value from the commodity out of which they are made, chiefly gold or silver

competition policy (**18**): policies aimed at decreasing monopoly power and increasing rivalry among sellers in markets

conditional convergence (**4**): the notion that economies converge to well-defined levels of economic prosperity (steady states) which are not identical, but depend on individual attributes of the nation or region concerned

conditionality (**19**): requirements imposed by the IMF on member-countries' macroeconomic policies for obtaining certain types of loans

consol (**14**): a bond, usually issued by governments, which pays a certain fixed payment each period forever (sometimes called **perpetuity**)

constant returns to scale (**3**): term describing a production function in which simultaneous equiproportional increases in the factors of production result in an equiproportional increase in output

consumer price index (**2**): an index of prices of a basket of goods representative of the consumption pattern of the 'average consumer', using fixed quantity weights in some base year

consumer surplus (**18**): the difference between the maximum amount that a consumer would be willing to pay for a specified quantity of good and what they must actually pay for it

consumption (**2**): goods and services produced and sold to households for the satisfaction of wants

consumption function (**8, 10**): a symbolic way of stating that the aggregate consumption is positively related to aggregate wealth and, if a significant proportion of households is constrained in credit markets, to disposable income

consumption – leisure trade-off (**5**): the fundamental determinant of the labour supply decision: in order to consume, we need income and therefore we need to work, which means giving up leisure time

consumption smoothing (8, 17): optimal choice by households to smooth out the impact of temporary disturbances to income on consumption plans by either borrowing (in the case of a negative shock) or saving (in the case of a positive shock)

contractionary monetary policy shock (10): a shift upward in monetary policy of the central bank described by the Taylor rule, due to an increase in the target or neutral interest rate

convergence clubs (4): groups of countries that experience convergence to similar levels of GDP or GNI per capita

convergence hypothesis (4): the hypothesis of a negative association between per capita growth and initial per capita GDP

coordination failure (1): situation occurring when agents (households, firms) fail to realize that their actions are interdependent, and that acting jointly might benefit all

copyrights (4): a legal right that prevents commercial usage by others of works like books, music, etc.

core or underlying inflation rate (12): the inflation rate taken into account during wage bargaining to anticipate future inflation or to recuperate losses from past inflation

countercyclical (1): term used to describe an economic variable when it is negatively correlated with the state of the economy; that is, it moves in the opposite direction to aggregate output over the business cycle

countercyclical fiscal policy (17): corrective device intended to keep the economy near its equilibrium level by increasing or decreasing aggregate demand via public spending or tax policies

covered interest rate parity (CIRP) (15): a no-arbitrage condition equating the difference between domestic and foreign interest rates to the forward exchange discount

credit default swaps (14): a type of derivative security which is based on a particular loan contract, typically a bond issued by a government, a bank or a company

credit rationing (8): a condition in loan markets in which there is excess demand for loans at the market interest rate

currency crises (15): episodes of sudden capital outflows from countries—most often which have fixed their exchange rates—leading to sharp losses of foreign exchange reserves held by the central bank and ultimately to a devaluation of the currency

current account (2): the sum of a country's trade in goods, services, and unilateral transfers with the rest of the world

cyclically adjusted budgets (17): budgets adjusted for the effect of the business cycle on tax revenues

deadweight loss of taxation (18): the loss of consumer and producer surplus which is caused by the introduction of taxes on goods and services, effectively driving a wedge between consumers' valuation and the cost of production

debt stabilization (17): the process of arresting explosive growth in the debt–GDP ratio, usually achieved by cutting government expenditures and raising taxes

decision lag (16): time lag in policy effectiveness needed by government to formulate policy

decreasing returns to scale (3): describes a production function for which an equiproportional increase in the factors of production results in a less than equiproportional increase in output; *see also* **constant returns to scale**

deflation (16): a period of sustained decrease in the general price level, or more generally a sustained decline in the inflation rate demand determined output: when suppliers produce whatever is demanded at a given price level

demand disturbance/shock (13, 16): a sudden exogenous shift in the level of aggregate demand at given levels of inflation, underlying inflation, and nominal interest rates

demand for money (6): the level of money, either narrow or broad, which households firms and governments choose to hold, given the level of economic activity, nominal interest rates, and the cost of moving between money and other assets

demand side (1): the analysis of spending decisions by economic agents

depreciation (capital) (2, 3, 11): the loss of original value of a physical asset owing to use, age, and economic obsolescence

depreciation (exchange rate) (6, 11): a market-determined decrease in the value of a currency; *see*: **appreciation, revaluation**

depreciation line (3): the straight line in the diagram of the Solow model without technical progress and population growth, which shows the investment per capita needed to maintain a constant capital stock per capita

derivatives (14): securities that derive their value from the behaviour of other underlying securities

derived demand (9): a demand for something which arises as a product of a demand for something else

desired demand function (10): total planned spending given the interest rate and real GDP

deterministic view of business cycles (16): the present depends mechanically on the economic history of the past

devaluation (11): decision by the monetary authority to reduce the value of the currency; *see*: **revaluation, appreciation, depreciation**

dichotomy principle (6): dichotomy is the delinking of the nominal and real sides of the economy; this follows from the monetary neutrality principle

diffusion (4): the process through which discoveries are progressively adopted by various industries

diminishing marginal productivity (3, 7): the tendency that, as the inputs into production are increased, the increments of output will decline

discounting (7, 14): valuing future goods or money in terms of goods or money today; *see also* **intertemporal price**

disinflation (13): a relatively rapid reduction in the inflation rate brought about by contractionary demand policy

distortionary taxation (18): *see*: **tax distortions**

diversification (14): the practice of holding wealth in a number of different assets, with the objective of averaging out the risk implied by any individual asset in the portfolio

dynamic inefficiency/efficiency (3): an economy is dynamically inefficient when a reduction of current savings can make all generations better off; it is dynamically efficient when future generations can be made better off only by reducing consumption (i.e. increasing savings) today

economic agents (1): term used to denote individual decision-makers, households, and firms

economic growth (1, 3): secular increases in the output of an economy, usually measured by the annual growth in GDP per capita

economic rents (18): returns to factors of production that exceed the minimum amount necessary to keep those factors of production in operation

effective exchange rate (6): an index consisting of a weighted average of a country's exchange rates *vis-à-vis* its main trading partners

effective labour (3): a measure of labour input which accounts for not only the number of hours worked but also for the effect of technical progress on the productivity of those hours

effectiveness lag (16): time lag resulting from a slow or delayed impact of economic policies on real activity

efficient market hypothesis (14): maintains that when markets are efficient, prices fully reflect all available information

efficiency wages (5): wages paid in excess of the marginal productivity of labour in order to induce sufficient effort on the part of the workers

elastic (5): generally, the sensitivity which the demand for something reacts to the price, in particular, when the demand for labour is sensitive to its price, the real wage, holding everything else constant

electoral business cycles (16): business cycles which result from governments' use of macroeconomic policies to boost their re-election prospects, implying that the economy should be booming and employment is high on election day and that in the aftermath of its election, the government tightens its policies

employers' associations (5): organizations of employers which represent their interests, especially in collective bargaining

endogenous and exogenous variables (1): endogenous variables are explained by economic principles; exogenous variables, in contrast, are determined outside the system under study

endogenous growth theory (4): in contrast with the theory of exogenous growth, which explains sustainable growth by exogenous technological advances, endogenous growth theory tracks down the sources of growth to the accumulation of factors of production, with particular emphasis on knowledge

endowment (5, 7): the exogenous resources that economic agents expect to have in the present and in the future

equilibrium GDP (10): the GDP level at which the desired demand for goods and services is equal to the supply

equilibrium unemployment (5): corresponds to the situation where the wage matches the collective preference of workers but leave some individual without jobs

equilibrium unemployment rate (5): the unemployment rate that occurs when employment and unemployment stabilize, i.e. when aggregate demand for labour is met by aggregate supply. Because labour supply may not perfectly reflect individuals' preferences, this unemployment may in part be involuntary (structural unemployment), but it may also reflect the efficiency of the labour market (frictional unemployment)

equilibrium (long-run) real exchange rate (15): the theoretical level of the real exchange rate (the nominal exchange rate doubly deflated by price indexes at home and abroad) necessary to enforce the national budget constraint with the rest of the world

equity – efficiency trade-off (17): the fact that improving equity among society's members often has a negative impact on the economy's efficiency

European Monetary Union (EMU) (19): the group of countries that share the same currency, the euro

European terms (6): one of two ways of quoting the exchange rate, here in units of domestic currency per one unit of the foreign currency (e.g. 7.8 Swedish krona or 1.1 Swiss franc for $1); *see also* **British terms**

excess demand (10): a market situation in which demand exceeds supply at prevailing prices

excess supply (10): a market situation in which the quantity supplied exceeds desired demand at prevailing prices

exchange market intervention (11): the central bank buys or sells its own currency against foreign currencies on the foreign exchange market in order to prevent unwanted exchange rate movements

exchange rate (1): the rate at which foreign money is traded for domestic money

exchange rate anchor (11): a strategy for pursuing monetary policy which fixes the nominal exchange rate to another currency in order to lower expectations of future inflation

Exchange Rate Mechanism (ERM) (19): the fixed exchange rate arrangement of the European Monetary System

exchange rate overshooting (15): a depreciation of the nominal exchange rate in response to an increase in the money supply, which exceeds, or overshoots, the extent implied by the principle of monetary neutrality

exchange rate regime (11): description of the exchange rate system adopted by a country: the exchange rate may be fixed, so that the central bank maintains the value of the domestic money in terms of another currency or group of currencies or it may be freely floating

expansionary monetary policy shocks (10): a shift downward in monetary policy of the central bank described by the Taylor rule, due to an decrease in the target or neutral interest rate

export function (10): function representing part of a country's foreign spending and therefore following its fluctuations—the greater the foreign spending, the greater will be exports

external competitiveness (6): the ability of countries to export goods to others at given levels of nominal wages, nominal prices, and nominal exchange rates

external terms of trade (6): the ratio of export to import prices, or how many units of imports are needed to purchase one unit of exports

externalities (17): activities that affect the welfare of economic agents not undertaking them directly

factors of production (1): inputs in the production process, such as labour, capital, or land, which create value added (in contrast to intermediary inputs)

fiat money (9): money which the state declares to be legal tender although its intrinsic value may be little or nothing

final and intermediate sales (2): final sales refer to sales of goods and services to the consumer or firm that will ultimately use them; intermediate sales refer to producers who use and transform these goods or services as part of their own production of goods and services

financial account (2): net sales of foreign assets by private domestic residents (a purchase by domestic residents worsens the financial account balance, a sale improves it)

financial intermediaries (9, 14): economic entities that collect funds from depositors and lend them to borrowers

financial intermediation (2): the channelling of savings of households by banks and other financial institutions to those willing to undertake physical investment

finding rate (5): the rate at which unemployed workers find a job, calculated as a ratio of job finds (per month or per year) to total unemployment

fiscal policy (1): the use of the government budget to affect the volume of national spending, or more generally to provide public goods and services, as well as to redistribute income

Fisher principle/equation (13): the decomposition of the nominal interest rate (i) into the sum of the real interest rate (r) and the expected rate of inflation (π^e)

fixed capital formation (7): *see:* **investment**

flows and stocks (2): a flow is an economic variable measured between two periods of time; a stock is a magnitude measured at a given time

foreign exchange market interventions (2): purchases and sales of foreign money in exchange for domestic money undertaken by monetary authorities

foreign exchange reserves (2, 11): foreign currencies held by the monetary authority for the purpose of intervening in the exchange markets

foreign or international rate of return (11): the total rate of return earned on domestic money, in per cent, when invested in a foreign asset over a short period (a month to a year), including gains

or losses due to movement in the exchange rate, which makes investors indifferent between investing at home and abroad

forward discount (15): when the forward price of foreign exchange is lower than the current spot price, implying an expected exchange rate depreciation

forward premium (15): when the forward price of foreign exchange exceeds the current spot price, implying an expected exchange rate appreciation

forward exchange rate (15): an exchange rate agreed upon today for a currency exchange that will occur at a future date

frictional unemployment (5): unemployment resulting from individuals' changing jobs or entering the labour force

Friedman critique (16): the view that inherent lags in decision, design, implementation, and effectiveness of activist monetary and fiscal policies may negate its influence on the business cycle or even increase its magnitude

fundamentals (15): factors driving the exchange rate; the net external position, and determinants of the primary current account as well as monetary conditions and the degree of price rigidity: in general, the underlying real factors that determine the value of an asset

GDP deflator (2): a (Paasche) price index for total value added of an economy, given by the nominal GDP divided by the real GDP (GDP valued at price of some base year)

GDP per capita (2): the ratio of GDP to population size

general equilibrium (10, 11, 13): condition of equilibrium applying simultaneously to several markets at the same time, recognizing the interdependencies between markets

global imbalances (7): large and lasting current account deficits and surpluses that emerged in the 2000s

gold exchange standard (19): the system established at the Bretton Woods conference in 1944 whereby gold was the fundamental standard of value, but for all currencies the gold parity was mediated by the dollar

gold standard (19): a system whereby a country defines its monetary unit in terms of gold

golden rule (3): proposition that per capita consumption is maximized in a growing economy at the point at which the marginal product of capital is equal to the growth rate

goods market equilibrium (10): the situation in which the desired demand equals supply

Gresham's Law (19): the proposition that money which is more valuable than its official exchange rate will disappear from circulation: 'bad money chases out the good'

gross domestic product (GDP) (1, 2): a location-based measure of a country's productive activity, corresponding to the value added generated by factors of production, both local and foreign-owned, within a country

gross investment (3): an economy's total expenditure on capital goods—equipment and machines, the construction of housing, and inventory changes—including those which are intended to replace losses due to wear, loss of value, or obsolescence

gross national income (GNI) (2): total value added produced by nationals, independently of whether they are residents or non-residents

growth traps (4): phases of economic development when low growth leads to low investment in physical, human and infrastructural capital, which in turn reduces growth prospects

hard pegs (13): a fixed exchange arrangement which intentionally makes it costly or even illegal to devalue, thereby increasing the regime's credibility

hedging (15): techniques used to protect oneself against foreign exchange fluctuations; more generally, any trading techniques used to eliminate risk

hollowing-out hypothesis (19): the hypothesis that the menu of exchange rate regimes has been narrowed to either fully floating rates or hard peg, implying that fixed-but-adjustable exchange rates are no longer feasible

household labour supply curve (5): the number of hours a household is willing to work as a function of the wage per hour

human capital (4, 17, 18): the education, training, and work experience acquired by individuals

human rights (4): the rights of individuals in a society to express views or religious beliefs, to associate with others, to engage in economic activity, and to be free from political persecution

Hume mechanism (19): the process by which trade imbalances were equilibrated under the gold standard system: a trade deficit (surplus) implies a reduction (increase) in gold and money supply, which leads to higher (lower) interest rates, to capital inflows (outflows), and to falling (rising) prices improving (worsening) the country's competitiveness

hyperinflation (1, 6): term used to describe periods of extremely high inflation, usually when the monthly rate exceeds 50%

imitation (4): process whereby technical discoveries are copied

implementation lag (16): time lag in policy effectiveness as a result of the time taken by parliaments and ministries to pass and originate legislation

import function (10): function representing part of domestic spending and therefore following its fluctuations: the greater domestic spending, the greater will be imports

impossible trilogy (19): the result that it is impossible to simultaneously operate a fixed exchange rate regime, allow full capital mobility, and conduct an independent monetary policy

impulse-propagation mechanism (16): mechanism that transforms shocks (impulses) into irregular oscillations like the business cycle

income effect (5): the portion of change in quantity demanded which is attributed to the change in real income that results from the price change

increasing returns to scale (3): a characteristic of the production function which occurs when a simultaneous equiproportional increase in the factors of production results in a more than equiproportional increase in output

index (1): a number that has no dimension (i.e. is not expressed in units such as DM, tons, hours, etc.); it is usually set to take a simple value like 1 or 100 at a specific date

indexation (12, 13): a provision in wage or other contracts by which nominal values are adjusted frequently to reflect changes in some price index and to maintain the real value of the contract's provisions

indifference curves (**5, 8**): a graphic representation of all possible combinations of two items that will yield equivalent utility (satisfaction)

industrial policies (**18**): these amount to official backing of national corporations or whole industries, taking on the form of subsidies, public orders, or trade policies

inelastic (**5**): insensitivity of demand to price, all other things equal

inflation (**1**): the sustained increase in prices over longer periods of time, as measured by the rate of change in a price index (an average of many or all prices in an economy)

inflation differential (**6**): the difference between the domestic and foreign inflation rates

inflation targeting (**9**): a policy approach taken by some central banks in which an inflation rate or band of inflation rates is explicitly and publicly announced

inflation-targeting strategy (**13, 16**): the central bank announces a target for the inflation rate that it aims to reach within 2–3 years, publishes its inflation forecast, and adjusts its policy in reaction to the difference between the target and the forecast

inflation tax (**17**): real revenue that the government obtains by inflation. Inflation erodes the real value of nominal assets and therefore may improve the financial condition of the government, reducing the value of its nominal liabilities

information asymmetry (**9**): a situation in which one party has better information than the other/s about the probability of an outcome, and all parties know it

insiders and outsiders (**5**): a distinction applied to workers who are already employed in long-term employment relationships

installation costs (**8**): the costs of installing new productive equipment

intellectual property rights (**4**): the rights of artists, authors, designers, inventors, or scientists to some of the economic profits their innovative or inventive activities may generate

interbank interest rate (**9**): the interest rate at which banks lend high-powered money (reserves) to one another

interbank market (**9**): a wholesale market for money, which brings commercial banks together

interest rate parity (**11**): the condition that interest rates are equalized across countries taking account of expected exchange rate changes

internal terms of trade (**6**): ratio between nontraded and traded good prices

international financial markets (IFM) line (**11**): the line in the open economy *IS–TR* diagram describing the interest rate at which net capital inflows are zero, i.e. when interest rate at home is equal to the required rate of return available abroad, measured in the domestic currency

international Fisher equation (**15**): uncovered interest parity and purchasing power parity imply that the real interest rates are equal across countries *ex ante*

International Monetary Fund (IMF) (**19**): an institution set up at the Bretton Woods conference in 1944 to promote international monetary cooperation and exchange rate stability, to establish a multilateral system of payments for current transactions, and to assist members facing balance of payments difficulties

intertemporal budget constraint (**7**): the relationship summarizing resources and opportunities available in the present and the future to a household for consumption; the present value of spending must be less than, or equal to, wealth

intertemporal price (**7**): the price of goods tomorrow in terms of goods today; how much we would be willing to pay for—or sell for—the good today for delivery at some future date

intertemporal trade (**7**): trade conducted by households and firms across time

interventionism (**1**): policy whereby a government supports, coordinates, and even controls certain aspects of private activity; *see*: **laissez-faire**

investment (**2, 7**): the acquisition of productive equipment for later use in production; also called fixed capital formation

investment function (8, 10): relationship between investment and its fundamental determinants: aggregate investment depends positively upon Tobin's q and GDP growth, and negatively upon the real interest rate

investment funds (14): a collection of assets, assembled by specialized financial institutions, in which investors can purchase shares

involuntary unemployment (5): includes those who wish to work at the current wage level but cannot find a job

IS curve (10): for given values of exogenous variables, the combinations of nominal interest rate i and real output (GDP) that are consistent with goods market equilibrium

job-finding rate (5): the average proportion of unemployed people who find a job during a given period, e.g. during a year

job matching (18): the matching of job offers of firms and unemployed workers

Keynesian assumption (10): the assumption that the evolution of the price level is insensitive to aggregate demand in the short run

(Keynesian) demand multiplier (10): a ratio indicating the effect of increases in exogenous components of aggregate demand on total aggregate demand

Keynesian revolution (1): the development of ideas and policies to deal with situations where price and/or wage rigidities lead to recessions; these ideas stand in opposition to (neo)classical economics, which holds that markets are able to take care of themselves

Keynesianism (16): the view that government demand management policy should play a key role in macroeconomic policy: Keynesians hold that markets suffer from imperfections—for example slow clearing of labour and product markets—which are responsible for the occasional underutilization of resources

labour (1): factor of production, usually measured in man-hours, i.e. the total number of hours worked in a firm, an industry, or a country

labour demand (5): the relationship linking the number of man-hours that firms wish to hire and the cost of labour

labour force (1, 5): the total number of individuals who are either working or actively looking for a job

labour force participation (5): the proportion of working-age people who are in the labour force

labour market institutions (5): formal and informal arrangements that regulate wage negotiations, working hours, health safety regulation, workers' influence, etc.

labour share (1): the fraction of national income or aggregate value added paid to labour as wages or other forms of compensation, including payments of firms to social insurance schemes on behalf of their employees

labour tax wedge (18): the difference between labour's cost to firms and wages actually received by workers

LAD line (13): The long-run aggregate demand curve, which states that inflation is ultimately set by demand, more precisely monetary policy

Laffer curve (18): the relationship between government tax revenues and the average tax rate: beyond some point, increases in tax rates are associated with decreases in tax revenues, because the distortionary effects outweigh the revenue gained

laissez-faire (1, 18): term used to describe the view that properly functioning markets will deliver the best possible social outcome, and that intervention by the government in economic affairs should be rejected; *see*: **interventionism**

Law of One Price (6): asserts that domestic and foreign prices are equal when converted in the same currency. It can apply good by good or to a basket of goods

learning-by-doing (4): the on-the-job adoption of new technologies

leisure (5): time spent not working

lender of last resort (9): the central bank, in its implicit commitment to protect bank customers by providing failing banks with sufficient monetary base to prevent collapse

life-cycle consumption (8): theory that consumption choices are made with a planning horizon equal to the individual's expected remaining lifetime; that an individual will build up savings during working years and exhaust them during retirement years

LM curve (**10**): for given values of the exogenous variables and the price level, the combinations of real output (GDP) and interest rates for which the money market is in equilibrium

logarithmic scale (**1**): on a normal scale, one moves up by the same distance when going through 1, 2, 3, etc. On a logarithmic scale, the same distance takes us to the squared value of the previous step; for example 10, 100, 10,000 are equally spaced up. A variable growing exponentially is plotted as a line

long run (**13**): The long run is what economists mean when they talk about the behaviour of an economy over a period of decades, rather than over short time spans of quarters or a few years

long-run equilibrium (**13**): the state of the economy (output and inflation) when aggregate demand equals aggregate supply and actual inflation is equal to underlying or expected inflation

macroeconomics (**1**): the study of the aggregate or average behaviour of the economy, as opposed to microeconomics, the behaviour of individual households, firms, and markets

marginal cost of capital (**8**): the cost of an additional increment to productive capacity

marginal productivity of capital (MPK) (**3, 8**): additional output produced by employing an additional unit of capital in the production process

marginal productivity of labour (**5**): additional output produced by employing an additional unit of labour in the production process

marginal rate of intertemporal substitution (**8**): describes how much of today's consumption a consumer is willing to exchange for tomorrow's consumption

marginal rate of substitution (**5, 8**): the rate at which one commodity can be substituted for another without changing the level of utility

market-clearing (**18**): term describing a market that works perfectly by equalling demand and supply at every instant

market failures (**18**): when markets are not functioning as in theory, for example because competition is imperfect with dominant players

or when all the relevant information is not available to all market participants

market liquidity (**14**): a financial market is liquid when it is easy at all times to find counterparts when selling or buying assets. The opposite case is that of shallow markets

market maker (**14**): traders or institutions that stand ready to deal in a particular asset

market power (**12**): the ability for producers to set a price that differs from those of close competitors. This is trivially the case of monopolists but can also occur when producers are able to differentiate their products (often using brand names), thus creating some limited monopoly power. The limit is that excessive prices may lead consumers to choose another brand. In this case, we talk of monopolistic competition

mark-up pricing (**12**): the percentage by which a firm increases the selling price of goods above the average or unit costs of production

Marshallian externality (**4**): an externality for which there is no market price

maturity (**14**): the length of time before an agreed-upon financial transaction will take place

maturity premium (**14**): the premium borrowers are willing to pay for borrowing over a longer period of time

maturity transformation (**9**): banks do maturity transformation when they borrow for a short term (e.g. they accept deposits from customers) and invest in long-term assets

median voter theorem (**16**): if voters' preferences are evenly spread along some dimension, then a political party's maximizing election strategy is to advocate policies that are most favoured by the median ('middle') voter

minimum wages (**5**): the lower bound set on wage rates that may be paid to workers, usually but not always by law

misalignment (**15**): a persistent deviation of the real exchange rate from its equilibrium value

monetary aggregates (**9**): various definitions of the money stock, differing largely by their degree of liquidity

monetary base (**9**): the sum of currency in the hands of the public and bank reserves

monetary economy (1): the part of the economy dealing with monetary and financial, nominal phenomena

monetary policy (1, 9, 14): actions taken by central banks to affect monetary and financial conditions in an economy

monetary policy autonomy (11): the ability of a central bank to decide and implement the interest rate that it wishes

monetary targeting (10): monetary policy which focuses on setting money aggregates such as M1 or M2 with no regard for level of interest rates

money growth targeting (9): a central bank strategy that sets the rate of growth of a chosen money stock aggregate (e.g. M1, M2, M3)

money illusion (12): term used to describe the failure to distinguish monetary from real magnitudes

money market (9): this is where banks and other financial institutions borrow from each other, usually for very short periods. Central banks may intervene on the money markets. Alternative names: interbank market, open market

money market equilibrium (10): equality of the exogenous and the central-bank-controlled money supply and the money demand that corresponds to a particular output level and exogenous transaction costs

money multiplier (9): the link between the monetary base and wider monetary aggregates

Mundell–Fleming model (11): the open economy version of the *IS–LM* model

N – 1 problem (19): in a fixed exchange rate system with N countries, the fact that $N - 1$ bilateral rates can be sufficient to determine all, leaving one degree of (monetary) independence

natural monopoly (18): occurs in industries exhibiting increasing returns (telecommunications, transport, etc.)

NDP (net domestic product) (2): in the national income accounts, GDP less depreciation

neoclassical (16): model claiming that flexible prices clear all markets even in the short run

neoclassical assumptions (12): the view that prices adjust even in the short run, so that the economy is always dichotomized

net investment (3): the increase in the capital stock taking into account depreciation

net taxes (2): the government's tax income from households and firms after transfers have been subtracted

neutral interest rate (9, 10, 13): the interest rate at which monetary policy is neither expansionary nor contractionary

neutrality of money/monetary neutrality (6): the principle that the money supply does not affect real variables such as real output or unemployment, but rather the price level

no-profit condition (14): the requirement that it is not possible to make an obvious profit without taking associated risks on financial markets

noise traders (14): irrational or misinformed traders who cause deviations of stock prices from their fundamental value for a long time

nominal exchange rate (6): the value of foreign currency in terms of domestic money

nominal GDP (2): total value added measured at current prices

nominal interest rate (13): an interest rate measured in terms of percentage per period of time paid on a nominal investment made in the local currency

non-excludable goods (4): a good is non-excludable when making it available to one person makes it available to all. An example is knowledge (e.g. understanding gravity or why Newton got hit on the head by a falling apple)

non-rivalrous goods (4): a good is non-rivalrous when its usage by one person does not detract from others' usage. Examples are clean air or knowledge

normative economics (1): economics that passes judgement or provides advice on policy actions; *see*: positive economics

official account (2): net transactions performed by the monetary authority on the foreign exchange market (net sales of foreign exchange)

Okun's Law (12): the observed inverse relationship between fluctuations of real GDP around its trend growth path and fluctuations of the unemployment rate around its equilibrium level

oil shock (12): a sharp increase in oil prices

open market operations (**9**): transactions undertaken by a central bank which exchanges securities for its own liabilities; these operations have the effect of supplying reserves to, or draining them from, the banking system

open position (**15**): a trader has an open position in a given asset when they stand to gain or lose if the asset price changes. The opposite, a cover position, can be arranged by committing to buy or sell the asset at a pre-arranged price

openness (**1**): the ratio of exports or imports—or the average of exports and exports—to GDP, which is a measure of the extent to which a country trades with the rest of the world

opportunity cost (**7, 8**): the value of a resource in its best alternative use

optimal capital stock (**8**): the stock of physical capital that maximizes the value of the firm, for which the marginal productivity of capital is equal to the marginal cost of investment

optimal currency area (**19**): a region for which no welfare loss is implied by the use of a common currency

output cost of disinflation (**13**): the sacrifice ratio, which compares the cumulated increase in the rate of unemployment with the reduction in inflation achieved over some period of time

output gap (**9, 12**): temporary deviations of GDP from its trend or equilibrium level

output – labour ratio (**3**): the ratio of output to the labour used to produce that output

overall balance (**2**): sum of the current and financial accounts (including errors and omissions), which by double-bookkeeping is the mirror image of interventions by the monetary authorities

overvalued (**15**): *see:* **undervalued**

parity/central parity (**19**): when the exchange rate is fixed vis-à-vis another currency, the monetary authorities declare the official value of the currency; this is called the parity. Usually, the exchange rate is allowed to vary around a value called the central parity

partisan business cycles (**16**): business cycles resulting from the succession in power of parties with different economic priorities and preferred policies; *see:* **political business cycles**

patents (**4**): a legal right granted to exclusive commercial use of an invention, normally for a limited period of time

PCA function (**10**): an expression describing how the difference between exports and imports is related to domestic spending, foreign spending, and the real exchange rate

pecuniary/non-pecuniary externalities (**18**): externalities that are/are not transmitted by the market's price mechanism

permanent income (**8**): the flow of income which, if constant, would deliver the same present value as the actual expected income path

perpetuity (**14**): a loan agreement with an infinite maturity; *see:* **consol**

persistence (**16**): long-lasting effect of a shock hitting the economy

personal disposable income (**2**): household net income from all sources after taxes have been paid and transfers received

person-hours (**5**): a measure of labour input which is equal to the number of people employed times the average number of hours spent working

Phillips curve (**12**): an empirical relationship linking the inflation rate negatively to the unemployment rate

Phillips trade-off (**12**): the notion that lower unemployment can be 'bought' at the price of a higher rate of inflation; or that higher unemployment is the price of a lower rate of inflation

physical capital (**2**): a factor of production consisting of durable inputs such as machines, buildings, computer hardware and software, and physical inventories

policy mix (**10**): the joint use of monetary and fiscal policies

political business cycles (**16**): business cycles resulting from the use of macroeconomic policies to improve the state of the economy just before elections; *see:* **partisan business cycles**

positive economics (**1**): the description and explanation of economic phenomena; *see:* **normative economics**

positive/negative externalities (**18**): an externality occurs when one's action has an impact on others.

It is positive when the effect on others goes in the same direction as on the agent at the source of the externality (e.g. reducing pollution). It is negative in the opposite case (e.g. using a seat in a public park)

PPP (purchasing power parity) line (**13**): a horizontal line corresponding to the foreign inflation rate, because at fixed exchange rates purchasing power parity rules out permanent differences between domestic and foreign inflation

present discounted value (**7**): the value of a stream of income or spending spread over time and valued at today's price; *see* **intertemporal price**

price flexibility (**12**): prices are flexible when they respond immediately and completely to any market disequilibrium

price level (**1**): the average level of prices in an economy

primary budget deficit (**7**): the budget deficit net of debt service (i.e. net of the payment of interest on the public debt)

primary current account (**7**): the current account less net interest payments (net investment income); alternatively, the difference between gross domestic product output and aggregate domestic spending when unilateral transfers are equal to zero

principle of monetary neutrality (**6**): asserts that nominal variables do not affect real variables

primary current account function (**10**): the relationship which relates the primary current account surplus to the real exchange rate σ (positively) to domestic GDP Y (negatively) and to foreign GDP Y^* (positively)

private income (**2**): income to the private sector which remains after taxes have been removed from, and transfers have been added to national income (more precisely, GDP plus net factor income earned abroad)

privatization (**18**): the sale or transfer of part or all of state-owned enterprises to the private sector

procyclical (**1**): an economic variable that is positively correlated with the state of the economy; that is, it moves in the same direction as aggregate output

producer surplus (**18**): difference between the price that a producer actually receives for a given quantity of goods and the amount corresponding to the minimum price at which they would be willing to supply the same quantity

product differentiation (**12**): a strategy used by firms to make consumers perceive their products as different from those of their competitors. A good example are cola drinks

production function (**3, 7**): theoretical relationship linking aggregate output to inputs of factors of production

productive efficiency (**17**): the optimal use of available productive resources

property rights (**4, 18**): rights to private ownership. The absence of effective enforcement of property rights stunts economic growth

public goods (**4, 17**): goods and services that are provided free of charge and the consumption of which by one person does not prevent the consumption by another person (characterized by non-excludability and non-rivalry)

public infrastructure (**4**): physical means collectively provided that raise a country's productive capacity. Some means are freely available (e.g. streets or public schools), others can be purchased (e.g. electric lines or trains)

q-theory of investment (**8**): theory linking investment to Tobin's q, the ratio of firms' market value to the replacement cost of installed capital

quota (IMF) (**19**): a country's voting and borrowing rights in the IMF, based on its initial deposit upon joining

Ramsey principle of public finance (**18**): principle that, for a given amount of revenue to be raised, goods with the most inelastic demands and supplies should be taxed most heavily in order to minimize overall loss of consumer and producer surplus in an economy

random walk (**8**): a variable that changes randomly from period to period, where the only change between its value today and its value tomorrow will be white noise and can be positive or negative

rate of depreciation (**3, 8**): the rate at which the capital stock loses economic value, either by becoming obsolete or by wear and tear, usually expressed as per cent per annum

rational expectations hypothesis (**7, 16**): hypothesis asserting that agents evaluate future events using all available information efficiently so that they do not make systematic forecasting errors

real business cycle theory (16): theory of the business cycle which explains economic fluctuations primarily as a consequence of technology shocks assuming price flexibility

real consumption wage (5): the ratio of nominal wages to the consumer price index; a measure of the price of leisure (or the return to work) in terms of consumption goods

real economy (1): term referring to the production and consumption of goods and services, and the incomes associated with productive activities; *see*: **monetary economy**

real GDP (2): total value added measured at constant prices, i.e. using prices observed in a reference year

real exchange rate (6, 15): the cost of foreign goods in terms of domestic goods, defined as the nominal exchange rate adjusted by prices at home and abroad

real interest rate (7, 13): the difference between the nominal interest rate and the expected rate of inflation

real shocks (10): exogenous shifts to the real level of economic activity, i.e. at a given level of interest rates or the price level

real wage rigidity (5): rigidity arising when unemployment fails to cause real wages to decline

realignment (11): a change in the official exchange rate parity

recessions (10): intervals of declining economic activity or output below trend potential output for an extended period

recognition lag (16): time lag in discovering that policy intervention is called for

relative price (5): the price of one good in terms of another, usually computed as the ratio of two nominal prices

relative purchasing power parity (6): situation occurring when the cost of the same basket of goods in different countries increases at the same rate once converted into a common currency

reserves ratio (9): the ratio of a commercial bank's reserves (vault cash or deposits at the central bank) to the total demand deposits it has issued

returns to scale (3): the impact on output of an increase in all inputs by the same proportion: if output increases equiproportionally, the production function is said to exhibit constant returns to scale; if output increases more or less than proportionally, we have respectively increasing or decreasing returns to scale

revaluation (11): decision by the monetary authority to increase the value of the currency; *see*: **devaluation, appreciation, depreciation**

Ricardian equivalence (7): hypothesis that the time profile of taxes needed to finance a given stream of government purchases has no effect on agents' intertemporal budget constraint and therefore on real spending and saving decisions; then public debt is not considered as private wealth

risk averse (14): behaviour characterized by a preference to avoid risk

risk premium (14): compensation above and beyond the expected rate of return on an asset required by agents to hold it

saving (2): postponement of consumption using some part of disposable personal income

saving schedule (3): the schedule shows how much a nation saves when the capital stock increases

Schumpeterian theory of innovation (4): the view that growth occurs because enterprising entrepreneurs constantly innovate

securitization (14): a financial procedure whereby an asset that is not traded (e.g. a housing loan) is transformed into a tradable asset, essentially through standardization

seigniorage (17): exploitation by the government of the monopoly power of the central bank to create money as a means of raising real resources

self-fulfilling attacks (19): exchange rate attacks that are not justified by the exchange rate fundamentals, but occur because, if they succeed, the authorities will relax monetary policy, proving the attack to be rational *ex post*

self-fulfilling crises (15): a crisis that occurs simply because it is expected to occur

separation rate (5): the rate at which employed workers become unemployed per unit of time; *see*: job-finding rate

sequencing (19): principles that indicate in which order a country that has long prevented the normal operation of markets and has at least partially isolated its economy can remove existing restraints and integrate itself in the world economy

share (14): a claim on a part of the profits or earnings of a firm after operating costs and interest have been paid

short-run equilibrium (13): the state of the economy when aggregate demand equals aggregate supply

Solow decomposition (3): the three-way decomposition of the sources of economic growth into capital accumulation, increase in labour utilization, and the Solow residual capturing technological progress

Solow growth model (3): a theory that analyses growth as being driven by exogenous technological change and the accumulation of factors of production

Solow residual (3): the part of GDP growth unexplained by the increase in factors of production and conventionally ascribed to technological progress

sovereign borrowing (7): borrowing undertaken by national governments vis-à-vis foreigners, usually in the form of bond issues or loans by international banks

special drawing rights (SDRs) (19): a reserve money created by the IMF in 1967 and allocated on the basis of quotas; used among central banks as an additional source of liquidity

speculative attacks (19): sudden loss of foreign exchange reserves of central banks, arising when exchange market participants anticipate an imminent devaluation

speculative bubbles (14): persistent deviations of market prices from their fundamental values

spot exchange rate (15): the exchange rate that applies to an immediate currency exchange

stagflation (12, 13): periods when both inflation and unemployment increase

steady state (3): a hypothetical state in which all variables have responded fully to exogenous changes in the environment

sterilized intervention/unsterilized intervention (11): actions undertaken by central banks to offset the impact of a foreign exchange intervention on the domestic money supply, usually a money market purchase or sale of securities in the same amount as the foreign exchange market intervention

stochastic view of business cycles (16): the view that business cycles do not respond to systematic inherent causes but to events that happen randomly

structural unemployment (5): unemployment arising as the result of a mismatch of demand and supply of labour

stylized facts (3): regularities in macroeconomic data which guide economists in their search for models to account for economic phenomena

substitution effect (5): the component of the total change in quantity demanded that is attributable to the change in relative prices

supply disturbance/shock (12, 16): a sudden exogenous increase in non-labour production costs

supply side (1, 18): the productive potential of an economy and the factors that determine its overall efficiency

swap (15): exchange of sums of money of the same currency but on different terms, for instance selling francs for delivery now while simultaneously buying them back for delivery in three months' time

systemic risk (9): the risk of a generalized collapse of the banking system, arising because banks and financial institutions hold large amounts of each other's liabilities

target interest rate (10, 13): the interest rate which the central bank would choose to set when output equals its trend or equilibrium level; is the anchor for the Taylor rule describing monetary policy; *see:* **neutral interest rate**

tax distortions (18): effects on real behaviour arising from the wedge that taxes introduce between the price received by the provider of a good or service and the price paid by its consumer

tax smoothing (17): the proposition that a government should not change tax rates in response to temporary causes of budget deficits, but should borrow instead

Taylor rule (9, 10): a simple description of how central banks set the interest rate in response to output fluctuations and to deviations of inflation from its desired rate

technological progress (**3**): the contribution to economic growth of technological change, usually captured by the rate of increase of total factor productivity

technological shocks (**16**): exogenous impulses, such as discoveries, inventions, product innovations, or process improvements, that alter the productivity of factors of production, change the environment of economic agents, and cause them to change their behaviour

time consistency problem (**18**): the possibility that a policy or a sequence of actions which is optimal before they are taken is no longer so afterwards, especially if other agents act in response to that policy or sequence of actions

Tobin's *q* (**8**): the ratio of the present value of the return from new investment to the cost of installed capital; often approximated as the ratio of share prices to the replacement price of equipment

total factor productivity (**3**): productivity in the production process that is attributable not to any particular factor of production, but to all; growth in total factor productivity is often measured as a weighted average of growth in average productivities of all factors of production

TR **curve** (**10**): a graphical representation of the Taylor rule, which states that central banks adjust the interest rate to reduce fluctuations in output and inflation

trade policies (**18**): policies designed to support a domestic product's sales through tariffs on foreign goods, or quotas on imports

trade union voluntary/involuntary unemployment (**5**): unemployment resulting from the fact that trade unions ask for higher real wages than if the market were perfectly competitive, which may be involuntary from the perspective of individuals

trade unions (**5**): organizations of workers formed for the purpose of taking collective action against their employers to obtain improvements of pay and other working conditions

trademark (**4**): the protected use of a name (brand) or graphic device (logo)

transmission channels of monetary policy (**14**): mechanisms by which monetary policy conducted by the central bank affect aggregate demand, including the direct effect of interest rates, asset prices, bank credit, and the exchange rate

trend (**1**): long-term tendency in a time series

Triffin paradox (**19**): the inconsistency of the US dollar (a national currency) as a world reserve currency with its gold backing: in order for internationally held dollar balances to grow with the world economy, the USA had to run balance of payment deficits over time which eventually outstripped its gold reserves

uncovered interest rate parity (UIRP) (**15**): the condition that rates of return on assets of comparable risk are equalized across countries once expected exchange rate changes are taken into account

underground economy (**2**): economic activities from which income earned is not reported and therefore is untaxed

underlying inflation rate (**12**): the inertial rate of inflation in an economy, which is driven by both expectations of future inflation as well as past expectations of present inflation based on earlier information and embedded in contracts and informal agreements

undervalued/overvalued (**15**): a currency is undervalued/overvalued when its exchange is below/above its long-run equilibrium value, or the level consistent with its long-run fundamentals

unemployment (**1, 5**): individuals without a job who are actively seeking work

unemployment benefit (**5**): financial assistance to those seeking a job but unable to find suitable employment

unemployment gap (**12**): the difference between the actual and equilibrium unemployment rate

unemployment rate (**1**): the ratio of the number of unemployed workers to total labour force

user cost of capital (**8**): the effective cost to a firm of using the production factor physical capital, including the opportunity cost of resources tied up in the capital, depreciation, changes in the value of capital, as well as tax treatment of these factors

utility (5, 8): the satisfaction that a consumer derives from the consumption of goods and services

value added (2): increase in the market value of a product at a particular stage of production; calculated by subtracting the value of all inputs bought from other firms from the value of the firm's output

vehicle currencies (15): currencies that are widely used to trade or save outside of the country that issued them

Volcker Rule (9): former Federal Reserve Chairman Paul Volcker proposal to prevent banks that accept deposits from getting involved in financially risky investments

voluntary unemployment (5): includes those who do not wish to work at the current wage level

vulnerabilities (19): economic or financial conditions that make a self-fulfilling crisis possible

wage bill (12): the sum of all gross wages and salary payments paid by firms to workers plus fringe benefits as well as contributions to social insurance funds (health care, pension, unemployment, etc.)

wage inflation (12): the annual rate of growth of nominal wages

welfare traps (18): situations where public subsidies—part of the welfare state—discourage private activities and keep recipients dependent on welfare payments

yield (14): the rate of return on an asset (measured in per cent per annum) based on the purchase price of that asset and the payments generated by the ownership of that asset

yield curve (14): a curve which represents how the interest rate changes according to the maturity of assets

zero lower bound (9): a situation where a central bank has brought its interest rate to 0%, and therefore cannot go lower

Index